The Accounting Primer

The Accounting Primer:

An Introduction to Financial Accounting

Thomas J. Burns
The Ohio State University

Harvey S. Hendrickson
Florida International University

McGraw-Hill Book Company

New York   St. Louis   San Francisco   Düsseldorf   Johannesburg
Kuala Lumpur   London   Mexico   Montreal   New Delhi   Panama
Rio de Janeiro   Singapore   Sydney   Toronto

The Accounting Primer: An Introduction to Financial Accounting

1 2 3 4 5 6 7 8 9 0 M U R M 7 9 8 7 6 5 4 3 2

This book was set in Helvetica by Black Dot, Inc., printed by The Murray Printing Company, and bound by Rand McNally & Company. The designer was J + M Condon, Inc.; the drawings were done by John Cordes, J. & R. Technical Services, Inc. The editor was Jack R. Crutchfield. Matt Martino supervised production.

Library of Congress Cataloging in Publication Data

Burns, Thomas Junior.
    The accounting primer.

    1. Accounting.   I. Hendrickson, Harvey S., joint
author.   II. Title.
HF5635.B969   657   72-39181
ISBN 0-07-009191-9

The following problems and questions have been adapted from those appearing in the Uniform Certified Public Accountant Examination and published by the American Institute of Certified Public Accountants, Inc., in the year indicated; all are reprinted by permission of the publisher.

Problem Number	Year Copyright by the American Institute of Certified Public Accountants, Inc.	Question Number	Year Copyright by the American Institute of Certified Public Accountants, Inc.
2–20	1971	4–15	1970
5–8	1956	5–10	1970
5–9	1956	7–10	1959
5–10	1956	8–6	1970
6–16	1969	9–10	1960
8–8	1971	9–12	1964
8–19	1960	10–8	1970
9–20	1971	11–7	1970
11–10	1953	12–20	1971
11–23	1971 and 1961		
12–10	1971		
12–11	1971		

To
our students
past and present,
particularly the good and the bad
but even the indifferent,
from whom we have learned

Contents

Preface

We suppose that everyone who writes a textbook plans to do something different. Our experience shows that most textbook writers do not succeed. The reader will have to judge for himself whether we are to be listed among those who do make some impact.

We can tell you only what we hoped to accomplish. *First,* we tried to stick to a single subject: financial accounting. We have avoided adding the one or two chapters on cost, taxes, managerial decision making, or what have you.

Second, we minimized the procedural aspects of the subject to an extent not usually deemed possible. Our basic technique is the T account. We do not use worksheets or special journals, and even the use of trial balances and financial statements is carefully moderated. We have tried to use figures most effectively. Where it did not seem necessary, we did not use figures. Where figures are used, we were careful to make them only as complex as necessary. When figures are large, we have omitted the 000's and put in a decimal point. Both the chapter material and the problems were prepared in this manner. Despite the minimization of the mechanics, the readers of this book should be able to keep books and understand thoroughly the framework of financial accounting.

Third, we have provided the material, as well as the space and time, to consider fully the currently prevailing theoretical structure of financial accounting. This is most unusual for a beginning book. Yet we feel very strongly, based on our own teaching experiences, that students of this conceptual book will understand the theory readily and will be better accounting students and accountants.

Fourth, we have tried to integrate both theory and procedure with practice. We have emphasized descriptions of the real world of accounting in Chapters 1 and 12, but some real world discussion is found in every chapter. The reader of this book will know what the CPA purports to do for the external users of financial statements. He will learn something of the nature of the auditing process and financial analysis. Contemporary and controversial topics in accounting, often neglected in elementary textbooks, are considered throughout. Deferred taxes, stock options, pension plans, and leases are a few discussed.

Fifth, this is the first beginning textbook in financial accounting suitable for undergraduates that has been developed around fund flows. Although we consider income statements to be flow statements and appropriate attention is given to income statements, more emphasis than usual is placed on working capital and cash fund-flow statements. This is in accord with contemporary thinking and practice. All predictions indicate that the significance and utility of these flows will be more appreciated in the future. Recently, the AICPA's Accounting Principles Board issued an opinion requiring that a fund-flow statement be included in every published financial report.

Sixth, this is the only accounting textbook at any level that specifies at the beginning all the various measurement techniques used in financial accounting. Apart from the conventional accounting and bookkeeping cycle, the emphasis is on actuarial mathematics, but the use of foreign exchange and general price-level indexes is considered too. Even the impact of the computer is analyzed. The subject of quantification or valuation is thus given major attention. Overall we have considered carefully the merits of direct valuation and show that indirect valuation may be a necessary substitute.

Last, this elementary text is dissimilar to most others because of its extensive footnotes, its chapter bibliographies, its glossary, and the eight appendixes, including one called "How to Study Accounting."

The reader is cautioned that the rigor of the book (except for the first chapter) requires a deliberate and careful reading (and re-reading) in order to be understood. Although problems and exercises are provided for all subjects covered, it is expected that the teacher and the student who expect to cover the entire book in a single course of conventional length should be prepared to select those topics that will be covered at a problem-solving level; it is the authors' conviction and experience that covering the other topics on a reading and discussion basis only is helpful, irrespective of whether the student will major in accounting. For students who will major in accounting, the early consideration of these topics will be helpful when the problem-solving level is attempted in later courses. For students who will not major in accounting, the exclusion of these topics precludes, perhaps permanently, the complete understanding of financial accounting. Chapters that require the most attention and probably should be considered at a problem-solving level are Chapters 2, 4, and 6; others that usually should be considered in this category are Chapters 3 and 9.

Whatever we have accomplished, our debt to others is unlimited. It is difficult for the authors of a textbook ever to acknowledge completely what they owe to others. First, we were undoubtedly influenced by the landmark textbooks of our generation. Many could be cited, but certainly those of William A. Paton should be mentioned. They have served as models for several generations of textbook writers. The textbooks of Maurice Moonitz (first with Charles Staehling and then with Louis Jordan) have been innovative in many ways. We should list too the theory textbook of Eldon Hendriksen, which was among the first to attempt a unified theoretical structure. Many other textbooks could be cited also, such as Jaedicke and Sprouse, for attention to fund flows; Mason, Davidson, and Schindler, for general analytical structure; and Fertig, Istvan, and Mottice, for attention to users.

We were also influenced significantly by our teachers, many of whom were not in accounting. Our greatest debt in this regard is to the many economics professors who taught us at several universities. As has been said many times before, economics is still the mother of accounting. Within the field of accounting, we owe the most to Carl A. Nelson, the George May Professor of Financial Accounting at Columbia University. While at the University of Minnesota he served as our doctoral dissertation committee chairman, and his influence on our lives has been remarkable. Our colleagues have been most helpful too. In this regard the encouragement received from Professors Carl Devine, Paul Fertig, Melvin Greenball, Robert Jaedicke, and Elzy McCollough is particularly noteworthy. Finally, we have been much influenced by the students we have had, whether at Stanford or Buffalo, at Lawrence or Michigan, at Southern Illinois or Minnesota, at Florida State or Ohio State. To all our students, even those not found in the classroom, this book is gratefully dedicated.

Special acknowledgments are made to Mrs. Gloria Irwin for her typing efforts, to Mrs. Kathie Dickhaut for her editorial assistance, and to our former students, Mr. Joseph R. Matson, MIT doctoral candidate; Professor Daniel L. Jensen, University of Illinois; Professor William Bentz, University of Kansas; Professor Philip Meyer, Boston University; and Mr. William Bottger, Ohio State University, for their specific suggestions.

Thomas J. Burns
Harvey S. Hendrickson

1 Accounting:
The Process
and Measurements

1

The World of Accounting: Accounting in Perspective

... sired four hundred years ago by a monk, and today damned by thousands of university students.*
HENRY RAND HATFIELD, 1923

Most public companies distribute their published accounting statements widely. They are made available to stockholders, potential investors, creditors, employees, customers, government agencies, and the general public. The flow of information to users outside the company is diagramed in Figure 1-1.

Criteria for Evaluating Financial Statements

The use and usefulness of accounting statements depends both on the user's skill in interpreting accounting data and on the information content of the statements. The accountant has little or no control over the skill of the user of accounting information; he is, however, responsible for the information contained in accounting statements. The American Accounting Association (AAA), an authoritative organization of accounting practitioners and teachers, has listed four criteria for determining what information should be reported in statements: relevance, quantifiability, verifiability, and freedom from bias. In essence, these criteria are the basis for justifying normative statements.

The AAA Committee provides the following clarification of *relevance:*

---

* Quoted from "An Historical Defense of Bookkeeping," a paper read before the American Association of University Instructors in Accounting (now the American Accounting Association) Dec. 29, 1923, and reprinted in *The Journal of Accountancy* (April 1924), p. 247.

Figure 1-1   *The flow of information to external users: summary.*

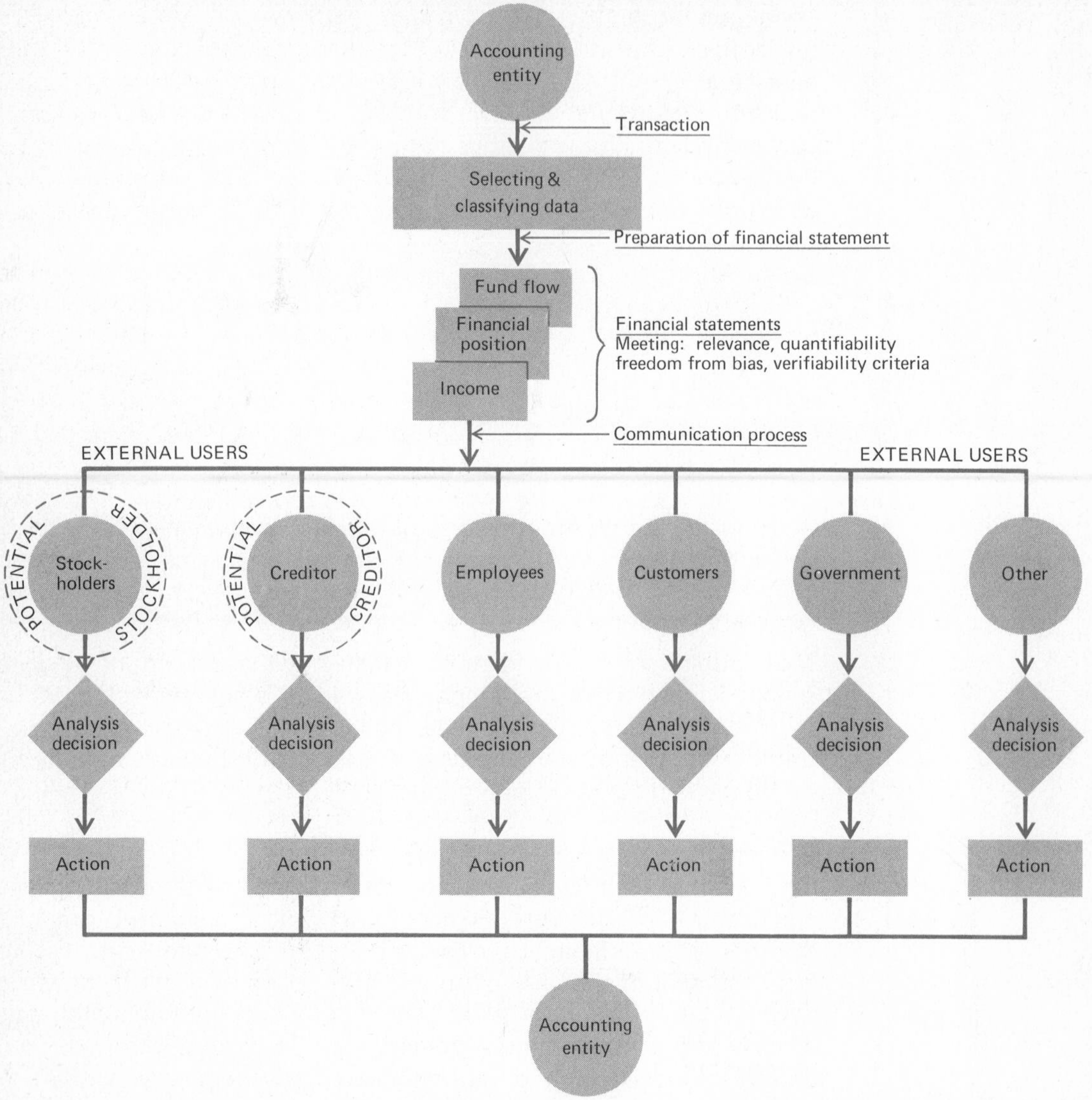

For information to meet the standard of relevance, it must bear upon or be usefully associated with the action it is designed to facilitate or the result it is desired to produce. This requires that either the information or the act of communicating it exert influence . . . on the designated actions.[1]

[1]American Accounting Association, *A Statement of Basic Accounting Theory* (Evanston, Illinois: 1966), p. 9.

Relevance is primary of the four criteria, and the AAA states that it is a necessary characteristic for all accounting information. It has been suggested that the relevance criterion is "user-dependent": the capability of any information or the act of communicating it to exert real or potential influence depends upon the external user's decision-making model. Consequently, the relevance of information can be judged only in terms of how the information is used in the decision-making process by present and potential investors, present and potential creditors, employees, customers, government, and other users.

The AAA identifies *quantifiability* as "the association of a number with a transaction or an activity where the numbers assigned obey prescribed arithmetic laws or procedures."[2] Since relevance is a qualitative dimension, quantifiability adds utility by providing an equivalent basis of comparison for objects or events. Quantifiability is much broader than just dollar valuation; and interval estimation is as legitimate as is point estimation.

Verifiability is "that attribute . . . which allows qualified individuals working independently of one another to develop essentially similar measures or conclusions from an examination of the same evidence, data, or records." Verifiability can be achieved only through "well-understood criteria . . . and consistency in the application of the criteria."[3] The most important business decisions are based upon analyses of accounting data; consequently, the reputation of every professional accountant weighs heavily on his ability to segregate significant facts from the mass of organizational data.

The *freedom from bias* criterion is aimed at eliminating from financial statements information that is beneficial to one or more groups of users while detrimental to others. The statements should have equal potential information content for all users.

Obviously, before the criteria of relevance, quantifiability, verifiability, and freedom from bias can be applied, accounting information must be developed and organized. A logical starting point for discussing the development of accounting information and, ultimately, the financial statement is to answer the question: What is accounting?

Definition of Accounting
In 1941, the American Institute of Certified Public Accountants (AICPA) defined accounting as the art of recording, classifying, summarizing, and interpreting financial *transactions* and events in money terms. However, the discipline has since developed to such an extent that this definition is now unduly restrictive, if not misleading.

[2]*Ibid.*, pp. 11–12.
[3]*Ibid.*, p. 10.

Accounting today is still based on *transactions*, but it has expanded. More specifically, it involves:

1. The timing of accounting through the recognition of transactions
2. The quantification of the results in monetary (or even physical) units
3. The processing and recording of the transactions (bookkeeping)
4. The systematic grouping and formal presentation of the recorded data (preparation of financial statements)
5. The review of the financial statements by an authoritative and publicly sanctioned body of public accountants
6. The reporting to external groups including stockholders, government, creditors, and the general public
7. The design of the system for the processing of transactions, the keeping of records, and the maintenance of internal checks
8. The feedback of the quantified, classified, and recorded data (internal reporting)
9. The projection of transactions (budgeting)
10. The functional studies of the organization (management services)[4]

Points 1 through 5 are really a more detailed description of the functions contained in the AICPA definition; points 6 through 10 show a wide expansion of the definition.

The narrow AICPA definition emphasizes the traditional score-keeping or record-keeping functions of the accountant. This book accepts the contemporary conception of accounting presented above. However, this broader scope of accounting is not entirely applicable directly to financial accounting; only points 1 through 7 that pertain directly to financial accounting will be considered in this book.

A transaction, a key concept in the definition of accounting, is an economic event or condition. Accountants select certain transactions as the basis for an entry in accounting records. An external (or business) transaction arises out of an event involving relationships between the enterprise (or accounting unit) and an outside person or firm. An internal (sometimes called an accounting) transaction arises out of the recognition of a condition; examples are periodic adjustments of money values.

The basic mechanics of accounting involves the recognition and recording of transactions. A transaction by definition exists, and is recorded when (1) its monetary values and (2) the amounts can be determined, when there is (3) sufficient evidence to verify its recording and it is (4) customary to do so.

The definition of accounting is the framework within which the

---

[4]This definition is based upon that found in Eric L. Kohler, *A Dictionary For Accountants*, 4th ed. (Englewood Cliffs, New Jersey: Prentice-Hall, Inc., 1970), pp. 7–8.

accounting profession operates. In the remaining sections of the chapter, the reader learns the ways in which the profession has been built around this framework.

The Purposes of Accounting and an Accounting (Information) System

Accounting extracts economic data from all parts of the enterprise, transforms these data into information for each company function or department, and integrates such information into reports and statements about the entire organization. The larger, more diverse, and more complex the enterprise, the more essential become the accounting controls. On the other hand, the manager of a small business may be very successful with a minimum of accounting routines since he personally can handle all activities of the firm.

It is possible to compare the accounting function to the human body's nervous system. If a person picks up a hot dish, the nervous system relays a message to the brain that pain is being suffered, and the body moves to stop the pain by dropping the dish.

Certain aspects of the accounting systems relay analogous messages to the corporate brain. For example, standard costing procedures will reveal any departure from standard. Thus, the accounting system alerts the manager to a deviation from planned results.

Human activity can be divided into at least three levels. There are accounting counterparts for each level. The lowest levels are mechanistic and routine. In a person, activities such as breathing and circulation of the blood are maintained subconsciously. In an organization, accounting carried on at this level is a recording function: routine data accumulation or bookkeeping. This is sometimes referred to as the *scorekeeping function* of accounting. The upper limit of this level might be thought of as learned automatic responses (equivalent to the body's nervous system reaction to the hot dish). Accounting (for example, standard cost systems) can function as this kind of automatic routine for certain organizational activities.

Systematic patterns of behavior, such as walking or talking, constitute a second level of human activity. Once these patterns of behavior are learned, the process continues with very little conscious effort as long as the body continues to function normally. Much of routine accounting also follows systematic patterns. Classifying and summarizing data and the preparation of conventional accounting statements through computerized bookkeeping systems are examples of this level of accounting activity.

The highest level of human activity involves conscious thought. This level extends from recognizing a problem situation to integrating one's experiences to interpret significant relationships and using insight and judgment to make a decision. Accounting's counterpart of these activities is the interpretation function, sometimes referred to as the *attention-directing* and *problem-solving* functions. These functions consist of extracting from the accounting data processing system the information necessary to raise substantive issues and to act in resolving problems.

Accounting as a control mechanism or information system can be performed at many levels; at a recording level, a processing level, or an interpretative level; or stated in another way, at a scorekeeping level, an attention-directing level, or a problem-solving or decision-making level. The importance of accounting (and accountants) in any organization can be correlated with that level of accounting which is given the most attention. If accounting is performed largely at the scorekeeping level, the contribution of accounting to the firm is probably minimal; if accounting is performed extensively at the problem-solving or decision-making level, its value is optimal.

How accountants report on the financial effects of past and future transactions and events is influenced, in part, by the nature or character of the organization being accounted for, and, perhaps more significantly, by the intended purposes of the financial reports rendered or the intended uses of the financial statements prepared. There are many possible major uses of the financial accounts. One of the best-known listings of such uses is the following:

1. As a report of stewardship
2. As a basis for fiscal policy
3. To determine the legality of dividends
4. As a guide to wise dividend action
5. As a basis for the granting of credit
6. As information for prospective investors in an enterprise
7. As a guide to the value of investments already made
8. As an aid to government supervision
9. As a basis for price or rate regulation
10. As a basis for taxation[5]

The purposes of an accounting system vary according to the levels at which its accountants operate. These, in turn, are dependent upon the variety of reports prepared, the kinds of entities involved, the different uses made of the reports, and, finally, the variety of abilities and skills demanded from accountants. What an accountant does is best understood in the light of what he has done in the past, a topic which is considered next.

[5]George O. May, *Financial Accounting* (New York: The Macmillan Company, 1943), p. 3. May (1875–1961) was widely known as the dean of American accounting. He became an English chartered accountant in 1897; joined the American firm of Price Waterhouse & Co.; and became senior partner in 1911.

The Historical Development of Accounting

As civilization has developed, so have the forms and functions of accounting. Progress of accounting in a particular nation seems to correlate directly with the extent to which that society develops its language, literature, and monetary system; fosters industry, commerce, and credit instruments; and recognizes ownership, particularly concepts of private property. Accounting exists in its most advanced state today where such instruments of civilization are most sophisticated.

The history of accounting, originating with the recording or bookkeeping function, is nearly as old as the history of man and has such antecedents as the art of writing, the use of arithmetic and of money, the development of commerce and trade, and the use of credit and capital. Of these antecedents, the use of arithmetic is probably the oldest and had its inception about 7000 B.C. in the era of Neolithic man. The oldest known accounting records are clay tablets about 5,000 years old, found in the Tigris-Euphrates Valley.

Before the introduction of coined money by the Greeks about 600 B.C., barter was the usual mode of trade, and domestic items such as animals, fields, or bushels of grain provided the units of exchange. The need for accounting developed as a society found it more and more useful and necessary to record producing and trading arrangements. The introduction of money facilitated trade, encouraged commerce, and fostered the growth of accounting.

For example, accounting was a fundamental factor in the achievements of the Roman Empire: The Roman legions maintained payroll and supporting records; the governmental machinery depended heavily upon accounting to control its people, territories, and other properties; the wealthy Roman general stressed accounting for stewardship purposes. In those centuries of signal fire and horseback communication, the Roman Empire's accounting system seems to be an important reason why the Roman way of life was superior to every other society of that time in administering both its military and its economic activities. Even Greek civilization, which was superior to Roman civilization in many other aspects, was clearly inferior in its administration and accounting. Stewardship accounting enabled Romans to know what they owned and what they were owed, as individuals and as an entire empire.

Both Roman and Greek accounting systems were individual records of receipts, payments, and debts. Neither civilization developed a general system of accounts because their principal purpose was to keep records of incoming and outgoing flows of tangible wealth rather than to measure income.

In the Middle Ages there was a rapid expansion of trade and com-

Figure 1–2　Stewardship accounting helped to create and expand the vast Roman Empire. (Encyclopedia Americana, international ed., vol. 23, p. 671, New York: Americana Corporation, 1965.)

merce as the serf replaced the slave, and economic expansion created a new focus on those engaged in trade and commerce. During this period the strategically located Italian city-states traded in the products of every country in the known world; merchants and traders organized partnerships and other agencies as well as credit instruments to facilitate their work.

In these city-states the supervision of long-term and long-distance enterprises, the development of manufacturing firms, and the need to control commerce and industry required more effective accounting than had existed previously. Records for inventories alone were inadequate for a complex, profit-motivated trading enterprise. A logical method of accounting, comprehensive enough to include all commercial transactions, was needed. Men developed double-entry bookkeeping before the fifteenth century to meet these accounting needs. Although refined by the double-entry system needs of economic enterprises of the following centuries, the double-entry system continues today as the analytical foundation of contemporary accounting.

The first book containing a complete description of double-entry bookkeeping appeared in Italy in 1494: *Everything about Arithmetic, Geometry, and Proportion*, by Luca Pacioli, a Franciscan friar, a university professor of mathematics, and a friend of Pope Julius II and Leonardo da Vinci. Although the accounting practice of almost 500 years ago bears little resemblance to that of today, Pacioli's ideas on such subjects as the accounting entity, consistency, materiality, and disclosure were similar to those of today. Accounting had developed to this extent at a time when chemistry consisted largely of alchemy; and when other modern disciplines, such as biology and medicine, effectively did not exist.

The Italian accounting and business practice rapidly spread to the rest of Europe, notably England. As the English and other Europeans expanded their trade, they developed more complex business institutions comparable to our present-day corporations to implement this commerce. For example, stockholders (rather than a few partners) owned the East India Companies of several European countries. Historians agree that the development of such concerns with their large profits was a key factor in creating the British Empire and other colonial powers. These institutions as well as the Industrial Revolution placed the greatest possible emphasis on the development of improved accounting systems. How else could the administrators of these trading companies exercise control over their agents in many lands, agents unable to return home for years if not decades? How else could the owners of manufacturing firms in the cottage industries supervise operations of employees working in their own cottages? By 1700 a London merchant wrote: "It is just as impossible for a merchant to be prosperous in trade without a knowledge of accounting as for a mariner to sail a ship to all parts of the globe without a knowledge of navigation."

More complex enterprises evolved from early trading and manufacturing companies: in England the limited company, and in the United States the corporation. Such companies made it possible to separate the ownership of a company from the management; in other words, the company's investors could divorce themselves from the operation of the company. These companies required a new kind of accounting. Companies had long engaged in examining and verifying their accounting records. The limited company and the corporation required an independent audit by an independent auditor not affiliated with the company, to ensure the stockholders (or the creditors) that the managers had done what they said they had.

The independent auditors came from the same country as the investors and/or the home offices of the companies; the audits were conducted in the country in which the business or office was located. A major consequence was the improvement of accounting in the foreign investment company and country to the higher standards that were practiced in the investing company and country. For several centuries when the European nations, notably Great Britain, dominated world trade, the independent auditors came from Europe. In the United States and such British Commonwealth countries as Australia, Canada, and New Zealand where Britain had major investments and interests, the auditors came from Great Britain, particularly Scotland. These auditors often spent months or years conducting the audits; many emigrated and became leading accountants and citizens of the investment country. In its most significant aspects, the development of American accounting (or for that matter, the accounting of India or Hong Kong) is due to the influence of these exported Scottish and English accountants. "It has been said by those who use Scotland's three great exports, golf, whiskey, and accountants, that the rewards of its golf are instant frustrations, the effects of its whiskey pass with the night, but the imprint of its accountants remains forever."[6]

In the twentieth century, American trade and investments have been or are the major force in much of the world. American auditors and American accounting have become prime exports. As British investments declined in Australia and other commonwealth nations, the influence of American capital and accounting grew. Great Britain and Italy now find that the development of American-oriented accounting practice parallels the rise of American-oriented industry and commerce within their own borders.

As the profession developed, it became necessary to regulate those who could practice accounting. The first college of accountants was located in Venice (about 1600); students had to undergo a six-year apprenticeship and pass an examination before graduating. In England in 1844, after a number of financial crises and bankruptcies, Parliament passed its first Companies Act which specified a yearly audit; this was the first of many governmental statutes and laws in many countries designed to improve accounting practice. In 1854, a society of Scottish accountants was formed, the first private professional organization to screen applicants before admitting them to membership and the first to have a significant influence on and responsibility for improving the standards and practice of accounting applicants before admitting them to membership. In the

[6]See T. A. Wise, "The Very Private World of Peat, Marwick, Mitchell," *Fortune* (July 1, 1966), p. 91.

United States today, the AICPA prepares and grades a uniform examination which is administered in conjunction with 54 state, district, and territorial boards of accounting twice a year to those aspiring to be Certified Public Accountants.

In the twentieth century there have been many significant influences on American accounting. Consolidations and mergers are increasing the complexity of enterprise structure. Wartime federal government price control and cost inspection also gave impetus to accounting. Government regulation of accounting began with the Hepburn Act in 1906. The act provided for uniform systems of accounts for United States railroads. Later came the effects of taxation, the Securities Exchange Act in the 1930s, and the adoption in 1933 of standards of accounting disclosure by the New York Stock Exchange.

Within accounting, there is a movement to emphasize flow statements: first the income statement, and now the working capital-flow statement (commonly referred to as the "fund" statement) and the cash-flow statement; and to deemphasize stock statements such as the balance sheet.

Educating professional accountants at universities and colleges, particularly the state universities, is emphasized. The AICPA and other accounting organizations strive to improve all aspects of accounting, particularly practice. Nonaccountants and nonbusinessmen too are becoming increasingly concerned with accounting. These are but a few of the many forces that are directly changing accounting. There are also forces external to the accounting discipline which force it to change. Such forces are most easily understood by examining the interaction of accounting with other disciplines.

How Accounting Interacts with Other Disciplines

As a discipline, accounting has been able to develop concepts that permit analysis of great masses of raw data which are useful in assessing both the status of the enterprise and the extent of its progress. Some of these concepts are indigenous to accounting; others are based upon different disciplines. Examples of the latter are the influence of law on the accounting concept of ownership and the close relationship between the accounting and economic concepts of income. Upon the basis of these borrowed concepts, which require considerable modification before they can be used, accounting must be considered a synthesized discipline.

Accounting, as is usual for a social science of an applied nature, overlaps and intermingles with many other disciplines. As the common information system of every type of enterprise—individual, business, or otherwise—it provides a technology suitable for making quantitative the inherent interrelations between enterprise capital and income; it systematically makes available to many interested parties significant data relevant to the resources and productive achievements of enterprises; and in so doing, it serves the public interest as an instrument of control. One accounting scholar suggests that at least three basic inquiries into other disciplines are necessary in order to study the foundations of accounting measurement: (1) *economic*, to determine what is measured; (2) *mathematical*, to illustrate the logical structure; and (3) *behavioral*, to examine the ways in which accountants and decision makers interact with each other through the measurement systems.[7]

Economics Because the information furnished by accountants is basically economic in nature, the relationship between accounting and economics is necessarily an indispensable one.[8] Both mine much the same raw material, namely economic events; both study the activities of individuals and business firms and are concerned with such concepts as income, expenditures, profits, capital, value, and prices. As one prominent economist, K. E. Boulding, has put it, "many of the basic concepts of economics are, in fact, derived from accounting practice, and many accounting practices have been devised in an attempt to answer what are essentially economic questions. The concept of profit (income), for instance, is essentially an accounting concept. A large amount of the activity of accountants consists in the attempt to measure it. The concept of profit (income) is likewise fundamental to economics."[9]

So important is this relationship between economics and accounting that the AICPA, in a 1967 study, *Horizons for a Profession*, concluded that

The beginning CPA who does not understand the tools of economic analysis and who is not able to deal with economic concepts in prose, diagrams, and mathematical equations can play only a limited role as an advisor to management.

The beginning CPA should . . . have knowledge of the . . . economic forces that affect the firm, their effects, and their interactions. For example, he should be aware of the relationship of price to demand, of the factor of elasticity, of the effect of . . . degrees of competition. He should understand cost behavior and the various concepts of cost (marginal, implicit, etc.), labor productivity, the theory and philosophy of government policies toward business.

[7]Yuji Ijiri, *The Foundations of Accounting Measurement: A Mathematical, Economic and Behavioral Inquiry* (Englewood Cliffs, New Jersey: Prentice-Hall, Inc., 1967) p. x.
[8]Most accounting courses first appeared in university curriculums as economics department offerings, and often in liberal arts colleges they are still listed this way.
[9]K. E. Boulding, "Economics and Accounting: The Uncongenial Twins," in W. T. Baxter and Sidney Davidson (eds.), *Studies in Accounting Theory* (Homewood, Illinois: Richard D. Irwin, Inc., 1962), p. 44.

These factors must be understood conceptually as they affect decision and policy making within the firm, and conversely as those decisions and policies in turn affect the economy.

Within this conceptual foundation of microeconomics, the beginning CPA should be familiar with the economists' approaches to analyses involving, for example, price equilibrium in relation to supply and demand behavior, and marginal revenue and cost behavior.[10]

The study indicates also that the junior accountant "should know some of the specific instruments of government control such as anti-trust machinery, regulation of public utilities, prohibitions on price discrimination, and restrictions on international capital movements through such means as the equalization tax and the taxation of the earnings of foreign subsidiaries."[11]

Microeconomics provides accounting with much of the theoretical foundation for its analytical techniques; macroeconomics provides accounting with perspective concerning its concepts and measurements. So closely interwoven are the two disciplines that it would be difficult to overstate the significance of economics to accounting.[12]

Law Another discipline, almost as closely related, is law. A knowledge of law, especially as it bears upon business, is necessary for an accountant to measure practically any item that is reported in financial statements. He must understand the legal implications of cash, receivables, patents, investments, plant, and equities. To express his opinion ("the auditor's certificate") about financial statements, he should consider the legal significance of numerous organizational arrangements (for example, corporation charters; union contracts; and lease, trust, and debt agreements) which are not explicitly measured and reported in the statements. An accountant finds legal knowledge vital in dealing with governmental agencies such as the Internal Revenue Service, the Securities and Exchange Commission (SEC), and the public service commissions.

Communications When 1,890 prominent accountants ranked 53 different subjects (including many accounting ones) in the order of their importance, only four nonaccounting subjects were ranked among the top ten: written and oral English ranked first; introduction to economics, introduction to business law, and algebra were among those ranked from fifth to tenth. Accounting basically is a

---

[10]Robert H. Roy and James H. MacNeill, *Horizons for a Profession* (New York: AICPA, 1967), p. 227.
[11]*Ibid.*
[12]Rather ironically, many economists, whether macro- or micro-, tend to depend on accounting information for their studies; yet it is not uncommon to find that such economists have never studied accounting.

communication system which conveys information as much by language as by figures. A competent accountant must transmit his information almost as much orally as in a written form. The successful accountant is one who spends at least as much time explaining his measurements as he does in making them.

Mathematics and statistics As stated earlier, mathematicians were instrumental centuries ago in setting up double-entry bookkeeping which underlies contemporary accounting. Until recently, however, little new mathematics had been introduced into accounting apart from a few isolated topics such as actuarial science (discussed in Chapter 2). Accounting, especially since World War II, has increased its use of mathematics and statistics.

This is most evident with the problems of sampling encountered both in the installation of financial information systems and in auditing, generally. The auditor who decided which of the thousands of accounts he should verify personally found that it was possible and worthwhile to present quantitative evidence about the accuracy and reliability of whatever sampling he undertook.

Accounting systems too have often incorporated mathematically derived decision rules, especially when these rules can be computer-programmed. In accounting systems work, particularly computerized information systems, accountants must work with models. Here knowledge of mathematics, statistics, and probabilities is essential.

Accounting practice becomes increasingly more quantitative; but even if certain quantitative techniques are utilized only occasionally in accounting practice, still an understanding of the techniques is essential to an accountant interested in maximizing the effectiveness of the accounting information system.

Behavioral sciences Although accounting is a discipline which services individuals as well as organizations, it is at the organizational level, especially in business enterprises, that accounting has been developed to the greatest extent. Consequently, it has proved to be most effective in such applications; and in these it warrants advanced study. If the United States were still a nation of country general stores and city "Mama and Papa" grocery stores, accounting would certainly be a less important discipline. The development of more extensive and sophisticated organizations has lifted accounting to its current level of prominence.[13]

Before there can be a system of accounting, there must be some conceptualization of the organization. The conceptualization of the organization which has been central (but was not essential) to the development of the financial accounting model is directly related to

[13]Perhaps it explains too why Aldous Huxley could imagine in his acclaimed science-fiction novel, *Brave New World,* that accountants would take over the world.

the "theory of the firm" of classical economics. It can be summarized as follows: The chief objective of a business enterprise is the maximization of the economic profits of the firm. Furthermore, this goal can be divided into subgoals for the various company divisions, and when these subgoals are additive, so that when the department maximizes its profit, the company maximizes its profits. Participants in the organization are motivated primarily by economic factors. The objective of management and ownership is to maximize the profits of the firm, and the firm's authority is based on its ability to provide economic rewards to the participants. Thus, the primary function of accounting measurement is to aid in the firm's process of profit maximization.

The traditional concept of the organization is basically economic, and its lack of emphasis on human behavior has resulted in numerous criticisms. These criticisms question the adequacy of economic profits as the sole significant explanation of an organization's behavior, and suggest that limitations on the decision-making process result in behavior that is best described as "satisficing" rather than "maximizing." Behavioral scientists have contributed to new conceptualizations of organization theories, which in turn have already exerted major influence in developing managerial accounting models and which promise to affect future financial accounting models in a major way. Behavioral science studies of communication, decision making, innovation, conflict, leadership, authority and accountability, learning, perception, and creativity are invaluable to accounting and accountants for the insight they provide.

In addition to its ties with economics, law, mathematics and statistics, and the behavioral sciences, accounting shares a common interest with any discipline that is organizationally oriented. Management, marketing, production, and finance are a few of these. The field of industrial engineering also overlaps considerably with accounting, particularly internal accounting. Both fields share similar problem interests and techniques, especially those that relate to computers and operations research. Also, both disciplines have a common interest in the newly emerging field of management science.

The test of any discipline is its usefulness to society; consequently, an examination of professional accounting seems to be in order. No glimpse of the accountant's world is complete without at least a working knowledge of his literature and of his professional organizations which dictate the modes and pace and direction of change.

The Accounting Profession(s)
For accounting professionals or practitioners the primary fields of interest are roughly classified as external and internal. In external accounting—usually considered to be the public practice of CPAs—

the accountant's focus of attention may be regarded as something of a "bird's-eye view." External accounting is akin to macroeconomics; like the macroeconomist, the external accountant measures many enterprises (even if, unlike the macroeconomist, he does not aggregate the measurements of all the firms in the economy). Internal accounting is generally considered to be the practice of accounting within a single enterprise, and is increasingly referred to as managerial accounting. The focus of the internal accountant is the "worm's-eye view." Internal accounting is akin to microeconomics; both measure the activities of segments of the single firm.

Usually governmental accounting has been regarded as a third field. Governmental accountants may be either externally oriented (the Federal Bureau of Investigation, the Internal Revenue Service), or internally oriented (the Defense Department, Atomic Energy Commission), or both externally and internally oriented (General Accounting Office). Actually the justification for classifying governmental accountants separately from other accountants (at least internal accountants) would seem to lie in what measurements are made, rather than whether measurements are made for one or many enterprises. Measurements of profits, earnings, or income are not customarily made for most government units (except for those operating as business firms), whereas such measurements often are regarded as the most important criterion of a business enterprise. This distinction fails to take into consideration that the accountants of many nonbusiness and nonindustrial enterprises other than governmental ones do not make earnings measurements. There was a time when few accountants were employed by these institutions. But today, since insurance companies, colleges, universities, foundations, and banks control much of the nation's wealth, they have learned to appreciate the value of using the accounting measurements of other enterprises and now use them for their own activities.

Within these two broad dichotomies, external or internal focus and profit or nonprofit measurements, there are many accountants who specialize mostly in one of four subareas: auditing, cost accounting, information systems (which includes computers), and income tax.

Public accounting Accountants in public practice are usually certified public accountants (CPAs) in the United States, Japan, and the Philippines; and chartered accountants in Canada, Great Britain, India, and many other countries. A certified public accountant in the United States is a professional accountant who has passed the uniform CPA examination (uniform throughout the country) and met the experience, educational, and other requirements stipulated by his state board of accountancy.

Although CPAs are sometimes involved in such publicity-attracting duties as the Miss America contest point tabulations and Academy Awards balloting, their services are nearly always much more substantive, and perhaps their work is almost as interesting. CPAs do not spend all of their time working with numbers; they have frequent conferences with clients about all sorts of business problems, and often travel to many parts of the country to observe the operations of different enterprises.

According to a recent AICPA study, the following are some of the many things that a CPA might commonly do in the course of his working days:

1. Set up or revise an accounting system for a business
2. Prepare plans for an audit
3. Discuss with a client the information obtained in an audit
4. Help prepare papers for registration of a stock issue with the SEC
5. Help a manufacturer develop a computerized cost accounting system which would give the required information for a government contract
6. Assist a client in obtaining a bank loan
7. Attend a committee meeting of his state professional society to discuss the proper solution of a new accounting problem
8. Plan a system of internal control designed to prevent fraud or embezzlement
9. Testify in court as an expert witness
10. Prepare a client's tax return or discuss his problems with a representative of the Internal Revenue Service
11. Prepare a monthly financial statement for a small business
12. Advise a client on his needs for working capital over the coming year
13. Review the financial report of the local community service organization

A CPA may become a specialist and engage only in certain kinds of accounting work. The three most widely recognized specialities (and most CPA firms of any size are organized along these lines into three sections or divisions) are: auditing, tax services, and management services. Within these areas a CPA can specialize further. An auditor could specialize in auditing certain industries (for example, distilleries or airlines); a tax specialist could specialize in gift and estate taxes or foreign taxes; and a CPA in management services could concentrate on actuarial consulting (for example, pension funds) or computer applications.

Typically a CPA works as an auditor; he examines financial reports and the data on which they are based. Although an auditor does engage in routine procedures such as proving cash balances and determining whether amounts owed by customers are correct and whether physical inventories actually correspond to what is stated in the books, the major part of his auditing duties is to determine whether the financial reports have been prepared in accordance with generally accepted accounting principles. He must exercise considerable professional judgment in making an audit. He or his firm must express a formal opinion as to whether the financial statements fairly present the financial condition of the client and the results of operations for the period covered. (The nature of auditing will be discussed further in Chapter 12.)

Whatever the scope and size of the business, accounting work in taxation requires considerable knowledge and skill. In complicated tax situations, there can be honest differences of professional opinion, and it is common for the federal government to be represented by Internal Revenue Service officials (who are usually accountants) and the taxpayer to be represented by a CPA and his firm. Usually such differences are settled by conferences, but sometimes they must be adjudicated in the courts. In recent decades, CPA tax specialists have come increasingly to advise businessmen concerning the probable tax consequences of contemplated business decisions. There may be substantial tax effects differences between using accelerated and straight-line depreciation methods, or between purchasing and leasing machinery and buildings.

A CPA in management services is engaged in business or management consulting. The scope and concept of management services differs considerably, even among large CPA firms, but generally in all firms such services constitute an ever-increasing percentage of the total services rendered. A CPA in management services may deal with marketing, organizational planning, personnel and recruiting, production, or any other type of problem that exists in an enterprise. Traditionally, however, management service CPAs have done most of their work in the areas of budgeting and cost accounting. With the advent of computers, they have expanded their areas of interest from control and systems to decision making. They employ recently developed techniques, commonly referred to as operations research, in which a number of different disciplines and mathematical and statistical models are used to illustrate relationships and to define and solve problems. A recent AICPA brochure indicates that management services may consist of any of the following duties: long-range planning, executive compensation, work simplification, job evaluation, plant layout, materials handling, shop methods, pricing policies and market analysis, financing, estate taxes (and estate planning), reorganizations and mergers, installation of pension and profit-sharing plans, renegotiation and termination of government contracts. This list, however, does not include all the services rendered by the management services divisions of CPA firms.

As an independent contractor, the practicing CPA finds himself working in an environment where his ethical and legal responsibilities are of the utmost importance at every stage of his work. This is in contrast to the internal accountant whose professional responsibilities, both social and legal, may be concerned chiefly with developing standards of behavior only in respect to his own company. The principal distinction between an internal accountant and a public accountant is not so much a matter of different duties but rather a difference in the type of responsibilities undertaken. The CPA has concentrated his concern traditionally on a company's public reports, such as the annual audit. The internal accountant (controller, cost accountant or analyst, or systems analyst) has ordinarily focused his attention primarily on accounting reports to be used within the company. It is dangerous to overemphasize this distinction because practicing CPAs (for example, in management services) have long been consulted on internal accounting problems; and internal auditors have been most helpful to independent CPAs in the conduct of public audits. Particularly in recent years this distinction has broken down as the duties of both external and internal accountants have expanded. Nevertheless, this crude distinction still is a reasonably valid one.

Internal accounting In general, the duties of an internal accountant are designed to accomplish any or all of the following objectives. His job is to provide management with the information needed for making intelligent decisions. He monitors the company's compliance with government regulations. In addition, he tries to increase the firm's efficiency and to prevent fraud. It is his primary responsibility to aid in the control of costs and in the meeting of planned profitability margins, as well as to establish the financial procedures and to measure and report the results of operations. The chief accountant for a company is usually called controller, treasurer, or financial vice-president. Other titles held by those who may be regarded as accountants are: assistant controller, chief accountant, plant accountant, internal auditor, systems analyst, financial analyst, budget accountant, cost accountant, computer specialist, and data processing specialist.

According to several surveys, more corporation chief executives in recent years have accounting-financial backgrounds than any other type of training. Many of the most prominent and successful corporations in the United States have (or had) accountants as presidents or chairmen of the board. Included are American Airlines, Caterpillar Tractor, Chrysler, Consolidated Edison, Crucible Steel, Ford, General Electric, General Foods, General Motors, General Telephone & Electronics, International Business Machines, International Telephone & Telegraph, Kennecott Copper, and 3-M. There are many more.

Accounting executives are forced, in the proper performance of their work, to develop a broad view of all the firm's operations. Their intimate and critical knowledge of every aspect of the business enables them to exert more major influence on decision making than perhaps anyone else except chief executives.

In addition, the kinds of major company decisions made in recent years have enhanced the position of financial officers. Decisions emphasizing financial factors and information have become much more important than formerly. More and more companies concentrate on cost-cutting programs; strive to raise or maintain their profit margins and the return on their invested capital; are forced to give major attention to the increasing complexity of the tax aspects of major corporate decisions; expand through corporate mergers and acquisitions and other ways which, in turn, have increased their demand for capital. Often an accountant's special area of interest plus his general knowledge as the company's information chief offers the critical background that a corporation seeks for its top executive.

The Activities of the Professional Organizations

There are numerous professional accounting organizations in the United States and abroad. The four most prominent organizations based in the United States are: the AICPA, the AAA, the National Association of Accountants, and the Financial Executives Institute. Although the AICPA is the most authoritative of the four, all have significant impact on the evolution of accounting and therefore merit the reader's consideration.

Each organization strives to improve accounting in numerous ways in accordance with its distinctive orientation. Each advises and consults on proposed governmental legislation which will have an impact upon accounting; each organization tries to improve its liaison with the principal users of accounting information, particularly those who have an organizational identity and a business orientation (for example, financial analysts, governmental agencies, bankers, and stock brokers). Each conducts liaison activity with the other three, as well as with other accounting organizations in the United States and abroad (for example, The Institute of Internal Auditors, the Federal Government Accountants Association, The Canadian Institute of Chartered Accountants, and The Institute of Chartered Accountants in England and Wales).

Each concerns itself with the professional needs of its members in many ways. The organizations publish magazines, on a monthly or quarterly basis, which contain articles on current professional issues; conduct courses and conferences designed to improve the professional qualifications of members; and sponsor a number of published research projects on various aspects of accounting. Each organization also devotes considerable effort toward improving the qualifications of those persons entering the accounting profession.

The oldest, largest, and most influential of these four organizations is the AICPA (founded as the American Association of Public Accountants in 1887). With its 80,000 membership limited to CPAs (except for international associates), it administers, through its Board of Examiners and Examinations Division, semiannual uniform examinations (in accounting practice, accounting theory, auditing, and business law) to qualified applicants for the CPA in all 50 states, the District of Columbia, Puerto Rico, Guam, and the Virgin Islands. The education and experience requirements for certification are specified by each state through law and its quasi-governmental body, the state board of accountancy. (See Appendix D for further details.) The AICPA also has put out numerous publications on accounting practice.

The AAA was founded in 1916 by university instructors of accounting, and it continues to be concerned chiefly with accounting education and university research. In addition to its regular members, it has several thousand associate student members. Among its relatively few publications, its 1940 monograph, *An Introduction to Corporate Accounting Standards* by Professors W. A. Paton and A. C. Littleton, which continues to be printed and studied, has been more influential than any other single accounting publication.

The National Association of Accountants (formerly the National Association of Cost Accountants) was organized in 1919. The organization's principle focus is internal accounting. An organization with a similar dedication is the Financial Executives Institute (formerly the Controllers Institute) which dates back to 1931. Its membership is limited to top corporate financial executives, such as financial vice-presidents, controllers, and treasurers.

An accountant is active in one or more professional organizations throughout his career for at least two reasons. First, he has a professional obligation to provide assistance in further developing accounting; second, the organization provides the individual (particularly through its journal) with an opportunity to continue his necessary lifelong professional education.

Periodical and Other Literature of Accounting: An Introduction

The earliest regular accounting periodical was the accountant's newspaper, *The Accountant,* which was started in 1874 in London. It is issued weekly and is distributed internationally. Although not true of *The Accountant,* most accounting periodicals are the official publications of the various accounting organizations. Because the journals speak for the entire organization, they are authoritative and often conservative as well. Some of the leading *financial* accounting periodicals in the English-speaking countries today, together with their sponsoring organizations and the year originated, are:

Accountancy (The Institute of Chartered Accountants in England and Wales, 1889)[14]
The Accountant's Magazine (The Institute of Chartered Accountants of Scotland, 1897)
Certified Accountants Journal (Association of Certified and Corporate Accountants, England, 1905)
The Journal of Accountancy (AICPA, 1905)
The Accountants' Journal (New Zealand Society of Accountants, 1922)
Canadian Chartered Accountant (The Canadian Institute of Chartered Accountants, 1911)
The Australian Accountant (Australian Society of Accountants, 1936)
The Chartered Accountant in Australia (The Institute of Chartered Accountants in Australia, 1930)

A closer look at two major accounting journals provides a feel for the different content and interest of accounting publications.

The Journal of Accountancy, aimed at the practicing CPA, carries official releases by the AICPA committees; important court decisions; trends in accounting practice; pending tax bills; reviews of accounting books and articles; questions and discussions of tax, accounting education, management services offered by CPAs, and the problems of implementing accounting principles. A CPA examination supplement to *The Journal* is issued twice a year and contains the text of a particular CPA examination together with unofficial answers to the questions. The major portion of each issue of *The Journal* is devoted to five or six articles of concern to practitioners. The articles range from accounting subjects of general interest (for example, development of an accounting principle or implementing an accounting practice) to those of interest to practitioners only (for example, how to administer a CPA office). Although *The Journal* contains much contemporary information on accounting, this information is essentially practical, is basically descriptive rather than theoretical, and is written primarily by practitioners.

The Accounting Review, a quarterly publication of the AAA, contains articles that are speculative and analytical, that almost always are theoretical, and that often are controversial. Although the sponsoring organization's membership consists of more than three times as many practitioners as teachers, most of *The Review* articles are written by the latter. Unlike *The Journal of Accountancy,* which has many counterparts, *The Review* for many years was the only promi-

---

[14]A new publication, *Accounting and Business Research,* was started by this organization in 1970.

nent journal of its type in the world. An English journal with a similar mission, *Accounting Research,* was published for 10 years ending in 1958. In the 1960s two new journals with similar objectives appeared: the semiannual *Journal of Accounting Research,* under the joint auspices of two universities (one American and one English), and the Australian biannual or semiannual, *Abacus.*

In the U.S. CPAs are organized by state, as well as nationally; nearly all the state organizations include "state society" in their titles. Each "state society" issues newsletters to its members; a few also issue monthly or quarterly journals containing articles of some quality. In addition, all the eight largest CPA firms issue periodicals that contain articles. The *Financial Executive* (published by the Financial Executives Institute) and *Management Accounting* (published by the National Association of Accountants) are prominent journals that contain articles on financial accounting (although they do not emphasize it). Also of interest is the American quarterly, *The Accountants Digest,* which publishes reviews of accounting articles and books from all countries. The *Accountants' Index,* an international bibliography of accounting articles and books, is published every two years by the AICPA, every year beginning with 1971.

Students of any profession must be familiar with its technical publications in addition to its periodicals. In a large number of countries (for example, West Germany) and for a few United States industries such as railroading and insurance, accounting is prescribed to a large extent by statute law. Accountants and accounting students must study the relevant statutes since the relevant professional accounting literature is likely to be limited. In other countries (for example, Great Britain) the latitude given to professional organizations has been very broad; the statutes deal in minimum reporting standards only. In such countries the literature of the professional organizations is exhaustive because the organizations often are directly engaged in raising accounting standards.[15]

The United States government has allowed more authority over financial reporting to be held by professional accounting organizations than has any other government. In acts of the 1930s the United States Government established the SEC with the authority to formulate accounting principles and practices for corporations whose stocks are listed with stock exchanges. This commission has permitted the AICPA to establish principles and standards of practice, retaining for itself an implicit veto power over any action of the AICPA. Both groups, the Commission and the Institute, issue pronouncements on accounting. The SEC has issued over 100 pronouncements

---

[15] Recently proposed amendments to the Companies Act of Great Britain would legislate accounting principles.

since 1937; these Accounting Series Releases are most often terse statements of Commission policy on technical accounting questions. The AICPA in a comparative manner, has issued eight terminology bulletins, 51 research bulletins (between 1939 and 1960), and about 20 *APB* Opinions since 1960. In the last decade, a dozen Accounting Research Studies have been published; these were commissioned to investigate problem areas before the issuance of an *APB* Opinion. Most of these monographs, ranging up to several hundred pages each, have had no more than two authors, whereas all other statements are committee efforts. Since the opinions and bulletins constitute the official policy announcements of the AICPA, they are, for most practical purposes, binding on all practicing CPAs. All other accounting periodicals and books in the United States either support these pronouncements or argue against them; consequently, the accounting student, as well as the practicing accountant, needs to be familiar with them. Other practitioner's organizations similar to the AICPA, publish policy statements in other countries.

In the United States the AAA, apart from *The Review,* has published both committee statements and individually authored monographs. Although these statements and monographs often do not directly influence the current accounting practice, their chief value is in structuring controversial ideas and theories to provide the basis for improving accounting practice. For example, as previously mentioned, the 1940 monograph, *An Introduction to Corporate Accounting Standards,* probably was the major influence on contemporary accounting practice in the decades after World War II. For those with a background in accounting there are several books on accounting that have been very influential, in addition to the periodicals, reports, and monographs mentioned.

Many recent accounting publications have stressed the impact of the computer in both accounting practice and research.

The Impact of Computers on Accounting
The computer promises to change our lives more drastically than the automobile, and at a much faster rate. This is particularly so for accountants whose measurements, systems, and reports have already changed much since the rather recent advent of the computer. Further change in accounting from "computer power" is anticipated. In every year since 1955, the number of installed computer systems in the United States has doubled: in 1956, the number was approximately 500; in 1975, it is likely to grow to 250,000.

Of the producing, selling, and staff functions of an enterprise, accounting was the first to utilize computers, and the one most affected.

In 1941, as indicated earlier, the AICPA defined accounting as the recording, classifying, and summarizing of financial transactions and interpreting these results. Although more contemporary definitions have expanded the scope of accounting, the AICPA definition is still the one most widely accepted, despite some disagreement over whether accounting includes an interpretive function.

Traditionally, the recording function means to write or enter in a book for the purpose of maintaining evidence. In accounting, this is essentially a clerical activity of preparing journal entries. When a bookkeeping system is computerized, the journals become stacks of punched cards (or tapes), which then may be transferred (posted later to tapes, disks, or drums which are the ledgers of this system). Data are transferred from a source document to a card by a keypunch operator or an optical scanner; thus the operator (or machine) performs the initial recording (bookkeeping) function. In a completely automated system all journals and ledgers are on the computer; in a semiautomatic system some journals and ledgers are kept manually while others are on the computer. However, even under a completely automated bookkeeping system, not all entries are based on standard source documents. For example, to make adjusting entries, the accountant must determine the entry and give a keypunch operator the entry to be punched. Although such entries are the most significant aspect of the recording function, the overall effect of the computer has been to relieve the accountant of most of the clerical work of his function.

Classification, the second traditional function, is the grouping of transactions or accounts under groups or classes which have systematic relations usually founded in common properties. Posting from journals to ledgers is one kind of classifying. With an automated system, the computer does the posting. However, as mentioned earlier, for a nonstandard transaction or for an internal or other transaction where there is no document as such, the accountant must give the appropriate entry to the keypunch operator. For these transactions the accountant continues to classify as before.

A financial statement consists of financial items classified according to certain criteria. If the information needed for a financial statement is in a form usable by the computer (cards or tape), and the individual records are sufficiently basic so that they possess the needed criteria, the properly instructed computer can do the classifying for a financial statement. In many companies some financial statements are prepared on the computer; it seems likely that these numbers (of both companies and statements) will increase. With the computer the accountant is able to reduce significantly his clerical role in classifying.

The computer has taken over the summarizing function too, limited only by the extent to which the bookkeeping is automated. With a fully computerized bookkeeping system, contemporary accountants do little summarizing. If the data are in machine-usable form, the computer can be instructed to perform addition, subtraction, multiplication, and division operations. With such a system the only summarizing the accountant performs is to add a relatively few numbers together to determine a figure that is not the output of one of the company's standard EDP systems.

These basic processes for developing accounting data are largely scorekeeping functions. Despite the help of clerks and bookkeepers, the typical accountant has traditionally devoted much of his attention and effort to these scorekeeping functions, often leaving him little time for interpretation. Now the accountant is able to free himself largely of these functions because of the speed and accuracy of the computer in performing numerical calculations. The time it takes a computer to add, subtract, multiply, or divide numbers is measured in microseconds (0.000001 of a second) or nanoseconds (0.000000001 of a second). These properties permit the accountant to work with huge quantities of data (relative to what could be handled manually with the aid of clerks) and still produce more accurate information. The accountant can also find the time to provide many useful new reports and studies.

For example, once the journals are on card or tape in a computerized bookkeeping system, they are posted to the ledgers (usually on tape) by computers. The element of human error is virtually eliminated, and the posting process is completed much faster than in a manual system. This means that the books can be closed and monthly statements prepared within a few hours or days after the end of the month, whereas previously several weeks were required. With computerized payroll accounting, human errors in calculating gross pay and the various deductions are virtually eliminated (once the data enter the system correctly), payrolls can be processed in a fraction of the time previously required (including the allocation of labor to the proper accounts), and special payroll information (for example, the average number of sick days taken by employees) can be produced quickly and accurately.

All this means that the computer has largely freed the accountant from clerical functions (that had previously predominated in his day-to-day activity) so that he now is able to concern himself with the design of the information and control systems and with the interpreting function—and to do this more effectively since the computer provides him with more and better data. Since the advent of the computer, the accountant is able to increase the time he devotes to the attention-directing and the problem-solving activities of the interpreting function. For the latter the accountant provides information that enables the company to select one solution among several alternatives. Attention-directing activity spotlights, interprets, and explains operations that are in most need of attention. Problem-solving activity involves searching for alternatives, studying of probable consequences, and reaching an objective decision based on the alternatives and consequences. Just as the computer has already relieved accountants of the routine recording, classifying, and summarizing function, it is likely to relieve them too of much of the routine attention-directing activity, thus enabling them to specialize more effectively in the more difficult interpreting tasks, providing information for problem solving. In the light of these implications, many of the clerical procedures of the traditional accounting functions have not been included in this book.

Summary
The history of accounting is nearly as old as the history of man, and the progress of accounting seems to correlate directly with the progress of civilization. The most highly developed nations need and use the most highly developed accounting systems. The earliest known accounting records were etched on clay tablets some 5,000 years ago. As nations expanded through conquest and colonization, they introduced accounting systems into new territories, spreading accounting worldwide. The scientific advancement and global expansion of trade and manufacturing have fostered the development of complex organizations, particularly during the twentieth century. These organizations require a wide variety of accounting information and skilled accountants to prepare it.

As the profession grew, it became necessary to regulate the practice of accounting to ensure the preparation of accurate and authoritative accounting information. Educational institutions developed courses in accounting; governments passed laws designed to improve the practice of accounting; and accountants formed professional organizations to set standards of practice, sponsor research, and improve communications, both through regular meetings and through the publication of journals, research monographs, and other information bulletins.

Accounting as it is practiced today has developed as a synthesized discipline drawing on the concepts of economics, mathematics, law, the behavioral sciences, communications, and statistics. It is also closely associated with the organization fields of management, marketing, production, finance, and industrial engineering, to cite a few.

In a general sense, accounting is considered the recording, classifying, summarizing, and interpreting of financial transactions and events in monetary terms. The development of computers has aided accountants in accomplishing their routinized tasks. This book deals specifically with the following accounting functions: the timing of accounting through the recognition of transactions (economic events or conditions); the quantification of results in monetary units; the processing and recording of transactions; the systematic grouping and formal presentation of recorded data; the review of financial statements by an authoritative and publicly sanctioned body of public accountants; the reporting to external groups including stockholders, government, creditors, and the general public; and the design of the system for the processing of transactions, the keeping of records, and the maintenance of internal checks.

The professional accountant may have an internal or external focus and may make profit (net income) or nonprofit measurements. The internal accountant practices within a single organization and is often referred to as a managerial accountant. The external accountant (usually the public accountant) compiles information about many organizations. Within these rough divisions are narrower specialties such as auditing, cost accounting, tax, and information systems design.

Regardless of his focus, what he measures, or his specialty, the accountant is concerned with the use and users of accounting information. He attempts to record, classify, summarize, and report accounting information which aids in the decision making of all interested in an organization. The decision maker can evaluate accounting information on the basis of four criteria: chiefly its relevance but also its verifiability, its quantifiability, and its freedom from bias.

A Selection of Supplementary Readings

American Accounting Association: *A Statement of Basic Accounting Theory,* Evanston, Illinois: 1966, pp. 1–36.

American Institute of Certified Public Accountants: "Review and Résumé," Accounting Terminology Bulletin No. 1. In *APB Accounting Principles,* vol. 2. New York, pp. 9503–9509.

Ashworth, John: *Careers in Accounting,* New York: Henry Z. Walck, Inc., 1963.

Biegler, John C.: "Key Objectives in Financial Reporting," *The Illinois CPA,* summer 1966, pp. 7–12.

Campfield, William L.: "Toward Resolving the Controversy over the Role of Accounting," *The Illinois CPA,* autumn 1965, pp. 13–16.

Carey, John L.: "The Origins of Modern Financial Reporting," *The Journal of Accountancy,* September 1969, pp. 35–48.

————: *The Rise of the Accounting Profession,* 2 vols. New York: American Institute of Certified Public Accountants, 1969–1970.

Cashin, James A.: *Careers and Opportunities in Accounting,* New York: E. P. Dutton & Co., Inc., 1965.

"Committee on Accounting History," Stephen A. Zeff, chairman. Supplement to vol. XLV, *The Accounting Review,* Evanston, Illinois: American Accounting Association, 1970, pp. 53–64.

de Roover, Raymond: "The Development of Accounting Prior to Luca Pacioli According to the Account-Books of Medieval Merchants." In A. C. Littleton and B. S. Yamey, eds., *Studies in the History of Accounting,* Homewood, Illinois: Richard D. Irwin, Inc., 1956, pp. 114–174.

Dryden, R. G.: "The Ancient and Honourable Art of Accounting," *The Chartered Accountant in Australia,* February 1969, pp. 754–762.

Edwards, James Don: "The Origin of Accounting," *The New York Certified Public Accountant,* August 1965, pp. 595–600.

Felt, Howard M.: "The Effort and Authority of the AICPA in the Development of 'Generally-accepted Accounting Principles,'" *The International Journal of Accounting Education and Research,* spring 1968, pp. 11–27.

Fertig, Paul E.: "A Statement of Basic Accounting Theory," *The New York Certified Public Accountant,* September 1967, pp. 663–671.

Frishkoff, Paul: "Capitalism and the Development of Bookkeeping: A Reconsideration," *The International Journal of Accounting Education and Research,* spring 1970, pp. 29–37.

Green, David, Jr.: "Evaluating the Accounting Literature," *The Accounting Review,* January 1966, pp. 52–64.

Gynther, Merle M.: "Disclosure to Investors—For the Amateur or the Professional?" *The Australian Accountant,* May 1968, pp. 268–274.

Jack, Sybil M.: "An Historical Defence of Single Entry Book-keeping," *Abacus,* December 1966, pp. 137–158.

Kaulback, Frank S., and Lawrence L. Vance: "The American Accounting Association," Education and Professional Training, *The Journal of Accountancy,* April 1969, pp. 85–87.

May, George O.: *Financial Accounting,* New York: The Macmillan Company, 1943, pp. 1–13.

Mobley, Sybil C.: "The Challenges of Socio-economic Accounting," *The Accounting Review,* October 1970, pp. 762–768.

Moonitz, Maurice: "Three Contributions to the Development of Accounting Principles Prior to 1930," *Journal of Accounting Research,* spring 1970, pp. 145–155.

Parker, R. H.: "Accounting History: A Select Bibliography," *Abacus,* September 1965, pp. 62–84.

————: "Three Topics in the History of Accounting," *The Accountant,* February 19, 1966, pp. 218–222.

Roy, Robert H., and James H. MacNeill: *Horizons for a Profession,* New York: American Institute of Certified Public Accountants, 1967, pp. 1–21, 31–42, 95–133, 191–267.

Ruggles, Richard, and Nancy Ruggles: "The Evolution and Present State of National Income Accounting," *The International Journal of Accounting Education and Research,* fall 1968, pp. 1–16.

Savoie, Leonard M.: "Financial Communication: The Public's Right to Know," *Financial Executive,* December 1968, p. 20.

Taylor, R. Emmett: "Luca Pacioli." In A. C. Littleton and B. S. Yamey, eds., *Studies in the History of Accounting,* Homewood, Illinois: Richard D. Irwin, Inc., 1956, pp. 175–184.

Teichrow, Daniel: "Business Information Systems and Accounting," *The Ohio CPA*, summer 1966, pp. 95–105.

Winjum, James: "Accounting in Its Age of Stagnation," *The Accounting Review*, October 1970, pp. 743–761.

Questions

1–1   For each of the following types of organization name parties other than management and owners who would be interested in relevant accounting information. Give reasons.

a. Service station
b. Labor union
c. City government
d. State university
e. Private college
f. Charitable organizations
g. Public utility
h. Manufacturing corporation listed on New York Stock Exchange
i. Family-owned corporation
j. Insurance company
k. Church

1–2   In his book *The Skills of the Economist,* p. 94, Kenneth Boulding writes that "accounting . . . is largely a by-product of the tax system and corporation law." What evidence exists to support Professor Boulding's view? Use either conceptual or procedural illustrations.

1–3   Good accountants advocate conservative practices for solving accounting problems. Evaluate the above statement. (NOTE: Conservatism in accounting refers to caution in preparing financial statements. Under conservatism, ordinarily where two or more equally acceptable alternatives are available, the one that results in smaller earnings or in smaller evaluation of assets is chosen.)

1–4   *Collectively, lawyers and CPA's provide services which cut across almost every facet of human endeavor. It is no accident, then, considering the interrelationship of financial and legal aspects of our society, that lawyers and CPA's are often concerned with similar problems, although perhaps viewed from different perspectives.**

a. Identify specific problems with which both accountants and lawyers are concerned.
b. How do lawyers and accountants differ in perspective? Economists and accountants?

*National Conference of Lawyers and Certified Public Accountants, "Lawyers and Certified Public Accountants: A Study of Interprofessional Relations," *The Journal of Accountancy*, August 1970, p. 65.

1–5   *Attempts to simulate the world of affairs in academic institutions almost always lack the essential ingredient of reality: the teaching of experience in the classroom is relatively very inefficient, classroom presentation is likely to be descriptive and the experiences taught never to be duplicated by the students in future professional practice. On this account, and for the con-*

*verse reason that inductive and deductive knowledge are much more teach-
able and subsequently much more useful, subjects dependent upon experience are the first to be winnowed out in the manner described. . . . Medical
training depends less upon the clinic than it once did, and engineering art
has given way to engineering science to a remarkable degree. Accounting,
we believe, is on the threshold of changes of this kind.**

What are the implications of this view for a procedural approach toward
teaching and learning accounting?

*Roy and MacNeill, *Horizons for a Profession*, New York: AICPA, 1967, p. 4.

1–6   *The accountancy profession thus developed in two separate, though related,
ways. Accountants in public practice drew their business from the increasing
complexity of company finance, from governmental action, particularly in
in the field of taxation, and from the widening basis of industrial investment.
In industry, accountants were concerned with the control of increasing
quantities of capital equipment and other productive factors, and with the
formation of management decisions.**

Give illustrations to substantiate the above viewpoint.

*Roy Sidebotham, *Introduction to the Theory and Context of Accounting*, Oxford: Pergamon Press
Ltd., 1965, p. 29.

1–7   Ghetto medicine and poverty law are regarded nowadays as new areas for
old professions. Indicate whether equivalent areas could be developed for
the accounting profession. Be specific about the concerns and tasks of
such activities. How would they differ from the traditional community service (e.g., Community Chest, church, Boy Scouts) provided by the professional
accountant?

1–8   It has been said that "accountancy is something of a maid of all work in
industry." Illustrate.

1–9   You have been assigned the task of debating the *affirmative* of the question:
Resolved, that the practice of accounting today is a "leech" on the organization. To what particular aspect or aspects of accounting would you direct
your attack? (A leech is someone who clings to another for gain.)

1–10   In his Introduction to *Studies in the History of Accounting*, B. S. Yamey suggests four possible explanations of how accounting has developed. These
are (1) individual genius, (2) the spirit of the Renaissance, (3) accident or
chance, and (4) changing business needs. Give possible examples for each
of the four, and indicate which explanations you believe to have been most
important.

1–11   *The function of accounting is (1) to measure the resources held by specific
entities (units); (2) to reflect the claims against and the interests in those
entities; (3) to measure the changes in those resources, claims, and interests;*

(4) to assign the changes to specifiable periods of time; and (5) to express the foregoing in terms of money as a common denominator. *

Contrast this concept of accounting with those given in the chapter.

* Maurice Moonitz, *The Basic Postulates of Accounting,* Accounting Research Study No. 1, New York: AICPA, 1961, p. 23.

1–12   Explain the historical development of accounting as a response to a relevance criterion.

1–13   Explain how a conflict might arise in trying to apply both the relevance criterion for information and any other accounting criterion or concept.

1–14   If possible, visit a business firm that has a computer. Inquire how the firm's accounting has changed since it was computerized. Prepare a report on your survey.

1–15   Before beginning this course (and reading this chapter), you probably had some impressions or opinions about accounting and accountants.
a. What were they?
b. Which ones were changed by Chapter 1, and how were they changed?

Problems

1–1   Prepare a diagram, flowchart, or schedule showing 5 (or 15) significant dates of major historical events in the development of contemporary accounting.

1–2   Go to the library and inspect the most recent issue of four accounting periodicals mentioned in this chapter. Write a paragraph about each one, describing its contents, or write a paragraph on the lead article in each one.

1–3

EASTMAN KODAK COMPANY OF NEW JERSEY AND ITS SUBSIDIARY COMPANIES
COMBINED BALANCE SHEET, 31st DECEMBER, 1902
(ROUNDED TO NEAREST THOUSAND)

(This is the first public annual report ever issued by this company. It consists of the position statement and the auditor's statement.)

Liabilities
Capital stock:

Preferred stock authorized, $10,000 *of which there has been issued*	$ 6,184	
Common stock authorized, 25,000 *of which there has been issued*	18,796	
	$24,980	
Less: Calls unpaid	979	$24,001

Capital stock of subsidiary companies outstanding			$ 2
Current liabilities:			
Accounts payable		$ 367	
Preferred stock dividends payable January 1st, 1903		84	
Common stock dividends payable January 1st, 1903		437	888
Surplus:			
Profits of combined companies for the six months ending December 31st, 1902		$ 1,488	
Deduct:			
Dividends and interest:			
3% on preferred stock	$ 151		
5% on common stock	806		
Interest on preferred warrants @ 6% P. A.	11		
Interest on common warrants @ 10% P. A.	51		
	$ 1,019		
On outstanding stock of subsidiary companies	0	1,019	469
			$25,360

Assets

Cost of property, including real estate, buildings, plant, machinery, patents and goodwill			$16,818
Current assets:			
Merchandise, materials and supplies		$ 2,208	
Accounts and bills receivable		892	
Railway bonds and other investments		1,428	
Call loans		500	
Cash at bank and on hand		3,514	8,542
			$25,360

We have examined the books of the Eastman Kodak Company of New Jersey and its subsidiary companies in America and England of the year ending December 31, 1902, and we have been furnished with certified returns from the European branches, the Kodak Gesellschmidt and the Society Anonyme Franchise for the same period, and certify that the balance sheet is correctly prepared therefrom.

We have satisfied ourselves that during the year only actual additions and extensions have been charged to Capital Account and that ample provision has been made for depreciation.

We are satisfied that the valuation of the Inventories of stock on hand as certified by the responsible officials have been carefully and accurately made at cost and that full provision has been made for Bad and Doubtful Accounts Receivable and for all ascertainable liabilities.

We have verified the cash and securities by actual inspection and by certificates from the depositories and are of the opinion that the stocks and bonds are fully worth the value at which they are stated in the Balance Sheet.

And we certify that in our opinion the Balance Sheet is properly drawn up so as to show true financial position of the company and its subsidiary companies, and the profits thereof for the half year ending at that date.

Sixth April, 1903   (Signed) Price Waterhouse & Co., Auditors

---

EASTMAN KODAK CO. AND SUBSIDIARY CO. IN THE U.S.
STATEMENT OF FINANCIAL CONDITION

Net Assets (in thousands)	December 26, 1972	December 27, 1971
Current assets:		
Cash	$ 27	$ 26
Marketable securities at cost (M.V. $320,750)	324	311
Receivables	185	165
Inventories	241	208
Prepaid charges applicable to future operations	5	5
Total current assets	$ 782	$715
Current liabilities:		
Payables	$ 178	$162
Taxes—income and other (less $115,000, U.S. government securities for 1972; $100,000 for 1971)	42	35
Cash dividends payable January 3, 1973 and 1972	65	54
Total current liabilities	$ 285	$251
Working capital	$ 497	$464
Properties:		
Buildings, machinery, and equipment at cost	$1,068	$958
Less: Reserve for depreciation	599	553
Net balance of depreciable assets	$ 469	$ 405
Land at cost	17	15
Net properties	$ 486	$420
Other items:		
Investments in subsidiary companies outside the U.S.	$ 44	$ 36
Sundry investments, receivables, and deposits	18	17
	$ 62	$ 53

Deduct:		
Contingent allotments	$ 7	$ 7
Deferred federal income tax	14	9
	$ 21	$ 16
Net assets	$1,024	$921

Ownership of Net Assets (in thousands)	December 26, 1972	December 27, 1971
Capital and retained earnings:		
Common stock ($5 par value, 180,000,000 shares authorized; Issued: 80,602,718 shares)		
Par value—paid in or transferred from retained earnings	$ 403	$403
Additional retained earnings transferred to capital	246	246
Balance of retained earnings used in the business	375	272
Total	$1,024	$921

Report of Independent Accountants
To the Board of Directors and Shareholders of Eastman Kodak Company:

In our opinion, the accompanying statement of financial condition and the related statement of earnings* present fairly the consolidated financial condition of Eastman Kodak Company and its subsidiary companies in the United States at December 26, 1972, and the results of their operations for the year then ended, in conformity with generally accepted accounting principles applied on a basis consistent with that of the preceding year.

Our examination of those statements, which we carried out as auditors elected at the annual meeting of shareholders held on April 27, 1972, was made in accordance with generally accepted auditing standards and accordingly included such tests of the accounting records and such other auditing procedures as we considered necessary in the circumstances.

February 16, 1973   Price Waterhouse & Co.

Answer the following questions:
1. What are the major differences in format between the 1902 statement and the 1972 statement? Terminology? Style? Accounting principles?
2. Using the major captions as terms for equations, prepare equations for each statement, and compare and contrast.
3. List individual account groupings appearing in the 1972 statement that did not appear in the 1902 statement, and speculate on their significance.
4. What are the differences in current assets between the two statements?

1-4

Using the above statements, answer the following questions:
1. Who were the likely users of the statements at the two dates?

*Not reprinted.

2. Which statement is easier to understand? Why?
3. What significant differences, if any, do you find between the auditors' opinions?
4. On the basis of the two statements presented, what other types of financial statements do you think might be presented. Defend your judgment.

1-5

Select an enterprise that you are knowledgeable about. Identify this organization, and specify its nature (indicating its business or objectives), scope and activities, employees, and the types of decisions it makes. What kinds of accounting information must be provided for this organization? If you do not know for certain (and are unable to find out), make a judgment. How is this information provided?

2

Valuation and the Measurement Process

Ideally, of course, it would be desirable to have direct *measures throughout. If we could by any means obtain future manufacturing and sales data in the forms and amounts that are later to eventuate, we should be able to prepare a balance sheet that would be an instrument of precision. We should be able in a true and realistic and reliable sense to disclose a financial condition with respect to the capital value of an enterprise.**

JOHN B. CANNING, 1929

When the basic structure of the accounting system is explained, often little attention is given to the underlying measurement process. Some knowledgeable accountants assert that since the traditional definition and model of accounting (which will be explained in Chapters 3 and 4) fail to explicitly include measurement, this is a task for others. In this view, the accountant's role is to record, classify, report, interpret, and verify (or attest) measurements, but not to measure. Other knowledgeable accountants assert that measurement is basic to the accounting process and that other accountants are remiss who fail to recognize their role and to accept their share of the responsibility for developing and improving measurement concepts and processes. Both groups, however, recognize that accountants cannot effectively perform their verification role without understanding measurement processes and concepts.

Measurement is the process by which numbers or numerical values are used to compare objects or events with other objects or events. The basic aspect of measurement is that it helps one to distinguish between the characteristics of objects or events. A less basic aspect of measurement is that it helps one to distinguish precisely between

*From *The Economics of Accountancy* (New York: The Ronald Press Company, 1929), p. 184.

the characteristics of objects or events. For example, if one wishes to distinguish between two poles that are identical except for length, which has been selected as the characteristic to be measured, then pole A can be distinguished from pole B if it is classified as the longer of the two. But one could distinguish precisely by selecting a measurement system and discovering or determining the lengths of the two poles. Merely determining that pole A is 5 feet long tells something very definite about it, but upon reflection one would obviously classify the system as a comparison. The pole is shorter than all objects that are more than 5 feet long. If one adds that pole B is 4 feet long, this also is a comparison statement, but specific comparisons now become possible between the two poles. In summary, measurement communicates information better by its precision.

Measurement is accomplished by quantifying information; quantitative information is more precise and less vague than nonquantitative (nonnumerical, often called qualitative) information. But even though it is nonquantitative, the latter must be communicated too. The communication capability for quantitative information has been increased in the past through measurement developments (described in Chapter 1). The communication capability for nonquantitative (or qualitative) information has been increased in the past through language developments. Further measurement and language developments may be expected. As was indicated in Chapter 1, accounting has developed over many centuries to apply measurement (and language) processes to facilitate organizational activities.[1]

Measurement in accounting is concerned primarily with providing information that is relevant for specified uses. Since measurement provides more information, accountants should measure, but their measurements must be relevant. The purpose of measurement here, too, is to facilitate comparisons and evaluations between and among objects, events, and entities (that usually are groups of objects and events). In financial accounting the major concern is to provide information about the entity that will be relevant to the needs of various interested individuals outside the entity (for example, current and potential owners, creditors, governments). This means that measurement is necessary to facilitate interfirm and intrafirm comparisons (see Chapter 3) as well as comparisons to other standards (such as management's promises) that the outside users may wish to make.

There are three fundamental steps in the financial accounting measurement process:

[1]For a further discussion of measurement, see Robert R. Sterling, *Theory of the Measurement of Enterprise Income* (Lawrence: The University Press of Kansas, 1970), pp. 65–115.

1. Selecting the relevant attribute, characteristic, or dimension of the object or event to be measured
2. Selecting the unit and scale of measure
3. Determining or discovering the number of units

The first step consists of deciding upon and describing the relevant attribute or dimension to be measured. In financial accounting that attribute usually is the value of the object or event, but there may be other relevant measures such as the number of units that can be produced in a month, the number of units ordered by customers for future delivery, or just the number of physical units of an item. Although the objective is to provide information relevant to outsiders, there are several valuations that might be given for an item. For example, information concerning the cost of an investment in marketable securities would be relevant for federal income tax purposes (because the taxable gain will be selling price less the cost) while information concerning the current market value of the securities might be relevant for other purposes.

The second measurement step usually does not cause major difficulty. It is essential that the unit selected be one that is commonly used and widely known. In addition, it is preferable that the unit be one that is commonly used to measure both services acquired and services used.

If the relevant attribute to be measured is the value of the object or event, then the relevant unit of measure is a monetary unit, usually that of the country in which the firm is operating—dollars in the United States.

Usually for objects and often for events where the attribute being measured is value, it is necessary to first select a physical or other nonmonetary unit of measure to which prices are applied to determine value. In other cases, where the relevant attribute to be measured is the quantity of an object or event, the relevant unit will also be a physical or other nonmonetary unit of measure. Examples of commonly used physical quantity measures for materials, supplies, and merchandise for sale are weight (pounds or tons); liquid measures (pints, quarts, gallons, or barrels); length (inches, feet, yards, or rods); surface area (square inches, feet, yards, or rods); volume (cubic inches, feet, or yards); containers (cartons, drums, or packages); or separate identifiable components or complete composite units (tires or automobiles).

A second group of quantity measures relate to units of time—minutes, hours, days, weeks, months, or years. In one type, the relevant attribute to be measured relates one or more services, objects, or events to a unit of time. Examples of this are services of employees, outside agencies, or leased equipment where specified services are to be furnished and are to be paid for at specified rates per unit of time. The second type of time quantity measures relates a bundle of services acquired at one point in time to the units of time during which portions of these services can be expected to be received. Examples of these are long-lived assets such as buildings and equipment, each of which is acquired at one moment of time but is expected to give specified services over many units of time. (As indicated above, buildings and machines also could be measured as physical quantities.)

A third group of quantity measures relates to performance units—the completion of some object or event. Examples of this are employees compensated on a piece-rate basis and salesmen's commissions or equipment services compensated on the basis of sales, production, or some other measure of output or performance.

The third step in the measurement process is to count, discover, or determine the number of units of the attribute of the object or event that is being measured. As was indicated earlier, this often is a two-stage process where the attribute being measured is the value of an object: first, determining the number of the appropriate nonmonetary units; second, applying the relevant price to these units and calculating their total value. The selection of the relevant price is a much discussed question in financial accounting and is the subject of the next section.

Valuation

Although several quantity measures may be relevant, accounting places greatest emphasis on monetary measures. The valuation process consists of the quantification of economic relationships, especially those of changes in cash. Since reporting upon these economic relationships is what accounting is all about, valuation is its central activity. Because of the difficulties associated with valuation measures, it has been suggested that these measures be dropped from accounting. But if this were done, how would income be measured? It is not an exaggeration to state that the objectives of valuation are in considerable part the objectives of accounting.

A shortcoming of valuation measures is that no single concept is applicable or relevant in all circumstances. The selection of a valuation measure (the price, or price per quantity measure discussed in the previous section) for a particular situation is highly dependent on who will use the information, and for what purpose. The concern of this chapter is with the valuation concepts that are most advantageous to external users of financial statements. For example, if current values based on what the firm expects to receive in cash by continuing its operations are larger than current liquidation values for individual assets and the entire firm, the expected values to be received are more relevant to the information needs of both creditors and stockholders because they will provide better measures of the future cash flows of the firm.

Accounting has been developed primarily for business organizations. Although nonbusiness organizations are very significant and numerous, most nonbusiness organizations resemble business firms in many ways, so that accounting ideas designed for business are applicable either directly or with slight modification to nonbusiness organizations. But the focus of this book is on the business organization, which also is emphasized in conventional financial accounting.

Business firms produce and/or distribute goods and services; since they are not chiefly consuming enterprises (as individuals frequently are), the relevant valuation measures for business enterprises are based upon exchange or conversion factors. A business firm operates in two types of markets, those in which it buys and those in which it sells. For those markets in which it makes purchases, input values or entry prices are relevant. For those markets in which it sells goods or services, output values or exit prices are relevant. Input values are the prices paid to obtain the resources necessary to operate the business; output values are the prices to be recovered by the firm in exchange for its products.

When accounts are converted to future cash flows, the process is called *direct valuation.* Commonly used terms for these cash flows are expected future output or exit prices, but current output or exit prices usually are considered to be acceptable substitutes. As already mentioned, external users of financial statements want to know the future cash flows of the business if possible; output or exit prices measure these cash flows *directly.* But direct valuation of all the accounts of a business is impossible, because most resources contribute jointly to the net cash flows.

If input or entry prices are used to measure value, the process is called *indirect valuation.* Given that the external users of financial statements want to know the future cash flows of the business; if such cannot be measured directly, measures of past cash flows may be helpful since past cash flows do have a bearing upon future cash flows. Input or entry prices, as measures of past cash flows, to some extent do constitute a measure of future cash flows, but the measure is indirect.

Direct Valuation
If direct valuation were always possible, it would be the preferable or ideal measure in nearly all accounting situations since users of financial statements find output or exit prices generally to be more

relevant information for decision-making purposes than input or entry prices. Indirect valuation, thus, is nearly always a *substitute* for the true preference of users; input or entry prices are acceptable to users only when output or exit prices are not available. It seems important to the authors that this distinction be stressed. Since most accounting valuation today is indirect, such indirect measures as cost often are assumed to be synonymous with value. With this misunderstanding, it is difficult to get direct valuation measures accepted even when such are possible. If direct valuation measures are not known to exist, of course, they are not considered; and indirect measures can be accepted more readily.

Direct valuation may be applied to the entire firm or to any one of the firm's accounts. It is applicable whenever the present value[2] of future cash receipts and disbursements associated with the firm or an account through exchange or conversion are definite and determinable. Such accounts as cash, receivables, payables, bonds, and mortgages are usually valued on this basis.

The problems of uncertainty are the chief drawback to more extensive use being made currently of direct valuation. If statistical or other methods of coping with this factor could be devised, presumably direct valuation could be applied more frequently. This uncertainty may take four different forms:

1. Uncertainty concerning the amount and timing of the future cash flows. Inventories are the most important type of account involving this type of uncertainty, because the firm does not have either oral or written promises from its future customers (as it does for receivables) to pay definite sums of money. Except for inventories produced for order, the firm often does not know when the inventories will be sold, or for how much, or when the customers will pay for them.
2. Uncertainty because of the difficulty of separating the cash flow for one account from that for other accounts. Although many resources of a firm contribute jointly[3] to the net cash flows of the firm, long-lived assets such as buildings and equipment are the major type of account involving this type of uncertainty. Some long-lived assets, such as goodwill (to be discussed in Chapter 7), cannot be identified separately.[4]

The final two types of uncertainty can be overcome to a considerable extent.

---

[2]The present value is determined by discounting the future cash receipts and disbursements to allow for the effects of interest—this topic will be explored at length in the next section of this chapter.

[3]In the usual situation, a combination of men, equipment, materials, etc., contributes jointly to the final product or service, often in proportions that cannot be varied so that the incremental or marginal contribution of each cannot be determined.

[4]Because resources make joint contributions and some assets lack a separate identity, the sum of the marginal (or incremental) net receipts associated with individual accounts will not equal the total net receipts from all products or services.

3. Uncertainty about the ability of customers (debtors) to keep their promises. This kind of uncertainty can be estimated reasonably well where
the number of debtors is large (as will be discussed in Chapter 5).
4. Uncertainty about the rate of interest, particularly for long-term receivables or payables. This difficulty usually can be overcome by reference
to the contract or the market (for rates experienced by others with similar
contracts).

Particularly for the external users of financial statements, it is
argued too that direct valuation may not be verifiable (even if relevant) on the grounds that the estimated cash flows (or adjustments
for risk) are determined subjectively; that is, they are the estimates,
often of interested persons, as contrasted to objectively determined
and verifiable cash flows that have occurred in market transactions.
Although direct valuation presents major problems in applications
to inventories and long-lived assets, it can be applied effectively
to any account category that has a short waiting period before the
account is converted into cash. In addition to the cash items, this
means that most receivables and payables can be and are valued on
this basis, because typically the collection period is short and/or
the interest rate is low.

To apply direct valuation, in addition to knowing the time periods
(or waiting periods) for the future cash flows, it also is necessary to
know the amounts of such receipts, and, of course, the interest
rate (usually called the discount rate), which is the actual or implicit
cost of waiting for the cash flow.

There are several other approaches to direct valuation. These
substitute measures are still of output or exit prices, but are at the
current time period rather than future time periods. These are: current output prices, current cash equivalents, and liquidation prices.
All these are prices that represent opportunities or alternatives that
the firm foregoes when it continues in business or continues to hold
particular assets.

The first, current output or exit prices, would tend to be available
when predicted future prices are not. Also current output prices are
often more relevant and usually more verifiable, because future
prices are mere forecasts or predictions. Current output prices
are effective for inventory when the discounted future cash receipts
cannot be calculated and current market prices usually can be determined (and discounted, if warranted, and netted of any future
costs yet to be incurred). However, in addition to the question of
whether a present price is an appropriate substitute for a future
price, current market prices are not applicable for all accounts, but
are really applicable only for those items that are to be sold. Thus
different valuation concepts must be applied to the accounts for

which current market prices are not applicable; and, as a result, different value measures would be used in the same set of accounts.

The other two approaches to direct valuation are based on the assumption that the firm will liquidate (that is, that it will not continue in business). For current cash equivalents[5] the assumption is that the liquidation will be an orderly one, so that each asset will be sold for an amount of cash equal to the current quoted market price for goods that are similar in kind and condition. For liquidation prices the assumption is that of a forced sale with large discounts from quoted market prices at amounts that sometimes are substantially below the firm's cost. The usual difficulty with both these methods is that if the firm does not partially or entirely liquidate, liquidation value information is not relevant. But such information is relevant to the firm in helping to decide (1) whether to continue in business or (2) whether to continue to hold or sell a particular asset. Both methods also overlook the possibility that the sales of several assets in combination or of the whole firm, even in liquidation, may have a different value than the total of the individual liquidation values for the different accounts. At least a portion of this difference occurs because some items, such as highly specialized equipment or most intangible assets (which, like goodwill, do not have a separate existence apart from the business) would be excluded since they do not have a current market price.

The Time Value of Money

In direct valuation, the time value of money or the interest factor constitutes the central variable. The time value of money is experienced by both individuals and firms in their business transactions. For example, if $1 is to be received a year hence, its present value to both creditor and debtor is less than $1. The difference between $1 and the present value of $1 expected a year from now is the interest (or discount, namely, interest in advance) factor or the time value of money. The longer that one would have to wait for the $1, the smaller would be its present value and the larger the interest factor.

The mathematics of interest was developed by actuaries for insurance companies; these formalized concepts are utilized in both

---

[5]Professor Raymond J. Chambers has advanced the term *current cash equivalent* as the one price or valuation concept that can be applied to all assets. He considers this to be the one type of contemporary information for business firms that is useful in making all judgments about the past, and all plans and choices for the future. That is, Chambers assumes that current cash equivalents are relevant for all future actions in markets, and thus are uniformly relevant at a point in time. He views past prices as not being relevant to future actions, and future prices as always being merely hypothetical. Thus, using current cash equivalents avoids the adding together of past, present, and future prices. For further discussions on this see Raymond J. Chambers, *Accounting, Evaluation and Economic Behavior* (Englewood Cliffs, New Jersey: Prentice-Hall, Inc., 1966), pp. 42–102 and "Second Thoughts on Continuously Contemporary Accounting," *Abacus* (September 1970), pp. 39–55.

accounting theory and practice, particularly in direct valuation. Basically there are four concepts: (1) simple interest, (2) compound interest, (3) the future value or amount of an ordinary annuity, and (4) the present value of an ordinary annuity. For ease in understanding, these concepts are discussed, first, by direct reasoning, and second, algebraically. For ease in application to problem solving, already computed tables of these values are shown in Appendix A.

Definitions of the following terms should help the reader in his understanding:

1. *Simple interest* is the time cost of money or the return on or growth of the beginning principal for *only one time period.* If it is applied for each time interval in a succession of periods (which is unusual), it is applied at a given rate per period, but only to the beginning principal, not to the principal that has grown as a result of previous interest additions. Interest is an increase in principal; simple interest usually applies only to short-term investments and loans.
2. *Compound interest* is distinguished from simple interest in only one way: it includes interest computed upon interest which has been added to the principal. Stated more formally, it is the return on or the growth in the principal for two or more time periods where the return in any period is added to the principal and earns a return in the next period. Compound interest has wide application in accounting measures for determining present valuations of future prospects and evaluating investment and borrowing decisions.
3. The *principal* is the existing value of the investment or loan contract which may or may not be its face value (or the amount stated in the contract).
4. An *annuity* is a loan to be repaid (or collected) in installments or an investment that will be partially recovered at regular time intervals. All the intervals are equal, but each interval may be for any time period. Compound interest is added to or subtracted from the principal once during each time period. An ordinary annuity is one in which equal payments or receipts (often called rents) occur at the end of each period; an annuity due has equal payments or receipts that occur at the beginning of each period so that interest continues for one period after the last payment or receipt. There also are open-end annuities and deferred annuities. The former are similar to the annuity due but remain open after the last receipt or payment for more than one period. A deferred annuity is one in which the receipts or payments begin two or more periods after the investment or loan is made.

Simple and compound interest Starting with simple interest, consider a 10 percent note, one promising to pay $1,000 at the end of four years and $100 interest annually. This annual interest of $100 could be received or paid each year without affecting the interest for the remaining years. With simple interest, if the annual interest amounts are not to be received or paid annually but are due with the principal at the maturity date, the amount of the investment or loan would increase each year by the amount of the interest on the initial principal as follows:

		Principal		
$1,000	$1,100	$1,200	$1,300	$1,400
0	1	2	3	4
		Year		

The amount of the investment or loan is increased only by the $100 a year since with the simple interest the annual rate is applied only to the beginning principal as follows:

Year	Beginning Principal	Interest Rate	Computations (Amount of Loan at Year End)
First	$1,000	10%	$1,000 + (1 × 10% × 1,000) = $1,100
Second	1,000	10	1,000 + (2 × 10% × 1,000) = 1,200
Third	1,000	10	1,000 + (3 × 10% × 1,000) = 1,300
Fourth	1,000	10	1,000 + (4 × 10% × 1,000) = 1,400

This computation could be simplified by adding the annual interest rate for each year to 1 and using it as a multiplier for each year as follows:

First:	$1,000 × 1.10 = $1,100
Second:	1,000 × 1.20 = 1,200
Third:	1,000 × 1.30 = 1,300
Fourth:	1,000 × 1.40 = 1,400

Since the rate of interest is customarily expressed as i, the above multipliers become $(1 + i)$, $(1 + 2i)$, $(1 + 3i)$, and $(1 + 4i)$.

The drawback of simple interest is that if each $100 is not withdrawn as it occurs, it does not become part of the principal or generate growth at the 10 percent rate for all successive years. In each year after the first one, the annual increase in principal should become larger by the amount of this interest on interest. Essentially this is the compound interest method as is demonstrated below:

		Year				
		1	2	3	4	
	$	$	$	$	0.10	The
				1.00	1.00	Com-
					1.00	pound-
			10.00	10.00	10.00	ing
					1.00	Proc-
				10.00	10.00	ess
					10.00	
I. Simple annual interest on beginning principal of $1,000		100.00	100.00	100.00	100.00	
II. Compound annual interest on beginning principal of $1,000 (annual increase in principal)		100.00	110.00	121.00	133.10	
III. Accumulated compound annual interest (total increase in principal)		100.00	210.00	331.00	464.10	
IV. Principal at end of each year (with beginning principal of $1,000)		1,100.00	1,210.00	1,331.00	1,464.10	

which can be summarized as follows:

Year	Annual Amount of Compound Interest	Accumulated Compound Interest	Principal at End of Year
0	-	-	$1,000.00
1	$100.00	$100.00	1,100.00
2	110.00	210.00	1,210.00
3	121.00	331.00	1,331.00
4	133.10	464.10	1,464.10

Once the concepts of interest (simple and compound) are understood, particularly how they are related (as shown in I and II), a shortcut can be developed using a multiplier. The multiplier 1.10 makes it unnecessary to calculate separately each year's increase at 10 percent and to add this amount to the principal value for next year's computation. For example, for the first year: $1,000 × 1.10 = $1,100; for the second year: $1,100 × 1.10 = $1,210; for the third year: $1,210 × 1.10 = $1,331; and for the fourth year: $1,331 × 1.10 = $1,464.10.

But an even easier procedure is available for arriving at the increased principal value at the end of the second or any other year in the series. If the 1.10 for the first year is multiplied by another 1.10 for the second year, we arrive at the amount $1.21, to which $1 would accumulate in two years at 10 percent. This amount, of 1.21, can be applied to our original principal of $1,000 to give a new principal of $1,210 at the end of two years. Tables showing the amount to which $1 will accumulate at various rates of interest at the end of various numbers of years have been prepared to reduce the amount of calculation required. Such a table, Amount of $1 Due in n Periods, is Table 1 of Appendix A. The main point of making a period multiplier out of 1 plus the interest rate $(1 + i)$ is that it automatically includes all the interest on interest (or compound interest) calculations shown in detail earlier. The table makes it possible to compute the amount of any principal by simple multiplication.

"Where there is time, there is interest" is a common expression. If we look at item IV in the compound interest method, the relationship between the principal at the beginning and at the end of a given number of periods can be established. First, the difference between the beginning balance of $1,000 and the ending balance of $1,464.10 is the increase in principal or the accumulated interest. Second, if $1,000 times 10 percent compounded annually increases to $1,464.10 in four years, then $1,000 must be the present value of $1,464.10 due four years later. If the latter is the value arrived at by multiplying $1,000 by $(1.10)^4$ (or 1.4641, if we use Table 1), then the present value of $1,000 can be derived from $1,464.10 by reversing the process—by dividing $1,464.10 by 1.10 four times in succession; or, if we use Table 1, by dividing by $(1.10)^4$ or 1.4641. In short, the ending principal is converted to the present value. For help in making this calculation by multiplication rather than division, see Table 3, Present Value of $1 Due in n Periods, in Appendix A.

In summary at this point, it has been shown that the values at the beginning and the end of the time periods can be equated by using the appropriate interest factor. That is, that at any given rate per period and for any given number of periods, the future amount of any present value can be determined by multiplying by $(1 + i)^n$, and the present value of any future amount can be determined by dividing by $(1 + i)^n$ or by multiplying by $1 ÷ (1 + i)^n$.

Ordinary annuities This relationship between the compound interest accumulation during a given number of years or other periods of time and the amount of an ordinary annuity (an ordinary series of equal annual amounts) for the same number of years is diagramed below (using our example):

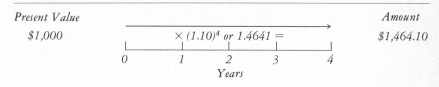

or by reversing the process: $1,000 = $1,464.10 ÷ (1.10)^4 or 1.4641. If $1 is used instead of $1,000:

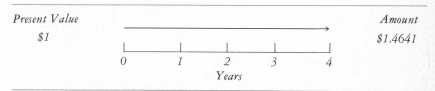

If the value of a dollar invested or loaned for four years at 10 percent per year increases to $1.4641, the amount of the increase must include the accumulated effect of the interest on interest at 10 percent earned for four years on the original $1.

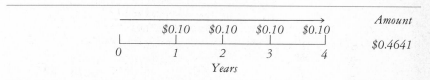

This shows as did the previous diagram, that $0.10 invested at the end of each year and accumulated at a 10 percent rate per year will grow to $0.4641 at the end of four years. It also constitutes an ordinary annuity of the amounts shown, and the accumulated amount at the end of the four years is the amount of such an annuity.

For convenience, ordinary annuity tables are based on an annuity of $1 per period. If each value amount in the previous diagram is multiplied by 10, the result would be the amount of an ordinary annuity of $1 per year as follows:

	Amount
(diagram: $1 at years 1, 2, 3, 4 over 0–4 Years)	$4.641

There are a number of ways of developing a formula for this process;

probably the simplest and most meaningful conceptual way would be to begin by recognizing that multiplying by 10 has the same effect as dividing through by 0.10, the interest rate in this example. The following results can be produced by dividing through by 0.10:

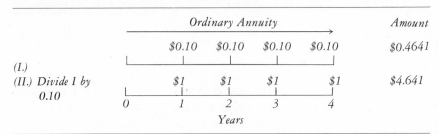

With these factors, it is now possible to establish a formula for computing the amount of any ordinary annuity at any given rate of interest. Such a formula consists of the amount of compound interest accumulated on the original $1 at the applicable interest rate divided by the appropriate interest rate. The amount in the numerator is always the accumulated growth in value of $1 for any given number of periods at any given rate of interest. To repeat, this numerator is always the *difference* between $1 at the beginning and the total amount to which it will accumulate at the end of the time periods. The complete formula for computing the amount of an ordinary annuity of $1 per period for n periods at interest rate i is $[(1+i)^n - 1] \div i$. To simplify calculations see Table 2, Amount of an Annuity of $1 per Period, in Appendix A.

The relationship between compound discount and the present value of an ordinary annuity is inherently the same as that between compound interest and the amount of an ordinary annuity, as is apparent in the earlier diagram reproduced as follows:

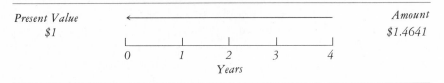

The present value of $1.4641 to be paid or received four years from now is $1; to bring the $1.4641 back to the $1, we divide $1.4641 by $(1.10)^4$ or 1.4641. In the same way, it is possible to determine what portion of the initial $1 would accumulate to the $1 at the end of the four years, and the remaining portion that would accumulate to the $0.4641. As before, divide each of the latter two amounts by $(1.10)^4$ or $1.4641 to derive the following:

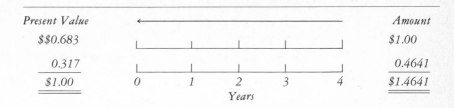

Present Value		Amount
$$0.683		$1.00
0.317		0.4641
$1.00	0 1 2 3 4	$1.4641

Years

The difference between any future sum and its present value at a given rate of interest is often called *compound discount* when the measurement is viewed as a subtraction from the future sum. It is also the amount by which the future amount must decrease at the stated interest rate in order to achieve the present value.

The total compound discount on the two separate future amounts is $0.4641; the discount on the $1 is $0.3170, and the discount on the $0.4641 is $0.1471. The $0.3170 is the present value of the accumulated discount, $0.4641, on the $1.4641 from the end of the four years at 10 percent. As observed previously, the present value of the compound discount, $0.3170, must also be the present value of an ordinary annuity; this can be shown by proving that $0.3170 is the present value of both I and II:

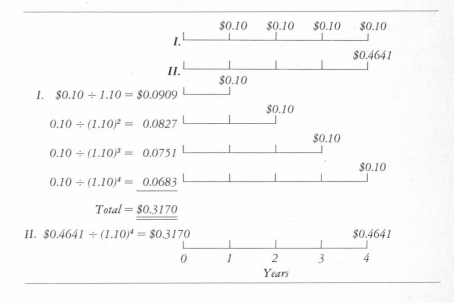

I. $0.10 ÷ 1.10 = $0.0909

0.10 ÷ (1.10)² = 0.0827

0.10 ÷ (1.10)³ = 0.0751

0.10 ÷ (1.10)⁴ = 0.0683

Total = $0.3170

II. $0.4641 ÷ (1.10)⁴ = $0.3170

Taking the second line of an earlier diagram and filling in the annuity amounts (simple interest on $1 for four years at 10 percent per year) yields the following:

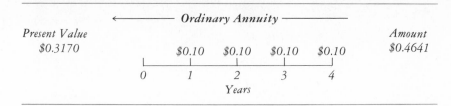

The formula for determining the present value of an ordinary annuity of $1 per period consists of the compound discount on $1 divided by the interest rate. Like the formula for the amount of an ordinary annuity, this formula must provide for any number of time periods and any rate of interest in order to be generally applicable. Thus, for this formula the future amount is always $1; tables are prepared which show the varying rates of interest. In this illustration the present value is $1 \div (1 + i)^n = \$1 \div (1.10)^4$, or $0.6830; and the compound discount is $\$1 - 0.6830$, or $0.3170, which when divided by 0.10 (as i) gives $3.17, as shown in the diagram. The formula for the present value of an ordinary annuity of $1 per period for n periods at interest rate i is $\dfrac{1 - \dfrac{1}{(1 + i)^n}}{i}$. To simplify calculations, see Table 4, Present Value of an Annuity of $1 per Period, in Appendix A.

In summary, the relationship between the present value and the amount of an ordinary annuity can be shown (along with their derivation) as follows:

	Present Value	Interest Compounded at 10% per Year for Four Years	Amount
1. Values, beginning and end	$1.00	0 1 2 3 4	$1.4641
2. Composed as explained of:			
a.	$0.6830		$1.00
b.	0.3170		0.4641
	$1.00		$1.4641
3. If value of 2a is deducted from $1.00	0.6830		1.00
4. Remainder is	$0.3170		$0.4641

5. *As shown before, this is* $0.3170

6. *Now, dividing through by an amount equal to rate (10% or 0.10)* $3.17

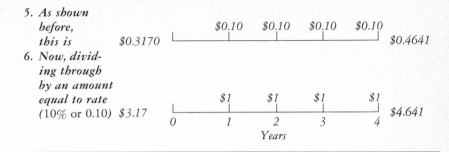

On each of the lines above:

The present value at the left end times $(1.10)^4$ or 1.4641 produces the value shown at the right end, and the amount at the right end divided by $(1.10)^4$ or 1.4641 produces the present value at the left end.

The values at both ends of the respective lines are equated at 10 percent per year for four years.

Lines 3, 4, 5, and 6 in succession present the steps in the calculation reflected in the ordinary annuity formulas.

Present Value of Ordinary Annuity (left end of lines)

$$\frac{1 - \dfrac{1}{(1+i)^n}}{i} \quad or \quad \frac{1 - \dfrac{1}{(1.10)^4}}{0.10} = \frac{1 - 0.6830}{0.10} = \frac{0.3170}{0.10} = \$3.17$$

Amount of Ordinary Annuity (right end of lines)

$$\frac{(1+i)^n - 1}{i} \quad or \quad \frac{(1.10)^4 - 1}{0.10} = \frac{1.4641 - 1}{0.10} = \frac{0.4641}{0.10} = \$4.641$$

As can be observed, the detailed presentation of the present value of an ordinary annuity formula could have been omitted, once the amount formula was developed. The lengthiness of the discussion was almost entirely due to avoiding the use of algebra. The present value formula is derived logically by rolling back the amount formula; consequently, the present value formula can be derived as follows:

---

1. *Amount formula* $\div (1+i)^n$ *or* $\left[\dfrac{(1+i)^n - 1}{i}\right]\left[\dfrac{1}{(1+i)^n}\right]$

which is:

$$2.\ \frac{(1+i)^n - 1}{i(1+i)^n}\ \ or\ \ \frac{1 - \dfrac{1}{(1+i)^n}}{i}$$

which is:

3. *The difference between the value of a sum due in the future and its present value divided by the interest rate (that is, the compound discount divided by the interest rate).*

By way of final summary, the close relationship among the four basic formulas is shown in Figure 2–1. By following either the inner or the outer ring we can see that if information is given for only one formula, the remaining three can be computed.

If these interest concepts are now presented algebraically, the four tables given in Appendix A are computed as follows:

Figure 2–1

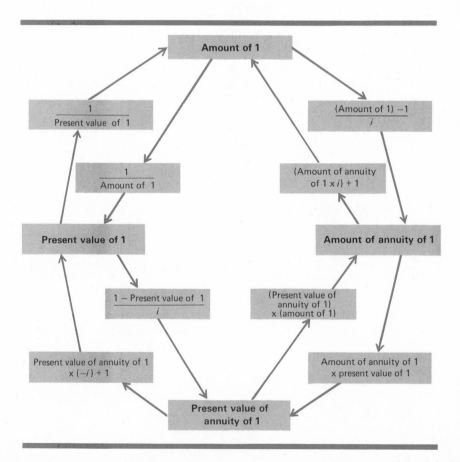

1. *Amount of $1* $= a_{\overline{n}|i} = [(1 + i)(1 + i) \cdots (1 + i)] = (1 + i)^n$

2. *Present value of $1* $= p_{\overline{n}|i} = \dfrac{1}{(1 + i)} \dfrac{1}{(1 + i)} \cdots \dfrac{1}{(1 + i)} = \dfrac{1}{(1 + i)^n} = (1 + i)^{-n}$

3. Amount of $1 per period (ordinary annuity) accumulated for *n* periods at interest rate *i*, $(A_{\overline{n}|i})$. Receipt or payment is assumed to be at the *end* of each period. Therefore, the last receipt or payment accumulates no interest, and the first accumulates interest for *n* − 1 periods, or

$$A_{\overline{n}|i} = 1 + (1 + i) + (1 + i)^2 + \cdots + (1 + i)^{n-1}$$

$$A_{\overline{n}|i} = \frac{(1 + i)^n - 1}{i}$$

4. Present value of $1 per period (ordinary annuity) discounted for *n* periods at interest *i*, $(P_{\overline{n}|i})$. Receipt or payment is at the *end* of each period. Therefore, the first payment is discounted for one period and the last payment for *n* periods, or

$$P_{\overline{n}|i} = (1 + i)^{-1} + (1 + i)^{-2} + \cdots + (1 + i)^{-n}$$

$$P_{\overline{n}|i} = \frac{1 - \dfrac{1}{(1 + i)^n}}{i} = \frac{1 - (1 + i)^{-n}}{i}$$

Variations of these concepts can be developed algebraically as follows:[6]

5. Amount of an annuity due of $1 per period accumulated for *n* periods at interest rate *i*. Receipt or payment is at the beginning of each period. Therefore, the last receipt or payment accumulates interest for *n* periods, or [with (x) denoting an annuity due]:

$$A_{\overline{n}|i}^{(x)} = (1 + i) + (1 + i)^2 + (1 + i)^3 + \cdots + (1 + i)^n$$

$$A_{\overline{n}|i}^{(x)} = \frac{(1 + i)^n - 1}{i}(1 + i)$$

$$= \frac{(1 + i)^{n+1} - 1}{i} - 1$$

6. Present value of an annuity due of $1 per period discounted for *n* periods at interest rate *i*. Receipt or payment is at the *beginning* of each period. Therefore, the first receipt or payment has a present value of $1, and the last is discounted for *n* − 1 periods, or

$$P_{\overline{n}|i}^{(x)} = 1 + (1 + i)^{-1} + (1 + i)^{-2} + \cdots + (1 + i)^{1-n}$$

$$P_{\overline{n}|i}^{(x)} = \frac{1 - (1 + i)^{-n}}{i}(1 + i)$$

$$= \frac{1 - (1 + i)^{1-n}}{i} + 1$$

[6]These may be omitted if desired.

7. Periodic payment that will grow to \$1 in n periods at interest rate i $\left(\dfrac{1}{A_{\overline{n}|i}}\right)$ when the direct payment is made at the *end* of the period. This sinking-fund formula follows directly from Equation 3, so that

$$\frac{1}{A_{\overline{n}|i}} = \frac{i}{(1+i)^n - 1}$$

8. The periodic payment necessary to extinguish a debt of \$1 in n periods at interest i (annuity worth \$1 today), $\dfrac{1}{P_{\overline{n}|i}}$. Payment is at the end of each period, and the formula follows directly from Equation 4 so that

$$\frac{1}{P_{\overline{n}|i}} = \frac{i}{1 - (1+i)^{-n}}$$

Indirect Valuation

As stated in an earlier section, direct valuation methods are nearly always better than indirect valuation methods for reporting financial information. This is so because the prices of goods and services to be sold as the product of the enterprise (output or exit prices) should provide more relevant information for external users of financial statements than the prices of goods and services acquired for re-sale or for further production (input or entry prices). Recognizing that direct valuation is preferable does not, however, preclude the substitution of indirect valuation for direct valuation when this be-comes necessary. On the other hand, accountants sometimes be-come so immersed with indirect valuation methods, especially his-torical cost, that they fail to consider anything else—even when there are no practical difficulties in using direct valuation. The chief argu-ment that can be made in favor of indirect valuation over direct valuation is that the former may be more verifiable. Sometimes, too, it is argued that indirect valuation does not result in the reporting of revenue before the good or service has been sold.

Basically, the best case for indirect valuation can be made in those situations where no stream of future cash receipts (or the equivalent) can be attached to the account being measured. As previously dis-cussed, the two chief asset categories in which this occurs are in-ventories and long-lived assets such as buildings and equipment. For inventories, there is uncertainty about the size and timing of the stream of future money flows; for the long-lived assets, there is uncertainty due to our inability to separate from the stream of future money flows those that are applicable to particular long-lived assets. In situations such as these, the valuation must be one inputed on an indirect basis, instead of the direct one of the present value of cash flows.

The basic technique for indirect valuation consists of measuring the present value of the future input prices or costs associated with the resource. Note that this measurement is really part of direct valuation which measures the present value of the discounted future net cash receipts (for example, future gross receipts less *future* input prices or *costs*) associated with the account. Where the waiting period before the costs are to be incurred is not long, discounting may not be required; this is the same point made for similar direct valuation situations. Where indirect valuation is applied in these situations, the input price or cost of acquisition may be a satisfactory equivalent for discounted future costs. For example, prepayments for insurance or rents often would cost the same if they were acquired when needed.

Many resources of a firm are purchased in advance of actual need, in order to reduce cost (for example, plant or inventories), to protect other investments (for example, leasehold improvements), or to make sure that the resources will be available when needed (plant and inventories again). When the firm has the choice between acquiring these resources separately or as a package, the approximation of discounted future costs may be the input price at date of acquisition. However, once these resources are acquired, the firm no longer has this choice; and it is rather unlikely that the equivalence of future expected costs of similar services and the current value of the asset resource (if such can be obtained) will continue long. In short, this valuation measure usually not only has the practical difficulties of direct valuation but also is subject to attack because it is the out-of-date historical cost.

Since the discounted future costs of indirect valuation often are both impractical and irrelevant, current input prices or current replacement costs are sometimes suggested as a substitute form of indirect valuation. These represent exchange prices that would be required currently to acquire an equivalent asset. If there is an exchange market for assets of the type being valued (and it is one in which the firm does or would acquire such assets), cost quotations from this market would constitute a current exchange price. In addition to the fact that such markets are not always available (although they may be available more often than historical cost advocates are willing to concede), this method of indirect valuation might not represent the current value to the firm for the particular asset, because of economic and technological changes. It also may not be a completely objective measure. But it does possess the following merits (as compared to historical costs, the substitute method for current costs): (1) it represents the appropriate indirect valuation basis for assets which the firm continues to acquire and to which it has not added value; (2) it facilitates separating from operating earnings the gains and losses that occur from holding assets often for purely speculative purposes; (3) current input prices or current replacement costs can be added logically since all are measured at the same point in time; and (4) such result in current input values being matched against current output prices (or revenues) on the income statement.

The valuation measure employed most frequently in accounting is *historical cost.* It is used so commonly that many accountants never discuss valuation but speak only of (historical) cost. It is defined as the exchange input or entry price for goods and services at the time such are acquired. It is measured by the cash outlay, indebtedness incurred, or the cash equivalent (where securities or other noncash assets are exchanged) at date of acquisition. It is later adjusted for a number of factors, a major one being a reduction (called depreciation) to reflect the portion of services received from buildings, equipment, and other plant assets.

Historical cost suffers from such shortcomings as becoming badly out of date over a period of time, of not being truly additive (where assets are acquired in periods that are far different in terms of time, prices, and technology), and of not recognizing holding gains and losses when they occur. Its chief virtue is that it is easy to verify. This assumes, of course, that the costs were the result of good judgment exercised by the entity—namely that the firm could not have purchased the same quality of services or goods at lower prices, or a better quality of goods or services for the same costs, and that these costs did represent the value of the goods and services to the firm at the date of acquisition. Neither of these assumptions is completely verifiable.

Four other indirect valuation methods which usually are applied to inventories could be discussed here; two of them—standard costing and direct costing—are classified as most useful to internal users of financial statements and therefore will not be considered in this book. The third—absorption costing—is relevant here, but because it usually is included and discussed as a part of managerial accounting, it too will not be discussed in this book. The fourth—the lower of cost or market (LOCOM)—will be taken up when inventories are discussed in Chapter 5.

Other Units of Measure

A major factor causing original input prices or historical costs to become outdated is the change over time in price levels and thus in the purchasing power of the monetary unit. Closely related to this for firms operating in more than one country are differences both at one time and over a period of time in price levels and purchasing power of the monetary units in these different countries. To fill the need for a stable, homogeneous unit of measure, accounting has developed at least three other measures which have considerable support, both in theory and, to a varying extent, in practice. These are general price indices, specific price indices, and foreign currency indices (or exchange rates).

Indices are statistical averages used to indicate common qualities inputed to a group of items. *A general price index* measures the proportional change over time in the prices of all goods and services. A *specific index* measures the change in the price structure or a proportional change over time in the prices of certain goods and services.[7] A *foreign currency index* measures the exchange relationship between a foreign currency and the domestic currency.

Of the three, the foreign currency index (or exchange) ratio, where applicable, is used extensively in practice. Most American accountants would convert Canadian dollars into United States dollars in preparing financial statements for a United States corporation, even if the exchange differences between these two currencies were not material. On the other hand, general price indices are not generally applied in preparing either corporate or governmental financial statements in the United States, even where changes in prices are far more significant than the value difference between United States and Canadian dollars. Thus far there appears to be little acceptance of the AICPA recommendation that supplementary financial statements be prepared using a general price index. In this area American accounting has failed to exercise leadership; in a number of foreign countries general price indices are applied in preparing financial statements. Specific price indices are employed to some extent in accounting in the United States. A special case of the specific price index is used when the historical cost basis of valuation is converted into the current replacement cost. Thus specific indices are another form of indirect valuation at or near current entry prices.

All three measures have been devised to cope with instability in prices and/or in the monetary unit. No monetary unit ever has been or ever will be a completely stable unit of measure or value. The real value of a dollar or any monetary unit is determined by its purchasing power or command over specific or all commodities and services on domestic or foreign markets. When prices fall, the purchasing power of the dollar or the monetary unit increases; when prices rise, the purchasing power of the dollar or the monetary unit decreases.

Sometimes called the "economic length" of the monetary unit or the dollar, a price index is a weighted-average relation between money and a given set of goods and services. In constructing any price index, there must be a base year or period for which a given set of goods and/or services is considered to have a value of 100

---

[7]In practice it is sometimes difficult to distinguish a structural (specific) price change from a general price change.

and which serves as a basis of comparison for all subsequent price changes. For example, if prices for the current period are 25 percent above those of the base period, the index for this period will be 125.

Several price indices are widely used in the United States in economic analysis, but not in accounting reports. These are the Consumer Price Index, the Wholesale Price Index, the Composite Construction Cost Index, and the Gross National Product Implicit Price Deflator. Only the GNP Implicit Price Deflator is considered to be appropriate for measuring general price-level changes; it measures the price change in all goods and services produced in a given year. Although the Consumer Price Index has been considered by many to be appropriate for measuring general price-level changes, it is in fact a specific index that measures the average change in retail prices of approximately 300 goods and services purchased by wage-earning families in the United States. The Consumer Price Index is reported monthly; the GNP Implicit Price Deflator is compiled quarterly. Since World War II, both have moved by the same magnitude and in the same direction. The Consumer Price Index has been used for many years in the escalator clauses of union wage contracts. The GNP Implicit Price Deflator was recommended by the AICPA's staff in its 1963 Accounting Research Study No. 6 and by the Accounting Principles Board in its Statement No. 3 as an appropriate index of general price-level changes. Ideally a separate price index should be constructed for the effect of a changing price level for every market on every accounting enterprise. In short, any general index has limitations.

Given the general acceptability of the indices discussed, the endless arguments among American accountants over which index should be used or the problems of preparing a general price index (such as selecting representative items and prices and attaching appropriate weights) seem to be only over details—significant details perhaps, but details that really seem to preclude the use of price indices in American accounting. This does not mean that a price index does not have to be adjusted from time to time because of changing attitudes of consumers and changing methods of production; consequently there must be periodic changes in the items included and the weights to be attached.

Given that the value of the United States dollar has declined substantially and almost continually since 1940, accounting statements based on indirect valuation could be misleading because they fail to recognize the changes in the purchasing power of the dollar. This is particularly so where comparative statements covering five- or ten-year periods are presented or where long-lived assets are a major resource of the firm.

The recognition of general price changes in accounting reports would not necessarily mean a change from the indirect basis of valuation, but it would tend to correct the most serious shortcomings of this approach. The recognition of specific price changes in accounting reports, however, by perceiving the significance of the present replacement values of individual assets, is closer to direct valuation than indirect valuation.

Although the price change and foreign currency measures are quite similar, American accounting practice is inconsistent: domestic general or specific price indices are used only in isolated instances; foreign currency indices, representing foreign prices, are practically always used where applicable. Since many American businesses now operate in worldwide markets, there are numerous situations in which foreign exchange indices are applied. Examples range from individual orders for goods or services bought or sold in foreign countries to branch offices or entire companies operated in foreign countries. In these transactions, the accounts of the foreign operation may be expressed in terms of a foreign currency; in order to prepare financial statements for American companies, these foreign currencies are compared to domestic currency by an index. Domestic transactions of varying dollars or monetary units *can be* restated through price indices, in terms of a single dollar or monetary unit. Foreign transactions of foreign currency *are* restated, through foreign currency indices (or exchange rates), in terms of a single monetary unit such as the dollar.

As with price indices, there is the problem of selecting the appropriate exchange rate since many foreign countries have both official and free market currency indices or rates of exchange. The instability of these measures complicates the selection. Where multiple rates exist, the AICPA has recommended that the most realistic rate or the free rate of exchange be used. Where more than one free market rate of exchange exists, the one most closely related to the remitting of profits from a foreign company is recommended.

There also is the problem of recognition of the gains or losses from applying these indices. For foreign currency translations, if the purchase and payment, and sale and collection, do not take place in the same period, the usual accounting practice is to recognize the *loss* in the period when a change in the index occurs, but to defer recognizing any *gain* until the cash is paid or received.

Since a foreign currency exchange rate tends to vary over time, there also is the problem of determining whether the rate to be applied should be as of the date the transaction occurred or as of the date the statement was prepared. The AICPA's position is that the latter rate should be used for current accounts on the position statement and for all income statement accounts. Some accountants have argued that a monetary (versus nonmonetary) rather than a current (versus noncurrent) distinction would be more appropriate for determining at what date the rate should be applied. The difference is that under the AICPA position there would be an exchange gain or loss from inventory (which is contrary to accepted practice), and that long-term liabilities would not be shown at their current realizable value (also contrary to accepted practice).

Although every transaction theoretically should be translated separately, the large volume of transactions often makes this impossible. Normally, simplifying averages are used. The AICPA recommends that when wide fluctuations have occurred, income statement accounts should be translated on the basis of a monthly average rate or a weighted average. If extremely wide fluctuations have occurred, the AICPA indicates that an end-of-period rate may be more realistic. Although foreign currency transactions are regularly translated to their dollar equivalent by American accountants, these transactions often may be excluded altogether if there are restrictions on the convertibility of capital or on the remittance of earnings from the foreign branch office or company. In general, this exclusion policy seems to be applied to excess. If foreign restrictions are reported in the statements, why exclude foreign transactions? It is inconsistent to exclude such transactions since the transactions of domestic branch offices and companies subject to similar constraints are included.

None of these three supplemental measures requires an alternative set of formal accounts, but each generally is regarded as an interpretive mechanism of valuation. The only special accounts required for any of the three measures are those for the gains and losses resulting from the application of the indices. The essential requirements for each measure are:

1. A classification of transaction values by dates incurred; and
2. A series of index numbers at the successive acquisition dates and the conversion date. For the general price index, these represent the purchasing power of the dollar for all goods and services. For the specific price index, these represent the purchasing power of the dollar for specific accounts, usually assets. For the foreign currency index, these represent the purchasing power of the dollar for a foreign currency.

The actual application of any of these measures can be cumbersome since the calculations, if done manually, can be fairly extensive, especially where the data of numerous transactions are converted or translated individually. However, most transactions can be aggregated on a monthly basis, and a monthly index can be applied. This means that all expenses for a particular month can be considered as a single transaction, for conversion purposes.

To illustrate these measures, a very simple example utilizing a general price index follows:

1. Comparative position statements for a corporation for the beginning and the end of a year are as follows:

Corporation
Position Statement
Year
(000's omitted)

Assets	Beginning	End	Equities	Beginning	End
Cash and receiv-			Current lia-		
ables	$ 50	$ 50	bilities	$ 50	$ 50
Inventories	25	25	Stockholders'		
Plant	200	225	equity	140	148
Less accumu-					
lated de-					
preciation	(85)	(102)			
	$190	$ 198		$190	$198

2. During the year, the revenues of the company were $150,000, expenses and taxes were $115,000, and dividends declared and paid were $10,000. The annual depreciation rate is 8.5 percent. The plant addition of $25,000 was made at the end of the year. The beginning plant was purchased six years earlier (or five years prior to the beginning of the year) when the price level was 125.
3. The general price index at the beginning of the year was 150, and there was no change during the year.
4. Under these circumstances all income statement data except for depreciation would be expressed in current dollars. The unconverted and converted income statement data will be as follows (000's omitted):

Corporation
Income Statement
Year
(000's omitted)

	Unconverted	Multiplier	Converted
Revenue	$150	150/150	$150.0
Expenses and taxes (except depre- ciation)	$115	150/150	$115.0
Depreciation	17	150/125	20.4
	$132		$135.4
Net income	$ 18 (Subtract depreciation increase of $3.4)		$ 14.6
Dividends	10		10.0
Net income retained	$ 8		$ 4.6

5. Converted position statements for the beginning and the end of the year are as follows (000's omitted):

Converted Position Statement

Assets	Beginning	End	Equities	Beginning	End
Cash and receivables	$ 50	$ 50.0	Current liabilities	$ 50	$ 50.0
Inventories	25	25.0			
Plant	240	265.0	Stockholders' equity	163	167.6
Less accumulated depreciation	(102)	(122.4)			
	$ 213	$ 217.6		$213	$217.6

NOTE: *The conversion multiplier for all accounts would be 150/150 except for the plant acquired six years earlier; this would be 150/125. The unconverted income retained is the difference between the unconverted beginning and ending stockholders' equity; and the converted income retained is the difference between the converted beginning and ending stockholders' equity. Note, too, the serious misstatement of earnings that results from the failure to record the decline in the value of the dollar in only one type of account where the recorded dollars are not converted to a common denominator in the preparation of financial statements.*

Summary

To perform his function effectively, the accountant must understand the process and concepts of measurement. Essentially, measurement helps to distinguish among characteristics of objects or events by using numbers or numerical values to compare one set of objects or events to another set of objects or events. Accounting, in general, applies measurement processes to facilitate organizational activities by providing information that is relevant for specific users. Financial accounting is concerned primarily with providing information about the entity to various interested individuals outside the firm. Measurement is necessary to provide the comparisons (e.g., intrafirm, interfirm, goals to accomplishments) which these users may wish to make.

Three major steps are basic to the financial accounting measurement process: selection of the attribute of the object or event to be measured; selection of the unit and scale of measurement; and determination of the number of units of the attribute measured. Accounting, which was developed primarily for business organizations, emphasizes monetary or valuation measures. Input values or entry prices are the prices that a business pays to obtain necessary resources; output values or exit prices are the prices that the business recovers in exchange for its products. The external users of financial statements want to know the future cash flow of the business. Output or exit prices measure these cash flows directly and are of greatest interest to external users. Input or entry prices measure future cash flows indirectly and may be substituted when output or exit prices are not available.

Direct valuation is applicable whenever the present value of future cash receipts and disbursements associated with the firm or an account within the firm are definite and determinable. Uncertainty about the amount and timing of future cash flows, the difficulty of separating the cash flow of one account from the cash flows of other accounts, uncertainty about the ability of customers to keep their promises, and uncertainty about rates of interest are all drawbacks to the direct valuation process.

The time value of money or the interest factor (the difference between the present value and the value expected a year from now) is the central variable in direct valuation. Four major concepts in the mathematics of interest are simple interest, compound interest, the future value (or amount) of an ordinary annuity, and the present value of an ordinary annuity. Appendix A provides tables useful in the application of these concepts, and Chapter 2 describes narratively and algebraically the way in which the tables were developed.

Substitution of indirect valuation for direct valuation becomes necessary in those situations where no stream of future cash receipts can be attached to the account being measured. The two primary asset categories in which this occurs are long-lived assets (e.g., buildings and equipment) and inventories. Indirect valuation measures the present value of the future input prices or costs associated with the resource.

The valuation measure most frequently used in accounting is historical cost, a form of indirect valuation. Historical cost is defined as the exchange input or entry price for goods and services at the time they are acquired. The chief merit of historical cost is its ease of verification. Its major defects are that it can become badly out-of-date; that it is not truly additive when resources are acquired in periods of different prices, time, and technology; and that it does not recognize holding gains and losses when they occur.

A major factor causing historical costs to become outdated is the change over time in the purchasing power of the monetary unit. For firms that operate in more than one country a related problem is differences in the price levels and purchasing power of monetary units used in these different countries.

General price indices, specific price indices, and foreign currency indices have been developed to provide stable, homogeneous units of measure. Even though the measures are quite similar, accountants are inconsistent in applying them. The foreign currency index, which measures the exchange relationship between a foreign currency and the domestic currency, is widely used by accountants. Accountants rarely apply either the general price index, which measures the proportional change over time in the prices of all goods and services, or the specific price index, which considers certain goods and services.

A Selection of Supplementary Readings

American Accounting Association: *A Statement of Basic Accounting Theory,* Evanston, Illinois: 1966, pp. 73–79.

American Institute of Certified Public Accountants: *Financial Statements Restated for General Price-level Changes,* Statement of the Accounting Principles Board No. 3. New York: 1969.

Bedford, Norton M.: "The Foundations of Accounting Measurement," Reviewer's Corner, *Journal of Accounting Research,* autumn 1968, pp. 270–282.

Bernstein, Leopold A.: "General Price Level Financial Statements—A Review of APB Statement No. 3," *The New York Certified Public Accountant,* January 1970, pp. 39–42.

Chambers, R. J.: "Asset Measurement and Valuation," *Cost and Management,* March–April 1971, pp. 30–35.

———: "Second Thoughts on Continuously Contemporary Accounting," *Abacus,* September 1970, pp. 39–55.

Churchman, C. West: "Why Measure?" In C. West Churchman and Philburn Ratoosh, eds., *Measurement Definitions and Theories,* New York: John Wiley & Sons, Inc., 1959, pp. 83–94.

Fertig, Paul E.: "Responsibility for Economic Measurements," *The Ohio CPA,* summer 1965, pp. 109–115.

Kist, LeRoy E.: "Accounting for Foreign Operations," *The Illinois CPA,* spring 1965, pp. 11–18.

Knortz, Herbert C.: "Bringing Accounting into Economic Measurements," *Financial Executive,* November 1967, p. 25.

Mattesich, Richard: "On the Perennial Misunderstanding of Asset Measurement by Means of 'Present Values'," *Cost and Management,* March–April 1970, pp. 29–31.

———: "On Further Misunderstandings about Asset 'Measurement' and Valuation: A Rejoinder to Chambers' Article," *Cost and Management,* March–April 1971, pp. 36–42.

Moonitz, Maurice: "Price-level Accounting and Scales of Measurement," *The Accounting Review,* July 1970, pp. 465–475.

Paton, W. A.: "Observations on Inflation from an Accounting Stance," *Journal of Accounting Research,* spring 1968, pp. 72–85.

"Report of the Committee on Foundations of Accounting Measurement." Yuji Ijiri, chairman. *Supplement to vol. XLVI, The Accounting Review.* Evanston, Illinois: American Accounting Association, 1971, pp. 1–48.

Rosen, L. S.: "Replacement Value Accounting and Historical Cost Accounting: A Comparison," *The Illinois CPA,* spring 1966, p. 7.

Rosenfield, Paul: "Accounting for Inflation—A Field Test," *The Journal of Accountancy,* June 1969, pp. 45–50.

Solomon, Kenneth Ira: "Current-cost Accounting," *The Illinois CPA,* autumn 1965, p. 171.

Staubus, George J.: "Current Cash Equivalent for Assets: A Dissent," *The Accounting Review,* October 1967, pp. 650–661.

Sterling, Robert R.: *Theory of the Measurement of Enterprise Income,* Lawrence: University Press of Kansas, 1970, pp. 39–115.

Wise, T. A.: "Those Uncertain Actuaries," *Fortune,* December 1965, p. 154 and January 1966, p. 164.
Wright, F. K.: "Capacity for Adaptation and the Asset Measurement Problem," *Abacus,* August 1967, pp. 74–79.

Questions

2–1   Does the rounding of dollar balances to the nearest $1,000, $10,000, or $100,000 introduce a degree of imprecision in accounting statements which decreases their usefulness?

2–2   Draw freehand graphs (using the horizontal axis for time and the vertical axis for dollars) of:
(1) The future value of a sum accumulating at some rate of compound interest for five time periods.
(2) The future value of the same sum accumulating at the same rate of simple interest for five time periods. Explain why they differ.

2–3   What is the relation between n and i in compound interest formulas?

2–4   Should an accountant in his role as a historian regard compound interest formulas as useful? As an analyst? Give illustrations.

2–5   Why should the accountant object to showing bond discount as an asset?

2–6   How can the difficulty of reporting on foreign operations carried on by a domestic firm be overcome?

2–7   Dayton's, an American company, has an account receivable of 5,000 British pounds which is to be paid in pounds. At the time the receivable was booked, the exchange rate for dollars and pounds was $2.80 for 1 pound. When the receivable was collected, the exchange rate had fallen to $2.75. Record the collection of the receivable.

2–8   Do you find any similarities between the use of the computer in accounting and actuarial mathematics (compound interest), price-level indices, and foreign exchange ratios? Any dissimilarities?

2–9   A finance company advertises: "Borrow $1,000 for a total cost of $50. You repay the loan in seven easy monthly installments of $150 each, the first one due one month after the loan." What is the rate of interest charged by the company?

2–10   Use the following choices to complete the schedule of compound interest formulas given on page 70:
    Possible choices for items 1 to 6:
a. A single deposit
b. A series of equal payments made at the end of each of n periods
    Possible choices for items 7 to 18:

c. Present deposit
d. Future amount
e. Periodic payment
f. Periodic deposit

Name of Formula	Other Names	Deposits or Payments	Given Element	Element to Be Ascertained	Mathematical Expression
Compound amount of 1	Compound interest table	(1)_____	(7)_____	(13)_____	$(1 + i)^n$
Present value of 1	Compound discount table	(2)_____	(8)_____	(14)_____	$\dfrac{1}{(1 + i)^n}$
Compound amount of 1 per period	Amount of ordinary annuity	(3)_____	(9)_____	(15)_____	$\dfrac{(1 + i)^n - 1}{i}$
Present value of 1 per period	Present value of ordinary annuity	(4)_____	(10)_____	(16)_____	$\dfrac{(1 + i)^n - 1}{i(1 + i)^n}$
Periodic payment accumulating to 1	Sinking-fund table, or rent of ordinary annuity	(5)_____	(11)_____	(17)_____	$\dfrac{i}{(1 + i)^n - 1}$
Periodic payment with present value of 1	Installment table	(6)_____	(12)_____	(18)_____	$\dfrac{i(1 + i)^n}{(1 + i)^n - 1}$

2–11   To what extent do you consider that the various valuation methods meet the information requirements of relevance, verifiability, freedom from bias, and quantifiability?

2–12   Without checking the tables in Appendix A, indicate in each of the following cases on a separate sheet of paper whether the numbers in the table will become lower or higher as the moves described are made. In all cases moving downward in a column represents an increase in the number of periods, whereas moving from left to right in any row represents successive increases in interest rates:

a. Moving from left to right in a single row in the table for the future value of an annuity

b. Moving downward in a single column in the table for the future value of one dollar

c. Moving downward in a single column in the table for the present value of an annuity

d. Moving from left to right in a single row in the table for the present value of one dollar

e. Moving from left to right in a single row in the table for the present value of an annuity

f. Moving downward in a single column in the table for the future value of an annuity

g. Moving downward in a single column in the table for the present value of one dollar

h. Moving from left to right in a single row in the table for the future value of one dollar

Problems

2-1

Compute the following to the nearest dollar:

a. Using only the table for $P_{\overline{n}|\,i}$, compute the present value of an annuity of $100,000 per quarter for 5 years at 20 percent interest compounded quarterly.

b. Using only the table for $A_{\overline{n}|\,i}$, compute the amount to which an annuity of $2,000 each six months will accumulate in 10 years at 2 percent interest compounded semiannually.

c. Compute by two different methods the amount of an annuity due at $1,500 per year for 10 years at 10 percent interest compounded annually.

d. Compute by two different methods the present value of an annuity due at $3,000 per year for 15 years at 5 percent.

2-2

For each of the following cases write a formula (that is, simply formulate a solution).

Case 1. Zsa Zsa Gabor has an opportunity to acquire a diamond necklace. If she owned the necklace, she could expect to rent it for various TV shows and theater plays, averaging $2,000 per year for 10 years, rent payable each year in advance. Personal property taxes on the necklace are $200 per year, payable at the end of each year. At the end of the tenth year Miss Gabor believes she can sell the necklace for $28,000. She would not undertake this investment unless she could earn an annual return of 10 percent. Determine the maximum amount that Miss Gabor should offer the present owner of the necklace, Mrs. Rex Bell.

Case 2. Nixon deposited $100 in a savings account in his daughter's name on the day she was born, and $100 on each birthday thereafter until she reached the age of eighteen, at which time he added a final deposit of $2,500. If the fund earned interest at 5 percent compounded annually, how much would be in the account on the daughter's eighteenth birthday?

Case 3. Onassis owed various debts totaling $9,500. On June 1 he arranged with a finance company to have the debts paid and to repay the finance company over three years by a series of six equal semiannual payments which could be applied first to interest and then to principal until the loan was retired. The finance company charges interest at 6 percent compounded semiannually. What payments will be required every six months?

Case 4. The Agnew Watch Company has an issue of bonds which must be retired at the end of 20 years. There are 80 bonds which must be called at a price of $1,050 per bond. The company wishes to plan for this retirement by investing an equal annual amount at the end of the first 10 years, and an equal annual amount twice as large at the end of each of the last 10 years, with the objective of having a fund sufficient to retire the bonds at the end of 20 years. The fund is expected to earn an annual rate of 6 percent. Determine the amount of the required annual investment during the first and second 10-year period.

2-3

Partial Tables

Periods	Table A	Table B	Table C	Table D	Table E	Table F
0			1.0000	1.0000		
1	1.0200	1.0000	0.9804	1.0200	1.0200	0.9804
2	0.5150	0.4950	0.9612	1.0404	2.0604	1.9416
3	0.3468	0.3268			3.1216	2.8839

The first three lines of several interest tables appear above. Assuming that complete tables are available in each instance, for each of the following items select from these incomplete tables (by letter) the one from which the amount required can be obtained *most directly.*

(1) The amount of interest that will accumulate on a single deposit by the end of a specified period

(2) The amount to which a single sum would accumulate at compound interest by the end of a specified period

(3) The amount that must be appropriated at the end of each of a specific number of years in order to provide for the accumulation at annually compounded interest of a certain sum of money

(4) The amount that must be deposited in a fund which will earn interest at a specified rate compounded annually, in order to make possible the withdrawal of certain equal sums annually over a specified period starting one year from the date of the deposit

(5) The amount, net of compound discount, which if paid now would settle a debt of a larger amount due at a specified future date

2-4

Using the appropriate table (from those in Appendix A), write the appropriate symbol for and compute (to nearest dollar) each of the following items:

(1) The present value of an annuity of $4,000 per year for 30 years at 4 percent compounded annually

(2) The present value of $50 every six months for 10 years, at 6 percent, compounded semiannually

(3) The amount to which $10 will accumulate in 5 years at 6 percent, compounded annually

(4) The present value of $10,000 due in 20 years at 4 percent, compounded semiannually

(5) The amount of an annuity of $500 every three months for five years at 8 percent compounded quarterly

2-5   In each of the following cases, determine i and n:
Case 1: 5 percent per year, for six years, compounded annually
Case 2: 6 percent per year, for five years, compounded semiannually
Case 3: 10 percent per year, for four years, compounded semiannually

2-6   Draw a graph showing the relationship between the present value of borrowing $20,000 (to be repaid $3,000 at the end of the first year, $10,000 at the end of the second year, and $12,000 at the end of the third year) and various effective rates of interest.

2-7   Find the interest rate i by interpolation in each of the following cases:
(1) $P_{\overline{3}|i} = \$2.7492$; (2) $A_{\overline{4}|i} = \$4.3424$.

2-8   Calculate the amount you would be willing to invest in order to earn 8 percent annually in a four-year enterprise for which it is known that cash receipts and cash disbursements would occur at the end of each year as follows (000's omitted):

		Cash	
Year	Receipts		Outlays
First	$60		$30
Second	80		50
Third	90		70
Fourth	60		30

2-9   The Sinatra family owns a mink ranch in Maryland. Although mink ranching is an extremely risky business (nearly one-third of the ranches have gone out of business in the last two years), it is potentially very profitable with good breeding stock.

The risks of mink farming are similar to those of any luxury industry. The product cannot be sold in periods when money is tight, and it is further subject to the vagaries of the fashion industry.

However, additional risks are involved in mink ranching, owing to the critical nature of the conditions necessary to raise mink. The animals mate in early spring, and whelp in late May or early June. They are ready to be pelted at seven months of age or in January of the next year. When they are weaned, they tend to eat a lot more and become a lot bigger, which means that it is expensive to keep them healthy. Also, at the time of weaning, the kittens must be inoculated against a variety of diseases. A further critical factor is that the animals must be pelted at a certain time to ensure that the quality of the fur is optimal. If pelting is done too early, the fur is not thick enough. If it is done too late, it loses color.

All these factors tend to increase the risks associated with mink ranching. Although the animals mate only once per year, they have an average of four kittens per litter.

The price received for the pelts varies. The record price for the particular strain produced on the Sinatra ranch was $2,700 per pelt, and the average price obtained in the sale to furriers is $2,300 per pelt. However, the mink ranches do not sell directly to furriers, but sell the uncured pelts to tanners, who cure and prepare the pelts for auction.

As a great deal of care and skill are required in curing the pelts, the price received by the ranchers averages only $1,500 per pelt. Also, because of the various factors outlined above, a rancher does not expect that all the kittens born in any one year will be sold. Approximately 1 in 100 dies before pelting. There is a further wastage of about 1 in 200 through mistiming of the pelting.

The breeding stock maintained on the Sinatra ranch is 500 males and 5,000 females. Each season each male services ten females and, each female produces an average of four kittens.

The age distribution of the breeding stock is outlined in Exhibit 2–1. Each male and female has an expected breeding life of only six seasons, and the first season occurs nine months after the animal's birth.

EXHIBIT 2–1
AGE DISTRIBUTION OF BREEDING STOCK AT JANUARY 1, 1972

Breeding Season	Number of Males	Historical Cost Per Mink	Number of Females	Historical Cost Per Mink
First	100	$500	1,000	$300
Second	100	500	1,000	300
Third	100	500	1,000	300
Fourth	100	500	1,000	300
Fifth	100	500	1,000	300
Sixth	. . .	. . . .	. . . .	. . .

Total value of males: $500 \times 500 = \$250,000$
Total value of females: $5,000 \times 300 = \$1,500,000$

The opportunity cost to the Sinatra family of their investment in the mink ranch is 4 percent. This is the return that they could obtain on their money if it were invested in a second mortgage. However, because of the greater uncertainties associated with mink ranching, it is thought that a 2 percent loading onto the opportunity costs represents a fair indication of the greater risk attached to the enterprise. Finally for a time horizon greater than one year, an additional percentage point per year should be added, to take account of the greater risks and uncertainties in the farther future.

The Sinatra family wants to know (1) whether it should value its minks at the historical cost (of the breeding stock plus feed and overhead costs distributed on a per mink basis) or on some other measure, (2) what should be the value of a kit at birth, (3) the value of each year's total brood, (4) the valuation of a breeding male at birth, and (5) the valuation of the breeding stock. How would you answer each of the Sinatra family's questions?

2–10   The Realty Co. is a large land-developing company headquartered in Florida. It is one of the most aggressive promoters of land sales in the United States, selling blocks of land for $1,000, sight unseen.

The company's salesmen operate throughout the United States and offer to sell lots for a $10 deposit (during the month of the sale) and $12.50 per month (starting the month after the month in which the deposit was made) for ten years. After the first year, the annual payment is $150 made at the end of the year, of which $50 represents profit.

They spend large amounts of money on advertising and development of the tracts of land that they sell, expending millions of dollars on roads, sewage, and land clearance.

In the last fiscal year, the company's cash inflow was approximately half the reported sales, due to the company's method of accounting for sales and profits. It sold 300 lots a month, or 3,600 lots for the year.

The procedure that the company follows is to record as sales in a particular year the total purchase prices of the lots sold in that year, most of which are to be paid for over ten years or more, rather than the actual cash amounts received.

The company's cash outflow is also normally in excess of the inflow, due to large first-year payments to salesmen and the lot-development costs. The difference is covered with debt financing at a 12 percent interest rate.

However, despite this cash deficit, the profit that the company ultimately expects to receive from the lot is recorded as earnings, after deducting future expenses and allowing for a small percentage of bad debt losses. Ignoring cash inflow of payments made on blocks purchases in earlier years, and given these data with respect to this year's operations:

(1) If the company is to continue with this method of recording, what would be a more appropriate sales figure?

(2) Since generally accepted accounting principles require that revenue be realized before it is recognized in the financial statements, what would be a more acceptable method of treatment, and what would be the reported profit under this method?

2–11   In April 1962, the Major League Baseball Player's Benefit Plan was amended to provide increased retirement benefits for baseball players, coaches, trainers, and team managers.

The benefits to be received on retirement were of two types—a fixed benefit, depending on the number of years of service given, and a variable benefit, depending on the amount earned annually by an invested fund, which the trustees expected to earn approximately 5 percent per annum.

The total benefit to be received was quite substantial. From the fixed benefit fund, a participant who began receiving benefits at age 65 would be paid $35 per month for each of the first 10 years of service, plus $20 a month for each additional year of service up to a maximum of 20 years total service.

From the variable benefit fund, on current earning power of the fund, a participant could expect to receive an additional $17 per month for each year of service up to a maximum of 10 years if he began receiving benefits at age 65.

Actuaries estimated that a man who reached 65 years of age could expect to live, on the average, for another 15 years. Life expectancy at younger ages was less than this. For example, a twenty-year-old had a life expectancy of 71 years, and a thirty-year-old had a life expectancy of 75 years.

The plan was funded by a levy on the participants of $2 for each day of the 172-day playing season, plus substantial percentages of the net gate receipts and broadcasting rights of World Series and All-Star Games.

The plan lists several classes of members and restricts membership to those participants classified as vested members, who are the only ones eligible to receive benefits upon retirement.

To become a vested member, a player, manager, coach, or trainer must give at least 5 years' service in one or more of these roles. If he gives less than 5 years' service, he is not eligible to receive benefits and may withdraw his contributions at any stage, upon which he will be paid 5 percent interest annually.

(1) What is the plan worth to a thirty-year-old player with 8 years of service, who is now giving up the game and intends to begin receiving benefits at 65?

(2) What value should be placed on the future benefits by a twenty-year-old rookie who is an average player and expects to play for 10 years?

(3) Would the twenty-year-old rookie in (2) be better off to participate in the fund or to invest in a 4 percent fund privately? [NOTE: Use 5% rate in (1) and (2).]

2-12   Design a problem involving the use of at least two interest tables found in Appendix A. Give some consideration to the originality of your problem. Indicate how you would go about solving the problem—what lines and columns of the table you would use, what you would add, subtract, multiply, divide, etc.

2-13   Suppose that a plant asset has a cost of $1,000 when the price index is 100. The next year the index is 110, and $110 depreciation is deducted in arriving at net income (10-year life). The next year the index is 120. Should depreciation be $120 or $130? Explain why.

2-14   At the beginning and at the end of a particular year, the accounts of a certain company show the following balances, in summary (000's omitted):

Debits	Begin.	End	Credits	Begin.	End
Cash and receivables	$50	$50	Current liabilities	$50	$50
Land	25	25	Stockholders' equity	140	143.5
Building	100	130	Building—allowance for depreciation	40	44
Trucks	100	100	Trucks—allowance for depreciation	45	67.5
	$275	$305		$275	$305

Land and buildings were acquired 10 years ago when the general price level was 80, and the present fleet of trucks was acquired two years ago when the index was 120. The index at the beginning of the current period is 160, and there is no change during this period. During the year the revenues of the company total $175,000, the cost of employee and other services and supplies acquired and used amounts to $110,000, and taxes total $25,000. The annual depreciation applicable for buildings is $4,000, and for trucks it is $22,500. During the year dividends of $10,000 were declared and paid, and an addition to the building was made at a cost of $30,000.

Prepare a price-level-adjusted position statement.

2–15

	December 31 (000's omitted)	
	1974	1975
Monetary assets	100	175
Liabilities	100	85
Price level (index)	100	200

Compute the purchasing power gain or loss.

2–16

Dr. Fager, a thoroughbred who won 18 of his 22 races for a total of $1,002,642 during his 28-month career, is being retired in perfect physical condition at the age of four. Most outstanding horses are retired after the age of five or six. William L. McKnight and John Nerud equal owners of Dr. Fager have sold 32 annual breeding rights for $100,000 per share to give him a projected value of $3.2 million. These breeding rights will be exercised at the average rate of $2\frac{1}{2}$ per month.

Dr. Fager's owners have invested so much in him ($500,000) that his loss would be disastrous. Nevertheless, Mr. McKnight and Mr. Nerud have been able to insure him for only $2.1 million by the use of Lloyds of London and six underwriters. Annual premiums payable in advance each year total $92,000; these are in addition to his present cost and have just been paid.

Although Dr. Fager has successfully mated with two ponies which are in foal, uncertainties remain. A stallion must mate with a mare an average of $2\frac{1}{2}$ times before getting her in foal; the average fluctuates with his ability to learn breeding techniques. If Dr. Fager's average is 2.5 or higher, such frequent breeding would be required that he might be worthless within one or two years. The probabilities are one out of four that this might be the case for Dr. Fager. Four years will be required to tell whether he can sire champions of his own quality. Before this time, the owners expect to sell additional breeding rights at the same price, one per month for the second, third, and fourth year. If Dr. Fager does not sire champions, his breeding rights will be worthless after the fourth year. If he does sire champions, the owners expect to sell and exercise annual breeding rights at the same price at the rate of one per month until he is ten years old.

(1) Compute Dr. Fager's value for the books of the McKnight-Nerud partnership, and show computations.
(2) Devise a plan for showing the periodic expiration of this value, together with your rationale. (NOTE: Use 6% rate.)

2–17

A store in Strasburg, Ohio, once referred to as the "world's largest country store," was closed in late August 1970 after operating since 1915. It auctioned off its remaining stock and fixtures. About 1,000 lamps from 1925, still bearing 25-cent price tags, sold for $20 apiece. Compute the net income on the sale of these lamps if 6 percent was the average interest rate for the period 1915 to the present.

2–18

You are preparing calendar-year financial statements for a company that has foreign subsidiaries. All transfers of funds are accomplished at the free market rate.

The following exchange rates are considered:
a. Official rate of currency exchange at December 31
b. Official rate of currency exchange at the date of payment or acquisition
c. Average rate of official currency exchange for the year
d. Average free market rate for each month or the year
e. Free market rate at December 31
f. Free market rate at the date of acquisition or payment

Among the foreign subsidiaries' accounts are the following:
a. Accounts Receivable, trade
b. Notes Payable to Bank (due January 1 of next year)
c. Inventory of Finished Goods, January 1 (shipped from domestic company)
d. Remittance from Domestic Company
e. Office Building

(1) In accordance with AICPA recommendations, indicate at which of the above exchange rates each account would be translated into United States dollars.
(2) Can you suggest any improvements on (1)? Explain.

2–19

On January 1, 1972, a firm held $10,000 in cash and owned property which had cost $50,000 when the firm was originally established on January 1, 1970, and which had accumulated depreciation of $10,000. The proprietor's capital was $50,000, and there were no other assets or liabilities. During 1972, the firm recorded revenue from the sale of services of $25,000, depreciation of $5,000, other expenses of $10,000, proprietorship withdrawals of $5,000. It may be assumed that sales and proprietorship withdrawals were recorded at the end of the year, and that any funds not distributed were used to augment cash balances. Relevant general price-level index numbers were:

January 1, 1970   100
January 1, 1972   120
Average 1972   125
December 31, 1972   130

Prepare financial statements for 1972 adjusted to the general price level prevailing at December 31, 1972. (NOTE: The adjusted balance of the retained earnings account should be calculated as a balancing item.)

2–20

The following are symbols relating to compound interest formulas:

$P_{\overline{n}|\,i}$ = present value of an annuity of n payments of $1 each at interest rate i per period

$p_{\overline{n}|\,i}$ = present value of $1 for n periods at interest rate i per period

$A_{\overline{n}|\,i}$ = future value of an annuity of n payments of $1 each at interest rate i per period

$a_{\overline{n}|\,i}$ = future value of $1 for n periods at interest rate i per period

R = periodic cash payment (or receipt)

(1) If one wishes to earn interest at an annual rate of 6 percent compounded quarterly on an investment that promises to pay the lump sum of $1,000 at the end of 6 years, the formula that could be used to compute the amount that should be paid now is

a. $1,000(A_{\overline{24}|\,.015})$
b. $1,000(a_{\overline{24}|\,.015})$
c. $1,000(P_{\overline{24}|\,.015})$
d. $1,000(p_{\overline{24}|\,.015})$
e. None of the above

(2) If one wishes to earn interest at the annual rate of 4 percent compounded semiannually on an investment contract that promises to pay $1,000 at the end of 20 years, along with semiannual interest payments of $25 (computed at an annual interest rate of 5 percent on the maturity amount), the formula that could be used to compute the amount that should be paid now is

a. $1,000(p_{\overline{20}|\,.04}) + $50(P_{\overline{20}|\,.04})$
b. $1,000(p_{\overline{40}|\,.02}) + $25(P_{\overline{40}|\,.02})$
c. $1,000(p_{\overline{20}|\,.05}) + $50(P_{\overline{20}|\,.05})$
d. $1,000(p_{\overline{40}|\,.05}) + $25(P_{\overline{40}|\,.05})$
e. None of the above

(3) On May 1, 1972, one wishes to know the amount of the equal payments that must be made semiannually beginning on November 1, 1972, in order to have a fund of $10,000 at the end of 20 years. If one is certain that the fund will earn interest at the annual rate of 6 percent compounded semiannually, a formula that could be used to compute the periodic payment is

a. $10,000 = R(A_{\overline{40}|\,.03})$
b. $10,000 = R(A_{\overline{20}|\,.06})$
c. $10,000 = R(P_{\overline{40}|\,.03})$
d. $10,000 = R(P_{\overline{20}|\,.06})$
e. None of the above

(4) On May 1, 1972, a new Corvette was purchased on a 4-year installment contract which required payments of $100 now and $100 on the first day of each month, with the last payment due on April 1, 1976. If the annual interest rate is 6 percent compounded monthly, the formula that could be used to compute the apparent cash price for the car is

a. $1,200(P_{\overline{4}|.06})$

b. $100(P_{\overline{47}|.005}) + \$100$

c. $100(P_{\overline{48}|.005})$

d. $100(p_{\overline{47}|.005}) + \$100$

e. None of the above

3

The Accounting Model and Financial Statements

It is the sufficient answer rather than the right answer which the accountant really seeks. Under these circumstances, however, it is important that we should know what the accountant's answer means, which means we should know what procedure he has employed.*
KENNETH E. BOULDING, 1962

Accountants have developed a framework or model of items concurrently labeled assumptions, conclusions, standards, principles, concepts, and postulates. Regardless of the terminology used, these items provide a basis for conventional financial accounting theory and practice: in this chapter they are called concepts. Some of the terms and underlying concepts may not be quickly understood, but their meaning will increase as they are integrated and applied in later sections. (In Chapter 12 the development of principles by the AICPA will be considered.)

The importance of understanding the accounting model cannot be overemphasized; it provides the framework for structuring, answering, and explaining questions relating to the recording of entries, the preparation of reports, and the analyzing of financial data. Although the exact nature of the accounting model has been represented differently by various individuals, the formulation in this book consists of four basic, generally applicable accounting concepts which will be considered next, and the accounting equation which will be discussed later in the chapter, after assets, liabilities, and equities have been introduced.

*From "Economics and Accounting: The Uncongenial Twins," in W. T. Baxter and Sidney Davidson, eds., *Studies in Accounting Theory* (Homewood, Illinois: Richard D. Irwin, Inc., 1962), pp. 53–54.

The Accounting Entity

The first accounting concept relates to the accounting unit or entity. All financial data are accumulated, reported, and analyzed for some unit, the boundaries of which must be established before the accounting system can be designed and the accounting process begun. The complete array of accounting units extends from the individual or household to the international organization, and includes charitable institutions, not-for-profit enterprises, and governmental units and agencies, as well as private businesses that normally are organized to earn a profit. Subunits of an enterprise, such as departments, divisions, or other areas of individual responsibility which qualify as cost or profit centers, are likely accounting units. However, these latter units are of major concern for internal managerial purposes, and will not be explored further in this book.

Major emphasis here will be on the accounting units that will facilitate the preparation of necessary, meaningful, and useful reports for external parties, including current and prospective owners and creditors and governmental agencies. For these users, the most commonly identified accounting entity is the business enterprise or activity. The entity usually is organized as a sole proprietorship, a partnership, or a corporation and is accounted for separately from the other activities of the owner or owners. When a single owner or group of owners are engaged in several different enterprises it usually is advantageous, for internal and often for legal purposes, to have a separate accounting system to reflect the affairs and activities of each identifiable business unit. The accounts of all or some of these separate systems may then be combined in ways which make reports and analyses more meaningful for external users.

Accounting units may be classified into four identifiable but overlapping entity concepts. The first of these relates to ownership, and the boundaries of the accounting entity established under this concept can be determined by the properties, obligations, and/or activities that are interrelated by virtue of their being owned by one or more individuals or groups. The second and most commonly used concept is the legal or statutory entity. The boundary of this accounting entity is identical with the legal entity (corporation, partnership, or sole proprietorship) formed under statutory or common law. A third concept relates to the economic entity. Under this concept the boundary of the accounting entity is established for a controlled, interrelated, and integrated economic activity—a managed economic unit.

A fourth concept relates to other socioeconomic entities of our environment. The best-known grouping in this category is an industry, in particular, the power and communications utility industries that are regulated respectively by the Federal Power Commission and the Federal Communications Commission. In given circumstances, each agency requires that the entire industry be accounted for as though it were a single unit. Another example of this might be the nation as a whole and the national income accounts which are compiled largely by summing the data from accounting reports of individual households and enterprises.

A first step in the financial accounting process, then, is to establish the boundaries of the accounting entity or entities for which the accounting system or systems will be designed and to which the other concepts of the accounting model will be applied.

Unit of Measure

A second accounting concept maintains that the unit of measure in the formal accounting system is the local monetary unit or money (for example, the dollar in the United States, the peso in Mexico). Although this does not preclude the use of nonmonetary measures in certain accounting records and reports, a physical unit, such as a pound, an inch, or a widget, usually lacks the universality to be appropriate for measuring and communicating useful information on the status or activities of an entire accounting unit.

It is often stated that accounting assumes that the monetary unit is stable (that is, that the dollar has a constant purchasing power over time); but the reader will recognize that such an assumption would not be realistic. Instead, accounting has chosen to ignore changes in the purchasing power of its monetary unit to some extent because of the failure to develop a widely acceptable, appropriate general index (or set of indices) of the changes in price level(s). As was indicated in Chapter 2, such an index has been identified (the Gross National Product Implicit Price Deflator), and both teachers of accounting and the AICPA have given substantial support to providing supplementary financial reports in which current purchasing power is the unit of measure.

Accounting Period

Another accounting concept relates to the rendering of (1) activity and performance reports (the major ones are income and fund-flow statements) for an *arbitrary* period of time, and (2) financial status reports at the last date of such a period. Reports may be compiled on major jobs, projects, contracts, or voyages for use within the firm, but external reports now are invariably prepared at regular time intervals.

The income or fund-flow measures tend to be more meaningful and more useful to external parties for analytical purposes when they are associated with a given period of time than when they are related to a job or project. For example, because of the high cost of compiling such information, it would be ridiculous to render a separate income report to outsiders for each major sale in a department store or for each job in a construction firm that has many contracts in progress. However, periodic performance reports would be useful in appraising the progress of the one-job-at-a-time firm whose contract extends over several years.

Because enterprise activity tends to be continuous, and the good or service that is provided to a customer on any given day usually is the result of operations that began a long time—often several years—before, increasing the length of the accounting period reduces the extent and difficulty of the measurement problems associated with rendering periodic financial reports. This is because a greater portion of the activities will then have been completed. For example, measuring the income of an enterprise for its entire lifetime is a rather simple task which can be done with complete certainty. It is reporting upon performance and financial status during the intermediate periods that presents the major measurement problems, but such timely reports are useful and necessary to decision making. These reports also provide the basis for most accounting activity.

It follows that reports of income tend to be more tentative as the time period is shortened. It has become almost a universal practice for the firm whose stock is traded on organized stock exchanges to render such reports at least once each year, and also to issue abbreviated reports at quarterly intervals.

Although most firms prepare annual reports at the end of the calendar year, a growing practice is the adoption of the natural business year as the accounting period. In effect, a 12-month period is chosen which ends (and begins) at a convenient time, preferably near the beginning of a slow season when regular activities and inventories are at a low point.

Objectivity and Verifiability
A fourth accounting concept concerns the need for selecting accounting measurements that can provide users of financial reports with relevant information that is reliable for decision making. There is substantial agreement among accountants that objective, verifiable, bias-free data are needed, but there is substantial disagreement concerning the meaning of the terms "objective," "verifiable," and "freedom from bias." The meaning that appears to be receiving increased acceptability and that has significance to accounting measurement theory will be used in this book. Measurements can be considered objective if they can be verified by several qualified experts and are also free from bias. As discussed in Chapter 1, verifiability is considered to be "that attribute of information which

allows qualified individuals working independently of one another to develop essentially similar measures or conclusions from an examination of the same evidence."[1]

The present discussion has referred to the basics of four accounting concepts—the accounting unit; the monetary measure; the time period; and objectivity, verifiability, freedom from bias—four concepts that will be applied further throughout the book.

Additional Concepts

Two additional concepts that have little relevance when the accounting is in terms of current values but are fundamental to traditional or conventional financial accounting which is based upon historical cost are matching and realization. Two less fundamental concepts to be considered here that also are generally applicable are consistency and disclosure.

Matching This concept states that income is determined by matching costs (resources used up) with revenues (resource inflows, usually cash or claims to cash). Income determination becomes a process of first recognizing the revenue when it is realized and then accumulating as expenses or deductions from revenues the values of assets used up and/or liabilities incurred directly or indirectly in bringing about the revenue. Many major financial accounting problems stem from the determination of income; these problems will be considered further in Chapters 4 and 9.

Realization The second concept is the recognition (recording) of revenue or gains or losses for the accounting unit at the time of realization. Although there is substantial disagreement concerning the meaning of "realization," this book will consider two primary criteria *as prerequisites* to its occurrence:

1. There must be objective evidence of the market value of the good or service; and
2. The earning process (in essence, the series of events that must be completed to create, furnish, and collect for the good or service or to cause the gain or loss to come into being) must be substantially completed, at least to the extent that the revenue is recognized.

For a retail enterprise, revenue normally would be realized, and recognized, when a sale is made, because this is the time when the good is transferred to the customer, and cash or claim to cash is received from him. Both criteria would be satisfied if cash or a claim to cash

[1] *A Statement of Basic Accounting Theory* (Evanston, Illinois: AAA, 1966), p. 10.

(receivable) is received and collection is assured and considered to be a minor step.

The concept of realization is an extremely important one which, when merged with the monetary unit concept, pinpoints historical cost as the conventional basis of valuation in accounting. Consequently, assets are calculated in terms of costs to the accounting unit, costs that are established and recorded at the time of acquisition. Nonmonetary assets, such as inventories, plant, and long-term investments, are recorded at cost, which may be adjusted downward to reflect declines in value or losses of usefulness. In other cases such assets, especially inventories, are carried at cost or adjusted cost until realization occurs and revenue is recognized (this usually involves a sale or an exchange transaction). Thus monetary assets, such as cash and receivables, reflect amounts realized and are no longer valued at cost. This is because cost, to enlarge upon the definition given in Chapters 1 and 2, is the amount of money paid (or to be paid) or the fair market value (cash value of the good if transferred in an arm's length transaction involving a willing buyer and a willing seller) of whatever was given up for the good, service, or right when it was initially acquired by and for the accounting unit. For assets which have been donated or for which the fair market value of whatever was given up is not readily available, cost becomes the fair market value of whatever was received.

Consistency Consistency refers to the application of accounting rules, methods, and procedures so as to avoid manipulating the end result and to facilitate comparisons over time and among different accounting entities. The accountant promotes consistency by encouraging the accounting unit to apply the same methods and procedures from period to period, in order to achieve uniformity. He permits changes to be made only to correct errors or to improve the accounting process or the meaningfulness of reported accounting data.

Disclosure Another secondary concept concerns the responsibility that the accountant has to present reports which fairly disclose the results of operations and/or the financial condition of the accounting unit, and which contain adequate factual information clearly expressed so as to not be misleading to the user. Ideally, accounting reports should reflect all the significant financial information (1) that is relevant to a given decision and (2) that can be understood by a given user or user group. This suggests three closely related and perhaps overlapping criteria of disclosure: (1) materiality, (2) adequacy, and (3) clarity.

Materiality is a statistical concept which implies that items that are not significant need not be taken seriously or, logically, that insignificant items cannot have a major impact on the entity. Having or not having knowledge of insignificant items should not influence decisions. Accounting, then, permits variations in the treatment of immaterial items, even though the concept of consistency is violated. For example, a gain or loss that relates directly to a prior period might be treated as a gain or loss of the period in which it was recognized if the amount was relatively small.

Adequacy of disclosure does not imply a need to give exhaustive details since to do this would tend to confuse the user by obscuring the major facts and relationships. Instead, reports should include only those data that are material and relevant to the decision of the given user or users. In many instances adequate disclosure requires the use of explanations to supplement the data appearing on the face of the statement. Such comments are of particular importance in elucidating (and, where appropriate, in stating the dollar amount of the effects of) the following practices: (1) using unusual or controversial procedures, (2) changing valuation bases and methods, or (3) reporting favorable or catastrophic events occurring soon after the accounting period has ended but before the reports are prepared.

Clarity requires the use of descriptions that are complete and understandable to an informed investor or a standard reader, who has been described as one who is interested enough to read carefully and who is reasonably well informed on financial matters, at least with respect to commonly used accounting and financial terminology. Thus, care should be taken in drafting statements to avoid words and expressions which, even though widely used, are likely to be misleading or vague. There has been improvement in the use of terminology in recent years, but many vague terms are still commonly used. Examples of these are "surplus" and "reserve."

Another aspect of disclosure relates to the continuity or going concern concept, for which theorists have many different interpretations. This concept often is explained as a logical extension to the accounting model of the fact that most firms (e.g., the typical corporation) are organized to operate for an indefinite period. But there is substantial disagreement as to whether continuity is an assumption, a condition, a prediction, or a relevant postulate. Your authors accept the view that the continuity concept is relevant to the presentation of information about the resources, obligations, and activities of the accounting unit that users need in making predictions of future activity. This is because the concept relates the present to the past and the future, so that in the case of a possible discontinuance of activity (e.g., a forced liquidation), the conventional accounting model would not apply, and the accountant should modify his presentation at least to the extent of disclosing the nature of the possible discontinuity in the activities of the accounting unit.

Definition and Classification of Assets

There are many definitions of an accounting asset, but the differences among them usually are slight. In general, the following three characteristics are implicit or explicit in most or all of the definitions:

1. An asset is an economic potential secured by law, from which there is a reasonable expectation that the accounting entity will receive a positive benefit or a service in the future.
2. An asset is the result of a financial transaction or economic event of the past, not the future.
3. The amount of the asset must be subject to calculation or close approximation in accordance with double-entry bookkeeping.

Normally, an asset is recognized only to the extent that there has been performance by at least one of the parties to the transaction agreement (that is, to the extent that the vendor or the intended recipient of the good or service has done something for the benefit of the other as a result of the agreement). A transaction need not necessarily precede the purchase of an asset (for example, changes occurring within an enterprise). Although most assets necessarily are tangible (or physical) in the sense that they can be seen, touched, or felt, assets can also be intangible (for example, goodwill). Furthermore, although assets ordinarily are measured in money, it is logically wrong to confuse the object measured, an accounting asset, with its measure, money values.

The weakest definitions of asset are stated in terms of

4. A specific basis of valuation (for example, cost)
5. Position on a statement (for example, on the left side)
6. Usual classification of the balance (for example, a debit)

Not all assets are valued on a cost basis; even in conventional financial accounting based on cost, some assets are valued at their selling price or on some other basis. Not all assets appear on the left side of a position statement, even where a horizontal format is used; in some countries they are listed on the right side.[2] Not all assets even have a debit balance.[3] Also in accounting an asset usually would not be recorded in connection with a wholly executory agreement (nonperformance on both sides) or beyond the extent to which either party has performed.

[2] A discussion of the position statement begins on page 94.
[3] A discussion of debits and credits begins on page 128.

Using the first three characteristics for a definition, the following are some of the major types of transactions that would give rise to an asset for an accounting unit:

1. Purchases of inventories, machinery, or other tangible (physical) goods to the extent that the goods have been received by the accounting unit or that such goods have been set aside by the vendor (seller) for the accounting unit, whether or not payment has been made
2. Purchases of patents, insurance coverage, licenses, services, and other intangibles (rights or services) to the extent that the vendor has performed his required service or that the accounting unit has made payment for the service or right to receive the service in the future

The following types of events *do not* give rise to accounting assets under these criteria:

1. Merely placing or receiving an order requiring the furnishing of a good, service, or right at a future date
2. Hiring an employee to begin work tomorrow
3. Having locational advantages or developing favorable relationships with employees, creditors, customers, or government

From these examples it is obvious that many assets created by economic events are not considered accounting assets and thus are not recorded. A major reason for this is the inability to measure or a lack of objective information concerning items that have not been purchased—or services that are to be performed over a period of time in the future by someone or something that the entity cannot own or has no intention of owning.

Classification of assets The criteria for assets relate to their operating characteristics and liquidity. The most liquid items, those that can be expected to be directly or indirectly converted into cash within one year or the operating cycle of the entity, whichever is longer, are classified as *current assets*. The operating cycle refers to the average time of the cash-to-cash cycle for the activities of the enterprise and may be diagramed for a retailing or wholesaling firm as follows:

Cash ⟶ *Inventory* ⟶ *Sale* ⟶ *Receivable* ⟶ *Cash*

For a manufacturing firm, the inventory stage would be expanded, and the following would be substituted:

Acquisition of Raw Materials, Labor, and Other Inputs ⟶ *Production Process* ⟶ *Finished Product*

Most enterprises have selected one year as the determining factor, regardless of the length of the operating cycle.

Current assets (normally classified in the order of their liquidity, with the most liquid listed first) include such items as cash (on hand or in the bank), readily marketable securities (held to earn a return on cash resources), amounts due from customers (accounts receivable), materials, supplies, and other goods on hand (inventories), and advance payments for such items as insurance or rent (prepaid or unexpired costs).

Items not classified properly as current assets are obviously noncurrent and are commonly separated into investments, plant, and other intangibles.

The *investments* category is used for those items of securities, long-term receivables, and other investments which (1) are neither readily marketable nor convertible into cash, or (2) may be readily marketable or convertible into cash, but which management does not intend to sell because it is holding them for longer-term investment or control purposes (for example, the cash surrender value of a life insurance policy or ownership investments in a subsidiary company). It is quite common for one corporation to buy a controlling interest[1] in one or more additional corporations for one or more of several purposes, such as to ensure a stable market for its output or to diversify so as to be less vulnerable to changing business conditions. Accounting for these investments will be discussed in Chapter 11.

Plant assets (often called long-lived or fixed assets) are normally classified in the order of their fixity (or permanence), with the most fixed (land) listed first. Included are items such as land, buildings, and equipment that have a useful life longer than one year (or the entity's operating cycle). Unlike current asset items such as inventories, which are physically converted in the production process or are sold and transferred to customers, the plant assets contribute to the performance of production, selling, or other functions or activities of the enterprise—they constitute the *physical* plant—thus, unless they are surplus or standby facilities, they cannot be sold without disrupting normal operations.

Included in the *other intangible assets* category are such items as patents, trademarks, and goodwill—all items that have a useful life longer than one year (or the entity's operating cycle) and that

---

[1] *Controlling interest* has legal and economic interpretations. The legal interpretation specifies ownership of 50 percent of the outstanding shares of voting stock plus one share. The economic interpretation usually specifies that a controlling interest enables the holder(s) to direct the operations of that corporation. The AICPA's Accounting Principles Board, in its Opinion No. 18, has concluded that an investment of 20 percent or more of the voting stock gives presumptive evidence that the investor has the ability to exercise significant influence over the operations of that corporation. The preferred accounting treatment is based on the economic interpretation.

do not fit neatly into one of the other categories. It should be recognized that although cash, receivables, prepayments, and investments are often considered to be tangible assets they are themselves, in fact, intangible since they are rights rather than physical goods.

Definition and Classification of Equities

The two major categories of equities normally grouped separately with subtotals for each are: (1) liabilities for the claims of creditors and (2) owners' or stockholders' equity for the residual claims of the owners.

Definition of liabilities In the most simplified sense, liabilities represent the debts of the accounting unit—the sources of its assets. A more complete definition of an accounting liability can be established by listing three characteristics:

1. A liability requires a future outlay of money, or an equivalent acceptable to the recipient.
2. A liability is the result of a financial transaction or economic event of the past, not the future.
3. The amount of the liability must be subject to calculation or close estimation (objectivity) and be based on double-entry bookkeeping.

This definition obviously excludes from accounting many items which in an economic sense might be considered to be liabilities, items such as next month's payroll, next year's purchase of inventory or plant assets, next month's borrowing from a bank—since these are future events. Possible awards of damages in a lawsuit currently in progress against the firm for an alleged infraction during the past are also excluded because of the impossibility of close estimation.

Included as accounting liabilities under this definition, however, are items that would traditionally be excluded by practicing accountants, such as amounts falling due in the future in connection with existing long-term leasehold (rental) contracts and, possibly, with long-term, fixed-dollar salary contracts.[5]

Classification of liabilities Liabilities normally are divided into two categories. First, *current liabilities* include those items which fall due and, thus, should be paid within one year (or the operating cycle of the entity). Another closely related, but more restrictive, definition states that current liabilities include those obligations whose liquidation is reasonably expected to require (1) the use of existing resources properly classified as current assets, or (2) the creation of

[5]For further discussion see Maurice Moonitz, "The Changing Concept of Liabilities," *The Journal of Accountancy*, May 1960, pp. 41–46.

other current liabilities.[6] This classification would include amounts owed to trade creditors for inventory purchases and the like (accounts payable), unpaid wages and salaries earned by employees (wages and salaries payable), various kinds of taxes (income taxes payable, withheld income taxes payable, payroll taxes payable, and property taxes payable), amounts owed on short-term loans from banks and other lending agencies (notes payable), amounts paid by customers for goods to be delivered or services rendered in the near future, and miscellaneous debts for goods or services that have been received (interest payable, rent payable, and dividends payable).

The second category, *long-term liabilities,* includes all liabilities of the entity not properly classifiable as current. Some of the items included would be amounts not due within one year (or the entity's operating cycle) on long-term borrowing (bonds, mortgages, notes, and contracts payable), estimated amounts due on new-product warranties, deferred income taxes, and leasehold liabilities.

Owners' equity Owners' equity includes those items that are necessary to reflect the status of the claims of the owners. The items included will vary somewhat, depending on the legal form of the entity (for example, sole proprietorship, partnership, or corporation).

If it were a sole proprietorship (owned by one individual), the following items would appear:

Individual's name, capital

If it were a partnership with two individuals as owners, the following items would appear:

Individual No. 1's name, capital
Individual No. 2's name, capital

Or if it were a corporation, there would be at least two items of stockholders' equity for a firm that has been in operation over a period of time:

Capital stock
Retained earnings[7]

Usually there is more than one capital stock item because the entity may have issued more than one class of stock (for example, common

---

[6]"Working Capital," Accounting Research Bulletin No. 43, Chapter 3, paragraph 7, in *APB Accounting Principles,* vol. 2 (New York: AICPA, 1971), p. 6011.
[7]If a sole proprietorship or a partnership retains earnings in the firm only temporarily, the account is called *current* or *drawing.*

and preferred). Capital stock items may be combined into a single item which might be called Capital Contributed by Stockholders. Retained earnings, too, are often subdivided into more than one item.

The Accounting Equation

Fundamental to the conventional accounting model is the equation which expresses the financial relationships of double-entry accounting and which may be manipulated just as any algebraic formula. The traditional form is:

Assets ($) = Liabilities ($) + Ownership ($)
which means
Assets ($) = Claims of Creditors ($) + Claims of Owners ($)

The equation may be transposed as follows:

Assets ($) − Claims of Creditors ($) = Claims of Owners ($)
or
Assets ($) − Claims of Owners ($) = Claims of Creditors ($)

The term *equity* is often substituted for *claim* so that we may speak of creditors' equity and owners' equity, or creditors' equity and stockholders' equity, or simply, equities. Thus, the equation becomes:

Assets ($) = Equities ($)

This form of the equation often is applicable in giant enterprises where it may be both difficult and unnecessary to clearly separate the claims of creditors from those of owners.

The equation often is modified to reflect the fact that all assets and liabilities of the accounting unit typically are subclassified as to whether they are current. Then the equation becomes:

Current Assets ($) + Noncurrent Assets ($) = Current Liabilities ($)
+ Noncurrent (or long-term) Liabilities ($) + Ownership ($)

As indicated earlier, *current* means conversion into cash within a year or the firm's operating cycle, whichever is longer, but usually a year.

Finally, the equation can be modified further to reflect the several major categories of noncurrent assets, such as investments, plant, and other intangibles. Thus:

Current Assets ($) + Investments ($) + Plant ($) + Other Intangibles ($) =
Current Liabilities ($) + Noncurrent Liabilities ($)
+ Ownership ($)

There are other versions of this equation. For example, in some countries the equation is reversed with the equities coming first; for certain types of enterprises there are other modifications of this equation too. In all versions it is convenient to express the relationships with equality signs. Nevertheless, it is important to note that all of them are identities or truisms, because the equality holds for all dollar amounts of assets and the claims against assets—each asset must have a claim or commitment—even though the interrelationship may not be traceable directly.

The Position Statement

The position statement (often called the statement of financial condition or, more commonly and traditionally, the balance sheet) provides information about the financial condition or status of the accounting unit at a given date. It is based upon the accounting equation. The statement sometimes is likened to a picture or a snapshot, which presents at a moment in time the firm's image of the cumulative effects of financial changes that have occurred from the initial organization of the accounting unit to the indicated moment. Thus, in conventional accounting it presents the end result of applying the accounting model in recording and classifying the

The Company
Position Statement
December 31, 1972
(000's omitted)
Vertical or Report
Format

Assets		
Current		*$1.7*
Investments		*0.5*
Plant		*2.5*
Intangibles		*0.3*
		$5.0

Equities		
Liabilities:		
Current	*$0.8*	
Long-term	*0.7*	
Total liabilities		*$1.5*
Stockholders' equity:		
Capital contributed		
by shareholders	*$2.7*	
Retained earnings	*0.8*	*3.5*
Total stockholders'		
equity		*$5.0*

financial events or transactions of the accounting unit for its entire life.[8]

The position statement offers two basic types of information: namely, stocks of resources (assets), and claims against those resources (equities). Assume, for illustration purposes, that the total assets of the accounting unit, a corporation, are $5,000; that its liabilities are $1,500; and, thus, that its stockholders' equity is $3,500. The position statement for the accounting unit might be presented in several different forms, of which the preceding, the vertical (or report) arrangement is one.

Published statements (or statements that are prepared for some problems in this book) normally will show the individual items in detail within each of the three major headings (assets, liabilities, and owners' equity) with additional subheadings. The subheadings used, as well as their organization within the major headings, will vary somewhat to reflect the situation and operating characteristics of the enterprise.

The preceding position statement for The Company would appear as follows when all items are listed using the horizontal (or account) format:

The Company
Position Statement
December 31, 1972
(000's omitted)
Horizontal or
Account Format

Assets			Equities		
Current:			*Current liabilities:*		
Cash on hand and in			Accounts payable	$0.2	
banks	$0.5		Wages and salaries		
Marketable securities	0.1		payable	0.1	
Accounts receivable	0.2		Income taxes payable	0.1	
Supplies	0.3		Withheld income		
Merchandise	0.5		taxes payable	0.1	
Prepayments	0.1	$1.7	Payroll taxes payable	0.1	
			Current obligations—		
			new product war-		
Investments:			ranties	0.1	
Cash surrender			Advances from cus-		
value of life in-			tomers	0.1	$0.8
surance policies	0.1				
Investment in af-					
filiated company	0.4	0.5			

[8]The careful reader will recognize that this may not be true if the accounting unit departs from conventional accounting with its indirect, historical cost basis of valuation and adopts a direct, current valuation approach.

Assets			*Equities*		
Plant:			*Long-term liabilities:*		
Land	$0.5		Bonds payable	$0.5	
Buildings	1.0		Deferred obligations		
Machinery, fixtures,			—new product		
and equipment	0.4		warranties	0.2	$0.7
Automobiles	0.6	$2.5	Total liabilities		1.5
			Stockholders' equity:		
Intangibles:			Capital contributed		
Patents	0.2		by stockholders	2.7	
Goodwill	0.1	0.3	Retained earnings	0.8	3.5
Total assets		$5.0	Total equities		$5.0

Elements of Income Determination

Before about 1930 the position statement received far greater attention than the income statement. Since then there has been general recognition that the position statement prepared in accordance with conventional or traditional accounting does not reflect the current value of assets, and that the value of an entity's assets or of the owners' equity depends largely upon income. Although it is the future income that is important, the incomes of current and past periods are useful as points of departure in predicting future income. Thus there is substantial agreement in considering the measurement of income to be the primary function of financial accounting.

There is, however, less agreement as to what income should comprise. Since this question will be explored more thoroughly in Chapter 9, for the present we will adopt the widely accepted view that in determining income the accountant should strive to measure the performance or relative efficiency of the entity for the period involved.

Revenue and expense In measuring performance, the accountant first recognizes the revenue of the period, and then matches this with the expenses or the values that have expired during the period directly or indirectly in earning the revenue. The net result of this matching of revenues and expenses will be income (or loss). This excess (or deficiency) should be a reasonable monetary measure of the performance during the period. It also represents the increase in net assets and in owners' equity as a result of this performance.

Revenues are the amounts received or to be received from the customer for the goods or services which the entity is supplying him. *Expenses,* on the other hand, are the values which have expired (the value of the assets used up and/or liabilities incurred) directly in furnishing the good or service to the customer, or indirectly with respect to the revenues but directly with respect to the entity and the time period for which the revenue is being accumulated.

Cash versus accrual basis (implicit in matching) One does not go far into a discussion of the conventional accounting concept of income without encountering the problem of the cash versus accrual basis of income determination. This problem relates to the recognition of revenues and/or expenses in the period in which the service or benefit is performed or received rather than when the cash is received or paid.

In its simplest and earliest form, the cash basis of income would have meant that revenues were recognized when cash was received, and expenses were recognized when cash was paid, whether or not the service had been performed or received. Although this approach may have some justification when there is complete uncertainty concerning the events of the future, it has little or no merit for most situations in the more stable economic environments, such as that of the United States, because it would tend to violate the concepts of matching and realization. Thus, the resulting income figures would tend not to be a good measure of performance for the period.

A more contemporary view of the cash basis would have revenues recognized on a cash basis, but the major value expirations (such as those related to inventories and plant assets) would be matched with the revenues, with the less important items being charged to expense as the cash is paid. This approach would be reasonable (1) if the collection step in the operating cycle is an extremely crucial one in which there is a high degree of uncertainty concerning the amount and/or time of collection, and (2) if the amount of expenses charged when the cash paid is not substantially different from the amount that should be matched with the revenues. (See Chapter 9 for a further discussion of the cash collection basis for recognizing revenue.)

Although a strict interpretation of the realization criteria might require the cash basis for revenue recognition in many circumstances, the matching concept requires the accrual of expenses in most instances, to avoid misleading income figures. First, the entity must determine the appropriate point at which realization occurs, so that the revenue may be recognized for its various lines of products or services. Second, it must establish guidelines appropriate for recognizing the expenses of earning the revenue.

The income statement The basic accountant's report on the entity's performance for the period, the income statement (sometimes called the profit and loss statement), may take one of several different forms:

the most common are the single-step and the multistep arrangements. In the single-step statement, all revenue items are shown
and the individual items summed; all the expenses are then itemized,
summed, and deducted as a single total, to derive the income figure
in one step. The multistep statement may have several different
arrangements, but there tends to be one or more revenue sections,
about three groups of expense items to reflect the major functions
performed by a manufacturing enterprise (acquisition and production, selling, and administration) with separate subtotals at each
section, and near the bottom of the statement a figure for income.
The 1972 revenue and expense data for The Company is recast into
two different forms in the following statements.

Single-step Form
The Company
Income Statement
Year Ended
December 31, 1972
(000's omitted)

Revenues:		
Sales	$2.4	
Interest	0.1	$2.5
Expenses:		
Cost of goods sold (merchandise expense)	1.2	
Salaries	0.3	
Depreciation*	0.2	
Advertising	0.1	
Insurance	0.1	
Miscellaneous	0.2	
Interest charges	0.1	
Income taxes	0.1	2.3
Net income		$0.2

The allocation of expired plant value to this period.

Multistep Form
The Company
Income Statement
Year Ended
December 31, 1972
(000's omitted)

Operating revenue:			
Sales			$2.4
Operating expenses:			
Cost of goods sold (merchandise expense)		1.2	
Gross margin on sales			$1.2
Selling:			
Salaries	$0.2		
Depreciation	0.1		
Advertising	0.1	$0.4	
Administrative:			
Salaries	0.1		
Depreciation	0.1		
Insurance	0.1		
Miscellaneous	0.2	0.5	
Total other operating expenses			0.9
Net operating income			0.3

Nonoperating:		
Interest revenue		$0.1
		0.4
Interest charges	$0.1	
Income taxes	0.1	0.2
Net income		$0.2

Another form that might be illustrated combines the statement of income with a reconciliation of retained earnings, which is often presented separately. The combination of the two illustrates that an income statement is a link between two position statements. Using the opening and closing figures for the income statement, this is as follows:

The Company Statement of Income and Retained Earnings For the Year 1972 (000's omitted)

Sales	$2.4
Less: Expenses (details)	2.2
Net income	0.2
Retained earnings, January 1, 1972	0.7
Dividends declared	0.1
Retained earnings, December 31, 1972	$0.8

Other Financial Reports

Although the income statement and the position statement traditionally have been the primary reports of financial accounting, they are commonly supplemented by a fund-flow statement. Like the income statement, the fund-flow statement is a report of a flow through the entity for a period of time. However, the fund-flow statement normally reports on changes in a fund, most commonly working capital (current assets less current liabilities), during a time period; whereas the income statement reports the changes in retained earnings between two position statements. Although the fund-flow statement, at least in skeleton form, usually can be prepared by reconstructing the events of a period from the data shown on both the income and position statements, the fund-flow statement provides answers to questions that cannot be answered directly from the income and position statements either individually or together. Examples of such questions are: What happened to net income for the period? How much was invested in new plant or other noncurrent assets during the period? How was this expansion financed? What were the proceeds of new bonds or capital stock issued during the period? Such fund-flow statements will be discussed in some depth in Chapter 6.

In addition, many firms not only include comparative position, income, and fund-flow statements for the current and immediately preceding year in their annual reports, but also provide statistical summaries of major items of financial data for a number of years.

Summary

The accounting model provides the framework for structuring and answering questions related to the recording of entries, the preparation of reports, and the analysis of financial data. The accounting model, as described in this book, consists of four major concepts and the accounting equation.

The four basic concepts of the accounting model are (1) the accounting entity, (2) the unit of measure, (3) the accounting period, and (4) the objectivity and verifiability of accounting data.

1. The boundaries of the unit to be measured must be established before the accounting system can be designed and applied. For external users of accounting statements the most commonly identified accounting entity is the business enterprise. The accounting entity may be classified according to ownership, legal, economic, or socioeconomic boundaries.
2. The normal unit of measure of the accounting system is the local monetary unit.
3. The accounting period is an arbitrary period of time for which meaningful reports are prepared. This time period might be one year, one quarter, or the operating (cash-to-cash) cycle of the entity.
4. The fourth basic concept of the accounting model requires that the accounting measurements selected be both objective and verifiable.

In the context of historical cost accounting, two other concepts, matching and realization, should be considered. The concept of matching states that income is determined by matching costs to revenues. The concept of realization states that revenue or gains or losses for the accounting unit are recognized at the time of realization, that is, at the time when there is objective evidence of the market value of the good or service and at the time when the earning process is substantially complete.

Two subsidiary concepts are that accounting procedures must be employed with consistency and that accounting reports must disclose fairly the results of the operations and the financial condition of the firm.

Fundamental to the conventional accounting model is the accounting equation. Its traditional form is: Assets (in dollars) = Liabilities (in dollars) + Ownership (in dollars). Liabilities means the claims or equity of creditors, and ownership means the claims or equity of owners, making it possible to state the equation as simply: Assets (in dollars) = Equities (in dollars).

An *asset* has three general characteristics: it has potential for future benefit or service to the accounting entity; it is the result of a past transaction; and its amount is subject to calculation or close approximation. Assets can be classified as current (those that can be expected to be converted into cash within the operating cycle of the firm) and long term. *Equities* are the sum of liabilities for the claims of creditors and owners' or stockholders' claims. Liabilities, the debts of the accounting entity, require a future outlay of money or the equivalent, are the result of past transactions, and must be able to be calculated or closely estimated and be based on double-entry bookkeeping. Liabilities, like assets, can be subdivided as current or long term.

The accounting equation is the basis for the preparation of the position statement of the firm, an accounting report that presents at a moment in time the cumulative effects of financial changes which have occurred since the initial organization of the accounting unit. It shows stocks of resources (assets) and claims against these resources (equities) at a particular moment in the life of the firm, and for many years it was considered the most important accounting report for external use. Recently the income statement has gained importance. To prepare the income statement, the accountant recognizes the revenues of the period (amounts received or to be received for goods and services) and matches these with expenses (values expired during the period directly or indirectly in the furnishing of goods or services). The result of this matching is income (or loss). Firms may also publish fund-flow statements; comparative statements of position, income, or fund flow; and statistical summaries of major items of financial data.

This chapter should be viewed as both an introduction and a résumé, to be reviewed after the study of each subsequent chapter, and, again, after completing the entire book. The four major accounting concepts and their subsidiary concepts plus the accounting equation constitute the conventional accounting model with which the reader should be thoroughly familiar by the time he finishes the book. However, he should not attempt exhaustive memorization at this point. Instead, he should follow the deductive development of these concepts into the theoretical and practical aspects of financial accounting. Thus, by the time he has completed study of the book, he should have a basis for understanding and evaluating the accounting process and accounting data.

A Selection of Supplementary Readings

American Accounting Association: *A Statement of Basic Accounting Theory*. Evanston, Illinois: 1966, pp. 7–36.
American Institute of Certified Public Accountants: *Basic Concepts and*

Accounting Principles Underlying Financial Statements of Business Enterprises, Statement of the Accounting Principles Board No. 4. New York: 1970.

Bedford, Norton M., and Toshio Iino: "Consistency Reexamined," *The Accounting Review,* July 1968, pp. 453–458.

Bernstein, Leopold A.: "Materiality—The Need for Guidelines," *The New York Certified Public Accountant,* July 1968, pp. 501–510.

Chambers, R. J.: "Uniformity in Accounting," *The New York Certified Public Accountant,* October 1967, pp. 747–754.

Hendrickson, H. S., and T. J. Burns: "The Accounting Unit." In Thomas J. Burns and Harvey S. Hendrickson, eds., *The Accounting Sampler.* New York: McGraw-Hill Book Company, 1967 and 1972.

Hendriksen, Eldon S.: *Accounting Theory,* rev. ed., Homewood, Illinois: Richard D. Irwin, Inc., 1970, pp. 92–121.

————: "Toward Greater Comparability through Uniformity of Accounting Principles," *The New York Certified Public Accountant,* February 1967, pp. 105–115.

Lall, R. M.: "An Enquiry into the Nature of Assets," *The New York Certified Public Accountant,* November 1968, pp. 793–797.

Moonitz, Maurice: "The Changing Concept of Liabilities," *The Journal of Accountancy,* May 1960, pp. 41–46.

Park, Colin, and John W. Gladson: *Working Capital.* New York: The Macmillan Company, 1963, pp. 32–48.

Sterling, Robert R.: "The Going Concern: An Examination," *The Accounting Review,* July 1968, pp. 481–502.

Wojdak, Joseph F.: "Levels of Objectivity in the Accounting Process," *The Accounting Review,* January 1970, pp. 88–97.

Questions

3–1

List ten examples of assets and five examples of equities.

3–2

a. Sales - Returns
b. Rent Received in Advance
c. Advances from Customers
d. Rent Payable
e. Advances to Suppliers

f. Income Taxes Withheld
g. Goodwill
h. Notes Receivable
i. Accounts Payable
j. Merchandise Inventory

Which of the above accounts appear on the position statement: (1) b c d e f g h i j; (2) b c d e f g j; (3) b c d e f g h; (4) b d e f g h i; (5) some other combination?

Which of the above accounts appear on the income statement: (1) b c d i j k; (2) a j; (3) a c d i j; (4) a b i; (5) some other combination?

3–3

Which of the following events is not recorded on the books?
(1) Delivery of merchandise paid for in advance
(2) Ordering $400 of merchandise
(3) Receipt of a fire insurance policy dated yesterday, invoice attached
(4) Inventory loss due to theft
(5) All the above are recorded on the books

3–4   A bus company sells coupon books redeemable for bus rides. On December 31, 1972, there are coupon books outstanding in the amount of $3,600. As accountant for the bus company you would treat the $3,600 as: (a) a current asset, (b) revenue for 1972, (c) a deferred charge, (d) a current liability, (e) an increase to ownership.

3–5   A sales memorandum book (or record of sales) shows a total of $6,000 for an accounting period, made up as follows: $1,000 received in cash, goods delivered; $3,000 sold on account, goods delivered; $1,000 paid in cash, but goods not yet delivered; and $1,000 for goods delivered in a prior period. It is estimated that $100 of the $3,000 will become uncollectible. Cost of goods sold amounts to one-half of gross sales. The gross margin for this period amounts to: (a) $2,000, (b) $1,900, (c) $1,950, (d) $2,900 (e) something else.

3–6   Indicate the net effect of these transactions on Assets, Liabilities, and Ownership for the current accounting period.
       a. Received $200 rent for the accounting period
       b. Purchased land for $1,000 cash; land is worth $3,000
       c. Owner withdrew $300 cash from the business for personal use
       d. Sold for $700 cash goods which cost $300
       e. Paid property taxes for prior year, already recorded as due, $500

       (1) The net effect on total assets: (a) $3,100, (b) $2,100, (c) $200 decrease, (d) $200 increase, (e) something else.
       (2) The net effect on total liabilities: (a) $300 increase, (b) $300 decrease, (c) $100 increase, (d) $400 increase, (e) something else.

3–7   Indicate the effect of each of the following transactions upon the total assets of a business by use of the appropriate phrase: "increase total assets," "decrease total assets," "no change in total assets."
       (1) Investment of cash by owner
       (2) Purchase of equipment at a price of $4,000, terms $1,000 cash and the balance payable on a six-months' note
       (3) Purchase of equipment for cash
       (4) Payment of a liability
       (5) Sale of an asset at a price equal to its booked value for cash
       (6) Sale of an asset at a price greater than its booked value; sale on account or for credit
       (7) Sale of an asset at a price less than its booked value; sale for cash
       (8) Collection of an account receivable
       (9) Purchased supplies on account
       (10) Borrowed money from a bank

3–8   State precisely what information is contained in the three-line heading of any financial statement and why this information is useful. Use the position statement (or balance sheet) as an example.

3–9   State whether each of the following is true, false, or doubtful. Give reasons.
       (1) Cash and ownership are the same.

(2) The recorded total assets of a firm occasionally may exceed the recorded total equities of the firm.

(3) If a firm owes taxes, the particular government is, in effect, providing resources for the firm.

(4) Net income is an increase in firm capital.

(5) Since long-term liabilities and ownership are both long-term equities, they may be considered as essentially identical.

3–10   Andy Williams who invested $10,000 of his own money in a small business renting TVs to hospital patients borrowed $5,000 from a bank for business use. At the end of his first year of operations, he found that there was $7,000 in his firm's bank account; his other assets were valued at $10,000. He owed his suppliers $3,000 and had repaid $2,000 of the bank loan. During the year he had paid himself a salary of $6,000.

(1) What can you conclude about his first year's operations?

(2) How could you use this information?

(3) What arguments would you use in trying to convince Mr. Williams to prepare records in addition to his checkbook?

3–11   Does a single position statement aid in determining the net change in ownership equity over time? Why?

3–12   Prepare a personal position statement for yourself as of this date. Prepare another position statement for yourself at the date you entered college. These statements should include not only what you owned but also any present value of your future as you see it. Be sure to show supporting calculations. Contrast the two statements.

Problems

3–1   On December 31 the position statement reports total assets of $44,000. One year earlier the position statement showed total assets of $54,000. Does this information show that the company suffered a loss of $10,000 during the year? Why or why not?

3–2   From the following information, compute net income for the year (000's omitted).

Total assets, January 1, 1973	$400.0
Total assets, December 31, 1973	440.8
Total liabilities, January 1, 1973	205.9
Total liabilities, December 31, 1973	212.6
Capital stock, January 1, 1973	175.0
Capital stock, December 31, 1973	200.0
Dividends declared during year	11.5

3–3   The following information was taken from the books and records of the Barry Goldwater Co. on December 31, 1973. (000's omitted):

Accounts payable	$ 6.8
Accounts receivable	10.4
Cash	1.4
Delivery equipment	19.0

Inventory of merchandise, December 31	$ 9.4
Land	10.0
Mortgage payable	11.5
Note payable	0.7
Notes receivable	1.4
Prepayments	0.4
B. Goldwater, capital	33.0

Prepare a classified position statement for the company as of December 31, 1973.

3-4   In the following diagram introduce dotted lines linking the two accounts whose amounts are changed by a specific transaction. Identify each transaction by number on the graph. For example, transaction 1 is the owner's cash investment in the enterprise. Continue to diagram the transactions given in Question 3-7.

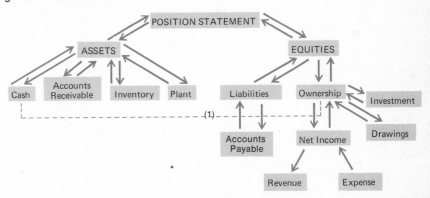

3-5   For each of the following transactions, indicate its effect on the position statement of *both* firms. Use the code, + for an increase, − for a decrease, and a 0 for no effect.

	The Arnold Co.			The Ziffel Co.		
	ASSETS	LIABILITIES	OWNERSHIP	ASSETS	LIABILITIES	OWNERSHIP
(1) The Arnold Co. purchases merchandise for $500 on account from the Ziffel Co.						
(2) The Ziffel Co. purchases equipment for $300 cash from the Arnold Co.						

	The Arnold Co.			The Ziffel Co.		
	ASSETS	LIABILITIES	OWNERSHIP	ASSETS	LIABILITIES	OWNERSHIP
(3) The Ziffel Co. purchases capital stock for $500 cash from the Arnold Co.						
(4) The Arnold Co. signs a contract agreeing to buy merchandise from Ziffel for a total price of $2,500.						
(5) A check for $100 in consideration of (4) is received by Ziffel from Arnold.						

3-6

Bachelor's Fantasy Position Statements:
September 15, 1972

By studying the successive position statements in the series shown below, determine what transactions or events have taken place. Prepare a list of these transactions by date of occurrence. (000's omitted on all statements.)

(1)	Assets		Ownership	
Cash		$25	H. Hefner, capital	$25

September 20, 1972

(2)	Assets		Equities	
Cash		$20	Mortgage payable	$10
Land		5	H. Hefner, capital	25
Building		10		
		$35		$35

September 21, 1972

(3)	Assets		Equities	
Cash		$10	Accounts payable	$ 3
Supplies		4	Mortgage payable	9
Land		5	H. Hefner, capital	25
Building		10		
Equipment		8		
		$37		$37

September 24, 1972

(4) Assets		Equities	
Cash	$ 9	Accounts payable	$ 2
Supplies	4	Mortgage payable	9
Land	5	H. Hefner, capital	25
Building	10		
Equipment	8		
	$36		$36

September 26, 1972

(5) Assets		Equities	
Cash	$ 9	Accounts payable	$ 2
Supplies	4	Mortgage payable	9
Accounts receivable	1	H. Hefner, capital	26
Land	5		
Building	10		
Equipment	8		
	$37		$37

September 27, 1972

(6) Assets		Equities	
Cash	$ 9	Accounts payable	$ 2
Supplies	3.5	Mortgage payable	9
Accounts receivable	1	H. Hefner, capital	25.5
Land	5		
Building	10		
Equipment	8		
	$36.5		$36.5

3–7

(1) Prepare a balance sheet from the following account balances (no owner investments or withdrawals were made during the period):

Accounts payable	$13
Accounts receivable	7
Building	24
Cash	9
Delivery equipment	10
Furniture	4
Intangibles	5
Inventory	29
Investment in bonds	5
Land	3
Mortgage payable	17
Notes payable	8
Notes receivable	4
Owners' equity	62

(2) Explain the probable nature of each item, and identify the event and kind of transaction in which it probably originated.

3-8

The assets and equities of the Maybelle Carter Company on June 30, 1972, were as follows (000's omitted):

Accounts payable	$13
Accounts receivable	8
Buildings	36
Cash in bank	7
Equipment	5
Interest payable	0.2
Inventory	11
Land	18
Long-term payable	10
Notes payable	9
Owners' equity	To be derived
Prepaid insurance	2
Wages payable	2

Prepare a report that will show total assets and equities, with the latter classified between creditors and owners.

3-9

Present the following comparative position statement information in another format: (000's omitted). Briefly defend your choice of format.

	Financial Position		Changes during Period	
	Beginning	Ending	Increase	Decrease
Assets:				
Cash	$ 6	$ 5		$1
Receivables	65	72	$ 7	
Inventories	150	145		5
Plant	50	55	5	
	271	277	12	6
Liabilities:				
Accounts payable	90	92	2	
Accrued items	40	45	5	
Notes payable	50	41		9
	180	178	7	9
Ownership:				
Capital stock	$ 91	$ 99	$ 8	

3-10

Mr. Clean began a business by investing $15,000 cash. The transactions were not completely recorded, but at the close of the year the ledger accounts showed the following balances.

Accounts payable	$4,500	Expenses	$ 900
Accounts receivable	4,500	Ownership withdrawals	1,000
Merchandise (This		Cash collected from cus-	
balance is the differ-		tomers during year	5,000
ence between purchases		Ownership, end of year	12,225
and sales)	5,000		

Prepare a position statement at the end of the period. What was the net income?

3-11

Each of the following six position statements was prepared immediately after the completion of a transaction (000's omitted). Identify each transaction, and explain fully.

Totie Fields' Parlor Position Statements:

January 1, 1972

(1)	Assets		Owners' Equity	
Cash	$25	T. Fields, capital		$25

January 5, 1972

(2)	Assets		Owners' Equity	
Cash	$20	T. Fields, capital		$25
Supplies	5			
	$25			$25

January 13, 1972

(3)	Assets		Owners' Equity	
Cash	$19	T. Fields, capital		$25
Supplies	5			
Prepaid advertising	1			
	$25			$25

January 16, 1972

(4)	Assets		Equities	
Cash	$19	Accounts payable		$ 1
Supplies	6	T. Fields, capital		25
Prepaid advertising	1			
	$26			$26

January 20, 1972	(5)	Assets		Equities	
	Cash	$19	Accounts payable		$ 1
	Accounts receivable	1	T. Fields, capital		26
	Supplies	6			
	Prepaid advertising	1			
		$27			$27

January 31, 1972	(6)	Assets		Equities	
	Cash	$19	Accounts payable		$ 1
	Accounts receivable	1	T. Fields, capital		25.5
	Supplies	6			
	Prepaid advertising	0.5			
		$26.5			$26.5

3–12

All figures in each of the following cases are in thousands (000's omitted). Calculate missing figures.

	Case I	Case II	Case III	Case IV
Beginning of period:				
Total assets	$?	$180	$220	$155
Total liabilities	40	60	20	75
End of period:				
Total assets	250	?	180	150
Total liabilities	70	35	30	65
Period:				
Revenues	200	90	260	140
Expenses	140	82	?	95
Dividends	20	20	0	20
Taxes	10	6	0	0
Interest	5	4	1	?
Assets received from shares issued	20	2	0	0
Assets given up for shares redeemed	35	5	0	5

3–13

The Great Pumpkin Position Statements: October 31 (000's omitted)

	1972	1973	1974
Cash items	$ 60	$100	$ 80
Receivables	38	46	42
Inventories	160	140	150
Prepayments	10	10	10
Plant	200	200	200
Plant: accumulated depreciation	(30)	(40)	(70)
Intangibles	2	2	2
	$440	$458	$414

Current payables	$104	$ 68	$ 80
Capital stock	200	200	200
Retained earnings	136	190	134
	$440	$458	$414

NOTE: *Exclusive of the cost of goods sold and depreciation, other expenses were $100,000. Inventory purchases totaled $400,000, $200,000 in each year. No dividends were declared or paid in the three years.*

Prepare income statements for 1973 and 1974.

3–14   Solve the following exercises:

(1) Currier invested $20,000 in a business. During the next ten years he invested an additional $5,000 and withdrew from the business $55,000. At the end of the ten-year period the assets of the business total $113,000, and the liabilities amount to $35,800. Determine the ten-year net income (or loss) of this business.

(2) The cash records of the Thomas Porter Hardware Store during a given month show cash collections from customers of $13,800 and cash sales of $9,870. At the beginning of the month the total amount due from customers was $5,180. The owner had written off as uncollectible $640 of customers' accounts during the month. Nothing is due from customers at the end of the month. From this information, determine the gross sales for the month.

(3) The Peter Rosenow Company has increased its merchandise inventory by $4,320 during the year and owes $5,900 more to suppliers than it did at the beginning of the year. During the year the company paid $20,300 to suppliers and $2,700 in transportation charges on merchandise, and bought $1,400 of merchandise for cash. Determine the company's cost of goods sold for the year.

3–15   Solve the following:

(1) A trial balance at the end of the year contains the following balances (000's omitted): Assets $100, Liabilities $30, Ownership $70. Withdrawals during the period were $10; investment was $6, and net income was $9. Put the trial balance figures into a T account. What were the ownership figures at the beginning and the end of the year?

(2) A trial balance at the end of the year contains the following balances (000's omitted): Assets $90, Liabilities $15, Ownership $56, Revenues $90, and Expenses $81. Withdrawals during the period were $3; investments were $16. Put the trial balance figures into a T account. What were the ownership figures at the beginning and the end of the year? How does this trial balance differ from that in (1) above?

3–16   Identify with a word or two the name (or use) of position statements prepared on the basis of the following equations:

1. $\Sigma A = \Sigma L + \Sigma SE$
2. $\Sigma SE = \Sigma A - \Sigma L$
3. $\Sigma A - \Sigma L = \Sigma SE$
4. $\Sigma A = \Sigma E$

3–17   Select the proper classification of each of the following accounts of the Don Meredith Company. Use the indicated numbers to show statement categories. If the account is *contra* or adjunct, place a X after the number.

Number	Category on Statement
1	Current Asset
2	Noncurrent Asset
3	Current Liability
4	Long-term Liability
5	Ownership
6	Revenue
7	Cost of Goods Manufactured and Sold
8	Selling and Administrative Expense
9	Nonoperating Revenue and Expense
10	Net Income Distribution

——— A. Accounts Receivable—Allowance for Bad Debts
——— B. Retained Earnings—Restricted for Contingencies
——— C. Plant—Allowance for Depreciation
——— D. Federal Income Taxes Payable
——— E. Sales—Sales Returns and Allowances
——— F. Retained Earnings—Restricted for Bond Retirement
——— G. Dividends Payable
——— H. Prepayments
——— I. Depreciation of Delivery Equipment
——— J. Interest Revenue
——— K. Interest Charges
——— L. Customers' Deposits
——— M. Gain on the Disposal of Plant
——— N. Notes Receivable
——— O. Bond Sinking Fund
——— P. Notes Payable
——— Q. Accounts Payable
——— R. Salaries Payable
——— S. Union Dues Withheld
——— T. Marketable Securities
——— U. Investment in Bonds
——— V. Intangibles
——— W. Prepaid Rent
——— X. Interest Payable
——— Y. Accounts Receivable

3–18   All figures in each of the following cases are in thousands (000's omitted). Calculate the missing figures.

	Case I	Case II	Case III	Case IV
Total assets, beginning of period	$100	$140	$210	$165
Total assets, end of period	125	135	190	180
Total liabilities, beginning of period	30	65	15	70
Total liabilities, end of period	60	40	25	60
Period revenue	150	?	240	125
Period expense	120	62	?	85
Period dividends	?	10	0	10
Assets received from shares issued during period	10	12	0	0
Assets given up for shares redeemed during period	25	5	0	?

3–19

Little Orphan Annie Enterprises Position Statements: December 31 (000's omitted)

a. The following position statements have been prepared under the accrual basis of accounting. Compute figures for blank lines.

		1972		1973
Assets				
Cash		$ —		$ 35
Accounts receivable		25		20
Inventory		20		25
Plant	50		50	
Less: Accumulated depreciation	10	40	15	35
		$		$115
Equities				
Accounts payable		$ 20		$ 25
Ownership		85		
		$105		$

b. 1. On the basis of the comparative position statements given above and that the cost of goods sold totaled $80,000, and that the owners made no additions or withdrawals during the year, fill out the following income statement for 1973.

Little Orphan Annie
Enterprises
Income Statement
for the Year 1973

Sales	$_____	*Show your computations*
Less: Cost of goods sold	_____	*of Cost of goods sold.*
Gross margin	_____	
Less: Depreciation $_____		
Other expenses _____20	_____	
Net income	=====	

2. Compute the net income under the cash basis:

Cash receipts	$_____
Less: Cash disbursements	_____
Cash basis net income	=====

Show in detail your computation of (a) the cash receipts and (b) the cash disbursements.

3-20   a. You are given the following information (all 000's omitted):

	Dittman Co.	Heimann Co.	Watson Co.
Cost of goods sold	$15	$18	?
Other expenses	9	?	$ 6
Net income	?	?	5
Sales	25	20	17
Ownership, December 31, 1972	?	24	40
Ownership, January 1, 1972	10	22	?
Owners' investments and withdrawals during 1975	0	0	0

Make the following computations:
(1) The net income of the Dittman Co. for 1972 was _____.
(2) The ownership on December 31, 1972, for the Dittman Co. is_____.
(3) The net income for the Heimann Co. for 1972 was
(4) The other expenses of the Heimann Co. was
(5) The ownership of the Watson Co. as of January 1, 1972, was

b. You are given the following information (all 000's omitted):

	Dittman Co.	Heimann Co.	Watson Co.
Assets, December 31, 1975	$106	$154	$52
Liabilities, December 31, 1975	?	42	15
Ownership, January 1, 1975	70	?	30
Ownership, December 31, 1975	90	?	?
Owners withdrawals during 1975	12	6	?
Additional owner's investment during 1975	21	0	2

Net operating income, 1975	*?*	*$ 15*	*?*
Revenue, 1975	*?*	*112*	*$60*
Expenses, 1975	*$72*	*?*	*45*

Compute:

(1) Liabilities of Dittman Co. on December 31, 1975 _____

(2) Revenues of Dittman Co. for 1975 _____

(3) Ownership of Heimann Co. on January 1, 1975 _____

(4) Expenses of Heimann Co. for 1975 _____

(5) Withdrawal of Watson's owners during 1975 _____

4 The Accounting Process and Control

Once upon a time there was an eminent accountant. Although his duties varied a great deal, there was always one activity that he did each day without fail. Each morning he came into his office, unlocked the center drawer of his desk, removed a small piece of paper, glanced at the paper, returned it, and relocked the drawer with the only key which he kept in his vest. As the years passed, he was promoted often finally becoming president and even chairman of the board of his company; he saw football and baseball games with the President of the United States; he married a television star; his portrait was painted by Peter Hurd; he entertained astronauts at dinner; he even became TIME's man of the year.

Then one day rich in honors and years, he died. After the funeral, several of his very closest and curious associates went to his office, unlocked the desk drawer, removed the paper, and on it they read:

THE DEBITS ARE ON THE SIDE NEXT TO THE WINDOW

Old accounting anecdote to be appreciated perhaps by young accounting students.*

The preparation of accounting reports to provide information useful to both external and internal parties begins with the design of a system for classifying and accumulating the necessary input data. Inherent in such a system should be a means of internal control which involves the coordination of the organization's methods and procedures to:

1. Encourage and measure employees' compliance with company policy
2. Facilitate the evaluation of operating efficiency
3. Ensure "internal checks" which
   a. Safeguard resources against waste, fraud, and inefficiency
   b. Promote accurate and valid records

A system that accomplishes these objectives involves not only the accounts and the procedures for the processing of the financial data, but also the selection and the assignment of personnel to perform the necessary tasks.

---

*Although this anecdote may convey the impression that debits and credits are an essential element of the accounting process, this is not so. They are only a *conventional* element of the accounting process.

In this chapter a representative set of accounts for a firm is developed using the conventional historical cost model; the firm's transactions for one month are processed; the built-in checks which aid in ensuring accurate and valid records are identified; and it is illustrated that reports prepared from these records do facilitate the evaluation of operating efficiency.

The Accounting Process

In many firms, especially small ones, one commonly encounters a set of financial data which consist primarily of a detailed record of the checking account, including all deposits and checks drawn. In addition, the firm may have a sales book; files of customer charge sales invoices and of supplier, bank, tax, and other creditor invoices and papers; and an annual compilation of inventories and plant assets. In order to determine the financial position of such a firm at any point in time or the year-to-date income, the transactions since the last set of statements were prepared must be reviewed and summarized, and inventories must be taken. The approach used, often called a single-entry system, is incomplete and usually inadequate for providing information quickly and efficiently.

On the other hand, the basic accounting model conventionally embraces a double-entry system which, if properly maintained, provides reliable up-to-date information very quickly and thus avoids most of the major handicaps of the manual, single-entry system.

The Accounting Cycle

The accounting cycle consists of a minimum of five essential steps which could be expanded to nine or ten if all the subroutines were listed separately:

1. Occurrence of the internal or external transaction—the economic event within the firm or with outsiders which provides the input data for the accounting system.
2. Classification of the transaction data and recording in chronological order—this is the journalizing step in a manual system.
3. Recording and accumulation of the classified data in ledger accounts—this is the posting step. The basic ledger account used in this book will be a T account, which is an abbreviated form of account often used for demonstrating the effect of a transaction or series of transactions. In the general form of the letter T, the space above the horizontal line is used for the name of the account, the space below is used for the amounts with debits entered to the left side of the vertical line, and credits entered on the right.
4. Preparation of position, income, fund-flow, and other financial statements, including trial balances taken to check the arithmetic accuracy of the records.
5. Closing of revenue, expense, and other nominal accounts at the end of

the period. The closing process, usually requiring both journalizing and posting, consists of transferring the balances in the nominal accounts (such as the revenue and expense accounts which accumulate detailed information for the income statement) to the real (position statement) account (retained earnings for a corporation) to which they relate.

Transaction Analysis

It is probably obvious from what has been stated that the accounting equation (Assets = Liabilities + Owners' Equity) for an enterprise is undergoing constant change as a result of internal and external transactions.

The following describes in outline form the principal types of transactions:

Transactions

External	*Internal*

1. Increases (or inflows) of assets:
   a. From stockholders* (cash and other items furnished in connection with the issuance of capital stock) —investments

   b. From creditors (cash, goods, and services furnished by lenders, employees, and suppliers)—investments

   c. From customers (cash, receivables, and other items given)—revenue transactions which increase stockholders' equity

   d. From donors (goods and services provided)—gifts

2. Decreases (or outflows) of assets:
   a. To stockholders (paying of cash dividends)— disinvestment†

---

*Stockholders are owners in the corporate form of business. Other forms of business have different owners. Partnerships have partners, and sole proprietorships have a single owner.
†If the date when the dividend is declared precedes the date when it is paid, the paying of dividends is actually a payment to a creditor (the claimant of a dividend payable).

    b. To creditors (payments on
       loans or for other goods
       and services provided by
       employees and suppliers)—
       disinvestment

    c. To customers and others | Many selling expenses are re-
(assets used up directly and | corded as internal transactions
indirectly in the furnishing | (e.g., cost of goods sold, depre-
of goods and services to | ciation and amortization of in-
customers)—expense trans- | tangibles) because it is not
actions which reduce stock- | possible to do otherwise. Many
holders' equity | of these are called adjusting
entries.

3. Substitutions

                          a. Asset for asset

Collection of cash from customers | Transfers from one account to
on their accounts and the purchase | another [such as the cost of raw
of items (such as inventories) for | materials or other assets being
cash paid before or at the time of | transferred to the production
purchase or the exchange of one | process (work in process) or the
asset for another. | cost of production completed being
transferred from work in process
to finished goods—usually these
are called adjusting entries].

                        b. Equity for equity

Declaration of dividends or the | Closing entries by which the bal-
recording of tax liabilities for | ances in revenue and expense
the current period (liability for | accounts are transferred to re-
stockholders' equity); the con- | tained earnings. (Strictly speaking,
version of a bond liability to | closing entries are not considered
capital stock; the issuance of a | transactions, even under a broad
stock dividend (transfer from | view of "transaction." If they
retained earnings to capital stock); | were, then a "transaction" would
the accruals of claims of outsiders | be identical to an "accounting
for goods or services used in | entry." However, for our pur-
connection with earning revenues | poses we consider closing entries
of the current period (expenses). | to be internal transactions.)

Clearly, accountants by themselves cannot create or eliminate
assets. Occasionally, they become involved in departures from the
conventional accounting model, such as the write-up or the write-
down of assets to their current values. The effect of such departures
is a major change which would require reflecting the amount of the
write-up in a separate account in stockholders' equity.

These transactions may be further classified in terms of their effects on the accounting equation. If one considers the equation to have three terms, there are nine possible types of basic changes which can be expressed algebraically as follows:

Assets	=	Liabilities	+	Owners' Equity
1. Increase	=	Increase		
2. Increase	=			Increase
3. (Increase = Decrease)				
4. Decrease	=	Decrease		
5. Decrease	=			Decrease
6.		Increase	=	Decrease
7.		Decrease	=	Increase
8.		(Increase = Decrease)		
9.				(Increase = Decrease)

All transactions that affect the position statement must either fall into one of these types or be a combination of two or more of them. All these types will be included in the following illustration, which includes both position and income statement accounts. Recall that revenue and expense accounts are merely detailed retained earnings accounts which are used to accumulate data for the income statement of a period.

Illustration—trading firm Corporation, Inc., was organized on January 1, 1972, and operations began immediately in its rented quarters which included a sales floor, a warehouse, and an office. The firm's accounting period is the calendar month. The following chart of accounts includes all the specific titles that the firm's accountant considers to be adequate for classifying and recording financial data for external purposes.[1]

[1]If Corporation, Inc., were a manufacturing firm, several of the accounts used would be different, to reflect that its operations are different. Instead of buying and selling merchandise (that was manufactured by other firms), it would buy raw materials and labor that would be combined into a product in its plant, consisting of land, buildings, machinery, and equipment that also must be bought or leased. Following the theory of production that states that values are created by changes in time, place, and form, the costs of all the resources used to complete the product are accumulated in accounting records that reflect or follow the progress of the product through the firm. These records (the cost accounts) reflect costs that follow the product from the point when the raw materials are purchased to the raw materials inventory, to the production process, to the finished goods inventory, and to the customer. While the goods are on hand in one of the inventory stages within the firm, their costs are assets, but these costs expire and become expenses (the cost of goods sold) at the time that revenue is recognized—usually this is at the time of the sale and transfer to the customer. The usual balance sheet (or real) accounts that differentiate a manufacturing firm from a trading firm are Raw Materials, Work in Process, and Finished Goods. These three accounts replace the Merchandise Inventory account(s) of a trading firm. As the materials and other items that contribute to the completion of the production process are transferred to the

Position Statement
Accounts

Assets	Equities
Current assets:	**Liabilities (current):**
Cash	Accounts payable
Accounts receivable	Wages and salaries payable
Merchandise inventory	Payroll taxes payable
Merchandise inventory—freight in	Withheld income taxes payable
Unexpired rent	Income taxes payable
	Dividends payable
Plant assets:	**Stockholders' equity:**
Furniture, fixtures, and equipment	Capital contributed by stock-
Furniture, fixtures, and equipment	holders
—accumulated depreciation	Retained earnings
Intangibles:	
Organization costs	

Income Statement
Accounts
(Details of Retained
Earnings Account)

Revenue:

Sales

Expenses:

Cost of goods sold
Other selling:
  Sales salaries
  Store rent
  Depreciation of store fixtures
  Miscellaneous

Administrative:

  Office salaries
  Office rent
  Depreciation of office furniture and equipment
  Miscellaneous

Income tax charge

production process, their costs also are transferred to Work in Process. In order to accumulate more detailed information, it is common for these individual costs to be classified into production cost accounts (which are detailed Work-in-Process accounts). Titles of commonly used production cost accounts for the costs of the items that go directly into the product are Raw Materials Used and Direct Labor, and for the overhead or indirect product costs are Supervision, Supplies Used, Factory Utilities, Factory Insurance, and Depreciation (or Rent) on Factory Building, Machinery, and Equipment. The production cost accounts are detailed work-in-process accounts, they are nominal accounts that are used during the period to accumulate data for production cost reports. At the end of the period, these costs would be transferred to the Work-in-Process Account. Production cost accounts are accounted for in the same manner as expenses (that is, they are increased by debits, decreased by credits), but they are asset, not equity, accounts.

The following are pertinent transactions in summary form for the month of January 1972:

1. 2,500 shares of capital stock were issued for cash of which $25,000 was promptly deposited in a checking account.
2. The following transactions were completed and the amounts paid by check:
   a. Lawyer's fees and related costs of forming the corporation, $500.
   b. Furniture, fixtures, and equipment acquired, $10,000.
   c. Rent for the three-month period of January 1–March 31, 1972, $1,500.
3. Ten sales and office employees were hired at various hourly and monthly wage and salary rates that are expected to average $3,500 per month.
4. a. Merchandise was purchased on account for $27,000 from a company.
   b. A freight bill of $270 for shipment of the above merchandise was received and paid by check.
5. Sales on account to customers total $26,000 for the month.
6. Wages and salaries earned during the month total $3,600. Of this amount, $2,000 represents earnings of sales employees, and $1,600 earnings of office and administrative employees.
7. Collections from customers total $23,000, all of which has been deposited in the bank.
8. The board of directors declared a cash dividend of $125.
9. The following additional checks were issued during the month:
   a. Company from whom merchandise was purchased (see transaction 4), $18,000.
   b. Employees' wages of $3,500 less $180 for Federal Insurance Contributions Act (FICA) tax and $660 for withheld federal and state income taxes, $2,660.
   c. Other office costs (repairs, utilities, etc.), $500.
   d. Other selling costs, $600.
   e. Payment for the dividend declared in transaction 8.
10. The company from whom merchandise is purchased (see transaction 4) accepts 500 shares of capital stock for $5,000 of its claims.
11. The company's share of payroll taxes is 3 percent for federal and state unemployment insurance and 5.2 percent for FICA benefits (adjusting entry).

12. Depreciation of furniture, fixtures, and equipment for the month was $100, of which $75 relates to the sales fixtures and $25 to the office furniture and fixtures.
13. Records indicate that merchandise having an invoice cost of $18,500 and applicable freight-in of $185 was sold and shipped to customers.
14. The rent expiration is recorded—of this $400 relates to the store and the balance to the office.

15. Estimated federal and state income taxes for the month are $550.

These transactions will be analyzed first in the following tabular form (the journalizing step):

Transaction Number	Increase or Decrease	Class of Account	Account Title	Amount
1	Increase	Asset	Cash	$25,000
	Increase	Owners' equity	Capital contributed by stockholders	25,000
2 a	Increase	Asset	Organization costs	500
	Decrease	Asset	Cash	500
b	Increase	Asset	Furniture, fixtures, and equipment	10,000
	Decrease	Asset	Cash	10,000
c	Increase	Asset	Unexpired rent	1,500
	Decrease	Asset	Cash	1,500
3	No effect—no more than a memorandum is necessary, because no one has performed as yet; thus, there has been no change in the equation.			
4 a	Increase	Asset	Merchandise inventory—	27,000
	Increase	Liability	Accounts payable —company	27,000
b	Increase	Asset	Merchandise inventory— freight in	270
	Decrease	Asset	Cash	270
5	Increase	Asset	Accounts receivable	26,000
	Increase	Owners' equity— retained earnings	Sales	26,000
6	Decrease*	Owners' equity— retained earnings	Sales salaries expense	2,000
	Decrease*	Owners' equity— retained earnings	Office salaries expense	1,600
	Increase	Liability	Wages and salaries payable	3,600
7	Increase	Asset	Cash	23,000
	Decrease	Asset	Accounts receivable	23,000
8	Decrease*	Owners' equity— retained earnings	Dividends declared	125
	Increase	Liability	Dividends payable	125
9 a	Decrease	Liability	Accounts payable —company	18,000
	Decrease	Asset	Cash	18,000
b	Decrease	Liability	Wages payable	3,500
	Increase	Liability	Payroll taxes payable	180
	Increase	Liability	Withheld income taxes payable	660
	Decrease	Asset	Cash	2,660
c	Decrease*	Owners' equity— retained earnings	Miscellaneous administrative expense	500
	Decrease	Asset	Cash	500

Transaction Number	Increase or Decrease	Class of Account	Account Title	Amount
d	Decrease*	Owners' equity— Retained earnings	Miscellaneous selling expense	600
	Decrease	Asset	Cash	600
e	Decrease	Liability	Dividends payable	125
	Decrease	Asset	Cash	125
10	Decrease	Liability	Accounts payable— company	5,000
	Increase	Owners' equity	Capital contributed by stockholders	5,000
11	Decrease*	Owners' equity— Retained earnings	Miscellaneous selling expense	164
	Decrease*	Owners' equity— Retained earnings	Miscellaneous administrative expense	131
	Increase	Liability	Payroll taxes payable	295
12	Decrease*	Owners' equity— Retained earnings	Depreciation of store fixtures	75
	Decrease*	Owners' equity— Retained earnings	Depreciation of office furniture and equipment	25
	Decrease†	Asset	Furniture, fixtures, and equipment— accumulated depreciation	100
13	Decrease*	Owners' equity— Retained earnings	Cost of goods sold	18,685
	Decrease	Asset	Merchandise inventory	18,500
			Merchandise inventory— freight in	185
14	Decrease*	Owners' equity— Retained earnings	Store rent expense	400
	Decrease*	Owners' equity— Retained earnings	Office rent expense	100
	Decrease	Asset	Unexpired rent	500
15	Decrease*	Owners' equity— Retained earnings	Income tax charge	550
	Increase	Liability	Income taxes payable	550

*Note that while the Retained Earnings account decreases, there is an increase in the respective expense account or income distribution account (Dividends Declared).

†Note that while there is an asset decrease, Furniture, Fixtures, and Equipment—Accumulated Depreciation increases because it is a contra-asset account—one that accumulates decreases in an asset account. This entry could have been recorded as a direct reduction in the asset account, Furniture, Fixtures, and Equipment.

The classified data for transactions 1 through 15 are now recorded (posted) in the respective T accounts of the general ledger as follows:

Corporation, Inc.
General Ledger
T Accounts

+	Cash		−
(1)	25,000	(2a)	500
(7)	23,000	(2b)	10,000
		(2c)	1,500
		(4b)	270
		(9a)	18,000
		(9b)	2,660
		(9c)	500
		(9d)	600
		(9e)	125
		✔	13,845
	48,000		48,000
✔	13,845		

+	Accounts Receivable		−
(5)	26,000	(7)	23,000
		✔	3,000
	26,000		26,000
✔	3,000		

+	Merchandise Inventory		−
(4a)	27,000	(13)	18,500
		✔	8,500
	27,000		27,000
✔	8,500		

+	Merchandise Inventory— Freight In		−
(4b)	270	(13)	185
		✔	85
	270		270
✔	85		

+	Unexpired Rent		−
(2c)	1,500	(14)	500
		✔	1,000
	1,500		1,500
✔	1,000		

+	Furniture, Fixtures, and Equipment		−
(2b)	10,000		

−	Furniture, Fixtures, and Equipment— Accumulated Depreciation		+
		(12)	100

+	Organization Costs		−
(2a)	500		

−	Accounts Payable		+
(9a)	18,000	(4a)	27,000
(10)	5,000		
✔	4,000		
	27,000		27,000
		✔	4,000

−	Wages and Salaries Payable		+
(9b)	3,500	(6)	3,600
✔	100		
	3,600		3,600
		✔	100

+ and − *denote side on which increases and decreases, respectively, are recorded.*

−	Payroll Taxes Payable	+
	(9b)	180
	(11)	295
	✔	475

+	Sales Salaries Expense	−
(6)	2,000	(C)	2,000

−	Withheld Income Taxes Payable	+
	(9b)	660

+	Store Rent Expense	−
(14)	400	(C)	400

−	Income Taxes Payable	+
	(15)	550

+	Depreciation of Store Fixtures	−
(12)	75	(C)	75

−	Dividends Payable	+
(9e)	125	(8)	125

+	Miscellaneous Selling Expense	−
(9d)	600	(C)	764
(11)	164		
	764		764

−	Capital Contributed by Stockholders	+
	(1)	25,000
	(10)	5,000
	✔	30,000

+	Office Salaries Expense	−
(6)	1,600	(D)	1,600

−	Retained Earnings	+
(F)	125	(G)	1,170
✔	1,045		
	1,170		1,170
		✔	1,045

+	Office Rent and Expense	−
(14)	100	(D)	100

−	Sales	+
(A)	26,000	(5)	26,000

+	Depreciation of Office Furniture and Equipment	−
(12)	25	(D)	25

+	Cost of Goods Sold	−
(13)	18,685	(B)	18,685

+ and − denote side on which increases and decreases, respectively, are recorded.

+	Miscellaneous Administrative Expense	−		−	Revenue and Expense Summary	+
(9 c)	500	(D)	631	(B)	18,685	(A)	26,000
(11)	131			(C)	3,239		
				(D)	2,356		
	631		631	(E)	550		
				(G)	1,170		
					26,000		26,000

+	Income Tax Charge	−
(15)	550	(E)	550

+	Dividends Declared	−
(8)	125	(F)	125

+ and − denote side on which increases and decreases, respectively, are recorded.

Traditionally, after the transactions for the accounting period are recorded, the balances of the general ledger accounts are computed, and a trial balance is prepared. A trial balance is merely a listing of accounts and their respective balances, which can be prepared at any time to test whether the accounts are in balance, a procedure that is unnecessary for the automated system. If the two money columns of the trial balance are equal, it is said that the accounts are in balance. Although this result gives a measure of control by suggesting that the data have been recorded accurately, it does not mean that all the individual accounts have correct balances: all of them may, in fact, have incorrect balances. This is an unlikely situation, but one that could arise either from misclassification in the initial analysis (during the journalizing step) and/or from posting the classified data to the incorrect account.

For Corporation, Inc., a trial balance could have been prepared after recording transaction 10; this would have been called an unadjusted trial balance. However, the following trial balance has been prepared to reflect the account balances after recording transaction 15, and might be called an adjusted trial balance. The headings for the money columns are not conventional, but they do reflect the ideas that have been introduced here. If the last dollar figure in a T account is in the left-hand money column, it reflects the account balance, the amount by which the entries in the left side of that account exceed those on the right. Similarly, if the last dollar figure is in the right-hand money column, it reflects that account's balance, the amount by which the entries on the right side of that account exceed those on the left.

The left column of the account is for debits, and the right column for credits. These two terms are fundamental terminology for recording transactions. A *debit,* recorded on the left side of an account (in certain countries, such as Switzerland, this relationship is re-

Corporation, Inc.
Trial Balance
January 31, 1972

Account Title	Left-hand Balances (Debits)	Right-hand Balances (Credits)
Cash	$13,845	
Accounts receivable	3,000	
Merchandise inventory	8,500	
Merchandise inventory—freight in	85	
Unexpired rent	1,000	
Furniture, fixtures, and equipment	10,000	
Furniture, fixtures, and equipment— accumulated depreciation		$ 100
Organization costs	500	
Accounts payable		4,000
Wages and salaries payable		100
Payroll taxes payable		475
Withheld income taxes payable		660
Income taxes payable		550
Dividends payable		
Capital contributed by stockholders		30,000
Retained earnings		
Sales		26,000
Cost of goods sold	18,685	
Sales salaries expense	2,000	
Store rent expense	400	
Depreciation of store fixtures	75	
Miscellaneous selling expense	764	
Office salaries expense	1,600	
Office rent expense	100	
Depreciation of office furniture and equipment expense	25	
Miscellaneous administrative expense	631	
Income tax charge	550	
Dividends declared	125	
	$61,885	$61,885

versed), is an accounting term indicating (1) an increase in an asset account, or (2) a decrease in an equity account. A *credit,* recorded on the right side of an account, indicates (1) an increase in an equity account, or (2) a decrease in an asset account. To verify these refer again to the + and − notations in the ledger accounts of the above illustration. Remember that the equity account, Retained Earnings for a corporation, is increased by increases in revenue accounts and is decreased by increases in expense accounts.

Thus far, examples of various types of accounts have been presented and summarized in the trial balance; the reader may be awed by the seemingly endless list of individual accounts. Actually, an exhaustive categorization of accounts by function provides a useful framework for identifying the relationships of the various accounts to the accounting cycle. First, those accounts that appear on the position statement can be listed in one of three subcategories: (1) asset accounts, (2) liability accounts, and (3) owners' equity accounts. Each of these subcategories typically is subdivided: assets into current and noncurrent; liabilities into current and noncurrent; and owners' equity into capital stock and retained earnings. The second major classification consists of those accounts that appear on the statement of income and retained earnings, and are typically subdivided into revenue, expense, and income distribution accounts, and accounts for gains and losses. The third primary classification is composed of temporary or suspense accounts which do not appear on any statement. One of these may be functional in the process of closing the income statement accounts in the ledger at the end of the accounting period. For example, all revenue and expense accounts would be closed, that is, their balances would be reduced to $0, and the balances would be transferred to the account, Revenue and Expense Summary, which in turn would be closed to the Retained Earnings account.

In addition to the three primary categories of accounts (position statement, income statement, and nominal), there are adjunct and contra accounts—valuation accounts that increase or offset the balances of other accounts on the position, income, or retained earnings statements. Consequently, an adjunct or contra account is always associated with a principal account so that information is maintained both in the principal account (for example, the balance of the principal accounts, Furniture, Fixtures, and Equipment and Merchandise Inventory), and in segregated increases in the principal account (for example, in the adjunct account, Merchandise Inventory—Freight In), or in segregated decreases to the principal account (for example, in the contra account, Furniture, Fixtures, and Equipment—Accumulated Depreciation). Direct debits and credits to the principal accounts would be feasible alternatives to using adjunct and contra accounts, but if this were done, information on both the principal accounts and the total increases or decreases would be lost.

Following the above classification scheme, the accounts in the trial balance can be categorized as follows:

I. Position statement accounts
  A. Asset accounts
    1. Current asset accounts
      a. Cash
      b. Accounts receivable
      c. Merchandise inventory
        Merchandise inventory—freight in (an adjunct account to Merchandise Inventory to reflect transportation charges separately)
      d. Unexpired rent
    2. Noncurrent asset accounts
      a. Furniture, fixtures, and equipment
        Furniture, fixtures, and equipment—accumulated depreciation (a contra account to Furniture, Fixtures, and Equipment)
      b. Organization costs (also classified as an intangible account)
  B. Liability accounts
    1. Current liabilities
      a. Accounts payable
      b. Wages and salaries payable
      c. Payroll taxes payable
      d. Withheld income taxes payable
      e. Income taxes payable
      f. Dividends payable
    2. Noncurrent liabilities
      a. Notes payable (not shown in example)
      b. Bonds payable (not shown in example)
  C. Owners' equity accounts
    1. Capital accounts
      Capital contributed by stockholders
    2. Retained earnings
II. Income statement accounts
  A. Revenue accounts
    Sales
  B. Expense accounts
    1. Cost of goods sold
    2. Sales salaries
    3. Store rent
    4. Depreciation of store fixtures
    5. Miscellaneous selling
    6. Office salaries
    7. Office rent
    8. Depreciation of office furniture and equipment
    9. Miscellaneous administrative
    10. Income tax charge

C. Gains
   Gain on disposal of property (not shown in example).
D. Losses
   Loss on disposal of property (not shown in example).
III. Temporary or suspense account
   Revenue and expense summary.

   The next step in the accounting cycle is the preparation of the financial statements. The income statement is normally prepared first from the revenue and expense accounts. The statement presented here also shows the income distribution account (Dividends Declared) and the ending balance of Retained Earnings, the reconciliation of which could also be shown in a separate statement or on the position statement—the important point being that these two statements are interrelated. On the statements presented here this interrelationship is through the Retained Earnings figure which appears not only on the income statement but also on the position statement.

   The position statement reflects the balances in the respective asset and equity accounts—except for the Retained Earnings figure, which, at this point (after recording transactions 1 to 15) is taken from the income statement.

Corporation, Inc.
Income and Retained
Earnings Statement
Month of January 1972

Sales			$26,000
Cost of goods sold			18,685
Gross margin on sales			7,315
Other expenses:			
Selling expenses:			
Sales salaries	$2,000		
Store rent	400		
Depreciation of store fixtures	75		
Miscellaneous	764	$3,239	
Administrative expenses:			
Office salaries	1,600		
Office rent	100		
Depreciation of office furniture and equipment	25		
Miscellaneous	631	2,356	5,595
			1,720
Income tax charge			550
Net income			1,170
Dividends declared			125
Retained earnings, January 31, 1972			$ 1,045

Corporation, Inc.
Position Statement
January 31, 1972

Assets			Equities		
Current:			*Current liabilities:*		
Cash	$13,845		Accounts payable		$ 4,000
Accounts receivable	3,000		Wages and salaries		
Merchandise inventory	8,500		payable		100
Merchandise inventory—			Payroll taxes		
freight in	85		payable		475
Unexpired rent	1,000		Withheld income		
			taxes payable		660
Total current assets	26,430		Income taxes		
			payable		550
Plant:			Total liabilities		5,785
Furniture, fixtures, and					
equipment	10,000				
Less accumulated depre-			*Stockholders' equity:*		
ciation	100				
Total plant assets	9,900		Capital con-		
			tributed by		
			stockholders	$30,000	
Intangibles:			Retained		
			earnings	1,045	
Organization costs	500		Total stock-		
			holders' equity		31,045
	$36,830				$36,830

The next step in the accounting cycle would be to recognize that the revenue and expense accounts have now served their purpose— the accumulating of detailed data on the entity's operations for the period—so that their balances may be transferred to the account to which they relate: Retained Earnings. In making the necessary entries or the closing of the accounts, as it is called, it is conventional to use an intermediate account, a clearing account, to avoid recording a large number of entries directly in the Retained Earnings account. This clearing account, called Revenue and Expense Summary in this illustration, is also often called Income Summary or Profit and Loss Summary. Referring to the T accounts shown on pages 126 to 127, you will note that the following closing entries have already been posted for these internal (or book) transactions.

By posting entries to the respective accounts, the balances in revenue and expense accounts were reduced to $0; double lines were drawn through them to indicate this and to permit their use in the next period, should that be desirable. Also note that the balance in the Retained Earnings account is now in agreement with that shown in both the Income and Retained Earnings Statement, and the Position Statement. The entire process described here would be repeated

Transaction Number	Increase or Decrease	Class of Account	Account Title (Retained Earnings)	Amount
A	Decrease	Equity	Sales	$26,000
	Increase	Equity	Revenue and expense summary	26,000
B	Decrease	Equity	Revenue and expense summary	18,685
	Increase*	Equity	Cost of goods sold	18,685
C	Decrease	Equity	Revenue and expense summary	3,239
	Increase*	Equity	Sales salaries expense	2,000
	Increase*	Equity	Store rent expense	400
	Increase*	Equity	Depreciation of store fixtures	75
	Increase*	Equity	Miscellaneous selling expense	764
D	Decrease	Equity	Revenue and expense summary	2,356
	Increase*	Equity	Office salaries expense	1,600
	Increase*	Equity	Office rent expense	100
	Increase*	Equity	Depreciation of office furniture and equipment	25
	Increase*	Equity	Miscellaneous administrative expense	631
E	Decrease	Equity	Revenue and expense summary	550
	Increase*	Equity	Income tax charge	550
F	Decrease	Equity	Retained earnings	125
	Increase*	Equity	Dividends declared	125
			(This entry is sometimes put through the Revenue and Expense Summary account)	
G	Decrease	Equity	Revenue and expense summary	1,170
	Increase	Equity	Retained earnings	1,170

*While the balance in the respective expense or income distribution account is reduced to $0, this has the effect of decreasing the equity account, Retained Earnings.

for this firm for the month of February and for each successive one-month accounting period.

Internal Transactions

The subject of internal transactions requires more discussion. Internal transactions may be classified not only as adjusting entries and closing entries but also as reversing entries. Of these, the adjusting entries are most significant and may be further classified as follows:

1. Allocations:
   a. Asset—expense
   b. Liability—revenue
2. Accruals:
   a. Asset—revenue
   b. Liability—expense
3. Correction of errors

As stated above, allocation adjusting entries may be of two types: asset—expense or liability—revenue. For each type there are two variations of entry: each account involved may be increased or decreased, depending on how the external transactions were recorded during the period.

A common type of adjustment is an asset—expense one where the asset is increased and the expense is decreased as a result of the entry. For example, the firm purchases a fire insurance policy. It may purchase insurance for three or more years in advance, as there is a considerable reduction in premium (or cost) if it does this instead of purchasing insurance yearly. Since the benefits of the policy will be received by the firm for three years instead of for only the current year, the cost of the policy will be recorded when purchased, as an asset. Although the firm could allocate one-third of the cost of the policy to expense when purchased (provided, of course, that the policy year and the accounting period coincide) and two-thirds to asset account, it is not customary to do so. Theoretically, the firm should record the total purchase in the account where there would be the least distortion (for example, asset for a three-year insurance policy purchased), provided no allocation is made when the purchase is made. In practice, large enterprises may decide arbitrarily, for control purposes, to record all purchases of one kind as assets, and all purchases of another kind as expenses. In our insurance policy example, where the cost of the policy is recorded as an asset, as time expires that portion of the cost which represents the expired benefits (time) should be allocated (or transferred) from the asset account to the expense account. If this is not done during the accounting period, it must be done at the end of the accounting period; otherwise the position statement would be overstated, and the net income understated, by the amount of the expired cost.

To summarize,

External Transaction	*Internal Transaction (adjusting entry at end of year)*

Debit—Unexpired insurance
   Credit—Cash
	Debit—Insurance expense
	   Credit—Unexpired insurance

Record purchase of 3-year insurance policy	Record 1-year expired premium

or if the policy were for only fifteen months, it would be recorded as follows:

External Transaction	Internal Transaction (adjusting entry at end of year)

Debit—Insurance expense
   Credit—Cash
Record purchase of 15-month
   insurance policy
	Debit—Unexpired insurance
	   Credit—Insurance expense
	Record 3 months of unexpired
	   insurance as asset

In addition to the insurance adjustment (which is illustrative of the adjustments often required for the prepayments category of asset), there are at least two other types of assets for which this allocation adjustment also may be required. The Inventory (asset)—Cost of Goods Sold (expense) allocation is one; the other is the long-lived asset—depreciation allocation. For long-lived assets that are depreciated, the reduction is not shown directly in the account but in a special contra account (as previously discussed). *Depreciation* refers to the allocation of the value of long-lived physical or tangible assets except for natural resources. *Depletion* refers to the allocation of the value of natural resources. *Amortization* is the allocation term used for long-lived intangible assets. For a manufacturing firm, the amount allocated to the period for long-lived assets may be recorded to the inventory account first before being expensed; for a non-manufacturing firm and for long-lived assets used in the selling and administrative activities of manufacturing firms, the allocation is directly to the appropriate expense.

The recognition of bad debts or uncollectible accounts from charge customers when such are estimated (as is customarily done instead of waiting until it is actually known which accounts are uncollectible) may be classified as an allocation adjustment too (although the income statement account to be adjusted preferably should be classified as contra revenue instead of expense). For further details of receivables adjustments see Chapter 5.

The less frequently encountered allocation is of the liability—revenue type. For example, the firm may occasionally receive or require payment from the customer in advance of delivering his goods or services; in a few kinds of businesses, such as the magazine or newspaper publisher, most customers pay in advance of receiving the good or service. In such circumstances (for the same reasoning as used in our insurance example), the firm usually will record the cash received in advance from the customer as a liability; at the end of the accounting period, an adjustment will be made to recognize the revenue earned (measured, for example, by the number of magazines and newspapers published) and to reduce the liability (for the number of magazines and newspapers paid for by the customer which have not yet been published).

It is possible that the customer advance may have been recorded initially as revenue; in this case, the end-of-period adjustment would be to recognize (and increase) the liability by decreasing the revenue account by the amount not yet earned.

Perhaps we should digress to point out the salient steps to follow when making an adjusting entry. They are three:

1. Identify the account whose balance should be adjusted (for example, Unexpired Insurance in our insurance illustration).
2. Calculate the correct balance of this account (cost of two year's insurance premium), and determine the difference (deduction in our illustration of the cost of one year's insurance premium) between the present balance and the correct balance; this is the amount of the adjusting entry.
3. Identify the related or companion account to the adjustment since this is double-entry bookkeeping (for example, in our insurance illustration, it is the Insurance Expense account).

The second basic type of adjusting entries is accruals. The term *accrue* (as suggested in Chapter 3) means to increase or to accumulate. Accruals in accounting occur when a contractual or benefit period does not coincide with the accounting period. There are two kinds of accruals: in one, there is the partial recognition of a revenue, together with its related asset; in the other, there is the partial recognition of an expense, together with its related liability. An example of each kind may be in order.

If the firm rents out a shed for a monthly rent payable on the first day of the next month, it will have at the end of its accounting period one month's rent earned but not yet received. The following adjustment consequently would be appropriate:

Debit—Rent receivable
  Credit—Rent revenue

This would be an example of an asset—revenue accrual adjustment. For an example of a liability—expense accrual adjustment, consider the same situation from the viewpoint of the firm using the rented shed; if we assume that its accounting period coincides with that of the firm that owns the shed, it has received the benefits of using the shed for a month without payment. The following adjusting entry would be in order for this firm:

Debit—Rent expense
  Credit—Rent payable

In addition to rent, accrual adjustments commonly are required for interest (cost of borrowing or lending money) or wages or salaries or commissions (where payment is not made at the end of the accounting period).

The third and final type of adjusting entry, correction of errors, is not a true adjusting entry. It usually is included because most errors are discovered and corrected at the end of the period when the other adjustments are being made. Corrections may involve any account since they relate to accounting errors of both commission and omission. Errors of omission, of course, are merely unrecorded transactions, and both types of errors should be corrected when discovered. For details of errors involving inventory, see Chapter 5. Closing entries may be classified as internal transactions too (as illustrated on page 132). There is no particular logic in any one way of preparing the entries to close out the income statement accounts and to record the net income (net loss) for the period.

For certain types of adjusting entries (except for those to correct errors) where asset or liability accounts were increased as a result of the adjusting entries, it may be desirable at the start of the new accounting period to make reversing entries in which all the debits are identical in account and amount with all the credits in a previous adjusting entry; and all the credits are identical in account and amount with all debits in the previous adjusting entry. Such reversing entries make it possible to record cash receipts and disbursements in the usual manner as though no adjusting entries were made at the end of the previous accounting period. To illustrate, provided such a reversing entry had been made, the firm renting out the shed could credit the rent for the last month of the previous year, received on the first day of the new year, to Rent Revenue, just as it would any other time it might receive such rent during the year. To repeat, such reversing entries may be recorded for any adjusting entry which increased any asset or liability account (but not, of course, any contra-asset or contra-liability account).

Internal Control[2]
The major ways in which an accounting system could provide for a system of internal control in Corporation, Inc., are as follows:

1. Training employees to comply with company policy:

---

[2]Although internal control sometimes is not considered part of financial accounting, it is helpful in understanding the accounting process.

Respective employees are made responsible for meeting sales quotas, expense budgets, and so on. The actual results are compiled by the accounting system and reported to the respective employees, their supervisors, and other interested managers. Financial rewards, promotions, and other means of recognition can be related to performance in accordance with established plans and policies.

2. Facilitating the evaluation of operating efficiency:
   a. The income statement provides a measure of *overall* performance and an index of efficiency. The data reported on the income statement for this period can be compared (1) to the data of this entity for past periods—intrafirm comparisons (not possible until next and succeeding periods for Corporation, Inc.); (2) to the data for other firms in the industry as reported by individual firms or trade associations—interfirm comparisons; and/or (3) to sales budgets, standards, or other quotas established within the firm.
   b. Data can be compiled in terms of subunits—departments or divisions, cost or profit centers—as well as in terms of the entire firm. Thus individuals can be made responsible for their performance, and deviations can be pinpointed more easily.

3. Providing an internal check to safeguard assets and to promote accurate, valid records:
   a. To promote unbiased, reliable records and reports, an operating department cannot control the accounting records for its own operations. In essence, the organization should be designed to adhere to the division of responsibilities principle. For example, the accounting department (a staff unit) should be separate from the operating departments (line units).
   b. To safeguard assets (and accuracy of records), it is essential that no one person control all aspects of the transaction (preparing invoices, collecting cash, keeping accounting records, handling merchandise, and so on). Thus control of operations, of assets, and of accounting records should be separated, and performed by different individuals. There should also be a division of duties within the accounting department so that the responsibility for authorizing or initiating a transaction is separated from responsibility for completing it.
   c. The system should have adequate methods, procedures, and forms to facilitate performance of the various activities of the firm (operations control), and to provide useful, accurate records and timely reports (accounting control).

The best system for accounting and control usually will be unique to the given entity. Thus, the system cannot be designed without a thorough study to determine the operating peculiarities and special needs of the entity. One will find, however, that there are some basic concepts which have general application. These include (1) the division of duties relating to operations, assets, and records among several people to safeguard assets (for example, to avoid the embezzlement of cash and other property), and to promote accurate records; (2) the assignment of responsibility and authority, with appropriate specialization and division of duties, for the accomplishment of all the firm's activities; and (3) a system of authorization and record procedures. These concepts are applied and illustrated in later chapters; the Appendix to Chapter 5, for example, considers the problems of controlling cash.

Summary

The accounting cycle consists of five essential steps: (1) the occurrence of an internal or external transaction; (2) the classification of transaction data and the recording of the data chronologically (journalizing); (3) the recording and accumulation of classified data in ledger accounts, in this book the T account (posting); (4) the preparation of position, income, fund-flow, and other financial statements; (5) the closing of revenue, expense, and other nominal accounts.

To carry out the accounting cycle it is necessary to analyze the internal and external transactions that cause constant change in the accounting equation of the firm. The principal types of transactions are: increases in assets from stockholders, from creditors, from customers, and from donors; decreases in assets to stockholders, to creditors, and to customers and others; and substitutions —asset for asset and equity for equity. These transactions may be further classified in terms of their algebraic effect on the accounting equation as diagramed on page 123.

Credit and debit are conventional terms in the vocabulary of recording transactions. A debit, recorded in the United States on the left side of an account, indicates an increase in an asset account or a decrease in an equity account. A credit, recorded in the United States on the right side of an account, indicates a decrease in an asset account and an increase in an equity account. It is important to remember that revenue and expense accounts are merely detailed retained earnings (equity) accounts and are used to accumulate data for the income statement of the period.

Each of the various accounts is related to the accounting cycle, and a classification of the accounts can help to clarify this relationship. The three subcategories of position statement accounts are asset accounts, liability accounts, and owners' equity accounts. Income and retained earnings statement accounts can be subdivided into accounts for revenues, expenses, and income distributions, and gains and losses. Accounts that do not appear on any statement are nominal accounts or temporary or suspense accounts. In addition, adjunct or contra accounts, which are valuation accounts used to increase or offset the balances of other accounts on the position, income, or retained earnings statements, are used in the accounting cycle.

During the accounting cycle both internal and external transactions are analyzed. Internal transactions may be classified as adjusting entries, closing entries, or reversing entries. Of the three, adjusting entries, which encompass allocations, accruals, and corrections of errors, are the most significant.

To illustrate the steps in the accounting process, a set of accounts for a firm was developed, and the firm's transactions during a specified period of time were processed.

Perhaps the most significant aspect of the accounting cycle is its ability to provide a system of internal control in the following ways: (1) The accounting process compiles the actual results of operations and serves as a measure of compliance to company policy. (2) The net income is a measure of overall performance and an index of efficiency. It can be used to make comparisons between various periods of the firm's operation, and to compare one firm to others in the same industry. Additionally, data can be compiled for subunits of the firm, to make similar comparisons. (3) The accounting process provides an internal check to safeguard assets through separation of control of assets, operations, and accounting records, and to promote accurate and valid records.

A Selection of Supplementary Readings

Allen, Brandt R.: "Computer Fraud," *Financial Executive*, May 1971, p. 38.

Arenberg, J. T.: "Accrual Accounting Made Easy," *Auditgram*, March 1966, p. 10.

Bedford, Norton M.: "The Need for an Extension of the Accrual Concept," *The Journal of Accountancy*, May 1965, pp. 29–33. Also see H. P. Hain and Norton M. Bedford: "Letters to the Journal," *The Journal of Accountancy*, October 1966, p. 20.

Chambers, R. J.: "Financial Information Systems," *The Australian Accountant*, August 1969, pp. 364–368.

Gorman, Thomas J.: "Corporate Financial Models in Planning and Control," *The Price Waterhouse Review*, summer 1970, pp. 40–53.

Harrowell, J. R.: "Financial Reporting," *The Chartered Accountant in Australia*, November 1967, pp. 402–407.

Hatfield, Henry Rand: "An Historical Defense of Bookkeeping," *The Journal of Accountancy*, April 1924, pp. 241–253.

Mason, Richard: "Management Information Systems: What They Are, What They Ought to Be," *Innovation*, no. 13, 1970, pp. 34–42.

Mitchell, R.: "Computer-based Systems and the Accounting Function," 2 parts, *The Accountant*, September 27, 1969, pp. 383–387, and October 4, 1969, pp. 420–424.

Newman, Maurice S.: "Building Internal Control into a Comprehensive Electronic Accounting System," *The New York Certified Public Accountant*, June 1966, pp. 433–442.

Willingham, John J., and Robert E. Malcolm: "Behavioral Exchange Data: The Key to Information Systems," *The Internal Auditor*, July–August 1970, pp. 33–45.

Woolley, P. J.: "The Use of Models in Accounting, Education and Training,"
Canadian Chartered Accountant, January 1968, pp. 72–75.
Young, Robert: "Internal Control in Electronic Data Processing Systems,"
The New York Certified Public Accountant, January 1967, pp. 45–50.

Questions

4–1 Indicate the net effect of these transactions on Assets, Liabilities, and Ownership for the current accounting period:
a. Purchased store equipment on account for $2,400, estimated life one year, no salvage value at the end of that time.
b. Used the above equipment for the current accounting period of one month.
c. Billed $2,100 to customers for services rendered (no sales of goods involved).
d. Returned merchandise to suppliers for $220 credit.
e. Paid $360 cash for insurance policy, policy period to begin in the future.

(1) The net effect on total assets: (a) $4,080 increase, (b) $4,440 increase, (c) $3,720 increase, (d) $4,300 increase, (e) something else
(2) The net effect on total liabilities: (a) $2,400 increase, (b) $220 decrease, (c) zero, (d) $2,200 increase, (e) something else
(3) The net effect on total ownership: (a) $1,540 increase, (b) $2,100 increase, (c) $1,740 increase, (d) $1,900 increase, (e) something else

4–2 The following occur in an accounting cycle:
a. Post closing trial balance
b. Journalizing
c. Posting
d. Reversing entries
e. Worksheet
f. Financial statements

What is their proper order: (a) cbfeda, (b) bcfead, (c) bcfeda, (d) bcefad, (e) cbefad?

4–3 Accounts Receivable—beginning of period $4,600, end of period $3,900.
Collections on accounts receivable—$27,400.
Accounts Payable—beginning of period $2,900, end of period $3,300.
Payments on accounts payable—$12,700.
Beginning Inventory—$5,100; Ending Inventory—$4,900.
Sales and purchases are all on account; all accounts payable are the result of purchases.

(1) Total sales amounted to: (a) $28,100, (b) $31,300, (c) $27,400, (d) $26,700, (e) something else.
(2) Total purchases amounted to: (a) $13,100, (b) $27,400, (c) $31,300, (d) $26,700, (e) $12,900, (f) something else.
(3) Total Assets $560,000; Plant $130,000; no long-term liabilities or intangibles. The current assets are twice the current liabilities. The ownership equity is: (a) $215,000, (b) $345,000, (c) $260,000, (d) $65,000, (e) something else.

(4) Office Salaries Payable has a balance of $150. The unpaid office salaries at the end of the period total $80. The adjusting entry (only one to be made) should be:
a. Debit Office Salaries Payable $80
b. Credit Office Salaries Payable $70
c. Debit Office Salaries $80
d. Debit Office Salaries $70
e. Credit Office Salaries $70

4-4   Indicate the net effect of these transactions on Assets, Liabilities, and Ownership for the current accounting period:
a. Purchased office supplies for $400 on account.
b. Used $100 of these supplies.
c. Sold merchandise which cost $200 on account for $500.
d. Collected $400 cash—$350 of it on accounts receivable, and $50 of it in prepayments for merchandise not yet ordered from this firm.
e. Estimated that $50 of accounts receivable may become uncollectible.

(1) The net effect on total assets: (a) $600 increase, (b) $1,300 increase, (c) $800 increase, (d) $550 increase, (e) something else
(2) The net effect on total liabilities: (a) $400 increase, (b) $450 increase, (c) $350 increase, (d) $300 increase, (e) something else
(3) The net effect on total ownership: (a) $150 increase, (b) $50 decrease, (c) $200 increase, (d) $250 increase, (e) something else

4-5   Indicate the net effect of these transactions on Assets, Liabilities, and Ownership for the current accounting period:
a. Received a credit memo of $1,000 from a creditor for defective merchandise; the goods are still in the inventory.
b. Ordered merchandise costing $2,100, to be delivered in the next accounting period.
c. Employees earned and were paid wages of $500, less $50 of withheld income tax.
d. Paid creditors $2,000.
e. Sold merchandise for $300 that cost $100.

(1) The net effect on total assets: (a) $3,550 decrease, (b) $3,150 decrease, (c) $2,550 decrease, (d) $2,150 decrease, (e) something else
(2) The net effect on total liabilities: (a) $850 decrease, (b) $900 increase, (c) $2,950 decrease, (d) $3,000 decrease, (e) something else
(3) The net effect on total ownership: (a) $300 decrease, (b) $200 increase, (c) $700 increase, (d) $1,200 increase, (e) something else

4-6   Given the following terms, you are to determine which groupings (1) to (5) are most closely related:
a. Expenses   e. Assets
b. Liabilities   f. Posting
c. Ledger   g. Position statement
d. Current assets   h. Working capital

i. Fiscal period
j. Current liabilities
k. Journal

l. Income statement
m. Revenue
n. Ownership

(1) ea, cfk, djh; (2) il, beh, amn; (3) gi, fge, ae; (4) bmn, gi, bel; (5) dgl, dfg, em.

4–7   Which of the following statements is correct?
(1) Closing and adjusting entries do not need to be made if a business is on a cash basis.
(2) Closing entries frequently involve several debits and credits to asset or liability accounts.
(3) The use of a worksheet eliminates the necessity of closing entries.
(4) If a business uses a fiscal year which is not a calendar year, closing entries need not be made at the end of the fiscal year.
(5) All of the above are incorrect.

4–8   Which of the following rules is incorrect? None or more than one can be incorrect.
(1) Credits are decreases in assets and decreases in expenses.
(2) Credits are decreases in contra assets and increases in liabilities.
(3) Debits are decreases in contra assets and decreases in ownership.
(4) Credits are decreases in expenses and decreases in contra assets.
(5) Debits are decreases in liabilities and increases in assets.

4–9   Determine the effect of the following events on the Assets, Liabilities, and Ownership, using the following classifications:
a. Increase one asset; decrease another asset.
b. Decrease an asset; decrease a liability.
c. Increase an asset; increase ownership.
d. Increase an asset; increase a liability.
e. Decrease an asset or increase a liability; decrease ownership.

(1) Purchase of raw materials on account
(2) Payment of the above materials
(3) Payment of freight bill for materials
(4) Use of raw materials
(5) Use of labor
(6) Payment of labor
(7) Purchase of factory equipment
(8) Use of factory equipment
(9) Purchase of insurance on factory equipment
(10) Use of insurance (i.e., passage of time)
(11) Completion of goods
(12) Sales of goods

4–10   Explain how items such as rent or interest may be involved in all four basic types of adjustments.

4–11   Are reversing entries ever essential? Useful? Give illustrations of three adjusting entries that might be reversed.

4–12   What is the minimum number of accounts that can change as the result of a transaction? Why?

4–13   In the following questions you are making the annual adjusting entries for the firm, based on its unadjusted account balances (where such are relevant) as of December 31, 1972, together with any necessary supplementary information. Only *one* entry is required for each situation.

(1) Wages Expense has a balance of $1,500; Prepaid Wages has a balance of $500. At this date, the company does not have any prepaid wages. The adjusting entry will be in the amount of: (a) $1,500, (b) $500, (c) $1,000, (d) $100, (e) some other amount.

(2) The company owes $100 for work performed since the last payday. The balance in wages expense after the adjusting entries in (1) and (2) will be (a) $2,100, (b) $2,000, (c) $1,600, (d) $1,500, (e) some other amount.

(3) The insurance expense for the period should be $240; Insurance Expense has a balance of $300. The adjusting entry should be to: (a) debit Insurance Expense $240, (b) credit Insurance Expense $240, (c) credit Insurance Expense $60, (d) debit Insurance Expense $60, (e) debit Insurance Expense $540.

(4) Supplies Inventory has a balance of $100; Supplies Expense has a balance of $200. At this date, the inventory is $150. The adjusting entry will include: (a) debit Supplies Expense $150, (b) credit Supplies Expense $50, (c) credit Supplies Expense $150, (d) debit Supplies Expense $50, (e) credit Supplies Inventory $150.

4–14   One professor has argued that instead of using debits and credits, one should use the terms left and right. Defend this viewpoint.

4–15   The following gross margin data are taken from the financial records of a company:

	Period Last	Period This
Sales	$300,000	$296,400
Cost of sales	200,000	203,300
Gross margin	$100,000	$ 93,100

(1) If it is known that volume declined 5 percent from that of the preceding period, then it is evident that selling prices:
   a. Increased 7 percent
   b. Increased 4 percent
   c. Increased 3.8 percent
   d. Decreased 3.6 percent

(2) If it is known that volume declined 5 percent from that of the preceding period, then it is evident that cost prices:
   a. Increased 7 percent
   b. Increased 6.5 percent

c. Increased 1.65 percent

d. Decreased 3.6 percent

(3) Suppose that volume increased 1.65 percent over that of the preceding period, then it is evident that cost prices:

a. Did not change

b. Declined 3.6 percent

c. Declined 5 percent

d. Declined 7 percent

(4) If the change in sales is partially accounted for by a 4 percent increase in selling prices, the amount of change in gross margin due to this single factor would be:

a. $15,600

b. $12,000

c. $11,400

d. $ 6,900

(5) If the change in cost of goods sold is partially accounted for by a 7 percent increase in cost prices, the amount of change in gross margin due to this single factor would be:

a. $14,000

b. $13,300

c. $ 6,900

d. $ 3,600

Problems

4-1

In each of the following T accounts indicate a routine transaction that would cause the effect recorded.

Accounts Receivable		Accounts Payable	
(1)	(2)	(3)	(4)

Building		Cash	
(5)	(6)	(7)	(8)

Land		Office Equipment	
(9)	(10)	(11)	(12)

Notes Payable		Inventory	
(13)	(14)	(15)	(16)

Capital Stock		Retained Earnings	
(17)	(18)	(19)	(20)

4-2

Routine transactions recorded for typical business enterprises are:

(1) Owners invest cash in enterprise

(2) Owners withdraw cash from enterprise

(3) Buy inventory on credit

(4) Buy plant for cash and long-term debt

(5) Deliver inventory to customers
(6) Depreciate plant
(7) Pay trade creditors
(8) Sell for cash
(9) Sell on credit
(10) Collect accounts receivable

Analyze these transactions and record them in T accounts, using the transaction number to code each entry.

4-3 A company owned by Andy and Flo Capp has the following ledger accounts as of October 31, 1972. Prepare a position statement as of October 31, 1972.

Cash			Accounts Payable	
12,000	13,000		13,000	4,000
330	700			100
3,000				1,200
800				12,000

Accounts Receivable			Taxes Payable	
250	3,000		700	950
4,000				
36,000				

Land			Mortgage Payable	
20,000				28,000

Building			Andy Capp, Capital	
32,000				20,000
				16,000

Equipment			Flo Capp, Capital	
14,000	330			20,000
	800			16,000

4-4 Brendan O'Regan of Shannon, Ireland, conducts a tourist business. As of February 15, 1972, the business ledger accounts were as follows. Determine the account balances and prepare a position statement as of that date.

Cash			Accounts Payable	
1,500	500		300	200
500	1,000		200	300
2,500	600		400	900
300	400			250
				500

Accounts Receivable		Wages Payable	
2,500	300		1,500
250			
250			
2,000			

Office Supplies		Notes Payable	
1,500		1,000	13,000
250			
250			

Office Equipment		Brendan O'Regan, Capital	
13,250			13,500

Delivery Equipment	
6,000	

4–5

Cash		Store Building		Capital Stock	
1		40			25

Accounts Receivable		Store Building— Accumulated Depreciation		Retained Earnings	
4			6		13.8

Accounts Receivable— Allowance for Uncollectible Accounts		Accounts Payable		Sales	
	0.1		0.5		35

Merchandise Inventory		Notes Payable		Salaries Expense	
30			5	10	

Unexpired Insurance		Interest Payable	
0.5			0.1

Adjusting entry data for December 31, 1973:
(1) Uncollectible accounts estimated at 2 percent of sales
(2) Unexpired insurance at December 31: $0.2
(3) Building depreciation 5 percent per year
(4) Note Payable dated November 1, 1973; interest at 12 percent annually
(5) Customer advance of $0.5 for 1975 delivery of merchandise credited to sales
(6) Merchandise on hand December 31: $10

Enter adjusting entries into T accounts, and prepare position and income statements.

4-6   For the series of independent transactions below, please indicate the effect of each transaction on the main categories of each statement, that is, the effect on total assets. Use + to indicate overstatement, − to indicate understatement, and 0 if there is no effect.

	Position Statement: December 31, 1972	Income Statement for the Year Ended December 31, 1972
(1) Acquisition of supplies for cash recorded as though purchased on account		
(2) Expired insurance not recorded		
(3) Failure to record cash sale		
(4) Failure to record charge sale		
(5) Failure to record receipt of cash from charge customer		

4-7   In the following matrix, each row is labeled with the name of an account or account class, and each column represents the effect of a specific kind of transaction on the account corresponding to the row. For each account or account class in every column, indicate the effect with + if there is an increase and − if there is a decrease. Note the example (0).

Transactions / Accounts	(0) Invest in enterprise	(1) Withdraw cash from enterprise	(2) Buy plant for cash	(3) Buy inventory on credit	(4) Pay trade creditors	(5) Sell on credit	(6) Sell for cash	(7) Deliver inventory	(8) Depreciate plant	(9) Collect from charge customers	(10) Amortize intangible	(11) Prepayments expense	(12) Record period taxes	(13) Pay period taxes	(14) Declare dividends	(15) Pay dividends	(16) Closing entries
Assets	+																
Liabilities																	
Ownership	+																
Cash	+																
Accounts receivable																	
Inventory																	
Prepayments																	
Plant																	
Intangibles																	
Accounts payable																	
Other payables																	
Capital stock	+																
Retained earnings																	
Revenues																	
Expenses																	

4-8 On the basis of the following information, enter appropriate adjusting entries into the relevant T accounts (000's omitted).

Prepaid Wages	Wages Payable	Wages Expense
	1.4	160

(1) At the end of the accounting period the firm had prepaid wages totaling $8.

Prepaid Rent	Rent Payable	Rent Expense
3		30

(2) The rent expense for the period is $36.

Merchandise Inventory	Cost of Goods Sold
85	280

(3) A physical count shows the ending merchandise inventory to be $96.

Supplies	Supplies Expense
1.8	6.4

(4) A physical count shows the supplies inventory to be $2.2.

Accounts Receivable	Accounts Receivable—Allowance for Bad Debts	Sales—Bad Debts
60	0.8	

(5) Of the period's sales of $100, it is estimated 1 percent will not be collected. Write-offs during the period were $3.

Plant	Plant—Accumulated Depreciation	Depreciation Expense
200	39	

(6) Depreciation charge for the period is $40.

Interest Charge	Interest Payable
3	

(7) Interest owed but not paid is $2.

Interest Revenue	Interest Receivable
3	

(8) Interest earned but not received is $2.

Prepaid Insurance	Insurance Expense
10	

(9) Insurance expense for the period is $3.

Sales	Advances from Customers
550	2.2

(10) Advances from customers at the end of the period is $2.

4-9   Analyze the following transactions by recording in T accounts. All transactions are for the same company.

No.	Amount	Event
1	$20,000	Owners invested cash in company; stock issued.
2	500	Company purchased office equipment for cash.
3	5,000	Company borrowed from bank or note.
4	4,000	Company sales: charge.
5	3,000	cash.
6	100	Company purchased office supplies: on account.
7	25	for cash.
8	300	Company engaged lawyer; paid his retainer for a year in advance.
9	100	Company engaged public accounting firm; agreed to pay $100 per month in advance. Paid first month.
10	125	Company paid for newspaper ads in advance.
11	2,000	Company collected on accounts receivable.
12	100	Company charged off accounts of customers which were not collectible.
13	2,500	Company made charge purchases of merchandise.
14	1,200	Company made payment for merchandise in 13.
15	1,500	Weekly payroll.
16	1,200	Company paid employees.

4-10   On the basis of the following information determine the amounts for the blank lines (000's omitted).

	Fudge Co.	Popsicle Co.	Mint Co.
Merchandise inventory, January 1, 1972	$ 20	_____	$ 64
Purchases	340	$ 462	
Cost of merchandise sold	_____	_____	600
Merchandise inventory, December 31, 1972	_____	80	72
Sales	400	580	_____
Other expenses	40	82	80
Net income	_____	58	24
Ownership, January 1, 1972	100	_____	240
Ownership, December 31, 1972	105	370	_____
Owner withdrawals	10	20	16

4-11   The following transactions illustrate the basic accounting cycle for a firm.
External Transactions (October 1–October 31):
(1) J. Gleason starts firm with $10,000 cash investment.
(2) Firm purchases goods for resale on account $6,000.
(3) Sells goods on account $9,000.

(4) Pays part-time clerks for services October 1–30: $500.
(5) Collects from customers $7,500.
(6) Pays creditors $4,500.
(7) Withdrawal by owner $200.

Internal Transactions (Adjusting entries—October 31):
 (8) Physical inventory: $1,500 goods on hand.
 (9) Records part-time clerical services for October 31: $30.

Closing Entries (October 31):
(10) Close out Sales to Revenue and Expense Summary.
(11) Close out two expense accounts to Revenue and Expense Summary.
(12) Close out Revenue and Expense Summary (Net Income) to Owner's Capital account.

Record the above transactions in T accounts (coded with transaction number), and prepare position and income statements.

4–12

In each of the following *unrelated* situations you are asked to prepare adjusting entries.

	Present Balance in Account	Required Balance in Account
(1) Advance from tenant	$ 500	$ 100
(2) Prepaid insurance	2,000	1,500
(3) Taxes payable	300	500
(4) Merchandise inventory	5,000	3,500
(5) Insurance expense	300	400
(6) Rent revenue	100	200
(7) Taxes	600	700
(8) Depreciation	0	500
(9) Rent payable	0	100
(10) Supplies expense	300	400

4–13

The following is a list of accounts. Draw up a chart, as illustrated below, identify each account as to type, and state whether the account is increased by a debit or a credit.

	Type of Account				Increased by	
	Asset	Liability	Revenue	Expense	Debit	Credit
(1) Advances by customers						
(2) Bonds payable						
(3) Building						
(4) Cash						
(5) Delivery equipment						
(6) Dividend payable						
(7) Goodwill						

	Type of Account				Increased by	
	Asset	Liability	Revenue	Expense	Debit	Credit
(8) Land						
(9) Merchandise inventory						
(10) Miscellaneous expenses						
(11) Notes payable						
(12) Notes receivable						
(13) Office salaries						
(14) Patents						
(15) Sales						
(16) Sales—discounts						
(17) Service revenue						
(18) Supplies expense						
(19) Unexpired insurance						
(20) U.S. government bonds						
(21) Taxes expense						
(22) Accounts receivable						
(23) Accounts payable						
(24) Cost of goods sold						
(25) Investment in stock						

4–14

Joe Miller, an excellent tailor, started a tailoring shop near a university on October 1. Using materials selected from samples he keeps in the shop, he makes suits only to customers' orders. When a customer orders a suit, Miller takes the measurements and then orders the required materials from manufacturers located in southern or eastern cities. The deposit required from the customer at the time when the suit is ordered is used to pay for the cloth. It takes a month from the time the customer orders a suit until it is completed and delivered. Then the customer is billed on 30-day terms for the balance owed.

During his first two months, Millers' records show the following:

	October	November
Deposits received	$ 800	$ 900
Cloth ordered and received	750	870
Cloth paid for	600	830
Customers' bills sent	1,200	1,400
Customers' collections on bills sent	300	950
Office expenses	450	500
Miller's salary	750	750
Cloth on hand at end of month	60*	210†
5-year equipment purchased	1,000	—
Supplies used	50	70

*For suit on which $75 deposit had been received.
†For overcoat on which $150 had been deposited.

Prepare monthly income statements, ignoring income taxes.

4-15

a. Determine the *revenue* earned and recorded by the Kasavubu Corporation during November, based upon the following. Show computations.
   (1) Kasavubu Corporation bonds with a face of $10,000 are issued for $9,500 cash.
   (2) United States bonds carried at a cost of $9,500 are sold for $9,600 cash.
   (3) Shares of Kasavubu Corporation stock with a par value of $9,500 are issued for $9,700 cash.
   (4) A customer, Colonel Mobutu, deposits $10,000 cash with a $20,000 order for goods.
   (5) A charge customer, Mr. P. Lumumba, signs a 6 percent 60-day $1,000 note dated November 30, 1972, in exchange for goods selling for $1,000.

b. Determine the amount of *expense* recorded by the same firm for the same period as a result of the following. Show computations.
   (6) Goods purchased during the month cost $2,000. On November 1 goods costing $600 were on hand. On November 30 goods costing $375 were still on hand.
   (7) Equipment with a six-month useful life was purchased on November 30 at a cost of $1,200.
   (8) A $3,000 three-year fire insurance policy for merchandise on hand was purchased at a cost of $36 on November 1.

4-16

The *New Frontiers* Corporation buys and sells goods on the usual terms. The firm's account balances are as follows (000's omitted):

	1973 October 1	1973 December 31
Accounts payable (for merchandise)	$ 27.5	$ 37.5
Accounts receivable	51.0	35.0
Accounts receivable—allowance for doubtful accounts	0.4	0.3
Accounts receivable—allowance for sales discounts	0.6	0.8
Cash	35.0	38.0
Capital stock	130.0	130.0
Corporation income taxes	0	10.0
Corporation income taxes payable	6.0	8.0
Dividends declared	0	6.0
Dividends payable	1.0	3.0
Equipment	140.0	150.0
Equipment—accumulated depreciation	7.1	10.0
Expense control (includes expenses to date for the period)	0	13.3
Income taxes withheld and payroll taxes payable	2.0	3.7
Interest charges	0	0.7
Interest payable	0.9	0.3
Merchandise—inventory, September 30, 1973	10.0	10.0

| | 1973 | |
	October 1	December 31
Merchandise—cost of goods sold	$ 0	$ 0
Merchandise—purchases	0	66.7
Merchandise—purchases—returns	0	3.0
Merchandise—purchases—freight in (paid by cash)	0	6.0
Merchandise—purchases—discounts lost	0	0.3
Notes payable	24.0	11.0
Retained earnings	34.0	34.0
Sales (only 10% were cash)	0	100.0
Sales—discounts	0	1.1
Sales—doubtful accounts	0	2.0
Sales—returns (on charge sales)	0	3.0
Sales—freight out (on charge sales)	0	1.0
Wages payable	2.5	1.5

Answer the following questions.
(1) If all end-of-the-period adjustments have already been entered in the accounts except to record the $15,000 ending inventory and to recognize the cost of goods sold, what is the period merchandise cost of goods sold?
(2) What is the net income for the period?
(3) How should the income statement for this period be dated?
(4) If the distribution of net income includes corporate income taxes, interest, and dividends, what was the amount of cash paid out for these purposes during the period?
(5) What would be the total stockholders' equity as of December 31, 1973?
(6) What was the amount of cash paid to the merchandise creditors during the period?
(7) What was the amount of cash collected from charge customers during the period?
(8) How should the position statement be dated?
(9) What account was debited when Sales—Freight Out was credited?
(10) *If we assume for this question only* that the firm had decided to estimate the ending inventory instead of counting the unsold merchandise and if the gross margin has averaged 40 percent *of the cost of the goods sold,* what would be the amount of estimated inventory?

4–17
The Downtown Window Cleaning Service was organized on September 1, 1974, and carried out the following seven transactions during the month:

Sept. 1   Mr. Dennis Frolin deposited $10,000 cash in the name of the business. Signed a lease for an office with monthly rent of $100. Rent for three months was paid in advance.
Purchased a three-year insurance policy for $504.
Purchased ladders and other equipment for a total of $2,400. A cash down payment of $1,400 was made, and a two-month note

bearing interest at 6 percent per year was given for the balance. The equipment was estimated to have a useful life of 10 years.

Sept. 2   Purchased 100 one-minute spot radio advertisements from radio station WIBA at $2.50 per spot announcement. The station was to report, at the end of each month, the number of spot announcements presented in that month.

Purchased washing supplies for $520, paying cash. Purchased additional supplies on credit, $210.

Sept. 3   Signed a contract with the Midwestern Bank for window washing services for its office building at $75 per week. The bank paid $500 in advance.

Sept. 14   Services billed for the first two-week period amounted to $2,100, exclusive of the payment from the bank. Collections in cash for the billed services amounted to $1,650. Cash collections for non-billed services, $200.

Biweekly wages to employees amounted to $1,135.

Sept. 15   Subleased part of office for $25 per month with rent for four months received in advance.

Sept. 28   Services billed for the second two-week period amounted to $2,075. Collections on services previously billed, $1,825. Cash collections for nonbilled services, $125.

Biweekly wages to employees amounted to $1,030.

Sept. 30   Mr. Frolin withdrew $450 for personal use. On September 27 he had an employee wash his car. The employee was paid $4.00 an hour and took $\frac{1}{2}$ hour to do this job.

Other Data:

(1) A statement from radio station WIBA noted that 44 one-minute spot announcements were made during September.

(2) Based on a physical count on September 30, the cost of washing supplies on hand amounted to $145.

(3) A statement was sent to the Midwestern Bank that five weekly services were rendered during the month of September.

(4) Services rendered to clients too late to be billed amounted to $125.

(5) Salaries earned by employees but not paid amounted to $95.

(6) Estimated uncollectible services were 1 percent of services billed during month.

Prepare:

a. Journal entries for all the September external transactions; and post to T accounts.

b. Trial balance as of September 30.

c. Adjusting entries (internal transactions); and post to T accounts.

d. Financial statements.

e. Closing entries: post and rule.

f. After-closing trial balance.

g. Any reversing entries that might be made.

4–18   Indicate, by drawing a circle around the × in the proper column, the effect of the following transactions (Increase—Decrease: Assets, Liabilities, and Ownership):

	Assets Increase	Assets Decrease	Liabilities Increase	Liabilities Decrease	Ownership Increase	Ownership Decrease
(1) Purchase of merchandise on account	×	×	×	×	×	×
(2) Investment in the business by the owner	×	×	×	×	×	×
(3) Purchase of a building for cash	×	×	×	×	×	×
(4) Purchase of an insurance policy for cash (3-year policy)	×	×	×	×	×	×
(5) Payment to a creditor	×	×	×	×	×	×
(6) Ownership withdraws merchandise	×	×	×	×	×	×
(7) Receipt of payment from debtors	×	×	×	×	×	×
(8) Payment of advance to a supplier	×	×	×	×	×	×
(9) Receipt of cash as an advance on an order by a customer	×	×	×	×	×	×
(10) The business borrows money on a short-term basis from the bank	×	×	×	×	×	×

4-19 *Ingemar Johansson Enterprises Trial Balance October 15, 1973 (000's omitted)*

Code Symbol	Account Title	Amount	Code Symbol	Account Title	Amount
(a)	Patents	$ 21.4	(x)	Advance from customer	$ 2.0
(b)	Advertising expense	0.1	(y)	Retained earnings, October 15, 1973	10.0
(c)	Office supplies expense	0.3			
(d)	Raw materials used	0.5	(z)	Income tax withheld	2.5
(e)	Depreciation of office equipment	0.5	(aa)	Income summary	0.0
(f)	Depreciation of factory equipment	1.0	(bb)	Payroll taxes payable	0.3
(g)	Unexpired insurance	1.5	(cc)	Wages and salaries payable	4.0
(h)	Factory supplies used	2.0	(dd)	Building—accumulated depreciation	4.0
(i)	Supplies on hand	0.5			
(j)	Factory labor costs	15.0	(ee)	Notes payable (due December 31, 1973)	5.0
(k)	Goodwill	0.1			
(l)	Building	10.0	(ff)	Accounts payable	12.0
(m)	Supervision	5.0	(gg)	Mortgage payable (due January 1, 1974)	20.0
(n)	Accounts receivable	20.0			
(o)	Marketable securities	15.0	(hh)	Capital stock—par	50.0
(p)	Office salaries	3.0	(ii)	Sales	45.0
(q)	Other factory costs	8.0			
(r)	Raw materials	5.0			
(s)	Equipment (net accumulated depreciation)	12.5			
(t)	Land	10.0			
(u)	Cash in bank	20.4			
(v)	Salesmen's salaries expense	1.0			
(w)	Capital stock—discount	2.0			
		$154.8			$154.8

Other Data:

Purchase orders outstanding $50

Inventories as of above date: Goods in process $1.2

Finished goods 1.8

Accounting period is fiscal year ending today.

On the basis of the above information, furnish the following items as they would appear on the various financial statements. (Code or label each figure utilized.)

(1) Third line of the heading on the: Income statement.

(2) Position statement.

(3) Total production costs.

(4) Cost of goods sold.

(5) Current assets (list in usual order of liquidity).

(6) Current liabilities.

(7) Plant.

(8) Stockholders' equity (on the *new* position statement).

(9) List code letters of contra accounts.

(10) List code letters of accounts that will be closed out as of above date.

4–20

The account balances shown on the books of the Delta Queen, a newly organized firm, on January 1, 1972, are as follows (000's omitted):

Accounts payable	$50
Advances from customers	0.5
Bonds payable	10
Capital stock	20
Cash	20
Plant	40
Raw materials inventory	15
Retained earnings	?

The following constitute all transactions for the month of January 1972:

(1) Raw material purchases on account	$ 78
(2) Obsolete raw materials which were discarded	14
(3) Raw material on hand at January 31, 1972	28
(4) Factory labor services incurred and payable during January	100
Less: FICA taxes withheld	5
Income taxes withheld	21
(5) Company payroll taxes for January:	
FICA	5
Unemployment	3
(6) Goods completing manufacturing process during January	140
(7) Advance collections received	0.3
(8) Advance collection satisfied	0.6
(9) Other sales for month on account (NOTE: Selling price is 50 percent greater than cost of item sold)	150

(10) *The bonds are retired on January 1 for:*	*9.8*
(11) *Depreciation on plant*	*4*
(12) *Collections on account*	*125*
(13) *Payment of debts*	*95*

a. Determine the Retained Earnings figure on January 1.
b. Using the T-account form, enter the beginning balances for those accounts having them, and make all appropriate entries needed for transactions 1 to 13 above in T accounts. Number entries.
c. Place a cross at the top of each T account that would be closed after an an Income Statement was prepared at January 31.

4-21

On December 31, 1973, James Coco's trial balance included the following items (000's omitted):

Accounts receivable	*$10*	*Accounts receivable—allowance for doubtful accounts*	*$0.5*
Store fixtures	*4*		
Store fixtures—accumulated depreciation	*1.5*	*Advertising expense*	*0.4*
Sales	*44*	*Notes receivable*	*4.5*
		Accrued interest payable	*0.5*

Prepare the adjusting entries needed to correctly reflect the following facts.
(1) Interest on notes payable was charged to expense. $20 of this applies to 1974.
(2) Interest accrued on notes receivable amounts to $20.
(3) Advertising materials on hand December 31, 1973, amounted to $75.
(4) Unpaid store rent for December is $200.
(5) Office supplies on hand amount to $25. All supplies purchased are charged to an asset account. Consumption this year totaled $545.
(6) Insurance is charged to an expense account when paid. Total payments this year were $300. The amount prepaid at year end is $150.
(7) Unpaid bills for electricity and telephone totaled $65.
(8) Sales salaries of $40 were unpaid; bonus to the office manager of $250 was to be paid in February 1974.
(9) Depreciation is $600 for year.
(10) The balance in the allowance for doubtful accounts should be $500 at year end.

4-22

Explain carefully, but briefly (i.e., overstates or understates) how the errors on page 160 made at the end of the current period affect the:
a. Current income statement
b. Next income statement
c. Current position statement
d. Next position statement

(1) Misstatement of merchandise inventory
(2) Misstatement of merchandise purchases
(3) Failure to record prepayments (or deferred costs)
(4) Failure to record accrued revenues (or accrued receivables)
(5) Overstatement of prepayments (or deferred costs)
(6) Failure to recognize revenue received in advance (Advances from Customers, Customers' Deposits, Unearned Revenue, Prepaid Revenue, Deferred Revenue)
(7) Overstatement of revenue received in advance
(8) Failure to record depreciation
(9) Failure to provide an allowance for bad debts
(10) Failure to recognize accrued liabilities or accrued expenses

4-23 List for each itemized figure in the following three accounts the names of the accounts in which the same figure would be recorded simultaneously.

Example:

	Machinery			*Answer:*
	(0) 1,000			*(0) Cash*

Accounts Receivable			*Income Summary*			*Accounts Payable*	
✔ 500	*(2) 5,500*	*(6) 6,000*	*(5) 10,000*	*(10) 3,000*	✔ 2,500
(1) 5,000	*(3) 500*	*(7) 300*		✔ 1,500	2,000
(4) 500		*(8) 2,400*		4,500	4,500
		(9) 1,300			✔ 1,500
6,000	6,000	10,000	10,000		

4-24 On January 1, 1973, the customers of the Industrial Nucleonics Corporation owed the firm a total of $93,194. Certain other customers had made advance payments at the time of placing an order for 1972 delivery; these payments, made in 1972, amounted to $6,254.

Cost incurred in 1972 which were not completely chargeable to 1972 revenue were:

Cost of merchandise on hand, December 31, 1972	*$73,614*
Cost of delivery trucks purchased January 2, 1972	
(Lifetime of trucks 4 years. Scrap value $1,200)	*8,400*

Cash received from customers during 1973 amounted to $1,378,580; of this amount $90,926 was collected for sales of 1972 and prior years. No advance payments were received during 1973. Goods delivered during 1973 for which payment was not received during 1973 had a sales price of $50,357. All goods on order January 1, 1973, were delivered during 1973.

Cash payments during 1973:	
For merchandise received in 1972	*$ 74,362*
For merchandise received in 1973	*871,652*
For freight on merchandise received in 1973	*24,202*

For employees' services received in 1973	$ 32,800
For rent for the period December 1, 1972 to January 31, 1974 at the rate of $400 per month	5,600
Costs incurred during 1973 for which no cash has yet been paid:	
Merchandise received in December 1973	21,994
Insurance policy covering the year July 1, 1973 to June 30, 1974 (There was no insurance in force during the first half of 1973.)	1,920

All the goods on hand January 1, 1973, and 75 percent of the goods purchased during 1973 were sold. Prepare a 1973 income statement, and show the amount due from customers at December 31, 1973.

4-25   Below you are given the accounts and balances appearing on the June 30, 1973 position statement for the Richard Borseth Company, a firm that closes its books and prepares statements monthly. You are also given the cash account page from the ledger for the month of June, together with the debit side of the seven adjusting entries made on June 30, and other information. Prepare the income statement for the month of June 1973.

June 30 Position Statement Balances:		*Debit Side of June 30 Adjusting Entries:*	
Accounts payable	$ 3,700	Advances from customers	$ 3,050
Accounts receivable	6,050	Cost of goods sold	110
Accounts receivable—allowance		Depreciation expense	45
for doubtful accounts	175	Insurance expense	150
Advances from customers	360	Rent revenue	185
R. Borseth, capital	24,940	Sales—doubtful accounts	65
Building and equipment	12,600	Supplies expense	55
Building and equipment—			
accumulated depreciation	3,800		
Cash	2,800		
Merchandise on hand	10,700		
Prepaid insurance	300		
Rent receivable	100		
Supplies on hand	425		

Cash

Beginning balance	$ 2,800	Accounts payable	$ 4,050
Cash sales of $2,150	2,107	Advances from customers	1,000
Accounts receivable	4,250	R. Borseth, current	250
Investment of Borseth	2,000	Miscellaneous expense	875
Rent revenue	350	New equipment	625
Advances from customers	300	Prepaid insurance	18
		Salaries	800
		Supplies expense	200
		Ending balance	3,989
	$11,807		$11,807

Other Information:
(1) Accounts Payable had credits during June of $3,350; Accounts Receivable had debits during June of $3,650.
(2) The company sublets part of its building; no Accounts Receivable were written off during June; and discounts are allowed only on cash sales.

4-26   Account balances of the Buckeye Corporation (000's omitted).

	November 22, 1973	November 21, 1974
Accounts payable	$ 60	$ 78
Accounts receivable	80	70
Accumulated depreciation	22	34
Capital stock	250	250
Cash	20	28
Dividends declared		4
Factory building	90	90
Factory cost of goods sold		172
Factory equipment	100	100
Finished goods	20	25
Land	40	40
Raw materials	35	55
Retained earnings	68	68
Sales		200
Selling and administrative expense		22
Wages payable	5	6
Work in process	20	30

Additional Information:
20 percent of the sales of the period were for cash; the rest were on account. Labor cost charged to work in process for the period was $70,000. Other labor services (entirely selling and administrative) cost $2,000 (part of the $22,000).
Overhead cost charged to work in process for the period was $35,000.

Answer the following questions:
(1) What was the net income for the period?
(2) Indicate how the income statement for the period should be dated.
(3) What was the amount of cash collected on account from charge customers during the period?
(4) What was the cost of goods completed during the period?
(5) What was the cost of materials put into production during the period?
(6) What was the cost of materials purchased during the period?
(7) What was the amount of cash paid to Accounts Payable creditors during the period?
(8) What was the amount of cash paid to employees and government tax agencies during the period?
(9) What was the amount of overhead cost, other than depreciation, incurred during the period?
(10) What is the total stockholders' equity on November 21, 1974?

(11) Assuming that the materials inventory at the end of the period had been $9,000 less and that all other inventories and purchases had been the same, would the net income have been greater or less and by what amount?

(12) Assuming that the selling and administrative expenses had been $2,000 greater, would the Factory Cost of Sales figure have been greater or less and by what amount?

(13) If the work in process inventory on November 22, 1973, had been $5,000 greater and all the inventories on November 21, 1974, had been as shown, would the cost of goods finished have been greater or less and by what amount?

4–27   In reviewing the records, you discover the following omissions. Compute an adjusted net income for each year.

	Accounting Year		
	1973	*1974*	*1975*
Reported net income	*$5,300*	*$6,100*	*$5,400*
Omissions from records			
(all at end of year):			
1. Accrued liabilities	*800*	*400*	*200*
2. Accrued receivables		*60*	*80*
3. Prepaid costs	*90*		*50*
4. Deferred revenue	*100*	*70*	*150*
5. Merchandise inventory	*150*		

4–28   For each of the following generic accounts, you are to record the generic account titles credited (or debited) when the specified generic account is debited (or credited) to record typical transactions. (Bizarre transactions are not to be considered.) Alongside each account list specific examples found most frequently.

o. Example
Contra—Asset

Asset	*Expense*
	Asset
	Revenue
	Contra—
	Revenue

a. *Adjunct—Asset*

o. 1. Accounts Receivable—Allowance for Bad Debts
  2. Plant—Accumulated Depreciation
  3. Accounts Receivable—Allowance for Sales Discounts
  4. Notes Receivable—Discount

a. 1. _____

   2. _____

   3. _____

   4. _____

b. *Adjunct—Liability*

b. 1. _____

2. _____

3. _____

4. _____

c. *Contra—Liability*

c. 1. _____

2. _____

3. _____

4. _____

d. *Adjunct—Ownership*

d. 1. _____

2. _____

3. _____

4. _____

e. *Contra—Ownership*

e. 1. _____

2. _____

3. _____

4. _____

f. *Adjunct—Revenue*

f. 1. _____

2. _____

3. _____

4. _____

g. *Contra—Revenue*

g. 1. _____

2. _____

3. _____

4. _____

h. *Adjunct—Expense*

h. 1. _____

   2. _____

   3. _____

   4. _____

i. *Contra—Expense*

i. 1. _____

   2. _____

   3. _____

   4. _____

4-29   The adjusting and closing entries, all dated as of December 31, 1972, are given below for a company on a calendar-year basis. Make reversing entries as of January 1, 1973.

	Debit	*Credit*
Sales—bad debts	$ 150	
Accounts receivable—allowance for bad debts		$ 150
Provide for estimated uncollectible accounts		
Interest receivable	15	
Interest revenue		15
Record interest revenue accrued		
Store supplies	160	
Store supplies expense		160
Adjust for store supplies on hand		
Depreciation expense	2,500	
Equipment—allowance for depreciation		2,500
Record annual depreciation		
Interest expense	20	
Interest payable		20
Adjust for unrecorded interest expense		
Salaries	276	
Salaries payable		276
Record accrued salaries		
Prepaid rent	1,200	
Rent expense		1,200
Adjust the Rent Expense account		
Insurance expense	1,000	
Unexpired insurance		1,000
Record insurance expired		
Income summary	8,000	
Inventory		8,000

Closeout opening inventory

Inventory	*$9,300*	
Income summary		*$9,300*

Record closing inventory

4-30

Following are three unadjusted trial balances. Only certain accounts have been included, but assume that all the accounts that are pertinent to the questions are given. The date on all the trial balances is December 31, 1972, and the accounting period in each case is one year. This information is to be used in answering questions (1) through (10).

A				*B*		
Merchandise				*Merchandise*		
inventory	*$80,000*			*inventory*	*$ 10,000*	
Prepaid insurance	*0*			*Supplies inventory*	*5,000*	
Supplies inventory	*500*			*Purchases*	*80,000*	
Accounts receivable		*$ 500*		*Supplies expense*	*0*	
Accounts receivable—						
allowance for bad						
debts	*250*			*Sales*		*$100,000*
Sales		*0*		*Customers' deposits*		*0*
Wages expense	*1,000*			*C*		
				Merchandise		
Wages payable		*500*		*inventory*	*$ 10,000*	
Supplies expense	*600*			*Cost of sales*	*100,000*	
Insurance expense	*360*			*Sales*		*$200,000*
Customers' deposits		*100,000*		*Wages payable*	*50,000*	
Cost of sales	*0*			*Wages expense*	*0*	
Sales—bad debts		*600*		*Supplies inventory*	*200*	
				Supplies used	*1,000*	

(1) In A, to which account were merchandise purchases charged?

(2) In B, if a customer paid in advance for an order, what account was credited?

(3) In A, which account was credited for sales?

(4) In C, is the Merchandise Inventory of $10,000 a beginning or an ending inventory?

(5) In A, will the adjustment for insurance be an adjustment for the portion of the asset used during the period, or an adjustment for the portion of the expense which was not used?

(6) In A, what account was credited for bad debt recoveries?

(7) In C, which account was credited for the cost of goods sold during the period?

(8) Which of the above trial balances will have to be adjusted to reflect properly the ending merchandise inventory?

(9) In A, the advances by customers must have been credited to what account?

(10) In A, explain the balance in the Accounts Receivable—Allowance for Bad Debts account?

4-31 The following table starts with the financial condition of the Muskie Manufacturing Company as of January 1, 1972, and ends with the financial status of the same firm a month later. All other lines show the effect of the transactions during the month (all figures represent thousands of dollars).

Transaction No.	(A)	+(B)	+(C)	+(D)	+(E)	+(F)	=(G)	+(H)	+(I)	+(J)	(K)	-(L)	=(M)
					Position Statement							*Income Statement*	
January 1, 1972	$2	+$6	+$10	+$3	+$18	+$0	=$3	+$6	+$20	+$10	$0	-$0	=$0
0	{+1 / -1												
1	+3										+3		
2	-1					+1							
3	-1		+1										
4		+3									+3		
5			+2					+2					
6	+4	-4											
7			+4					+5				+1	
8	-4							{-5 / +1					
9			+2		-3							+1	
10	+5							+5					
11	+5								{+4 / +1				
12			{+3 / -3										
13													
14			+1 {+6 / -6	-2								+1	
15			-3									+3	
16							-1				+1		
17	+1						+1						
18	-3				+10			+7					
Closing Entries, February 1, 1972	$11	+$5	+$17	+$1	+$25	+$1	=$6	+$18	+$25	+$1 +$11	7	-6	=1

Assets ($60) = Equities ($60)

(1) Name, in order, the major categories of position statement accounts (Letters A to J) and income statement accounts (Letters K to M). (Four letters represent the current asset categories.)

(2) Identify (in a few words) the set of eighteen (18) *nonduplicate* transactions which would give the results shown, indicating the accounts involved and the nature of the changes.

Sample Answers:
(1) (A) represents the *cash* items (which are the first assets listed where the liquidity ordering is followed).
(2) Transaction (0) is a deposit of cash in the bank account.
Increase (Debit) Cash in Bank.
Decrease (Credit) Cash on Hand.

4–32

Lars Eric Lindblad operates the H.M.S. *Lindblad Explorer,* first ship built for cruises to the Antarctic, the Seychelles, and the Galapagos. The transactions given below occurred during June 1972.

1972
June 1 Lindblad deposited $400,000 in a bank account in the name of the business, Lar–Eric, Inc.
June 2 Title of ship was transferred to the business. It was valued at $6,000,000.
June 3 New equipment costing $25,000 was purchased for the ship, a cash payment of $15,000 was made, and a promissory note was issued for the balance.
June 4 Purchased additional equipment costing $10,000 for the ship; a cash payment of $5,000 was made, with the balance to be paid in 10 days.
June 6 Sold some equipment for the amount of its historical cost. Down payment of $2,000 received in cash; the $3,000 balance is due within 30 days.
June 11 Returned some equipment to vendor; amount owed vendor reduced by $800.
June 14 Paid balance due on equipment purchased June 4.
June 15 Purchased $10,000 of supplies, paying cash.
    15 Paid $2,500 on note.

(1) Journalize the above transactions.
(2) Post to ledger accounts and determine the balances.
(3) Prepare a position statement.

2 Measuring Fund Flows

5 Analysis of Working Capital

A current asset is one which is readily convertible into cash and which, by its nature, probably will be converted into cash. Such assets are often spoken of as being liquid, and this adjective is a good one, since it conveys the impression of a ready convertibility and implies "flowing," as in a stream.*

STEPHEN GILMAN, 1916

During the twentieth century various proposals for asset classification have been given consideration. Much attention has been given to classifications based on dichotomies such as "operating-nonoperating" and "essential-nonessential to continuing operations." However, the asset classification that has been most strongly supported is the one that distinguishes between resources as claims that are reported as specified sums of money (monetary assets) and those that are not reported as specified sums of money (nonmonetary assets). This dichotomy emphasizes a key distinction between assets, a division between liquid or uncommitted assets (monetary assets) and committed or deferred charges to operations (nonmonetary assets, usually measured as unexpired costs).

This proposed classification makes clear the basic difference between those assets with which the firm has already created revenue (through the delivery of goods or services to customers) and those with which the firm has yet to generate revenue. The classification provides a basis for uniform valuation within the two categories of assets. Monetary assets are valued on the basis of their expected

*From *Principles of Accounting* (Chicago: LaSalle Extension University, 1916), pp. 157–158.

cash flow; nonmonetary assets are valued on the basis of their cost.[1] This distinction also clarifies the complementary relationship between position statements and fund-flow statements, if the fund is defined as monetary assets or net monetary assets.

Nonmonetary assets may be classified further into those that will expire in future operations (inventories, prepayments, long-lived plant and equipment, and limited-life intangibles) and those that will not expire in future operations (land and unlimited-life intangibles such as organization costs and permanent investments in stocks). This latter classification is based on the assumption that the firm will not go out of business or dispose of so-called "permanent" investment. In this connection, proposed changes in the treatment of liabilities are not as significant. One method would entail subdivision on the basis of due dates (rather than the current-noncurrent classification); another would classify on the basis of those liabilities that originate from normal operations and those that do not (but are a part of the longer-range financing of the organization).

Monetary Current Assets

Monetary assets are classified as current assets since they are intended to be used in current operations within the operating cycle of the company or one year, whichever is longer. But they are distinguished from other current assets in that they are claims to a fixed number of dollars of general purchasing power. Usually they constitute contracts, formal or informal, specifying that an external individual or organization will pay the company a given amount of money on a stipulated date (or within a specified time period). For instance, cash is expressed in terms of its value, which is both current and definite.

Among the net monetary asset accounts, (cash, marketable securities, and receivables less the current liabilities), surely the most significant are the cash accounts. The flows into and out of these accounts are the basic transactions for any firm. These cash events are the basis for accounting measurements and business decisions since no other resource of the entity commands readily transferable general purchasing power to the same extent that cash does.

Most accounting measurements, whether of revenue, expenses, or the distribution of net income, or of assets or liabilities, are based

---

[1] The careful reader may question whether the monetary-nonmonetary classification and the suggested valuation bases are appropriate for all types of business entities and situations. The answer to this probably is: No, because the proposal is most suitable for manufacturing and trading firms in which selling is the crucial step in the operating cycle (most businesses would be included in this class), so that revenue is recognized at the time of sale. The proposal is least suitable for the many firms in which production is the crucial step in the operating cycle (included here are firms that mine or process precious metals, produce many agricultural products, or enter fixed price contracts before beginning a construction project that may not be completed for several years), so that revenue is recognized at the time of production. (For a more complete discussion of this, see Chapter 9.)

on cash flows. The conventional measure of revenue is the amount of the cash anticipated from sales. The usual measure of expense is the actual cash outlay or the anticipated cash outlay (indebtedness incurred) for resources utilized by the entity in creating revenue. The usual distribution of net income is in the form of cash payments to the owners (cash dividends for stockholders). Accounting accruals are measured by allocations of past or anticipated future cash receipts or payments to the current period, whereas deferrals are measured by allocations of past or anticipated future cash receipts or payments to one or more future periods. The discounted, expected net cash receipts to be derived from the asset (its present value) constitute its basic accounting measure. The expected cash payments are the basic measure of a liability.

Monetary investments Although accounting for the cash accounts is most significant, these procedures are quite simple. For this reason they are discussed in the Appendix to this chapter. The other categories of monetary assets are monetary securities (sometimes bonds held for temporary investment) and receivables. Both represent claims to a fixed number of dollars; as such, both should be valued on the basis of the discounted value of the cash to be received. The accounting for temporary investments in bonds or their equivalent (monetary securities) is simple. Although there should be an adjustment for the discount when appropriate, and an adjustment to reflect a change in the uncertainty about collection, the bond contract stipulates the interest rate, and collection is usually assured for investments in high-grade securities.

Listed as Marketable Securities on a position statement, these temporary investments in bonds are usually valued in practice on the lower-of-cost-or-market basis (Locom, which will be described in the discussion on inventories). It is contended that cost is the most relevant valuation basis for considering the gains or losses when the bonds are sold. During the period when these bonds are held, the usual practice is to record any loss (when the current market price is less than the cost), because the bonds should not be shown in excess of their current realizable value, but not to record any gain (when the cost is less than the market price), because, it is argued, the gain is unrealized and transitory.

In recent years, there has been some increased support in practice for valuing monetary investments at current market prices instead of amortizing the premium or discount to reflect maturity value (although premiums may still be amortized because of favorable tax effects). Current market prices reflect that the securities will be sold in the near future (and not at maturity). They also reflect changes in the market rate of interest (instead of continuing to amortize the premium or discount at the issue rate of interest).

In 1962, Professors Sprouse and Moonitz advocated that monetary securities be measured by their current market prices because these prices:

1. Provide better and more relevant information (by including holding gains and losses)
2. Provide identical values for identical securities (instead of different costs) valued on the same basis as the other monetary assets
3. Are verifiable (usually to the extent that cost prices are verifiable)[2]

In 1967 the Companies Act of Great Britain required all British companies to measure marketable securities on the basis of their market value. In the United States, however, without such a requirement, the cost basis for the valuation of marketable securities predominates. Of 600 companies whose 1969 financial statements were surveyed, 398 held marketable securities temporarily, and only 30 of these stated the market value (although 227 other companies indicated that the basis of valuation of marketable securities approximated market).[3] If the amortization of cost provides a valuation basis roughly equivalent to the current market price, the cost basis of valuation would be acceptable. However, without such a qualifier, if the cost measurement is used, the current market price should be shown parenthetically or in a footnote. In May 1971 the AICPA's Accounting Principles Board (APB) held public hearings on whether marketable ownership equity securities should be accounted for at current market value or at historical cost.

Nonmonetary investments held temporarily (such as investments in common stocks) under the current-noncurrent classification dichotomy are usually combined with temporary monetary investments. They may be liquidated for cash whenever needed but are similar in that they cannot be estimated by discounting a future maturity value (or adjusted for collection uncertainties). Such investments are valued at either cost or Locom; a strong case can be made for valuing them at current market prices.

For both temporary monetary and nonmonetary investments (generally held as secondary cash sources), there are the accounting problems of the revenues (interest or dividends) created by these resources. Interest revenue usually is accrued and recorded in the period in which it is earned; dividend revenue usually is not accrued but is recorded in the period in which it is paid to the company (although there is no good reason why it should not be estimated and accrued). Since the accounting for these securities is similar to that for long-term investments, see Chapter 8 on this subject, particularly regarding the sale of investments.

[2]Robert T. Sprouse and Maurice Moonitz, *A Tentative Set of Broad Accounting Principles for Business Enterprises,* Accounting Research Study No. 3 (New York: AICPA, 1962), p. 25.
[3]See *Accounting Trends and Techniques: Annual Survey of Accounting Practices Followed in 600 Stockholders' Reports,* 24th ed. (New York: AICPA, 1970), pp. 44–45.

Accounts receivable In accounting, receivables may include either accounts (oral and implied promises to pay) or notes (written promises to pay). These monetary assets, usually classified as current, must; (1) arise from typical sale transactions and (2) be collectible within the usual credit period allowed customers by the firm (an aspect of the operating cycle). Unless nominal, any credit sale transactions to other than the usual customers (for example, officers and employees) or for which the terms of sale vary from the firm's usual credit practice should be segregated in special receivable accounts. Although accounts receivable and notes receivable often are combined for statement purposes, unusual characteristics of the latter may warrant their separate listing.

As indicated earlier, the uncollected balances owed by customers should be valued at their present values, namely, the discounted value of the cash to be received in the future. Since the cash is not available until after a waiting period, receivables should not be measured at their maturity value. What should be the interest rate? Usually the market rate for credit of equal risk should be used.[4] Although there may be some merit in using the firm's opportunity cost which may approximate the firm's cost of capital rate or its internal rate of return, the actual cost of granting credit to customers may be insignificant (or even negative, because there may be material losses of revenue without the extension of credit in an economy where such is the usual practice). In the usual receivable situation, the discount usually is not significant, and therefore may be ignored. Otherwise, it should be deducted from both the related receivables and revenue.

Uncollectible accounts Another problem in measuring receivables (and related revenues) concerns the uncertainty of collection. Which customers will not pay their accounts when due? Ever? The usual procedure is to deduct from the receivable an estimate of the amount that will not be collected. This is referred to as an allowance for uncollectible accounts (or doubtful accounts or bad debts), and it is a contra-asset (or contra-receivable) account, sometimes referred to as a valuation account. For statistical reasons, this estimate is more likely to be accurate when it is based on a large number of receivables rather than on a few. Actually the most accurate measure of the deduction from the receivable may be calculated by "aging the receivables," wherein each receivable is reviewed and classified

[4]But since there may be a large variety of possible transactions, one specific rate may not be applicable to all situations. The objective is to approximate the interest rate that would have been negotiated between an independent borrower and an independent lender for a similar transaction with comparable terms in which the alternatives open to the purchaser were either to pay cash or to give a note bearing the prevailing rate of interest to maturity. The appropriate rate of interest normally will be equal to or greater than the rate at which the creditor could obtain similar financing from other sources at the transaction date. For a further discussion of this, see AICPA, Opinions of the Accounting Principles Board No. 21, "Interest on Receivables and Payables" (New York: 1971).

by age (or length of time unpaid) and other characteristics. Such classifications are most helpful in determining the amount that will be collected. For example, very few receivables are paid within much less than 30 days after the sale is made, and very few receivables (in the typical situation) are ever collected after six months.

On the other hand, the computation of the corresponding deduction from the revenue account (properly referred to as a contra-revenue account, Sales—Uncollectible Accounts, Sales—Doubtful Accounts, or Sales—Bad Debts) is most accurate when estimated as a percentage of the period's credit sales. This estimate should be based upon the past experience of the firm adjusted, of course, for any current changes. This deduction should not be listed on the income statement as an expense, although it is often treated that way in practice. It is not correct to classify uncollectible accounts in this way if it is accepted that credit losses are inherent in credit sales rather than a result of a second transaction that occurs after the sale. If the contra-asset account balance for receivables is computed by "aging the receivables" (or by taking a predetermined percentage of receivables) and the contra-revenue account is calculated by applying a predetermined percentage to the credit sales of the period, two different figures may result. If the difference is nominal, the figure prepared for the contra asset may be used (although this is not the balancing figure but the adjustment figure necessary to give the required balance); if this difference is significant, it should be listed in a separate account and reported separately on the income statement as a correction of prior periods' income. The adjusting entry (in general journal format) under these circumstances would be as follows:

	Debit	Credit
Sales—uncollectible accounts (estimate computed as a predetermined percentage of credit sales)	××	
Accounts receivable—allowance for uncollectible accounts (estimate computed by "aging" or as predetermined percentage of receivables and increased or decreased for any preadjustment balance in the Allowance account)		××
Correction of prior periods' income— adjustment for uncollectible accounts estimate	×× *or*	××

This entry when posted to the appropriate ledger accounts should appear as follows:

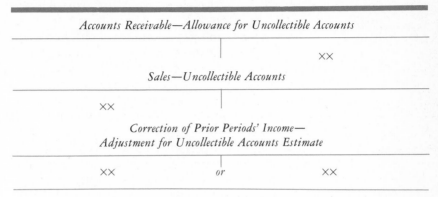

Under an allowance method for estimating uncollectible accounts, the actual write-off of the uncollectible account is made against the contra-asset allowance account as follows, since it was charged to the contra-revenue account (and deducted from the period's income) when the estimate was recorded:

	Debit	Credit
Accounts receivable—allowance for uncollectible accounts	××	
Accounts receivable		××

The write-off of a specific account found to be uncollectible would be posted as follows:

Accounts Receivable—Allowance for Uncollectible Accounts

××	✔ Balance

Accounts Receivable

Balance ✔	××

This procedure, usually referred to as the *direct* write-off of uncollectible accounts, is not regarded as acceptable accounting (unless the amounts involved are not material), since without the earlier estimate both the receivable and revenue of the prior period in which the sale was recorded have been overstated. The adjustment does correct the receivable balance to the extent that it was in error because of this specific receivable but understates the period revenue and net income (unless the sale was recorded in the same period).

Occasionally an account that was written off as uncollectible is later collected. If the write-off and the recovery occur within the same accounting period, the debits would be to Cash (and Accounts Receivable) and the credits to Accounts Receivable—Allowance for Uncollectible Accounts (and Accounts Receivable). If the write-off and the recovery occur in separate accounting periods, the credit would be to Correction of Prior Periods' Income—Recovery of Account Previously Written Off instead of to Accounts Receivable—Allowance for Uncollectible Accounts, in order to correct the net income for the earlier period. Although the bad-debt problem usually arises with accounts receivable, it may arise with other receivables. When it does, treatment is essentially the same as with accounts receivable.

Cash discounts Unfortunately many terms used in accounting have more than one meaning. Such a term is discount. In the earlier discussion of receivables, it was indicated that the measurements should be discounted ones; here a *discount* is considered to be a compensation to be received for waiting. A second meaning of the term *discount,* also in connection with receivables, is that it is an allowance given for the settlement of a debt before it is due.[5] Such allowances are called (1) trade or quantity and (2) cash discounts. The former are allowed regardless of whether the debt is paid before it is due and are given to customers on the basis of their classification (wholesaler or retailer) or because of the large quantity ordered at one time; these discounts are deducted in arriving at the invoice price before billing the customers and are unaffected by the date of payment. Since trade discounts are not recorded in the accounts, they should not be confused with cash discounts but sometimes trade discounts are distinguished as being any discount exceeding 2 percent.

Cash discounts are included in the customer billings and are amounts allowed for the prompt settlement of a debt arising out of a sale. Usually this period is 10 days but sometimes longer periods of time are permitted.

Three methods are used in accounting for cash discounts. The traditional way, the gross method, widely used in practice, is to record cash discounts taken (by customers paying promptly) as miscellaneous expense (or contra revenue). This method, like the direct write-off of uncollectible accounts, is not regarded as an acceptable method of accounting when material amounts of cash discounts are taken in a period other than when the sale was made.

[5]Other meanings in connection with notes and capital stock will be considered later.

The second and third methods, the adjusted gross method and the net method, have considerable theoretical support. Both the adjusted gross and the net methods will lead to the same revenue (and receivable) except that figures may not be shown in the same places in the financial statements under both methods. Under the adjusted gross method, separate contra accounts (receivable and revenue) are used for recording cash discounts; under the net method (net of cash discounts), the cash discounts are netted before recording the credit sale and are booked only if not taken by the customer.

Under the adjusted gross method, the deduction from receivables at the end of the period (Accounts Receivable—Allowance for Cash Discounts) should include an estimate of cash discounts which it is expected from past experience that customers will be able to deduct when paying their outstanding accounts. It is this estimate that must be recorded to convert the gross to the adjusted gross method. Under this method, the deduction from sales revenue (Sales—Cash Discounts) will include all cash discounts pertaining to sales revenues of this year, whether or not actual collection has been made. The deduction will consist of actual cash discounts taken on this year's sales, plus an estimate of cash discounts which customers will take next period when paying accounts receivable arising out of this year's sales.

Under the net method (net of cash discounts), additions must be made at the end of the period, directly to accounts receivable (for the estimate of cash discounts on outstanding accounts which will not be taken by customers when they remit next period), and indirectly to sales revenue (through an adjunct account, Sales—Cash Discounts Not Taken[6] for the estimate of cash discounts on outstanding accounts which will not be taken by customers when they remit next period).

The entries under both methods are illustrated below:

No.	Date	Transaction	Adjusted Gross Debit	Adjusted Gross Credit	Net Debit	Net Credit
1	December 25	$100 charge sale; terms— 2%/10 days, net/30 days:				
		Accounts receivable	$100		$98	
		Sales		$100		$98

[6]Some authors show this incorrectly as miscellaneous revenue or the discounts taken as miscellaneous expense on the dubious grounds that the prompt settlement of a receivable is a prepayment, while payment after the end of the discount period is "normal."

No.	Date	Transaction	Adjusted Gross Debit	Adjusted Gross Credit	Net Debit	Net Credit
2	December 30	Part payment on previous sale:				
		Cash	$49		$49	
		Sales—cash discounts	1			
		Accounts receivable		$50		$49
3	December 31	Estimate $\frac{1}{2}$ of balance will be paid within discount period:				
		Sales—cash discounts	0.5			
		Accounts receivable— allowance for cash discounts		0.5		
		Accounts receivable			0.5	
		Sales—cash discounts not taken				0.5

which will be posted to accounts as follows:

Adjusted Gross Method

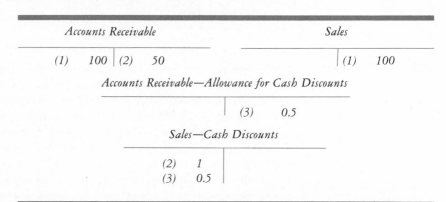

Net Method

which will appear on the two financial statements as follows:

Position Statement

	Adjusted Gross	Net
Accounts receivable	$50	$49.5
Less cash discounts	0.5	
Net receivable	$49.5	$49.5

Income Statement

	Adjusted Gross	*Net*
Sales	$100	$98
Less cash discounts taken	1.5	
Add cash discounts not taken		0.5
Net sales	$ 98.5	$98.5

Cash discounts on purchases also may be accounted for properly by either the adjusted gross or the net method; for the sake of brevity, this analysis is not shown. There has been a trend in recent years toward the use of the net method instead of the adjusted gross method, on the grounds that recording cash discounts not taken on purchases is more significant information for controlling internal activities than recording those taken. In addition to considering financial charges, uncollectibles, and cash discounts, sales returns may be estimated and deducted from receivables. Since the accounting for sales returns is similar to that already discussed, it will not be analyzed here, but the entries to be made when the adjusted gross method is used are illustrated in the Appendix to Chapter 6.

Notes receivable There are several special features of accounting for notes receivable. One, the interest on interest-bearing notes is accrued in separate accounts, interest receivable and interest revenue. The mechanics for this will be discussed more fully in connection with bond investments; the accounting for bond interest and note interest is very similar. Two, the firm may sell (or discount) its customers' notes to a bank before the notes mature in order to realize cash. This is the reason why, in business law, notes are called negotiable instruments. In this process the bank discounts the note and refers to the note as a "discount" (where interest has been deducted in advance—this is another accounting use of the term).

The formula for computing such a discount is $D = MV \cdot R \cdot T$, where D = discount, MV = maturity value—interest plus principal of the note, R = annual discount rate, and T = time (in years) left on the note before maturity. The formula for computing simple interest by way of contrast is $I = P \cdot R \cdot T$, where I = interest, P = principal or face of the note, R = interest rate, and T = time (in years) that the note will run to maturity. The proceeds of a discounted note is $PR = MV - D$, where PR = proceeds, MV = maturity value = interest plus principal of the note, and D = discount. Some variations are possible in these computations, depending often on how exact a measure of the year is used (12 months, 365 days, and so on).

When a firm sells a customer's promissory note to its bank, it is possible that the bank "discount" will exceed the accrued interest on the note; consequently, in this situation, the firm will record a financing charge (or loss on discounting). Usually, however, the discounting charge is less than the interest, and the former is netted against the latter. When the firm sells the customer's note to its bank, it may close out the appropriate note receivable account. In this situation, however, the firm usually has a contingent liability: if the customer fails to pay the bank when the note becomes due, the firm must do so.

Such a guaranty endorsement by the firm of the customer note discounted at the bank sometimes is recorded in a contra-asset account (Notes Receivable—Discounted) despite its contingent liability nature. This account has a simple cycle. It is opened when the note is discounted; it is closed when the note becomes due, regardless of whether the customer pays the bank.

Contingent liabilities are obligations resulting from a past transaction or another economic event that the firm may have to consider as a consequence of a future event which is possible but not probable. If the future event were probable, the obligation would be booked as a real liability. When it is not probable but possible, it is classified as a contingent liability. The actual treatment may depend on whether an expected value would be more or less relevant to statement users. Another common example of a contingent liability is a pending lawsuit against the company for damages. Usually contingent liabilities are not entered on the books, but are disclosed in footnotes to the position statement.

Monetary Current Liabilities

Although, as indicated earlier, monetary assets may be considered collectively or gross, they usually are discussed in net terms, that is, less monetary current liabilities. As indicated in Chapter 3 liabilities, for accounting purposes, must have four characteristics: (1) they involve future money outlays or their equivalents; (2) they are the result of past external transactions not future ones; (3) they must be subject to calculation or close estimation; and (4) they must be based on double-entry bookkeeping.[7] Most current liabilities are monetary and clearly possess these four qualities. When the liability is an open account to be paid within a short period of time (for example, usually accounts payable), the present value approximates the maturity value, and the discount can be disregarded. However, liabilities should be recorded at their present value when the discount is significant. This applies to both explicit interest-

[7]See Maurice Moonitz, "The Changing Concept of Liabilities," *The Journal of Accountancy* (May 1960) pp. 41–46.

bearing and implicit interest-bearing (noninterest-bearing) notes. Unfortunately this sometimes is disregarded in practice, with the note shown at maturity value and the discount booked as a bogus asset, Prepaid Interest. Usually the basis for the recognition of the liability is the prior need to book an asset or an expense. With a loss, however, the prior need becomes the booking of the liability itself. Generally assets and liabilities should not be offset against each other;[8] a marginal exception is in those situations where specified government securities are acceptable for taxes owed. Accrued liabilities for wages, taxes, interest, etc., are not significantly different from other liabilities. The former are for services received continuously but recorded at convenient intervals, usually at the end of the accounting period.

As indicated in Chapter 3, a current liability must be payable out of current assets or transferred to revenue within one year, or the operating cycle of the firm, whichever is greater. The operating cycle is the length of time that it takes the firm to acquire or manufacture goods or services and turn these back into cash.

Usually the current liabilities that present the greatest problems are those that arise from advance payments by customers. Although these obligations may be monetary (where the repayment must be in a given number of dollars or the equivalent goods or services), often they are only in terms of some agreed quantity and quality of the goods to be furnished or of the services to be performed, but not in terms of the monetary value of these goods or services.

As so often is the case, the language camouflages the nature of the problem. Instead of the unambiguous Advances from Customers, such terms as Deferred Income, Deferred Revenue, Unearned Income, Reserve for ———, and Deferred Credits are frequently used in practice. If accountants would recognize that it is confusing to describe position statement accounts in terms used for income statement accounts (and vice versa), the first three would be avoided. The last two (Deferred Credits and Reserve for ———) are examples of accounting jargon which convey little or no meaning to accountants, much less to users of financial statements. Their use is essentially an attempt to avoid classification. (In addition to credits and reserves, other terms of this sort are surplus and charges.)

The use of the three income statement terms for Advances From Customers is an attempt to relate the advance to revenue-producing or income-earning activities of the future. But it is not possible to relate advances with either costs incurred or costs to be incurred. The only occasion for a future outlay of cash directly to the customer would be if the goods or services were not provided, and the ad-

---

[8]See AICPA APB Opinion No. 10 "Omnibus Opinion-1966" (New York: 1966).

vance would have to be returned. Since the obligation to provide these goods or services is part of the normal operating cycle, and the result of the advance (apart from the reason for it, which may be to avoid losses from uncollectible accounts) is a current financing transaction, the advance typically is a current liability. Occasionally Deferred Income or Deferred Revenue may be used to describe a situation in which no advance was made but the reporting of revenue is deferred, it is contended, because of uncertainties regarding additional expenses or collection. Usually, however, estimates of these uncertainties can be made and the revenue reported. The real rationale for these classifications is to conceal the smoothing[9] of net income.

The conventional classification of position statement assets and liabilities consists in separating those that constitute current assets or working capital or net current assets (current assets minus current liabilities) from those that do not. *Working capital* is measured as the difference between the current assets and the current liabilities, where *current,* as indicated earlier, is conceived to be one year or the operating cycle, whichever is longer. Working capital, therefore, consists of the net monetary assets plus inventories and prepayments. This classification is the conventional accounting presentation of what constitute acceptable liquidity and circulation concepts for the typical firm.

During the latter half of the nineteenth century and the early decades of the twentieth, bankers, as creditors, were the principal external users of financial statements. As such, bankers were primarily interested in a "pounce" approach to the position statement (or in those resources that were capable of being realizable quickly in cash). In response to this type of pressure, the working capital concept evolved for the balance sheet, although a special-purpose and separate Statement of Affairs has long been prepared by accountants for just this liquidity purpose for firms involved in bankruptcy and liquidation proceedings. Of course, today other users of financial statements also have an interest in the firm's liquidity or solvency.

A secondary factor in the evolution of the working capital concept is the turnover rate of assets and liabilities. Dividing assets and liabilities according to the velocity of their turnover on a current basis provides guidelines for the users of financial statements. Further discussion of how the working capital concept is used in accounting will be found in Chapters 6 and 12.

Two principal criticisms of the working capital classification are: (1) there are inherent inconsistencies in its application and (2) it is

---

[9]"Smoothing" is the "managing" of the net income reported in each period so that increases are reduced to provide a "cushion" for possible decreases that may occur later.

not well suited for presentation in the position statement, which is not after all a statement of liquidity.

The first of these shortcomings could be remedied if concepts of current assets and liabilities in practice could be modified along the following lines:

1. Inventories should not be classified as current if it is anticipated that they will be sold to installment buyers and that the resulting receivable will not qualify as a current asset.
2. Assets should not be classified as current if their cost will attach to long-lived property.
3. If a prepayment is considered current (as it is), the entire cost of a productive asset with a similar life expectancy should be considered current too (which presently it is not).
4. If the next year's payment of long-term debt is considered current (as it is), the next year's depreciation or amortization of the assets acquired with this debt (or otherwise) should be classified as current too (which it is not).

The second shortcoming is more difficult to remedy since the time factor essential to judging liquidity is missing from position statements. Flow statements (not stock or static statements such as the balance sheet) are surely better vehicles for judging liquidity. Since working capital (or cash) fund-flow statements are rapidly becoming as primary in accounting as position and income statements (the latter being the traditional flow statement), this kind of criticism may be alleviated. In summary, however, a monetary classification of assets and liabilities would seem to provide more relevant information for most firms than the current classification which is used widely in practice.

Nonmonetary Current Assets

Inventories are intrinsic in two major accounting measurements: working capital and net income. For the former, the objective of inventory measurement is to report the cash, or cash equivalent, that will flow from the sale of merchandise. This includes the prediction of future cash inflows from sales and of future cash outflows for the purchase of merchandise. For the latter, the objective of inventory measurement for most firms is to attempt to match costs with related revenues in the determination of income.

In magnitude, inventories often are one of the most significant resources of the firm. There are five different types of inventories which may be shown separately on financial statements: merchandise, materials, work (or goods) in process, finished goods, and supplies. The first is used by retailing or wholesaling firms; the next three are used by manufacturing firms; the last category is es-

EXHIBIT 5-1
SUMMARY SCHEDULE
TO COMPARE
FOUR METHODS FOR MEASURING INVENTORY QUANTITIES

Method	Type	Measurement	Application
1. Periodic	Physical	End of period usually at cost; losses included in cost of goods sold.	Prerequisite to audit and presentation of unqualified published financial statements.
2. Perpetual	Book	Continuous from records usually at cost; losses included in inventory until actual quantities are verified by a physical count.	Interim statements.
3. Gross profit	Book	Special from records at selling price converted to cost by multiplying by cost-selling price ratio from previous periods.	Estimate quantity when count not possible; also test to verify other methods.
4. Retail	Physical	End of period count at selling prices converted to cost by multiplying by current period cost-selling price ratio. Selling price of goods available for sale minus period sales equals book inventory at retail.	Department stores or firms where perpetual or periodic methods using physical output units are not possible or desirable. Similar to perpetual except that the physical unit is the selling price.

Methods 2, 3, and 4 require regular physical count of the inventory in hand for verification purposes.

sentially auxiliary materials which are present in all these firms. Sometimes supplies are classified as a prepayment (instead of inventory) because they are not to be sold.

Inventories are measured differently from other current assets, both the monetary ones and the prepayments. Monetary assets can be computed by discounting the expected cash receipts; this cannot be done for inventories even if their future sales prices can be forecast (which is not always possible), since the timing of cash receipts from the future sale of inventories is not usually predictable. In terms of their future returns, prepayments cannot be measured separately since they are not revenue; there are no prices for these services as there are for inventories. (Inventories require other resources too before they can earn revenue.)

Measurement of inventories There are two major problems in the measurement of inventories. First, what is the number of units? Second, how should these units be valued? This is the process by which dollars (or other currencies in other countries) are assigned to each inventory item or unit.

Measurement of inventories at cost There are four common methods by which the quantities of inventories are computed. Only one of the four is truly independent, since the use of any of the other three methods is improved if combined with the fourth method. These methods are the periodic (or the physical), the perpetual (or the book), the gross margin (or the gross profit), and the retail. The last two are valuation methods too.

The *periodic method,* the independent one, requires a physical count of all items in the inventory. This actual physical check is needed by practically all organizations as a part of the verification process. If the firm uses only the periodic method for determining inventory quantities (and prices as well), the net cost of merchandise purchased during the period is charged to Cost of Goods Sold expense and the end-of-period adjusting entries to record the inventory are as follows:

	Debit	Credit
Inventory (as of end-of-period date)	×	
Cost of goods sold		×
Record new periodic inventory		
Cost of goods sold	×	
Inventory (as of previous period's end-of-period date)		×
Closeout previous periodic inventory		

Although it would be possible to make a single entry adjusting the old inventory balance to the new inventory figure, it is customary for control purposes to record the adjustment in two entries.

With the periodic method, losses due to theft and other causes are hidden in the Cost of Goods Sold expense account (so no separate theft expense is recorded for the period). In short, the inventory is computed directly; the expense is the residual figure of the total values associated with the goods sold and lost during the period. This method of periodically checking inventory quantities must be used by professional auditors before they are able to certify without qualification the inventory figures shown in published financial statements.

With the *perpetual method,* the inventory records are kept in such a manner as to make it possible to know the balance of merchandise on hand or to compute an up-to-date inventory figure at any time. With identifiable high-value or unique inventory items (such as diamond necklaces), this is often particularly desirable. With this method it is possible (although not required) to record the inventory expense for each sale at the time of sale; this is different from the periodic inventory method in which the inventory expense associated with all period sales is not recorded until the end of the period. Since thousands of distinct items may be included in inventory, perpetual records may become very cumbersome and expensive to manipulate manually. However, computer applications often make the method both feasible and desirable. The chief value of this method for financial accounting purposes is to provide inventory figures for interim reports. To isolate losses which tend to be concealed in the inventory account, a physical count of all inventory items is made from time to time and compared to the inventory record during each period and a complete end-of-period inventory is taken occasionally.

The third and fourth methods differ from the first two in that aggregate relationships are used instead of the summation of individual items. The first of these, the *gross margin method* (usually referred to as the gross profit method), is based on the recorded sales for the period. The sales prices are converted to the cost figures by multiplying by a cost-selling price ratio (which is an average of this ratio for previous periods). This method has particular merit in those situations in which the inventory has been destroyed by fire or stolen and it is not possible to make a physical count. It is commonly used to approximate the inventory when other methods are not possible or practicable (or, perhaps, as a verification of other methods). Its shortcoming, in addition to lacking a provision for a physical count, is that the ratio used is based upon relationships of previous periods instead of the current one. (See Exhibit 5-2.)

The fourth method, the *retail method,* does use the current period's cost-selling price ratio (see line A in Exhibit 5-2) in converting to cost the inventory taken at retail prices. In addition, the retail method also is a perpetual method because an up-to-date inventory can be completed at any time as follows (before making the conversion to cost):

B. *Goods for Sale at Retail Prices — Period Sales = Inventory at Retail Prices*

Under the gross margin method (where the conversion to cost has already taken place) the computation is as follows:

D. *Goods for Sale at Cost Prices — Estimated Cost of Sales = Inventory at Cost Prices.*

EXHIBIT 5–2

A COMPARISON OF METHODS OF COMPUTATION FOR
THE RETAIL METHOD VERSUS THE GROSS MARGIN METHOD
(000's OMITTED)

Retail Method

Goods available for sale during period at cost			$28.0	70%
Original markup		$12.8		
Additional markup	$0.8			
Additional markup cancellations	0.2	0.6		
		13.4		
Markdowns	1.7			
Markdown cancellations	0.3	1.4		
A. Current period net markup				
or gross margin			12.0	30%
Goods for sale at retail prices			40.0	100%
Less period sales (net of returns)			29.0	
B. Inventory at retail prices			11.0	
Margin included in inventory				
(30% of 11.0 = 3.3)			3.3	
Inventory at cost (approximate)			$ 7.7	

Gross Margin Method

Previous period (or periods') sales (net)	$60.0	100%
Previous period (or periods') cost of		
goods sold (net)	36.0	60%
C. Previous period (or periods') gross margin	$24.0	40%
Goods available for sale during period at cost	$28.0	
Less estimated cost of goods sold (60% of 29 = 17.4)	17.4	
D. Inventory at cost (approximate)	$10.6	

NOTE: For the retail method, a more current ratio would be determined if only purchases for the year were considered; but this presents a problem of allocating markups and markdowns between the beginning inventory and purchases. If the inventory taken on the retail method basis is to be valued to reflect the lower of cost or market, markdowns should be excluded, thus computing lowest ratio possible. There is doubt, however, that this would reflect market as replacement cost.

When the retail method is used, a physical count of the inventory on hand is taken and valued on the basis of the selling price tags attached to the merchandise, thus permitting the use of the firm's sales personnel in valuing the inventory. (Usually inventory items valued on a cost basis are coded with letters that must be converted to numbers in order to determine cost; or the cost information is considered conficential, requiring higher-level personnel to value the inventory.) For interim statements, it is possible to estimate the inventory from the records after computing the cost-selling price ratio, without taking a physical count. Without such a count, losses would be an unknown part of the inventory account as under the perpetual method; with a count the amount of loss could be determined and recorded separately.

There are a number of technical questions about what to include in the inventory counts. Consider goods in transit either to or from the firm; goods ordered and segregated for the firm (by the vendor) or for the firm's customer; goods acquired on approval or conditionally, on consignment (in or out); pledged goods; and advances on buying or selling orders.[10]

Goods in transit, under a strict legal interpretation, namely, the passing of title, include all merchandise consigned to customers and all purchased merchandise being transported (if the freight is paid by the purchaser); such would be included in inventory. In order to comply with the legal interpretation, a firm will sometimes delay the completion of the inventory count until a few days after the end of the period when merchandise purchased will have been received and merchandise sold will have been shipped. In practice, a firm may *consistently* omit goods in transit in taking inventory.

Goods ordered and segregated for the entity (by the vendor) are ordinarily treated differently from goods earmarked for particular customers. The latter are included in the inventory whereas the former are not. Goods being purchased on approval basis or on conditional sales contracts are treated both ways in practice; the conventional treatment is to exclude the former and include the latter. Goods out on consignment to the firm's agents are included, whereas goods received on consignment are excluded. Goods pledged for special purpose are included with a footnote to the position statement specifying the pledge. Although advances from customers or to creditors sometimes are considered in practice to be part of the inventory, such monetary accounts should be classified as receivables or payables.

In the broadest sense all resources of the firm, even the monetary assets, could be considered inventory since all are needed to earn revenue. In accounting, only one (or two) resources are considered inventoriable. Where merchandise is acquired for resale, only the net[11] invoice value of the goods and occasionally the transportation-

---

[10]Underlying these questions is the accounting entity issue; for a further discussion see Chapter 11.
[11]As was explained earlier, the same accounting alternatives exist for recording cash discounts on purchases as for recording cash discounts on sales. To save space, they are not outlined here. Recording the purchases at net and only the purchase discounts lost has the greatest merit since this alternative isolates the loss due to inefficient management or insufficient cash. Recording the purchase discounts lost has the following advantages: (1) if the discounts are not taken, the net method discloses the lost discount rather than concealing it; (2) it is most convenient since no adjustment is required when the bulk of invoices are paid within the discount period (a profitable practice of efficiently managed, well-financed firms); and (3) it puts the computation of purchases and inventories on the same basis as the cash outgo.

in service (and very rarely the storage and handling services) are inventoriable.

With goods that are manufactured by the firm, the value of the raw materials and of the service of workmen utilized directly in producing goods and of the other resources most clearly associated with the production function usually are inventoried. All other values incurred for the selling and administrative functions of the organization (with minor exceptions, such as the prepayment) are considered to expire with the period. For example, the corporation president who may spend 90 percent of his time planning future production and sales will have *100 percent of the salary paid* for his services charged to expense in the current period.

Such understatement of inventories does suggest major implications about the measurement of both working capital and net income. However, at the present time it is not possible to include in inventory the value of administrative services, since no acceptable method has been developed to trace connections and make reasonable allocations. Although much of the selling activity usually takes place at the time when the revenue is recognized (the related values expire at the time of sale and are not inventoriable), the remainder of selling services are similar to those of administration. No appropriate technique exists for attaching to inventories the value of administrative and, to some extent, selling services. Taxes and interest are intrinsically *period* values and are not inventoriable. Taxes other than those levied on sales or income usually are classified in practice as an indirect manufacturing value (where the firm produces its own goods), and as such are inventoriable. Interest, on the other hand, should be excluded from inventory, in order to be consistent with the practice of separating financial services from other services, and should never be shown as a prepayment (as indicated earlier, to do so would be a mistake, since interest collected in advance constitutes part of the liability, the debt instrument's discount).

In addition to the possible magnitude of an error in taking or recording inventories, such errors have a special significance. They affect both income and the change in working capital for not one but two periods.

For example, if the end-of-period inventory is overstated, both the working capital at the *end* of the period and the change in working capital *for* the period will be overstated (both by the same amount). Furthermore, since the ending working capital would be the beginning working capital figure for the next period, the change in working capital for the next period would be understated, but the ending balance of working capital would not be affected by this error.

The effect of an error in the end-of-period inventory upon income would be the same as upon the change in working capital. For the first period, the overstatement of inventory would cause the cost

---

EXHIBIT 5-3

A COMPARISON OF

INVENTORIABLE RESOURCES VERSUS PERIOD RESOURCES

	Resources Acquired Line		Revenue Recognized Line
Merchandise (where goods are purchased for resale)			
Net invoice price			
Transportation—in			
Storage or handling	*Inventoriable Resources*	*Expired Resources*	
Production (where goods are manufactured)			
Direct materials			
Direct labor			
Indirect manufacturing			
Selling	.... >		
Salesmen	.... >		
Advertising	.... >		
Transportation—out	.... >		
Other	.... >		
Administrative	.... >		
Executives	.... >		
Accounting	.... >		
Other	.... >		
Taxes	.... >		
Interest	.... >		

---

of goods sold to be understated and the income to be overstated. For the second period, where the opening inventory would be overstated, the cost of goods would be overstated, and the income understated. Note that the end-of-period inventory error affects both flow statements (income and funds) for two periods (by the same amount, but in opposite directions); but the stock or static (position) statements for the end of only the first period.

Current value Probably the most valuable rule for avoiding errors in taking and recording inventory is to establish a precise inventory date and to include the effect of all transactions up to and including that date, and exclude all transactions thereafter—auditors refer to these practices as "observing the cutoff."

In measuring inventory, the most difficult problem usually is to determine not the quantity of units but the value to be assigned to each unit. From an accounting theory standpoint (as discussed in Chapter 2), inventory should be valued like receivables (on the basis of the present value of the cash receipts that will be generated). Since this valuation method requires that the firm be able to predict both the timing and the amounts of the selling price and cash receipts, it is practiced rarely because these conditions often are not known with reasonable certainty. However, when the merchandise is sold under contract with stipulated prices and assured dates and amounts of payment, the inventory should be valued in this fashion.

The entry for recording inventory valued on this basis is as follows:

With this basis of valuing inventory, all costs associated with the inventory would be classified as current period expenses. When a claim exists against the customer, a receivable should be opened by a transfer from the inventory account.

When the sales price is known and it is expected that the cash will be collected in a short time and without significant losses, the inventory may be valued at current selling prices. This is possible when contracts provide payments immediately or in the near future (so that the discount factor is insignificant), and when selling and collection costs also are insignificant. Mining firms that produce gold or silver to be sold at fixed prices in the government-controlled market value their inventory at selling prices since their selling costs are negligible and there is little delay or uncertainty concerning collection. The entry for recording inventory (and the associated entries) is the same as the one already described.

When there are considerable selling activities (or other activities in addition to those of production), the inventory may be valued at net realizable value.[12] In addition to a known sales price and a short collection period, this method necessitates estimating all additional costs to complete, sell, deliver, and collect for the product. Apart from the difficulty of making the estimates, it seems implicit in this method that the profit associated with the activities yet to be performed probably should be estimated too. This would constitute a further difficulty. The basic entry to record the inventory under this method would be to the same two accounts; the estimated future costs in connection with the product would be recorded as a period expense (and credited to a liability or contra-asset account).

[12]Net realizable value is not an alternative valuation measure to sales price but only a more general one. Sales price is incorporated as a special measure when future selling outlays are expected to be zero.

EXHIBIT 5-4
SUMMARY SCHEDULE TO COMPARE
INPUT VERSUS OUTPUT METHODS OF INVENTORY VALUATION

Method	Conditions for Application	Exclusions from Reported Revenue
Output Values		
1. Discounted money receipts	a. Know sales price b. Know timing of cash receipts	Interest
2. Current selling prices	a. Know sales price b. Short collection period	None
3. Net realizable	a. Know sales price b. Short collection period c. Know or be able to predict costs of selling and collecting	Portion of gross revenue attributable to selling and collecting
Input Values (substitutes for output values)		
1. Historical cost	a. Revenue not yet earned b. Highly uncertain selling prices	Operating revenue and gains or losses from specific price changes (until time of sale)
2. Current replacement cost	a. Revenue not yet earned b. Highly uncertain selling price c. Current costs objectively measurable	Operating revenue not segregated from gains or losses from specific price changes
3. Net realizable less normal profit margin	Approximation of replacement cost or as minimum valuation when it is above replacement cost	Normal gross margin deferred
4. Lower of cost or market	Without much theoretical justification, but widely practiced	Gains from specific price changes not segregated; also operating revenue reported only at time of sale

Format adapted from Eldon S. Hendriksen, Accounting Theory, rev. ed. (Homewood, Illinois: Richard D. Irwin, Inc., 1970), p. 331. (Standard cost and normal-stock bases omitted.) Despite the impression that may be drawn from above, not all classes of inventory are intended for sale: e.g., supplies.

Few inventories are valued at the present time on the basis of any output method; this is due in part, at least, to a failure to understand that such methods are in accord with what accounting purports to be all about; consequently, all other inventory valuation methods (input values) are only substitutes or surrogates for inventory output value measures. Since this logic is not reflected in current practice, the result is that input or cost value measures for inventories are presented as though they were satisfactory. Consequently, research to improve accounting by improving the output methods has not been encouraged.

The AAA, the AICPA, and other American and foreign accounting groups have long accepted cost as the primary valuation method for inventories, and usually consider anything but the cost method (or the lower of cost or market for the AICPA) to be the exception—where cost data are unavailable or undependable (or where cost figures are decidedly higher than net realizable values).

As indicated earlier *cost* usually is defined in terms of the historical cost that has resulted from an exchange transaction for inventory (or other nonmonetary or non-cash assets). Historical cost is measured by the cash outlay or by the indebtedness incurred (or in unusual circumstances, by other cash equivalents). In the context of this discussion, cost refers to the total of the *inventory* at a particular point in time; cost is also used to refer to the price paid for a *single unit* of inventory acquired at a particular point in time, to the *average price* paid per unit of inventory acquired during a specified period of time, and to the total of inventory *purchases* during a specified period of time.

Advocates of the historical cost valuation method argue that:

1. Cost is verifiable and not subject to bias since it is based upon a past exchange transaction; hence, it is less disputable than data provided under other valuation methods.
2. Cost is the best measure of the value of merchandise and raw materials because mere acquisition by the firm does not add to their value.
3. Cost is a reasonable substitute for output values when such are uncertain.
4. Cost is the only method that is completely structured on the double-entry bookkeeping method and that permits the complete identification and tracing of each change.
5. Cost does provide data that decision makers regard as helpful since history often is a good basis for predicting the future.
6. Cost is in line with the spirit of maintaining an orderly valuation system completely accepted by millions of individuals.
7. Cost is the least expensive among all valuation methods now in existence or proposed.

Those that oppose cost as a valuation method offer the following arguments:

1. Costs incurred at different dates are not comparable or additive.
2. Costs do not reflect changes in prices or the value added by the firm, especially for work-in-process or finished goods inventories.
3. Cost provides for a mismatching since current revenues are matched not with current but with historical cost.
4. Cost computations are not simple but often involve arbitrary allocations which are misleading.

Even if historical cost is accepted as the appropriate basis of valuation, the problem remains of determining how the cost flows of the inventory should be measured. This determination would be facilitated by considering the objectives of associating costs with inventory. These are:

1. Costs should be identified as closely as possible with each inventoriable unit to facilitate: (a) the matching of specific unit costs with their revenue, and (b) the identification of cost with specific units in inventory.
2. The firm should be viewed as having a continuous series of transactions instead of a series of separate and independent transactions. Thus, the emphasis is upon economic flows (not physical flows), because the primary emphasis in current accounting practice is upon matching and net income determination and not upon the stock of inventory itself.
3. The inventory should be valued on a current basis (which conflicts with the first and second objectives).
4. It is desirable to identify gains and losses from price changes and separate the income earned by buying and holding from that earned by selling.

The most realistic way to measure the cost flow would be to label or tag each unit in such a way that it would be identifiable or traceable throughout its history with the firm. When one unit can be distinguished from another, this is possible; and when the units have a high value and are unique, this may be practical. However, for most goods, it is neither possible nor practical to measure cost in this fashion. In addition, this method lends itself to income smoothing (defined on page 184) because homogeneous units may have quite different costs so that when a sale is made, the manager can select low-cost units if he wishes to report a higher net income, or high-cost units if he wishes to report a lower net income. The method also lends itself to reporting misleading information when many arbitrary allocations are involved in the costing of specific units, as when there are substantial amounts of shipping costs and cash discounts which apply to groups of units and not to single units. Furthermore, this method does not facilitate the fourth objective of cost association—the identification of gains and losses from price changes.

Consequently, in most situations other methods of measuring cost must be used instead of specific identification. In evaluating these alternative methods, it may be worthwhile to consider assumptions about cost flows, since every method (including specific identification) is based on one of three assumptions. These may be described as the *pool,* the *procession,* and the *bypass* assumptions. Under the first assumption all cost factors pour into the top of a tank; after a complete intermingling, they emerge through a faucet. The weighted-average and moving weighted-average methods of measuring historical cost are based on this assumption.

EXHIBIT 5–5
SUMMARY SCHEDULE
TO COMPARE
FIVE METHODS FOR COMPUTING HISTORICAL COSTS

Method	*Objective*	*Condition for Application*	*Working Capital (Position Statement) (Fund-flow Statement)*	*Net Income (Income Statement)*
1. *Specific identification*	*Specific matching*	*Identifiable high-value or unique units*		
Substitutes for Specific Identification (Nos. 2–5)				
2. *Weighted average*	*Single representative price*	*Periodic inventory only*		
3. *Moving weighted average*	*Single price with greater weight to recent purchases*	*Perpetual inventory only*	*Recent costs*	*Highest when prices rise*
4. *First-in, first-out (Fifo)*	*Approximate specific matching*	*Assumes oldest goods (costs) sold first*	*Recent costs*	*Highest when prices rise*
5. *Last-in, first-out (Lifo)*	*Matches current costs with current revenue*	*Assumes newest goods (costs) sold first*	*Old costs*	*Lowest when prices rise (usually)*

NOTE: This list is not all-inclusive. Such methods as standard are omitted. However, those listed are the ones used most extensively.

The second assumption is that of a procession of well-trained cost soldiers, each one in place according to seniority, with the oldest soldiers in front and the youngest bringing up the rear. The first-in, first-out (or Fifo) method of costing is based on this assumption.

The third or bypass assumption considers it necessary for the firm to have a complete inventory on its shelves and its bins *before* it can function. After its sample—safety or basic—stock of merchandise is complete, any subsequent purchases are for sales purposes. The last-in, first-out (Lifo) method is based on this assumption.

The most popular alternative to specific identification in theory and in practice is Fifo (see Exhibit 5–6). It achieves the first objective, does quite well with both the second and third, and only clearly fails the fourth objective. For most types of goods in most industries it tends to approximate specific identification, but it is superior to specific identification since it is not subject to managerial manipulation. It may present inventory in terms of recent costs, and although

it does not match current costs with current revenues, it does a reasonable matching job since it tends to approximate the usual physical
flow of goods in which the oldest units are used first. But it does
not facilitate the identification of gains and losses from price changes,
and occasionally there are practical difficulties in its application.[13]

The method that has never been popular in theory and that has
shown some decline in practice in recent years is Lifo. The principal
impetus for its use has been its general acceptance for income tax
returns. It has been permissible (provided that the firm also uses it
in company statements) since 1939 when it was added to the Internal
Revenue Code, and 1947 when a Tax Court decision expanded its
coverage to include inventories such as those in a clothing store
where the records are maintained in terms of retail prices because
continuing identification of specific physical unit descriptions would
be impossible.[14]

This method achieves only one of the four stipulated objectives
and that in a limited way only. Lifo assumes a cost flow that is contrary to the usual flow of goods. Despite its attempt at matching current costs against current revenue, it usually does not provide good
matching unless both purchases and sales occur regularly in approximately the same quantities. Except for a few types of inventories
such as coal piles or hardware items that are stored in bins, Lifo
does not approximate specific identification. If inventories are material and if the method has been used for several years, during which
inventory values have increased (or decreased) substantially, working
capital computations are worthless since the inventory valuation
usually is hopelessly out of date. Lifo also makes no provision for
recognizing unrealized gains and losses arising from specific
changes (which are concealed by the over- or undervaluation of the
inventory).[15]

Of those discussed, the average methods are the most neutral
in terms of the effect on both working capital and income. With a
high turnover of merchandise and frequent purchases, however,
weighted averages may approximate Fifo. Also it should be recognized that all the methods will give the same results if purchase and
selling prices are constant.

Under the weighted-average method, all inventory is considered
commingled, and no particular inventory is retained. The inventory is
priced on the basis of the average prices paid for the goods weighted

[13]These may occur when many lots are purchased during the period at different prices, or when
goods are returned to stock after subsequent lots have been sold. See Eldon S. Hendriksen, *Accounting Theory*, rev. ed. (Homewood, Illinois, Richard D. Irwin, Inc., 1970), p. 340.
[14]The Lifo method, however, may not be combined with Locom for income tax reporting purposes.
[15]Another consequence of using Lifo is that it permits net income to be manipulated if the base
inventory quantities become depleted. When this occurs, management can decide either to replace the depleted inventories so that the current costs would be charged to the Cost of Goods
Sold or to not replace the inventories so that the old Lifo cost, much higher or lower than the current ones, would be charged to the Cost of Goods Sold.

EXHIBIT 5-6

A COMPARISON OF

METHODS PRACTICED FOR DETERMINING INVENTORY COST

	Number of Companies	
Methods	*1969*	*1955*
Specific identification	24	9
Average	202	146
First-in, first-out (Fifo)	276	138
Last-in, first-out (Lifo)	153	202
Replacement (or current)	16	4
Other	89	78
	760	577

NOTE: *The above information was extracted from Accounting Trends and Techniques: Annual Survey of Accounting Practices Followed in 600 Stockholders' Reports, 24th ed. (New York: AICPA, 1970), p. 56. The number of methods used in 1969 exceeds the number of companies surveyed since some companies used more than one method; and in 1955 some companies did not report the method used.*

---

according to the quantity purchased at each price. The results from this method for both inventory valuation and income determination usually rank between the results obtained under Fifo and those obtained under Lifo, since under this method prices will lag behind the market. When a perpetual inventory is maintained, the weighted-average method becomes a moving weighted-average method. Under the latter method the lag behind current prices is diminished since more emphasis is placed on recent prices.

None of the historical cost methods facilitates the separate identification of gains and losses from price changes. In order to accomplish this objective, the replacement cost method must be followed. This method is based on the current input value of the inventory.[16] It eliminates the need for any assumption regarding the flow of merchandise (which is necessary for the various historical cost methods). It not only permits the matching of current costs with current revenues, but it also reports the current value of inventory for working capital purposes. It facilitates the identification and separation of the holding gains and losses from the trading gains and losses. Properties claimed for replacement costs are: verifiability, freedom from bias (if prices are obtained from current quotations or purchases), additivity, consistency, and, of course, relevance.

Much support for the replacement cost method has been shown in the past decade. The following con arguments are often presented:

---

[16]In addition to being defined as the current input value of nonmonetary assets, this term also is used in accounting to mean either the historical cost restated to reflect specific current purchasing power of the dollar or physically invested capital.

EXHIBIT 5-7
A COMPARISON OF THE
METHODS PRACTICED TO PRICE INVENTORIES

Basis	1969	1955
Lower of cost or market	511	471
Cost-oriented	161	285
Market-oriented	26	30
Other	9	26
	707	812

SOURCE: *Accounting Trends and Techniques: Annual Survey of Accounting Practices Followed in 600 Stockholders' Reports (New York: AICPA, 1970), p. 53. In 1969, 499 out of the 600 companies stated one basis only; 96 stated more than one basis; and 5 stated no basis or had no inventories.*

Replacement costs are not available for many types of merchandise (seasonal, style, and those that are partially obsolete or are produced by obsolete methods). This method would result in the recognition of unrealized holding gains. Changes in costs are not *always* reflected in selling prices, and the firm would not *always* have acquired the merchandise if it had to pay current costs. When replacement costs are not available, they may be estimated sometimes by subtracting a normal gross margin from the estimated selling price, less a normal markup. In order for these to approximate current costs, there must be a direct relationship between costs and selling prices, and the normal markup must apply to the items being valued.

As can be seen from Exhibit 5-7, the most popular method in practice is neither an output- nor an input-value method, but a hybrid one called the lower of cost of market (Locom). Developed long ago to provide creditors with the lowest probable conversion value of inventory, it is used not only to present a conservative working capital figure, but also to provide a conservative net income figure, since it recognizes losses whenever any evidence exists that such are possible, and defers gains until such are realized beyond a reasonable doubt. Although without any support in accounting theory (a situation of long standing),[17] the method continues to be used extensively. Advocates of replacement cost argue that Locom should be eliminated in favor of replacement cost. No real disagreement exists among accountants: (1) that Locom is most unconservative in income statements of future periods when prices recover and previously written-down inventories must be charged to ex-

[17]But this method has some support in utility theory where the consequences of failure far outweigh the consequences of success.

pense, and (2) that it is inconsistent because it may use one valuation basis one year and another the next.

Despite its many shortcomings, this method has been recognized by the AICPA, the AAA, the SEC, and most foreign accounting organizations for its practicality (for charging investor losses to the period in which they are incurred and valuing inventory on the basis of what it will realize in the future). Locom requires that the inventory be priced at the lower of the two values: cost or market. *Market* is defined for this method by the AICPA as the current replacement cost (by purchase or by reproduction) except that:

1. Market should not exceed the net realizable value (the ceiling)—that is, the estimated selling price in the ordinary course of business less reasonably predictable costs of completion and disposal.
2. Market should not be less than net realizable value reduced by an allowance for an approximately normal profit margin (the floor).

In short, market means current replacement cost within the specified range; if the value is not within the range, the floor or ceiling is used as the measure of market. This method can be applied to individual inventory items, categories within the inventory, or the entire inventory. In any application, the first step is to price the item, category, or entire inventory at both cost and market; and the second is to select the lowest price. The highest valuation is achieved by valuing the inventory as a whole; the lowest (and most conservative) by valuing each item separately. When prices have fallen substantially, it is possible to show both the cost and the "market" in the position statement where the Locom is applied by opening the following contra-asset account:

Inventory—Allowance for Actual Decline in Inventory Value

	×

The corresponding debit should be made to a loss account rather than to the Cost of Goods Sold expense account.

Prepayments The second category of current nonmonetary assets consists of claims to future services obtained by prepayments. Typically such items are for insurance, rent, property taxes, and sometimes for supplies (although the last should be listed with the inventories), or, erroneously, for interest (which should be shown as a contra-liability account). Insurance and taxes on property might better be classified as adjuncts to the related property; but since they are current items, they are listed separately. These assets usually are described as prepaid expenses; since the distinction between

an asset and an expense is a fundamental classification in accounting, this carelessness is unfortunate. Advances to vendors would be
a more appropriate description. Typically these assets are valued
on a historical cost basis (although other alternatives are available),
and are amortized on the assumption that the services and benefits
are received continually over a specific time period (the straight-
line method).

Sequence format Given that working capital constitutes an important measurement, the position statement can be prepared for
showing this amount. The format is called *sequence,* and the statement equation is as follows:

$$(CA - CL = WC) + (NCA - NCL) = OE$$

where CA = current assets
        CL = current liabilities
      WC = working capital
   NCA = noncurrent assets
   NCL = noncurrent liabilities
     OE = ownership equities

Summary

Among those alternative asset classifications proposed as a replacement for the current-noncurrent dichotomy, the monetary-
nonmonetary one has received most support. This classification
would provide for uniform valuation within the two categories of
assets; the present classification does not provide such uniformity
principally for inventories and prepayments.

Monetary assets are classified on the basis of their expected cash
flow; all qualify as current since they are intended to be used in
current operations within the operating cycle of the company or
one year, whichever is longer. But unlike nonmonetary current
assets, they are claims to a fixed number of dollars of general purchasing power. Among these, cash, marketable securities, and
receivables less the current liabilities, surely the most significant
(if most simple) are the cash accounts since most accounting measurements are based on cash flows. Marketable securities, whether
monetary or nonmonetary, are usually valued at cost; but a strong
case can be made for valuing both at current market prices.

Ordinary receivables, either accounts or notes, must arise from
typical sales transactions and be collectible within the usual credit
period allowed customers by the firm. The uncollected balances
owed by customers should be valued at their present values, namely,
the discounted value of the cash to be received in the future. The
usual practice is to deduct from the receivable an estimate of the

amount that will not be collected, or an allowance for uncollectible accounts. The corresponding amount should be reported on the income statement as a deduction from the revenue. This estimate is most accurate from an income statement viewpoint when based on a percentage of the period's credit sales; from the position statement viewpoint the estimate may be most accurate when the receivables are "aged."

Cash discounts are amounts allowed for the prompt settlement of debts arising out of sales. Of the three methods (gross, adjusted gross, and net) practiced for the accounting of cash discounts, the preferred methods are the adjusted gross and net. Discount also refers to interest deducted in advance on notes. When a firm sells a note to a bank, the interest may be deducted in advance. In this situation the firm has a contingent liability (since if the note is not paid at maturity to the bank, it must be paid by the firm).

Liabilities have four characteristics: (1) they involve future money outlays or their equivalents; (2) they are the result of past external transactions, not future ones; (3) they must be subject to calculation or close estimation; and (4) they must be based on double-entry bookkeeping. Although most current liabilities are monetary, those that arise from advance payments by customers present the greatest problems.

Working capital is measured as the difference between the current assets and the current liabilities. It consists of the net monetary assets plus inventories and prepayments. For the typical firm, this classification is considered to constitute acceptable liquidity and circulation concepts.

Intrinsic in computing working capital and net income, inventories are not usually measured by discounting the expected cash receipts since the timing of cash receipts from the future sale of inventories usually is not predictable. There are four methods by which the quantities of inventories are computed: periodic, perpetual, gross margin, and retail. Errors in taking or recording inventories affect both income and the change in working capital for two periods. In taking and recording inventory one can avoid errors by "observing the cutoff." The most difficult problem in measuring inventory is to assign the value per unit; the valuation in practice usually is on a cost basis. Where specific identification is not feasible, inventory is costed on the basis of one of three assumptions about cost flows. The most popular methods of costing based on one or another of these assumptions are Fifo, Lifo, and weighted average. In practice, the most popular method is Locom, despite its many shortcomings. Market is measured for this method as not less than net realizable value reduced by an allowance for an approximately normal profit margin (the floor) and not more than the estimated selling price in the ordinary course of business less reasonably predictable costs of completion and disposal (the ceiling). The second category of current nonmonetary assets, prepayments, is usually valued on an historical cost basis.

If the position statement is prepared to show working capital, the format is called sequence.

A Selection of Supplementary Readings

American Institute of Certified Public Accountants: "Restatement and Revision of Accounting Research Bulletins," Accounting Research Bulletin No. 43, chap. 3, "Working Capital," and chap. 4, "Inventory Pricing." In *APB Accounting Principles,* vol. 2. New York, pp. 6010–6018.

Battista, George L., and Gerald R. Crowningshield: "Inventories at Realizable Values?" *NAA Bulletin* (now *Management Accounting*), May 1965, pp. 31–43.

Chambers, R. J.: "Financial Information and the Securities Market," *Abacus,* September 1965, pp. 3–30.

Copeland, Ronald M., Joseph F. Wojdak, and John K. Shank: "Use LIFO to Offset Inflation," *Harvard Business Review,* May–June 1971, pp. 91–100.

Goldberg, L.: "A Note on Current Assets," *Abacus,* September 1965, pp. 31–45.

Holmes, William: "The Market Value of Inventories: A Review," *The Journal of Accountancy,* March 1964, pp. 55–59.

Huizingh, William: *Working Capital Classification.* Ann Arbor: The University of Michigan, 1967, pp. 109–121.

Hylton, Delmer P.: "Improving Inventory Presentation in Financial Statements," *The New York Certified Public Accountant,* August 1965, pp. 583–589.

Lacey, Frederick B.: "How Accountants Can Fight Organized Crime," *World,* Peat, Marwick, Mitchell & Co., Summer 1970, pp. 3–5.

Moonitz, Maurice: "The Changing Concept of Liabilities," *The Journal of Accountancy,* May 1960, pp. 41–46.

Most, Kenneth S.: "The Value of Inventories," *Journal of Accounting Research,* Spring 1967, pp. 39–50.

Mueller, Gerhard G.: "Valuing Inventories at Other than Historical Costs— Some International Differences," *Journal of Accounting Research,* Autumn 1964, pp. 148–157.

Parker, R. H.: "Lower of Cost and Market in Britain and the United States: An Historical Survey," *Abacus,* December 1965, pp. 156–172.

Stamp, Edward: "A Note on Current Assets," *Abacus,* December 1965, pp. 188–189.

Staubus, George: "Determinants of the Value of Accounting Procedures," *Abacus,* December 1970, pp. 105–119.

Sterling, Robert R.: "Conservatism: The Fundamental Principle of Valuation in Traditional Accounting," *Abacus,* December 1967, pp. 109–132.

_____: "In Defence of Accounting in the United States," *Abacus,* December 1966, pp. 180–183.

Appendix to Chapter 5

The cash holdings of even the largest corporation may vary considerably, because of the state of the economy, the nature of the industry, and the policies and habits of the firm. For instance, a few years ago among the 500 largest industrial corporations (which are surveyed annually by *Fortune* magazine) the "cash and equivalents" varied from $1.75 million (or 0.74 percent of assets) for J.I. Case to about $96 million (or 44.5 percent of assets) for Curtiss-Wright (see below).

Cash and Equivalents

Company (a partial listing)	Cash (in millions of dollars)	Percent of Assets
Who Has the Cash?		
Curtiss-Wright	$ 96.252	44.5
Maytag	63.821	42.8
Libbey-Owens-Ford	88.227	30.3
Zenith Radio	77.465	30.0
Pabst Brewing	47.915	29.9
Hunt Foods & Industries	133.988	29.1
Avon Products	70.764	29.0
U.S. Steel	1,550.941	27.0
Eastman Kodak	451.170	27.0
Proctor & Gamble	372.046	26.7
Coca-Cola	171.976	25.9
New York Times	20.993	25.7
. . . And Who Hasn't?		
Hewlitt-Packard	2.268	1.55
Hart Schaffner & Marx	1.445	1.31
Libby, McNeill & Libby	2.588	1.13
Case (J.I.)	1.755	0.74

Adapted from "Personal Investing," Fortune (July 1967), p. 170.

Petty Cash

Since most cash is transferred by bank check, accounting for currency and coins usually is not difficult. Firms keep petty cash funds consisting of currency and coins; these are convenient for miscellaneous cash disbursements. For each such fund, an account is kept in the usual manner. Although it is possible to keep such a fund so that its balance may vary considerably from period to period, for internal control purposes most firms maintain such funds on an *imprest* basis or with a stipulated, unchanging balance from period to period. As might be expected, cash is the type of asset that must be controlled most carefully by the firm, and having a stipulated balance for a petty cash fund is an effective way of facilitating such control. With such a control, the sum of the currency and coins in the petty cash fund plus the cash disbursements made from the fund should always be equal to the stipulated balance. The fund normally is opened by a check drawn against the firm's checking account; to replenish the fund, an additional check is drawn and charged to the various accounts for which the cash disbursements were made. These entries (in general journal form) are as follows:

Opening Entry	Debit	Credit	Replenishing Entry	Debit	Credit
Petty cash	500		Selling expenses	10	
Cash in bank		500	Administrative expenses	5	
			Miscellaneous expense	5	
			Cash in bank		20

and a T account for Petty Cash, after these two entries had been posted, would be as follows:

Petty Cash

Opening entry	500	

It would be possible for the above account to remain unchanged for many periods since the replenishment of this fund does not change the petty cash amount. The exceptions would be if the fund balance were to be increased or decreased because of a change in the amount needed, or if disbursements had been made from the fund at the end of the accounting period and the fund had not been replenished. In the latter situation it would be necessary to record these disbursements, as well as the actual cash balance in the account, in order to prepare financial statements for the period. Presumably, in this situation, the replenishment would be made at the start of the new accounting period. Except for amounts, the entry would be the same as the one used to open the account. It is also possible, of course, for the firm to increase the stated balance of the fund if the fund activity warrants it—or to decrease it or even close it if the need for the fund diminishes.

The other cash accounts (checking and savings) do not have stipulated balances, although well-managed companies do prepare cash budgets (essentially plans for cash receipts and cash disbursements) which enable these companies to predict their cash balances. Such budgeting or planning enables management to avoid both temporary insolvency (where the company does not have cash to pay its bills) and excessive cash holdings (where the company is foregoing revenue-creating activities).

Usually the variety and volume of cash transfers by check make checking accounts the firm's single most significant set of accounts. For example, if one has access to the detail of these accounts plus information on the inventories, it usually is possible to reconstruct all the other major accounts. In practice, this sometimes becomes necessary because the accounting records are destroyed or disappear.

Since the cash holdings of a firm are its most liquid resource, and thus most vulnerable to theft or other misappropriation, it is vital that the entity have effective internal control of cash. One control device is to have different individuals responsible for different cash activities. For instance, the person who opens the mail and sorts out cash received in this manner should not be the same person who prepares the bank checking account deposits, and the person who prepares the checks should be still a third individual. Large corporations open numerous checking accounts and restrict each account to specified types of cash transactions to facilitate the exercise of effective internal control. Such procedures are difficult to install in small companies (where the cash holdings do not warrant numerous accounts, and where only one or two individuals are involved in the record keeping); this explains why cash embezzlements seem to be more common in small concerns.

Cash in Bank

The auditor reviews the records of cash more carefully than he does those of any other company resource. He is particularly knowledgeable about the various ways in which cash shortages may be concealed. Two common ways of concealing such shortages are referred to as "kiting" and "lapping." The former usually is considered to be the act of drawing and cashing an unrecorded check on one bank and depositing it in another; the latter is the theft of cash received from one customer whose account is credited at a later date by the theft of cash received from another customer.

The most frequently prepared cash statement is a monthly one prepared to reconcile the cash balance reported on the bank statement with the one shown on the company books. It is possible to prepare such a statement by starting with either the bank statement balance or the book balance and adjusting to arrive at the other balance. The major shortcoming of such an approach is that neither balance is likely to be the adjusted or correct balance (cash surely is not the account to be misstated or omitted from the statement). Consequently the cash reconciliation statement format most favored is one that does show both the book balance and the bank statement balance adjusted to the correct balance.

The bank statement balance typically does not reflect all the cash deposits because the bank statement period does not coincide with that of the entity. It will not reflect all the checks written during the period because many of these will be in the process of being cleared among the many banks or will not have been presented to the bank for payment. These two discrepancies constitute the two major sources of the difference between the book balance and the bank statement balance. The adjustments made to the book balance (apart from corrections of errors) also involve charges to the account made by the bank via credit or debit memorandums. For example, the bank may have collected cash for the firm or loaned cash to the firm (both of which would increase the book balance), or the bank may have returned a customer's NSF (Not Sufficient Funds) check deposited by the firm but charged back to the firm's account when the customer's bank returned it. The bank might also record a service charge for handling the checking account for the firm.

Since it is possible for the firm and/or the bank to have made errors in recording transactions for the account, the reconcilement process may involve corrective additions to or subtractions from both balances.

The actual clerical process which underlies the preparation of the reconciliation statement consists of the following:

1. Verifying the canceled checks (accompanying the bank statement) which have been presented for payment to the bank against the accounting record which lists the checks written during the period in order to identify the outstanding checks. The sum of the outstanding checks constitutes a deduction from the bank statement balance. The accounting record will show all checks written, usually in a check register or a cash disbursements journal (although sometimes such detail may be shown in the ledger account).
2. Comparing the bank deposits (as shown on the bank statement and the bank deposit receipts) with the receipts shown in the cash receipts journal (or perhaps the ledger account) to isolate deposits in transit.
3. Usually in this process, special debit and credit memorandums shown on the bank statement will be identified. The actual memorandums may be sent with the bank statement or received earlier. If these special memos have not been the basis for previously recorded adjustments on the books, they are the basis for adjusting the book balance.
4. Finally, if the adjusted book balance does not coincide with the adjusted bank statement balance, all cash records should be reviewed for errors. In this process, separate reconciliation statements of checks canceled with checks written, and of bank deposits with cash receipts, may be helpful.

The adjusted balance format for a cash reconciliation statement is as follows:

Company
Bank Reconciliation
Statement
For the Period
Ended _____
(Account Form)

Bank statement balance, date	×	*Book balance, date*	×
Add: Deposits in transit	+ ×	*Add: Bank credit memos*	+ ×
	×		×
Less: Outstanding checks	− ×	*Less: Bank debit memos*	− ×
Adjusted balance, date	×	*Adjusted balance, date*	×

NOTE: *If errors were made, they could, depending on the errors, necessitate both plus and minus adjustments to either balance.*

Another merit of this reconciliation statement format is that it separates those adjustments that require entries on the part of the firm (those made to the Cash in Bank account per books, or on the right side) from those adjustments that do not require adjusting entries on the part of the firm (those made to the balance of the bank statement, or on the left side). The Cash in Bank account is adjusted at the end of the period normally only on the basis of a bank reconciliation statement.

Questions

5–1

(1) A company discounted its own note at the bank on December 26. This was not recorded on the books. The effect of this omission on the December statements was to:

a. Understate assets, understate liabilities
b. Understate assets, understate liabilities, overstate ownership
c. Overstate ownership, understate liabilities
d. Something else

(2) The effect of a company discounting a noninterest-bearing note receivable on position accounts is:

a. No change in assets, increase liabilities, decrease ownership
b. Increase assets, increase liabilities, decrease ownership
c. Increase assets, increase liabilities, no change in ownership
d. Increase assets, increase liabilities, increase ownership
e. Decrease assets, decrease ownership
f. Something else

5–2

Given the following figures, what is the working capital? Merchandise Inventory, averages 12 months to sell, $13,000; Cash $40,000; Office Supplies $2,100; Investment in Subsidiary Company $4,000; Unexpired Insurance $2,000; Accounts Receivable $26,000; Accounts Payable $41,000; Notes Payable $12,000—due in equal amounts over the next 12 years.

(1) $41,000, (2) $30,100, (3) $42,100, (4) $28,000, (5) $41,100.

5–3

The Cash in Bank balance is $3,145, while the bank statement shows a balance of $7,530. There were deposits in transit of $1,420, bank charges not recorded on the books of $10, a deposit of $360 that the bank credited to the account in error, and a check which cleared the bank at (and made out for) $580 but was entered in the books at $850.

(1) The total of outstanding checks is
    a. $4,205
    b. $5,185
    c. $4,545
    d. $3,185
    e. Something else

(2) The corrected cash balance is
    a. $4,205
    b. 5,185
    c. 4,545
    d. 3,185
    e. Something else

5–4

(1) The method of determining the cost of the inventory which attempts to assign "current costs" to "current revenues" is: (a) Lifo; (b) Fifo; (c) average cost; (d) Locom; (e) none of these.

(2) The Locom basis of valuing inventories results in: (a) a relatively high value, (b) the gross margin being overstated when prices go up, (c) stating inventory at current liquidation value, (d) the gross profit being understated when prices go down, (e) the proper measurement of cost of goods sold.

(3) Use of the Lifo method: (a) results in an understatement of current assets in times of rising prices; (b) should be adopted when prices are at their peak; (c) reflects the most recent cost in inventory; (d) charges revenue with highest cost in times of falling prices; (e) none of the above is correct.

(4) A business operates on the perpetual inventory method and has not taken a physical inventory. Net Sales totaled $78,000, Gross Margin, $40,000; and Net Income, $2,000. The adjusting journal entry for inventory included:
    a. A credit of $38,000 to purchases
    b. A credit of $38,000 to merchandise inventory
    c. A debit of $38,000 to cost of goods sold
    d. Some other amount to some account
    e. No entry needed

5–5

(1) The Lifo method of costing inventories (a) cannot be used where the inventory is made up of perishable goods, (b) prices the ending inventory at market, (c) results in lower profits (than use of Fifo) during a period of price declines, (d) usually excludes from the net income computation those profits that cannot be realized in cash, (e) corresponds with the usual physical flow of goods.

(2) Gross margin in past periods has averaged 35 percent. In the current period goods available for sale amounted to $500,000 at selling price and $350,000 at cost. Sales were $300,000. The position statement should have an inventory of (a) $50,000, (b) $90,000, (c) $150,000, (d) $155,000, (e) $200,000.

(3) Locom (a) has not been justified on the grounds of conservatism, (b) lowers the profits of a period in which price increases have taken place, (c) is rarely used in accounting, (d) is not often used for plant, (e) means cost or selling price whichever is lower.

(4) The Fifo method of pricing inventories (a) assumes that the newest goods are sold first, (b) assumes that the goods first received are in the inventory, (c) will show a relatively high (compared to Lifo) cost of goods sold during periods of rising prices, (d) costs inventory at recent costs, (e) requires the use of a perpetual inventory.

(5) Showing purchase discounts taken as revenue on the income statement (a) may result in the showing of revenues before the goods are sold, (b) automatically reveals the discounts lost, (c) understates liabilities, (d) results in accounts payable being shown net, (e) understates assets.

5-6   Following is an analysis of the one inventory item (gizmo) for the month of January:

January		Number of Units	Unit Cost
1	Balance	100	2.00
5	Purchased	300	2.10
16	Purchased	400	2.10
28	Purchased	200	2.20
8	Sold	200	
20	Sold	300	
29	Sold	200	

(1) Assuming the use of the periodic inventory method, the inventory count of January 31 totals 300 gizmos. The cost of the inventory using the weighted-average cost method would be: (a) $630, (b) $640.50, (c) $633, (d) $660, (e) none of these.

(2) The WEP Company's opening inventory consisted of 20,000 units at $4. Assume the following facts:

Purchases		Issued	
June 1	5,000 @ $3	June 10	1,000 units
June 8	5,000 @ $5	June 18	3,000 units
June 29	5,000 @ $4	June 30	2,000 units

If the closing inventory is valued at $115,000, the inventory method that has been used is (a) Fifo, (b) weighted average, (c) Lifo, (d) impossible to determine.

(3) Assuming that the accounting period ending December 31, 1972 was one of rising prices, the method of arriving at original cost which would propably result in the highest cost assigned to the inventory on hand would be: (a) Lifo, (b) Fifo, (c) average cost, (d) Locom, (e) none of these.

(4) Under a periodic inventory system, pricing the inventory at Locom: (a)

results in a position statement figure which is considered conservative; (b) tends to reflect unrealized gains in the income statement in times of rising prices; (c) will result in a lower net income figure; (d) is conservative on the position and income statements in the current year, but tends to shift inventory profits into prior years; (e) none of the above is correct.

(5) The gross margin method of estimating inventory: (a) provides accurate data on the number of units in inventory; (b) is of doubtful validity if the nature of the business is changing; (c) is more accurate than a perpetual inventory system; (d) provides management with valuable information about changes in the rate of gross margin; (e) does none of the above.

5-7

Beginning inventory	*1,000 units*	*@ $1.00 per unit*
Purchases	*500*	*@ 2.00*
	500	*@ 1.00*
	500	*@ 3.00*
Sales	*1,200 units*	

(1) The ending inventory under Fifo (periodic) is: (a) $2,050, (b) $1,600, (c) $2,275, (d) $2,600, (e) $2,000.

(2) The ending inventory under the weighted average (peridoc) is: (a) $2,080, (b) $1,600, (c) $2,275, (d) $2,600, (e) $2,000.

(3) The ending inventory under Lifo (periodic) is: (a) $2,080, (b) $1,600, (c) $2,275, (d) $2,600, (e) $2,000.

(4) The December 31, 1970, inventory is overstated by $1,600; the December 31, 1971, inventory is overstated by $900, and the December 31, 1972, inventory is overstated by $400. The 1972 net income is: (a) overstated by $2,000, (b) overstated by $1,500, (c) understated by $400, (d) understated by $1,300, (e) understated by $500.

5-8

The Thurber Co. had an inventory of 1,000 units at $1 per unit on January 1, 1972. It made the following purchases and sales during January:

January 6	*Purchased*	*500 units @ $1.10 each*
14	*Sold*	*800 units*
24	*Purchased*	*1,000 units @ 0.90 each*
27	*Sold*	*600 units*

(1) The inventory on January 31, 1972, under Fifo (periodic) would be: (a) $990, (b) $1,010, (c) $1,060, (d) $1,100, (e) none of the above.

(2) The inventory on January 31, 1972, under Lifo (periodic) would be: (a) $1,010, (b) $1,060, (c) $1,100, (d) $1,110, (e) none of the above.

(3) The inventory on January 31, 1972, under weighted average (periodic) would be (to the nearest dollar): (a) $1,010, (b) $1,110, (c) $1,050, (d) $1,078, (e) none of the above.

(4) Lifo, Fifo, and weighted average are methods used to: (a) arrive at Locom, (b) obtain selling price, (c) value inventory at replacement cost, (d) determine cost, (e) do none of the above.

(5) If the ending inventory were understated by an error, the effect would

be: (a) to understate the cost of goods sold, (b) no effect on net income, (c) to understate the gross margin, (d) to overstate the net income, (e) none of the above.

5-9   In view of the major emphasis that the realization concept places on the convertibility of assets into cash, discuss the advisability or desirability of showing the probabilities of all classes of assets being realized or converted into cash. Identify any assets where this is done.

5-10   The following data concerning the retail inventory method are taken from the financial records of the Arlene Golonka Company.

	Cost	Retail
Beginning inventory	$18,600	$ 30,000
Purchases	91,000	154,000
Freight in	1,400	—
Net markups	—	1,000
Net markdowns	—	1,740
Sales	—	156,760

(1) The ending inventory at retail should be
  a. $28,240
  b. $27,980
  c. $27,240
  d. $26,500

(2) If the ending inventory is to be valued at approximately the lower of cost or market, the calculation of the cost to retail ratio should be based on goods available for sale at (1) cost and (2) retail, respectively, of
  a. $111,000 and $186,740
  b. $111,000 and $185,000
  c. $111,000 and $182,260
  d. $109,600 and $184,000

(3) If the ending inventory for the current period at cost amounts to $15,900, it appears that the rate of markup for the current period as compared to that for the preceding period was
  a. The same
  b. Higher than before
  c. Lower than before
  d. Indeterminate

(4) If the foregoing figures are verified and a count of the ending inventory reveals that merchandise actually on hand amounts to $25,000 at retail, ignoring tax consequences the business has:
  a. Realized a windfall gain of approximately $1,500
  b. Sustained a loss in terms of cost of approximately $900
  c. Sustained a loss in terms of cost of approximately $1,500
  d. Experienced no gain or loss as there is close coincidence of the inventories

(5) If the Lifo inventory method were used in conjunction with the data, the ending inventory at cost would be:
   a. $16,430
   b. $16,060
   c. $15,980
   d. $15,900

5-11   Compare the effects of employing Fifo versus Lifo in a period of *rising prices:* (a) on the firm's period income statement and its position statement and (b) on the firm's industry and the economy. Compare the effects on (a) and (b) in a period of *falling prices.*

5-12   Examine critically the recommendation that inventory should be valued at the lower of net realizable value or current replacement cost.

5-13   To what extent do you consider that alternative methods of inventory (or other asset) valuation should be permitted in published financial statements?

Problems

5-1   The following exercise is useful for establishing differences between the Fifo and Lifo methods of determining the historical cost of inventories.

The firm has been operating for at least two periods and employs perpetual inventory records; both the quantity of units sold and the quantity of units purchased during the period are greater than the quantity of units in the beginning inventory for each period of operation.

If either Fifo or Lifo is used, all prices contained in the ending inventory or cost of goods sold and not contained in the beginning inventory are prices of the current period. Quantities are not affected by a change in the historical cost valuation method.

(1) If the *quantity* of inventory has *increased* throughout the period (insert the words *none, some,* or *all* in the following blanks):
   a. Then _____ of the prices contained in the beginning Lifo inventory are contained in the Lifo cost of goods sold.
   b. Then _____ of the prices contained in the beginning Lifo inventory are contained in the ending Lifo inventory.
   c. Then _____ of the prices contained in the beginning Fifo inventory are contained in the Fifo cost of goods sold.
   d. Then _____ of the prices contained in the beginning Fifo inventory are contained in the ending Fifo inventory.

(2) If the *quantity* of inventory has *decreased* throughout the period (insert the words *none, some,* or *all* in the following blanks):
   a. Then _____ of the prices contained in the beginning Lifo inventory are contained in the Lifo ending inventory.
   b. Then _____ of the prices contained in the beginning Lifo inventory are contained in the Lifo cost of goods sold.
   c. Then _____ of the prices contained in the beginning Fifo inventory are contained in the Fifo cost of goods sold.
   d. Then _____ of the prices contained in the beginning Fifo inventory are contained in the ending Fifo inventory.

(3) If cost prices have always been *rising* (insert the phrases *less than* or *greater than* in the following blanks):
   a. Then all the prices in the beginning Lifo inventory are either _____ or equal to the prices in the beginning Fifo inventory.
   b. Then all the prices in the ending Lifo inventory are either _____ or equal to the prices in the ending Fifo inventory.
(4) If cost prices have always been falling (insert the phrase *less than* or *greater than* in the following blanks):
   a. Then all the prices in the beginning Lifo inventory are either _____ or equal to the prices in the beginning Fifo inventory;
   b. Then all the prices in the ending Lifo inventory are either _____ or equal to the prices in the ending Fifo inventory.

5-2   One of your clients asks you to indicate the proper unit price in accordance with the Locom rule. Indicate the unit value that should be used to price each of the items in the inventory, and explain your selection so that the distinction between *replacement cost* and *net realizable value* is apparent.

Unit Number	Historical Cost	Sales Price	Replacement Cost	Estimated Completion and Selling Cost	Normal Profit
1	1.96	2.40	1.86	0.21	0.36
2	4.30	5.35	4.36	0.42	0.88
3	1.50	1.60	1.20	0.20	0.40
4	0.50	0.75	0.48	0.05	0.10
5	3.00	3.50	2.75	0.35	0.70
6	7.00	9.00	6.50	0.75	1.40
7	1.55	1.40	1.37	0.10	0.18
8	1.90	1.95	2.00	0.20	0.41
9	5.00	6.50	5.10	0.50	1.05
10	1.25	1.35	1.33	0.12	0.17
11	1.15	1.50	1.12	0.05	0.03
12	8.60	10.70	8.72	0.84	1.76
13	0.25	0.38	0.24	0.03	0.05
14	6.25	8.50	2.35	0.25	0.75
15	10.00	15.00	9.50	2.00	0.75

5-3   After studying Locom, you decide to consider using it for your firm. The following five situations often occur in your firm. Please consider each situation separately, and determine whether a loss has been incurred; and if so, the amount. Also show how the loss would be recorded and what disposition would be made of it on the financial statements.
(1) The selling price of product *X* has declined from $1.25 to $1.00 while the cost of acquiring the product is unchanged at $0.18.
(2) The selling price of product *T* has remained unchanged at $10. Its cost, however, has declined from $4 to $3.
(3) The selling price and the cost price of product *Y* have declined from $5 to $4 and from $4 to $3, respectively.

(4) The company expects a price decline of $5 in the purchase price of product *E* during the next accounting period; however, as yet, there has been no change in either selling or purchase price.

(5) The firm has agreed to pay for product *R* next year at a price of $10. The firm has to lower its selling price to reflect the current market price of $9.

5–4   A firm is interested in using the retail method to estimate inventory value. Data from the current year's operations are listed below.

		(000's omitted)
	At Cost	*At Retail*
Purchases	$40	$75
Sales, gross		60
Net markups		4
Net markdowns (regular)		5.5
Markdowns for special sales		3
Beginning inventory	9	13
Employee discount		0.6
Transportation costs	3	
Sales—returns		0.4
Sales—doubtful accounts		0.1

Shrinkage is estimated to be 0.5 percent of goods available for sale at retail. Compute inventory, and explain the method.

5–5   Indicate the implications of the following end-of-the-period inventory errors on income and position statements:

(1) Merchandise received, on hand, and properly recorded initially is overlooked in the physical count.

(2) Merchandise received, on hand, and properly recorded initially is counted twice by the inventory crew.

(3) Merchandise on hand (or in transit to the firm) at the inventory date has *not* been recorded or counted.

(4) Merchandise on hand has not been recorded but is counted.

(5) Merchandise sold to customers is recorded, but was counted since it was not delivered.

5–6   The Howard Hughes Store has used the lower of cost (Fifo) or market as a basis for pricing inventory. Its net income record is (000's omitted):

1973	$ 6.3
1974	11.2
1975	13.5
1976	(6.6)
1977	9.6

The business was started in 1973.

Inventories according to the books and as repriced under two other bases are (000's omitted):

	Locom	Fifo	Lifo
1973	$30.0	$30.0	$30.0
1974	37.4	37.4	33.4
1975	47.5	47.5	38.4
1976	23.4	28.6	26.0
1977	29.4	29.4	28.1

(1) Determine the net income in each of the five years if inventories had been priced on a Fifo basis.
(2) Determine the net income in each of the five years if inventories had been priced on a Lifo basis.

5–7   The Shirley MacLaine Company uses the retail inventory method, calculating the cost-selling price ratio after adding markups but before subtracting markdowns.

Information for 1973 is (000's omitted):

Inventory, January 1, 1973: Cost	$ 9.725
Selling price	16.450
Purchases: Cost	107.315
Selling price	181.540
Freight in	2.36
Markups	1.01
Markdowns	4.56
Sales	179.36

Determine the cost of the December 31, 1973 inventory and the cost of goods sold.

5–8   Information concerning balances on hand, purchases, and sales of a toy for the Sherlock Holmes Corporation are given in the following table.

Date	Received	Issued	Balance	Unit Price	Received	Issued	Balance
Jan. 1			100	1.50			$150
24	300		400	1.56	$468		
Feb. 8		80	320				
Mar. 6		140	180				
June 11	150		330	1.60	240		
Aug. 18		130	200				
Sept. 6		110	90				
Oct. 15	150		240	1.70	255		
Dec. 29		140	100				

(1) If a perpetual inventory record of the toy is operated on a Fifo basis, it will show a *closing inventory* of what amount?

(2) If a perpetual inventory record of the toy is operated on a Lifo basis, it will show a *closing inventory* of what amount?

(3) *Assume that no perpetual inventory is maintained for material and that quantities are obtained by* an annual physical count. The accounting records show information concerning *purchases,* but not concerning *issues.* On this assumption the *closing inventory* on a *Fifo* basis will be what amount?

(4) With the same assumptions as in question (3) the *closing inventory* on a *Lifo* basis will be what amount?

Potential answers to questions (1) to (4):
a. $150
b. $152
c. $156
d. $160
e. $170
f. Answer not given

(5) If a perpetual inventory record of material is operated on a moving average basis, it will show a closing inventory that is:
a. Lower than on the Lifo basis
b. Lower than on the Fifo basis
c. Higher than on the Fifo basis
d. Answer not given

5–9   The Arthur C. Doyle Corporation *began business on January 1, 1972.* Information about its inventories under different valuation methods is shown below. Using this information, *you are to choose the phrase that best answers each of the following questions.*

December 31	Lifo Cost	Fifo Cost	Market (Replacement Cost)	Locom
1972	$10,200	$10,000	$ 9,600	$ 8,900
1973	9,100	9,000	8,800	8,500
1974	10,300	11,000	12,000	10,900

(1) The inventory basis that *shows the highest net income for 1972 is?*

(2) The inventory basis that *shows the highest net income for 1973 is?*

(3) The inventory basis that *shows the lowest net income for three years combined is?*

(4) For the year 1973, *how much higher* or *lower* would profits be on *the Fifo cost basis* than on the Locom *basis?*

(5) On the basis of the information given, it appears that the *movement of prices* for the items in the inventory was:
a. Up in 1972 and down in 1974
b. Up in both 1972 and 1974

    c. Down in 1972 and up in 1974
    d. Down in both 1972 and 1974

5-10

Possible answers:

a. Fifo

b. Lifo

c. Specific identification

d. Standard cost

e. Base stock

f. Retail

g. Market price of product less cost of disposition

h. Weighted-average cost

i. Common cost

j. Average cost

k. Answer not given

For each of the following questions, choose the best answer from those listed above:

(1) An inventory method that developed from consideration of the flow of costs rather than the flow of goods is:

(2) An inventory method that is designed to approximate inventory valuation at the lower of cost or market is:

(3) In situations where there is a rapid inventory turnover, an inventory method that produces almost the same results as the Fifo method is:

(4) An inventory method that necessitates the keeping of a perpetual inventory record is:

(5) An inventory method that may be used for federal income tax purposes only if it is used for general accounting purposes is:

(6) In a period of rising prices, the inventory on the position statement is valued nearest to current cost when the inventory method being used is:

5-11

The Minnesota Fats Company has available the following information for one of the items in its inventory:

Purchases:	January 2		1,300 @ $1.50
	March 1		1,500 @ $1.60
	June 1		1,200 @ $1.70
Sales:	January	400	
	February	500	
	March	600	
	April	500	
	May	300	
	June	700	

Determine the cost of the June 30 inventory and the cost of goods sold by each of the following methods (carry all calculations to the nearest dollar):

(1) Costing those sold in each of the six months by the use of:

    a. Fifo

    b. Lifo

    c. Moving average

(2) Costing the June 30 inventory by the use of:

    a. Fifo

    b. Lifo

    c. Weighted average

5-12

(1) The Justine Store management, suspecting a salesman (with exclusive control of the top hat department) of theft, made a surprise inventory of his department on January 20, 1973. The retail value of the hat inventory was $4,400. In the past, the company has experienced losses due to customer theft, damage, etc., but the total of these has never exceeded 10 percent of *total sales*.

Top hat department data disclosed in records:

Inventory December 31:	*At retail*	*$4,950*
	At cost	*3,400*
Purchases:	*At retail*	*1,650*
	At cost	*1,170*
Sales		*1,600*
Purchases—transportation in		*80*
Purchases—discounts		*30*

Compute the apparent loss to the company at cost due to employee theft during the first 20 days of 1973.

(2) A cloak manufacturing firm, turning out only one grade of cloak, was robbed of 300 cloaks and 1,000 yards of woolen cloth on the night of February 18. From January 1 to February 18, 3,000 cloaks were produced, and 4,500 were sold. Twenty thousand yards of woolen cloth were used. Purchases during the same period were 18,750 yards of woolen cloth at $0.50 per yard.

Manufacturing cost per unit was: Materials, $3.33, Processing, $3.50; Total, $6.83.

Inventory taken *after* the theft was: 1,250 cloaks; 6,250 yards woolen cloth.

Give the detail, in units, of the beginning inventory.

5-13

Jesse James held a 90-day 5 percent note receivable for $650, dated September 7. On October 3 of the same year he discounted the note at 6 percent at the Cheyenne National Bank. Determine the following regarding the note:
(1) Date due
(2) Maturity value
(3) Discount period
(4) Amount of discount
(5) Proceeds
(6) Interest revenue or charge upon discounting the note

5-14

(1) State the effect of each of the following errors upon the position and the income statements of the current period and the succeeding period:
  a. The company fails to record a sale of merchandise on account; goods sold are excluded in recording the ending inventory.
  b. The company fails to record a sale of merchandise on account but the goods sold are included in recording the ending inventory.

    c. The company fails to record a purchase of merchandise on account; goods purchased are included in recording the ending inventory.

    d. The company fails to record a purchase of merchandise on account; goods purchased are not recognized in recording the ending inventory.

    e. The ending inventory is overstated as the result of a miscount of goods on hand.

    f. The ending inventory is overstated as the result of inclusion of goods held on a consignment basis and never recognized as a purchase.

(2) The following errors are discovered at the beginning of 1974 in auditing the accounts of the Presley Sales Corporation. Give the entry to correct each error, assuming that perpetual inventory records are not maintained.

    a. The company failed to record a charge sale of $210 at the end of 1973. The merchandise had been shipped and was not included in the ending inventory. The sale was recorded in 1974 when cash was collected from the customer.

    b. The company failed to recognize $400 due from a consignee as a result of goods sold by this party at the end of 1973. The consignee had failed to report the sale of consigned goods, and the company included goods of $260 relating to the consignment sale in goods on consignment.

    c. The company failed to make an entry for a credit purchase of $60 at the end of 1973, although it included this merchandise in the inventory account. The purchase was recorded when payment was made to the creditor in 1974.

    d. The company failed to recognize a credit purchase of $1,350 at the end of 1973 and also failed to include the goods purchased in the ending inventory. The purchase was recorded when payment was made to the creditor in 1974.

    e. The company overlooked goods of $360 in the physical count of goods at the end of 1973.

(3) The Sands Co. adjusted and closed its books at the end of 1973 with the summary of 1973 activities showing a net loss of $1,215. The following errors relating to 1973 are discovered upon an audit of the books of the company made in March 1974. Prepare adjusting entries.

    a. Merchandise costing $1,650 was recorded as a purchase at the end of 1973 but was not included in the ending inventory since it was received on January 9, 1974.

    b. Merchandise costing $315 was received in 1973 and included in the ending inventory; however, the entry recording the purchase was made on January 4, 1974 when the invoice was received.

    c. 500 units of commodity Z costing $6.15 per unit were recorded at a per-unit cost of $1.65 in summarizing the ending inventory.

    d. Goods in the hands of a consignee costing $6,000 were included in the inventory; however, goods costing $1,450 had been sold as of December 31, and the sale was not recorded until January 31 when the consignee made a remittance of $1,750 on this item.

    e. Merchandise costing $368, sold at $490, and shipped on December 31, 1973, was not included in the ending inventory; however, the sale was not recorded until January 12, 1974 when the customer made payment on the sale.

5-15 The Clyde Fitch Corporation commenced business on January 1, 1973. Information about its inventories under different valuation methods is shown below (with 000's omitted). Using these data, show which inventory basis will give the lowest net income for the two years combined. How much higher or lower would the net income be?

	Valuation Techniques		
Inventory Dates	*No. 1*	*No. 2*	*No. 3*
December 31, 1973	*$20.4*	*$20*	*$19.2*
December 31, 1974	*9.2*	*8.8*	*8.6*

5-16 The Igor Stravinsky Company commenced business on January 1, 1973. Using the following information (with 000's omitted) about its inventories under different valuation methods, show which basis will give the lowest net income for the two years combined. How much higher or lower would the net income be?

	Valuation Techniques		
Inventory Dates	*No. 1*	*No. 2*	*No. 3*
December 31, 1973	*$18.4*	*$17.2*	*$17.6*
December 31, 1974	*40.8*	*38.4*	*40.0*

5-17 All the merchandise of The Hair Hunters' Beauty Salon was destroyed by fire on April 10, 1973. Sales and merchandise data for the calendar year to date of fire were as follows (000's omitted):

Sales	*$87*
Sales—returns	*3*
Merchandise inventory, January 1	*23.6*
Purchases—freight in	*0.9*
Purchases	*40*
Purchases—returns	*1.7*

Compute the estimated fire loss, assuming that selling prices have averaged 160 percent of cost of goods sold.

5-18 From the following information, compute the cost valuation of the ending inventory on both the retail inventory and the gross margin methods (with 000's omitted):

Selling price of all merchandise available for sale	*$33*
Purchase price of all 8,250 units acquired and available for sale	*7*

Freight in on purchases	*1.5*
Purchases—returns, allowances, and discounts	*0.25*
Sales—discounts	*0.5*
Selling price of 2,000 unsold units	*8*

Based on previous experience, it is estimated that gross margin has averaged 20 percent of net sales. It is assumed that all available units of merchandise not in the ending inventory are sold at the established selling price.

5–19   From the following information, prepare an income statement for the Fyodor Dostovevsky Corporation for the year ending December 31, 1973 (000's omitted).

Cash	*$ 40*	*Selling expense*	*$ 20*
Factory supplies used	*10*	*Work in process,*	
Work in process,		*January 1, 1973*	*25*
December 31, 1973	*20*	*Production costs for year*	*125*
Sales	*200*	*Unexpired insurance*	*25*
FICA tax payable	*17*	*Rent expense (sales office)*	*6*
Miscellaneous office expense	*2*	*Retained earnings,*	
Advances from customers	*5*	*December 31, 1973*	*130*
Depreciation on factory		*Office salaries*	*15*
building	*10*	*Depreciation on office*	
Retained earnings,		*equipment*	*3*
January 1, 1973	*100*	*Finished parts,*	
Finished parts,		*December 31, 1973*	*56*
January 1, 1973	*50*	*Cost of goods sold*	*?*
Factory labor costs	*60*	*Net income*	*?*

NOTE: No dividends were declared or paid, nor did any other changes take place in stockholders' equity during the year. Production costs include Factory Supplies Used, Depreciation on Factory Building, and Factory Labor Costs.

5–20   Given that beginning and ending work-in-process inventories are zero, that the beginning finished goods inventory is zero, and that one-half of the goods produced during the period are sold, what would be the effect on each of the items below if an expense were handled as a production cost? Consider the effect as overstating, understating, or not affecting.
a. Net income for the period
b. Assets at the end of the period
c. Liabilities at the end of the period
d. Ownership at the end of the period

5–21   Compute the missing figures in each of the following unrelated situations (000's omitted).

(1) Sales salaries	*$ 25*
Raw materials used	*75*
Office equipment depreciation	*5*
Other factory costs	*30*
Beginning work-in-process inventory	*15*

Delivery truck expenses	$ 3
Ending work in process inventory	20
Factory labor costs	100
Cost of parts finished during the period	?

(2) *Furniture and fixtures*	$ 40.0
Notes receivable	5.0
Cash	10.0
Rent deposits by tenants	8.0
Accounts receivable	12.0
Neil Simon, capital	26.0
Inventories	15.0
Accounts payable	14.5
M. Stapleton, capital	?
Total assets	89.5
Contracts payable	11.0
Unexpired insurance	?

5–22

(1) Calculate the ending inventory at cost and the cost of goods sold from the following information (000's omitted).

	Cost	Selling Price
Opening inventory	$ 60.0	$ 82
Purchases	220.0	328
Purchases—returns	0.6	1
Freight in	$ 20.0	
Markdowns	22.6	
Markups	8.4	
Sales		310

(2) From the following information estimate the value of the inventory on hand December 31, 1973 (000's omitted).

Inventory, January 1, 1973	
(at cost)	$ 60.0
Purchases	60.2
Freight in	0.7
Purchases—returns	0.9
Sales	110.0
Sales—returns and allowances	5.0
Sales, 1968–1972	1,200.0
Cost of sales, 1968–1972	800.0

(3) From the following information compute the cost of goods sold for December and the value of the inventory on December 30, using the Lifo method with perpetual inventory records.

		Units	Unit Price
December 2	Inventory	500	$1.00
8	Purchased	1,000	1.20
15	Issued	200	
22	Issued	800	
29	Purchased	500	1.10

5-23

The John Glenn Corporation has purchased the following:

	Period	Units	Price
1973:	Jan. 1–Mar. 31	21,000	$21.00
	Apr. 1–June 30	34,000	22.00
	July 1–Sept. 30	27,000	23.00
	Oct. 1–Dec. 31	6,000	24.00
1974:	Jan. 1–Mar. 31	24,000	25.00

The inventory as of January 1, 1973 consisted of 12,000 units priced at $19.00 per unit.
Sales during 1973 totaled 80,000 units.

The following are gross margin summaries for 1973 (000's omitted).

	A	B	C	D
Sales	$2,800.0	$2,800.0	$2,800.0	$2,800.0
Cost of goods sold	1,745.6	1,716.0	2,000.0	1,786.0
	1,054.4	1,084.0	800.0	1,014.0

After making appropriate computations for each letter, indicate what inventory method was used to calculate cost of goods sold.

5-24

A company started business January 1. All sales are charged on terms of 2/10, n/30. Each of the company's three accountants prepare separate sets of statements as follows:

	Accountant No. 1	Accountant No. 2	Accountant No. 3
Income Statement			
(revenue section only)			
Sales	$40,000	(1)$ _____	(2)$ _____
Sales—discounts	(695)		(3)$ _____
Sales—lapsed discounts	_____	(4)$ _____	
Net sales	39,305	(5)$ _____	(6)$ _____

	Accountant No. 1	Accountant No. 2	Accountant No. 3
Position Statement *(receivables section only)*			
Accounts Receivable	(7)$ _____	(9)$ _____	$1,800
Less: Allowance for sales discounts			$ (36)
	(8)$ _____	(10)$ _____	$1,764

(1) Complete the above statements for these accountants (list appropriate amounts for numbers 1 to 10).
(2) Identify the technique used by each accountant.
(3) Identify by *number* the accountant who used the technique that records discounts only when taken, regardless of when the corresponding sales were recorded.

5–25   From the information given below you are to use one way to explain why the cash balance has increased only $5,000 when the net income for the year is $10,000. You may do this by (1) starting with the beginning $5,000 cash balance, adding receipts and subtracting cash disbursements, and ending with the $8,700 ending balance; (2) starting with the $10,000 net income, add back non-cash expenses, and subtract non-cash revenue and cash expenditures not included as expenses of the period, and end up with the $3,700 increase in cash figures; or (3) pointing out the items in the position and income statements that have an effect upon the cash account. Be sure to give the account title for each figure that you use in your reconciliation. (000's omitted.)

	Position Statements December 31 1974	1975	Income Statement 1975		
Cash	$ 5	$ 10	Sales		$100
			Inventory,		
Accounts receivable	15	25	January 1	$10	
Merchandise inventory	10	15	Purchases	80	
				90	
Plant—net	200	190	Inventory,		
	$230	$240	December 31	15	75
			Gross margin		25
Accounts payable	$ 6	$ 5	Other Expenses		
Wages payable		1	Wages	$ 5	
Capital stock	200	200	Depreciation	10	15
Retained earnings	24	34			
	$230	$240	Net income		$ 10

5–26   Two companies owned by two brothers are identical in every respect except for a difference in their accounting for inventories.* Both use a periodic inventory; however, one company costs its inventory on a Lifo basis and the other on a Fifo basis. Below is a record of the first few months of the companies' operations. During any one month both costs and quantities move only in one direction; this occurs only at the beginning of each month.

Month	Ending No. of Inventory Units	Price per Unit
January	10	$10
February	20	10
March	20	12
April	25	13
May	20	14
June	10	15

Compare the ending inventory accounts of the two companies.

*Purchases and sales are made uniformly throughout the year by both companies. Both buy from and sell to similar sources in similar quantities and at similar prices at similar times. Purchases during a month are approximately four times those of the ending inventory.

6 Fund-flow Statements: Cash, Net Monetary Assets, and Working Capital

---

Note that not just one but a wide variety of flow statements or concepts may be constructed on the basis of the same basic data. The statement of income (flow) has traditionally been emphasized, almost to the exclusion of other useful flows, such as (working capital) funds flow and cash flow.*
ROBERT K. JAEDICKE and ROBERT T. SPROUSE, 1965

Accounting reports on the financial *flows* of the firm generally are regarded as more significant measures than accounting reports on its financial stocks. The term *fund* or *funds* is used in many different ways in accounting, but here it will be used in two ways. It may refer to the stock of one type or class of asset (for example, to the several cash accounts or to monetary assets), or it may refer to two or more classes of assets and/or liabilities (for example, current assets less current liabilities). Although flow reports may be made for a one asset fund (such as petty cash), accounting fund-flow statements usually refer to the multiclass type of report.

Definitions, History, and Practice
Among the possible definitions of a fund for fund-flow statement purposes the more frequently used are: cash items (as defined here, this includes temporary or marketable securities), net short-term monetary (or quick) assets (cash items and receivables less current liabilities), and working capital (current assets less current liabilities). Closely related to these definitions of funds are the all-financial-resources and all-changes-in-financial position concepts. Although these concepts usually are applied with the working capital definition, they may be applied with cash or other relevant definitions. However, it requires the reporting on the fund-flow statement of all *significant*

---

*From *Accounting Flows: Income, Funds, and Cash* (Englewood Cliffs, New Jersey: Prentice-Hall, Inc., 1965), p. 6.

transactions, even those that affect only non-fund accounts—such as the issuance of capital stock or long-term liabilities for noncurrent assets, or substitute-type transactions like the conversion of long-term liabilities into capital stock—and when the cash definition is used, this includes changes within working capital—such as a significant decline in (liquid) cash that is largely or entirely offset by an increase in (less-liquid) inventory. It would be possible to use as a fund any combination of assets (and/or equity) accounts that one deemed significant, but only the ones mentioned here have considerable acceptance.[1]

Although the first fund-flow statement did not appear in an accounting textbook until 1908,[2] fund-flow statements were published occasionally by companies in the second half of the nineteenth century.[3] Despite their basic importance, annual reports of firms often did not include such statements until recently. One of the more striking changes in accounting in the past decade has been the increased popularity of this type of statement. The information content provided by fund flows has seemed to become more apparent to users; its relative freedom from bias and its verifiability are becoming more appreciated by both users and auditors. Of the 600 largest United States corporations surveyed in 1955, 21 percent (or 124) presented fund-flow statements; in 1969, 91 percent (or 548) included such statements in their annual reports.[4]

The greatest impetus behind this increased emphasis on fund-flow statements came from the AICPA in Opinions of the Accounting Principles Board No. 3, "The Statement of Source and Application of Funds," published in 1963. The most significant recommendations made by APB Opinion No. 3 were that a fund-flow statement (or funds statement) should be presented as supplementary information in financial reports and that the statement should apply the all-financial-resources concept.[5] In a new opinion, APB Opinion No. 19, "Reporting Changes in Financial Position," the AICPA APB has made a fund-

[1]Not acceptable for accounting purposes but a popular shortcut definition of a cash fund flow for "quick and dirty" analysis is net income plus depreciation. It assumes, usually quite incorrectly, that these two items approximate the change in working capital from operations.

[2]W. M. Cole, *Accounts: Their Construction and Interpretation* (Boston: Houghton Mifflin Company, 1908), pp. 97–102.

[3]L. S. Rosen and Don T. DeCoster, "'Funds' Statements: A Historical Perspective," *The Accounting Review* (January 1969), p. 125.

[4]*Accounting Trends & Techniques: Annual Survey of Accounting Practices Followed in 600 Stockholders' Reports*, 24th ed. (New York: AICPA, 1970), p. 267.

[5]Other recommendations in this Opinion, such as that comparative fund-flow statements be presented, that "funds provided by operations" be presented in such a manner as to imply that depreciation is an increase in funds, and that the title of the statement be "Statement of Source and Application of Funds" have been well received, according to Philip E. Fess and Jerry Weygandt in "The Funds Statement: Trends and Recommendations," *The New York Certified Public Accountant* (February 1969), pp. 120–124. That the second recommendation has been followed is most unfortunate. Other recommendations, such as that cumulative fund-flow statements be presented or that the all-financial-resources concept of funds be used apparently have no more than limited acceptance.

flow statement mandatory for published financial reports covering fiscal periods ending after September 30, 1971. Thus the utility and the significance of these statements is likely to increase even more.

Of the various definitions of funds that might be employed, the one most widely used by accountants (probably because it is considered to be the most significant) is working capital. In recent years, however, considerable attention has been given to the cash definition of funds. Although the AICPA recommended the use of the all-financial-resources concept in its APB Opinion No. 3, this part of the Opinion apparently has not been influential; in its new APB Opinion No. 19, the only traditional fund definitions mentioned are cash and working capital. Although the all-financial-resources concept also is not mentioned in the New Opinion, the ideas underlying the concept are clearly present in the requirement that the statement be based on a broad concept embracing all changes in financial position.[6] Of the 548 companies referred to earlier that included fund-flow statements in their 1969 annual reports, 33 statements were prepared on a cash basis, 5 were based on other definitions, and the remaining accounted for changes in working capital only. If an accounting fund-flow statement did not specify its definition of fund, one can assume that it was prepared on a working capital basis (or on a working capital basis applying the all-financial-resources concept). The title would be more descriptive and consequently more useful if it stated the fund definition (that is, Cash Flow Statement, Working Capital Flow Statement, etc.). However, APB Opinion No. 3 did not include a recommendation that the definition of fund be included in the statement title, and this omission has not been corrected in the new Opinion on this subject. Of the two titles recommended in No. 3 the one having the widest acceptance was "Statement of Source and Application of Funds" (in 242 of the 548 statements in the 1969 annual reports). APB Opinion No. 19 recommends that the title be "Statement of Changes in Financial Position." Both this title and the commonly used one that was recommended in the earlier Opinion would be improved if the fund definition were specified.

Fund-flow Transaction Analysis

For the purpose of preparing a fund-flow statement, all transactions occurring during the statement period should be classified in one of three ways:

1. Transactions that changed only accounts that are included in the defined fund.

---

[6]"Reporting Changes in Financial Position," Opinions of the Accounting Principles Board No. 19 (New York: AICPA, 1971), p. 374.

2. Transactions that changed one or more accounts that are included in the defined fund, and one or more accounts that are not included.
3. Transactions that changed only accounts that are not included in the defined fund.

Since transactions of the first category involve changes only in accounts comprising the fund, these flows generally are not reported directly on the fund-flow statement. They are usually reported on a supporting schedule as internal changes in the composition of the fund. The body of the fund-flow statement is a report on what caused the external change in the fund for the period or which non-fund accounts caused changes in the fund accounts. Such information is found in the second category of transactions. The final or third category of transactions (those causing change only in non-fund accounts) may or may not be employed in the preparation of a fund-flow statement. Ordinarily such transactions are not used since they do not change fund accounts. If they are significant, however, they should be considered when the all-changes-in-financial-position concept is applied. A common example of a transaction that would not be considered under any concept discussed here is the declaration and issue of stock dividends which would decrease retained earnings and increase the capital stock outstanding accounts, neither of which is considered a fund account. Sometimes transactions in this category are substantive as, for example, when bonds are refinanced (one issue of bonds is exchanged for another). Such transactions rightly may be regarded as important flow information and, if so, they must be considered when the all-changes-in-financial-position concept is applied. Under strict adherence to the fund definition, each transaction in this third category is examined to see whether it represents a flow of sufficient importance to be reported.

The basic transactions of the second category (those recorded in both fund and non-fund accounts) are as follows:

Transactions

Increases in Funds	Decreases in Funds
1. Period revenues (including gifts and gains from disposal of fund assets)	1. Period expenses (including taxes and losses on disposal of fund assets)
2. Investments by creditors and owners	2. Retirement of investments
3. Disposal of non-fund assets	3. Acquisition of non-fund assets
4. Net decrease in funds	*or* 4. Net increase in funds

Restated in terms of specific accounts, these transactions are classified as follows:

Increases in Funds	Decreases in Funds
1. Increases in sales and gains from disposal of fund assets accounts	1. Increase in expenses, losses from disposal of fund assets, and taxes accounts
2. Increases in non-fund equities (liability or ownership) accounts	2. Decreases in non-fund equities (liability or ownership) accounts
3. Decreases in non-fund asset accounts	3. Increases in non-fund asset accounts
4. Net decrease in funds *or*	4. Net increase in funds

Statement Formats

The transactions and the changes in specific accounts are listed above in an *account format* for an asset; this means that the increases or debits are shown on the left side, and the credits or decreases are shown on the right. The net change in funds is the balancing figure in the account. When this format for presenting a fund-flow statement is used, it is called the *balanced account* form. This simple format for a fund-flow statement is the oldest in general use; it is, of course, very similar to the account format for a position statement (or balance sheet). Other formats that are used include the following.

The *complete report format* shows the change in the fund as the difference between increases and decreases. This report format shows revenues as increases, and expenses as decreases. It has the merit of directing attention to the net change in the funds.

The *long-form analytical type* of fund statement attempts to match specific increases with specific decreases (or sources with uses). If this is possible, this approach provides more information to the user. The format is illustrated as follows:

Net sales and other revenues		$ xx
Less current outlays for expenses, taxes,		
and losses (including interest)		−xx
Funds provided from operations		$ xx
Less income distribution to stockholders		
(cash dividends)		−xx
Funds available from net income		$ xx
Add disposals of non-fund assets		+xx
Funds available from net income and disposals		$ xx
Financing issuance of capital stocks		
and long-term debt	$ xx	
Less retirement of stocks		
and bonds	−xx	xx

Funds available for expansion and investment		$ xx
Less expansion—plant, equipment, and	$ xx	
noncurrent investments	xx	−xx
Increase in working capital		$ xx

NOTE: *A decrease in working capital would appear after Financing.*

The two most popular formats for fund statement presentation are variations of the report form; apparently they are favored because they can be prepared more quickly than the other formats. However, many users have difficulty interpreting the resulting statement. These are the *remainder type* and the *reconciling type* of the report form. In each, the report gives a net income figure from the period income Statement, and adjusts it to show the net change in funds from operations, before listing the other increases and decreases. The saving of time in preparation comes from the comparatively few adjustments that must be made to the income figure, as contrasted with recording on the fund statement each revenue and each expense and other current outlay. Unfortunately, the time saved by the accountant preparing the report formats of the fund statement is usually more than offset by the user's difficulty in understanding the statement, since the rules for adjusting the income figure are different from those for presenting fund increases and decreases.

Under the remainder type, the net income figure is given first with the net change in funds shown as the last figure in the statement. Under the reconciling type, the beginning fund balance is given first with the net change in funds shown as a difference and added (or subtracted) to give the ending fund balance as the last figure on the statement. The *account* format of the fund-flow statement may also be varied to adjust the income figure from the income statement instead of reporting directly each revenue and each current outlay for expenses, losses, and taxes.

For instructional purposes it is desirable to adhere to one format, and so the *account* format will be used hereafter. Since the net income variation is the most popular in practice, it will be the one discussed. The regular account method will be stressed as it is the most logical and readily understood approach.

In practice, accountants prepare fund-flow statements from worksheets; this is the same procedural device that they commonly use to prepare any type of statement. Although the worksheet procedure has considerable merit for a professional accountant, it has major drawbacks for a beginning accounting student. It is cumbersome for the typically short introductory problem and places heavy emphasis on memorization of procedures (rather than on an understanding of the analysis) since no underlying rationale for a specific work-sheet approach appears to be generally accepted in practice or theory.

This book therefore deliberately avoids the use of worksheets; instead the use of T accounts will be emphasized. Under double-entry bookkeeping, the accounts are kept in basically the same way in all firms. Furthermore, this uniformity of account record keeping is invaluable in enabling anyone to comprehend the fundamental ideas of financial accounting. Since a student of accounting may encounter many different worksheet techniques, perhaps he should wait until he is affiliated with a firm so that he need learn only one worksheet technique.

Steps in Preparing Statements

In preparing fund-flow statements there are three primary steps. First, the fund definition to be used must be established. As in the earlier discussion, this is usually either working capital (favored by professional accountants) or cash (favored by many business-men) instead of net-quick assets which emphasizes the difference between the monetary and nonmonetary accounts. The net-quick assets concept seems to come closest to resolving the dispute over which fund definition is most relevant for a business or other or-ganization, because the basic dichotomy to be recognized in pre-paring a fund statement is the separation of those account flows that occur more rapidly from those that occur more slowly. Thus the accountants' argument over which definition of fund is most relevant for a business is similar to the economists' argument over which concept of cash is most relevant for the banking system or the entire economy. The traditional accounting decision on the rele-vant definition of a fund for a firm is working capital. For the typical firm, accountants have long maintained that dividing accounts into current and noncurrent categories is the most useful classification for both position and fund-flow statement purposes.

Unfortunately, for many firms the turnover of inventories and pre-paid items does not correspond closely to the turnover of cash, receivables, and current liabilities; thus, the most relevant distinc-tion often would appear to be a monetary rather than a current one. The definition of funds that is adopted for statement purposes auto-matically determines whether an account flow is to be emphasized on the statement.

Under a working capital fund definition, those flows of non-working capital accounts (noncurrent assets and equities) that have altered the working capital accounts are emphasized (or reported directly on the statement). Under an acid-test fund definition, those flows of nonmonetary accounts that have altered the monetary accounts are emphasized. When an all-changes-in-financial-position concept is applied, no distinction is drawn between the two, and all significant non-fund account flows are reported with approximately equal emphasis. Even so, probably the cash definition of funds is easiest to apply since the distinction between the cash accounts and the non-cash accounts seems most obvious; the cash-flow fund statement reports how the flows from the non-cash accounts have affected the cash flow.

After a fund definition has been adopted, all period transactions must be classified into those that have changed only fund accounts, those that have changed only non-fund accounts, and those that have changed both non-fund and fund accounts. Except under the all-changes-in-financial-position concept, only the last category is reported on the fund-flow statement; and thus only these transactions need to be considered directly in preparing a fund-flow statement. These transactions are reported on the fund-flow statement by describing the nature of the non-fund account flow. The effect of these transactions on the fund account flow is reflected only in the net change in funds on the statement, and in summary form for each fund account in a supplementary schedule if desired. The final step in the three-step process is the selection of a reporting format for statement purposes.

The most difficult of the three steps is the second one, the classifying of the period transactions in order to determine which ones are to be reported directly on the fund-flow statement. The basic records for this purpose are the ledger accounts of the period. First, each account must be classified as being either a fund account or a non-fund account; second, each type of transaction involving a non-fund account transaction must be further identified as to whether the other accounts altered by this transaction were fund or non-fund accounts. If the latter, the transaction may be disregarded except under the all-changes-in-financial-position concept of funds which requires that all such transactions be examined individually to see whether their underlying significance merits disclosure on the fund-flow statement.

The required calculations may be simplified if the income and position statements have already been prepared and if the position statement is in the comparative format which shows for each account not only the balances of both the previous and current periods but also the net change. If the position statements have not been prepared in this format, the period changes must be determined for each account directly from the ledger (from comparative trial balances or from a comparison of the position statements at the beginning and the end of the period). Once the period changes for each account have been determined, and each account has been classified into one of the three transaction categories, the following analysis should be undertaken.

First, summarize the changes that occurred during the period in the balances of the defined fund accounts to determine the direction (increase or decrease) and the amount of the net change in the fund balance during the period. After doing this, these accounts may be disregarded unless one prepares a supplementary schedule of the changes in the defined fund account balances or unless the all-changes-in-financial-position concept is applied and the changes in some of the individual accounts are so significant as to require reporting.

Second, for the remaining or non-fund accounts, determine which changes had a corresponding change in a fund account; these transactions are reported directly on the fund-flow statement. As indicated earlier, reporting of significant changes in non-fund accounts is optional. Where these transactions are significant, the authors favor, and the all changes-in-financial-position concept requires, their inclusion.

In addition to this there are two additional complicating factors in the preparation of fund-flow statements. One is that the change in a non-fund account during the period may be a net, instead of a gross, change. A net change means that during the period the non-fund account was affected by one or more of both the inflow and outflow *types* of transactions rather than that the change was due entirely to either the inflow or the outflow type of transaction. The net change in a non-fund account must be analyzed further to determine the gross change resulting from each of the two or more types of transactions that altered the non-fund account. Fortunately, even for the large corporation, only a few accounts are affected by both types of transactions. The most common example (and often the only one) occurs when the company has both acquired and disposed of plant and/or equipment in the same period, and the net change in one or more of these accounts is the difference between the two different types of transactions.

The final complicating factor relates to the selection of the format for statement presentation. As mentioned earlier, the format used most frequently in practice (whether of the report or account variety) shows first the net change in funds from operations which is derived indirectly by adjusting the net income figure. This adjustment process is accomplished by *adding back* to Net Income the amount(s) of those transactions which involved only non-fund accounts that increased expenses or losses or that decreased revenues or gains on the income statement and by *deducting* from Income the amount(s) of the transaction(s) which involved only non-fund accounts that decreased expenses or losses or that increased revenues or gains on the income statement. Examples of the *former* (losses on the disposal of noncurrent assets and depreciation, depletion, and amortizations of noncurrent assets and of bond liability discount or of a bond investment premium) are much more numerous than the *latter* (gains on the disposal of noncurrent assets and amortization of a bond liability premium or of a bond investment asset discount).

The preparation of several fund-flow statements is illustrated in the Appendix to this chapter. The illustrations are an important part of the chapter and have been placed in the Appendix only to save space. The Appendix must be carefully studied in order to grasp the concepts in this chapter.

Cash Fund-flow Statement

A fund-flow statement using the cash definition should be the easiest of the fund definitions to understand and to prepare; after all, it is simply a report explaining the increases and decreases in the cash account for the period or the summary of changes in the various cash accounts if more than one exists. However, as the following illustrations will show, the cash fund-flow statement is not the easiest to prepare, because there are fewer accounts within the cash definition; thus, there would tend to be more external accounts and more changes to consider. If one has access to the ledger of the company, one could summarize the inflows and outflows in the cash, petty cash, and marketable securities accounts; rearrange these flows according to the statement format selected; and the cash fund-flow statement could be prepared.

Your understanding of the cash fund-flow analysis will be enhanced greatly if you have a mental picture of the flows—the relationships and interrelationships (interfaces), depicted in Figure 6-1, of what is reported on a cash fund-flow statement. One should keep in mind that not all selling and administrative expenses, new investments in plant, interest, income taxes, and dividends are paid in cash immediately.

Unfortunately, access to the cash account or other accounts is rarely available to the financial analyst or the user of financial statements. Sometimes it also is not available to the professional accountant. However, everyone who professes to know something about accounting or wishes to analyze (in summary form) the transactions of an entity for a period should know how to prepare a fund-flow statement when the accounts are not available.

The usual approach is to utilize comparative position statements (for the beginning and the end of the period) and the income statement for the period. If the changes in the position statement accounts have not been recorded on the comparative position statement, these calculations must be made first.

Figure 6-1 *Cash flow through a business.*

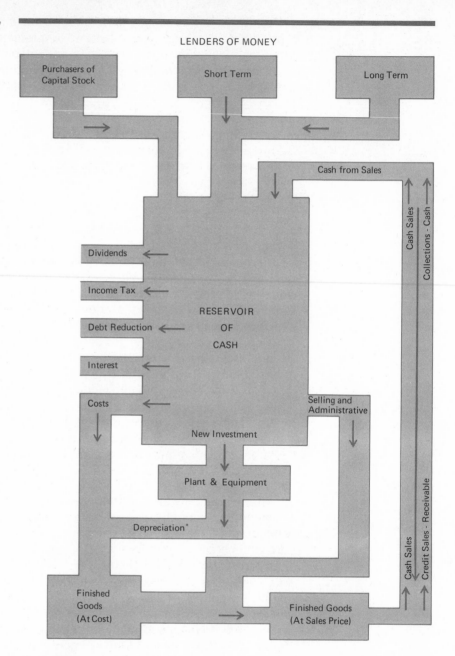

Adapted from chart in J. A. Griswold, Cash Flow through a Business *(Hanover, N.H.: Amos Tuck School of Business Administration, 1955), p. 2; and reprinted in Colin Park and John W. Gladson,* Working Capital *(New York: The Macmillan Co., 1963), p. 50.*
Unlike the others, depreciation only simulates a cash flow; only when the plant and equipment are replaced will an actual cash flow result. For a further discussion of depreciation, see Chap. 7.

Next, these changes may be recorded in various T account formats as a preliminary to preparing the actual statement. For example, the changes in the fund accounts may be recorded in a T account in order to determine the net change in funds for the period. For a cash definition of fund, this account would be titled Net Cash Change (Internal). As one might expect, the T account rules here for this account are the same as for an asset.

The next step is somewhat more elaborate. It requires the preparation of a T account for each remaining account on both the position statement (or balance sheet) and the income statement, in short every non-fund account the balance of which has changed during the period.

The next step is to isolate those non-fund accounts whose changes are related to changes in the Cash account. Each of these non-fund accounts should be closed out by entering the change-balance figure on the side opposite the change balance of the non-fund account and then transferring this amount to a new account called Cash Fund Flow (External). When all these transfers have been made, the Cash Fund Flow (External) account will reflect the context of the formal cash fund-flow statement and, thus, will be the basis for its preparation.

The final step before preparing the cash fund-flow statement is to transfer the balance in the Cash Fund Flow (External) account to the Net Cash Change (Internal) account, thereby closing both these accounts.

The process is essentially one of dividing these changes into two categories: those that represent transactions affecting both cash and non-cash accounts (these become the cash fund-flow statement) and those that represent transactions which affect only non-cash accounts (which should be eliminated if a strict conception of cash is used for the fund-flow statement).

By applying your knowledge of account relationships in the double-entry system to an inspection of the other financial statements (position and income), you can identify the summary transactions for the period which caused changes in a cash account (and thus should be reported on the cash fund-flow statement) or which caused non-cash changes. All this can be accomplished quickly with practice, without having access to either the ledger (to inspect the accounts) or to the journals (to identify the transactions). See the Appendix to this chapter for illustrations.

In summary, the cash fund-flow statement is a statement of cash receipts and disbursements. The title is not the one used most frequently. As stated earlier, the one most widely used in practice (and in textbooks) is Source and Application of Funds. Although there are many variations to this title, most of them use synonyms for one or more of the significant terms. There are at least two major defects to such a title: (1) The words "source" and "application" do not communicate change as precisely as do "increase" and "decrease"; and (2) the term "funds" does not indicate which definition of funds has been used (although in practice "funds" usually is interpreted to mean working capital). Since the title used in the Appendix illustrations (Cash Fund-flow Statement) avoids such shortcomings, it is highly recommended. The student of accounting should remember that accounting statements are prepared for use largely by non-professionals; therefore precision of language in the preparation of such statements is at least as important as precision of figures.

Net Short-term Monetary Asset and Working Capital Fund-flow Statements

The Appendix to this chapter contains illustrations of statements based on two additional definitions of funds: net short-term monetary assets and working capital concept. As was discussed earlier, the net short-term monetary assets statement is based on the excess of current monetary assets (cash, petty cash, marketable securities, and net accounts receivable) over current liabilities. The working capital definition of funds is the excess of current assets over current liabilities.

The preparation of fund-flow statements is an excellent process for testing one's knowledge of account relationships and the mechanics of the accrual basis of accounting. For this reason, the working capital definition of funds may be favored for pedagogical purposes since there is considerable overlap between this concept and the accrual basis of accounting. Accountants, however, usually find that the merits of the working capital definition of funds (as contrasted to other definitions, including cash) lie in its stress upon the less frequent transactions occurring between the organization and outsiders and in its provision of a liquidity perspective which is more typical and general.

Cash and Working Capital (All-changes-in-financial-position) Fund-flow Statements

The three fund definitions illustrated in the Appendix, cash, net short-term monetary, and working capital, for fund-flow statements (as well as the income statement, which might be regarded as another fund-flow statement[7]) present the causes of flows in a definition of a company's liquidity. The all-changes-in-financial-position concept has a slightly different objective, namely, to report all significant financial transactions for the period. The all-changes-in-financial-

[7]See George J. Staubus, "Alternative Asset Flow Concepts," *The Accounting Review* (July 1966), pp. 397–412.

position concept of funds used in this book includes such transactions as the acquisition of property in exchange for stock or bonds (and refinancing) but when the cash definition is used, the statement should also report significant changes in other working capital accounts. See the Appendix for an illustration.

Kinds of Information on Fund-flow Statement

What kinds of information are revealed by a fund-flow statement? The kinds of specific information provided by a fund-flow statement not disclosed (or at least not disclosed as effectively) on a position or an income statement are:

1. The major increases in the fund: operations (that is, adjusted income), loans, and stockholder investments
2. The major decreases in the fund: cash dividends, plant (and other long-lived) acquisitions or expansions, and debt and/or stock retirements
3. The relationship between the increase in the fund resulting from operations (that is, adjusted net income) and its disposition (cash dividends and net income retained)
4. The impact of decreases in the fund on its overall balance
5. The internal changes in the composition of the fund (for example, the changes in the current assets and the current liabilities comprising working capital)

Several kinds of general information which may be provided by a fund-flow statement consist of:

1. The trend of the financial strength (or weakness) of the organization
2. Indication of the impact of increases and decreases in the fund upon future dividend-paying ability
3. Disclosure of the company's financial habits (or its management's financial attitudes[8]

Summary

One of the most striking changes in accounting during the past decade has been the increased popularity of the fund-flow statement. In fact, the AICPA now requires a fund-flow statement for published financial reports covering fiscal periods ending after September 30, 1971.

It would be possible to use as a fund any combination of asset and/or equity accounts deemed significant; however, only cash, net short-term monetary assets, and working capital funds have considerable acceptance. Of these, firms consider working capital most significant, and accountants use it most widely.

[8]See Charles T. Horngren, "Increasing the Utility of Financial Statements," *The Journal of Accountancy* (July 1959), pp. 39–46, for results of a survey among professional financial analysts supporting these uses.

The fund-flow statement provides specific information not available in an income or position statement. This information includes (1) the major increases in the fund, (2) the major decreases in the fund, (3) the relationship between the increase in the fund resulting from operations and its disposition, and (4) the internal changes in the composition of the fund.

There are three primary steps in preparing a fund-flow statement: (1) The fund definition to be used must be established. (2) All period transactions must be classified into *(a)* those that have changed only fund accounts, *(b)* those that have changed both fund and non-fund accounts, and *(c)* those that have changed only non-fund accounts. (3) The format for reporting the fund-flow statement must be selected. Possible choices are the account format, the complete report format, and the long-form analytical format.

The most difficult step in the preparation of the fund-flow statement is the classification of transactions to determine which will be reported. Transactions that change only fund accounts generally are reported on a supporting schedule to the fund statement instead of on the statement itself. Those transactions that changed both fund and non-fund accounts constitute the body of the fund-flow statement since this is essentially a report of what non-fund accounts caused changes in fund accounts. Transactions that caused changes in only non-fund accounts usually are not considered unless the all-financial-resources or all-changes-in-financial-position concept is applied in the preparation of the fund-flow statement. The all-changes-in-financial-position concept (now recommended by the AICPA) requires that all transactions, including those that affect only non-fund accounts, be considered individually, to determine whether their significance merits their disclosure on the fund-flow statement.

In the Appendix to Chapter 6, examples of cash, net short-term monetary asset, working capital, and working capital (all-changes-in-financial-position) fund-flow statements are presented. The cash fund-flow statement is the reporting of all increases and decreases in the cash account for the period. The net short-term monetary assets statement is based on the excess of current monetary assets over current liabilities. The working capital statement reports the excess of current assets over current liabilities.

An examination of the fund-flow statements in the Appendix and an understanding of their preparation should demonstrate why the information that such statements provide can disclose the company's financial habits, indicate the impact of increases and decreases in the fund upon future dividend-paying abilities, and show the trend of the financial strength or weakness of the organization.

It should be noted that the titles of the fund-flow statements in the Appendix are not the same as titles of similar statements used in practice. Businesses generally title their fund-flow statements "Statement of Source and Application of Funds" and the AICPA now recommends that it be titled "Statement of Changes in Financial Positions." The titles would be more useful if the fund definition (cash, working capital, etc.) used in preparation of the statement were included in the title, as has been done in the Appendix.

A Selection of Supplementary Readings

American Institute of Certified Public Accountants: "The Statement of Source and Application of Funds," Opinions of the Accounting Principles Board No. 3. New York: 1963.

_____: "Reporting Changes in Financial Position," Opinions of the Accounting Principles Board No. 19. New York: 1971.

Anton, Hector R.: *Accounting for the Flow of Funds.* Boston: Houghton Mifflin Company, 1962, especially pp. 29–39.

Drebin, Allan R.: "'Cash-flowitis': Malady or Syndrome?" *Journal of Accounting Research,* Spring 1964, pp. 25–34.

Fess, Philip E.: "Improving Working Capital Analysis," *The New York Certified Public Accountant,* July 1967, pp. 506–512.

Fess, Philip E., and Jerry J. Weygandt: "Cash Flow Presentations—Trends, Recommendations," *The Journal of Accountancy,* August 1969, pp. 52–59.

_____: "The Funds Statement: Trends and Recommendations," *The New York Certified Public Accountant,* February 1969, pp. 120–124.

"Funds Flow Statements—Why and How?" *Accountancy,* September 1970, pp. 644–649.

Hobbs, James B.: "Double-entry and Working Capital Analysis," The Teachers' Clinic, *The Accounting Review,* October 1966, pp. 763–767.

Horngren, Charles T.: "The Funds Statement and Its Use by Analysts," *The Journal of Accountancy,* January 1956, pp. 55–59.

_____: "Increasing the Utility of Financial Statements," *The Journal of Accountancy,* July 1959, pp. 39–46.

Käfor, Karl, and V. K. Zimmerman: "Notes on the Evolution of the Statement of Sources and Applications of Funds," *The International Journal of Accounting* Education and Research, Spring 1967, pp. 89–121.

Park, Colin, and John W. Gladson: *Working Capital.* New York: The Macmillan Company, 1963, pp. 1–8, 14–19, 53–99.

Paton, William A.: "The 'Cash-flow' Illusion," *The Accounting Review,* April 1963, pp. 243–251.

Rosen, L. S.: "Funds Statement Concepts": part I, "History and Cash Reports"; part II, "The Liquidity Perspective"; part III, "The Perspective of Interentity Transactions"; Education and Training; *Canadian Chartered Accountant,* October, November, and December 1968, pp. 275–277, 369–372, 445–449.

Rosen, L. S., and Don T. DeCoster: "'Funds' Statements: A Historical Perspective," *The Accounting Review,* January 1969, pp. 124–136.

Schornack, John J.: "Signs of the Times in Financial Reporting: The Development of the Funds Statement," *The Illinois CPA,* autumn 1966, pp. 1–10.

Staubus, George J.: "Alternative Asset Flow Concepts," *The Accounting Review*, July 1966, pp. 397–412.

Trumbull, Wendell P.: "Developing the Funds Statement as the Third Major Financial Statement," *NAA Bulletin* (now *Management Accounting*), April 1963, pp. 21–31.

Appendix to Chapter Six

The following data for a company are used to illustrate the preparation of fund-flow statements. Statements will be prepared under the following definitions of funds: cash, net short-term monetary assets, and working capital.

Transactions for the year with all figures in thousands (000's and dates omitted) are as follows:

Transactions

A. Sales: charge $490; cash $10
B. Collections on charge sales: $499
C. Write-off of uncollectible accounts: $1
D. Estimated uncollectible accounts: $1
E. Disposal of marketable securities with a book value of $2 for $3
F. Cash transferred to bond sinking fund: $5
G. Retained earnings appropriated for bond retirement: $5
H. Purchases for inventories: charge $350 (including discount of $2); cash $2
I. Payments on charge purchases (after deducting discounts of $1): $339
J. End-of-year inventories: $35
K.* Amortization of discount on investment in bonds: $0.1
L.† Amortizations: tools $1; goodwill $0.5
M. Depreciation: buildings $1; equipment $2
N. Payment: income tax liability $40
O. Other payments: salaries (including accrued liability) $70; other selling and administrative expenses (excluding salaries) $20
P. Petty cash end-of-period expenses: $0.5
Q. Expired prepaids: $0.5
R.* Amortization of premium on bond liability: $0.1
S. Cash received as interest on investment: $2
T. Cash disbursed for interest on bond liability (including accrual of $1): $2
U. Cash dividends: declared $15; paid $10
V. Additional shares having a market value of $3 and a par value of $2 were issued to stockholders as a stock dividend.
W. Equipment: purchases $10; cash from disposals $5 (with a book value of $3 and accumulated depreciation of $1)
X. End-of-year accruals: salaries $5; income taxes $45; bond interest charge $1; bond interest revenue $0.5
Y. Building: cash from disposal $2 (with a book value of $4 and accumulated depreciation of $1)
Z. Closing entries

---

*Discussed in Chapter 8.
†Goodwill is discussed in Chapter 7.

T Accounts

Cash

✔	10	(F)	5
(A)	10	(H)	2
(B)	499	(I)	339
(E)	3	(N)	40
(S)	2	(O)	90
(W)	5	(T)	2
(Y)	2	(U)	10
		(W)	10
		✔	33
	531		531
✔	33		

Petty Cash

✔	1.0	(P)	0.5
		✔	0.5
	1.0		1.0
✔	0.5		

Marketable Securities

✔	5	(E)	2
		✔	3
	5		5
✔	3		

Accounts Receivable

✔	20	(B)	499
(A)	490	(C)	1
		✔	10
	510		510
✔	10		

Interest Receivable

(X)	0.5	

Accounts Receivable— Allowance for Doubtful Accounts

(C)	1	✔	2
✔	2	(D)	1
	3		3
		✔	2

Inventories

✔	30	(J)	345
(H)	350	✔	35
	380		380
✔	35		

Prepaids

✔	1.0	(Q)	0.5
		✔	0.5
	1.0		1.0
✔	0.5		

Investment in Bonds

✔	10.0	
(K)	0.1	
	10.1	

Bond Sinking Fund

✔	5	
(F)	5	
	10	

Land

✔	5	

Buildings

✔	30	(Y)	5
		✔	25
	30		30
✔	25		

Equipment

✔	40	(W)	4
(W)	10	✔	46
	50		50
✔	46		

Equipment— Accumulated Depreciation

(W)	1	✔	10
✔	11	(M)	2
	12		12
		✔	11

Buildings— Accumulated Depreciation

(Y)	1	✔	5
✔	5	(M)	1
	6		6
		✔	5

Goodwill

✔	3.0	(L)	0.5
		✔	2.5
	3.0		3.0
✔	2.5		

Organization Costs

✔	2

Tools

✔	5	(L)	1
		✔	4
	5		5
✔	4		

Accounts Payable—Allowance for Cash Discounts

✔		1	(I)	1
(H)		2	✔	2
		3		3
✔		2		

Accounts Payable

(I)	340	✔	20
✔	30	(H)	350
	370		370
		✔	30

Salaries Payable

(O)	3	✔	3
		(X)	5

Dividends Payable

(U)	10	(U)	15
✔	5		
	15		15
		✔	5

Taxes Payable

(N)	40	✔	1
✔	6	(X)	45
	46		46
		✔	6

Interest Payable

(T)	1	✔	1
		(X)	1

Notes Payable*

✔	5

Bonds Payable

✔	30

Bonds Payable—Premium

(R)	0.1	✔	1.0
✔	0.9		
	1.0		1.0
		✔	0.9

Capital Stock—Par

		✔	50
		(V)	2
			52

Capital Stock—Premium

		✔	25
		(V)	1
			26

Retained Earnings Appropriated for Bond Retirement

		✔	5
		(G)	5
			10

*Noninterest bearing.

Retained Earnings—Unappropriated

(G)	5.0	✔	10.0
(U)	15.0	(Z₆)	13.2
(V)	3.0		
✔	0.2		
	23.2		23.2
		✔	0.2

Sales

(Z₁)	500	(A)	500

Sales—Doubtful Accounts

(D)	1	(Z₁)	1

Interest Revenue

(Z₂)	2.6	(K)	0.1
		(S)	2.0
		(X)	0.5
	2.6		2.6

Gain on Disposal of Marketable Securities

(Z₂)	1	(E)	1

Gain on Disposal of Equipment

(Z₂)	2	(W)	2

Selling and Administrative Expense

(L)	1.5	(Z₄)	97.5
(M)	3.0		
(O)	87.0		
(P)	0.5		
(Q)	0.5		
(X)	5.0		
	97.5		97.5

Cost of Goods Sold

(J)	345	(Z₃)	345

Loss on Disposal of Building

(Y)	2	(Z₅)	2

Taxes

(X)	45	(Z₅)	45

Interest Charges

(T)	1.0	(R)	0.1
(X)	1.0	(Z₅)	1.9
	2.0		2.0

Income Statement Summary

(Z₃)	345.0	(Z₁)	499.0
(Z₄)	97.5	(Z₂)	5.6
(Z₅)	48.9		
(Z₆)	13.2		
	504.6		504.6

Company
Trial Balance
End of Year

	First Year (after closing)		Second Year (before closing)	
	Debit	*Credit*	*Debit*	*Credit*
Cash	$ 10		$ 33.0	
Petty cash	1		0.5	
Marketable securities	5		3.0	
Accounts receivable	20		10.0	
Accounts receivable—allowance for doubtful accounts		$ 2		$ 2.0
Interest receivable			0.5	
Inventories	30		35.0	
Prepaids	1		0.5	
Investment in bonds	10		10.1	
Bond sinking fund	5		10.0	
Land	5		5.0	
Buildings	30		25.0	
Buildings—accumulated depreciation		5		5.0
Equipment	40		46.0	
Equipment—accumulated depreciation		10		11.0
Tools	5		4.0	
Goodwill	3		2.5	
Organization costs	2		2.0	
Accounts payable		20		30.0
Accounts payable—allowance for cash discounts	1		2.0	
Salaries payable		3		5.0
Dividends payable				5.0
Taxes payable		1		6.0
Interest payable		1		1.0
Notes payable		5		5.0
Bonds payable		30		30.0
Bonds payable—premium		1		0.9
Capital stock—par		50		52.0
Capital stock—premium		25		26.0
Retained earnings appropriated for bond retirement		5		10.0
Retained earnings—unappropriated		10	13.0	
Sales				500.0
Sales—doubtful accounts			1.0	
Interest revenue				2.6
Gain on disposal of marketable securities				1.0
Gain on disposal of equipment				2.0
Cost of goods sold			345.0	
Selling and administrative expense			97.5	

	First Year (after closing)		Second Year (before closing)	
	Debit	Credit	Debit	Credit
Loss on disposal of building			2.0	
Taxes			45.0	
Interest charges			1.9	
	$168	$168	$694.5	$694.5

Company
Statement of Income
and Retained Earnings
For Second Year

	Debit	Credit
Revenue:		
Sales	$500	
Less doubtful accounts	1	$499.0
Interest		2.6
Gains on disposals:		
Marketable securities	1	
Equipment*	2	3.0 $504.6
Expenses, taxes, interest, and losses:		
Cost of goods sold	345.0	
Selling and administration†	97.5	
Loss on disposal of building*	2.0	
Interest charges	1.9	
Taxes	45.0	491.4
Net income for period		13.2
Add beginning retained earnings		10.0
		23.2
Less: Appropriation for bond retirement	5.0	
Cash dividends	15.0	
Stock dividends	3.0	23.0
Ending retained earnings		$ 0.2

*Book value of equipment was $3; of buildings $4.
†Includes depreciation on equipment of $2; on building of $1.

Company
Comparative Position Statements
End of Year (Account Form)

Assets	First Year		Second Year		Increases (Decreases)	
Current:						
Cash	$10		$33.0		$ 23.0	
Petty cash	1		0.5		(0.5)	
Marketable securities	5	$ 16	3.0	$ 36.5	(2.0)	$20.5

Comparative Position Statements (Continued)

Assets	First Year		Second Year		Increases (Decreases)	
Receivables:					$(10.0)	
Accounts	$20		$10.0			
Less doubtful accounts	2	18	2.0	$ 8.0	$(10.0)	
Interest			0.5	8.5	0.5	(9.5)
Inventories		30		35.0		5.0
Prepaids		1		0.5		(0.5)
		$ 65		$ 80.5		$15.5
Long-term investments:						
Investments in bonds	$10		10.1		0.1	
Bond sinking fund	5	15	10.0	20.1	5.0	5.1
Plant:						
Land	$ 5		$ 5.0			
Buildings	$30		$25		$(5.0)	
Less accumulated depreciation	5	25	5	20.0		(5.0)
Equipment	$40		$46		$ 6.0	
Less accumulated depreciation	10	30	11	35.0	(1.0)	5.0
Tools	5	65	4.0	64.0	(1.0)	(1.0)
Intangibles:					$ (0.5)	
Goodwill	3		2.5			
Organization costs	2	5	2.0	4.5		(0.5)
		$150		$169.1		$19.1
Equities						
Current Liabilities:						
Payables:						
Accounts	$20		$30.0		$10.0	
Less cash discounts	1	$ 19	2.0	$ 28.0	1.0	$ 9.0
Salaries		3		5.0		2.0
Dividends				5.0		5.0
Taxes		1		6.0		5.0
Interest		1		1.0		
		$ 24		45.0		$21.0
Long-term liabilities:						
Note	$ 5		$ 5.0			
Bond	$30		$30.0			
Add premium	1	31	0.9	30.9	$(0.1)	(0.1)
		36		35.9		
		$ 60		$ 80.9		$20.9
Ownership:						
Capital stock:						
Par	$50		$52.0		2.0	
Premium	25	$75	26.0	$78.0	1.0	$3.0

Comparative Position Statements (Continued)

Equities	First Year			Second Year			Increases (Decreases)		
Retained earnings:									
Appropriated for bond retirement	$ 5			$10.0			$ 5.0		
Unappropriated	10	15	90	0.2	10.2	88.2	(9.8)	(4.8)	$ (1.8)
			$150			$169.1			$19.1

The Preparation of a Cash Fund-flow Statement

1. Determine the net change in funds according to the definition of fund selected for statement preparation. For example, the changes in the cash accounts may be recorded as below, to determine the net change in cash funds for the period.

Net Cash Change (Internal)

Debit (increases)	*Credit (decreases)*	
Cash 23.0	Petty Cash	0.5
	Marketable Securities	2.0
	✔	20.5
23.0	23.0	
✔ 20.5		

2. Prepare T accounts for every non-fund account the balance of which has changed during the period, and record the net change in each account.

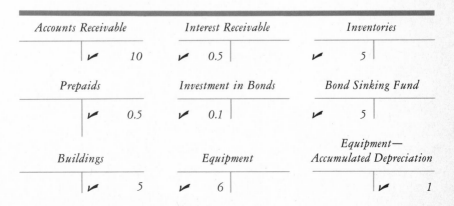

Accounts Receivable	*Interest Receivable*	*Inventories*
✔ 10	✔ 0.5	✔ 5

Prepaids	*Investment in Bonds*	*Bond Sinking Fund*
✔ 0.5	✔ 0.1	✔ 5

Buildings	*Equipment*	*Equipment— Accumulated Depreciation*
✔ 5	✔ 6	✔ 1

Tools		Goodwill		Accounts Payable	
	✔ 1		✔ 0.5		✔ 10

Accounts Payable— Allowance for Cash Discounts		Salaries Payable		Dividends Payable	
✔ 1			✔ 2		✔ 5

Taxes Payable		Bonds Payable—Premium		Capital Stock—Par	
	✔ 5	✔ 0.1			✔ 2

Capital Stock—Premium		Retained Earnings Appropriated for Bond Retirement		Retained Earnings— Unappropriated	
	✔ 1		✔ 5	✔ 9.8	

Sales		Sales—Doubtful Accounts		Interest Revenue	
	✔ 500	✔ 1			✔ 2.6

Gain on Disposal of Marketable Securities		Gains on Disposal of Equipment		Cost of Goods Sold	
	✔ 1		✔ 2	✔ 345	

Selling and Administrative Expense		Loss on Disposal of of Building		Taxes	
✔ 97.5		✔ 2		✔ 45	

Interest Charges	
✔ 1.9	

3. Identify those transactions that caused changes in a cash account or caused non-cash changes, and make appropriate entries in the T accounts.

The first revenue account, Sales, is closely related to the contra-revenue account, Sales—Doubtful Accounts, and to the non-cash asset account, Accounts Receivable. The decline of $10 in Accounts Receivable (since there is no change in the Accounts Receivable—Allowance for Doubtful Accounts balance) indicates that $10 of the opening balance was collected during the period in addition to the net sales figure. Our entry is as follows:

Accounts Receivable			Sales			Sales—Doubtful Accounts		
(a)	10	✔ 10	(a)	500	✔ 500	✔	1	(a) 1

Cash Fund Flow (External)

(a)	509	Sales and Collections on Accounts Receivable

Interest Revenue, is closely related to the non-cash asset accounts, Interest Receivable and Investment in Bonds. The increase of $0.5 in Interest Receivable implies that $0.5 of the $2.6 Interest Revenue was not received in cash during the period. The other account related to Interest Revenue is Investment in Bonds which increased $0.1 (which could have occurred only by amortizing discount on the bonds); this $0.1 of Interest Revenue will not be received in cash until the bonds are sold or surrendered for their face amount at maturity.

Interest Receivable			Investment in Bonds			Interest Revenue		
✔	0.5	(b) 0.5	✔	0.1	(b) 0.1	(b) 2.6	✔	2.6

Cash Fund Flow (External)

(a)	509	Sales and Collections on Accounts Receivable
(b)	2	Interest Revenue

The next revenue account is the Gain on the Disposal of Marketable Securities. Since Marketable Securities are regarded as cash, this is easy to analyze: no other non-cash accounts can be involved, this can be closed out.

Gain on Disposal of Marketable Securities			Cash Fund Flow (External)		
(c)	1	✔ 1	(a)	509	Sales and Collections on Accounts Receivable
			(b)	2	Interest Revenue
			(c)	1	Gain on Disposal of Marketable Securities

The next and last revenue account, Gain on Disposal of Equipment, however, is more difficult to analyze for at least two reasons.

First, when we inspect the change in the Equipment account, we note that the change represents an increase although a disposal would be recorded as a decrease. Apparently the change in the Equipment account is net (not gross), and we shall have to analyze it and the related accounts further to determine the gross increase (acquisitions) and gross decrease (disposals). The second difficulty is that Gain on Disposal of Equipment is only part of the cash proceeds received from the disposal. Although it is technically correct to list the gain as part of revenues on the fund-flow statement, it would be a better statement if the total proceeds from the disposal were shown as a single increase of cash on the statement.

Equipment			Equipment—Accumulated Depreciation		
✔	6		(d_1) Depreciation	2	✔ 1
(d_2) Disposal	4	(d_3) 10 Purchase			(d_2) 1
	10	10		2	2

Selling and Administrative Expense			Gain on Disposal of Equipment		
✔	97.5	(d_1) 2 Depreciation on Equipment	(d_2)	2	✔ 2

Cash Fund Flow (External)

		(a)	509	Sales and Collections on Accounts Receivable
		(b)	2	Interest Revenue
		(c)	1	Gain on Disposal of Marketable Securities
Acquisitions:				
(d_3) Equipment	10	(d_2)	5	Disposal of Equipment

From the income statement we learn that the net increase to the Equipment—Accumulated Depreciation was $2; since the related account is Selling and Administrative Expense, a non-cash account, we make an entry into these two accounts, reversing the original entry (d_1). Now we can see by inspection that the net decrease in the Equipment—Accumulated Depreciation account must have been $1; this logically must have been the accumulated depreciation on the disposed equipment. However, we would have difficulty analyzing the increase in the equipment account further if we were not told on the income statement that the book value of the disposed equipment was $3 (since otherwise we have two unknown accounts, the cash proceeds and the book value of the disposed property). If the book value is $3, and the accumulated depreciation is $1, then the original cost value of the equipment was $4. It follows that the cash proceeds were $5 [because the Gain was $2, see entry (d_2)]. After computing the original value of the disposed equipment, it is possible to deduce that the purchase of equipment for the period was $10 [see entry (d_3)].

Next, if we sum the change in Inventories, an increase of $5, and the increase in the Cost of Goods Sold, $345, and deduct the net increase in Accounts Payable of $9 (Accounts Payable $10 less the increase in the contra account, Accounts Payable—Allowance for Cash Discount $1), we conclude that $341 was disbursed in cash for goods [see entry (e)].

Inventories		*Accounts Payable*		*Accounts Payable—Allowance for Cash Discount*	
✔ 5	(e) 5	(e) 10	✔ 10	✔ 1	(e) 1

Cost of Goods Sold		*Cash Fund Flow (External)*			
✔ 345	(e) 345	Current Outlays:			
		(e) Cost of Goods Sold 341	(a) 509	Sales and Collections on Accounts Receivable	
			(b) 2	Interest Revenue	
			(c) 1	Gain on Disposal of Marketable Securities	
		Acquisitions:			
		(d_3) Equipment 10	(d_2) 5	Disposal of Equipment	

Next, consider Selling and Administrative Expense which is related to the non-cash accounts (in addition to Equipment—Accumulated Depreciation), Prepaids, Buildings, Buildings—Accumulated Depreciation, Loss on Disposal of Building, Tools, Goodwill, and Salaries Payable as follows:

Prepaids		*Buildings*		*Buildings—Accumulated Depreciation*	
(f) 0.5	✔ 0.5	(g_2) 5	✔ 5	(g_1) 1	(g_2) 1

Tools		*Goodwill*		*Loss on Disposal of Building*	
(h) 1	✔ 1	(h) 0.5	✔ 0.5	✔ 2	(g_2) 2

Salaries Payable		
(i)	2 ✔	2 ✔

Selling and Administrative Expense			
	97.5	(d_1)	2	Depreciation on Equipment
		(f)	0.5	Prepaids
		(g_1)	1	Depreciation on Buildings
		(h)	1.5	Tools and Goodwill
		(i)	2	Salaries Payable
		(j)	90.5	
	97.5		97.5	

Cash Fund Flow (External)

Current Outlays:				
(e) Cost of Goods Sold	341	(a)	509	Sales and Collections on Accounts Receivable
		(b)	2	Interest Revenue
(j) Selling and Administration	90.5	(c)	1	Gain on Disposal of Marketable Securities
Acquisitions:				
(d_3) Equipment	10	(d_2)	5	Disposal of Equipment
		(g_2)	2	Disposal of Building

Next, consider the remaining income statement accounts, Taxes (which is related to the non-fund account, Taxes Payable) and Interest Charges [which is related to the non-fund accounts, Interest Payable, Bonds Payable—Premium (and Bonds Payable, which may be ignored)] and the closely related accounts, Retained Earnings—Unappropriated (which is related to Dividends Payable, Retained Earnings Appropriated for Bond Retirement, Capital Stock—Par and Capital Stock—Premium). If we add the net income for the year to the Retained Earnings—Unappropriated, this account is balanced too.

Taxes		
✔ 45	(k_1)	5
	(k_2)	40
45		45

Taxes Payable		
(k_1)	5	✔ 5

Dividends Payable		
(k_5) Dividend Declared	15	✔ 5
		(k_6) 10 Dividend Paid
	15	15

Bonds Payable—Premium		
✔ 0.1	(k_3)	0.1

Interest Charges		
✔	1.9	(k_4) 2
(k_3)	0.1	
	2.0	2

Capital Stock—Par

(i_2)	2	✔	2

Capital Stock—Premium

(i_2)	1	✔	1

Retained Earnings Appropriated for Bond Retirement

(i_1)	5	✔	5

Retained Earnings Unappropriated

✔		9.8	(k_5) 15	Dividend Declared
			(i_1) 5	Appropriation for
Net Income				Bond Retirement
for Year		13.2	(i_2) 3	Stock Dividend
		23.0	23	

Cash Fund Flow (External)

Current Outlays:					
(e)	Cost of Goods Sold	341.0	(a)	509	Sales and Collections
(j)	Selling and Administration	90.5			on Accounts Receivable
(k_2)	Taxes Paid	40.0	(b)	2	Interest Revenue
(k_4)	Interest Paid	2.0	(c)	1	Gain on Disposal of
(k_6)	Dividend Paid	10.0			Marketable Securities
Acquisitions:			(d_2)	5	Disposal of Equipment
(d_3)	Equipment	10.0	(g_2)	2	Disposal of Building

Then, the last account, Bond Sinking Fund:

Bond Sinking Fund

✔	5	(m)	5

Cash Fund Flow (External)

(e)	Cost of Goods Sold	341.0	(a)	509	Sales and Collections
(j)	Selling and Administration	90.5			on Accounts Receivable
(k_2)	Taxes Paid	40.0	(b)	2	Interest Revenue
(k_4)	Interest Paid	2.0	(c)	1	Gain on Disposal of
(k_6)	Dividend Paid	10.0			Marketable Securities
Acquisitions:			(d_2)	5	Disposal of Equipment
(d_3)	Equipment	10.0	(g_2)	2	Disposal of Building
(m)	Bond Sinking Fund Deposit	5.0			

Finally if we add the net cash increase $20.5 [transferred from the T account Net Cash Change (Internal)], we will have balanced our Cash Fund Flow (External) account as follows:

Cash Fund Flow (External)

Current Outlays:					
(e)	Cost of Goods Sold	341.0	(a)	509	Sales and Collections
(j)	Selling and Administration	90.5			on Accounts Receivable
(k₂)	Taxes Paid	40.0	(b)	2	Interest Revenue
(k₄)	Interest Paid	2.0	(c)	1	Gain on Disposal of
(k₆)	Dividend Paid	10.0			Marketable Securities
	Acquisitions		(d₂)	5	Disposal of Equipment
(d₃)	Equipment	10.0	(g₂)	2	Disposal of Building
(m)	Bond Sinking Fund Deposit	5.0			
	Net Cash Increase	20.5			
		519.0		519	

This T account is the basis for preparing the following cash fund-flow statement using the complete report format:

Company
Cash Fund-flow
Statement
for Year 2
(000's omitted)

Increases in Cash			Decreases in Cash		
From revenues:			Current outlays:		
Sales and collections			Cost of goods sold		$341.0
on accounts receivable		$509	Selling and		
			administration		90.5
Interest		2	Interest charges		2.0
Gain on disposal of			Income taxes		40.0
marketable securities		1			473.5
		512			
			Dividends paid		10.0
From disposals:			Acquisitions:		
Equipment	$5		Equipment	$10	
Building	2	7	Bond sinking fund		
			deposit	5	15.0
			Net increase in cash		
			(see schedule)		20.5
		$519			$519.0

Company
Net Increase in
Cash Schedule
for Year 2
(000's omitted)

	End of Year 1	End of Year 2	Increase (Decrease)
Cash	$10	$33.0	$23.0
Petty cash	1	0.5	(0.5)
Marketable securities	5	3.0	(2.0)
Net increase in cash	$16	$36.5	$20.5

The following long-form analytical format for the cash fund-flow statement is preferred, because it reports operations on a cash fund basis, thus giving another measure of the company's performance for the period:

Company
Cash Fund-flow
Statement
for Year 2
(000's omitted)

Increases in Cash			Decreases in Cash		
From operations:			*Dividends paid*		$10.0
Revenues:			*Acquisitions:*		
Sales and collections	$509		Equipment	$10	
Interest	2		Bond sinking fund		
Gain on disposal of			deposit	5	15.0
marketable securities	1	$512.0			
Current outlays:					
Cost of goods sold	341.0				
Selling and					
administration	90.5				
Interest paid	2.0				
Income taxes	40.0	473.5			
Cash from current					
operations		38.5			
Other increases:					
From disposals:					
Equipment	5				
Building	2	7.0	Net increase in cash		20.5
		$ 45.5			$45.5

As explained earlier, however, the most frequently used format for presenting a fund-flow statement starts with a net income figure (from the income statement of the period) and adjusts it by adding back those deductions on the income statement that did not require the outlay of cash, and by deducting those additions on the income statement that did not provide cash.

The procedure given here can be modified easily to provide for the preparation of a cash fund-flow statement on this basis by using a Net Income T account (and thus eliminating all the income statement accounts) and making the adjustments to this account in the following manner:

		Net Income			
(b)	Interest Revenue	0.6	✔	13.2	
(d₂)	Gain on Disposal of		(a)	10.0	Collections
	Equipment	2.0	(d₁)	2.0	Depreciation on
(k₄)	Interest Charge	0.1			Equipment
			(e)	4.0	Cost of Goods Sold

	Net Income (Continued)			
		(f)	0.5	Prepaids
		(g₁)	1.0	Depreciation on Buildings
		(g₂)	2.0	Loss on Disposal of Building
		(h)	1.5	Tools and Goodwill
		(i)	2.0	Salaries
✔	38.5	(k₁)	5.0	Taxes
	41.2		41.2	
		✔	38.5	Net Increase in Cash from Operations

which can be presented in statement remainder type account format, as follows:

*Company
Cash Fund-flow
Statement
for Year 2*

Increases in Cash			Decreases in Cash		
From operations:			Dividends paid		$10.0
Net income		$13.2	Acquisitions:		
Add back deductions not requiring cash outlays:			Equipment	$10	
Collections of accounts receivable	$10		Bond sinking fund deposit	5	15.0
Taxes	5				
Cost of goods sold	4				
Depreciation	3				
Salaries	2				
Loss on disposal of building	2				
Tools, goodwill, and prepaids	2	28.0			
		41.2			
Less for additions not providing cash:					
Interest revenue	0.6				
Gain on disposal of equipment	2.0				
Interest charges	0.1	2.7			
Cash provided from current operations		38.5			
From disposals:					
Equipment	5.0				
Building	2.0	7.0	Net increase in cash		20.5
		$45.5			$45.5

The major shortcoming of this statement is that it tends to convey to the reader the false impression that the cash of the firm was increased through recording depreciation and amortizing goodwill. Despite this misleading impression, this format continues to be used because it can be prepared in less time by the professional accountant (if not the student of accounting). The major shortcoming of this format could be corrected if only the Cash Provided from Current Operations was included on the statement (and the details of how it was computed were omitted).

The Preparation of a Net Short-term Monetary Assets Fund-flow Statement

Net Short-term Monetary Assets Fund-flow Statement

Net Short-term Monetary Assets Change (Internal)

	Debit		Credit
Cash	23.0	Petty Cash	0.5
Interest Receivable	0.5	Marketable Securities	2.0
Accounts Payable—Allowance		Accounts Receivable	10.0
for Cash Discounts	1.0	Accounts Payable	10.0
		Salaries Payable	2.0
		Dividends Payable	5.0
✔	10.0	Taxes Payable	5.0
	34.5		34.5

	✔ Net Decrease in Net Short-term Monetary Assets	10.0

and:

Inventories				*Prepaids*			*Investment in Bonds*	
✔ 5	(e)	5	(f)	0.5	✔ 0.5	✔ 0.1	(b)	0.1

Bond Sinking Fund			*Buildings*			*Equipment*		
✔ 5	(m)	5	(g₂) 5	✔ 5	✔	6	(d₃) 10	Purchase
					(d₂) Disposal	4		
						10	10	

Buildings— Accumulated Depreciation

(g₁)	1	(g₂)	1

Equipment—Accumulated Depreciation				Tools			Goodwill		
(d_1) Depreciation	2	✔	1	(h) 1	✔	1	(h) 0.5	✔	0.5
		(d_2)	1 Disposal						
	2		2						

Bonds Payable—Premium				Capital Stock—Par				Capital Stock—Premium			
✔	0.1	(k_3)	0.1	(i_2)	2	✔	2	(i_2)	1	✔	1

Retained Earnings Appropriated for Bond Retirement

(i_1)	5	✔	5

Retained Earnings Unappropriated

✔		9.8	(k_5)	15.0 Dividend Declared
			(i_1)	5.0 Appropriation for Bond Retirement
Net Income for Year		13.2	(i_2)	3.0 Stock Dividend
		23.0		23.0

Net Income

(b)	Interest Revenue	0.1	✔	13.2	
(d_2)	Gain on Disposal of Equipment	2.0	(d_1)	2.0	Depreciation on Equipment
(e)	Cost of Goods Sold	5.0	(f)	0.5	Prepaids
(k_3)	Interest Charge	0.1	(g_1)	1.0	Depreciation on Building
✔		13.0	(g_2)	2.0	Loss on Disposal of Building
			(h)	1.5	Tools and Goodwill
		20.2		20.2	
			✔	13.0	Net Increase in Net Short-term Monetary Assets from Operations

Net Short-term Monetary Assets Fund Flow (External)

(k_5)	Dividend Declared	15.0	✔	13.0	Net Increase in Net Short-term Monetary
(d_3)	Equipment Purchase	10.0			

(m)	Bond Sinking Fund Deposit	5.0			Assets from Operations
			(d_2)	5.0	Disposal of Equipment
			(g_2)	2.0	Disposal of Building
				10.0	Net Decrease in Net Short-term Monetary Assets
		30.0		30.0	

Company
Net Short-term
Monetary Assets
Fund-flow Statement
for Year 2
(000's omitted)

Increases in Net Short-term Monetary Assets			Decreases in Net Short-term Monetary Assets		
From operations:		$13	Dividends		$15
From disposals:			Acquisitions:		
Equipment	$5		Equipment	$10	
Building	2	7	Bond sinking fund		
Net decrease in net short-term (monetary) assets		10	deposit	5	15
		$30			$30

Company
Net Decrease in Net
Short-term Monetary
Assets Schedule
for Year 2
(000's omitted)

	Balances End of Year 1	End of Year 2	Increase (Decrease)
Cash	$10	$33.0	$ 23.0
Petty cash	1	0.5	(.5)
Marketable securities	5	3.0	(2.0)
Accounts receivable	20	10.0	(10.0)
Accounts receivable—allowance for doubtful accounts	2	2.0	
Interests receivable		0.5	0.5
	$34	$45.0	$ 11.0
Accounts payable	$20	$30.0	$ 10.0
Accounts payable—allowance for cash discounts	(1)	(2.0)	(1.0)
Salaries payable	3	5.0	2.0
Dividends payable		5.0	5.0
Taxes payable	1	6.0	5.0
Interest payable	1	1.0	
	$24	$45.0	$ 21.0
Net decrease in net short-term monetary assets	$14	$ 0.0	$(10.0)

Note that the remainder type account format statement above lists only the final figure from operations, thus avoiding the chief criticism of the income-adjusted approach [namely, that when these adjustments are shown on the fund-flow statement, the impression is created that such are increases (and decreases) of funds], while retaining its merit by not repeating income statement data.

The Preparation of a Working Capital Fund-flow Statement

Working Capital Change (Internal)

Cash	23.0	Petty Cash	0.5
Interest Receivable	0.5	Marketable Securities	2.0
Inventories	5.0	Accounts Receivable	10.0
Accounts Payable—Allowance		Prepaids	0.5
for Cash Discounts	1.0	Accounts Payable	10.0
		Salaries Payable	2.0
		Dividends Payable	5.0
✔	5.5	Taxes Payable	5.0
	35.0		35.0

✔ Net Decrease in Working Capital   5.5

Investment in Bonds		Bond Sinking Fund		Buildings	
✔ 0.1	(b) 0.1	✔ 5	(m) 5	(g₂) 5	✔ 5

Buildings—Accumulated Depreciation		Equipment		Tools	
(g₁) 1	(g₂) 1	✔ 6	(d₃) 10 Pur-	(b) 1	✔ 1
		(d₂) Dis-	chase		
		posal 4		Goodwill	
		10	10	(b) 0.5	✔ 0.5

Equipment—Accumulated Depreciation		Bonds Payable—Premium		Capital Stock—Par	
(d₁) Depre-	✔ 1	✔ 0.1	(k₃) 0.1	(i₂) 2	✔ 2
ciation 2	(d₂) 1 Dis-				
	posal				
2	2				

Capital Stock—Premium

(i_2)	1	✔	1

Retained Earnings Appropriated for Bond Retirement

(i_1)	5	✔	5

Retained Earnings—Unappropriated

✔		9.8	(k_5)	15 Dividend Declared
			(i_1)	5 Appropriated for Bond
Income for				Retirement
Year		13.2	(i_2)	3
		23.0		23

Net Income

(b)	Interest Revenue	0.1	✔	13.2	
(d_2)	Gain on Disposal of Equipment	2.0	(d_1)	2.0	Depreciation on Equipment
(k_3)	Interest Charge	0.1	(g_1)	1.0	Depreciation on Building
✔	Net Increase in Working Capital from Operations	17.5	(g_2)	2.0	Loss on Disposal of Building
			(h)	1.5	Tools and Goodwill
		19.7		19.7	
			✔	17.5	Net Increase in Working Capital from Operations

Working Capital Fund Flow (External)

(k_5)	Dividends Declared	15.0		17.5	Net Increase in Working Capital from Operations
(d_3)	Equipment Purchase	10.0	(d_2)	5.0	Disposal of Equipment
(m)	Bond Sinking Fund Deposit	5.0	(g_2)	2.0	Disposal of Building
				5.5	Net Decrease in Working Capital
		30.0		30.0	

Company
Working Capital
Fund-flow Statement
for Year 2
(000's omitted)

Increases in Working Capital			Decreases in Working Capital		
From operations		$17.5	Dividends declared		$15
From disposals:			Acquisitions:		
Equipment	$5		Equipment	$10	
Building	2	7.0	Bond sinking fund	5	15
Net decrease in working			deposit		
capital		5.5			
		$30.0			$30

Company
Net Decrease
in Working Capital
Schedule for Year 2
(000's omitted)

	Balances		
	End of Year 1	End of Year 2	Increases (Decreases)
Cash	$10	$33.0	$ 23.0
Petty cash fund	1	0.5	(0.5)
Marketable securities	5	3.0	(2.0)
Accounts receivable	20	10.0	(10.0)
Accounts receivable allowance for doubtful accounts	(2)	(2.0)	
Interest receivable		0.5	0.5
Inventories	30	35.0	5.0
Prepaids	1	0.5	(0.5)
	65	80.5	15.5
Accounts payable	20	30.0	10.0
Accounts payable—allowance for cash discounts	(1)	(2.0)	(1.0)
Salaries payable	3	5.0	2.0
Dividends payable		5.0	5.0
Taxes payable	1	6.0	5.0
Interest payable	1	1.0	
	24	45.0	21.0
Net decrease in working capital	$41	$35.5	$ (5.5)

Applications of the All-changes-in-financial-position Concept A concept that may be applied to any definition of the fund is the all-changes-in-financial-position concept. As presented in the AICPA's APB Opinion No. 19, a fund-flow statement applying this concept to the working capital definition would differ from the preceding statement and schedule in only two respects (assuming that the gains or losses on disposal on building or equipment are not extraordinary items): (1) the statement title would be Statement of Changes in Financial Position and (2) the Increases in Working Capital section would begin with Net Income and add back (or deduct) income statement items that did not change working capital (as was illustrated earlier using the cash definition).

If the preceding working capital fund-flow statement had used the format that begins with the revenues (as was illustrated for the cash definition) the statement would conform except in title to an alternate format that is considered acceptable in APB Opinion No. 19.

If the all-changes-in-financial-position concept as recommended in APB Opinion No. 19 had been applied to the cash fund-flow statement using either the format beginning with net income or with revenue, there would be a different title and another change. Changes in the other working capital accounts could be listed in the body of the statement. Since this modification is a simple one, it will not be illustrated.

The illustrations given here conform so closely to the recommendations of APB Opinion No. 19 because the Company situation does not include important transactions that affect only non-fund accounts (e.g., the issuance of capital stock for plant assets or the conversion of bonds payable into capital stock).

Questions

6-1

	December 31 (000's omitted) 1972	1973
Current assets	$100	$130
Plant	80	100
Plant—accumulated depreciation	(20)	(24)
	$160	$206
Current liabilities	$ 60	$ 49
Bonds payable		49
Capital stock	90	97
Retained earnings	10	11
	$160	$206

Data for 1973:   Net income $6
                 Depreciation   4
                 Dividends   5

The bonds were sold on December 31, 1973; no depreciable property was disposed of during the period.

(1) The working capital made available from operations was: (a) $1, (b) $5, (c) $6, (d) $10, (e) $25

(2) The increase in working capital was: (a) $9, (b) $10, (c) $25, (d) $41, (e) $46

(3) The sale of bonds provided working capital amounting to: (a) $49, (b) $50, (c) $51, (d) $54, (e) $58

(4) Working capital is supplied by: (a) issuance of stock dividends, (b) amortization of goodwill, (c) depreciation on office equipment, (d) depletion of natural resource, (e) none of these.

6-2   The senior vice-president of the Bank of America National Trust and Savings Association, in describing the evaluation of accounting data, stated recently that an attempt is made to determine the extent to which a customer's current assets "can be converted into cash to pay back the loan and other liabilities in the regular course of business." In this connection, he states that other items such as the cash surrender of life insurance and real estate not used in the business are also evaluated. If this type of evaluation is general among credit analysts, define the concept of fund flow that they would find most useful.

6-3   Accountants are upset when depreciation is classified as an increase in working capital. Explain: (1) why this is regarded as an error, (2) how accountants often give the impression that this classification is correct, and (3) under what special circumstances depreciation may actually provide for an increase in working capital.

6-4   Only those transactions that affect *both* working capital and nonworking capital accounts should be reported in the body of the working capital fund-flow statement. According to this rule: (1) List the transactions (and the accounts that are changed) which should be reported on the fund-flow statement. (2) List the substantive transactions (and the accounts that are changed) which should not be reported on the fund-flow statement.

6-5   Explain the relationship between depreciation and working capital.

6-6   If one were to define a fund as Retained Earnings, what kind of fund-flow statement would be generated?

6-7

Position Statement, January 1, 1972 (000's omitted)		Working Capital Fund-flow Statement For 1972 (000's omitted)		
Current assets:	$20	Balance, January 1, 1972		$17
Buildings	13	Increases:		
Buildings—accumulated		Operations:		
depreciation	(3)	Net income	$20	
Equipment	23	Loss on sale of equipment	3	
Equipment—accumulated		Depreciation on buildings	1	
depreciation	(2)	Depreciation on equipment	1	25
Organization cost	4	Issue of stock		5
	$55	Disposal of equipment		7
				54

Position Statement, January 1, 1972 (000's omitted) (Continued)		Working Capital Fund-flow Statement For 1972 (000's omitted) (Continued)		
Current liabilities:	$ 3	Decreases:		
Capital stock	5	Dividends	$ 6	
Retained earnings	47	Purchases: Land	2	
	$55	Buildings	4	
		Equipment	12	$24
		Balance, December 31, 1972		$30

Total assets on the December 31, 1972 position statement are $71. Accumulated depreciation on the equipment sold was $1. Organization cost of $1 was charged directly to retained earnings in error.

(1) When the equipment was sold, the equipment account was credited for an amount between: (a) $0 and $2, (b) $6 and $8, (c) $10 and $12, (d) $13 and $15, (e) over $16.

(2) The current assets on December 31, 1972 are: (a) $10–15, (b) $16–21, (c) $22–27, (d) $28–33, (e) over $33.

(3) The balance in retained earnings on December 31, 1972 is: (a) $45–50, (b) $51–56, (c) $57–62, (d) $63–68, (e) $69–74.

(4) Capital stock account(s) on December 31, 1972 is: (a) $5, (b) $6, (c) $10, (d) $12, (e) $15.

(5) Organization cost: (a) at the end of the year cannot be determined, (b) should have appeared in the working capital fund-flow statement as an addition to net income, (c) should have appeared in the working capital fund-flow statement as a deduction from net income, (d) should not be added to net income in this case, (e) does not affect retained earnings.

(6) Loss on disposal of equipment: (a) appears on the income statement, (b) appears as a direct charge to Retained Earnings, (c) is not an increase in working capital but a provision of working capital, (d) is not a decrease in working capital but rather a use of working capital, (e) is none of the above.

(7) Net income for the period was: (a) $20, (b) $15, (c) $25, (d) $19, (e) $22.

6–8   For a working capital fund-flow statement, transactions 1 to 5 are to be classified according to one of the following categories:

a. A transaction that represents an *increase* in working capital.

b. A transaction that represents a *decrease* in working capital.

c. A transaction that requires an *addition* to net income in determining the working capital made available from normal operations.

d. A transaction that requires a *deduction* from net income in determining the working capital made available from normal operations.

e. None of the above categories is applicable.

(1) Annual estimation of depreciation on delivery equipment
(2) Collection of accounts receivable
(3) Sale of capital stock
(4) Annual amortization of premium on bond payable
(5) Annual deposit of cash in a bond retirement fund as required by the bond

6-9   Prepare a one-page essay evaluating the application of the all-changes-in-financial-position concept to the conventional working capital fund-flow statement.

6-10   Specify what transactions would be treated differently when the all-changes-in-financial-position concept is applied to a conventional working capital fund-flow statement. Illustrate.

6-11   When adjusting the net income (net loss) to determine the increase in working capital from operations, determine which of the following items are added back (AB) or deducted (D). Prepare solution on a separate sheet of paper.

	Reported Net Income	Reported Net Loss
(1) Depreciation	_____	_____
(2) Depletion	_____	_____
(3) Amortization of intangible	_____	_____
(4) Amortization of unamortized bond payable discount	_____	_____
(5) Amortization of unamortized bond payable premium	_____	_____
(6) Gains on disposal of noncurrent assets	_____	_____
(7) Losses on disposal of noncurrent assets	_____	_____
(8) Gains on disposal of current assets	_____	_____
(9) Losses on disposal of current assets	_____	_____
(10) Amortization of bonds receivable premium	_____	_____

6-12   Accountants consider working capital to be a very useful concept. Do you agree? Consider the problems of defining and measuring it.

Problems

6-1

Prepare a statement of working capital fund flow for the year 1971.

*Comparative Balance
Sheets
December 31
(000's omitted)*

	1970	1971
Current assets	$ 37.5	$ 30.00
Land	22.5	34.00
Buildings (net)	75.0	87.75
Machinery and equipment (net)	112.5	75.00
	$247.5	$226.75
Current liabilities	$ 15.0	$ 22.00
Bonds payable	90.0	60.00
Preferred stock	45.0	30.00
Common stock	75.0	90.00
Retained earnings	22.5	24.75
	$247.5	$226.75

*Retained Earnings
Analysis
(000's omitted)*

Balance, January 1, 1971		$22.50
Net income for 1971		27.25
		49.75
Dividends:		
Cash	$10	
Stock	15	25.00
Balance, December 31, 1971		$24.75

Depreciation during 1971:	
On buildings	$ 2.25
On machinery and equipment	22.50

There were no purchases of machinery and equipment, and the sales of machinery and equipment took place at book value. There were no sales of buildings.

6-2

You are given the following working capital fund-flow statement for the calendar year 1973, together with a balance sheet at December 31, 1972, for the Baiman Co. Using this information, you are to prepare a balance sheet at December 31, 1973

Baiman Co. Balance Sheet December 31, 1972		(000's omitted)	Baiman Co. Working Capital Fund-flow Statement For Year Ended December 31, 1973		
Current assets	$16		Beginning working capital		$12
Land	3		Increases:		
Buildings—	15		Operations:		
accumulated depreciation	(3)		Net income	$16	
Equipment—	21		Loss on sale		
accumulated depreciation	(2)		of equipment	3	
	$50		Depreciation		
			on buildings	1	
			Depreciation		
Current liabilities	$ 4		on equipment	1	$21
Capital stock	10				
Retained earnings	36		Sales: Capital stock	5	
	$50		Equipment	7	33
					45
			Decreases:		
			Payment of dividends	6	
			Purchases: Land	2	
			Buildings	4	
			Equipment	7	19
			Ending working capital		$26

Total assets on the December 31, 1973 balance sheet are $70; $0.5 depreciation had accumulated on equipment that was sold.

6–3

The Cleverley Corporation Comparative Balance Sheets December 31 (000's omitted)

	1972	1973
Current assets	$46.0	$ 64.0
Investments	12.0	7.8
Machinery	6.0	9.0
Building	17.0	23.0
Land	10.0	13.0
Patents	3.5	3.2
	$94.5	$120.0
Current liabilities	$ 8.0	$ 10.0
Mortgage payable	15.0	13.5
Accumulated depreciation:		
Machinery	1.0	2.5
Building	4.0	6.0
Capital stock	50.0	60.0
Retained earnings	16.5	28.0
	$94.5	$120.0

Additional information:
(1) Dividends paid amounted to $5.
(2) A portion of the investments was sold at a gain of $1.5.
(3) Machinery with a cost of $1.2 and accumulated depreciation of $0.8 was sold at a gain of $0.7.

Prepare a working capital fund-flow statement for 1973.

6-4 From the following information, prepare a cash-flow statement for 1973 (000's omitted).

	January 1	December 31
Cash	$ 721	$ 218
Accounts receivable	1,436	2,223
Temporary investments	2,000	
Prepaid assets	141	214
Inventories	3,876	6,421
Investment in subsidiary company—at cost	2,400	3,400
Land	861	883
Buildings	5,473	8,321
Buildings—accumulated depreciation	(2,121)	(2,430)
Equipment	3,418	5,621
Equipment—accumulated depreciation	(1,420)	(1,810)
	$16,785	$23,061
Accounts payable	$ 423	$ 760
Miscellaneous accrued payables	213	311
Income taxes payable	100	500
Mortgage payable	1,000	2,400
Bonds payable—issued at face value	6,000	8,000
Capital stock—$10 par	1,000	1,100
Capital stock—premium	3,500	4,030
Retained earnings	4,549	5,960
	$16,785	$23,061

Additional notes:
(1) Equipment junked—cost $165,000, accumulated depreciation $140,000
(2) Equipment traded—cost $88,000, accumulated depreciation $23,000, trade-in value $100,000
(3) Building sold—cost $141,000, accumulated depreciation $38,000, sales price $218,000
(4) 10 percent stock dividend paid during year—based on the par value of the stock
(5) Cash dividends paid amounting to $2 per share outstanding on December 31, 1973

6-5 The following are the comparative postclosing trial balances of the Krull Corporation as of December 31 (000's omitted).

	1970	1971
Cash	$ 65.0	$ 45.0
Accounts receivable (net)	35.0	25.0
Inventories	30.0	28.0
Prepaids	8.0	9.0
Investments	47.0	34.0
Land	4.0	5.0
Buildings	90.0	120.0
Equipment	79.0	90.0
Patents	14.1	12.8
	$372.1	$368.8
Accounts payable	$ 55.0	$ 37.0
Accrued payables	4.0	6.0
Federal income taxes payable	10.0	3.0
Buildings—accumulated depreciation	45.0	40.5
Equipment—accumulated depreciation	39.0	42.0
Bonds payable	50.0	50.0
Common stock	100.0	125.0
Retained earnings	69.1	65.3
	$372.1	$368.8

Prepare a net short-term monetary assets fund-flow statement for 1971 using the following supplemental data:

(1) Dividends declared during the period amounted to $12.

(2) Equipment having an original cost of $9 and accumulated depreciation of $6 was sold at a gain of $15.

(3) Part of the long-term investments was disposed of at a gain of $25.

(4) A building that originally cost $20 and had accumulated depreciation of $13.5 was sold at a loss of $3.

(5) No patents were bought or sold during 1971.

6-6

Frolin Corporation
Trial Balances
December 31
(000's omitted)

	Postclosing Trial Balance, 1971	Adjusted Trial Balance, 1972
Cash	$ 2,000	$ 3,000
Accounts receivable	8,000	7,000
Allowance for bad debts	(500)	(400)
Inventory	12,000	11,000
Plant	24,000	25,000
Plant—accumulated depreciation	(10,500)	(12,100)
Depreciation expense	-0-	2,500
Other operating expenses	-0-	11,000
Sales—bad debts	-0-	200
	$ 35,000	$ 47,200

	Postclosing Trial Balance, 1971	Adjusted Trial Balance, 1972
Accounts payable	$ 2,000	$ 3,000
Bonds payable	10,000	-0-
Capital stock	19,000	22,000
Retained earnings	4,000	4,000
Sales	-0-	18,000
Gain on sale of plant	-0-	200
	$ 35,000	$ 47,200

During the year, plant with an original cost of $2,000 and accumulated depreciation of $900, was sold for $1,300. The bonds were retired at book value on January 1, 1973. Prepare a net-quick asset fund-flow statement.

6-7   You are given the following working capital fund-flow statement for the calendar year 1975, together with a balance sheet at December 31, 1974. Using this information, prepare a statement of financial position at December 31, 1975.

Balance Sheet December 31, 1974		Working Capital Fund-flow Statement For 1975		
Current assets	$17,000	Beginning working capital		$ 4,500
Land	4,000	Increases:		
Buildings (net)	14,390	Sales: Bonds	$20,000	
Machinery and		Stock	10,000	
equipment (net)	19,110	Equipment	1,420	31,420
Goodwill	4,000			35,920
	$58,500			
		Decreases:		
Current liabilities	$12,500	Net operating loss	$3,000	
Capital stock	30,000	Depreciation on		
Retained earnings	16,000	machinery and equipment	(500)	
	$58,500	Depreciation on buildings	(400)	
		Loss on equipment sale	(1,900)	200
		Dividends		2,000
		Purchases: Land		2,000
		Machinery and equipment		1,300	5,500
		Ending working capital		$30,420

Goodwill of $1,000 was written off during the year, directly to Retained Earnings. Total equities on the December 31, 1975, balance sheet are $71,580.

6-8   The following are the changes in the account balances of Pearl Bailey's hardware business for the fiscal year ended January 31, 1971 (000's omitted):

Cash	$ 48.0
Accounts receivable	(8.0)
Accounts receivable—allowance for uncollectible accounts	(0.2)
Inventory	(15.0)
Equipment	25.0
Equipment—accumulated depreciation	10.0
Accounts payable	(5.0)
Accrued liabilities	0.4
P. Bailey, capital	44.8

The parentheses denote a decrease in the debit or credit balance normal to a given account.

Accounts receivable of $1 were written off as uncollectible. Equipment costing $7.5 was sold for $3, resulting in a loss of $0.6. Net income, including the loss on sale of equipment amounted to $64.8.

(1) Prepare a working capital fund-flow statement.
(2) Prepare a cash fund-flow statement.

6-9   Using the information presented below for the Agora Company, prepare a working capital fund-flow statement.

Excerpt from Position Statements

	1971 Debit	1971 Credit	1972 Debit	1972 Credit
Land	$15,000		$ 16,000	
Building	30,000		31,500	
Equipment	7,100		7,450	
Mortgage notes payable		$10,000		$ 9,000
Buildings and equipment— accumulated depreciation		20,000		20,650
Capital stock		50,000		52,000
Capital resulting from land write-up				1,000
Retained earnings		17,000		18,400
Working capital	44,900		46,100	
	$97,000	$97,000	$101,050	$101,050

Retained Earnings Account

Stock Dividend	$ 500	Initial Balance	$17,000
Cash Dividend	1,000	Net Income for Year	2,900
Final Balance	18,400		
	$19,900		$19,900

Depreciation was charged during the year as follows: building $400, delivery equipment $500. A new roof was put on the building, and other extraordinary repairs were made at a cost of $250, which was charged in error to the Accumulated Depreciation account.

6–10   An accounting student was asked to prepare a cash-flow statement from the following balance sheets, income statement, and additional information. His cash-flow statement is shown. Prepare a corrected statement.

Balance Sheets
1974

	January 1	December 31
Assets		
Current assets		
Cash	$ 5,000	$ 7,000
Accounts receivable	10,000	9,000
Merchandise inventory	12,000	11,000
Prepaid rent	1,000	1,500
Total	28,000	28,500
Buildings and equipment (net)	100,000	102,000
Total assets	$128,000	$130,500

Income Statement
For 1974

Revenue		$ 56,000
Expenses:		
Cost of goods sold	$30,000	
Wages	11,000	
Rent	2,000	
Depreciation	7,000	
Taxes	2,500	52,500
		3,500
Interest charges	1,000	
Dividend (in cash)	500	1,500
Change in retained earnings		$ 2,000

Additional information:
(1) All sales and purchases of merchandise are on account.
(2) Short-term notes in the amount of $2,000 (exclusive of interest) were repaid during the year.
(3) No common stock was repurchased, and no new long-term notes were issued during the year.

Cash-flow Statement

	As Prepared	As Corrected
Inflows:		
Customers	$56,000	$_____
Short-term notes	2,000	_____
Long-term notes payable	7,000	_____
Common stock	8,000	_____
Total inflows	$73,000	$_____
Outflows:		
Merchandise	$29,500	$_____
Wages	11,000	_____
Rent	2,000	_____
Buildings and equipment	7,000	_____
Interest	1,000	_____
Taxes	2,500	_____
Short-term notes payable	2,000	_____
Long-term notes payable	-0-	_____
Dividends	500	_____
Total outflows	$55,500	$_____
Net inflow or (outflow)	$17,500	$_____

6–11

*The Veritas Est Lux Co.
Statement
Showing Causes of
Net Changes in
Working Capital
for 1972*

Funds obtained from:		
Operations (net income transferred to retained earnings)		$179,001
Current assets used up in year's operations:		
Cash on hand and in banks	$ 33,427	
Postal stamps	20	33,447
Increase in common stock outstanding		30,000
		$242,448
Funds applied to:		
Payment of cash dividends		$ 35,442
Declaration of stock dividends (not yet issued)		27,400
Additional investments:		
Accounts receivable—trade	$ 10,005	
Notes receivable—trade	2,500	
Inventories	101,442	
Marketable securities	10,440	
Cash surrender value of life insurance	1,141	
Long-lived assets (net increase)	15,142	
Patents	20,000	
Prepaid costs	2,452	163,122
Payments of bond maturities		10,000
Reduction in current liabilities		6,484
		$242,448

On the basis of the preceding statement:
(1) Prepare a revised statement.
(2) List specific items which the data supplied lead you to believe (a) should have been included in the statement or (b) should have been excluded from the statement. For each item you mention, give your reason for inclusion or exclusion, and state how you would treat the item. (Note: The major effort here should be devoted to considering the *function* and *content* of the statement with form relevant only insofar as it is essential to the statement's function. There should be some consideration of what definition of funds would be most relevant.)

6–12 Note that each of the following five *fund-flow* statements is based upon a different definition of funds and uses a different statement format.

Form I. Working Capital Fund-flow Statement—Long-form Analytical Type

Net sales and other revenues	X (A)
Current outlays for expenses, taxes, and interest	−X (B)
Funds provided from operations	X
Income distribution to stockholders	−X (C)
Funds available from earnings	X
Disposal of noncurrent assets and miscellaneous	+X (D)
Funds available from earnings, disposals, and	X
miscellaneous financing	+X (E)
	X
Funds available for expansion and investment	−X (F)
Increase in working capital	X (G)

Form II. Net Short-term Monetary (or Quick) Assets Fund-flow Statement—Report Form Remainder Type

Additions to net short-term monetary assets:

Net income	X		
Addbacks	+X (H)		
Deductions	−X (I)	X	
Other		X (J)	X

Deductions from net short-term monetary assets:

Distribution of net income to bondholders, government, and stockholders		X (K)	
Other		X (L)	X
Change in net short-term monetary assets			X (M)

Form III. Cash (and Marketable Securities) Fund-flow Statement—Complete Report Form

Funds provided: Revenues	X (N)	
Other	X (O)	X

Funds applied: Expenses, interest, taxes, dividends,

etc.   X (P)

Other   X (Q)   X

Change in cash (and marketable securities)   X (R)

Form IV. Cash Fund-flow Statement—Reconciling Report Form

Net cash, beginning of period   X

Increases: Net income after interest and taxes   X

Addbacks   +X (S)

Deductions   −X (T)   X

Other   X (U)   X

Decreases: Distribution of net income   X (V)

Other   X (W)   X

Net cash, end of period   X (Y)

Form V. All-changes-in-financial-position (Working Capital) Fund-flow Statement—Balanced Account Form

Sources:	Net income	X		*Dispositions:*	Dividends	X *(cc)*
	Addbacks	+X *(Z)*			Other	X *(dd)*
	Deductions	−X *(aa)*	X			
	Other		X *(bb)*			
			X			X

For each of the following transactions, for each definition and format of the fund statement, indicate by *letter* in the blank spaces following the list where the effect would be registered. If there is no effect, leave the space blank. The "all-inclusive" concept of net income statement has been prepared.

Transactions

(1) Declaration of stock dividends (not yet issued).

(2) Issued preferred stock in exchange for equipment.

(3) Bad debts (under allowance method) estimated for period. Small amount written off.

(4) Gain on disposal of old machinery.

(5) Payment of cash dividends (previously declared).

(6) After the retirement of an officer, the insurance policy on his life was canceled, and a cash settlement was received by the firm. These proceeds were in excess of the book value of the policy.

(7) Sales Discounts lapsed and not taken by customers. (Sales recorded at net originally.)

(8) Estimated income taxes for period. Part of these are to be deferred for several years.

(9) Amortization of Bonds Payable—Premium.

(10) Loss on Sale of Marketable Securities.
(11) Two-year notes issued at discount for organization costs.
(12) Inventories—Allowance for Decline in Inventory Value was increased.
(13) Amortization of discount on Notes Receivable.
(14) Liability for maintenance service reduced as service is performed. Service has been guaranteed for two years.
(15) Decrease in Retained Earnings Appropriated for Self-insurance.
(16) Discount amortized on Investment in Bonds.
(17) The book value of marketable securities was reduced in accordance with the Locom.
(18) Note Receivable discounted at bank was dishonored at maturity date.
(19) Company had changed from Lifo to Fifo inventory method during current year. Prices had fallen since adopted Lifo.
(20) Goodwill was decreased.

	I	II	III	IV	V
(1)					
(2)					
(3)					
(4)					
(5)					
(6)					
(7)					
(8)					
(9)					
(10)					
(11)					
(12)					
(13)					
(14)					
(15)					
(16)					
(17)					
(18)					
(19)					
(20)					

6–13

Unable to account verbally to his directors for the discrepancy between the projected net income and the projected working capital changes for his corporation, the president asks you to assist him in preparing the written report explaining the difference. Prepare a Working Capital Fund-flow statement.

The net changes (decreases are in parenthesis) in the two primary statement accounts, as projected for the year 1972 (000's omitted), are as follows:

Cash	$ (25)	Accounts receivable—	
Marketable securities	75	allowance for uncollectibles	$ 5
Accounts receivable	10	Plant—accumulated depreciation	59
Inventories	50	Accounts payable	25

Current prepayments	$ 5	Accrued liabilities	$ 45
Land	50	Bonds outstanding (5%) (net)	550
Plant	150	Preferred stock (6%)	(400)
Organization costs	8	Capital from common shareholders	500
		Retained earnings appropriated	
		for casualties	(25)
		Retained earnings unappropriated	(495)
Cost of product sold	1,450	Sales	2,510
Other expenses	600		
Loss on retirements	25		
Corporation income taxes	250		
Interest charges	6		
Preferred dividends (cash)	28		
Common dividends (cash)	92		

From the footnotes, additional data are disclosed:

Depreciation:	Expensed	$106.5	Cash outlays:	Preferred stock	$420
	Inventoried	30.0	(partial)	Interest charges	5
	Retirements	77.5		Corporation income	
Cash receipts:	Retirements	30.0		taxes	260
(partial)	Bonds—par	560.0		Preferred dividends	24
	Common stock	0.0		Common dividends	95

6–14

David Levine Company Statement of Causes of Changes in Working Capital for Year Ended December 31, 1972 (000's omitted)

Funds obtained from:		
Operations (net income transferred to retained earnings)		$180
Decrease of current assets during year:		
Cash on hand and in banks	$33	
Accounts receivable	50	83
Sale of common stock		100
		$363

Funds applied to:	
Payment of cash dividends	$ 35
Declaration of stock dividends (not yet issued)	31
Investment in additions to:	
Inventories	139
Plant (net increase)	85
Prepayments	3
Payment of bond maturities	50
Reduction in current liabilities	20
	$363

You are to criticize the above statement in respect mainly to its function and content. Include in your discussion *specific* items that you believe: (1) should have been included on the statement, (2) should have been excluded from the statement.

6-15   The following are comparative position statements presented to the board of directors for the David Frye Company at its meeting of January 15, 1972.

	December 31 (000's omitted)	
	1971	1972
Assets		
Current:		
Cash	$ 10	$ 28
Accounts receivable	26	30
Inventories	43	17
	79	75
Property, plant, and equipment:		
Land	25	20
Buildings	45	45
Machinery and tools	100	96
	170	161
Less: Accumulated depreciation	7	2
	163	159
Patents	6	6
Goodwill	25	25
	$273	$265
Equities		
Current liabilities:		
Notes payable	$ 2	$ 35
Accounts payable	19	16
	21	51
Bonds payable	20	
Stockholders' equity:		
Capital stock	200	200
Retained earnings	32	14
	$273	$265

Additional information:
(1) The land decrease resulted from an appraisal.
(2) Net income was $22,000 on the income statement.
(3) The directors state to the auditor that they are unable to ascertain what has become of the net income for the year.

Construct a working capital fund-flow statement and account for any difference between working capital provided by current operations and $22,000. For *each* item you mention, give your reason for inclusion or exclusion, and state how you would treat the item.

6–16

The following fund-flow statement was prepared by the company controller under the broadest concept of funds, one that includes all significant transactions providing or requiring funds, namely, the all-changes-in-financial-position concept of funds and the working capital definition of funds.

Soul Company
Statement of Source and
Application of Funds
For 1972
(000's omitted)

Funds provided by:	
Contribution of plant site by the City of Baton	
Rouge (Note 1)	*$115*
Net income after extraordinary items per income	
statement (Note 2)	*75*
Issuance of note payable—due 1972	*60*
Depreciation and amortization	*50*
Deferred income taxes referring to accelerated	
depreciation	*10*
Sale of equipment—book value (Note 3)	*5*
	$315

Funds applied to:	
Acquisition of future plant site (Note 1)	*$250*
Increase in working capital	*30*
Cash dividends declared (but not paid)	*20*
Acquisition of equipment	*15*
	$315

Notes:
(1) Plant site donated by the city valued by the board of directors at $115; adjoining property purchased for $135.
(2) Research and development expenditures were considered abnormal in 1972; these totaled $25 and were reported as expenses.
(3) The gain of $3 on the disposal of equipment (with a book value of $5) was included as an extraordinary item on the income statement.

Without revising the statement, identify the weaknesses in presentation and disclosure of the above statement; indicate what you consider the proper treatment of each item.

6–17

Prepare fund-flow statements for Budweiser, using three different definitions of funds.

Budweiser Corporation
Comparative
Position Statements
December 31
(000's omitted)

	1972	1973	*Increase (Decrease)*
Assets			
Cash	$ 10.0	$ 12.0	$ 2.0
Accounts receivable (net)	28.0	28.0	0.0
Inventory	44.0	16.0	(28.0)

	1972	1973	Increase (Decrease)
Prepayments	1.3	1.5	0.2
Land	8.0	16.0	8.0
Building and equipment	60.0	96.0	36.0
Building and equipment—			
Accumulated depreciation	(20.0)	(22.0)	(2.0)
	$131.3	$147.5	$ 16.2
Equities			
Accounts payable	$ 44.0	$ 44.0	$ 0.0
Income taxes payable	2.2	2.0	0.2
Capital stock	74.0	60.0	14.0
Retained earnings	27.3	25.3	2.0
	$147.5	$131.3	$ 16.2

Data from the income statement: sales $420, net income after taxes $14, cost of goods sold $320, depreciation $10, wages and salaries $40, and a gain of $2 on a truck sale. The dividends declared and paid were $12.

    The only asset sold during the year was the truck. It cost $12 and it was sold for $6; accumulated depreciation on it was $8.

6–18

The board of directors of the Jim Ryun Company is disturbed that the company's cash and working capital balances at the end of 1972 are substantially lower than they were at the beginning, despite the fact that the net income was $175 before taxes of $88.25. The position and income statements are as follows:

Jim Ryun Company
Position Statements
December 31
(000's omitted)

	1971	1972	Increase (Decrease)
Assets			
Cash in bank	$ 64.50	$ 21.0	$ (43.50)
Accounts receivable (net)	42.75	66.5	23.75
Inventories	76.25	96.0	19.75
Plant (net)	130.00	250.0	120.00
Prepayments	8.60	12.5	3.90
	$322.10	$446.0	$123.90
Equities			
Accounts payable	$110.5	$131.50	$ 21.00
Income taxes payable	30.9	88.25	57.35
Dividends payable		15.00	15.00
Mortgage payable	62.5		(62.50)
Capital stock	50.0	75.00	25.00
Retained earnings	68.2	136.25	68.05
	$322.1	$446.00	$123.90

Net sales		$1,650.00
Cost of sales	$1,325.00	
Selling and administration	145.00	
Loss	5.00	
Income taxes	88.25	1,563.25
Net income		86.75
Dividends declared		18.70
Retained earnings retained		68.05
Retained earnings at beginning of year		68.20
Retained earnings at end of year		$ 136.25

Other data (000's omitted):
(1) Depreciation: Accumulated at beginning of year $80
                  Accumulated at end of year $90
                  For year $35: Cost of Sales $28;
                                Selling and Administration $7
(2) Machinery costing $15, which was one-half depreciated, was sold for $2.5 in cash during year.
(3) Receivables written off during the year amounted to $1.15. The balance in the Allowance for Bad Debts account was 5 percent of the gross receivables at the beginning and end of the year.
(4) All reductions of prepayments and all increases in short-term payables are applicable to selling and administration (rather than to cost of sales).

Prepare cash fund-flow and working capital fund-flow statements.

6–19
*University of
Minnesota
Fund-flow Statement
for Year Ended
June 30, 1970
(000's omitted)*

	General Operations and Maintenance Fund	Restricted Funds	Auxiliary Services Fund
Source of Funds for Current Operations			
From the State			
State appropriation	$ 66,936		
For the general support of instructional, research, and administrative departments, and maintenance of instructional buildings and grounds. Includes income from Permanent University Fund of $1,952.			
Indigent patients		$ 2,002	
Cost of the indigent patients at the University of Minnesota Hospitals—cost shared by counties.			
Special projects and research		13,305	
Includes appropriations that enable the University to perform special projects requested by various interested groups of			

	General Operations and Maintenance Fund	Restricted Funds	Auxiliary Services Fund
citizens of the State such as Agricultural Extension, General Agricultural Research, Medical Research, Psychopathic and Child Psychiatric Hospitals, Hospital Rehabilitation Center, Livestock Sanitary Board, and many other programs. Special appropriation for Educational equipment and library acquisitions were appropriated as part of the General Operations and Maintenance Fund but are included in the Restricted Funds in the financial report. Total appropriation was $1,500.			
Student tuition and fees Includes collegiate, Extension Division, and Summer Session tuition and fees for all campuses.	$23,614	$191	
Sales and services Includes hospital and dental infirmary receipts, sale of bulletins and agricultural products, receipts from the operation of University Theatre, The Cancer Detection Center, and other receipts.	13,747	24,841	
Auxiliary services Includes income from such activities as dormitories, dining halls, married student housing, printing, laundry, University Press, and Health Service.			$31,740
Federal government Instruction, Agricultural Research and Extension.		4,363	
Sponsored research, training programs and Institutes, and other projects.		44,702	
Corporations, foundations, individuals, and Other Gifts, Grants, and Research Contracts and income from Endowment.		15,120	
Intercollegiate athletics Includes Duluth, Morris, and Crookston.			1,875
Totals	$104,297	$104,524	$33,615

	General Operations and Maintenance Fund	Restricted Funds	Auxiliary Services Fund
Uses of Funds for Current Operations			
Administration	$ 3,666	$ 428	
The expenses of the offices of the Presidents, the Business Office, the Office of Civil Service Personnel, the Storehouses, and other general administrative offices.			
General expense	16,084	734	
The expenses of the offices of the Office of Student Affairs and Admissions and Records, the cost of staff insurance and retirement, intercampus bus, truck service, general bulletins and publications, convocations, and other services of a general expense character.			
Instruction and department research	51,099	16,053	$ 24
The expense of college instruction and departmental research, including instructional trust funds. Special appropriation for Educational Equipment was appropriated as part of the General Operations and Maintenance Fund but is included in the Restricted Funds in the Financial Report. Total expenditures were $370.			
Libraries	3,625	621	
Special appropriation for Library Acquisitions was appropriated as part of the General Operations and Maintenance Fund but is included in the Restricted Funds in the financial report. Total expenditures were $322.			
Organized activities relating to instructional departments	2,530	26,547	
Includes the cost of operating University Hospitals, University High School, the University Theatre, and other related activities.			

	General Operations and Maintenance Fund	Restricted Funds	Auxiliary Services Fund
Extension and public services *Includes activities such as the General Extension Division, Agricultural Extension, Museum of Natural History.*	$6,223	$14,289	
Budgeted and sponsored research *Includes the Agricultural Experiment Stations, the Mines Experiment Station, and all sponsored research.*	3,987	38,426	
Physical plant operations *The expenses of maintaining and operating the buildings and other improvements on all campuses.*	12,614	581	181
Auxiliary services *Includes expenditures for such activities as dormitories, dining halls, married student housing, printing, laundry, University Press, and Health Service.*	10	23	31,280
Student aid *Includes Fellowships, Scholarships, and Prizes.*	97	6,130	
Transfers, increase in obligations, and other adjustments	4,362	692	2,130
Totals	$104,297	$104,524	$33,615

(1) What definition of fund is used in the preceding statement?
(2) Identify differences between this statement and those discussed in Chapter 6.

6-20 Complete the following fund-flow statement from the information given in the balance sheets, income statement, and other data below by writing the numbers and letters on your solution paper and inserting the proper figures and words. Each letter indicates a caption; each number indicates a possible figure. (NOTE: Not all numbered items necessarily require figures.)

(a) _____

The Meschuginner
Corporation
Working Capital
Fund-flow Statement
(all 000's omitted)

Additions to Working Capital:

Operations: Net Income Fund-flow Statement $124

Add: (b) _____

      (1) _____ $ _____

      (2) _____ $ _____

      (3) _____ $ _____

      (4) _____ $ _____

      (5) _____ $ _____ $ _____

Deduct: (c) _____

      (6) _____ $ _____

      (7) _____ $ _____

      (8) _____ $ _____ $ _____

      Funds from Operations $

      Other

      (9) _____ $ _____

     (10) _____ $ _____

     (11) _____ $ _____

     (12) _____ $ _____ $ _____

            Total Additions $

Deductions from Working Capital:

     (d) _____

   (13) Income Taxes $ _____

   (14) Interest $ _____

   (15) Cash Dividends $ _____ $ _____

      Other

   (16) _____ $ _____

   (17) _____ $ _____

   (18) _____ $ _____

   (19) _____ $ _____ $ _____

           Total Deductions $ _____

(e) _____ in Working Capital $ _____
    (Increase or Decrease)

(20) Working Capital: January 1 $ _____
            December 31 $ _____ $ _____

Comparative
Balance Sheets
December 31
(000's omitted)

	1972	1973	Increase (Decrease)
Assets			
Current	$ 293	$ 319	$ 26
Investments	5	7	2
Bond sinking fund	3	4	1
Plant	319	390	71
Plant—accumulated depreciation	(138)	(144)	(6)
Plant—accumulated depletion	(10)	(20)	(10)
Patents	10	9	(1)
Goodwill	6	4	(2)
	$ 488	$ 569	$ 81
Equities			
Current liabilities	$ 159	$ 170	$ 11
Bonds—8% mortgage—par	80	80	
Bonds—7% debenture—par (issued December 31)		3	3
Bonds payable—premium	5	6	1
Capital stock—par $100	130	110	(20)
Capital stock—discount	(8)	(6)	2
Retained earnings appropriated for bond retirement	3	4	1
Retained earnings—unappropriated	119	202	83
	$ 488	$ 569	$ 81

Condensed
Income Statement Data
for Year Ended
December 31, 1973
(000's omitted)

Revenue:		
Sales	$172.5	
Interest earned	3.0	
Gain on trade-in of truck	1.0	
Sinking fund	0.5	$177
Deductions:		
Expenses	50	
Loss from embezzlement of cash	2	
Loss on abandoned plant	1	53
Net income		124
Corporate income taxes	11	
Interest charges	6	
Dividends	23	40
Net income retained		$ 84

Other data:

(1) The only noncurrent assets retired were:
    (a) A building costing $21,000 with $20,000 of accumulated depreciation was abandoned.
    (b) A truck costing $6,000 with accumulated depreciation of $4,000 was traded in on a new truck.

(2) Corporate income tax paid $8,500.
    Dividends paid $25,000. Stock issued par $5,000.

(3) Cost of investments purchased $1,500.

6–21

Working Capital
Fund-flow Statement
Report Format

Increases:
Net income (includes nonoperating
  items and with both taxes and interest
  considered as expenses:
  + Addbacks (a)
  − Deductions (b)
  Funds from operations
  Other Funds (c)
    Total increases
Decreases: (d)
Change in working capital (e)
  where (e) = internal changes in working capital

I. Indicate where, if anywhere, each of the following would appear on the above.

_____ (1) Amortization of bonds payable—premium
_____ (2) Amortization of bonds payable—discount
_____ (3) Gain on disposal of long-term investments
_____ (4) Loss on disposal of long-term investments
_____ (5) Loss on disposal of marketable securities
_____ (6) Gain on disposal of marketable securities
_____ (7) Amortization of bonds receivable—premium (investment in bonds)
_____ (8) Amortization of bonds receivable—discount (investment in bonds)
_____ (9) Estimate of bad debt losses
_____ (10) Write-off of bad debt losses of (9)
_____ (11) Declaration of stock dividend
_____ (12) Declaration of cash dividend
_____ (13) Payment of cash dividend in (12)
_____ (14) Payment of stock dividend in (11)
_____ (15) Depletion of natural resources
_____ (16) Retained earnings appropriated for fire loss
_____ (17) Building destroyed by fire
_____ (18) Building (in 17) replaced
_____ (19) Depreciation reflected in increased inventory
_____ (20) Bonds converted into stock

_____ (21) Amortization of goodwill
_____ (22) Increase in retained earnings appropriated for contingencies
_____ (23) Refund of corporate income taxes
_____ (24) Reappraisal increase in plant
_____ (25) Collection of accounts receivable

II. Indicate changes in answers if fund defined is: cash, net short-term monetary assets, and working capital using the all-changes-in-financial-position concept.

3 Measuring Financial Position and Income Flow

7　Long-term Assets

> *. . . it is feasible to approach these problems by reconstructing the most perfect conditions under which accounting could be practiced, and by determining what the ideal aim of accounting should be under such conditions. After this has been done, it can be determined how far present conditions vary from perfect conditions and what compromises this variance necessitates in the practical accomplishment of the ideal aim. In this manner one may, by not losing sight of the ideal aim, make as few concessions to expediency as practicable, and thus stay as close to the ideal aim as present conditions will permit.**
> KENNETH MacNEAL, 1939

The principal classes of long-term assets and liabilities consist of both monetary and nonmonetary assets and monetary liabilities. The nonmonetary accounts, on which this chapter focuses are land, plant, equipment (sometimes all three are referred to as plant), and the accounts traditionally referred to as intangibles. The monetary accounts to be considered in Chapter 8 are those for long-term investments in bonds, sinking funds, leases, pensions, and bond liabilities. Position statement accounts resulting from tax allocation will also be considered in Chapter 8, but long-term investments in stocks will be deferred until Chapter 11.

The greatest diversity of valuation and reporting methods in accounting is found among these noncurrent accounts. For the monetary accounts, direct valuation techniques (based upon input prices, not output prices) are ordinarily employed. For most nonmonetary accounts, historical cost is the usual basis of indirect valuation. Because of the comparatively long lifetime of these accounts, the chief problem is how to amortize their value over their lifetime for matching purposes in the determination of income; for this process a wide

*From *Truth in Accounting* (Philadelphia: University of Pennsylvania Press, 1939), pp. 174–175.

variety of methods are used. Some of these accounts, land, for example, have been kept basically in the same manner for hundreds of years. Others, such as leases, pensions, and deferred income taxes, have come into existence only in recent decades. Some accounts are kept in precise detail (for example, equipment), while others, notably certain intangibles such as goodwill, usually are not accounted for.

Acquisition and Retirement Problems of Owned Property

Plant (or land, buildings, and equipment) assets, apart from possessing the qualities of all assets, have some additional characteristics of their own. These are their physical attributes and their nonmonetary nature. Owned property is not directly converted into cash but only provides services which are converted into money. As mentioned previously, there are three categories of owned property which are common to enterprises. These are land, buildings, and equipment. Tools is a possible fourth category, although its treatment, if not its classification, is more akin to inventories than to plant. The plant categories of assets are classified as noncurrent, even when less than one year remains to be received from the specific asset. With the exception of land, the lifetime of plant assets, although long term, still is limited (or finite).

There is fairly general agreement in practice and to some extent in theory that plant should be valued at acquisition or historical cost.[1] As discussed in Chapter 2, property rights are not monetary (with the exception of leases). This means that it is not possible to trace any incoming cash flows for the firm to a specific plant asset. Since the initial plant typically is acquired before the firm begins to earn revenue, the firm presumably has not added to the plant's value at the date of acquisition. Therefore, its input value or entry price— historical cost—is not only the feasible but also the most relevant basis of valuation at that time. The historical cost valuation basis for plant at acquisition usually is verifiable and free from bias since it resulted from a marketplace transaction by the firm.

As discussed in Chapter 5, there are other input valuation bases besides historical cost. Current input value is often considered, since the current value of the annual services provided by an asset is measured most accurately by the current costs of equivalent services. But such costs may not be relevant (since this is not an efficient way to obtain them) or even available. Sometimes replacement costs are considered, since this is regarded as a current input concept. It is a method of adjusting for changes in prices. However, if the firm did not have the plant, there is usually little evidence that the firm

---

[1]See Eldon S. Hendriksen, *Accounting Theory*, rev. ed. (Homewood, Illinois: Richard D. Irwin, Inc., 1970), p. 362.

would pay the current replacement cost. Furthermore, it is almost impossible to take into consideration the effect of technological innovation.

A major disagreement seems to exist over what should be included in the historical cost of plant. There is general agreement, however, that plant cost includes the net invoice price (gross invoice price less any trade and cash discount), the transportation costs (if material), and any costs to start the plant operating (if material), such as installation and test-run costs. Costs to start the plant operating are any payments required to get it either to the location where it will be used or into condition so that it may function as intended. If there is any delay in paying for the plant which eliminates cash discounts or requires an interest payment, these events are considered not in costing the asset but as separate financing charges. The authors support this view because the net invoice price is the maximum price that should be paid by efficient management. Even if the lowest initial cost (or an invoice price net discounts and interest) is not the most efficient one for a particular firm, more relevant accounting information would be provided where operating costs (which is what plant assets become as they are utilized) are separated from financing costs (which are not deferred beyond the period in which they are incurred). Consequently the total invoice payment need not be the appropriate plant cost unless interest is not included.

Most of the disagreement over whether interest on financing should be considered part of plant cost occurs when the firm constructs the plant building (or machine) instead of purchasing it. If interest is to be interpreted as a distribution—instead of a determinant—of income, this problem would not exist. But if interest is interpreted as a determinant, apart from considering it as a financing charge, two other views might be taken of it in the construction of plant: One is to charge to plant cost the interest actually paid or due on amounts borrowed for the specific purpose of constructing the

---

EXHIBIT 7-1

A CLASSIFICATION OF PLANT COSTS

AS TO ASSET OR EXPENSE

Purchased Plant Asset		Expenses, Charges, or Losses	
Invoice Price	Trade Discounts	Repairs	
		Maintenance	
If Material [Transportation Installation Test Run	Cash Discounts	Depreciation	
		Insurance	
		Taxes	
		Interest	

asset, up to the date that the plant is ready for use; another is to charge to plant cost a normal interest on all funds used specifically for constructing the asset, up to the date that the plant is ready for use. In the view of the authors, only the last of these two views has any applicability, and this is limited to regulated industries. The maximum income that the firm is permitted to earn is based on total capitalization. Implicit in the first view of including interest in plant cost is the assumption that debt (rather than owner) equity is used to finance construction; because of interdependencies and the joint use of the asset cash, generally it is difficult or impossible to trace specific fund sources to their specific uses.

Special acquisition problems When buildings are purchased, they are acquired with surrounding land in what is called a "basket" purchase. Since the life of land usually is infinite, it is desirable to separate the cost of the land from the cost of the building. The "basket" price can be divided between the land and the building in proportion to a ratio based on their separate current market or assessed values. Book values of the properties as shown on the books of the previous owner usually are irrelevant for this purpose; they would perpetuate the valuation errors made by the previous owners including differences resulting from price changes. Although land usually has an unlimited life, improvements made to the land sometimes have a limited life. In these situations, the costs of the land improvements should be segregated in a separate account to facilitate their amortization. Assessed values are shown on the records of the property tax assessor.

Sometimes buildings and land are acquired, and the buildings are demolished. If this was intended when the purchase was made, the costs of removing the old buildings should be charged to the land account. If the intent was to use the old building as a part of the new building, the removal costs may be charged to the new building account. If the intended purpose was to use both the land and buildings, the later costs of demolishing the buildings can be charged as a period loss. The best support for this position is evidence that the old buildings were used in the operations of the company before being destroyed.

Apart from the question of interest, there is some controversy over the overhead to be allocated to self-constructed assets when a firm constructs its own plant. There are several views on this issue; those having the most support are to include charges for variable overhead (or the additional overhead incurred as a result of the construction) when there were no beneficial alternative uses for the facilities used, or to include charges for a full share of all overhead on a full cost basis when there were beneficial alternative uses for these facilities.

Retirement problems When a plant asset is retired or sold, the appropriate accounts should be closed, and a book gain or loss determined. Any proceeds from the disposal should be reflected in the gain or loss. For example, if a company car held for several years is sold, the entry to record the disposal of the car, provided that the cash proceeds from the disposal exceed the book value (car cost less accumulated depreciation to date), would be:

	Debit	Credit
Cash	×	
Car—accumulated depreciation	×	
Car		×
Gain on disposal of car		×
To record disposal of car		

If the cash proceeds received are less than the book value, a loss account would be substituted for the gain account in the above entry. Note that the gain or loss on disposal is the difference between the proceeds and the book value.

The above illustration assumes that the date of disposal coincides with the date when depreciation is recorded. Since depreciation is usually recorded as an end-of-period adjusting entry, this assumption would not ordinarily be valid. Instead, before recording the disposal, it would be necessary to make an adjusting entry to record the depreciation on the car during the period before the date of disposal. Part-year depreciation, as is likely to be required in this situation, would be measured to the nearest month rather than in days (or sometimes arbitrarily as one-half year) on both retirements and acquisitions.

Sometimes firms will trade in old cars (or other equipment) for new ones. There are two methods of recording trade-ins: the accounting method and the income tax method. Under the accounting method, a book gain or loss on the trade-in is recorded; under the income tax method, no such gain or loss is recorded. To illustrate, entries under each method are shown below:

Accounting Method

	Debit	Credit
Car (new)	×	
Car—accumulated depreciation (old)	×	
Cash		×
Car (old)		×
Gain on trade-in of old car		×
To record trade-in of old car and record new car		

Income Tax Method

	Debit	Credit
Car (new)	×	
Car—accumulated depreciation (old)	×	
Cash		×
Car (old)		×
To record trade-in of old car and record new car		

Accountants must be careful to accept the trade-in allowance stipulated by the vendor only when it is a valid value of the old asset. Often the dealer will inflate this allowance in order to set a special price for the new asset. The disposing firm should establish the market price of the old asset instead of accepting the dealer's trade-in allowance as equivalent in value. Since well-established second-hand markets exist for many plant assets (for example, cars), this value often can be determined quite readily.

As the names imply, the accounting method is preferred by accountants, and the income tax method is used for income tax return purposes. The merit of the accounting method is that it avoids the distortion possible under the income tax method. This distortion comes about when the book values of newly acquired assets vary substantially from their market prices because of the inclusion in the accounts of gains or losses from previous trade-ins (that is, where the trade-in allowance is substantially greater than the market value of the old asset). The only theoretical support for the income tax method is its use where plant assets are grouped together and accounted for as a group instead of as separate items. If plant assets are to be accounted for on a group basis, they should be homogeneous in service and value. When they are considered as a group, depreciation charges should be computed for the group as a whole, and no book gain or loss determined until the entire group has been disposed of.

Depreciation (and Depletion)
In plant accounting the main emphasis is placed on accounting for depreciation. Its significance is due to its importance in income determination rather than its relevance to fund flow. As we have seen, however, depreciation often appears as a misleading item on some forms of fund-flow statements; 79 companies out of 600 in 1969 showed depreciation as a separate item only in their fund-flow statements.[2]

In APB Opinion No. 12, the AICPA has recommended that the following depreciation information be disclosed in the financial statements or footnotes: the period expenses; the balances of major

[2]See AICPA's *Accounting Trends & Techniques: Annual Survey of Accounting Practices Followed in 600 Stockholders' Reports*, 24th ed. (New York: AICPA, 1970), p. 184.

classes of depreciable assets; the balances of accumulated depreciation, either by classes or in total; and a general description of the method(s) used.

Among the several concepts of depreciation, two have received the most attention. The primary one is that depreciation is an allocation of cost according to the revenues or benefits to be received each year. This is the AICPA's position, and this concept stresses cost allocation (over the asset's useful life in a systematic and logical manner) and realization. The second concept, a broader one, generally supported by the AAA but not in practice, stresses measurement of the decline in value of the asset instead of the amount of cost to be allocated. Since the first concept results in rather arbitrary allocations and the second, although more defensible, usually is found to be unmeasurable, depreciation accounting is a major cause of the dissatisfaction with the income statement. Some have argued for fund-flow statements other than income because no depreciation allocations would be required.

To compute conventional depreciation, it is necessary to know the asset's cost, its service life, and the scrap value, if any, at the end of its service life. Usually all three are considered to be constant throughout the service life of the asset; hence no changes are considered unless significant clerical or measurement errors are discovered. Conventional accounting depreciation is a process of allocation, not one of valuation.

In computing depreciation, especially in the determination of the service life and in the selection of the method, it is important to consider the causes of depreciation. These are:

1. Physical wear and tear due to use or to the action of the elements
2. Unusual damage due to varying the level of maintenance as well as to accidents
3. Technological obsolescence due to inventions and technical improvements
4. Economic obsolescence, often referred to as inadequacy for the intended purpose, due to economic progress and changes such as internal growth of one firm or external changes

The careful reader will note that the first and second of these are most closely related to use, whereas the third and fourth are most closely related to the passage of time.

Of the many methods used to compute depreciation, most companies use the straight-line method, as can be seen in Exhibit 7–2, and there is recent evidence showing that this number is increasing.[3]

---

[3]See Paul Frishkoff, "Some Recent Trends in Accounting Changes," *Journal of Accounting Research* (spring, 1970), who reports: "Depreciation accounting changes, almost all of them from accelerated methods to straight line, increased some three-fold from 1967 to 1969" (p. 142).

In addition to the straight-line method, there are three other types of cost allocation depreciation. Each type is distinguished from the others on the basis of the way in which the amount of the periodic charge against revenue is determined. For the straight-line method, the amount of the depreciation charge is determined by multiplying the asset's depreciable cost by a constant percentage (the reciprocal of the asset's service life), to yield a charge that is the same or constant for each period over the service life. For the other three types, this periodic charge is decreasing, increasing, or variable. Another way of putting this is to state that three types of methods are a function of time, and the fourth is a function of use.

The method of depreciation selected by a firm usually is based on whether the pattern of depreciation charges seems reasonable for the asset and the firm. Unfortunately, the selection of a method in the past too often has been influenced by its income tax effects. (Although different methods may be used on tax returns than in the statements, many companies prefer to use one method for both purposes.) Although the income tax and causal factors predominate in accounting practice, there are other factors that should be considered. In practice, these are often disregarded (on the grounds that their effects are minor), or even ignored. The other factors include: (1) expected repairs and maintenance costs, (2) expected changes in revenues and operating efficiency (which may be coupled with the degree of uncertainty regarding the later periods of an asset's life, and obsolescence), and (3) the interest factor (or the necessity of waiting for a long period to recover the asset investment). Although it would be possible to determine the combined expectations of each of these variables, as well as to recognize the firm's past experience,

EXHIBIT 7-2

DEPRECIATION METHODS

USED BY 600 CORPORATIONS IN 1968 AND IN 1969

Method Used	Number	
	1969	1968
Straight line	534	451
Declining balance	90	77
Sum-of-the-years digits	56	50
Other methods or not specified	134	116
	814*	694

Adapted from Accounting Trends & Techniques: Annual Survey of Accounting Practices Followed in 600 Stockholders' Reports, 24th ed. (New York: AICPA, 1970), p. 187.
*Some companies use more than one method.

EXHIBIT 7–3
CONDITIONS FOR COMMON DEPRECIATION METHODS
(CLASSIFIED ON THE BASIS OF PERIOD CHARGES)

Charge per Period	Methods	Function of Time	Use	Repairs and Maintenance	Revenues and Operating Efficiency
Constant	Straight line	×		Constant	Constant
Decreasing	Sum-of-the-years digits or Double-declining balance	×		Increasing	Decreasing
Increasing	Annuity or Sinking fund	×		Constant/ Decreasing	Constant/ Increasing
Variable	Production or Revenue		×	Proportional	Proportional

and derive a mathematical equation for computing depreciation for each major category of asset for every firm, this is not done, despite the obvious relevance of such an approach. Instead each firm uses one or more of the standardized equations shown in the preceding table.

Method	Depreciation	Rate	Base

Straight line:

$$D = \frac{1}{n} \times (C - S)$$

where D = periodic depreciation charge
n = number of periods
C = cost
S = salvage, scrap, or liquidation value

Method	Depreciation	Rate	Base

Double-declining balance:

$$D \quad = \quad \frac{2}{n} \quad \times \quad (C-AD)$$

where AD = accumulated depreciation

Sum-of-the-years digits:

$$D \quad = \quad \frac{t}{\frac{n(n+1)}{2}} \quad \times \quad (C-S)$$

where t = remaining periods

Annuity:

$$D \quad = \quad \frac{1}{P_{\overline{n}|i}} \quad [C - (p_{\overline{n}|i})S]$$

where $P_{\overline{n}|i}$ = present value of an annuity of \$1 per period =

$$\frac{1 - \frac{1}{(1+i)^n}}{i}$$

$p_{\overline{n}|i}$ = present value of \$1 due in n periods = $\dfrac{1}{(1-i)^n}$

Sinking fund:

$$D \quad = \quad \frac{1}{A_{\overline{n}|i}} \quad \times \quad (C-S)$$

where $A_{\overline{n}|i}$ = amount of an annuity of \$1 per period =
$\dfrac{(1+i)^n - 1}{i}$

Production:

$$D \quad = \quad \frac{U_p}{U_t} \quad \times \quad (C-S)$$

where U_p = units produced during the period
U_t = total units expected to be produced by the asset during its lifetime

Revenue:

$$D \quad = \quad \frac{R_p}{R_t} \quad \times \quad (C-S)$$

where R_p = net revenue contributed by the asset for a period
R_t = net revenue contributed by the asset for all periods during the life of the plant asset

If assets are acquired during the year, less than a full year's depreciation may be computed for the first and last years of their service life. The accepted solution is to compute the amount of depreciation for each full year in the life of one asset and then prorate each full year's depreciation between the two accounting years. This technique is applicable to all time-based depreciation methods, but the major problem is with the sum-of-the-years-digits method. For example, assume the following:

Asset cost, May 1, 1972 $2,100
Estimated service life   5 years
Estimated salvage value $300

The calculation of depreciation under the two decreasing-charge methods is as follows:

Double-declining Balance Year	Depreciation	Sum-of-the-years Digits Year	Depreciation
Depreciation for full year in indicated year of asset's life:			
1 (40% of $2,100) =	$840	1 (5/15 × $1,800) =	$600
2 (40% of $2,100 − 840) =	504	2 (4/15 × $1,800) =	480
Depreciation for period May 1, 1972 to December 31, 1972:			
2/3 (8 months) × $840 =	$560	2/3 (8 months) × $600 =	$400
Depreciation for 1973:			
1/3 (4 months) × $840 =	$280	1/3 (4 months) × $600 =	$200
2/3 (8 months) × $504 =	336	2/3 (8 months) × $480 =	320
	$616		$520
Alternate Calculation for 1973:			
40% × ($2,100 − 560) =	$616		

The straight-line method emphasizes economic obsolescence instead of physical wear and tear. Its chief merit seems to be that it is easily understood and computed. When an asset contributes a constant amount of net services (revenues after deducting repairs and maintenance costs) per period, this method gives an increasing rate of return (based on the diminishing nondepreciated cost). It gives logical results only if the depreciation factors are substantially constant or offset each other and the discount rate is zero.

The main impetus for the decreasing charge methods, sometimes called accelerated depreciation, was the liberalization in 1954 of the United States Internal Revenue Code. The decreasing charge methods pattern of depreciation fits assets whose revenues and operating efficiency decline over time while repairs and maintenance costs are constant or increasing. Under both methods of decreasing charge presented, the asset book value is reduced more in the early years than in the last years of the asset's life. The rationale for the larger depreciation amounts in the earlier periods is that services available now are worth more than those available in the future. The interest factor is not considered directly in these methods.

However, with increasing charge methods the interest factor is central. Under the annuity method, the assumption is that the initial cost represents the present value of a stipulated number of years of services from which must be deducted the present value of the expected salvage value at the end of the asset's life. The use of the two present value tables (explained in Chapter 2) is required.

Interest Revenue would be credited with the return on investment at the stipulated interest rate, and the difference between the depreciation charge and the interest revenue would be credited to Plant—Accumulated Depreciation as follows:

	Debit	Credit
Depreciation charge	×	
Interest revenue		×
Plant—accumulated depreciation		×

Since the Interest Revenue would decline each period (because the book value of the asset declines), the depreciation charge in effect (gross depreciation charges minus the interest revenue) would increase each period.

Under the sinking-fund method, periodic depreciation is measured by the hypothetical sinking-fund deposit which, if invested at a given rate of interest for each period, will accumulate to the depreciable cost of the plant asset at the date of retirement.

This method emphasizes asset replacement and financing, factors that generally are not considered to be among the objectives of depreciation accounting. Although the deposit for each period would be the same, the interest would increase for each period thus, in effect, increasing the period depreciation charge as follows:

	Debit	Credit
Depreciation charge	×	
Interest expense	×	
Plant—accumulated depreciation		×

Both methods will yield the same net effects on both the income and position statements, providing that the depreciation charge is

---

EXHIBIT 7-4
COMPARISON OF
ANNUITY AND SINKING FUND METHODS

Annuity	*Sinking Fund*
Depreciation	*Depreciation*
Less: *Interest revenue*	**Plus:** *Interest expense*
Increase to	*Increase to*
accumulated depreciation =	*accumulated depreciation*

---

a period expense (rather than a production overhead cost which is added to the value of inventories or self-constructed assets).[4]

Unfortunately few plant assets function in such a way that any of these methods fit the situation precisely. Very few assets provide services with constant or increasing value over time while the repairs and maintenance costs and operating efficiency remain constant. Exceptions are found in regulated industries, such as public utilities, where these methods are used. The principal application of an increasing charge depreciation method would seem to be the financing method of reporting leases for the lessor.[5]

In the variable method, depreciation is a function of use, rather than of time. Use may be measured in either production units or revenue contribution. The variable method is applicable if the physical aspects of depreciation are more significant than the economic ones, such as obsolescence. Apart from ignoring such factors as repairs and maintenance, revenues, and operating efficiency, the weakness of this method lies in the difficulty of anticipating early obsolescence.

[4]The interest method has been advanced to overcome this problem.

$$D = \frac{1}{A_{\overline{n}|i}} \times (C - S) + i(AD)$$

$$= \frac{1}{P_{\overline{n}|i}} \times [C - (p_{\overline{n}|i})S] - i(C - AD)$$

where $i(AD)$ = interest rate times accumulated depreciation at beginning of the period

This is an increasing charge depreciation method in which the depreciation charge is equal to the credit to Accumulated Depreciation in the annuity and sinking fund methods. It is not complicated by recording imputed interest (revenue in the annuity method and expense in the sinking-fund method). This method is a combination of the annuity and sinking-fund methods.
[5]Essentially this method is an increasing charge depreciation method. The cash rent received each period net the interest revenue (computed on the beginning of the period book value) constitutes the return of investment. As the book value becomes smaller the interest portion of the rent becomes smaller and period by period the return becomes larger so that the rate of return remains constant. For further details, see Chapter 8.

Besides the cost allocation methods of depreciation, there are three others that have limited application. The first is the inventory (or appraisal) method, which is used for tools. As the term implies, depreciation results from observing or taking inventory. The second and third are the retirement and replacement methods used by railroads and other public utilities in depreciating ties, rails, and other assets. Under the retirement method, the original cost of assets is charged to depreciation when they are retired. Under the replacement method, the original cost is retained for position statement purposes while the cost of replacements is charged as depreciation. These three methods essentially are position statement approaches, are not systematic, and tend to result in overstated depreciation charges and understated asset values. In addition, these methods provide opportunities for smoothing income by timing of retirements and replacements. For nonprofit organizations, depreciation is usually not computed because conventional net income statements are not prepared.

Depletion

Depletion refers to the cost allocation process for natural resources in accounting while depreciation is the similar process for other physical plant assets. Unlike depreciated plant which retains its physical qualities, depleted assets are consumed during the process. When the ore is removed from the mine or the trees are cut in the forest, the natural resource is wasted or removed physically.

The depletion base is the total cost of acquiring and developing the property, less any residual value of the land after the wasting assets have been depleted. Although any of the depreciation methods discussed could be applied to depletion, a variable charge method is commonly used. Similar to the production depreciation method, the depletion rate is the ratio of the number of units recovered during the period to the expected total number of units to be recovered from the property. If the base is multiplied by the period rate, the depletion charge for the period can be determined. If the depletion base is divided by the expected total number of recoverable units, a depletion cost per unit can be calculated. Although decreasing charge methods would appear to have merit, they are not used. Since depletion is a function of physical output and not of time, the straight-line method is not relevant.

As an alternative to cost depletion, the Internal Revenue Service permits the taxpayer to use percentage depletion on his tax returns if it is more advantageous to him. This consists of a stipulated percentage of the gross income (revenue) received from the sale of natural resource units without regard to the cost or the number of units removed. The only limit to percentage depletion is that depletion may not exceed 50 percent of taxable income (computed before deducting depletion) from the resource. Not suitable for accounting purposes, percentage depletion is a subsidy to natural resource owners to encourage exploration.

Repairs and Maintenance

The pattern of repairs and maintenance costs for a plant asset during its lifetime also should be considered in selecting a depreciation method. Maintenance refers to the usual and normal upkeep necessary to keep assets in efficient, effective operating condition; this includes normal recurring repairs. Generally "repairs" refers to restoring the plant asset to its normal full-capacity condition without changing its expected service life or capacity. Specifically, repairs include the adjusting or restoring of component parts of the asset or the minor replacement of asset parts. Usually the repairs and maintenance costs are charged to expense in the period in which they are incurred. Since these costs usually increase (often considerably) as the asset becomes older, each period does not carry an equal proportion of the asset's lifetime repairs and maintenance costs. Sometimes, too, these costs may be delayed for several periods, which makes them even more irregular.

For these reasons, special contra-asset accounts to plant sometimes are set up, to which are credited for each period the appropriate share of these costs as estimated for the lifetime of the asset. Such a periodic adjusting entry would be as follows:

	Debit	Credit
Repairs and maintenance expense	×	
Plant—accumulated repairs and		
maintenance		×
To record estimated repairs and maintenance		
expenses for the period		

When the actual repairs and maintenance costs are incurred they would be charged to the contra account as follows:

	Debit	Credit
Plant—accumulated repairs and		
maintenance	×	
Cash		×
To record actual repairs and maintenance expense		

During the lifetime of the plant asset this account would reflect both types of transactions, and when the asset is scrapped or liquidated, this contra account would be closed, along with the plant asset account and the other contra account for accumulated depreciation. This approach is usually discredited in practice. It is considered to be too subjective, and it results in recognizing a contra account that meets neither the criteria for a liability nor the criteria for a true contra asset because it relates to future rather than present or past costs.

Other costs incurred over the lifetime of an asset are referred to as additions, improvements, betterments, and major replacements. Often these are difficult to distinguish and treat properly. The following three guidelines, however, usually provide some help in clarifying these situations:

1. If these costs are material and extend the lifetime or capacity of the plant asset (either quantitatively or qualitatively) beyond its original status, they should be set up and depreciated separately over the extended lifetime or capacity.
2. If these costs restore the lifetime or the capacity of the plant asset back to its original status, those original costs that have been replaced should be removed from the plant account, and the new costs should be charged to the account.
3. If it is not possible to identify the original cost of the specific property of the plant asset that has been restored, the new costs may be charged against the contra account for accumulated depreciation.

Intangibles

As already explained, intangible is a quality that describes most assets except for inventories and plant; however, in accounting, franchises, patents, copyrights, trademarks, trade names, goodwill, and organization costs usually are the only assets classified as intangibles on the position statement. Receivables, prepayments, investments, leases, and pensions, all of which do not have a physical existence, are not classified as intangibles. Intangibles in an accounting statement sense are classified as noncurrent and usually are almost impossible to associate with specific revenues or periods. Although many tangible assets have value in alternative uses in this or other firms, most accounting intangibles do not, to the extent that it is difficult or impossible to separate them from the plant, other property, or the firm. Probably their most notable characteristic, however, is the extreme degree of uncertainty as to the timing and amount that affect the value of their future benefits. Trademarks and trade names usually are intangible assets that are developed to sustain demand for the firm's products; patents and copyrights are intangible assets that usually reflect how the firm produces its supply of products. Goodwill or organization costs may affect either or both the demand for or the supply of the firm's products.

Although the above presentation has stressed the differentiating characteristics of accounting intangibles, it should be recognized that these assets are probably more similar to than different from other assets in many important respects, especially other intangibles such as the several types of prepayments. Many patents and copyrights do have alternative uses and can be sold; there may be no more uncertainty with respect to the future benefits to be received from a copyright or a patent than from a new piece of highly specialized equipment that may become valueless in the indefinite future as a result of technological or economic changes. Neither tangibles nor intangibles are homogeneous groups, so that both groups overlap in terms of the degree of uncertainty concerning their future benefits and the extent of their alternative uses. Probably the area of greatest similarity is that the firm usually has the same objective (or intent) when it invests in intangible assets as when it invests in tangible assets, namely, to facilitate the earning of revenue and a net income.

However, because of their uncertainty and their nature, intangibles usually are recorded on the basis of indirect valuation, or historical costs. Typically the costs of many intangibles are treated as period expenses, particularly when they are acquired gradually over the years by annual expenditures. This practice is supported by some theorists including the Australian, Raymond Chambers, who argues that nonseverable [cannot be exchanged (as in a sale), converted (as in production), or otherwise separated (as in a gift)] intangibles should not be listed as assets since they are not measurable in terms of a current cash equivalent.

Probably the depression of the 1930s has had the greatest impact on the contemporary treatment of intangibles. During that era the many corporations that went bankrupt frequently found when disposing of their assets that their intangibles were valueless. Practicing accountants appear to have been so deeply impressed by this experience that they sometimes seem to go to unnecessary lengths to avoid recording intangibles as assets, particularly those developed over a period of time. The general omission of intangibles from the position statement seems inconsistent with the rather detailed accounting treatment of plant assets.[6] In fairness to accountants, however, there is little evidence to indicate that external users find intangibles reported as assets to be relevant. Some, such as bankers, are known to disregard such information.

Another practice, much criticized, is to value intangibles at a nominal $1 on the position statement.[7] If it is not possible to value intangibles adequately in monetary terms, they might be described in foot-

[6]The prevailing practice only recognizes goodwill in a consolidated entity. For details, see Chapter 11.

[7]W. Wolff in "Accounting for Intangibles," *Canadian Chartered Accountant* (October 1967), pp. 255–259, reports that in a survey of the 1964 annual reports of 325 Canadian companies, less than a third (103) reported intangible assets and a third of these (36) reported the intangibles at a nominal value of $1.

notes to the statements with comments concerning the total amounts expended for these purposes and the current (and, possibly, expected future) benefits.

The valuation of goodwill has received considerable attention in accounting literature. One view is that company goodwill represents a master valuation account (an adjunct account to all assets), which reports the value of the firm beyond what is allocated to the other assets. Another concept is that goodwill represents the present value of the expected superior future earnings (net cash inflows) which result from advantageous relationships that the enterprise enjoys with any or all of those associated with it. These may include consumers, governments, suppliers, employees, and creditors. Although many methods of valuing goodwill have been considered, measurement based on superior earnings has received the greatest support. This type of goodwill measurement rests on the assumption that any superior earnings (those in excess of average or normal earnings) of the firm are due to goodwill. After estimating the next period(s) revenues, expenses, and income, the required income is computed by applying the firm's or industry's normal earnings rate to the amount of booked net assets adjusted to current market values. The difference between anticipated income and required income is the superior earnings attributable to goodwill that will be realized during the next year. If the appropriate interest rate and the limited number of years that such superior earnings might continue are estimated, the proper interest factor can be selected from the table for the present value of an annuity of $1 per period for n periods at i interest per period (Appendix A) and applied to the superior earnings figure; the result would approximate the present value of goodwill.

If intangibles are purchased and paid for in large lump sums, they are usually classified as assets with limited or unlimited lives. If the intangibles have limited lifetimes, there is the accounting allocation problems of assigning portions of intangible cost to the periodic revenue. The usual practice is to amortize over the legal or economic life, whichever is shorter. Ordinarily this is the economic lifetime. When intangibles are amortized, the amortized amount is written off directly against the asset account instead of added to a contra account; since each intangible is unique, its total cost is not comparable to that of the others. Nevertheless, the reporting of accumulated amortization would at least focus attention upon the proper accounting for intangibles.

The AICPA's position on goodwill and other intangibles has not been one of leadership; in general, it accepts the prevailing practice. For example, in APB Opinion No. 17[8] it concludes that even intangi-

[8]Opinions of the Accounting Principles Board No. 17, "Intangible Assets" (New York: AICPA, August 1970).

bles with indeterminate life must be amortized; the force of this requirement would seem to support, if not encourage, rapid write-offs. If assets such as organization costs do have unlimited life, amortization would be inappropriate; in fact, the value of some intangible assets may increase over time. Nevertheless, the APB did reject in this Opinion the extreme position taken in the AICPA Accounting Research Study No. 10, *Accounting for Goodwill*,[9] which recommended that goodwill should never be shown as an asset or amortized, but instead should be recognized when purchased and deducted from stockholders' equity. The committee instead reaffirmed the validity of the matching-process concept for intangibles.

EXHIBIT 7–5
R. G. BARRY CORPORATION AND SUBSIDIARIES
FINANCIAL AND HUMAN RESOURCE ACCOUNTING STATEMENTS*
FOR 1969 (000'S OMITTED)

Balance Sheet

	Financial and Human Resources	Financial Only
Assets		
Current assets	$10,004	$10,004
Net property, plant, and equipment	1,771	1,771
Net investment in human resources	986	
Other	1,295	1,295
	$14,056	$13,070
Liabilities and Stockholders' Equity		
Current liabilities	$ 5,716	$ 5,716
Long-term debt	1,936	1,936
Deferred compensation	62	62
Deferred federal income taxes as a result of appropriation for human resources†	493	
Stockholders equity:		
Capital stock	879	879
Additional capital	1,736	1,736
Retained earnings:		
Financial	2,741	2,741
Appropriation for human resources†	493	
Total stockholders' equity	5,849	5,356
	$14,056	$13,070

[9]George R. Catlett and Norman O. Olson, Accounting Research Study No. 10, *Accounting for Goodwill* (New York: AICPA, 1969).

Statement of Income

	EXHIBIT 7–5 (Cont.)	
	Financial and Human Resources	Financial Only
Net sales	$25,310	$25,310
Cost of sales	16,276	16,276
Gross margin	9,034	9,034
Selling, general, and administrative expenses	6,737	6,737
Operating income	2,297	2,297
Other deductions	953	953
Net income before federal income taxes	1,344	1,344
Human resource expenses applicable to future periods	174	
Adjusted income before federal income taxes	1,518	1,344
Federal income taxes	731	644
Income	$ 787	$ 700

This is a reproduction of the statements that were published as the 1969 financial report of this Columbus, Ohio, firm; the statements, even excluding human resource accounting, were not certified by its auditors. The figures have been rounded to the nearest thousand.
†*Deferred Taxes is discussed starting on page 357. Restrictions of Retained Earnings is discussed starting on page 471.*

The costs of developing management are expensed in the period in which they are incurred, despite the recognition that any company's future is dependent largely upon management's actions and decisions. In the past several years experiments have been carried on with several companies in an area called *human resource accounting.* With this approach, outlay costs for recruiting, acquiring, training, familiarizing, and developing management personnel are accumulated and recorded as an intangible asset when the outlays have expected value beyond the current accounting period. The basic outlays in connection with acquiring and integrating new management people are to be amortized over the period for which it is expected that the company will benefit. Investments made for training or development are to be amortized over a much shorter period of time. Since human resource accounting is in the preliminary and experimental stage, it remains to be seen whether an effective pattern of amortization can be developed for such assets. The information potential offered by these experiments is, of course, considerable. Actual statements incorporating human resource accounting are compared with conventional statements in Exhibit 7–5.

Summary

The greatest diversity of valuation and reporting methods in accounting is found among noncurrent accounts. This chapter has focused on the long-term nonmonetary assets: *plant* (or owned property) including land, buildings, and equipment; and *intangibles.* An indirect valuation method, normally historical cost, is generally used to value these assets.

Problems associated with accounting for the acquisition and retirement of plant assets include method of valuation, what to include as the historical cost of the asset (if this is the valuation technique selected), separation of land and building when purchased together, allocation of costs of demolishing a building, allocation of retirement gain or loss, and determination of depreciation. Accounting has placed primary emphasis on the problems of accounting for depreciation.

Two depreciation concepts are considered: allocation of costs according to revenues to be received each year, and measurement of the decline in the value of the asset. Since the latter is usually found to be unmeasurable, conventional accounting for depreciation stresses the cost allocation over the asset's useful life in a systematic and logical manner and realization.

There are at least seven common methods of depreciation. Five methods—straight line (constant charge per period), sum-of-the-years digits or double-declining balance (decreasing charge per period), and annuity or sinking fund (increasing charge per period)—are most closely related to the passage of time. The production or revenue methods of depreciation (variable charge per period) are most closely related to use. The most commonly used method is the straight-line method. The standard equations that firms use to compute depreciation, employing one method or a combination of methods, are listed on pages 304 to 305.

In addition to the cost allocation methods of depreciation listed above, three other methods exist which have limited application. They are inventory method, which is used for tools and results from observing inventory; the retirement method, under which the original cost of assets is claimed to depreciation when the assets are retired; and the replacement method, under which the cost of replacement is charged as depreciation.

Depletion is the cost allocation process for natural resources. Depleted assets, unlike depreciated plant assets, are completely consumed and have no salvage value. Although any of the depreciation methods could be applied to depletion, a variable charge per period is commonly used.

In selecting a depreciation method it is important to consider maintenance and repair costs. Usually these costs are charged to expense in the period in which they are incurred.

The second category of long-term nonmonetary assets considered in Chapter 7 is intangibles. In accounting, only franchises, patents, copyrights, trademarks, trade names, goodwill, and organization costs are classified as intangibles, although the term itself could logically apply to any asset (e.g., prepayments, leases, receivables) which does not have a physical existence. The most notable property of accounting intangibles probably is the extreme uncertainty about the timing and amount that affect their future benefits. Because of this uncertainty, intangibles are usually recorded using the indirect valuation method, historical cost.

Of the valuation problems associated with intangibles, the valuation of goodwill has perhaps received the most attention in the accounting literature. Two views predominate: that goodwill should be accounted for as the value of the firm beyond what is allocated to other assets, and that goodwill represents the present value of expected superior earnings resulting from the advantageous relationships that enterprise enjoys with those associated with it.

A Selection of Supplementary Readings

American Institute of Certified Public Accountants: "Restatement and Revision of Accounting Research Bulletins," Accounting Research Bulletin No. 43, chap. 5, "Intangible Assets"; chap. 9, "Depreciation." In *APB Accounting Principles,* vol. 2. New York, pp. 6018–6020, 6031–6035.

_____ : "Declining Balance Depreciation," Accounting Research Bulletin No. 44 (revised). In *APB Accounting Principles,* vol. 2. New York, pp. 6067–6069.

_____ : "New Depreciation Guidelines and Rules," Opinions of the Accounting Principles Board No. 1. New York: 1962.

_____ : "Status of Accounting Research Bulletins," Opinions of the Accounting Principles Board No. 6. New York: 1965.

_____ : "Intangible Assets," Opinions of the Accounting Principles Board No. 17. New York: 1970.

_____ : "Review and Résumé," Accounting Terminology Bulletin No. 1. In *APB Accounting Principles,* vol. 2. New York, pp. 9510–9513.

Battista, George L.: "The Selling and Administrative Expenses Dilemma," *Management Accounting,* November 1965, pp. 3–8.

Baxter, W. T.: "Asset Lives: Choice of Optimum Length," *Accountancy,* August 1966, pp. 537–544.

_____ : "Depreciating Assets: The Forward-looking Approach to Value," *Abacus,* December 1970, pp. 120–131.

Beams, Floyd A.: "The Case against the Indirect Deduction of Depreciation," *The New York Certified Public Accountant,* December 1968, pp. 871–877.

Beaton, D. C.: "Replacement Value and Depreciation," *The Accountant,* July 9, 1966, pp. 37–39.

Brief, Richard P.: "Depreciation Theory in Historical Perspective," *The Accountant,* Nov. 26, 1970, pp. 737–739.

Brummet, R. Lee: "Accounting for Human Resources," *The New York Certified Public Accountant,* July 1970, pp. 547–555.

Brummet, R. Lee, Eric G. Flamholtz, and William C. Pyle: "Human Resource Measurement—A Challenge for Accountants," *The Accounting Review,* April 1968, pp. 217–224.

Catlett, George R., and Norman O. Olson: *Accounting for Goodwill,* Accounting Research Study No. 10. New York: AICPA, 1968, pp. 8–21, 74–89.

Duncan, Wilbur S.: "Accounting Research Study No. 10—'Accounting for Goodwill'—A Summary of Its Conclusions," *The New York Certified Public Accountant,* June 1969, pp. 429–436.

Heath, John, Jr.: "What Is Value?" *Financial Executive,* June 1971, pp. 13–15.

Likert, Rensis, and William C. Pyle: "Human Resource Accounting," *Financial Analysts Journal,* January–February 1971, pp. 75–84.

Milburn, J. A.: "A Look at Problems in Research and Development Accounting," *Canadian Chartered Accountant,* June 1968, pp. 404–408.

Most, Kenneth S.: "Depreciation in Economic and Accounting Theories," *The Accountant,* Feb. 25, 1971, pp. 237–240.

Myers, John H.: "Depreciation Disclosure," *The Journal of Accountancy,* November 1965, pp. 36–40.

Nethercott, L. J.: "Depreciation under Changing Price Levels," *The Australian Accountant,* September 1970, pp. 391–393.

Piaker, Philip M.: "'Non-accounting' for Goodwill—A Critical Analysis of Accounting Research Study No. 10," *The New York Certified Public Accountant,* November 1969, pp. 837–843.

Pick, John: "Concepts of Depreciation—Business Enterprises," *The New York Certified Public Accountant,* May 1970, pp. 369–380.

Pyle, William C.: "Human Resource Accounting," *Financial Analysts Journal,* September–October 1970, pp. 69–78.

Rothstein, Eugene L.: "Problems in the Treatment of Research and Development Costs," *Management Accounting,* November 1965, pp. 9–12.

Skinner, Allen: "Accounting for R & D Costs," *Management Accounting,* May 1971, p. 29.

Solomon, Kenneth Ira, and Howard G. Kaplan: "Research and Development Costs," *The Illinois CPA,* summer 1968, pp. 7–11.

Staubus, George J.: "Asset Lives: Three Comments," *Accountancy,* October 1967, pp. 658–660.

Summers, E. L., and C. H. Griffin: "Another Look at Depreciation Policies," *Cost and Management,* September–October 1969, pp. 20–24.

Thomas, Arthur L.: *The Allocation Problem in Financial Accounting Theory,* Studies in Accounting Research No. 3, Evanston, Illinois: American Accounting Association, 1969, pp. 1–29, 70–82.

Van Horn, Lawrence G.: "Accelerated Depreciation—A Tax Benefit, but Harmful Accounting," *The New York Certified Public Accountant,* May 1967, pp. 346–353.

Williams, Michael D.: "Asset Valuation and Recognition," *Cost and Management,* July–August 1969, pp. 33–40.

Winter, J. C.: "Accelerated Depreciation—A Victim of Its Own Success?"

The New York Certified Public Accountant, October 1967, pp. 774–781.

Wolff, W.: "Accounting for Intangibles," *Canadian Chartered Accountant,* October 1967, pp. 255–259.

Wolk, Harry I.: "Current Value Depreciation: A Conceptual Clarification," *The Accounting Review,* July 1970, pp. 544–552.

Woodruff, R. L.: "Human Resource Accounting," *Canadian Chartered Accountant,* September 1970, pp. 156–161.

Questions

7–1
(1) Repairs are:
   a. Expenses under 100 percent
   b. Expenditures to combat wear and tear
   c. Same as replacements
   d. Adjustments to depreciation
   e. Maintenance expenditures not prolonging the asset's life
(2) The following is *not* a repair:
   a. A machine is painted.
   b. Tires are replaced on an auto.
   c. A building is repaired after being knocked out to permit a new machine to be installed.
   d. A new tile floor in the office.
   e. New gears for an auto transmission.
(3) A manufacturing company uses an Accumulated Repairs account which had a balance of $450 at the beginning of the fourth year of the related asset's life. The life was estimated at ten years, and repairs totaling $90 had been charged against accumulated repairs during the first three years. During the fourth year, repairs on the asset cost $165, and were debited to Accumulated Repairs. The entry to record repair expenses at the end of the fourth year should include a debit to repair expense of: (a) $120, (b) $150, (c) $165, (d) $180, (e) something else.
(4) The use of accelerated depreciation and the repair "reserve" method, together, tend to:
   a. Increase profits in the early life of the asset
   b. Equalize periodic costs of a long-lived asset over its life
   c. Increase expenses in the early life of the asset
   d. More than one of the above
   e. None of the above

7–2
A firm purchases an asset at a cost of $3,000 on January 1, 1972. Life is estimated as five years or 7,500 hours of use. Scrap value of zero is anticipated. During 1972 it was used 2,000 hours.
(1) Under the straight-line method, depreciation for 1972 will be between: (a) $300 and $500, (b) $500 and $700, (c) $700 and $900, (d) $900 and $1,100, (e) $1,100 and $1,300.
(2) Under the working hours method, depreciation for 1972 will be between: (a) $300 and $500, (b) $500 and $700, (c) $700 and $900, (d) $900 and $1,100, (e) $1,100 and $1,300.
(3) Under the sum-of-the-years-digits method depreciation for 1972 will be between: (a) $300 and $500, (b) $500 and $700, (c) $700 and $900, (d) $900 and $1,100, (e) $1,100 and $1,300.

(4) Under the declining-balance method with a rate twice that under the straight-line method, depreciation for *1973 (the second year)* will be between: (a) $300 and $500, (b) $500 and $700, (c) $700 and $900, (d) $900 and $1,100, (e) $1,100 and $1,300.

7-3 (1) A machine is purchased on January 1, 1970. Its cost is $5,000, estimated life 10 years, salvage value $200. On January 1, 1978, the machine is overhauled at a cost of $1,000. Its life is estimated to end on December 31, 1982; salvage value of zero is expected. Depreciation for 1978 would be (a) $432, (b) $480, (c) $680, (d) $392, (e) $540.

(2) An asset with a cost of $4,000 is depreciated at a straight-line rate of 10 percent. On January 1, 1972, a repair of $600 is debited to the asset account. The result for 1972 is (a) net income is overstated $540, (b) net income is understated $600, (c) net income is overstated $600, (d) net income is understated $60, (e) net income is correctly stated.

(3) An asset is purchased on January 1, 1972. Its cost is $5,000, estimated life 10 years, salvage value zero. On January 1, 1978, an expenditure of $1,600 is made. Efficiency of the asset but not its life is increased. Total depreciation for 1978 would be: (a) $500, (b) $400, (c) $660, (d) $900, (e) $820.

(4) Accounting depreciation: (a) measures the amount of the asset that has worn away during the period, (b) measures the amount by which the value of an asset has declined during a period, (c) estimates the cost of the services given up by the asset during the period, (d) does not take into account the factor of obsolescence, (e) is a method to provide funds to replace the asset.

7-4 (1) An asset is purchased on January 1, 1972, at a cost of $2,000. Its life is estimated at four years with a $400 salvage value. On January 1, 1976, it has a value of $600 and is traded for a new asset, with an additional cash payment of $2,100. The life of the new asset is estimated at four years with a $700 salvage value. Depreciation for 1976 would be (a) $350, (b) $500, (c) $550, (d) $400, (e) $100.

(2) Salvage value and life are estimates. Reported net incomes for the early years of life will be decreased as a result of: (a) low estimates of both, (b) low estimates of salvage value and high estimate of life, (c) high estimate of salvage value and low estimate of life, (d) high estimates of both, (e) using the actual salvage value and actual life.

(3) If an allowance for repairs is maintained, the expenditure for repairs is debited to: (a) the Asset account, (b) the Allowance account, (c) an Expense account, (d) the Accumulated Depreciation account, (e) Retained Earnings.

(4) Additions to plant are ordinarily debited to: (a) the Asset account, (b) the Allowance account, (c) an Expense account, (d) the Accumulated Depreciation account, (e) Retained Earnings.

7-5 (1) An asset cost $20,000 and has a life of five years and salvage value of $5,000.
Using the straight-line method, depreciation expense the *second* year will be (a) $1,000, (b) $2,000, (c) $3,000, (d) $4,000, (e) $5,000.

(2) For the above asset, the depreciation the second year, if the sum-of-the-years-digits method is used, will be (a) $1,000, (b) $2,000, (c) $3,000, (d) $4,000, (e) $5,000.

(3) An asset cost $20,000 and has a life of five years. If the declining-balance method is used (with a rate twice that of the straight-line method), depreciation the second year will be (a) $4,000, (b) $3,200, (c) $8,000, (d) $4,800, (e) $1,800.

(4) An asset which cost $6,000 and for which accumulated depreciation is $5,000 is sold for $600. The result is a (a) loss of $5,400, (b) loss of $4,400, (c) net income of $600, (d) loss of $5,000, (e) loss of $400.

(5) Accumulated depreciation should be shown on the position statement as (a) an asset, (b) a deduction from an asset, (c) a liability, (d) a deduction from a liability, (e) an ownership item.

7-6   Rudy Vallee purchased a jet airplane at the beginning of the year at a cost of $380,000. Salvage value was $20,000, estimated life five years, estimated life-time in flying hours 100,000 hours. The plane was operated 5,000 hours the first year, and 7,500 hours the second year. Compute depreciation by various methods for the first and second years, and select a method that you deem most appropriate in this situation and give reasons for your choice.

7-7   For each of the various depreciation methods, how are the following factors considered?
a. The original cost of the asset
b. The current replacement value of the asset
c. Obsolescence
d. The life of the asset
e. The flow of services from the asset
f. The asset's disposal or scrap value

7-8   An escort company owns four business autos. These autos have *no scrap value* and are depreciated on a *straight-line* basis. (Each figure in the following accounts represents an entry, not a balance.) Give estimated service life for each auto.

Automobiles		Automobiles—Accumulated Depreciation	
1970		1970	
July 1, Alpha Romeo	$2,500	December 31	$ 125
1971		1971	
January 2, MG	4,000	December 31	650
1972		1972	
May 1, Thunderbird	4,800	December 31	1,450
1973		1973	
January 3, Jaguar	5,000	December 31	2,350

7-9   What is accounting for depreciation, and what is its objective?

7-10

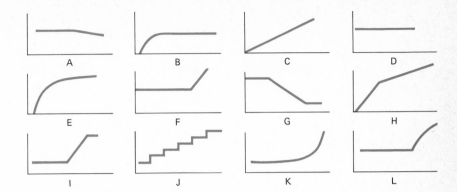

A. Write the letter of the graph above which matches the depreciation or other cost given below. The vertical axes of the graphs represent total dollars of expense, and the horizontal axes represent production. In each case the zero point is at the intersection of the two axes.

(1) Depreciation of equipment, where the amount of depreciation charged is computed by the machine-hour method.

(2) Depreciation of equipment, where the amount is computed by the straight-line method. When the depreciation rate was established, it was anticipated that the obsolescence factor would be greater than the wear and tear factor.

(3) Salaries of repairmen, where one repairman is needed for every 1,000 machine-hours or less (i.e., 0 to 1,000 hours requires one repairman, 1,001 to 2,000 hours requires two repairmen, etc.).

(4) Electricity bill—a flat fixed charge, plus a variable cost after a certain number of kilowatt-hours is used.

(5) Cost of raw material used.

B. Identify a specific cost or expense for every graph not associated with a specific cost or expense in part A.

7-11

Some of the sources of intangible assets (and liabilities) are knowledge, image, contacts, human values, and synergy (an intangible that results from a combination of tangible assets).

(1) Give two illustrations for each source.

(2) For each, indicate how it might be measured.

(3) For each, what is the present accounting practice?

7-12

"Question. Can you touch an account? Answer. You can touch the debtor."* How does the answer provide some support for the accounting definition of "intangible"?

7-13

In the calculation of accounting depreciation as it is conventionally measured, of what importance are the following factors:

*Testimony of George O. May as reprinted in Bishop Carleton Hunt, ed., *Twenty-five Years of Accounting Responsibility, 1911–1936* (New York: Price Waterhouse & Co., 1936), vol. 1, p. 246.

(1) The original cost of the asset
(2) The current replacement value of the asset
(3) Inflation and changing prices
(4) Obsolescence
(5) The flow of services that the asset yields
(6) The life of the asset
(7) The asset's resale or scrap value

7-14   Is it possible to define the value of a single asset that is part of an integrated group of assets? Consider a pump on an oil pipeline; if the pump breaks down, the entire pipeline ceases to operate.

7-15   From a student's examination paper on the measurement of cost: "Cost can be measured in many ways. It can be measured by cash outlay or indebtedness incurred. If cash is not the means of exchange, the cash equivalent can be used. If you exchange one asset for another (not cash), cost can be measured by the fair market value of the asset received or given up. Fair market value is an objective value: a price that could be obtained on an open market which is free from bias. The New York Stock Exchange is an example of a market which could be used to determine fair market value. In the absence of fair market value, fair value can be used. Fair value is a range of values with liquidation price being the minimum, and replacement or reproduction costs adjusted for depreciation being the upper limit. Fair market value is more objective, and it should be preferred. Fair market value is a closer 'cash equivalent' than fair value, and the result is a better valuation of assets." Do you agree? If so, what are the implications for the AAA criteria?

Problems

7-1   Johnny Cash operates a number of trucks used in his construction business. A five-year life and no salvage value are used for depreciation purposes. Straight-line depreciation is used for all trucks acquired in 1972 and earlier years, and sum-of-the-years digits for all acquired in 1973 and after. Data on trucks in operation on January 1, 1976, follow:

Truck	Cost	Date Acquired	Accumulated Depreciation 12/31/75
1	$3,000	1/4/70	$3,000.00
2	3,600	4/25/71	3,360.00
3	3,900	5/11/72	2,860.00
4	4,050	6/12/73	2,902.50
5	4,200	9/9/74	1,773.33
6	3,900	10/1/75	325.00

On all trucks purchased or retired before the fifteenth of the month, a full month's depreciation is charged; if the truck is purchased or retired after the fifteenth, no depreciation is charged for that month.

Sum-of-the-years-digits depreciation has been calculated in this manner (truck 4):

First year:	5/15 × $4,050 = $1,350	
1973:	7/12 × 1,350 =	$787.50
1974:	5/12 × 1,350 =	562.50

Second year:	4/15 × 4,050 = $1,080	
1974:	7/12 × 1,080 =	$630.00
1975:	5/12 × 1,080 =	450.00

Third year:	3/15 × 4,050 = $ 810	
1975:	7/12 × 810 =	$472.50

(1) Prepare journal entries for the following transactions which occurred during 1976.

February 10	Truck 1 was sold for $400.
March 28	Truck 2 was traded in on truck 7. The cost of the new truck was $4,500. A trade-in allowance of $300 was received.
May 25	Truck 3 was damaged in an accident. The damaged truck was sold for $100.
May 28	Truck 8 was purchased for $4,500.
July 10	Truck 4 was traded in on truck 9. The cost of the new truck was $4,500. A trade-in allowance of $700 was received.

(2) Prepare a schedule showing the 1976 depreciation for each of the nine trucks.

7-2

A company has competed successfully for many years with other companies in its industry. The company, like its major competitors, has averaged about 25 percent gross margin on sales. The company's success lies mainly in its ability to keep operating expenses lower.

The company, through extensive research, has developed and patented a new product. The patent, which gives the company exclusive production rights, has been assigned a development cost of $510,000.

The company's chief accountant seeks advice on how to amortize the patent cost. The tax consultant suggested that a life of five years would probably be allowed by the Internal Revenue Service for income tax purposes. The patent attorney indicated that the legal life of the patent is 17 years but that, with slight modifications proposed by the research department, the patent could be renewed for an additional 17 years, a total of 34 years in all. The company's marketing research expert has expressed the opinion that the patent would permit the company to make a gross margin, on the new product, of 45 percent for the first four years; for the next four years the gross margin would be about 35 percent; after eight years the gross margin would drop to the industry level of 25 percent. The president's secretary, an extremely attractive young lady, suggest 10 years because "it divides so easy."

(1) Over what life would you suggest that the patent cost be amortized? Why?
(2) What criterion or criteria should govern the method used? (Continued)

(3) Calculate the amortization cost for the first full *year* of its use.

(4) Illustrate, by general journal entry, the patent amortization for the first month of the patent's use.

(5) Give a pro-forma illustration of the position statement presentation of this patent at the end of the first full year of its use.

7-3

A four-wheel drive truck was acquired by Ernie Hemingway for $5,000 on July 1, 1972. The truck was to be used only in hauling merchandise from the warehouse to the store. The truck was estimated to have a five-year life and a trade-in value at the end of that time of $800. During this time, it was anticipated that the truck would make 45,000 trips (from the warehouse to the store) and operate a total of 18,000 hours. The net income (before depreciation) expected to be realized during the life of the truck was $1,200,000. During the remainder of 1972, the truck operated 3,000 hours and made 5,000 trips. The net income (before depreciation) realized during this time was $200,000. The truck, the only one owned by Ernie Hemingway, had an appraised valuation of $4,500 on December 31, 1972.

(1) Compute depreciation for 1972 by as many methods as you can that are consistent, based on time. Identify each by name, and distinguish among the methods between those giving larger write-off than straight line in early years of life, and those giving smaller write-off than straight line in early years of life.

(2) Compute depreciation for 1972 by as many methods as you can that are consistent, based on use.

7-4

(1) In general, how do you decide whether to record an acquisition as an asset or expense?

(2) The table below summarizes the acquisitions of a firm on January 1, 1972. The accounting period is the calendar year, and the services of each acquisition are uniformly distributed (in a straight-line fashion) over the useful life. Indicate whether you would record each item as an asset or as an expense at the date of acquisition. Company policy is to classify expenditures of $50 or less as expenses.

Acquisition	Cost	Useful Life in Years
a. Delivery truck	$4,500	5
b. Special equipment for delivery truck	600	5
c. Tires for delivery truck	400	1/2
d. Special equipment for delivery truck	60	2 1/2
e. Sign for delivery truck	30	5
f. Office chair	100	3
g. Office desk	250	5

(3) If you decide to classify an acquisition as an asset, then how do you decide whether to classify it separately or with another asset for the purposes of applying depreciation procedures?

(4) Indicate which of the above acquisitions could be grouped together (treated as a single asset) for purposes of applying depreciation rules.

(5) Under what conditions would your answer in (4) be different? What would it be, and why would it change?

7-5   The Marcus Aurelius Corporation wishes to use a "repair reserve" procedure for a machine purchased May 1, 1972 that cost $24,000 with total repairs estimated at $3,600 over its nine-year life. On November 1, 1972 repairs of $300 were incurred. Record the appropriate general journal entries (without explanation) for both November 1 and December 31 (the end of the accounting period). Ignore depreciation.

7-6   Diverse approaches have been made to depreciation and income measurement. Is income earned when (1) the cost of the asset has been recovered, (2) funds to replace equipment have been recovered, or (3) funds to allow expansion to keep up with the industry have been recovered? Concentrate on usefulness criterion. What difficulties are encountered with concept (2)?

7-7   Two concerns have been in business for the same number of years. They started with the same capital; average earnings and dividends have been the same during the years of operation. Does it necessarily follow that the goodwill of one company is the same as the other. Explain your answer.

7-8   The chief engineer of a company suggested in a conference of the company's executives that the accountants should speed up depreciation on the machinery in Department 3 because improvements are making these machines obsolete very rapidly and a replacement fund big enough to cover the replacement is wanted.
   Explain the accounting concept of depreciation, giving special attention to the issues raised by the chief engineer.

7-9   In evaluating depreciation methods, select from the following statements those that you could logically defend.
(1) Depreciation is a sunk cost.
(2) Straight-line depreciation gives an increasing rate of return on the company's capital investment.
(3) The allowing of accelerated depreciation for tax purposes is an indirect means of subsidizing business investment.
(4) In public utilities, it is possible to argue that depreciation based on income is closely related to the economic productivity of the asset.
(5) Under the declining-balance method, the total cost of the asset will never be completely depreciated.

7-10   After a great deal of investigating investment opportunities, Stanley Baiman had decided to purchase a liquor store location in New York in 1960. It cost $100,000 with net fixtures valued at $15,000, and the original legal cost of the license was $5,000; its gross sales for the previous year were $200,000.
   Several things influenced this decision. The existence of court-enforceable fair trade laws in that state meant that he would not have to face price competition. Although this was a distinct advantage, the major factor was a state law which strictly limited the number of licenses to operate such stores.

The number of licenses was frozen, and the same law restricted the distance between stores to 1,500 feet.

Thus, the business seemed to virtually guarantee an income. However, owing to the above laws, the only method of entry was to purchase an existing license, all of which sold at a substantial premium.

(1) Should $80,000, the premium above the legal cost of the franchise, be amortized? If so, by what methods?

(2) In 1964, the Reform Liquor Law was passed in New York. This law permitted an increase in the number of licenses issued, lifted price controls, and did away with the distance requirement between stores. Large department stores obtained licenses and began price cutting by using liquor as a "loss leader" to attract customers. Should Mr. Baiman change the way he accounts for the franchise premium?

7-11   Assume that you propose to buy the Belafonte Corporation and that in this connection it is necessary to make a valuation of the enterprise.

The following data regarding the Belafonte Corporation are compiled:

(1) Average level of revenues for the past three years is $900,000; it is estimated that the average for the next five years will be 10 percent higher. Average of all charges except depreciation and income taxes is $600,000; the average of the same factors for the next five years is estimated at $630,000.

(2) Current liabilities, not including explicit interest, have averaged $150,000 for the past three years and now stand at this figure; no major change in this condition is expected for the future. Net book value of current assets is now $400,000; the amount is a fair representation of current values except in the case of inventories which are recorded at $20,000 less than their present value.

(3) Net book value of existing plant assets is now $900,000, and net appraised value of these resources is $1,200,000; average depreciation charge for the past three years based on current replacement cost would exceed average charge booked ($51,000) by $15,000. Organization costs incurred when the Belafonte Corporation was formed, amounting to $20,000, were written off improperly; no other intangibles appear on the books, although the company markets products under trade names and has a favorable position in the industry. Income taxes for the future are estimated at 50 percent of the net.

(4) Capital-attracting rate of return on booked resources required in this situation is estimated at 7 percent; it is assumed that the company can earn this rate on these booked resources indefinitely. Superior earnings are assumed to be assured for a period of five years.

Compute the value of goodwill.

7-12   In January 1973 the Ngo Corporation purchased land, together with a building standing on it, as a site for a new plant. During 1973 the corporation constructed the plant with its own labor, facilities, and equipment. All transactions relating to the above properties were charged to the account Real Estate—New. As the new accountant for the company, you have recommended that they reclassify all items in this account to one of the following accounts:

a. Land account
b. Buildings account
c. Revenue (or gain) account
d. Expense (or loss) account
e. Some other account

Indicate to which one or more of the five types of accounts listed above you would transfer each of the following items. Whenever the answer is (e), name the account.

(1) Contract price of "basket" purchase (land and building)
(2) Legal fees relating to conveyance of title
(3) Invoice cost of materials and supplies used in construction
(4) Direct costs arising from demolition of old buildings
(5) Discounts received for early payment of (3)
(6) Total discount and issue costs on bonds issued during year (bond proceeds were used to finance construction)
(7) Interest charge to end of year on bonds mentioned in (6) above
(8) Cost of building permits and licenses
(9) Total cost of excavation
(10) Premiums for insurance against natural hazards during construction
(11) Net cost of tool shed erected for use in constructing new building
(12) Installation costs for newly acquired machinery installed in new buildings
(13) Proceeds from sale of materials salvaged from razing old buildings
(14) Special municipal assessments for sidewalk and street paving necessitated by changed use of property
(15) Cost of old building demolished

7-13   As the operator of a foreign car rental service, you acquire the following automobiles on the first day of your accounting period:

Model	Cost	Estimated Salvage	Estimated Life (Years)
Alfa Romeo	$ 3,519	$ 519	3
Jaguar	4,452	1,452	4
Mercedes-Benz	5,020	1,020	5
Porsche	5,700	700	5
Rolls-Royce	13,995	1,995	12

(1) Name two depreciation methods that give decreasing periodic charges, and compute first-year depreciation for the Jaguar by the method giving the largest charge.
(2) The Rolls-Royce is traded (in the middle of the seventh year) for two dozen golf carts and motor scooters costing $500 apiece. Record appropriately, provided the trade-in allowance is $7,500. (Do not use the *income tax* method; assume *straight-line* depreciation, and assume that the balance owed is paid in cash.)

(3) a. The Porsche is sold outright at the end of the first year. This vehicle is to be depreciated on the basis of use; it has operated 54,000 miles of the 540,000 miles of anticipated use. Record the sale if a 6 percent 60-day $5,000 note is accepted.

b. For the following two accounts, identify precisely one transaction which would cause the following accounting effects:

Example:	Answer:
0. Mortgage Payable—Credit	0. Borrowed money,
1. Machinery—Accumulated Repairs—Credit	and pledged real
2. Bond Sinking-fund Interest Revenue—Debit	estate

(4) a. You discount the note [with recourse received in (3a)] 20 days later in settlement of your account with TV Thompson at a 6 percent rate. Record.

b. Give the entry (entries) for your firm if the note is not paid at maturity. (Assume a $5 bank service.)

(5) You borrow $1,200 on the firm's 5 percent 30-day note discounted by your bank at 4 percent. Record. Also record the necessary adjusting entry 15 days later at the end of the accounting period.

(6) After depreciating the Mercedes-Benz for three years on a *straight-line* basis, you decide that the car's service life will be twice what you originally estimated. Compute the depreciation charge for the fourth year by the best method, and make the necessary entries.

(7) You replace the tires and motor on the Alfa Romeo (after two years) at a cash cost of $500, thus partially rehabilitating the car. Record if:

a. The cost of the discarded tires and motor are known to have been $450, or

b. Their cost is unknown.

7–14　　This problem consists of nine questions which require journal entries as answers (without explanation). Assume that the accounting period is the calendar year and that any necessary entries have *not* been made for the current year.

(1) A firm wishes to use a "repair reserve" method for a machine purchased January 2, 1973 that costs $12,000 with total repairs estimated at $3,500 over its 10-year life. During 1973 repairs of $125 were debited to repair expense. Make the December 31, 1973 entry that is needed.

(2) You are given the following data in chronological order:

Beginning inventory	25 units @ $10.00 each
Purchase	30 units @ 11.00
Sale	10 units
Purchase	20 units @ 12.00

Make the complete journal entry needed for a cash sale of 45 units at $20 each, using Lifo perpetual.

(3) Using the same data as in (2) above, journalize using Fifo perpetual.

(4) You are given the following account balances: Merchandise Inventory $2,100 (2,100 units); Purchases $6,200 (1,300 units @ $2.00 in May and

1,200 units @ $3.00 in September). Give the journal entry to close and adjust, assuming an ending inventory of 2,500 units, Lifo.

(5) You are given the following account balances: Merchandise Inventory $250 (20 units): Purchases $13,200 (900 units), Purchases—Freight In $450, Purchases—Returns $110 (10 units), Purchases—Discounts $260, and ending inventory of 100 units. Make the entry to adjust and close, using a weighted-average method, Locom, with market of $17 per unit.

(6) A machine purchased January 1, 1973 for $4,400, with estimated life of five years and $400 salvage value, depreciated on a straight-line basis and was traded for a new machine costing $7,100 on June 30, 1973, with a cash payment of $5,000. Give the entry at June 30, 1973.

(7) A machine purchased January 1, 1973 for $6,000 with estimated life of five years and zero salvage, is to be depreciated on the sum-of-the-years-digits method. The machine is sold for $2,000 on December 31, 1976. Prepare the necessary entries at that date.

(8) A machine purchased January 1, 1973 for $10,000 with estimated life of 10 years and zero salvage, is to be depreciated on the declining-balance method with a rate of twice that of the straight-line method. The machine is sold for $3,000 on January 2, 1977. Make the necessary journal entries at that date, disregarding 1977 depreciation.

7-15

A slot machine is purchased on January 3, 1973. Records of cost and past depreciation are lost, but it is known that depreciation has been calculated at 10 percent of the balance of the machine account. The December 31, 1975 balance of the machine account of $10,692 represents cost less depreciation to date, on the declining-balance method. (If the machine had cost $100 on January 3, 1973, its ledger balance would be $90 at the end of 1973, $81 at the end of 1974, and $72.90 at the end of 1975.) The estimated life of the machine is 10 years from date of purchase.

Prepare the adjusting entry to be made on December 31, 1975 to show depreciation expense and to correct the accounts if the sum-of-the-years-digits method is to be used.

7-16

A Flextooth Crusher was purchased on July 1, 1973; the invoice price was $5,200. Freight charges were $325, and installation costs $150. The cash discount of 2 percent was taken.

The life of the machine was estimated at 10 years. Total repairs were estimated at $2,300. Straight-line depreciation and an accumulated repairs account are to be used. On December 1, 1974, $500 was paid for repairs. On January 1, 1975, $1,000 was paid for modifying the machine to permit an increase in output without increasing the life of the machine. On November 13, 1976, the machine was sold for $700. The Accumulated Repairs account had a credit balance of $75.

Prepare the entries regarding the above on the following dates:

a. July 1, 1973
b. December 31, 1973—end of accounting year
c. December 1, 1974
d. January 1, 1975
e. November 13, 1976

7-17

After exploration and geophysical surveys costing $1,500,000, a company acquires rights to mine a given property in 1973 under the following terms:
a. A cash payment of $500,000.
b. A royalty of $25,000 per year for 12 years.
c. At a cost of about $500,000, the property will be restored to its present appearance, all mine shafts permanently sealed, and all equipment removed at the end of 12 years.
d. Equipment to be installed at a cost of $2,000,000.
e. Roads and bridges to be built at a cost of $75,000.
f. Mine tunnels and shafts to be constructed at a total cost of $900,000 or $75,000 per year.
g. Expected mine output in thousands of tons:

Year	Output	Year	Output	Year	Output
1973	5	1978	28	1982	17
1974	20	1979	24	1983	20
1975	28	1980	20	1984	15
1976	30	1981	18	1985	5
1977	20				

Consider the accounting problems related to the lettered items; outline how you would account for this mine, and give appropriate journal entries for 1973, 1974, and 1985.

7-18

A company acquired and placed in service a machine as of January 1, 1973 at a cost of $10,000. Depreciation was computed on the straight-line basis with an expected salvage of $1,500 and an expected life of 4 years. Depreciation had been properly accumulated to December 31, 1975.

Early in 1976 the machine manufacturer produced a greatly improved model; this was offered to the company at: (a) list $10,000, (b) cash without trade-in $8,500, and (c) cash with trade-in $7,500. Accepting the third alternative, the company received its new machine on July 1, 1976.
(1) What various values might be assigned to the new machine? Show supporting calculations for each value, and give arguments for and against its use.
(2) Show journal entries under each alternative.

7-19

A company ships its liquor product in State of Ohio containers that cost $4.50 each. Customers are billed $6 each for the containers, which is refunded if the container is returned in good condition. The company's past experience is that 50 percent of the containers shipped are never returned for refund and that, on the average, containers are good for about four shipments. Containers have a scrap value of $0.50 each when retired from service. The company buys 600 containers per month and carries an average inventory of 1,800 containers. Shipments average 15,000 containers per year.

State two major assumptions that must be made in order for the system to work. One is to determine when a container is sold, and two is how to estimate the book value of the containers not returned. Defend both your assumptions as to why they are more reasonable than any other pair of assumptions based on the information given.

List the titles of the special accounts that you think would be necessary to account for these containers most effectively. For each account, state under (a) precisely how it would be listed on either the income statement or position statement. State under item (b) precisely how it would be treated in preparing a working capital fund-flow statement [namely, whether any change would be treated as (1) internal working capital change; (2) external working capital change, whether increase or decrease; and (3) an adjustment to net income, whether an addition of a deduction]. State under item (c) the titles of accounts that would be credited when this account is debited, and also those that would be debited when this account is credited (as below):

Account No. 1. Title: _____

       a.
       b. 1.
          2.
          3.
       c.

Give illustrative journal entries for the following transactions to show how your method would work:

A. Shipped 1,200 containers to customers.
B. The expected number of containers are to be returned for credit.
C. The expected number of containers will not be returned.
D. Depreciation on 1,200 containers shipped.
E. 50 containers are scrapped.
F. Purchased 600 new containers.
G. ⎫
   ⎬ Supply your own transactions.
H. ⎭

7-20

The Audie Murphy Corporation reported net income for 1972, 1973, and 1974 in the following amounts:

1972	$25,000
1973	$33,000
1974	$17,000

An examination of the records of this corporation for 1972 and 1973 disclosed the following information:

(1) In 1972, a machine was constructed by the corporation in its own plant. The total cost of construction was $11,000. A similar machine, if purchased through the usual trade sources, would have cost $14,000, and the firm used this amount in recording the machine in its accounts. The excess of the recorded cost over the cost of construction was credited to Gain on Construction of Machinery. The corporation has recorded depreciation on this machine at an annual rate of 10 percent since July 1, 1972, the date the machine was placed in service.

(2) In 1973, the company increased the balance of the Land account by $12,000, representing the excess of the estimated replacement cost of

the corporation's plant site over the original cost thereof. The amount of $12,000 was credited to Miscellaneous Revenue.

Prepare a schedule showing the computation of the correct net income for 1972, 1973, and 1974, according to accepted accounting principles. What do you consider as the correct incomes in the three years?

8 Bonds and the New Assets and Liabilities

*Accounting can rise no higher in the scale of certainty than the events which it reflects. . . . There are no doubt some who regard intangible assets as unreal and favor writing them off on this account—but if once the view is accepted that value depends on expectations for the future, the proposal is either invalid or applicable almost equally to tangible assets. Indeed, experience shows that intangible are often more enduring than tangible values.**

GEORGE O. MAY, date unknown

The discussion of long-lived assets and liabilities continues in this chapter. In Chapter 7 nonmonetary accounts for plant and intangibles were considered; in this chapter those of a monetary nature will be analyzed. These consist of bonds (both as investments and liabilities), leases, and pensions. Finally accounts resulting from income tax allocation and the investment credit will be reviewed briefly.

Bond Investments and Liabilities

The principal example of a long-term liability (to the debtor) and a long-term investment (to the investor) is a bond contract. Although long-term investments may be in stocks as well as in bonds, only bonds will be considered here. (Stocks will be considered in Chapter 11.) Occasionally, some bonds may be classified as current (for example, marketable securities). Usually both long-term investments and long-term liabilities, such as bonds, are regarded as the most current of the noncurrent accounts. Thus, a long-term investment in bonds is listed on the position statement between the current and the plant and intangible assets. Bonds and other long-term

*From Paul Grady, editor, *Memoirs and Accounting Thought of George O. May* (New York: The Ronald Press Company, 1962), pp. 294–295.

liabilities are listed after current liabilities but, of course, before the ownership equity accounts.

In contrast to the usual verbal or implied contractual arrangements of short-term investments and obligations, bonds and other long-term investments and obligations are usually written contracts which specify the rights and obligations of both the lenders and the debtors; these include the due dates, the amount(s) or rate of interest payments, the maturity date, and the property pledged as security. If the bonds are secured by liens on real property, they are called mortgage bonds. If the bonds are secured by the trust deposit of stocks and other securities, they are called collateral bonds. If liens on equipment are given, they are called equipment bonds. Usually only long-term property is pledged. If the bonds are secured only by the general reputation of the issuing company, they are called debentures, the only type of bond issued by most large corporations. Bonds on which interest is payable only if earned are referred to as income bonds but are seldom issued.

As explained in Chapter 2, bonds are the principal accounting example of assets and liabilities valued on a direct valuation basis at the date of acquisition or issue. Bond contracts involve future events that can be predicted and evaluated accurately and objectively. Both lenders and debtors do expect to carry out the terms of the contract exactly as specified. A major area of uncertainty is whether the issuer will default; this risk is reflected in the price that the lender paid for the bond. Other areas of uncertainty include price-level changes which affect the purchasing power of the interest and principal payments to be received by the lender.

Since there is a single payment (or receipt) when a bond contract is purchased (or issued), there is a tendency to think of bond contracts exclusively in terms of this cash flow. This is incorrect since a bond contract consists of two types of cash flows, and the payment (or receipt) at the date of purchase (or issue) is simply the sum of the present value of these two types of future cash flows. The two kinds of future cash flows in a bond contract are:

1. The face value of the bond, a fixed sum due at the maturity date.
2. The periodic interest at the rate and times specified in the contract. Although the rate given and expressed as a percentage of the face value is an annual rate, the payments are usually made semiannually.

Based on the discussion in Chapter 2, the reader will recognize that the present values of these two kinds of future payments (receipts) are expressed as $1 \div (1 + i)^n$ for each $1 of the first, and as $\{1 - [1 \div (1 + i)^n]\} \div i$ for each $1 of the second. More precisely, the present value of a bond contract can be computed by adding the present value of the maturity amount (the face value times the present value of $1 due in n periods:

$$p_{\overline{n}|i} = \frac{1}{(1+i)^n}$$

as expressed in the table in Appendix A) to the present value of the interest payments (the amount of one interest payment times the present value of an annuity of $1 per period:

$$P_{\overline{n}|i} = \frac{1 - [1 \div (1+i)^n]}{i}$$

as expressed in the table in Appendix A).

In computing the present value of the bond at issue, or its market price, it is necessary to recognize that two interest rates are involved in a bond contract. One is the *nominal* or coupon rate (set by the borrower), which is stated in the bond contract; this is used to compute the amount of cash interest usually paid (or received) every six months. The other is the *effective* or yield rate (set through the operation of the investment market); this reflects the market interest rate for bond issues of this term with adjustments for the expected risk, and is used to compute the market price of the bond or its present value at the date of issue.

Although it is unlikely that both the nominal and effective interest rates would be the same, this is nevertheless possible. In such an event, the face value of the bond also would be its present value. For example, if a $10,000 10-year bond[1] were issued with semi-annual interest payments at a nominal and effective interest rate of 6 percent, its present value would be computed as follows (with interest factors taken from the two present value tables in Appendix A):

Present value of maturity amount:
  $10,000 \times p_{\overline{20}|3\%}$ = $10,000 \times 0.5537$
     (*3% for 20 periods since 6 months is 1/2 year,*
     the rate would be 1/2 the annual rate) $ 5,537

Present value of nominal interest payments:[2]
  $300 \times P_{\overline{20}|3\%}$ = 300×14.8775 4,463

     Present value = maturity amount $10,000

Typically, however, the effective or yield rate of interest is different from the nominal or coupon rate. If the effective rate is greater than the nominal rate, the bond is said to sell (or be issued) at a *discount*.

---

[1]Industrial bonds are rarely issued in such small amounts, but for illustrative purposes smaller figures are easier to work with.
[2]Rounded to nearest dollar.

If the effective rate is less than the nominal rate, the bond is said to sell (or be issued) at a *premium.* Examples of both situations follow.

If the effective rate in the example above were 8 percent, the cash proceeds or present value of the bond at date of issue would be:

Present value of maturity amount:
$$\$10,000 \times p_{\overline{20}|4\%} = \$10,000 \times 0.4564 \qquad\qquad \$4,564$$

Present value of nominal interest payments:[3]
$$\$300 \times P_{\overline{20}|4\%} = \$300 \times 13.5903 \qquad\qquad \underline{4,077}$$

Present value of bond contract $\underline{\underline{\$8,641}}$

If the effective rate were 4 percent, the cash proceeds or present value at date of issue would be:

Present value of maturity amount:
$$\$10,000 \times p_{\overline{20}|2\%} = \$10,000 \times 0.6730 \qquad\qquad \$\ 6,730$$

Present value of nominal interest payments:[3]
$$\$300 \times P_{\overline{20}|2\%} = \$300 \times 16.3514 \qquad\qquad \underline{4,905}$$

Present value of bond contract $\underline{\underline{\$11,635}}$

If only one present-value interest table were available, the present value of the bond contract still could be computed by using whatever present-value table is available.

If only the present value of $1 due in *n* periods table were available, the present value of the bond contract with an effective rate of 4 percent would be calculated as follows:

Present value of maturity amount:
$$\$10,000 \times p_{\overline{20}|2\%} = \$10,000 \times 0.6730 \qquad\qquad \$\ 6,730$$

Present value of nominal interest payments:[4]

$$\underset{\substack{(maturity \\ value)}}{\$10,000} - \underset{\substack{(present \\ value\ of \\ maturity \\ amount)}}{\$6,730} = \$3,270 \times \dfrac{3\%\ (nominal\ rate)}{2\%\ (effective\ rate)} \qquad 4,905$$

     $\underline{}$

     $\underline{\underline{\$11,635}}$

If only the present value of an annuity of $1 per period table were

---

[3]Rounded to nearest dollar.
[4]As an alternative (as shown in Chapter 2), the present value of an annuity of $1 per period could be determined easily from the present value of $1 for *n* periods:

$$\frac{1 - [1 \div (1.02)^{20}]}{0.02} = \frac{1 - 0.6730}{0.02} = 16.3500$$

available, the present value of the bond contract would be computed as follows:

Maturity amount of bond	$10,000
Plus[5] the present value of the difference between what the semiannual interest payments would be at the nominal rate (0.03 × $10,000) and at the effective rate (0.02 × $10,000) discounted at the effective rate:	
$\$300 - 200 = \$100 \times P_{\overline{20}|2\%} = \$100 \times 16.3514$	1,635
	$11,635

If the present value of the maturity amount and the present value of the future stated or coupon interest amounts of the bond contract were reported separately on the position statement for both long-term bond investments and long-term bond liabilities, much of the confusion about the nature of the bond contract might be avoided. Conceptually the bond asset or liability should be shown on the position statement immediately after issuance as follows:

	If Purchased (Sold) to Yield		
	4%	*6%*	*8%*
Bonds receivable (or payable)—			
Face amount $10,000, maturing in 10 years	$ 6,730	$ 5,537	$4,564
Bonds receivable (or payable)—			
semiannual interest amount $300	4,905	4,463	4,077
Total present value of bond	$11,635	$10,000	$8,641

The above presentation, although not followed in practice, would communicate clearly the meaning of the liability amounts for bonds (or notes).

In practice, however, the bond investment is reported as a single amount, whereas two accounts are used to accomplish this for the bond liability.

Using the same example, the asset would be reported by the lender as follows:

	If Purchased to Yield		
	4%	*6%*	*8%*
Investment in long-term bonds	$11,635	$10,000	$8,641

---

[5]If the effective interest rate were greater than the nominal rate, the difference would be deducted, not added.

while the liability would be reported by the debtor as follows:

| | If Sold to Yield | | |
	4%	6%	8%
Bond payable	$10,000	$10,000	$10,000
Plus premium (or less discount)	1,635		(1,359)
	$11,635	$10,000	$ 8,641

Both of these presentations obscure the two distinct cash flows in-volved in a bond contract, the result of a traditional overemphasis on the face value of a bond, together with a failure to recognize the true nature of a bond. Occasionally the discount is reported as pre-paid interest and classified completely in error as an asset by the borrower and as a liability by the investor. The discount under all circumstances is neither a prepayment of cost by the debtor (for ex-ample, prepaid insurance) nor an advance to the investor (customer's deposits). Instead, the discount is the present value at the effective interest rate of the periodic excess of the effective interest over the nominal interest, which remains uncollected by the bondholder and unpaid by the issuing firm until the due date of the bond. Thus the amount of the discount represents unpaid or future interest which is not paid until the date of maturity, not prepaid interest.

Occasionally the bond premium has been recorded by the issuer as revenue at the time of issuance. This is clearly incorrect because at no stage during the lifetime of the bond does the premium con-stitute revenue to the issuer. Instead, the premium represents the present value at the effective rate of the periodic excess of the nom-inal interest over the effective interest, which is returned by the issu-ing company to the bondholder over the bond's lifetime as part of the periodic interest payment. This is shown clearly in the earlier illus-tration (page 339), in which the present value of the bond contract is shown when the only table available is the present value of an annuity of $1 per period.

Accounting practice also often lumps the discount with the various other costs incurred with issuing bonds. If material, these costs should be recorded as an asset and amortized as bond issue ex-penses over the lifetime of the bonds.

During the bonds' lifetime, accounting for bonds is concerned chiefly with interest. The interest charge (revenue) in any specific accounting period is the nominal interest payment (receipt) plus any amortization of discount or less any amortization of premium. The present (or carrying) value of the asset (or liability) at any statement date is reported as the maturity value of the bond less any unamor-tized discount or plus any unamortized premium (which *indirectly,* of course, is the summation of the two values of the bond).[6] The amortization process (similar to the depreciation or depletion process, except that intangibles are involved) consists of allocating to the periodic nominal or cash interest the appropriate portion of the total discount (or deducting from the nominal interest the appropriate portion of the premium). The result of the amortization process is to convert the interest receipt (or payment), which is at the nominal interest rate, into interest revenue (or expense), which is at the effective or yield interest rate.

Two methods of amortization are in common use. The one with most merit is the *interest* method; under it, the present value of the bond at the beginning of the period is multiplied by the effective interest rate, and the difference between this effective interest and the nominal interest is the amount of period amortization. The chief advantage of this method is that it results in a periodic interest revenue (or expense), which is based on the same (initial) effective interest rate (and the present value of the bond at the beginning of each period) over the bond's lifetime.

The second method, the one used by most firms and the one that must be used in federal income tax returns, is the straight-line method, discussed earlier in connection with depreciation. This traditional method, although more easily computed and understood than the interest one, gives a varying ratio of interest expense to the bond's book value over the bond's lifetime, since a uniform amount of premium or discount is amortized in each period.

The AICPA in its APB Opinion No. 12 accepts the interest method as a theoretically sound and acceptable method.

A special problem of accounting for interest arises when the bonds are issued between interest payment dates. When this occurs, the accrued interest from the last interest payment date to the date of issue is "sold" with the bond. This interest is recorded as a separate and current liability, Interest Payable, by the issuer or as a separate and current asset, Interest Receivable, by the bondholder. At the next interest payment date, these interest accounts would be closed, and the balance of the payment (receipt) reported as current-period interest charge (interest revenue).

One type of bond contract provides for the repayment of the face or maturity amount of the bond over its lifetime in a series of periodic installments; this is called a *serial bond*. Although the interest method of amortization could be used for any discount or premium on serial bonds [for example, by viewing each installment and the related interest receipts (or payments) as a separate bond issue], the *bonds*

---

[6]It should be recognized that if the market interest rate for this type of security has changed since the date of issue, the present (or carrying) value of the asset (or liability) will be different from its current (market) value.

outstanding method typically is employed with this type of bond. This method is an adequate substitute for the interest method. If the regular straight-line method were applied to a serial bond issue, sizable distortions in periodic interest could result, with a corresponding impact on periodic income. With the bonds-outstanding method, the amount of amortization is a constant amount per period for each dollar of face value of the bonds outstanding at the beginning of the period. Under this method the amount of premium or discount to be amortized during a period is equal to the dollar amount of bonds outstanding at the beginning of the period, multiplied by the quotient of the total amount of premium or discount to be amortized over the life of the bonds, divided by the sum of the dollar amount of bonds outstanding at the beginning of each year during the life of the bonds. This can be applied to the amount of bonds outstanding in any particular period for the amortization for that period.[7]

As mentioned earlier, nominal bond interest is usually paid (or received) semiannually. The amortization may be recorded at each interest date or deferred until every second interest date if statements are prepared annually and if the bond year corresponds with the accounting year. If the interest year and the accounting year do not coincide, the adjusting entries for interest at the end of the accounting year must include the appropriate amount of amortization (in order that the nominal interest be converted to the effective interest).

When bonds are retired, any gain or loss on retirement to either the issuer or the investor should be recorded on his respective set of books. Sometimes bond issues are retired by a process of refunding; this means that the old issue is exchanged for the new issue. If the old bond issue is refunded before it matures, there may be unamortized discount or premium (plus issue costs on the books of the issuer) at the date of refunding. Sometimes too, a call premium, a special inducement in price, is stipulated in the bond contract to

---

[7]For example, if a five-year six percent serial bond with a face value of $10,000 was issued at $9,700, with $2,000 to be retired at the end of each year, the amortization each year per $1 of bonds outstanding at the beginning of the year would be $300/$30,000 = $0.01 (or $10 per $1,000). Thus the discount amortization would be $100 for the first year, $80 for the second, $60 for the third, $40 for the fourth, and $20 for the fifth and last year. The sum of the bonds outstanding is computed as follows:

Beginning of:	
1st year	$10,000
2d year	8,000
3d year	6,000
4th year	4,000
5th year	2,000
	$30,000

compensate bondholders for the trouble, costs, and possibly lost interest, in the event that the bonds are called for payment by the issuer before the regular maturity date.

There are three methods of accounting for the unamortized amounts on the old issue: (1) to recognize any gain or loss at the date of refunding, (2) to continue to amortize these amounts over what would have been the lifetime of the old bond issue, and (3) to extend the period for amortization over the lifetime of the new issue.

In the viewpoint of the authors, the first method is preferable to the others for unregulated enterprises. Such unamortized amounts as well as any call premium are the costs of terminating a disadvantageous contract; as such, they are expired since they relate to past transactions and events. Such amounts do not represent part of the current value of the new issue since a change in the market price of interest occurred before the refunding.

On this issue the position of the Internal Revenue Service for once is in accordance with good accounting theory and practice. Although the first is the prevailing practice, the AICPA has given support to all three methods.

Our previous example of a 6 percent bond (with a 10-year life and with interest payable semiannually) can be used to illustrate bond accounting under various assumptions as to the effective interest rate and methods of amortization for both the investor and the debtor. In our illustration, the bond year is assumed to coincide with the accounting calendar year, and the figures are rounded to the nearest $1 (for convenience).

Three transactions are recorded in the appropriate T accounts:

A The issue as of January 1
B The six months' interest as of July 1
C The second six months' interest as of January (which would be recorded as of December 31 since this is the end of the accounting year)

If the bond is issued at a 6 percent effective rate, the T accounts for the investor would appear as follows after the three transactions have been recorded:

	Investor		
Cash	*Investment in Bond*	*Interest Receivable*	*Interest Revenue*
✔ ———	(A) 10,000		(B) 300
(A) 10,000		(C) 300	(C) 300
(B) 300			

and for the issuing corporation:

Debtor

Cash		Bonds Payable	Interest Payable	Interest Charge
(A) 10,000	(B) 300	(A) 10,000	(C) 300	(B) 300
				(C) 300

If the bond is issued at a 4 percent effective interest rate and the premium is amortized by the interest method, the T accounts for the investor would appear as follows after the three transactions had been recorded:

Investor

Cash		Interest Receivable	Investment in Bond		Interest Revenue
✔ ——	(A) 11,635	(C) 300	(A) 11,635	(B) 67	(B) 233
(B) 300				(C) 69	(C) 231

and for the issuing corporation:

Debtor

Cash		Interest Payable	Bond Payable
✔ ——	(B) 300	(C) 300	(A) 10,000
(A) 11,635			

Bond Payable—Premium		Interest Charges
(B) 67	(A) 1,635	(B) 233
(C) 69		(C) 231

If the bond is issued at an 8 percent effective interest rate and the discount is amortized by the interest method, the T accounts for the investor would appear as follows after the three transactions have been recorded:

Investor

Cash		Interest Receivable	Investment in Bond	Interest Revenue
✔ ——	(A) 8,641	(C) 300	(A) 8,641	(B) 346
(B) 300			(B) 46	(C) 347
			(C) 47	

and for the issuing corporation:

	Cash			Debtor Bond Payable				Bond Payable—Discount	
✔ ——		(B)	300	(A) 10,000		(A)	1,359	(B)	46
(A) 8,641								(C)	47

	Interest Payable			Interest Charge	
	(C)	300	(B)	346	
			(C)	347	

Our illustration provides some support for the contention that unless the effective interest rate is significantly different from the nominal interest rate, the straight-line method of amortization (which results in the amortization of the average amount of premium or discount per period) will approximate the interest method. In our example, even though the rates are an entire percentage point apart, the differences are not significant. In the premium illustration, straight-line amortization would be $1,635/20 or $82 for each of the 20 semi-annual periods, as compared with $67 and $68 for the first and second periods under the interest method. In the discount illustration, the straight-line amortization would be $1,359/20 or $68 in each of the 20 periods, as compared to $46 and $47 in the first and second periods under the interest method.

Sinking Funds
In addition to the installment approach provided for in the serial bond, bond contracts also contain other provisions for their retirement. These provisions may be of two types; both have the objective of reducing the lender's risk of loss and require action on the part of the debtor corporation. The first provides for periodic deposits of cash into a segregated fund which is to be used to retire the bonds, and the second provides for periodic reservations (or restrictions) of retained earnings to inform stockholders that the retained earnings, when so restricted, are not available for dividend declarations. Either or both types of provisions may be found in a single bond contract. The first type of provision tends to afford more protection than the second, because it requires the earmarking of cash which is necessary to retire the bonds; however, if a retained earnings reservation actually results in smaller dividends being paid, the debtor firm will have more net assets available for other uses, such as bond retirement, than it would otherwise. This type of provision will be

considered in Chapter 11, along with accounting for retained earnings.

When cash is reserved for a specific purpose such as the future retirement of bonds, it cannot be regarded as unrestricted cash. Instead, it is classified with long-term investments, as the most current of the noncurrent assets. Accounts that contain this cash restricted for special purposes are referred to as *sinking funds.* As discussed in Chapter 7, an interest method of depreciation is based on the sinking-fund concept. The fund may be maintained in the firm or given over to the control of a trustee. Since the retirement of bonds usually takes place only over a number of years, it is expected that the cash deposits will be invested during the waiting period, and any earnings will remain with the fund. Sometimes the sinking-fund provision will reduce the amount of periodic deposit required by the amount of the estimated earnings from the sinking fund. The periodic deposits in the fund are recorded as a transfer of cash; any net income (or expenses) of the fund will be entered as an increase (or decrease) in the fund and as periodic revenue (or expense), which is reported on the current income statement. When the bonds are retired, the sinking-fund investments must be converted into cash before the bond liability is retired unless, as is sometimes done, the cash was used to reacquire these bonds before maturity. Any excess of sinking-fund cash is returned to unrestricted cash while any deficiency in sinking-fund cash is covered by an additional transfer from unrestricted cash.

The New Assets and Liabilities

Although many long-term assets and liabilities have been accounted for since the corporate form of organization was developed in the nineteenth century, there are three major types that have evolved largely since World War II. These are leases, pensions, and income tax allocations. The problems with these comparatively new accounts are essentially the same ones discussed with the more familiar accounts. These relate to their nature, their reporting, their valuation, and their timing. With income tax allocations the problem is whether emphasis should be placed on flows or stocks. For pensions, changes in valuation are the focus. For leases, the emphasis is on income and revenue association or other fund flows such as cash or working capital. Although the problems relating to these accounts are familiar ones, there seems to be considerable confusion about their treatment. The confusion may be attributed to their newness.

Leased assets and applicable liabilities In accounting practice, a major distinction is made between assets that are owned and assets that are leased. Ownership rights are those of possession, use, and disposal; lease rights are those of possession and use but not of disposal. Under these circumstances a company which leases another's property (the lessee) under a noncancelable long-term contract will show the value of neither the lease asset nor the lease liability on the position statement. Yet, if the same company had purchased the property, it would be recorded as an asset regardless of how it was to be paid for. Also, if the lessee had prepaid the rents, a lease asset would be booked.

Compared to purchasing, leasing offers a number of advantages to the lessee. These are:

1. A method of raising funds for the acquisition of assets above and beyond funds available through direct borrowing
2. A way of avoiding the various problems of ownership, not only those of asset obsolescence, but also sometimes those of administration (for example, maintenance and record keeping)
3. A means of providing property that cannot be obtained through outright purchasing (for example, a computer) or that is needed only temporarily

In some situations, these advantages may weigh less than certain disadvantages such as the high cost of lease financing and the lack of residual rights (that is, no rights in the leased property after the lease ends).

In many lease contracts the property can be purchased for a nominal sum at the end of the lease. In practice, if it can be established clearly that the lease contract is a purchase, both the asset and the liability must be recorded; otherwise, even if material, the long-term lease contract is reported only in a footnote. Thus, for accounting practice purposes, there are two types of leases: lease purchase agreements and lease nonpurchase agreements (or executory leases).

Accepting prevailing practice, the AICPA has not changed its basic position on leased property in over 20 years;[8] in its APB Opinion No. 5, it continues to recommend essentially what it had recommended earlier, that leased property need be reported only in footnotes (giving the amounts of the annual rents and other obligations).[9] Although the Opinion provides nominally for the recording of leases as assets where a purchase takes place, the force of the Opinion serves to make it very difficult to demonstrate that a purchase has occurred.

---

[8]But the APB is again reviewing lease accounting and held public hearings on the subject in October 1971.

[9]Such a footnote might be worded as follows:

Lease Commitments. At December 31, 1972, the corporation was obligated under existing noncancelable leases for the use of real property with approximate minimum annual rentals as follows (000's omitted): 1973: $1,000; 1974: $900; 1975: $750; 1976–1990:$200 per year. The corporation must pay all taxes, insurance, and other operating costs on most of these leases, in addition to the rental payments. As these existing leases expire, it is likely that they will be renewed or replaced.

It takes the highly illogical position that a purchase cannot occur under a lease contract unless the payments for the use of the property exceed the decrease in the service value of the property rights (that is, where the lessee increases its equity in the assets and any residual value of the assets at the end of the "lease" belongs to the lessee or can be acquired for a nominal amount). But owned property, when acquired, is recorded as an asset, together with the related liabilities, irrespective of how the payments are made. Frequently, owned property may be sold or even abandoned before it is fully paid for. Therefore, this distinction does not seem to be valid.

There are practical problems in computing the value of leased property. For example, consider a company leasing property for 25 years at an annual rent of $10,000 under a contract in which all the rights received under the lease are property rights (which means that the lessee is responsible for repairs, insurance, taxes, and maintenance of the leased property). Here, the AICPA would recommend that the lease be booked as a purchase. The problem would be solved if the alternative cash price for the property were known because usually this would be an appropriate measure of its value. If the alternative cash price in this example were $90,770, it could also be determined that the interest rate implicit in the lease contract would be 10 percent. This is done by equating the $90,770 with the present value of an annuity of 25 rents of $10,000, and then solving for the interest rate, using the tables in Appendix A. On the other hand, if the cash price is not known, the lessee must determine an appropriate interest rate; for this example, it will be assumed to be 10 percent. The valuation would be the present value of the 25 annual rents discounted at 10 percent. The interest factor for the present value of an annuity of $1 per period (see Appendix A) is 9.0770 which, multiplied by the $10,000, gives a present value of the lease contract of $90,770. The lease asset and liability could be recorded at this value.

The selection of a proper interest rate may cause some problems. Also, the lessor (or the party owning the property) may make the payments for insurance, taxes, repairs, and maintenance on the property instead of the lessee. In this situation the annual payment would be both for the property rights and for these other services. Since these other services (or obligations) are accounted for separately from property rights where owned property is involved, presumably this also should be done for leased property. This would necessitate the very difficult division of the annual payment into the payment for property rights and the payment for services yet to be performed.

The problem of the appropriate interest rate could be solved by using an appropriate market rate, which could be the general rate of interest applicable for long-term borrowing by firms of similar risk, or the rate that the particular firm may have experienced recently in receiving long-term loans.

(assets) and obligations (liabilities) on position statements, and (3) allocation of pension costs to periodic income statements.

The third problem is the one that usually causes most difficulty. The total costs of a pension program are uncertain since the amount to be paid usually depends upon future events regarding employees and the amount that the fund can earn. However, with the aid of the methods applied by actuaries these uncertainties can be resolved. As with other long-term commitments, it should be remembered that the allocation process is not related to the method by which the asset is financed. Unlike other long-term assets, but similar to leases, the costs of pension programs are measured in terms of future cash flows, not past ones. Although the objective of pension amortization is the same as with depreciation, depletion, or other amortization—to accomplish matching—this is impossible to achieve. In matching, the cost expiration is to be matched with the revenue contribution—if not specifically, then at least by period. With existing methods this is not possible for pension funds. The best that can be done is to allocate the values in a systematic fashion, and to prevent the charges to pension expenses from fluctuating widely from period to period without there also being changes in pension cost variables.

The costs associated with pension plans are divided into three groups. These are *prior service costs* (for services performed before the inception of the plan or a change in plan benefits); *current* (or normal) *costs* (for the annual pension cost assigned to each year following the inception of the pension plan or a change in the plan); and the *actuarial gains and losses* (which arise from investment gains and losses or changes in interest rates and represent the difference between the actuarial assumptions and the actual conditions affecting the final pension cost).

Several accounting alternatives for prior service costs have been proposed: (1) charge the entire amount to expense in the period when the plan is adopted or changed, as either operating or extraordinary charges; (2) allocate the amount over the future service lives of employees who were active when the plan was adopted or changed, or over the period during which benefits are expected from the adoption or alteration of the plan; and (3) ignore the prior service costs by not accounting for them. Of the three alternatives, the second one, allocation, has received the most support. Charging the entire amount to the current period is rejected because such costs are costs of prior periods, not in an accounting sense (since no benefit was received), but only in an actuarial sense (since pension benefits include allowances for employee services received before the adoption of the plan). Ignoring the prior service costs is rejected on

the grounds that these costs do exist and should be reported, even if full funding is not necessary.[10]

In APB Opinion No. 8, the AICPA recommends that the prior service cost be amortized over periods ranging from 10 to 40 years. However, this recommendation is proposed as an alternative to not recognizing past service costs beyond the interest on the unfunded past service costs.[11] This latter provision (and the one found most frequently in practice) confuses the costs of the pension plan with the extent to which it is financed.

For the current service costs, APB Opinion No. 8 again seems to confuse cost allocation with financing since it proposes that the allocation be based on an actuarial cost (or financing) method. All the actuarial cost methods include an interest factor equal to the assumed earning rate on the pension fund. Under these methods, however, the periodic charge may be constant, increasing, or decreasing. Of these, perhaps the one providing the constant charge per period has the most merit because the revenue contribution of a pension plan cannot be measured. With results similar to the straight-line method of depreciation, the *projected benefit cost* method consists of a level normal cost, equal to a constant sum for each individual (depending on the age of the employee when he is hired or on when the plan is started), which when invested at the anticipated rate will achieve the required benefit cost at retirement. With this method, the total cost will stay level if the benefit cost was computed correctly (which means that there must be no unexpected change in plan benefits).

Another method is the *accrued benefit–unit credit* approach, under which the pension benefit for each employee is to be funded as it accrues and the normal cost equals the present discounted value of his retirement benefit earned as a result of his service in the current year. The benefit accrual and the normal cost for each succeeding year will increase because it will be discounted for a shorter period of time. The rationale for this method is that the longer the service, the higher the compensation, and since pension cost is a form of compensation, it also should increase over time. Under some plans, however, this factor is recognized directly by relating pension cost to salary level, instead of indirectly via the investment earning rate. Under the accrued benefit method, the periodic alloca-

---

[10]There are at least three possible methods by which a company might pay out assets to its funding agency or fund its pension plan. These are: *full actuarial funding* during the employment period (that is, the present discounted value of all future pension benefits for every employee covered), *terminal funding* at the time when the individual employee retires (that is, the present discounted value of all future pension benefits for the retiring individual), and *pay-as-you-go funding* after retirement (that is, actual pension payments to retired employees).

[11]Except that this amount may be adjusted upward when the pension fund plus stipulated pension related costs are less than the actuarially computed value of the vested benefits.

tion may become quite level for a mature employee group when the salaries (if benefits are related to salaries), average age, number, and turnover of employees all remain constant. Despite any termination date specified in a union contract or other possibility of cancellation, the typical pension program is likely to continue as long as the company does. Consequently, the economic view prevails, not the legal one; this means that all pension expenses should be accrued, and the accrual should not be limited to only those costs that become legal liabilities.

APB Opinion No. 8 does exclude some of the most objectionable approaches to accounting for pensions by stating (1) that a pension plan should be accounted for as though the company will continue to provide benefits beyond its legal obligation, which may be limited to the extent of assets in the fund, and (2) that the entire cost of benefit payments to be made ultimately should be charged to expense instead of to retained earnings. Even so, it requires, as a minimum, the accrual only of costs representing little or no more than the company's legal liability, and permits the smoothing of this effect over several years. With actuarial gains and losses, APB Opinion No. 8 permits spreading (over 10 to 20 years) or averaging, both of which result in smoothing of income. Many firms recognize any gains or losses by adjusting the pension costs of the current period.

The accounting for pensions is very similar to that for leases. If the periodic outlays for pension funding are classified as expenses, the journal entry would be as follows:

	Debit	Credit
Pension expense	×	
Cash		×
To record periodic pension expense		

If the outlay had not been made at the end of the accounting period, it would be recorded as an adjusting entry with the credit to a payable. If the pension plan is "capitalized" (that is, recorded as an asset and a liability), the following entry would be made:

	Debit	Credit
Pension asset	×	
Pension liability		×
To record present discounted value of		
pension program		

Subsequent periodic entries would be made to show changes in the pension asset and liability accounts and to record periodic pension expense and funding. If the periodic funding of the pension is recognized, the following entry would be made:

	Debit	Credit
Interest expense	×	
Pension liability	×	
Cash		×
To record funding of pension:		
Funding payment ×		
Less: Interest ×		
Reduction of liability ×		

If the periodic amortization of the pension is recognized, the following entry would be made (on an effective interest basis):

	Debit	Credit
Amortization charge or expense	×	
Pension asset—accumulated amortization		×
To record periodic amortization:		
Funding payment ×		
Less: Interest ×		
Reduction of asset ×		

The above entry assumes that the amortization of the pension cost coincides with its funding. If it does not, the amortization could be recorded on other bases such as straight line.

Inasmuch as wage and salary contracts are not capitalized, it also does not seem appropriate to capitalize the present value of future pension benefits and obligations since the latter, of course, are a part of the former. Under APB Opinion No. 8, the difference between the amount charged as current pension cost and the amount funded should be reported as an asset or as a liability, as the case may be; or, if the vested benefit rights[12] of employees exceed the sum of the accrued liability and the pension fund, the excess should be reported as both an asset and a liability. Since liabilities conventionally are reported when obligations exist, irrespective of their legal status, the latter recommendation is inconsistent.

Of significance, however, is the extent to which the pension program is being funded. This should be described in the footnotes and should include information on prior service costs, if these are segregated. Furthermore, any type of fund-flow statement should

---

[12]A pension benefit is called vested when the right to receive it is no longer contingent on being employed under the plan.

identify the annual disbursements that are made into the pension fund.

Income tax allocation Income tax allocation has received perhaps more attention in practice and theory than have leases and pensions. In accounting, income tax allocation means apportioning federal income taxes between different periods or different statements (or sections of a statement). There are three types of differences between accounting income and taxable income (as reported on the federal income tax return). The first type is permanent differences which do not give rise to tax allocation. These differences arise from legislative restrictions or allowances, which do not have a bearing upon accounting income. For example, interest on municipal bonds is excluded from taxable income (and hence is exempt from federal income taxation, except in connection with the minimum tax provision of the Tax Reform Act of 1969). Such interest, however, is always accounting revenue in the period in which it is earned by the bondholder. Another example is the percentage depletion allowances (mentioned in Chapter 7).

The second type of difference is temporary; these result in intraperiod (or interstatement and sometimes intersectional) tax allocation. They arise either when losses or gains are charged or credited directly to retained earnings, or when taxable items are reported in different sections of the income statement (for example, an operating income section less applicable income taxes, and an extraordinary items section less applicable income taxes). The number of situations that arise under the former has declined sharply since APB Opinion No. 9 was issued. As will be explained in Chapter 9, the emphasis of this Opinion was on restricting income statements to the all-inclusive concept. A multistep income statement (as required under APB Opinion No. 9) lists the nonoperating or extraordinary items in a separate section, so that the income tax is divided into that for operating transactions and that for nonoperating transactions. Since only the income statement and the retained earnings statement (which often is combined with the income statement) for the same period are affected, there is no dispute over intraperiod income tax allocation.

Under intraperiod allocation, if the allocation is between statements, in the entry recording the estimated tax charge for the period the charge must be divided between the loss or gain account that appears in the retained earnings statement (or in the extraordinary items section) and the income tax expense account that appears on the income statement (in the income before extraordinary items section). If the allocation is only between sections of the income statement, the tax may be divided as the statement is prepared and not reflected in separate accounts.

The third type of differences also is temporary—differences that result in interperiod income tax allocation. These arise when transactions are reported on the income statement in a different period (or periods) from the period when they are reported on the income tax return. The confusion and controversy over tax allocation is concerned with this third type of difference.

There are four kinds of interperiod tax differences. Two result from revenues or expenses that are reported on the current income statements but are deferred for income tax purposes. The other two result from revenues or expenses that are reported on the current tax returns but are deferred for accounting statement purposes. Examples of the first two are (1) revenues reported on a sales basis for income statement purposes, and on a cash collection basis for tax return purposes, and (2) expenses reported on the estimated warranty expense (the accrual) basis for income statement purposes, and on the actual warranty cost incurred (cash) basis for tax return purposes. Examples of the other two are (3) advances from customers (which constitute revenue for tax return purposes but are deferred for accounting statement purposes), and (4) accelerated depreciation for tax returns while straight line is used on the statements. Examples 1 and 4 under tax allocation require that a deferred income tax credit (classified as a liability) be computed for the difference; examples 2 and 3 under tax allocation require that a deferred income tax charge (classified as an asset) be established for the difference.

Under interperiod allocation, when income is taxable during the current period, but is not recognized until later on the income statement, there is a deferral of the tax charge (or prepaid taxes). Under tax allocation, when income is recognized now on the income statement but deferred for tax return purposes, there is an accrual of the tax credit (or a tax liability). In both these situations, as in all instances when either interperiod or intraperiod income tax allocation is involved, the basic idea is to let the income tax follow the income.

Entries illustrating the four examples are:

	Debit	Credit
For (1) and (4):		
Income tax charge	×	
(*income statement amount*)		
Deferred income tax credit		×
(*difference or accrual*)		
Cash (or income taxes payable)		×
(*amount of tax due per tax*		
return)		

	Debit	Credit
For (2) and (3):		
Deferred income tax charge	×	
(difference or deferral)		
Income tax charge	×	
(income statement amount)		
Cash (or income taxes payable)		×
(amount of tax due per tax		
return)		

The controversy over interperiod allocation is concerned with: (1) In what kind of situation is it appropriate? (2) Given that it is appropriate, how should it be reported in the financial statements? By the latter we mean: Should it be partial or complete (referred to by the AICPA as comprehensive); and what tax rate should be used? In APB Opinion No. 11, the AICPA supports comprehensive interperiod tax allocation, on the grounds that the matching process should be applied to income taxes as it is to other expenses. Even if income taxes were reclassified as a distribution of income, comprehensive allocation would still be appropriate.

The AICPA Opinion states that comprehensive tax allocation should be used so that the tax expense of any period would include the tax effects of all statement revenues, expenses, and losses. The Opinion also states that between the dates when the tax differences arise and when they reverse, they should be recorded as deferred charges and deferred credits; and that the tax rate at the time of reporting the initial difference should be used throughout the periods in which tax allocation has effects.

By contrast, under partial tax allocation, prepaid or accrual income taxes are recognized only for those nonrecurring or infrequent situations where the reversal will take place within a determinable, relatively short time (of, say, five years). In example 4 above, the tax difference between straight-line and accelerated depreciation would never be paid as long as the firm follows a policy of replacing its assets at the ends of their service lives. Should the firm also increase its investment in depreciable assets, the deferred tax credit will constitute an increasing payable balance not requiring payment. Although one can argue that a part of the old difference is reversed each year and a new amount added, if the firm ceases operations usually the reversal would not be completed.[13] Also, if the complete

---

[13]This is not always correct since, if this happens, the firm may have to pay a larger capital gains tax if it used accelerated tax depreciation than if it used straight-line tax depreciation on depreciable assets sold at time of liquidation.

reversal will take place only over a long period of time, the present value of these distant amounts would tend to be insignificant. For these three reasons, the case for partial allocation over comprehensive allocations seems compelling.

Complete tax allocation is often challenged on the grounds that deferred charges or prepaid taxes lack the usual properties of assets, because future benefits are not assured. Another argument against tax allocation is that future tax rates are highly uncertain and subject to change, as are tax laws generally. If income tax rates decline, the reversal also would not be completed. There is also uncertainty about the firm's future, for example, prepaid taxes will never be applied if the firm does not earn income. A major argument against tax allocation is that it obscures the firm's cash flow, because only under conventional accrual accounting without tax allocation does the tax obligation measure the current effect on cash flow. Notwithstanding the previous arguments against comprehensive tax allocation, its main defect is that it lacks sufficient practical application to be evaluated properly.

The net-of-tax concept of income tax allocation has been advanced as an alternative to the deferral or liability concepts. Under it, tax allocation is reported as a contra asset (instead of as prepaid taxes or deferred charges). The rationale underlying this concept relates to what is probably the strongest theoretical argument for a compromise solution to the interperiod income tax allocation controversy. This argument is that a major benefit (or service) to be received from the investment in an asset is its tax benefit (its deductibility in determining the amount of income tax due), and that there should be some accounting recognition of the fact that this benefit has been received (as where depreciation is computed, using an accelerated method for the tax return and the straight-line method for accounting statements). Closely related to this is the assumption that adjusting the historical value of an asset for its tax effect would also result in a more current position statement valuation. But if this were to be accomplished, many more factors besides tax effects would have to be considered.

Investment Credit

Related to the problems of tax allocation and deferred income tax liabilities is the accounting for the investment credit. In order to encourage businesses to purchase certain machinery and equipment, the United States government has permitted the purchaser of such property to reduce the amount of federal income tax payable for the year when the property was acquired by a certain percentage of the cost of the property. This permanent reduction in income tax payable or tax credit is called the *investment credit*.

Although the calculation of the investment credit is not particularly difficult, the accounting for it is our concern.[14] The company entitled to an investment credit will always take the credit as a reduction of the federal income tax that it owes for the year when the qualified property was acquired.

The accounting issue concerns the accounting period(s) in which to recognize the investment credit as a reduction of income tax expense on the income statement. There are two principal methods of recording the investment credit. These are: (1) the *flow-through* method (or cash-basis accounting method), and (2) the *allocation* method (or accrual-basis accounting method). Under the former method, the entire credit is reported as a reduction of income tax on the income statement in the year when the credit is allowed for tax purposes. The supporting rationale is that current period taxes are reduced by current period purchases of property, and therefore current period tax expense should be reduced accordingly. Under the latter method, the investment credit is allocated so as to reduce reported income tax expense on the income statements equally over the entire life of the acquired assets. The supporting rationale for allocation is that the investment credit influenced the decision to acquire the depreciable assets, and that these assets generate revenue over several future accounting periods. In two APB Opinions, the AICPA has come to allow either method.[15] Under the *flow-through* method, the income tax on the income statement is net the investment credit. Under the *allocation* method, the investment credit is shown as a contra to plant (or as a liability). The investment credit is amortized over the years when the qualified property is used as a reduction in periodic depreciation (or as a reduction in periodic income tax).

Summary

The discussion of long-term assets and liabilities begun in Chapter 7 is continued here. The focus is on the long-term monetary accounts of bonds, leases, and pensions.

Bonds are the principal accounting example of assets and liabilities valued on a direct valuation basis at date of acquisition since the bond contract eliminates most areas of uncertainty. It is impor-

---

[14]The investment credit is 7 percent of the entire cost of *qualified* depreciable property if the property has an estimated life of eight years or longer. Qualified depreciable assets include new machinery, equipment, and other tangible personal property (but not real estate property such as buildings and land). If the estimated life is less than eight years, lower percentages apply. If the lessor elects, the lessee may claim it for new leased property. There are limits on the amount of the investment credit; in the initial year, it can be taken against the first $25,000 of tax payable plus half of any tax payable over $25,000.
[15]For further details see Chapter 12.

tant to recognize in the valuation of bonds that the bond contract consists of two types of future cash flows in addition to the principal of the bond: the amount to be paid or received at maturity, and the periodic interest. Two interest rates are involved in the bond contract: the nominal or coupon rate set by the borrower, and the effective or yield rate set through the operation of the investment market. If the effective rate exceeds the nominal rate, the bond is issued at a discount; if the effective rate is less than the nominal rate, the bond is issued at a premium.

Accounting for bonds is concerned primarily with interest. The interest charge (revenue) is the nominal interest payment (receipt) plus any amortization of discount or less any amortization of premium. The result of amortization is to convert interest receipt (or payment) at the nominal interest rate into interest revenue (or expense) at the effective or yield rate. The preferred method of amortization is the interest method, and the common method of amortization is the straight-line method.

Bond contracts can contain provision for the retirement of the bonds. Serial bonds provide for repayment of the face value of the bonds over their lifetime in a series of periodic installments. In addition, there are two other types of retirement provisions. One provides for periodic deposits of cash into a segregated fund which is used to retire the bonds; the other provides for periodic reservations of retained earnings. The accounts that contain cash thus restricted or reserved are called sinking funds.

Three major long-term monetary assets and liabilities have evolved largely since World War II: leases, pensions, and income tax allocations. Their newness has generated considerable confusion about their treatment for accounting purposes.

Leased assets are distinguished from owned assets by the rights associated with each. Both involve the rights of possession and use, but only owned assets also provide the rights of disposal. There are two types of leases: lease purchase agreements, and executory leases (lease nonpurchase agreements). Questions concerning the method of reporting leased property on financial statements are associated partly with the problems of computing the value of leased property. Currently, long-term leased properties can be reported in footnotes to the position statement or in the body of the statement. Generally, long-term leases are reported in footnotes of the position statement of the lessee. In terms of the lessor, the financing method is used to record the lessor's rights when the lessee pays all expenses related to the use of the property; the operating method is used when the lessor pays these expenses.

In accounting for a pension plan, the basic considerations are disclosure of the terms of the program, reporting of rights (assets) or obligations (liabilities), and allocation of pension costs to periodic income statements. The private pension plan typically requires periodic deposits into a pension trust sinking fund and specifies rules for determining the time and amount of pension payments to retired employees. The costs associated with the pension fund are prior service cost, current costs, and actuarial gains and losses.

The third "new asset and liability" considered in Chapter 8 is income tax allocations and the related topic of investment credit. Income tax allocation in accounting is the apportionment of federal income taxes among different periods, statements, or sections of a statement. Controversy over income tax allocation centers around determining the situations in which income tax allocation may be appropriate and how tax allocations should be reported in financial statements.

When the federal government permits a purchaser of machinery and equipment to reduce the amount of income tax payable for the year when the property was acquired by a certain percent of the cost of the property, the reduction or tax credit is called an *investment credit.* In accounting for investment credit the primary concern is when to recognize the credit on the income statement.

A Selection of Supplementary Readings

Abrams, Reuben W.: "Accounting for the Cost of Pension Plans and Deferred Compensation Contracts," *The New York Certified Public Accountant,* April 1970, pp. 300–307.

Alvin, Gerald: "Resolving the Inconsistency in Accounting for Leases," *The New York Certified Public Accountant,* March 1970, pp. 223–230.

American Institute of Certified Public Accountants: "Reporting of Leases in Financial Statements of Lessee," Opinions of the Accounting Principles Board No. 5. New York: 1964.

———: "Accounting for Leases in Financial Statements of Lessors," Opinions of the Accounting Principles Board No. 7. New York: 1966.

———: "Accounting for the Cost of Pension Plans," Opinions of the Accounting Principles Board No. 8. New York: 1966.

———: "Accounting for Income Taxes," Opinions of the Accounting Principles Board No. 11. New York: 1967.

———: "Omnibus Opinion—1967," Opinions of the Accounting Principles Board No. 12. New York: 1967.

———: "Accounting for Convertible Debt and Debt Issued with Stock Purchase Warrants," Opinions of the Accounting Principles Board No. 14. New York: 1969.

Anton, Hector R.: "Accounting for Bond Liabilities," *The Journal of Accountancy,* September 1956, pp. 53–56.

Axelson, Kenneth S.: "Needed: A Generally Accepted Method for Measuring Lease Commitments," *Financial Executive,* July 1971, p. 40.

Bevis, Herman W.: "Contingencies and Probabilities in Financial Statements," *The Journal of Accountancy,* October 1968, pp. 37–45.

Corcoran, Eileen T.: "Reporting of Leases," *Financial Analysts Journal,* January–February 1968, pp. 29–35.

Cotton, W. D. J.: "Lease Financing," parts I and II, *Accountants' Journal,* November and December 1967, pp. 132–139, 172–181.

Dewhirst, John F.: "A Conceptual Approach to Pension Accounting," *The Accounting Review,* April 1971, pp. 365–373.

Dreher, William A.: "Alternatives Available under APB Opinion No. 8: An Actuary's View," *The Journal of Accountancy,* September 1967, pp. 37–51.

Gilling, Donald M.: "Accounting for Leases; The Fundamental Question," *Accountants' Journal,* March 1970, pp. 283–286.

Hall, William D.: "Current Problems in Accounting for Leases," *The Journal of Accountancy,* November 1967, pp. 35–42.

Halliwell, Paul D.: "Basic Principles of Pension Funding and APB Opinion No. 8," *Management Accounting,* July 1969, p. 15.

Hawkins, David F.: "Controversial Accounting Changes," *Harvard Business Review,* March–April 1968, p. 20.

———: "Objectives, not Rules for Lease Accounting," *Financial Executive,* November 1970, p. 30.

Hicks, Ernest L.: *Accounting for the Cost of Pension Plans,* Accounting Research Study No. 8. New York: AICPA, 1965, pp. 1–30, 138–148.

Hueffner, Ronald J.: "A Debt Approach to Lease Accounting," *Financial Executive,* March 1970, p. 30.

Hylton, Delmer P.: "What *Is* the Balance Sheet?" *The New York Certified Public Accountant,* June 1970, pp. 485–491.

Jenkins, David O.: "Purchase or Cancellable Lease: Which Is Better?" *Financial Executive,* April 1970, pp. 26–31.

Kaye, Lloyd S.: "The Role of Management Decision in Pension Funding," *Financial Executive,* June 1971, p. 22.

Kelley, Raymond L.: "Leasing as Viewed by a Banker," *The Illinois CPA,* summer 1966, pp. 17–22.

Langenderfer, Harold Q.: "Accrued Past-service Pension Costs Should Be Capitalized," *The New York Certified Public Accountant,* February 1971, p. 137.

Mellman, Martin, and Leopold A. Bernstein: "Lease Capitalization under APB Opinion No. 5," *The New York Certified Public Accountant,* February 1966, pp. 115–122.

Moore, Carl L.: "Deferred Income Tax—Is It a Liability?" *The New York Certified Public Accountant,* February 1970, pp. 130–138.

Myers, John H.: *Reporting of Leases in Financial Statements,* Accounting Research Study No. 4. New York: AICPA, 1962, pp. 1–67.

Norgaard, Corine T.: "Financial Implications of Comprehensive Income Tax Allocation," *Financial Analysts Journal,* January–February 1969, pp. 81–85.

Philips, G. Edward: "Pension Liabilities and Assets," *The Accounting Review,* January 1968, pp. 10–17.

Phoenix, Julius W., Jr., and William D. Bosse: "Accounting for the Cost of Pension Plans—APB Opinion No. 8," *The Journal of Accountancy,* August 1967, pp. 27–37.

Seago, W. E.: "Accounting for Pension Costs—An Illustrative Case," *The New York Certified Public Accountant,* June 1971, pp. 425–432.

Simmons, Maurice O.: "New Light on Actuarial Cost Methods," *Financial Executive,* July 1968, p. 69.

Spacek, Leonard: "The Case for Income-tax Deferral," *The New York Certified Public Accountant,* April 1968, pp. 271–276.

Sprouse, Robert T.: "Accounting for What-you-may-call-its," *The Journal of Accountancy,* October 1966, pp. 45–53.

Stevenson, Richard A., and Joe Lavely: "Why a Bond Warrant Issue?" *Financial Executive,* June 1970, pp. 16–21.

Vatter, W. J.: "Accounting for Leases," *Journal of Accounting Research,* autumn 1966, pp. 133–148.

Waugh, James B.: "The Interperiod Allocation of Corporate Income Taxes: A Proposal," *The Accounting Review,* July 1968, pp. 535–539.

Wharton, H. M.: "Capitalization of Leases: The Case Against," *Accountants' Journal,* March 1970, pp. 286–287.

Willy, W. J.: "Leasing as Viewed by a CPA," *The Illinois CPA,* summer 1966, pp. 13–16.

Wise, T. A.: "Those Uncertain Actuaries," parts I and II, *Fortune,* December 1965 and January 1966, pp. 154 and 164.

Zises, Alvin: "Law and Order in Lease Accounting," *Financial Executive,* July 1970, p. 46.

Questions

8–1

On March 1, 1972, the Klug Company issued bonds with a face value of $100,000 for $110,000 cash. These bonds promise annual interest of 6 percent. The interest is payable semiannually on March 1 and September 1. The bonds were to be repaid on March 1, 1982. Record the entries that should be made on the following dates: March 1, 1972; September 1, 1972; December 31, 1972. Amortize on a straight-line basis.

8–2

On January 1, 1975, the Heaton Company issued bonds with a face value of $1,000,000 for $900,000 cash. These bonds promise annual interest of 4 percent, payable semiannually on January 1 and July 1. The bonds were to be repaid on January 1, 1985. On January 1, 1980, the bonds were reacquired for $1,011,000. Make the journal entries for January 1, 1975 and January 1, 1980. Amortize on a straight-line basis.

8–3

"Specifically, I do not think the loan officer is going to be able to eliminate from his areas of interest and concern the accounting principles and practices of his particular borrower, *no matter what happens in the effort to narrow the differences in these practices and principles.*"*

What are the implications of this view upon such issues as booking leases and deferred taxes as liabilities?

*Herman W. Bevis, *Accounting and Auditing Comparability: Fact and Fiction,* an address before the Fall Conference of the Robert Morris Associates, Houston, Texas, November 15, 1965. New York: Price Waterhouse & Co., 1966, p. 15.

8-4   The AAA Committee, in its ASOBAT (1966), recommended "the reporting of all long-term leases, material and nonrepetitive purchase commitments, pension plans, and executive compensation contracts including stock options or deferred payments and the like in dollar terms in the regular framework of the statements." Describe the problems (procedural, format, disclosure) that will be encountered in carrying out this recommendation.

8-5   How do you think lease rights and obligations should be reported in the balance sheet of the lessee? Briefly evaluate alternative methods of accounting for leases in circumstances where rentals are paid periodically throughout the term of the lease.

8-6   Select the best choice for each of the following:
(1) A contingent liability:
    a. Has a most probable value of zero, but may require a payment if a given future event occurs.
    b. Definitely exists as a liability, but its amount and/or due date are indeterminate.
    c. Is commonly associated with operating loss carry-forwards.
    d. Is not disclosed in the financial statements.
(2) An example of an item that is not a liability is:
    a. Dividends payable in stock.
    b. Advances from customers on contract.
    c. Accrued estimated warranty costs.
    d. The portion of long-term debt due within one year.
(3) Convertible subordinated debentures:
    a. Have priority over other indebtedness.
    b. Are usually secured by a first or second mortgage.
    c. Pay interest only in the event that earnings are sufficient to cover the interest.
    d. Can be exchanged for other securities.

8-7   Under which of the following circumstances would a CPA consider that a leasehold might require recognition on the tenant's books?
(1) The tenant has made a payment to purchase leasehold rights from a preceding lessee. The amount should be amortized over the appropriate period.
(2) The tenant made a large advance rental payment or paid a bonus when the lease was arranged. The amount should be amortized over the appropriate period.
(3) There are substantial penalties for nonrenewal of the lease. If the lease is not to be renewed, the liability and the related cost should be recognized.
(4) There are heavy estimated costs of reconditioning or restoring leased facilities at the termination of the lease. The liability should be accumulated over the life of the lessee by charges to leasehold expense.

8-8   Classify the following arguments as supporting or opposing income tax allocation.

(1) Allocation of taxes involves a form of income normalizing or smoothing.

(2) The amount of income taxes attributable to income is not reasonably determinable.

(3) Tax allocation is the treatment of income taxes on an accrual basis consistent with the accounting for other items.

(4) Tax allocation is in accordance with major emphasis on the income statement.

(5) Income taxes are not necessarily a cost because they are paid only if period revenues exceed period costs; therefore, tax payments are somewhat akin to dividend payments.

(6) A better matching of revenues and expenses is accomplished.

(7) Material amounts included in the income statement are not considered in computing income tax liability.

(8) With continued expansion of depreciable assets, the deferred tax applicable to accelerated depreciation will not be payable.

(9) In situations in which the timing differs for accounting and tax purposes, there will be a balancing out of the dollar differences; thus, the periodic differences will cancel out in time.

(10) It is difficult to fit the deferred income tax accounts into the standard definitions of assets and liabilities, for they do not represent things of value owned or legal obligations.

8–9   With regard to the problem of accounting for pension cost, explain the significance of each of the following items on corporate financial statements: deferred pension cost, current service cost, past service cost, and trustee's fees.

8–10   Select the letter of the answer choice which best completes each statement. Mark only one answer for each numbered statement.

(1) With respect to the allocation of income taxes, it is recommended that:

   a. Because of the difficulty in making allocations and because of the uncertainty of tax rates, no allocation should be attempted.

   b. Because income taxes are an expense, they should be allocated to income and retained earnings accounts of the same period, but they should not be allocated to other accounts which will affect the income of other periods.

   c. Allocation of income taxes should be made as long as the amount shown for income taxes in the income statement is not increased beyond the amount of the tax estimated to be actually payable.

   d. Because income taxes are an expense, they should be allocated to income and other accounts affecting the income of the current period or affecting the income of the current and future periods.

   e. None of the above.

(2) When a pension plan is first adopted, the costs based on past services of employees should be treated as follows:

   a. They should be charged on the income statement in the years in which they are paid.

   b. They should not be charged on the income statement because the services were received in the past.

    c. They should be charged to operations of the current and future periods on a systematic amortization basis.

    d. They should be carried on the books indefinitely as long as the pension plan is in existence.

    e. None of the above.

(3) When bonds have been refunded, the preferred treatment for unamortized discount, issue cost, and redemption premium on these bonds is as follows:

    a. They should be written off directly on the income statement.

    b. They should be amortized over the remaining years of the original life of the issue retired.

    c. They should be amortized over the life of the new issue.

    d. They should be carried on the books as an asset.

    e. None of the above.

8-11   Select the letter of the answer choice which best completes each statement. Mark only one answer for each numbered statement.

(1) An argument against capitalizing leaseholds on the tenant's books is as follows:

    a. Liabilities exist under the leasehold and should be revealed to outside investors.

    b. Disclosure of the liability by footnote might be properly related, by the reader of financial statement, to the overall financial structure of the firm.

    c. An investor could make better comparisons of companies leasing and companies purchasing facilities.

    d. Leasing is an alternative to purchasing and perhaps to borrowing; capitalization would recognize this fact.

    e. Computation of return on capital by regulated industries might be distorted.

(2) An argument for capitalizing leaseholds on the tenant's books is as follows:

    a. The facilities are not actually owned by the tenant, and recording the leasehold might be deceptive.

    b. A large fixed rental obligation should be of paramount interest to an investor.

    c. The tax deductibility of rental payment might be impaired because the leasehold amortization would differ from cash payments.

    d. Authorities do not agree either on the method of computation or on the method of presentation.

    e. Investors would place a lower valuation on the firm because the overall rate of return on total assets would be reduced.

8-12   Prepare a one-page essay on the following excerpt from J. C. Penny Company's Annual Report for 1968: "Accumulated tax effects (the deferred tax liabilities) are shown in the balance sheet as deferred credits. These amounts are not liabilities and in the normal course of business may never be paid."

8-13   Prepare a brief essay on the following excerpt from Bird & Son's Annual Report for 1967:

Federal income tax regulations provide for special definitions of the net income upon which taxes payable are based. Such definitions include permission to elect to accelerate the recognition of depreciation expense. The effect of the company having made this election has been the immediate reduction of tax burdens and the corresponding conversion of cash resources for other use in the business. The income statement includes a charge equivalent to the current net tax reduction resulting from the election to define taxable net income on this basis; the accumulated tax reduction, representing conserved cash resources employed in the business, is set forth separately in the balance sheet. In the absence of changed conditions, the funds provided by the accumulated tax reduction will be retained for use in the business indefinitely.

8–14   If the characteristics of a liability are considered to be: a future outlay of money, results from transactions of the past, subject to calculation or close estimation, and double-entry bookkeeping, which of these would cause an accountant the most difficulty in recording pension liabilities, and why?

8–15   It is contended that three possible methods of depreciation and related tax treatment are acceptable today: namely, straight line for books, and accelerated for tax returns *with or without tax allocation,* and accelerated for both books and tax returns. Give an illustration of what is meant by tax allocation in this situation.

Problems

8–1

Bonds Payable	*Bond Payable—Premium*	*Bond Interest Charges*
4/1/72 $1,000	4/1/72 $100	10/1/72 $30

(1) The 10-year 6 percent bond with interest payable semiannually (October 1 and April 1) of the Chicago East Company was issued on April 1, 1972. It is the only bond liability that the company has.
   a. The total bond interest expense for the year 1972 (with straight-line amortization) is $_____ .
   b. The actual cash paid out in interest in 1972 is $_____ .
   c. The cash proceeds of the bond issue on April 1, 1972 are $_____ .
   d. The total bond liability on April 1, 1972 is $_____ .
   e. The market rate of interest was (higher) (lower) on April 1, 1972 than the stated or nominal rate.
   f. If the bond was issued on June 1, 1972 (dated April 1, 1972) at a premium of $100 plus accrued interest, what would be the cash proceeds of the bond issue on June 1, 1972?
   g. Estimate the market rate of interest on this bond. _____
(2) Indicate whether any of the following are constants for all periods under the effective interest cost (or compound interest) method of amortizing bond discount.
   a. The amount by which the bond discount is reduced
   b. The interest paid to the bondholder
   c. The interest cost as shown on the income statement

d. The interest rate (as calculated from the statements)

e. The bond liability shown on the position statement

8-2

General Data:

(1) All bonds sold by GM Co. to GE Co.

(2) Both firms account on a calendar-year basis. (No reversing entries are made.)

(3) Face value of each bond issue: $1,000 (straight-line amortization used).

(4) All bonds have a 10-year life and bear 6 percent nominal interest payable semiannually on April 1 and October 1.

Transactions

1	8/1/72	Sale debenture (A) at face plus accrued interest. Brokerage commission $116. Sinking-fund principal repayment provisions: Reserve $100 in cash every January 1, except for the first year when only $50 is to be contributed.
2	10/1/72	Paid interest (A).
3		Sale real estate mortgage bond (B) @ 97.
4		Sale collateral trust bond (C) @ 103.
5, 6, 7	12/31/72	Adjustments: (A), (B), (C).
8	1/1/73	Sinking fund deposit (A).
9, 10, 11	4/1/73	Interest payments: (A), (B), (C).
12	5/1/73	Call mortgage bond (B) @ $105 plus accrued interest.

Record transactions above in T accounts for GM Co. Do the same thing for GE Co.

8-3

On January 1, 1966, the Buckeye Corporation secured a 50-year lease on a building, agreeing to pay a rental of $100,000 payable January 1 of each year.

On January 1, 1976, Badger, Inc., purchases Buckeye's right in the lease. The purchase is made on the following basis:

(1) It is agreed that the rental value of the building is $150,000 per year.

(2) It is agreed that a 5 percent interest rate is to be used.

(3) Badger is to pay a lump sum to Buckeye on January 1, 1976, and $100,000 each year for nine years starting January 1, 1977, in full payment for Buckeye's right under the lease.

(4) Buckeye retains the obligation to pay $100,000 annually on its initial lease.

     a. How much will Badger pay Buckeye on January 1, 1976?

     b. What entries will Badger make during 1976 in accordance with conventional practice?

     c. What entries will Badger make during 1976 considering effective interest?

NOTE: Assume that financial statements are prepared only at year end. If the student has time, he might prepare entries for Badger for 1977 and 1978.

8-4

The following footnote appeared in the current financial statements of a large corporation:

In 1971 a property was sold for $1,536,000 and leased back. The lease on a net basis is for 20 years at an annual rental of $170,000. The loss of $128,000 on the sale is being amortized over the period of the lease.

(1) Show the journal entry that must have been made at the time the lease transaction was completed.
(2) Which elements of the 1971 income statement and the December 31, 1971 position statement would be different if the lease had been capitalized? Explain. (Ignore any differences in reporting income taxes that might arise.)

NOTE: The interest rate implicitly associated with the lease is approximately 10 percent compounded semiannually.

8-5

For each account used in recording bond transactions, you are to open a T account, and show how related accounts are altered for each change in the account. For an example, see Bonds Payable below:

Bonds Payable

Cash (when retired)	Cash Bonds Payable—Discount (when issued)

Use the following accounts:
(1) Bonds Payable—Premium
(2) Bonds Payable—Discount
(3) Bond Interest Charges (or Expense)
(4) Bond Interest Payable
(5) Bond Issue Costs
(6) Bond Sinking Fund
(7) Bond Sinking Fund Revenue
(8) Retained Earnings—Appropriated for Bond Retirement
(9) Investment in Bonds
(10) Bond Interest Revenue
(11) Bond Interest Receivable

8-6

The 1969 annual report of a hotels-motels company contains the following note to its position statement:

At January 2, 1970 (position statement date), the Company had entered into long-term leases covering land . . . and buildings. Minimum annual rentals required thereby aggregated approximately $8,200,000 . . . also are miscellaneous lease agreements requiring annual rentals . . . of which $1,047,000 is applicable to long-term leases. These leases have terms of 50 years. The unexpended balances of commitments are not reflected in the position statement.

The total assets of the company are in excess of $550 million. The average implicit interest rate in the leases is 6 percent. Leases are rental contracts for the use of specified property.

By how much should the assets be written up if the leases are recorded as assets?

8-7

The annual report of a construction company contains a note to its financial statements under the term "commitments." The company has total assets of approximately $200 million.

The note reads, in part: "The company's subsidiaries have ground leases in connection with buildings in operation which require annual rental payments . . . aggregating approximately $3,340,000. Of the aggregate annual rentals, $206,000 applies to a base expiring within 20 years, and $3,134,000 applies to a lease expiring within 50 years."

The interest rate implicit in both lease contracts is 8 percent per annum, and the company simply records the rental payments in its income statement as an expense of the period. What other method for the evaluation of these leases might be more realistic, and, if this were used, by how much would the assets and liabilities be increased?

8-8

On January 1, 1973 the Buckeye Corporation issued for $1,106,775 its 20-year 8 percent bonds which have a maturity value of $1,000,000 and pay interest semiannually on January 1 and July 1. Bond issue costs were not material in amount. The following are three presentations of the long-term liability section of the position statements that might be used for these bonds at the issue date:

---

1. *Bonds payable—principal (maturing January 1, 1993)*   *$1,000,000*
   Bonds payable—interest ($40,000 per period for 40 periods)   *1,600,000*
   Total bond liability   *$2,600,000*

---

2. *Bonds payable (maturing January 1, 1993)*   *$1,000,000*
   Bonds payable—premium   *106,775*
   Total bond liability   *$1,106,775*

---

3. *Bonds payable—principal (face value $1,000,000 maturing*
      January 1, 1993)   *$ 252,572**
   Bonds payable—interest (semiannual payment $40,000)   *854,203†*
        $1,106,775

---

*The present value of $1,000,000 due at the end of 40 (six-month) periods at the yield rate of 3 1/2% per period.
†The present value of $40,000 per period for 40 (six-month) periods at the yield rate of 3 1/2% per period.

(1) Discuss the conceptual merit(s) of each of the date-of-issue position statement presentations shown above for these bonds.
(2) Explain why investors would pay $1,106,775 for bonds that have a maturity value of only $1,000,000.

(3) Assuming that a discount rate is needed to compute the carrying value of the obligations arising from a bond issue at any date during the life of the bonds, discuss the conceptual merit(s) of using for this purpose:
   a. The coupon or nominal rate
   b. The effective or yield rate at date of issue
(4) If the obligations arising from these bonds are to be carried at their present value, computed by means of the current market rate of interest, how would the bond valuation at dates following the date of issue be affected by an increase or a decrease in the market rate of interest?

8-9

On January 1, 1973 the Vicki Tim Company, issued 10-year bonds, maturity value $100,000 at 95 (that is, at 95 percent of the face value). The bonds bear interest at 8 percent per annum, payable on December 31 of each year. The bond indenture stipulates that a bond sinking fund be set up, to which shall be transferred equal annual amounts, the sum of which will be sufficient to retire the bonds at the maturity date (assume a zero rate of return on the sinking fund). The indenture also stipulates that each year retained earnings should be restricted for the retirement of bonds. Write the journal entries necessary in the years of issue and maturity.

8-10

A $100,000 10-year bond with a coupon rate of 5 percent is issued for $92,560 (that is, the yield is 6 percent) on January 1, 1972. Interest is to be paid on July 1 and January 1. Prepare all necessary entries for 1972, considering that the company is on a calendar-year basis.

8-11

On September 30, 1973 the LBJ Corporation acquired $10,000 of 6 percent semiannual interest Kennedy Company bonds maturing on August 1, 1980. On December 31, 1973 the LBJ Corporation made the following entry:

	Debit	Credit
Interest receivable	$250	
Investment in Kennedy Company bonds	45	
Interest revenue		$295

Reproduce the journal entry that was made to record the purchase of the bonds on September 30, 1973.

8-12

Four interest tables are shown in Appendix A. Show exactly how each may be used to determine the amount that should be paid for a $1,000 20-year 8 percent bond that promises to pay interest semiannually, if an annual yield of 7 percent is desired.

8-13

On January 1 a company purchased $100,000 of 5 percent bonds of another company for $113,780 to yield 4 percent over the 20 years to maturity, interest payable semiannually. On June 30 it sold $100,000 of its own 4 percent bonds for $93,450 to yield 4.5 percent over 20 years. Its accounting period is the calendar year; it uses the straight-line method of amortizing premium and discount. The company had total depreciation expense for the year of $210,000; it had net income of $453,200 after unusual gains of $3,500 and losses of $8,700—both from sale of long-lived assets. Calculate, in detail, the funds provided by operations.

8-14

On September 1, 1972, 10 bonds are issued at 95 (percent of face value); these bonds are 20-year $1,000 par 6 percent with interest payable on March 1 and September 1. The company keeps its books on a calendar-year basis.

Determine:
(1) The annual deduction from revenue for interest.
(2) The annual payment of cash to bondholders.
(3) The actual amount of the long-term liability on the date of issue.
(4) The issuance of bonds at a discount indicates that the market rate of interest is (greater) (less) than the rate printed on the bond.
(5) The entries on September 1, 1972; December 31, 1972; and March 1, 1973.

8-15

The Wald Corporation issued $100,000 6 percent second-mortgage 10-year bonds on October 1, 1972, at $102.36 (for each $100 face). These bonds were dated August 1, 1972. Interest is payable semiannually, on February 1 and August 1. The company closes its books annually on December 31 of each year and amortizes on an average cost basis. From this information, answer the following questions:
(1) What was the entire amount of the proceeds received from the sale of these bonds?
(2) What will be the balance of the Interest Charges account as of December 31, 1972?
(3) What will be the balance of the Premium account as of December 31, 1972?
(4) How much interest was paid in cash to bondholders in 1972?
(5) What will be the balance of the Interest Payable account as of December 31, 1972?
(6) What will be the balance of the Interest Charges account as of December 31, 1972 (after closing)?
(7) What is the effective interest rate on these bonds? (State at least whether it is above or below 6 percent.)

8-16

(1) After incorporating, the firm (now known as The Basil Demetomos Corporation) issues 6 percent 10-year debentures (dated August 1, 1973) on October 31, 1973: face $500,000, issue price 94 (percent of face value) plus accrued interest. Interest is payable semiannually, on February 1 and August 1.
  Amortization is calculated on a uniform charge per period basis. Compute the cash proceeds of the issue, and show how both the interest and principal would appear two months later on the firm's position statement as of December 31, 1973.
(2) If the entire issue in (1) was purchased by The Ryder Smith Company on December 31, 1973, how would the bond accounts appear on that firm's position statement as of the same date?
(3) On the basis of the information given in (1), determine the following for the issuing firm:

a. The actual cash paid out in interest in 1974.
b. The amount of bond interest charges to be shown on the 1974 income statement.
c. The approximate effective interest rate.
d. In the amortization of discount or premium, by the effective-interest method, which gives a decreasing interest charge per period? Why?

8–17 Prepare all *1973* interest transactions journalized (except for closing entries) for the Humbert Humbert Corporation relevant to its $500,000 7 percent bonds issued at face value on January 1, 1972. Interest payments are made every six calendar months; the corporation's accounting periods end February 28 and August 31. The corporation does not make reversing entries, and records accruals only at the end of each accounting period.

8–18 The Never-on-Sunday Bottle Club decided to build a new building and to finance it by selling mortgage bonds. On January 1, 1972 the club issued bonds with par value of $100,000 bearing interest at 7 percent payable semiannually, January 1 and July 1, in a 6 percent market. The NOSBC received $103,000 for the bonds. The bonds mature in five years; the firm is on a calendar-year basis.
(1) Record the issuance of the bonds.
(2) Record the full interest charges for the first half of 1972 by (a) the straight-line and (b) the effective-interest methods.
(3) Record (1) and (2) above for the firm that purchased the bonds. (This firm is also on a calendar-year basis.)
(4) Show how and where the bond accounts would appear on the statements of both firms.

8–19 A company has just acquired all the capital stock of another corporation and has asked you to audit the position statement of the latter as of date of acquisition. In the course of your examination, you determine that the company has a noncontributory pension plan and has charged to expense all payments made to the pension trust. There is no special provision in the pension plan which limits the company liability to an amount equal to assets in trust. The independent actuaries employed by the company have furnished you with the following summary of past service liability as of the audit date (000's omitted.):

	Accrued Liability	*Assets in Trust*	*Net Liability*
For presently retired employees	$1,189	$425	$764
For employees eligible to retire at their own option	477	——	477
For employees under retirement age	1,569	——	1,569
	$3,235	$425	$2,810

Discuss the factors to be considered in making adjustments to properly reflect the above.

8-20   Shown below are excerpts from the financial statements of Inland Steel for two recent consecutive years. Also included is a footnote from the second-year financial statements.

From Consolidated Statement of Financial Position (000's omitted)

	December 31	
	Second year	First year
Current liabilities:		
Federal taxes on income	$24,634	$29,885
Other liabilities:		
Deferred income—investment tax credit	21,454	18,354

From Consolidated Income Statement (000's omitted)

	For Year Ended December 31	
	Second year	First year
Deduction:		
Deferral of investment tax credit, less amortization	$ 3,100	$ 3,773

NOTE 1: **FEDERAL INCOME TAX.** *The investment tax credit is being taken into income over the depreciable lives of the assets to which the credits are related. The amount of the credit included in income was $2,661,000, or 15 cents per share for the first year, and $3,447,000 or 19 cents per share for the second year.*

(1) What method is Inland using in accounting for the investment credit? Briefly describe an alternative method which would result in a different net income figure.
(2) If Inland had used an alternative method, what amount would have appeared for net income for the second year? Show all calculations.

9

Fund Flow: Income Recognition under Certainty and Uncertainty

. . . a man's income . . . (is) the maximum value which he can consume during a week, and still expect to be as well off at the end of the week as he was at the beginning.*
J. R. HICKS, English Economist, 1939

Introduction to Hicks' Concept of Money Income
under Conditions of Certainty

Accountants are not the only professionals concerned with income measures; economists also are. Income as defined by accountants is called *accounting income;* income as defined by economists is called *economic income.* Since there are as many concepts of economic income as there are of accounting income, it is as difficult to generalize about economic income as it is about accounting income. Both the economist and the accountant would prefer to measure the results of operating an enterprise when its lifetime is over; however, economic concepts of income tend to depend to a considerable extent upon assumptions as to complete information and *certainty* about the future. On the other hand, the accountant is committed to dividing up the lifetime of the enterprise into time periods, and as each period lapses, to measure results; accounting income thus must cope directly with *uncertainty.* Nevertheless, the economic concepts of income have had a considerable impact upon accounting.

The concept of economic income most influential in contemporary accounting is the one developed in 1939 by the English economist, J. R. Hicks, and adapted for the corporation by the American econo-

*From *Value and Capital* (London: Oxford University Press, 1939), p. 172.

mist, Sidney Alexander.[1] Hicks' definition of income (given in the prologue to this chapter) is the amount that a man can consume during a period and still remain as well off at the period's end as he was at the period's beginning. For the corporation, Alexander interpreted this concept to mean the amount that the firm could distribute to shareholders during a period and still maintain the same residual ownership equity at the end of the period as it had at the start of the period. This still does not solve the problem of what "well-offness" means to the enterprise. Is it defined in terms of money and of current cash equivalents (or net realizable value or fair market value)? This "well-offness" value is usually defined as being the amount that a *willing* buyer would pay in an arm's-length transaction to a *willing* seller (or the value that would be arrived at in a perfect market). Or is it defined in terms of expectations, of either future money receipts or future real income (the goods and services that the enterprise can consume)? Or is it defined in stocks of physical goods or consumption goods? Is it perhaps the firm's position in the industry (no. 1, no. 2, and so on)? All these interpretations have received some support for each may be of value to some users at some time for some particular purpose. Usually, however, "well-offness" is considered to be cash flows when the future interest rates are assumed to be known (such that the enterprise is indifferent at this interest rate to receiving future money or current money).

This type of economic approach to determining income could be called a *position* (or balance sheet) *statement approach* for obvious reasons. Under this concept, income for a specific period is determined by comparing the value of ownership equity at the end of the period with that at the beginning of the period (and considering owners' investments and dividends). Since period income begins only after some measure of ownership (or capital) equity is maintained, this approach is sometimes referred to as the "capital maintenance" approach to determining income. Although capital maintenance (or position statement or economic) approaches to income have been developed on the basis of the market value of the total enterprise (or the market values of specific assets or liabilities), the basic approach is considered one of capitalizing the income of the firm or determining the present value of the future net cash flows of the firm from customer collections, outlays for equipment, and other cash-flow sequences. As discussed in Chapter 2, this requires advance knowledge of three things: (1) the amounts, (2) the timing of these amounts, and

---

[1]Sidney Alexander, "Income Measurement in a Dynamic Economy," *Five Monographs on Business Income* (New York: AICPA, 1950), as revised by David Solomons in *Studies in Accounting Theory* 2d ed., W. T. Baxter and Sidney Davidson, eds. (Homewood, Illinois: Richard D. Irwin, Inc., 1962), pp. 126–200.

(3) the interest rates. None of these is easy, or frequently even possible, to determine in advance. However, this approach is the basis for both the accrual and allocation types of end-of-period adjustments; and it also is used commonly in the valuation of both short- and long-term receivables and payables, occasionally in the valuation of individual assets, and rarely for the valuation of the entire firm.[2]

This approach can be better understood perhaps when it is applied over the lifetime of a firm about which everything is known. In this case of complete certainty, only direct valuation would be used, since all assets and liabilities would be valued on the basis of a known future flow of cash. All assets (which would be receivables) and liabilities would increase at a predetermined rate, which would be the same for all enterprises. Assets would decrease only when converted into cash or withdrawn from the enterprise. Liabilities would decrease only when paid. Therefore, period income would become the period interest on the investment in the enterprise or the period growth in ownership (provided that current period owner investments and withdrawals would be equal, which is not, of course, the usual situation).

This concept is illustrated below for a four-year enterprise whose owners are satisfied with a 10 percent rate of return on their investment or a 10 percent net income rate. The amounts of the changes in the values of the assets and liabilities for each year are shown after the year's money receipts and disbursements have actually been received or paid. It is assumed not only that all cash receipts and cash disbursements are known in advance, but also that they are uniformly spaced to occur at the end of each successive year. In the four position statements (one for the end of each year), the income for each year is shown as the last figure in that year's "Revenue, Expense, and Income Increase" column and is marked with an asterisk (*).

As shown in Exhibit 9–1, the firm has earned total income of $4,172 over its four-year lifetime (or $1,582 for the first year, $1,341 for the second year, $976 for the third year, and $273 for the fourth year).[3]

---

[2]It should not be inferred from the foregoing that the "change-in-net-asset-value" approach to income definition is *only* used in connection with the capitalized-income or market-value approaches. It can also be used *to* define the all-inclusive concept of income under conventional valuation rules. The change-in-net-asset-value approach is *not* a unique income concept but a way of expressing *any* all-inclusive approach to income.

[3]The proof of these calculations can be shown as follows:

Total cash receipts	$45,000	
Total cash disbursements	25,000	$20,000
Total investment		15,828
Total income for four years		$ 4,172

EXHIBIT 9-1
FIRM UNDER COMPLETE CERTAINTY
POSITION STATEMENTS AND NET INCOME*

	Year 1			Year 2		
	Beginning	Increasing	Decreasing	Beginning	Increasing	Decreasing
Assets	$ 8,182	$ 818	$9,000			
	9,090	909		$ 9,999	$1,001	$11,000
	11,269	1,127		12,396	1,240	
	6,830	683		7,513	751	
	$35,371	$3,537	$9,000	$29,908	$2,992	$11,000
Liabilities	$ 4,545	$ 455	$5,000			
	4,958	496		$ 5,454	$ 546	$ 6,000
	5,259	526		5,785	579	
	4,781	478		5,259	526	
	$19,543	$1,955	$5,000	$16,498	$1,651	$ 6,000
Ownership	$ 3,637	$ 363	$4,000			
	4,132	413		$ 4,545	$ 455	$ 5,000
	6,010	601		6,611	661	
	2,049	205		2,254	225	
	$15,828	$1,582	$4,000	$13,410	$1,341	$ 5,000

	Year 3			Year 4			
	Beginning	Increasing	Decreasing	Beginning	Increasing	Decreasing	Ending
Assets	$13,636	$1,364	$15,000				
	8,264	826		$9,090	$910	$10,000	
	$21,900	$2,190	$15,000	$9,090	$910	$10,000	
Liabilities	$ 6,364	$ 636	$ 7,000				
	5,785	578		$6,363	$637	$ 7,000	
	$12,149	$1,214	$ 7,000	$6,363	$637	$ 7,000	
Ownership	$ 7,272	$ 728	$ 8,000				
	2,479	248		$2,727	$273	$ 3,000	
	$ 9,751	$ 976	$ 8,000	$2,727	$273	$ 3,000	

*All figures are rounded to the nearest dollar.

Also, from Exhibit 9-1 the summary of cash receipts and cash disbursements for the four-year period is as shown in Exhibit 9-2.

EXHIBIT 9–2
FIRM UNDER COMPLETE CERTAINTY
SUMMARY OF CASH RECEIPTS AND CASH DISBURSEMENTS
(000'S OMITTED)

	Beginning	Year 1	2	3	4	Total Cash Flows
Assets:						
Expected receipts	$35.371	$9	$11	$15	$10	$45
Liabilities:						
Expected disbursements	19.543	5	6	7	7	25
Ownership	$15.828	$4	$ 5	$ 8	$ 3	$20

If this information were presented in T accounts, it would appear as

Assets		Liabilities		Ownership	
35,371	9,000	5,000	19,543	4,000	15,828
3,537	✔ 29,908	✔ 16,498	1,955	✔ 13,410	1,582
38,908	38,908	21,498	21,498	17,410	17,410
✔ 29,908	11,000	6,000	✔ 16,498	5,000	✔ 13,410
2,992	✔ 21,900	✔ 12,149	1,651	✔ 9,751	1,341
32,900	32,900	18,149	18,149	14,751	14,751
✔ 21,900	15,000	7,000	✔ 12,149	8,000	✔ 9,751
2,190	✔ 9,090	✔ 6,363	1,214	✔ 2,727	976
24,090	24,090	13,363	13,363	10,727	10,727
✔ 9,090	10,000	7,000	✔ 6,363	3,000	✔ 2,727
910			637		273
10.000	10,000	7,000	7,000	3,000	3,000

The entry to record the original investment in the company would be as follows:

	Debit	Credit
Cash	$15,828	
Ownership equity		$15,828
Assets	35,371	
Liabilities		19,543
Cash		15,828

The entries at the end of the first year would be as follows:

	Debit	Credit
Assets (10% of $35,371)	$ 3,537	
Ownership equity		$ 3,537
To record the increase in assets and ownership		
Ownership	1,954	
Liabilities (10% of $19,543)		1,954
To record the increase in liabilities and decrease in ownership		
Cash	9,000	
Assets		9,000
To record the receipt of cash		
Liabilities	5,000	
Ownership	4,000	
Cash		9,000
To record the cash disbursement		

The difference between the cash receipts and cash disbursements in each period ($4,000 the first year) would be withdrawn by the owners since it is not needed by the enterprise, and if it was continued in the business, the return on investment would fall below the required 10 percent (unless the firm invested in another 10 percent project). Entries for the second, third, and fourth years would be the same as for the first year (except for the original investment entry).

By this time the reader should recognize the relationship between the calculations made in Exhibit 9-1 and the discussion of direct valuation and actuarial arithmetic in Chapter 2. Each item in the schedule is set out to show the number of time intervals between the beginning and the point in time that each event occurs. For each prospective event, the receipt of cash or the disbursement of cash, its value at the beginning must be that amount which will increase at a 10 percent annual rate to the amount of the event. For example, the first cash receipt is valued at $8,182 which multiplied by 10 percent gives $818. This amount added to the beginning amount equals $9,000 or the cash receipt at the end of the first year ($8,182 × 1.10 = $9,000 or $8,182 = $9,000 ÷ 1.10). This process gives the present value of the receipt (or disbursement) due at the end of the first period. Based on this discussion, the reader should recognize that much of the foregoing time-consuming and laborious computation required for Exhibit 9-1 could have been avoided by using Table 3, Present Value of $1 Due in *n* Periods (see Appendix A).

Although the approach to income determination, described here and in Chapter 2, does have some applicability in preparing routine income statements, an approach based on changes in value over time does not seem broadly applicable at present. External users of financial statements in particular advance this negative view.

Such subjectively prepared statements would be unacceptable, it is argued, since external users would be totally dependent on management's ability to report estimates realistically and managers would have to repress their emotional opinions regarding future cash flow. This type of argument fails to recognize that portions of the income statement are already prepared with this and other subjective approaches.[4]

Consideration of Problems Relating to Income under Uncertainty
In order to cope with the measurement of income under uncertainty (the prevailing situation in most businesses), a second approach has been developed by accountants. This approach, accounting income, predominates in the preparation of conventional statements. It was described generally in Chapter 3 as consisting of matching expenses with the revenues reported for the period. This "matching" process is based on an operational or transactions approach. Income, instead of being based primarily upon changes in expected cash flows or the passage of time, is usually recognized upon the occurrence of certain preselected activities or transactions.

The accounting approach to determining income is often identified with discrete events.[5] Such events may be of many different types and may be related to income determination only in its broadest sense. It may be argued effectively that turning on the neon sign to advertise the business or even turning the key in the door of the business are revenue-producing activities. Usually, however, the events considered to be associated with earning revenue are narrowed to the following ones (the first seven may be identified directly with the steps in an entity's operating cycle described in Chapter 4):

1. The purchase of goods and services for later production and/or sale
2. The progress of goods toward completion of the production process
3. The completion of the production of goods
4. The receipt of orders for goods or services

---

[4]For a discussion of objectivity, in contrast to subjectivity, see Chapter 3.
[5]An exception to this point is depreciation. Depreciation is not a "discrete event," but it is an element in the accounting approach to determining income.

5. The delivery (or furnishing or making available of) the goods or services to the customer
6. The transfer of legal title of the goods or services to the customer
7. The collection of cash or its equivalent from the customer
8. The expiration of the product warranty or guarantee (which might be considered a part or an extension of step 4)
9. The physical growth (accretion) of a readily marketable commodity
10. The increase in the market value (appreciation) of a readily marketable good or right

With accounting income, the first major problem is to determine when revenues should be recognized and recorded in the accounts. It is generally accepted that revenues should be recorded as soon as they are *realized*. Accounting *realization* is considered to have occurred as indicated in Chapter 3 when:

1. The values associated with all the revenue and related revenue-producing activities are measurable (that is, there must be objective evidence of the market value of the good or service).
2. The major revenue-producing activities of the firm are substantially completed. In accounting, this means that most of the values associated with these activities must have been incurred as well as most of the work.

Although accounting realization does not specify clearly what has to be realized or even whose realization is to be used, it usually is interpreted to mean the accountant's knowledge that cash will be received. Of the ten possible revenue-recording events previously detailed, only the production, delivery, and collection events are considered as practical points for recognition of revenue by the accountant. Of these, the delivery of goods or services (or the sale) is the conventional point for revenue recognition.

For the typical business it is argued that the delivery of the goods or services to the customer is the key revenue-producing activity. Before the time that this takes place, the firm does not really know to whom it can sell the good or service or even for how much. After that time, the legal transfer of title usually is not a problem even when it does not pass with delivery. Additionally, under our credit economy, the costs associated with collection and any guarantee can be measured reasonably well. For these reasons, the point of sale (or delivery) is the usual basis for recognizing revenue.

There are two other practical possibilities, however. For some enterprises, it may be possible to recognize revenue while the good is being produced or when the good or service has been produced. Under the production basis of recognizing revenue, the price (and often the customer) for the good or service needs to be known in advance of the sale; under these circumstances, the delivery of goods or point of sale constitutes a relatively minor revenue-producing activity. As long as the costs associated with delivery or sale can be measured, the point of revenue realization can be moved back to the production event. Gold-mining is the classic example of an industry that recognizes revenue on the basis of production. When the goods or services are being produced under contract, it is possible to recognize revenue on the basis of the percentage of the contract certified as complete (which corresponds to the percentage of the contract cost incurred). This is called the "percentage of completion" basis of recognizing revenue, which is frequently used by construction firms, and is, of course, closely related to the production basis.

As our economy has been maturing into a primarily credit one, recognizing revenue at the point of collection has been declining in importance and relevance. Nevertheless, those enterprises that sell goods or services with high profit margins to customers who are poor credit risks still find it necessary to defer recognizing revenue until the cash is collected, since both the amounts that will be collected and the values associated with collection may not be predictable in advance, and the work involved in collecting may be significant. Firms selling on an installment basis also may find it necessary to use this basis of recognizing revenue.

The following illustration compares the three different methods of recognizing revenue: the production basis, the sale basis, and the collection basis. A firm beginning business with cash of $5,000 has produced 100 units at a unit cash cost of $100; 75 units are sold at a unit price of $150 with cash selling costs of $15 per unit and cash collection costs of $10 per unit; and of the 75 units sold, 60 have been paid for, 10 are to be paid for later, and 2.5 will not be paid for. Neither the costs, the selling price, nor the uncollectible rate ($3\frac{1}{3}$ percent) are expected to change.

In summary, the income per unit is as follows:

Unit selling price	$150	
Less uncollectible	5	$145
Unit costs: Production	100	
Selling	15	
Collection	10	125
Unit income		$ 20

The following T accounts illustrate the recording differences under the three methods.

Production Basis
(100 units)

Cash

✓	5,000	10,000	(A)
(E)	9,000	1,125	(C)
		600	(D)
		2,275	✓
	14,000	14,000	
✓	2,275		

Accounts Receivable

(B)	11,250	9,000	(E)
		2,250	✓
	11,250	11,250	
✓	2,250		

Accounts Receivable— Allowance for Uncollectibles

	375 (F)

Accounts Receivable— Allowance for Future Collection Costs

	150 (D)

Inventory

(A)	15,000	11,250	(B)
		375	(C)
		250	(D)
		125	(F)
		3,000	✓
	15,000	15,000	
✓	3,000		

Cost of Goods Produced

(A)	10,000	10,000	(II)

Other Expenses

(C)	1,500	2,500	(II)
(D)	1,000		
	2,500	2,500	

Revenue—Production

(I)	15,000	15,000	(A)

Revenue—Production Uncollectibles

(F)	500	500 (I)

Income Summary

(I)	500	15,000	(I)
(II)	12,500		
Net income	2,000		
	15,000	15,000	

Code for Transactions:
(A) Production (includes cost of goods produced):
   (Production: 100 @ $150)
   (Costs: 100 @ $100)
(B) Sales:
   (Sales: 75 @ $150)
(C) Selling costs:
   (Incurred: 75 @ $15 = $1,125)
   (To be incurred: 25 @ $15 =   375)
                              $1,500

Code for Closing Entries:
(I) Close out revenue accounts
(II) Close out expense accounts

(D)   *Collection costs:*
    (Incurred: *60 @ $10 = $ 600)*
    (To be incurred on goods sold: 15 @ $10 =   150)
    (To be incurred on goods in
        inventory: *25 @ $10 =   250)*
                                      $1,000)

(E)   *Collections:*
    (60 @ $150)

(F)   *Uncollectibles:*
    (On sales: $0.03\frac{1}{3} \times \$11,250)
    (On goods in inventory: $0.03\frac{1}{3} \times \$3,750)

Sales Basis (75 units)

Cash

✔ 5,000	10,000 (A)
(E) 9,000	1,125 (C)
	600 (D)
	2,275 ✔
14,000	14,000
✔ 2,275	

Accounts Receivable

(B) 11,250	9,000 (E)
	2,250 ✔
11,250	11,250
✔ 2,250	

Accounts Receivable— Allowance for Uncollectibles

	375 (F)

Inventory

(A) 10,000	7,500 (B)
	2,500 ✔
10,000	10,000
✔ 2,500	

Cost of Goods Sold

(B) 7,500	7,500 (II)

Accounts Receivable— Allowance for Future Collection Costs

	150 (D)

Revenue—Sales

(I) 11,250	11,250 (B)

Revenue—Sales Uncollectibles

(F) 375	375 (I)

Other Expenses

(C) 1,125	1,875 (II)
(D) 750	
1,875	1,875

Income Summary

(I) 375	11,250 (I)
(II) 9,375	
Net Income 1,500	
11,250	11,250

Code for Transactions:	Code for Closing Entries:
(A) Production: (100 units @ $100)	(I) Close out revenue accounts
(B) Sales (includes cost of sales): (Sales: 75 @ $150) (Costs: 75 @ $100)	(II) Close out expense accounts
(C) Selling costs: (75 @ $15)	
(D) Collection costs: (Incurred: 60 @ $10 = $600) (To be incurred: 15 @ $10 = 150) $750)	
(E) Collections: (60 @ $150)	
(F) Uncollectibles: $(0.03\frac{1}{3} \times 11{,}250)$	

Collection Basis (60 units)

Cash

✔	5,000	10,000	(A)
(E)	9,000	1,125	(C)
		600	(D)
		2,275	✔
	14,000	14,000	
✔	2,275		

Accounts Receivable

(B)	7,500	7,500	(E)
(C)	1,125	1,725	✔
(D)	600		
	9,225	9,225	
✔	1,725		

Accounts Receivable—Allowance for Uncollectibles

	300	(F)

Revenue—Collections

(I)	9,000	9,000	(E)

Inventory

(A)	10,000	7,500	(B)
		2,500	✔
	10,000	10,000	
✔	2,500		

Cost of Goods for Which Cash Collected

(E)	6,000	6,000	(II)

Income Summary

(I)	300	9,000	(I)
(II)	6,000		
(II)	1,500		
Net income	1,200		
	9,000	9,000	

Revenue—Collections Uncollectibles

(F)	300	300	(I)

Other Expenses

(E)	1,500	1,500	(II)

Code for Transactions:
(A) Production:
     (100 @ $100)
(B) Sales:
     (Costs: 75 @ $100)
(C) Selling costs:
     (75 @ $15)
(D) Collection costs:
     (60 × $10)
(E) Collections:
     Debit to:
     (Cost of goods for which cash collected: 60 @ $100 = $6,000)
     Debit to:
     (Other expenses: selling and collection
      costs on goods for which cash collected: 60 @ $ 25 = 1,500)
     Credit to:
     (Accounts receivable: $7,500)
     (Margin: 60 × $ 25 = 1,500)
     Debit to cash and credit to revenue: 60 × $150 = $9,000
(F) Uncollectibles:
     (0.03 $\frac{1}{3}$ × $9,000)

Code for Closing Entries:
(I)   Close out revenue accounts
(II) Close out expense accounts

*Although it would seem more logical here to base uncollectibles on receivables or total sales on account, instead of on revenue already collected, this example is made consistent with the others.

For this illustration, comparative income statements would be as follows:

Firm
Income Statement
for the Period

| | Event for Recognizing Revenue | | |
	Production	Sales	Collection
Revenue	$15,000	$11,250	$9,000
Less uncollectibles	500	375	300
Net revenue	14,500	10,875	8,700
Expenses:			
Goods	10,000	7,500	6,000
Selling	1,500	1,125	900
Collection	1,000	750	600
	12,500	9,375	7,500
Net income	$ 2,000	$ 1,500	$1,200

Comparative position statements would be as follows:

Firm
Position Statement
End of Period

| | Event for Recognizing Revenue | | |
	Production	Sales	Collection
Current assets:			
Cash	$2,275	$2,275	$2,275
Accounts receivable	2,250	2,250	1,725
Less: Collection costs	(150)	(150)	
Uncollectibles	(375)	(375)	(300)
Net receivable	1,725	1,725	1,425
Inventory	3,000	2,500	2,500
	$7,000	$6,500	$6,200
Ownership:			
Beginning	$5,000	$5,000	$5,000
Income	2,000	1,500	1,200
	$7,000	$6,500	$6,200

The reader may compare the differences in the valuation of receivables and inventories under the three methods on the schedule below. *Net selling price* is the same as net realizable value discussed in Chapter 5 and is defined as the cash to be received in the future less related costs (such as those of selling or collection) to be incurred in the future. Two valuations, cost for receivables under the collection method for recognizing revenue, and net selling price for inventories under the production method, are marked with arrows. The reason for this is to remind the reader how they differ from the conventional sales basis for recognizing revenue. It should be noted that this illustration differs from current accounting practice in two respects. First, to record future collection, collection costs as expenses in the period in which the revenue is recognized under the production and sales bases carry the matching process one step further than is customary in current practice where no recognition would be made of these estimates. Second, in current practice, under

---

EXHIBIT 9–3
THE VALUATION OF RECEIVABLES AND INVENTORIES UNDER
THREE COMMON METHODS OF RECOGNIZING REVENUE

Revenue	Receivables	Inventories
Recognized at time of:		
Production	Net selling price $\longrightarrow$	Net selling price
Sales	Net selling price	Cost
Collection $\longrightarrow$	Cost	Cost

the collection basis, the selling costs incurred on goods sold for which collections have not been received would be charged to expense instead of to the asset account, Accounts Receivable, as is done here.

Expense Concepts

Under the matching process, expenses are goods or services that have been used or consumed in the creation of revenue. Expenses are measured by the value of the expired goods or services given up in producing revenue; usually this means historical cost measured by the cash outlay, indebtedness incurred, or the cash equivalent. Occasionally expenses may be valued on a current or an opportunity cost basis. As discussed in Chapter 5, it is not possible to associate specific expenses with specific revenues (except for some production or merchandise costs); thus, the substitute criterion for determining expenses is costs expended during the account period. All those values that have expired or have been consumed *during the period* and are associated with earning revenue are termed expenses.

Although income usually is defined as "revenues less expenses," losses are reported on the income statement too; they can be distinguished from expenses in that the losses are values that have expired during the period without earning any revenue. If the total amount of expenses exceeds the total amount of revenues reported on the income statement, the excess of expenses over revenues also is termed a loss (or deficit) rather than income. Thus the term "loss" has two meanings, one for individual transactions or events, and another for the aggregate of all transactions and events reported on the period income statement.

Also, as discussed in Chapter 5, it is necessary not to confuse contra-revenue accounts with expenses. The former are reductions of gross revenues that are not realized; examples are: Sales—Returns and Allowances, Sales—Uncollectibles, and Sales—Cash Discounts. The one most frequently misclassified, Sales—Uncollectibles (or Sales—Bad Debts) should not be defined as an expiration of goods or services (or measured in cost terms) because this is usually more closely related to the credit sale, the credit-granting transaction, than to a second event occurring after the sale, a change in the credit standing of the customer. The costs incurred in issuing the enterprise's capital stock also are not period expenses because issuing corporate stock is a financing transaction, not a revenue-creating one.

As shown in Chapter 4, expenses are usually classified on the income statement according to the major functions of the enterprise (production, selling, and administration), but this classification is not relevant to external users since it does not facilitate their evaluating the contributions of the several functions or making forecasts about the firm. More meaningful classifications of expenses for external users might be according to the timing of cash flows (past versus current or future) or according to whether the expenses are fixed or vary with changes in production or sales volume.

Classifications of Revenue-producing Activities

Along with the possible variations in classification of income statement items concerning when revenue should be considered realized, there are also several methods of classifying the types of revenue-producing activities that should be reported on the income statement. Three major variations are: the current operating concept (or the "dirty surplus"), the all-inclusive concept (or the "clean surplus"), and the AICPA approach which is closely related to the all-inclusive concept.

Under the current operating concept, current, operating, and normal events (or changes) are reported separately from nonoperating, noncurrent, and nonnormal events. The latter are either segregated in a separate section of the income statement or are omitted from the income statement entirely and recorded instead directly to the Retained Earnings or related ownership accounts. The rationale is to distinguish clearly between those events that are related to activities and revenues of the current period and those related to other changes in ownership. Sometimes the operating-nonoperating dichotomy is confused with the recurring-nonrecurring dichotomy, but they are not identical. For example, the cost of overtime labor in a rush period is an operating event but not necessarily a recurring one. In certain geographic areas, the costs of the annual flood relate to a recurring event, but this is not an operating activity.

The objective of the current operating concept is to compute a more efficient net income measure, one that can be used more effectively to compare the current period's performance of the business and its management, not only with its performance in previous periods, but also with the income of other firms in the industry or elsewhere. Under this approach, the values of productive factors acquired in prior periods are included if they are used in creating revenue for the current period. With nonoperating, nonnormal, and noncurrent activities included, it is much more difficult to compute a single income that is an effective measure of current period efficiency. Although these classifications of the enterprise's activities are difficult to apply, it is argued that the accountant is more skilled to do the classifying than anyone else. In practice, however, this concept has not been effective. As enterprises have grown, it has become almost impossible to establish workable criteria for these classifications. The result has been that this concept has been much abused in practice, being frequently used to manipulate the net income measure in accordance with the wishes of the firm's management, to "manage" reported income of which the so-called "smoothing" of income technique is an example.

Partially for this reason, the all-inclusive (or "clean surplus") concept has received considerable authoritative support. The AAA has recommended this concept three times (in its 1936, 1941, and 1948 statements). Professors Sprouse and Moonitz give it some support too in their 1962 AICPA-sponsored Accounting Research Study No. 3. Under this approach, all transactions that change ownership during the period resulting from changes in assets or liabilities (except for dividend declarations and other capital retirement or investment transactions) are reported on the income statement. The objective of the all-inclusive concept is to measure income over a series of years (instead of a single year) to emphasize that the income of a period is less important than the trend of period income over time and to show the trend in operating efficiency. This concept is also an aid in predicting future performance. By not omitting any type of revenue-producing (or loss) activity, this concept is less subject to income smoothing, and the arbitrary distinctions of the current operating concept are avoided. Since all income-producing transactions are reported on the same statement, this concept probably is more easily verified and understood by the external reader, too. Also, over time, the annually reported net income will total to the enterprise's entire income to date. Notwithstanding its basic assumption that the reader is more capable than the accountant of classifying the reported data for his needs, the all-inclusive concept has much merit.

In 1966 with the intent, presumably, of requiring that the all-inclusive concept be followed in practice, the AICPA issued APB Opinion No. 9. Although this Opinion does not completely embrace the all-inclusive concept, it does require that all revenue-producing changes recognized during the period be included except for certain adjustments of net income for prior years. Examples of prior period adjustments to be excluded are given as: (1) the nonrecurring adjustments of income taxes; (2) the results of renegotiation proceedings or rate cases; and (3) the results of litigation. Any adjustment of the prior period should be excluded where the economic events occurred in the past and where no meaningful measure was possible at the time. Further clarification of the prior period definition would be useful although the force of the Opinion seems to preclude all but a very few types of exceptional adjustments. The Opinion also required that extraordinary items (defined imprecisely as material, nonrecurring items) should be segregated at the bottom of the income statement. Another authoritative body, the federal Securities and Exchange Commission, effectively requires that the all-inclusive concept be practiced. For practical purposes, the authoritative organizations in the United States that have taken stands support the all-inclusive concept.

Possible Divisions of Income

After resolving the problems of determining income, there remains the problem of how the income should be divided. These are not separate problems since the determinants of income cannot be the distributions of net income and vice versa. Who are the recipients of the net income? Accountants have never clearly identified which of the various groups associated with the enterprise should be considered income recipients. Consequently, there are at least five possible answers to this question, each of which has some support.

The first view, the value-added approach, includes the broadest range of income recipients. Under it, employees, governments, creditors, and owners receive income. When this concept is applied, the period wages and salaries (for employees), the period taxes (for governments), and the period interest charges (for creditors) are classified along with the period dividends (for owners) as distributions, not determinants, of income. For the many giant American corporations, this approach would seem to have much merit since these corporations do have broad economic and social significance. Although this viewpoint is rarely formally recognized in the income statement accounts, it is occasionally recognized in the annual report, often as part of the president's letter.

Under the second approach, the employees are classified as outsiders, and their wages and salaries are classified as expenses; otherwise the approach is identical to the value-added one. For the third viewpoint, that of all (long-term) investors, the only change is to classify income taxes as an expense. With the fourth viewpoint, that of all stockholders, interest charges become an expense. Under the final viewpoint, that of common stockholders, dividends declared on preferred stock also become an expense, leaving only the dividends declared on common stock as a distribution of income.

The five approaches are summarized in the T accounts shown on page 395.

The classification of interest charges as a distribution rather than a determinant of income has much merit. For many corporations, the distinctions between creditors and owners are fuzzy, particularly where owner and management are separate groups. To include interest charges with dividends, thus segregating all financial charges as distributions, provides a clearer income figure, one that permits better comparisons with other firms since the effects of different financial (capital) structures are excluded. However, in practice (as illustrated in Chapters 3 and 4), interest is usually classified as an expense.

With the income of the enterprise approach, income taxes are classified as a distribution of income. Although income taxes are neither a financial nor an operating charge, their exclusion in determining income is realistic and can be justified on the grounds that income taxes are not controllable by the company, and, of course, governments do provide numerous benefits including the stable environment without which firms could not continue. External users of financial statements, such as investors, do seem to make decisions on the basis of after-tax income; and income taxes do seem to be directly considered in setting prices and making other internal de-

Five Approaches to Income Distribution

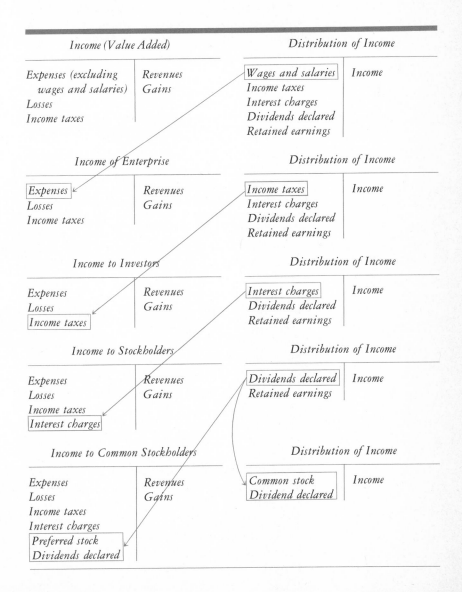

cisions. Finally, it is not consistent to classify government as a recipient while disregarding the general public and, particularly, employees.[6]

The argument for including the preferred stock dividends as a deduction in determining income is based upon the similarity of preferred stock dividends to interest. Conventionally, interest is regarded as a payment for the use of money, whereas profit, in a "pure" sense, is an extra payment for innovation or entrepreneurship. Accounting income does not provide for any division of the payments to owners between interest and "pure" profit;[7] thus dividends consist of both. Since dividends to preferred stockholders often would be made up largely of interest payments rather than "pure" profit payments, such dividends might be more appropriately classified with interest charges than with dividends to common stockholders.

The direct argument for showing all income as distributed only to common stockholders is a pragmatic one, based on the widely accepted view that income to common stockholders is the single most important figure on the statement because the report is prepared primarily for them. The figures quoted most frequently from income statement data are the dividends declared and the income per share of common stock. This approach has been broadened and improved in recent years by including not only the current common stockholders but also other equity holders who have special rights permitting them to become common stockholders. For example, many issues of long-term debt and preferred stock include contractual agreements giving the right of conversion to common shares. In two statements, APB Opinions Nos. 9 and 15, the AICPA has required that the effect of possible conversions be considered in computing income per share of common stock.

Although the distribution of net income is important information which should be reported on the income statement along with the determination of income, it usually is not so reported. With the more traditional views of income distribution, the dividend declarations are reported on the retained earnings statement. Even so, the reporting on the supplementary statement is more likely to be overlooked, and, of course, with the broader views of distribution, it is possible that certain items might be omitted. One solution is to present a three-section income statement consisting of: (1) the determination of income including extraordinary items—first section; (2) the distribution of income—second section; and (3) the reconciliation of

---

[6]Also, if income taxes are classified as a distribution of net income, the income tax allocation question, discussed in Chapter 8, is no longer a relevant one.
[7]This has been attempted at various times without success. One major problem, of course, is to determine what rate of interest should be used.

retained earnings—third section. Under this format, the retained earnings statement is combined with the traditional income statement, thus ensuring that no income item is omitted. Also, because there is merit in each of the five views of income distribution, it may be desirable to combine the five, or as many as desired, on the single statement rather than reporting only a single view.

This can be accomplished as follows:

Income ("value added")	x
Less wages and salaries	$-x$
Income of enterprise	x
Less income taxes	$-x$
Income to investors	x
Less interest charges	$-x$
Income to stockholders	x
Less preferred stock cash dividends	$-x$
Income to common stockholders	x
Less common stock cash dividends	$-x$
Income retained	x
Retained earnings beginning	$+x$
Retained earnings end	x

Income—an Overview

The concepts of income that are most relevant to accounting have been explained in this chapter. To overlook the effects of federal income tax laws and of taxable income which have directly influenced accounting practice might be a basis for criticism. The impact of taxes on long-lived assets and liabilities, including the associated income statement effect, was discussed in Chapters 7 and 8. Except for these isolated instances, the legal concepts of taxation seem to have little to do with the objectives of accounting income determination. Probably a more valid charge would be that the psychic income concepts (namely, the satisfaction of human wants such as power, prestige, and other social and psychological wants) are not taken into consideration. Only money income or the increases in the monetary valuation of enterprise resources have been mentioned owing to space constraints and the focus of this textbook.

There still is a great deal of disagreement over the valuation, recognition, and reporting aspects of income determination. The conventional income statement is a compromise statement. It combines both direct and indirect valuation and utilizes both economic and accounting concepts, namely, the capital maintenance and transactions approaches. The impact of uncertainty and the inability at present to deal with it adequately are the chief reasons for the compromise. Because of uncertainty, it has not become possible to determine income so as to achieve a complete matching of revenues and expenses in any specific sense. Such matching is possible only in the sense of allocating to a given period the value of revenue recognized for the period along with the value of goods and services deemed to have expired before the same point in time.

Another reason for the compromise approach is the numerous and sometimes conflicting objectives of income reporting. Since the return *on* money capital is quite different from the return *of* money capital, the statement should be careful to report only income transactions and to exclude other capital transactions.

This is difficult to achieve in many situations. The statement is also expected to provide the information needed for all kinds of decisions, both external and internal, these information needs varying from measures of past and present performance and efficiency of the firm and its management to planning and organizing the future of the firm. It does not seem reasonable to expect that one statement can serve all the objectives of accounting effectively, yet this often has seemed to be what is expected.

Since compromise solutions are usually not popular ones, and since the efforts to improve the statement such as publishing comparative statements and the recommendations of the AICPA's APB Opinion No. 9 thus far have had only minor effects, considerable discontent with the statement remains. The most practical suggestion for improving the statement is that several different types of income, utilizing different valuation and reporting methods, be recognized on the single period statement or on several statements for the same period. Under this approach, external users could select the information that was most relevant to their objectives. Other proposals have recommended supplementing the published statements with various internal reports, such as budgets, thus giving the external users more information with which to overcome the decision-making defects of the income statement. Despite its numerous shortcomings and the barrage of criticisms to which it is subjected, the income statement is still regarded as the single most valuable accounting report by all the groups who use financial statements, including external users.

Summary

The J. R. Hicks concept of economic income as modified by Sidney Alexander has been influential in determining accounting income. Under this concept, periodic income is determined by comparing the difference between position statements after some measure of ownership is obtained. Not easy or often even possible, this approach is the basis for both the accrual and allocation types of end-of-period adjustments, and it also is used commonly in the valuation of both short-term and long-term receivables and payables.

The second approach to measuring income under uncertainty, the prevailing situation in most businesses, predominates in conventional accounting. This transactions approach is identified with discrete events. In order to *realize* (receive cash from) revenue, (1) the values associated with all the revenue and related revenue-producing activities must be measurable, and (2) the major revenue-producing activities of the firm must be substantially completed. Only the production, delivery, and collection events are considered as practical points for the recognition of revenue by the accountant. The conventional point of revenue recognition is the delivery of goods or services. With these three methods the value of receivables and inventories may vary. Receivables are costed under the collection basis; inventories are valued at the net selling price (or net realizable value) under the production method.

Expenses, under the matching process, are goods or services that have been used or consumed in the creation of revenue. Expenses are usually measured by the cash outlay, indebtedness incurred, or the cash equivalent. Since it is not usually possible to associate specific expenses with specific revenues (except for some production or merchandise costs), the substitute or period criterion for matching in determining expenses is utilized. Expenses are all values associated with earning revenue that have expired or have been consumed during the period; losses are values that have expired during the period without earning any revenue or where the total amount of expenses exceeds the total amount of revenues reported on the income statement. Although expenses are usually classified on the income statement according to the major functions of the enterprise (production, selling, and administration), more meaningful classifications of expenses for external users might be according to the timing of cash flows or according to whether or not they vary with changes in production or sales volume.

As for the type of revenue-producing activities that should be reported on the income statement, three major variations are possible: the current operating, the all-inclusive, and the AICPA approach. The last mentioned approximates the all-inclusive approach except for excluding a very few types of exceptional prior period adjustments. Under the AICPA approach, extraordinary items are to be segregated at the bottom of the statement. The all-inclusive concept has been supported by all authoritative United States organizations taking a stand.

In considering the question of how the income should be divided, there are at least several answers as to which groups should be considered income recipients. These are: (1) the value-added approach, (2) the value-added approach with employees excluded, (3) all long-term investors except the government, (4) all stockholders, and (5) only common stockholders. Despite the importance of information on the distribution of net income, this item is usually left off the income statement and relegated to a supplementary statement, the retained earnings statement. One way to avoid overlooking this information is to present a three-section income statement (in which the distribution of income is the second section). Despite shortcomings and criticisms of the income statement, it is still regarded as the single most valuable accounting report by all financial statement users.

A Selection of Supplementary Readings

Alexander, Sidney S.: "Income Measurement in a Dynamic Economy," *Five Monographs on Business Income.* New York: AICPA, 1950. Revised by David Solomons and included in W. T. Baxter and Sidney Davidson, eds., *Studies in Accounting Theory,* 2d ed. Homewood, Illinois: Richard D. Irwin, Inc. 1962, pp. 126–200.

American Institute of Certified Public Accountants: "Reporting the Results of Operations," Opinions of the Accounting Principles Board No. 9. New York: 1966.

———: "Earnings per Share," Opinions of the Accounting Principles Board No. 15. New York: 1969.

Bruns, William J., Jr.: "Accounting Information and Decision-making: Some Behavioral Hypotheses," *The Accounting Review,* July 1968, pp. 469–480.

Chambers, R. J.: "New Pathways in Accounting Thought and Action," *Accountants' Journal,* July 1968, pp. 434–441.

Cowan, T. K.: "The Profit Illusion," *Accountants' Journal,* November 1967, pp. 140–143.

Frishkoff, Paul: "Some Recent Trends in Accounting Changes," *Journal of Accounting Research,* Spring 1970, pp. 141–144.

Hatfield, Henry Rand: "An Accountant's Adventures in Wonderland," *The Journal of Accountancy,* December 1940, pp. 527–532.

Husband, George R.: "That Thing Which the Accountant Calls Income," *The Accounting Review,* July 1946, pp. 247–254.

Hylton, Delmer P.: "On Matching Revenue with Expense," *The Accounting Review,* October 1965, pp. 824–828.

Kirkman, P. R. A.: "Errors in Profit Measurement in a Period of Inflation," *Certified Accountants Journal,* April 1971, p. 193.

Kosiol, Erich E.: "A Proposal for a General Concept of Cost," *The International Journal of Accounting Education and Research,* Fall 1967, pp. 1–19.

Mathews, R. L.: "Income, Price Changes and the Valuation Controversy in Accounting," *The Accounting Review,* July 1968, pp. 509–516.

May, George O.: "The Valuation of Goodwill," excerpt from testimony, *In the Matter of the Estate of E. P. Hatch, Deceased* (Lord & Taylor), 1912.

McCosker, Joseph S.: "Backlog Reporting: Challenge to Accountants," *The Journal of Accountancy,* May 1969, pp. 53–60.

Mitchell, Bert N.: "A Comparison of Accounting and Economic Concepts of Business Income," *The New York Certified Public Accountant,* October 1967, pp. 762–772.

Myers, John H.: "The Critical Event and Recognition of Net Profit," *The Accounting Review,* October 1959, pp. 528–532.

Nelson, Carl L.: "An Accountant's View of Profit Measurement," in Harold W. Stevenson and J. Russell Nelson, eds., *Profits in the Modern Economy.* Minneapolis: University of Minnesota Press, 1967, pp. 73–81.

Pacter, Paul A.: "APB Opinion No. 15: Some Basic Examples," *The New York Certified Public Accountant,* August 1970, pp. 638–646.

Ross, Howard: "Is It Better to Be Precisely Wrong Than Vaguely Right?" *Financial Executive,* June 1971, pp. 8–12.

Serfass, William D., Jr.: "The Accountant's Role in the Preparation of Public Corporation Reports," *The New York Certified Public Accountant,* August 1965, pp. 590–594.

Shwayder, Keith: "A Critique of Economic Income as an Accounting Concept," *Abacus,* August 1967, pp. 23–35.

Snavely, Howard J., and Allan H. Savage: "Clean Surplus vs. Current Operating Performance—Gaps in APB Opinion No. 9," *The New York Certified Public Accountant,* February 1970, pp. 124–129.

Solomons, David: "Economic and Accounting Concepts of Income," *The Accounting Review,* July 1961, pp. 374–397.

Sterling, Robert R.: *Theory of the Measurement of Enterprise Income.* Lawrence: The University Press of Kansas, 1970, pp. 117–189.

Thomas, Arthur L.: *The Allocation Problem in Financial Accounting Theory,* Studies in Accounting Research No. 3. Evanston, Illinois: American Accounting Association, 1969, pp. 83–105.

Vance, Lawrence L.: "The Case for Current Costs," *Accountancy,* April 1971, pp. 183–189.

Walker, Lauren M., Gerhard G. Mueller, and Fawzi G. Dimian: "Significant Events in the Development of the Realization Concept in the United States," *The Accountant's Magazine,* August 1970, pp. 357–360.

Witte, Arthur E.: "Signs of the Times in Financial Reporting: The Statement of Income," *The Illinois CPA,* Autumn 1966, pp. 11–17.

Questions

9–1   What interpretations can be given to the term "as well off as"? For an investor, which interpretation seems most relevant for the determination of net income?

9–2   If it is true that "accounting income and economic income will never be in agreement," why is it important for accountants to understand something about the income concepts of economists? Also cite areas of disagreement.

9–3   *The reputable accountant never loses sight of the fact that his income statements are influential in matters of dividend policy. Income, for him, is perhaps only what may be reported safely to unsophisticated directors as income. He aims, it would seem, never to ascertain what income is, in any really definable sense, but rather to devise rules of calculation which will make the result a minimum or at least give large answers only in the future. Con-*

ventional accounting, moreover, not only employs a procedure with a mark-edly conservative bias but promptly repudiates this procedure whenever it shows signs of working the other way.*

*Henry C. Simons, economist, in *Personal Income Taxation* (Chicago: University of Chicago Press, 1938), p. 81.

Comment and illustrate.

9–4

(1) At which of the following points of time would it usually be proper to recognize revenue? (a) For a manufacturer when an order is received, (b) for a retailer when a customer pays cash to apply on his account, (c) for a retailer when the merchandise increases in value, (d) for a transit company when tokens are received for a ride, (e) for a magazine publisher when a subscription is received.

(2) Receipt of cash before revenue is earned results in: (a) a debit to the Prepayment Asset account when the cash is received, (b) a credit to the Customers' Deposits account when the cash is received, (c) a credit to the Prepayment Asset account when the revenue is earned, (d) a credit to the Customers' Deposits account when the revenue is earned, (e) an adjustment to Retained Earnings.

(3) The recognition of revenue on the basis of production is appropriate in which of the following types of business? (a) A manufacturing company that sells on the installment plan, (b) a cigarette manufacturer, (c) a ship-building firm that is building an aircraft carrier, (d) a manufacturer of men's suits, (e) all of the above.

(4) Which of the following transactions involves the recognition of revenue by a retailer? (a) The issue of bonds, (b) the collection of cash on accounts receivable, (c) the borrowing of money at the bank on a 90-day 7 percent promissory note, (d) the sale of merchandise on account, (e) none of these.

(5) The Jarring Company signs a contract with the Thant Company for the construction of a $400,000 building. The accountant for the Jarring Company would treat this as: (a) a debit to Construction in Progress, and a credit to Contracts Payable; (b) a debit to Building, and a credit to Contracts Payable; (c) a debit to Construction Receivable, and a credit to Accounts Payable; (d) a debit to Purchases, and a credit to Accounts Payable; (e) no entry is necessary.

9–5

The following data apply to the first year of operation of a firm:

Production　　10,000 units at a cost of $5 per unit
Sales　　　　　9,000 units at a price of $10 per unit
Collections from customers, $60,000

For present purposes it will be assumed that there are no selling expenses.

(1) If revenue is recognized at the time of production, the revenue will be: (a) $50,000, (b) $60,000, (c) $90,000, (d) $100,000, (e) $110,000.

(2) If revenue is recognized at the time of production, the net income will be: (a) $10,000, (b) $30,000, (c) $40,000, (d) $45,000, (e) $50,000.

(3) If revenue is recognized at the time of sale the net income will be: (a) $10,000, (b) $30,000, (c) $45,000, (d) $50,000, (e) $90,000.

(4) If revenue is recognized when cash is received, the revenue will be: (a) $50,000, (b) $60,000, (c) $90,000, (d) $30,000, (e) $10,000.

(5) The costs to be carried forward to be charged against revenue of future periods will be the highest if revenue is recognized at the time of: (a) production, (b) payment of production costs, (c) sale, (d) collection of cash, (e) closing the books.

9–6   "Net Income is a behavioral variable as much as it is an economic variable. Net Income therefore depends upon your point of view and what you want to do about it." Explain how you think an accountant would respond to this statement. An economist.

9–7   The notion of maintaining capital intact is often used to define income. What are the various concepts of capital that are used in this context?

9–8   For each of the following methods of valuing inventory, state the point at which revenue was realized, and give an example or illustration of the correct usage of each:
(1) Inventory recorded at cost
(2) Inventory recorded at the net figure of selling price less costs to complete
(3) Inventory recorded at selling price

9–9   The following items have been criticized as improperly matching costs with revenues. Briefly discuss each item from the standpoint of matching costs with revenues, and suggest corrective or alternative means of presenting the financial information:
(1) Valuation of inventories at the lower of cost or market
(2) Receiving and handling expense
(3) Bad debt expense
(4) Cash discounts on purchases as revenue

9–10   The general ledger of a corporation engaged in the development and production of television programs for commercial sponsorship contains the following accounts before amortization at the end of the current year:

Account	Balance (Debit)
"All in the Family"	$151,000
"On the LBJ Ranch"	29,000
"The Mary Tyler Moore Show"	35,000
"The James Taylor Hour"	8,000

An examination of contracts and records reveals the following:
(1) The first and third accounts above represent the total cost of completed programs that were televised during the accounting period just ended. Under the terms of an existing contract, "All in the Family" will be rerun during the next accounting period, at a fee equal to 80 percent of the fee for the first televising of the program. The first-run contract earned

$500,000 of revenue. The contract with the sponsor of "The Mary Tyler Moore Show" provides that he may, at his option, rerun the program during the next season at a fee of 50 percent on the first televising of the program.

(2) The balance in "On the LBJ Ranch" account is the cost of a new program which has just been completed and is being considered by several companies for commercial sponsorship.

(3) The balance in "The James Taylor Hour" account represents the cost of a partially completed program for a projected series that has been abandoned.

How would you report each of the first four accounts in the financial statements?

9–11   How can one argue that a bank should recognize revenue at the time when the bank makes the loan?

9–12   Identify the numbered components in the following breakeven chart according to the code given below:

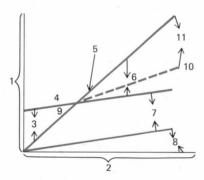

1. _____	A. Net Income
2. _____	B. Total Revenues
3. _____	C. Dividends Declared
4. _____	D. Units of Revenue—Sales
5. _____	E. Breakeven Point
6. _____	F. Cost of Goods Sold
7. _____	G. Total Expenses
8. _____	H. Net Loss
9. _____	I. Dollars of Revenue—Sales
10. _____	J. Selling and Administrative Expenses
11. _____	K. Earnings Retained

Problems

9–1   A firm produces a product at a cost of $6.00 per unit, all of which is paid at the time of production. It costs $3.00 per unit to sell the product, all of which is paid at the time when the product is sold. The sales price is $10.00 per unit. All sales are on account.

During the first year of operation the firm expects to produce 400,000 units; sell 360,000 and collect $1,000,000 from its customers.

During the second year it expects to produce 300,000 units, sell 340,000, and collect $2,100,000 from its customers. It has not determined when it will recognize revenue.

You are asked to consider the effect of various possibilities.

(1) Suppose that the firm recognizes revenue at the time of production.
   a. State the effect of producing one unit on the various assets and equities.
   b. State the effect of selling one unit on the various assets and equities.
   c. State the effect of collecting $5.00 on the various assets and equities.
   d. What will be the income for the first year?
   e. What will be the income for the second year?
(2) Suppose that the firm recognizes revenue at the time of sale. Follow instructions a, b, c, d, e.
(3) Suppose that it recognizes revenue at the time when cash is collected from the customer. Follow instructions a, b, c, d, e.

9-2

As part of its public relations program, a company sells books of admission tickets to the community theater for $10 per book. Each book contains 10 tickets good for admission any time from October through March. The regular admission price is $1.25. The company prepares the following statements for its ticket sales for October and November:

	October	November
Sales	$3,250	$6,500
Expenses	1,890	2,900
Net income	$1,360	$3,600

Sales includes the cash received from the sale of coupon books during each month. The number of books sold is 100 in October, and 350 in November; 630 and 2,310 tickets from the coupon books had been presented for admission in the two months, respectively. No entries had been made for the tickets. If you do not agree with this treatment, show how you would report these transactions on the income and the position statements.

9-3

For each of the following situations, make the journal entries that must have been made to reflect the extraordinary items:

a.

Walt Disney
Productions
Income Statement
(000's omitted)

Income before nonrecurring item	$10,367
Life insurance proceeds (Note 8)	900
Net income for the year	$11,267

NOTE 8. *Life insurance proceeds of $1,500,000 were received during the fiscal year under life insurance contracts which the company maintained on Walt Disney. The excess of $900,000 over the cash surrender value of $600,000 at October 1 has been reported separately.*

b.
W. R. Grace & Co.
Income Statement
(000's omitted)

Income before extraordinary items	*$47,481*
Extraordinary items, net of related U.S.	
income taxes (Note 1)	*3,996*
	$51,477

NOTE 1. In May, the company sold its investment in the Ruberoid Co. to General Airline & Film Corporation for $29,980,000. The gain on this transaction of $1,700,000, net of related income taxes of $566,000, has been shown as an extraordinary item in the income statement. As of December 29, the company sold its interest in Andretta-Werke Weber & Bandow G.M.B.H., a wholly owned subsidiary operating in West Germany. The estimated effect of this transaction on an after-tax basis is $2,296,000 and has also been shown as an extraordinary item in the income statement. Additional information reveals that the proceeds on the sale of Andretta-Werke Weber & Bandow G.M.B.H. was $22,800,000, and that the income tax related to this transaction was $517,000. As of statement date, the income tax on both sales had not actually been paid in cash.

9–4

On January 1, 1972, you bought a herd of 100 calves with the intention of holding the herd for four years and at the end of that period selling them as beef cattle. You paid $100 each for the calves. The events from January 1, 1972 to January 1, 1976 are summarized below:

Year	Size of Herd	Average Weight (lb) of Each Calf (at beginning of year)	Cost of Feed Purchased and Used
1972	*100*	*200*	*$5,000*
1973	*100*	*350*	*6,500*
1974	*100*	*550*	*6,500*
1975	*100*	*800*	*7,000*
1976	*100*	*1,000*	

The market price per pound for beef throughout the period was (on January 1 of each year): 1972: $0.49; 1973: $0.61; 1974: $0.58; 1975; $0.65; and 1976: $0.72. Each price is net of any transportation costs.

Although you purchased all your feed, you did rent a plot of land for $1,000 per year on a yearly basis. You erected some temporary buildings, built some fences, and purchased some feeding equipment at the same time that you purchased the herd. These items cost you $3,200, and you judged their useful life to be about eight years, or about long enough to be used for two herd cycles, which was the period of time you intended to stay in business. You planned to use straight-line depreciation. At the end of 1975 you could have sold the cattle at auction at an average price of $0.70 per pound. Instead, on January 1, 1976, you contracted with a local meat-packer to slaughter the cattle, process the meat, and sell the processed output to wholesale meat dealers. The total selling value of the finished product was $95,000. The meat-packer paid for all the costs incurred in slaughtering, processing, and selling and charged you a fee of $26,000 for handling the entire transaction.

Calculate the amount of net income for each year, 1972 to 1976, assuming that (1) revenue is recognized only on the basis of the sale, and (2) revenue is recognized on the basis of market movements and growth. Under each set of conditions calculate the amount of the inventory that would be reflected on the position statement at the end of each year. For 1976 show the net income associated with slaughtering the herd. Do not be concerned with that portion of 1976 revenue associated with a possible second herd of calves.

9–5 You are to advise the Holden Caulfield, Jr. firm on how to recognize revenue on an uncompleted $1,000,000 two-year contract dated the first day of the company's accounting year and payable in two annual installments. It was estimated that 15 percent of the contract price would be net income and that 60 percent of the contract costs had been incurred at the end of the first year. Compute the first-year revenue, expenses, and net income that might be booked under three different techniques; select the one you think most defensible, and give your criteria.

9–6 A company started operations in 1971 with cash of $100,000 and capital stock of $100,000. During the year it produced 20,000 wigs at a cost of $10 each (all paid for in cash). It sold 15,000 of these for $20 each, all sales being on account. During 1971 the cash received on accounts receivable totaled $200,000. Selling costs during the period were $45,000 (all paid in cash).

Put an X in the column headed with the method that would produce the final balance given for the account. More than one X is possible!

		Revenue Recognized at		
Account and Balance (in thousands)		Production	Sale	Cash Received
1. Cash	$ 55			
2. Inventory	85			
3. Sales	400			
4. Sales	300			
5. Cost of Goods Sold	150			
6. Net Income	70			
7. Selling Expense	45			
8. Accounts Receivable	100			
		(1)	(2)	(3)

What would be necessary for the net income in column (1) to be the same as columns (2) and (3) combined?

9–7 A company purchased a tract of unimproved land for $13,280. This land was improved and then subdivided into building lots at an additional cost of $7,600. These building lots were all of the same size, but owing to differences in location, were offered for sale at different prices, as noted below:

Group	No. of Lots	Price per Lot
1	12	$1,200
2	18	900
3	6	700

Operating expenses for the year connected with this project totaled $8,700.

Lots remaining unsold at year end were as follows: 4 in group 1, 6 in group 2, and 1 in group 3.

Prepare the income statement for this project for this period.

9–8

A company agrees to buy an electronic gauge from the Columbus Company, paying $10,000 down and $10,000 annually for 14 years. In making this agreement the company assumed that it had a credit rating justifying a 4 percent interest rate, but the Columbus Company used a 6 percent rate of interest in its calculations. The companies did not discuss a cash price for this gauge, and there is not a market for such gauges elsewhere.

(1) Show calculations to compute the amount of sales to be shown on Columbus' books.

(2) What is the cost of the gauge on the purchasing company's books?

9–9

A manufacturing company makes widgets. At the beginning of 1970 it was expected that throughout all future time the company would be able to manufacture 100,000 widgets a year and sell them for $325,000, with expenditures as follows:

Materials	$110,000
Labor	105,000
Machinery	12,000
Other production costs	90,000
	$317,000

On January 1, 1972, the firm's position statement was as follows:

Cash	$ 2,000
Raw materials (for 5,000 widgets)	5,000
Finished goods (1,000 widgets)	3,000
Plant ($100,000–$55,000)	45,000
	$55,000

The cash is the minimum necessary. The raw materials have a replacement cost of $5,500. The finished goods have a replacement cost of $3.17 and a selling price of $3.25. There are no selling costs.

During the year 1972, the following events occurred:

Sales (110,000 @ $3.25)	$357,500
Materials purchased (for 110,600 widgets @ $1.10)	121,660
Labor used (for 110,100 widgets @ $1.05)	115,605
Machine purchased	12,000
Other production costs	100,000

Expectations at the end of the period:

Sales (110,000 @ $3.25)	*$357,500*
Materials (110,000 @ $1.10)	*121,000*
Labor (110,000 @ $1.05)	*115,500*
Machinery	*12,000*
Other costs	*100,000*

Cash dividends were paid to decrease the cash balance to $2,200.

At the beginning and end of the period, the machinery had a value of $63,296. These are 10 machines, ranging in age from 1 to 10 years. Costs of operating the machines are constant over the 10-year period. The machines have a life of 10 years. Calculate three types of net income. The interest rate is 10 percent.

9–10   A construction company has received $400,000 in cash by issuing capital stock. It has a contract to construct a $4,000,000 building on the following terms: There will be a monthly estimate of the value of the completed portion, and 90 percent of the estimate is to be paid to the company by the twentieth of the following month with the remaining 10 percent ($400,000) to be paid within 30 days after the building is completed. The total cost for the building is estimated to be $3,720,000.

During the first year completion to the extent of $1,600,000 was certified ($200,000 in December). Total cost of the work (paid in cash) was $1,480,000; total cash received, $1,260,000 (90 percent of $1,400,000).

Prepare income and position statements if revenue is recognized: (a) as a percentage of completion, and (b) at time of completion.

9–11   The Matt Dillon Company owns 100 shares of the Chester Manufacturing Company and 100 shares of the Festus Stores, Inc. Data on these investments (on a per share basis) are:

	Chester	*Festus*
Cost, 1970	*80.25*	*60.75*
Market value, January 1, 1972	*83.50*	*64.50*
Earnings, 1972	*6.43*	*5.25*
Dividends, 1972	*3.50*	*3.00*
Market value, December 31, 1972	*87.12*	*69.25*

The Kitty Investment Company owns 100 shares of Saloon, Inc., and 100 shares of Doc Stores, Inc. Data on these investments are:

	Saloon	*Doc*
Cost, 1970	*70.50*	*43.50*
Market value, January 1, 1972	*68.25*	*41.25*
Earnings, 1972	*5.43*	*3.80*
Dividends, 1972	*5.00*	*3.75*
Market value, December 31, 1972	*64.25*	*39.50*

The Arness Investment Company had the same portfolio as Dillon, but sold its stock on December 31.

Compare the net income of the three companies (Dillon, Kitty, and Arness), using the following three methods for recognizing revenue: (a) dividends received, (b) earnings, and (c) dividends received plus increase in the market value of the stock. Defend your selection of the preferable method.

9–12 A furniture company that had received $700,000 by issuing stock made installment sales of $800,000 during its first year of operation. Cash purchases of furniture were $580,000. Cost of goods sold was $480,000. Selling and administrative costs (paid in cash) associated with these sales were $220,000; collections were $120,000.

During the second year, installment sales were $1,200,000, while cost of goods sold was $720,000, with cash purchases of $750,000, and administrative costs (paid in cash) were $260,000. Collections on first-year sales were $260,000, and on second year $200,000. Determine net income for both years by the most appropriate method, and give rationale.

9–13 A wheat producer stores his wheat in a grain elevator and receives a warehouse receipt for it. He sells wheat at times based on two factors: his need for cash, and his forecast of the market. When should he recognize revenue?

9–14 Steamship companies classify revenue and expense primarily by ship and voyage; each voyage of each ship is considered separately. Instead of net income being determined for a period of time, it is computed for each voyage, with all revenues from voyages in progress being deferred, and all costs associated with voyages in progress classified as prepayments. Defend this practice by comparing it with the other alternatives available.

9–15 You are considering starting a grocery store as of January 2, 1972. You have $100,000 of your own funds to invest in the business and can borrow money at 6 percent from your uncle. You estimate that you will need to pay a total of $60,000 for a building ($34,000), equipment ($16,000), and land ($10,000) as of this date, and that an additional $32,000 must be paid for inventory then too. Your estimate of operations for the first three years (in thousands) is as follows:

	Year		
	1	2	3
Sales	$160	$240	$320
Purchases	150	212	278
Salaries and other	32	40	48
Depreciation	4	4	4

You believe that this growth would permit you to sell the business (excluding the cash) on December 31, 1974, for $100,000 cash (with the buyer assuming any outstanding bank loan).

You assume that all cash receipts and disbursements for each year are made at the end of the year and that all purchases and sales are for cash only. You will need a $10,000 cash balance on hand at the beginning of each year (with interest on any bank loan to be paid annually at the end of the year). Selling prices (without markups or markdowns) are set at 125 percent of cost. Income taxes are at a 25 percent rate. You do not wish to start the store unless you can earn at least 10 percent on your own and borrowed funds. Should you enter the business? Use appropriate computations to support your answer.

9–16   Compute the amount of (1) periodic revenue, (2) periodic net income, (3) end-of-period inventory, and (4) end-of-period receivables if revenue is recognized at the time of: (a) production, (b) sale (to dealer), (c) sale (to dealer's customer), and (d) cash collection, based upon the following first-period operating transactions for the Aristotle Onassis Corporation:

I. Production: 2,000,000 units at the following costs: Depreciation, $750,000; and other, $5,250,000.

II. Shipments to dealers: 900,000 units billed at $7,200,000.

III. Under a three-year contract, a shipping firm had agreed to haul 2,700,000 units for a total cost of $270,000, half of which had been paid in advance—$135,000. There are no administrative or other selling expenses.

IV. Dealers reported selling product for which they had been billed $5,400,000.

V. Dealers remitted cash to company: $4,500,000.

9–17   Cary Grant is a citrus grower in Florida. Although the fruit is picked and sold during only January and February, Grant incurred expenses throughout the year for the care and upkeep of the orchards. In 1971 Grant received $36,000 in both January and February from the cash sales of fruit. His labor costs were $1,000 each month throughout the year; utilities and other expired costs amounted to $24,000 annually. What was Grant's income for the month of April?

9–18   The January 1, 1972, position statement of a mining company is (in millions): cash $1; mine $5 = capital stock $6.

During 1972 the company records the following transactions: It mined 100,000 ounces of gold at a cost of $30.00 per ounce; of this amount $5.00 per ounce is depletion cost, with the remaining costs being paid in cash. It sold and delivered 60,000 ounces of gold at a price of $35.00 per ounce. Delivery costs paid were $30,000. It collected $1,750,000 (for 50,000 ounces).

Prepare financial statements if revenue is recognized at time of: (a) production, (b) sale, and (c) receipt of cash from customers.

9–19   A company owns several United States government series E bonds purchased at a discount from face value; e.g., a $100 bond costs $75 initially. Then, as time passes, the bond increases in value as interest builds up. If the bond is held to maturity (eight years and eleven months) the investing company will have earned 5 percent annual return. At any time during the period the bond can be redeemed according to a schedule of values. This schedule, however, does not build up at a constant 5 percent rate since the redemption value increases slowly in the early years and more rapidly in the last years.

(1) What do you think constitutes the realization of revenue in the situation, and why?

(2) With the following redemption schedule available, show how you would calculate the revenue for the second year. Assume that three $100 bonds were acquired at the beginning of the accounting year.

End of Year	Redemption Value
First	$78.00
Second	81.60
Third	85.60

9–20   The Rodger Vadim Farm, a corporation, produced the following in its first year of operations:

	Bushels	Selling Price per Bushel
Oats	6,000	$1.40
Wheat	9,000	2.40

During the year it sold two-thirds of the grain produced and collected three-fourths of the selling price on the grain sold; the balance is to be collected in equal amounts during each of the following years.

Additional data for the first year:

Wealth at beginning of year 1	$100,000.00
Wealth at end of year 1	115,000.00
Depreciation on productive plant	3,000.00
Other production costs (cash)	4,500.00
Miscellaneous administrative costs (cash)	3,600.00
Grain storage costs	0.00
Selling and delivery costs (incurred and paid at time of sale), per bushel	0.10
Additional stockholder investments during year 1	0.00
Dividends paid to stockholders during year 1	10,000.00
Income taxes	0.00

The Roger Vadim Farm is enthusiastic about the accountant's concept of matching costs and revenues; it wishes to match all costs with revenue.

(1) Recently the president was introduced to a noted British economist who convinced him that the accountant's accrual approach to measuring income in fact was merely a partial accrual, and that full accrual would require consideration of changes in "wealth," which was defined as "the present value of expected net future receipts." Following this, it

was suggested that a full accrual income for a period would be determined to be the amount that could be spent during a period while
leaving wealth unchanged. Income measured in this way for the first
year would be:
a. $30,000
b. $25,000
c. $20,000
d. $15,000
e. None of the above

(2) If revenues were recognized when the production is complete (i.e., inventory is carried at net selling price), income computed in accordance
with the farm's matching objective for the first year would be:
a. $21,600
b. $17,900
c. $17,400
d. $ 7,400
e. None of the above

(3) If revenue were recognized on the cash-collection basis, income computed in accordance with the farm's matching objective for the first year
would be:
a. $8,700
b. $6,300
c. $4,400
d. $2,900
e. None of the above

(4) If revenue were recognized on the sales basis, income computed in accordance with the farm's matching objective for the first year would be:
a. $10,400
b. $ 9,900
c. $ 9,400
d. $ 7,400
e. None of the above

9–21

Ayrshire Collieries Corporation's income statement reports net income, and
net income after deducting provision for price-level depreciation.

(1) Which of these income figures does Ayrshire use in reporting earnings
per share?

(2) Which of these income figures do you consider to be more meaningful
in evaluating the potential earning power of Ayrshire? in comparing
the performance of Ayrshire with other corporations in the same industry? Explain.

(3) How would you explain the provision for price-level depreciation reported by Ayrshire?

(4) In what way(s) is the provision for price-level depreciation consistent
and/or inconsistent with the related accounts reported in Ayrshire's
position statement?

Ayrshire Collieries
Financial Highlights
Fiscal Years Ended
June 30
(000's omitted)

	1971	1970
Sales of coal and coke	$49,055.00	$46,373.00
Net income after all deductions	2,847.00	3,524.00
Per share*	3.67	4.55
Dividends paid	758.00	722.00
Per share†	1.00	1.00
Stock dividend	2%	5%
Working capital:		
Current assets	$13,371.00	$14,670.00
Current liabilities	7,179.00	6,320.00
	$ 6,192.00	$ 8,350.00
Operations:		
Number of mines	10	11
Production-tons of coal:		
Ayrshire mines (including 50% of Gibraltar tonnage)	6,761	6,153

*Current basis of 774,947 shares.
†On basis of shares then outstanding.

Ayrshire Collieries
Position Statement
Fiscal Years Ended
June 30
(000's omitted)

Assets	1971	1970
Current assets:		
Cash	$ 4,201	$ 5,292
U.S. government securities, at cost	1,851	3,103
Accounts receivable, less reserve	6,785	5,778
Coal and other products, at market or less	534	497
	13,371	14,670
Property, plant, and equipment at cost:		
Operating property	42,104	31,002
Less accumulated depreciation and depletion	26,657	18,927
	15,447	12,075
Construction in process	3,419	9,386
Undeveloped coal lands	7,675	5,168
	26,541	26,629
Investments	4,211	5,425
Prepaid and deferred charges:		
Repair parts and supplies	2,312	1,998
Advance royalties	2,180	1,168
Other	1,154	782
	5,646	3,948
	$49,769	$50,672

Equities	1971	1970
Current liabilities:		
Accounts payable and accrued	$ 3,234	$ 3,093
Federal income taxes	1,258	1,381
Current requirements on long-term obligations	2,687	1,846
	7,179	6,320
Long-term obligations:		
Notes payable:		
$4\frac{1}{2}\%$ first mortgage and collateral trust notes, due serially to 1976		1,820
$4\frac{1}{2}\%$ unsecured notes, due serially to 1976	2,400	3,000
Installment purchase contracts	3,610	2,236
Equipment purchase contracts due serially to 1976	2,056	
Other	75	69
	8,141	7,125
Reserves:		
Work stoppage	300	300
Deferred federal income taxes	100	162
	400	462
Stockholders' equity:		
Common stock, par value $3 per share, authorized 800,000 shares; issued and outstanding 774,947 and 760,034 shares, respectively	2,325	2,280
Paid-in capital	8,000	7,250
Capital maintained by recognition of price-level depreciation (see note on statement of income)	2,587	2,378
Retained earnings	21,137	24,857
	34,049	36,765
	$49,769	$50,672

Ayrshire Collieries
Income Statement
Fiscal Years Ended
June 30
(000's omitted)

	1971	1970
Revenues:		
Sales of coal and coke	$49,055	$46,373
Income from other products, royalties, interest,		
rentals, etc.	1,421	1,606
	$50,476	$47,979
Expenses:		
Coal and coke purchased for resale	$25,011	$24,899
Coal production costs	14,560	12,117
Depreciation and depletion	2,098	1,654
Selling, administrative, and general	3,864	3,648
Interest	237	146
Federal income taxes	1,650	1,796
	47,420	44,260
Net income	3,056	3,719
Provision for price-level depreciation (see Note)	209	196
Net income, after deducting provision for price-		
level depreciation	$ 2,847	$ 3,523

NOTE: The provision for price-level depreciation represents the excess of depreciation cost measured by the current purchasing power of the dollar over depreciation cost measured by the purchasing power of the dollar at the dates of acquisition or contraction of the companies' depreciable property. Reference is made to the opinion of Arthur Andersen & Co. for approval of this accounting.

10

Analysis of Owners' Equity: Partnerships and Proprietorships

Thus the right-hand side of the balance sheet is entirely composed of claims against or rights over the left-hand side. "Is it not then true," it will be askt, "that the right-hand side is entirely composed of liabilities?" The answer to this is that the rights of others, or the liabilities, differ materially from the rights of the proprietor, in the following respects.

(1) The rights of the proprietor involve dominion over the assets and power to use them as he pleases even to alienating them; while the creditor cannot interfere with him or them except in extraordinary circumstances.

(2) The right of the creditor is limited to a definit sum which does not shrink when the assets shrink, while that of the proprietor is of an elastic value.

(3) Losses, expenses and shrinkage fall upon the proprietor alone, and profits, revenue and increase of value benefit him alone, not his creditors.

For these reasons the proprietary interest cannot be treated like the liabilities . . . .

. . . Surely The Business does not stand in the same relation to its proprietors or its capitalists as to its "other" liabilities. It would seem more appropriate to say that it is "owned by" than "owes" the proprietors.*
Charles Ezra Sprague, 1907

Except for the greater variety and complexity of accounts found in the more complicated forms of business enterprise, accounting for assets and liabilities seems quite similar for any business. Perhaps this is so because in practice assets and liabilities are both defined and measured quite separately and with little concern for the owners' equity factor in the position statement equation. Thus ownership equity is

*From *The Philosophy of Accounts* (New York: 1907), pp. 46–47, 49.

measured largely as a residual or as the difference between the aggregate assets and the aggregate liabilities. It thus would be easy to record ownership on a single-entry basis. However, in conventional financial accounting the same rules of double-entry bookkeeping are observed in recording transactions in the ownership accounts as in all other equity accounts.

In this chapter the characteristics of the proprietorship and the partnership will be reviewed. Chapter 11 will focus on the characteristics of the corporation. As in previous chapters, the special valuation, reporting, and control problems will be emphasized. Ownership will be considered from the point of view of both the enterprise and the owners themselves.

Although investments in and withdrawals of ownership are recorded directly in ownership accounts, most of the basic periodic change in ownership accounts is attributed to income that is directly related to the periodic changes in assets and liabilities. Revenue and and expense accounts, gain and loss accounts, are elaborations of ownership. Revenues and gains represent increases in ownership resulting from increases in assets or decreases in liabilities; expenses and losses represent decreases in ownership resulting from decreases in assets or increases in liabilities.

The claims of owners have lower legal priorities than those of creditors. This applies to both those payments that are made periodically and those that are made at maturity or liquidation dates. For example, bondholders are entitled to receive periodic interest payments before stockholders receive cash dividends. The maturity date and maturity amount are known for bondholders and constitute a legal obligation whereas for owners no such date and value exist; payments to stockholders are dependent on the availability of cash and do not constitute legal obligations, except when the enterprise is in liquidation. Then, the owner has a legal claim to the residual after all creditors have been paid.[1]

The basic rights of ownership are four: (1) the right to manage or to be represented in management; (2) the right to share in the income of the enterprise; (3) the right to make additional investments in the enterprise if such are required in order to maintain the existing proportion of ownership; and (4) the right to share in the residual proceeds if the enterprise is liquidated.

The Proprietorship

The simplest accounting theory about ownership is the proprietary theory. The position statement equation $\Sigma A - \Sigma L = \Sigma OE$ (or ΣP) expresses this theory; it focuses upon the proprietor and any changes

---

[1]After dividends are declared, stockholders have a legal claim to the amount declared. But this claim is that of a creditor, not an owner.

in his accounts. Under this concept, ownership is the sum of the proprietor's original and subsequent investments in the enterprise, plus income, less withdrawals or losses. The all-inclusive income statement is based on this concept, since net income includes all items affecting proprietorship except for the proprietor's investments in and withdrawals from the enterprise. Thus net income, under the proprietary theory, is added to the personal capital accounts of the owners. Although this theory can be applied to corporations, particularly in net income per share computations, it is most applicable to sole proprietorships and partnerships.

Under proprietary theory, accounting for ownership in a sole proprietorship requires only one or possibly two accounts. These are a capital account for permanent investments in the enterprise and a current or drawing account for temporary investments in and withdrawals from the enterprise. The latter is increased through income and decreased through withdrawals and losses. Often, the current or drawing account is kept open only during the period, and is closed into the capital account when statements are prepared. The name of the owner is included in the title of each owner's account for the proprietorship (e.g., Joe Namath, Capital).

Joe Namath, Capital

Withdrawals (credit is to Cash or other assets) *Loss (credit is to Revenue and Expense Summary)*	*Investment (debit is to Cash or other assets)* *Income (debit is to Revenue and Expense Summary)*

Partnerships

Accounting for ownership in a partnership requires the same kinds of account(s) as for a sole proprietorship, except that there must be a separate capital (and possibly a current) account for each partner. However, there are a few special problems in accounting for ownership when the enterprise has more than one owner.

Before we consider these problems, the distinguishing characteristics of a partnership should be identified. The first is the ease and convenience with which a partnership can be started. As with a sole proprietorship, a partnership can be formed quickly with little cost. The second characteristic is the limited life of a partnership, especially compared to that of a corporation. A partnership is dissolved legally by the (1) death, (2) retirement, (3) bankruptcy, or (4) incapacity of a partner, or (5) the admission of a new one. Although partnerships sometimes are unstable and short-lived, they can be stable and long-lived when the management plans it that way. For example, large public accounting partnerships are little affected by the retirement or admission of partners since the firm plans to continue, irrespective of the status of an individual partner. Thus, the limited life characteristic is more indicative of a legal aspect of all partnerships than of the actual substance of particular partnerships.

Besides (1) its ease of formation and (2) its typically limited life, a partnership also may be characterized by (3) the unlimited liability of each partner or owner, (4) its mutual agency or the right of each partner to act for and obligate the partnership, (5) the co-ownership of partnership property and partnership income.

Unlimited liability means that each partner is personally liable for the debts of a partnership. In the event that the partnership becomes insolvent or liquidates, this characteristic becomes most significant for partners with personal assets. Sometimes a limited partnership is established; this means that the limited partners may not have a personal liability for the obligations of the partnership. The partner or partners who have unlimited liability to the creditors of the partnership are called *general partners.* If a partnership is composed entirely of general partners, it is called a general partnership; if it has one or more limited partners, it is called a limited partnership.

Each partner has the right to commit the partnership to binding contracts. This mutual agency characteristic ordinarily does not extend beyond acts performed within the normal scope of partnership business operations. With the co-ownership of partnership property characteristic, the individual partner does not have a claim against any specific partnership asset, even if he contributed it to the partnership. Each partner, too, has the right to participate in partnership earnings as stipulated in the partnership agreement (or equally with other partners in the absence of such a stipulation).

In order to avoid disputes among partners, those forming a partnership prepare written partnership agreements which recognize the special characteristics of partnerships. These articles of copartnership should include: (1) the starting date and the duration of the partnership; (2) the plan for sharing profits and losses; (3) the capital contributed by each partner; (4) the name and nature of the partnership, including the duties, rights, and names of each partner; and (5) the length of the accounting period, the nature of the accounting records and statements, and the arrangements for periodic audits by outside accountants. Other equally important provisions might be for the arbitration of disputes among the partners and plans for the liquidation of the partnership. These latter provisions should stipulate valuation procedures to be used especially for intangibles such as goodwill. Provisions for insurance on the lives of the partners also should be included in the articles.

Other features of a partnership can be cited. Under present federal income tax law, a partnership files an income tax return but it does not pay an income tax. Instead all partners must include their share of all taxable partnership income in their personal income tax returns, even if the income has not been distributed. Another feature is the practice of reporting any salary payments to partners for their services as managers or employees as distributions of income (rather than expenses) of the partnership. Although the measurement of partnership income may be somewhat invalidated by this practice, especially for interfirm comparisons, it avoids the problem that arises when such payments are set at a level that is unrealistic relative to the value of services received. Other support for this practice is found in the traditional legal view that a partnership is an association of individuals in which a partner is not an employee but an owner. Existing income tax rules require that this practice be followed, too, on income tax returns. However, for internal evaluation purposes, reasonable expenses may be allowed for such services, so as to make the statements comparable with other corporate enterprises.

The special reporting problems associated with a partnership may be divided into three categories:

1. The formation of a partnership including the admission of a partner into an existing partnership
2. The distribution of the partnership's periodic income or losses during the lifetime of the partnership
3. The liquidation of the partnership

In all three categories of problems, the accountant must carefully distinguish between two sets of relationships among the partners. The first is expressed in the ratio of the amounts of capital contributed and maintained by the partners; the second is the ratio by which the partners share partnership income or losses. If not specified in the partnership agreement, the capital ratio can be determined by inspecting the capital accounts, and the profit and loss ratio consists of equal shares to each partner, regardless of the capital ratios.

Income and loss agreements Income and loss agreements among partners may be based on three factors: (1) the ratio of partner capital; (2) the quality and the quantity of partner services contributed; and (3) miscellaneous factors such as prestige, contacts, special talents, or expertise that a partner may bring to the partnership or the personal financial risk of the wealthiest partner(s).

The first factor, the capital ratio, is based on the current capital balances rather than the original capital contribution. It does not include loans made by partners to the partnership. There are two basic problems in distributing income and losses on the basis of the partners' investments. First, what should be the measure of the investment during the earning period? Second, what is the relevant rate of return, or imputed interest, on the partner's investment? If the investments remain relatively constant during the period, the ending capital account balance can be used as the base without distortion. If the investments have fluctuated during the period, the simple average of the beginning and ending balances of the capital account might be used. Better still would be a weighted average of the monthly balances. The rate for the imputed interest often is called the firm's cost of capital, and may be its borrowing, lending, or earning rate. The investment base and rate should be stipulated in advance in the written partnership agreement to avoid disputes later. The written agreement also provides the opportunity to specify penalties for the partner who fails to maintain a minimum investment and to indicate whether balances in current or drawing accounts should be considered as capital for profit allocation purposes.

As imputed interest is considered to be the return on the partners' capital investments, imputed salaries are the return for the partners' services. The amounts for imputed salaries are set in advance of the period, although arrangements for bonuses can be made dependent on the outcome of the period. Both the abilities of the working partners and their working hours need to be considered; a partner who does not work openly for the partnership enterprise is called a silent partner. Presumably these imputed salaries should be based on the value of similar services or what the services would cost in another similar enterprise.

The miscellaneous factors considered in an income and loss sharing ratio are prestige or contacts and risk. Although prestige or contacts may be considered as part of a partner's services and allowed for in the imputed salary figure or the income and loss sharing percentage, it may be desirable to make separate allocations for these factors. Individual partners may enjoy great professional prestige and be widely known among various groups (for example, in the 1960s Richard Nixon was accepted into an existing New York law firm, which was then renamed with Nixon listed first). Such professional qualities or other talents or expertise may attract many persons to do business with the partnership who otherwise would not do so. If this is so, the partnership should recognize the value of these special services in distributing its income. There is also the risk factor. Because of the unlimited personal liability that general partners have for the debts of the partnership, the personal risk for a wealthy partner is considerably higher than for a partner without wealth. This is particularly true if the partnership activities are subject to high risk. If the partnership is unable to pay its debts, the wealthy partner will have to pay them, whereas the less wealthy partner may be unable to do so; for this reason, a wealthy partner may choose to become a limited partner.

In applying a partnership income and loss sharing plan to the partnership net income for the period, distributions are made according to the plan, even when the net income to be distributed is less than the sum of the stipulated distributions. To illustrate, consider a partnership with two partners, O. K. Simpson and S. Agnew who have agreed to share income as follows: (1) to impute 10 percent interest on their average partnership capital balances; (2) to distribute imputed salaries of $50,000 and $10,000, respectively; and (3) to distribute any residual equally. For the current year, the partnership income was $50,000 with average capital balances of $100,000 for Simpson and of $25,000 for Agnew. The distribution of income would be as follows:

	Partnership	O. K. Simpson	S. Agnew
Average capital	$125,000	$100,000	$25,000
Income	$ 50,000		
Interest rate		10%	10%
Less interest on investment	12,500	$ 10,000	$ 2,500
	$ 37,500		
Less salaries	60,000	50,000	10,000
Deficit	$ (22,500)		
		$ 60,000	$12,500
Less charge-back of deficit	22,500	11,250	11,250
Distribution of income		$ 48,750	$ 1,250

In summary, the capital ratio is only one of two or three factors to be considered in determining the income-sharing ratio or agreement. Under these circumstances, the two ratios ordinarily should differ. Only occasionally will the two ratios coincide. When this occurs, the accounting for partnership ownership will be simplified.

Admission of a partner When new partners are admitted to an existing partnership or when a present partner retires from a partnership, valuation problems may arise. For example when non-cash assets are contributed by a new partner, their value must be determined. Whenever possible, current market values should be established from existing markets for similar assets rather than by appraisal. Similar valuation problems may be encountered when a partner retires from the firm.

The admission of a new partner into an existing firm may occur by transfer when the new partner *purchases* part or all of the interest of an existing partner, or by *investment* when the new partner invests directly in the firm, thus increasing the firm's resources. The former is recorded on the existing partnership books by transferring the interest from the selling partner's capital account to a new capital account for the entering partner.

When a new partner invests directly into an existing firm, the exact entry made usually depends upon the interpretation of the circumstances. When the investment exactly equals the book value of the interest acquired, only one entry is required. In those rare circumstances, the simple entry would be to record an increase in assets and an increase in ownership in the new partner's capital account. However, the investment usually is greater or less than the book value of the interest acquired. Since the book values of the existing partnership are not likely to be current market values, the new partner would be expected to invest an amount different from the book value of the interest that he acquires. Another explanation for the difference between the investment and the book value of the interest acquired would be that either the previous partners or the new partner would realize a gain on the admission.

If the investment differs from the book value, there are three different interpretations and methods for recording the transaction. First, the difference can result from the book values of the tangible assets being less or greater than the current values of these assets. This interpretation is called the *revaluation* method. Second, the difference can result from unrecorded intangibles from the previous partnership or the new partner. This interpretation is called the *goodwill* method. Finally the difference can result from a gain to the previous partners or to the new partner. This interpretation is called the *bonus* method.

In order to illustrate these methods, consider the following situation. L. Alcindor and O. Robertson, partners in an existing firm, decide to admit P. Maravich as an equal partner. Alcindor and Robertson share earnings and losses equally and have capital balances of $10,000 and $5,000 respectively. If Maravich invested $7,500, he would contribute an amount exactly equal to the book value of the one-third interest that he acquires. The entry to record his admission would be as follows:

	Debit	Credit
Cash	$7,500	
P. Maravich, capital		$7,500
To record admission of new partner		

If Maravich contributes $10,000 in cash to the new partnership for his one-third interest, the entry or entries to record his admission may be any one of the following, depending on the interpretation (where the accounting records of the existing firm will continue to be used[2]):

1. If the book value of the tangible assets of the previous partnership is less than their market value:

	Debit	Credit
Individual assets*	$5,000	
L. Alcindor, capital		$2,500
D. Robertson, capital		2,500
To record revaluation of previous partnership assets		

*Where it is not possible immediately to revalue specific assets, an adjunct account for all assets, Assets—Adjustment for Revaluation, might be used temporarily.

Calculation: The required investment of $10,000 = $\frac{1}{3}$; therefore, $20,000 = $\frac{2}{3}$. $20,000 (actual value of previous partnership assets) − $15,000 (book value of previous partnership asset) = $5,000 (or revaluation writeup required). $5,000 ÷ 2 (since previous partners share income and losses equally) = $2,500.

	Debit	Credit
Cash	$10,000	
P. Maravich, capital		$10,000
To record admission of new partner.		

2. If there are unrecorded intangibles (for example, goodwill) for the previous partnership:

	Debit	Credit
Intangibles (or goodwill)	$5,000	
L. Alcindor, capital		$2,500
O. Robertson, capital		2,500
To record intangibles for previous partnership		

Calculation: Same as in (1)

	Debit	Credit
Cash	$10,000	
P. Maravich, capital		$10,000
To record admission of new partner		

3. If the partnership does not wish to recognize the unrecorded intangible value (for example, because of the second class treatment given such assets) or if there is a gain or bonus for the partners in the previous partnership (for example, the existing partnership may appear to be a great success so that Maravich is anxious to join—often this is a case of a will-

[2]When new accounting records are opened for the new partnership, the entries given here normally would be recorded in the accounts of the existing firm so that the initial entry would be to record a trial balance which includes the partnership accounts of all partners in the new firm.

ing buyer versus an unwilling seller so that recording goodwill may not be appropriate):

	Debit	Credit
Cash	*$10,000*	
P. Maravich, capital		*$8,334*
L. Alcindor, capital		*833*
O. Robertson, capital		*833*
To record admission of new partner		
and gain to previous partners		

Calculation: The capital of the new partnership ($15,000 + $10,000) = $\frac{3}{3}$. Therefore, $8,334 (rounded) = $\frac{1}{3}$. $10,000 (actual investment by new partner) − $8,334 (required investment by new partner) = $1,666 difference, bonus or gain to the old partners.

With the same situation except that Maravich invests $6,000 for a one-third interest, the previous entries would be as follows:

4. If the book value of the tangible assets of the previous partnership is greater than their market value:

	Debit	Credit
L. Alcindor, capital	*$1,500*	
O. Robertson, capital	*1,500*	
Individual assets *		*$3,000*
To record revaluation of previous partnership assets		

*A contra account, Assets—Allowance for Revaluation, could be used temporarily.

Calculation: The required investment = $6,000 = $\frac{1}{3}$. Therefore, $12,000 = $\frac{2}{3}$. $15,000 (book value of previous partnership) − $12,000 (current value of previous partnership) = $3,000 (difference or overvaluation).

	Debit	Credit
Cash	*$6,000*	
P. Maravich, Capital		*$6,000*
To record admission of new partner		

5. If the new partner contributes intangibles or goodwill along with his cash investment:

	Debit	Credit
Cash	*$6,000*	
Goodwill	*1,500*	
P. Maravich, capital		*$7,500*
To record admission of new partner		

Calculation: The existing capital = $15,000 = $\frac{2}{3}$. Therefore, with $7,500 (required investment) and $6,000 (actual investment), the difference is $1,500 (or the goodwill contributed by the new partner).

6. If there is a gain or bonus for the new partner and a loss to old partners:

	Debit	Credit
Cash	*$6,000*	
L. Alcindor, capital	*500*	
O. Robertson, capital	*500*	
P. Maravich, capital		*$7,000*
To record admission of new partner		
with gain to new partner		

Calculation: The capital of the new partnership (15,000 + $6,000) = $21,000 = $\frac{3}{3}$. Therefore, $\frac{1}{3}$ = $7,000 (new partner's capital) − $6,000 (required investment of new partner) = $1,000 (bonus or gain to new partner) = loss to old partners. $1,000 ÷ 2 = $500 (loss to each old partner).

In summary, where the tangible investment differs from the book value of the interest acquired, the admission of a new partner may be recorded by the *revaluation* method (1 and 4), the *goodwill* method (2 and 5), or the *bonus* method (3 and 6). Of the three methods, the *revaluation* and *goodwill* methods are basically similar; the only difference is that the former refers to tangible assets while the latter refers to intangible assets. With the *bonus* method, there is one feature which makes it unpopular. The bonus or gain for one partner is permanently deducted from the investment of another partner. If the partnership is dissolved shortly after the admission of a new partner, this means that each partner will receive a return based on his capital account balance at that time, and not on his original investment. In line with the previous discussion, any gain, revaluation, or devaluation to the previous partners from the admission of a new partner is divided in accordance with the previous partners' income-sharing ratio instead of their capital ratio. The retirement of a partner is treated similarly to the admission of a new partner; it may be recorded on the basis of the revaluation of the tangible or intangible assets or as a gain on retirement.

Partnership liquidation Many enterprises come to an end before achieving their initial goals. Some forms of enterprise, such as partnerships, are inherently more subject to endings than others.

When a firm has ended its regular activities and is in the process of disposing of its assets, whether piecemeal or as a unit, the firm is said to be in *liquidation.* After an enterprise has completed the winding up of its activities by selling its assets, paying its liabilities, and distributing the remaining cash to its owners, it is said to be *liquidated.*

When an enterprise decides to liquidate, the end-of-period adjusting and closing entries should be made so that the income for the final period is recorded. The liquidation process may be completed quickly, particularly if the firm is sold as a unit; or it may require several months or even years. The length of time that it takes to liquidate depends on a number of factors such as the kinds and amounts of assets that are to be disposed of on a piecemeal basis, or difficulties and problems encountered in making final settlements with creditors, employees, customers, or others. Since each general partner has an unlimited personal liability for the debts of the partnership, any unpaid creditors may collect from the personal assets of such partners. If the liquidation process does not take long, the firm will try to settle with the partners in one payment. If the liquidation process is delayed, usually the firm will make installment payments to the partners during the liquidation process instead of waiting to make a single payment at the end of the liquidation.

In partnership liquidations, sometimes there is confusion about the status of a partner's loan to the firm. The Uniform Partnership Act states that partners' loans have priority over partners' capital balances for order of payments. It is customary in liquidation proceedings, however, to combine any partner's loan balances with his capital balance since the existence of a partner's loan account will not advance the time of payment to any partner during the liquidation process. If a partner has an actual or potential deficiency in his capital account, the credit balance in his loan account must be offset against the deficiency. This right of offset effectively nullifies the priority provision of the Uniform Partnership Act.

In liquidation, each partner is entitled to receive as a settlement the balance of his capital and loan accounts plus his share of any income or gain on the disposal of the firm's assets (or minus his share of any deficiency or loss on the disposal of the firm's assets). For a one-payment liquidation, there are two rules to observe:

1. Before any partner is entitled to any payments, all creditors must be paid in full.
2. Before any cash is distributed to any partner, the entire actual loss or gain from the disposal of assets must be distributed to the partner's account according to the partnership's income- and loss-sharing ratio.

The first rule is self-explanatory since the liquidation claims of all creditors have priority over all liquidation claims of the partners, even when partners have made loans to the firm. The second rule is needed to prevent overpayments to a partner or partners. If a partner receives an overpayment, he may be able to refund it. But often this may not be possible. The result is that his partners will receive less in liquidation than their ownership equity or share more loss than they should under the profit and loss ratio.

For an installment basis liquidation, the same two rules are in force except that the second rule is amended to include not only actual but also potential losses. Under an installment basis liquidation, potential losses represent the book values of any assets that have not been liquidated at the date of the installment payment. If the distribution of potential losses causes a deficiency in a partner's capital account, this deficiency is reallocated against the other partners' capital accounts. This treatment of a deficiency resulting from a potential loss is in contrast to the treatment of a deficiency resulting from an actual loss. The partner with a deficiency resulting from an actual loss would be expected to make it good. Only if he was unable to do so would the deficiency be reallocated among the remaining partners.

If the income- and loss-sharing ratio is proportional to the balance of the partner's capital accounts, the second rule can be ignored since the capital ratio equals the income- and loss-sharing ratio. After this equality is achieved during an installment liquidation, the second rule can be ignored. But usually, as explained earlier, this is not the situation. Therefore gains and losses must be distributed first, on the income and loss basis, before cash on the capital (and loan) account balances is distributed.

The following is an illustration of accounting for partnership liquidations.

A partnership has three partners who share equally in income and losses. The partnership position statement on the day they decide to liquidate is as follows:

The Partnership Position Statement December 31, 1972 (000's omitted)

Assets		Equities	
Cash	$ 10	Accounts payable	$ 20
Accounts receivable—net	15	Loan payable (to Picasso)	10
Inventories	25	Picasso, capital	40
Plant—net	40	Cézanne, capital	20
Patent	10	Matisse, capital	10
	$100		$100

The partners retained the cash and were able to dispose of the other partnership assets for $49,000 cash, with the understanding that the purchaser would pay the accounts payable creditors. Since the book value of the partnership net assets other than cash is $70,000 (total assets of $100,000, minus accounts payable of $20,000 and cash of $10,000; or the partner's balances of $10,000, $40,000, $20,000, and $10,000, less the undistributed cash of $10,000), the loss is $21,000, which would be charged in equal thirds against the partners' balances as follows:

The Partnership Liquidation Schedule December 31, 1972 (000's omitted)

	Nets Assets	Picasso, Capital and Loan	Cézanne, Capital	Matisse, Capital
Balances before liquidation	$80	$50	$20	$10
Less loss	21	7	7	7
	59	43	13	3
Less cash	59	43	13	3
	$ 0	$ 0	$ 0	$ 0

If the partners were unable to dispose of the enterprise as a package but had to dispose of the assets piecemeal and make their own settlement with the creditors, the liquidation would be treated quite differently. Under these circumstances, assume that the partners disposed of the receivables for $12,000 cash, which combined with the cash on hand of $10,000 provided for a first installment payment of $22,000; next, the inventories realized $24,000 cash, which constituted the second installment payment; the third payment consisted of the cash proceeds from the patent of $15,000; and the last payment of $36,000 was the result of deducting, from the $37,000 in cash received for the plant, the $1,000 of costs incurred in liquidating.

The Partnership First Installment Payment Schedule (000's omitted)

	Assets	Accounts Payable	Picasso, Capital and Loan	Cézanne, Capital	Matisse, Capital
Balances, before liquidation	$100	$20	$50	$20	$ 10
First installment	22				
Actual and potential loss	$ 78		26	26	26
			24	(6)	(16)
Reallocate deficiencies	—		−22	6	16
Allocation of first installment		$20	$ 2	0	0

Note that the actual and potential losses are distributed to the capital accounts before the cash installment is distributed. Since these deficiencies are caused by possible or potential losses, and not actual losses, Cézanne and Matisse would not be expected to contribute personal assets to cover them. Although the actual losses of $3,000 on accounts receivable could be charged off first before the possible losses of $75,000, the cash distribution would not be altered.

The Partnership Second Installment Payment Schedule (000's omitted)

	Assets	Picasso, Capital and Loan	Cézanne, Capital	Matisse, Capital
Balances before second installment	$78	$48	$20	$10
Second installment	−24			
Actual and potential loss	$54	−18	−18	−18
		30	2	(8)
Reallocate Matisse's deficiency		− 4	− 4	8
		26	(2)	$ 0
Reallocate Cézanne's deficiency		− 2	2	
Allocation of second installment		$24	$ 0	

Although this installment helps to convert the partners' capital ratio into the income and loss ratio of equal shares, the conversion is not complete since Picasso and Cézanne still have balances that are twice as large as that of Matisse.

The Partnership Third Installment Payment Schedule (000's omitted)

	Assets	Picasso, Capital	Cézanne, Capital	Matisse, Capital
Balances before third installment	$54	$24.0	$20.0	$10
Third installment	15			
Actual and potential losses	$39	13.0	13.0	13
		11.0	7.0	(3)
Reallocate Matisse's deficiency		−1.5	−1.5	3
Allocation of third installment		$ 9.5	$ 5.5	$ 0

The Partnership
Fourth Installment
Payment Schedule
(000's omitted)

	Assets	Picasso, Capital	Cézanne, Capital	Matisse, Capital
Balances before fourth installment	$39	$14.5	$14.5	$10
Fourth installment	36			
Actual loss	$ 3	1.0	1.0	1
Allocation of fourth installment		$13.5	$13.5	$ 9

In summary, the partnership liquidation is as follows:

The Partnership
Summary
Liquidation Schedule
(000's omitted)

	Assets	Accounts Payable	Picasso, Capital	Cézanne, Capital	Matisse, Capital
Balances before liquidation	$100	$20	$50.0	$20.0	$10
First installment	22	20	2.0		
	78		48.0	20.0	10
Second installment	24		24.0		
	54		24.0	20.0	10
Third installment	15		9.5	5.5	
	39		14.5	14.5	10
Fourth installment	36		13.5	13.5	9
Actual loss	$ 3		$ 1.0	$ 1.0	$ 1

The Partnership
Summary
Liquidation Schedule
Actual Gains
and Losses
Separated as Incurred
(000's omitted)

	Assets	Accounts Payable	Picasso, Capital and Loan	Cézanne, Capital	Matisse, Capital
	$100	$20	$50.00	$20.00	$10.00
Actual loss on receivables	3		1.00	1.00	1.00
	97	$20	49.00	19.00	9.00
First installment	22	20	2.00		
	75	$ 0	47.00	19.00	9.00
Actual loss on inventory	1		0.33	0.33	0.34
	74		46.67	18.67	8.66
Second installment	24		24.00		
	50		22.67	18.67	8.66
Actual gain on patent	5		1.67	1.67	1.66
Balances	$55		$24.34	$20.34	$10.32

	Assets	Accounts Payable	Picasso, Capital and Loan	Cézanne, Capital	Matisse, Capital
Balances carried forward	$55		$24.34	$20.34	$10.32
Third installment	15		9.50	5.50	
	40		14.84	14.84	10.32
Actual loss on plant	4		1.34	1.34	1.32
	36		13.50	13.50	9.00
Fourth installment	$ 36		$13.50	$13.50	$ 9.00

Summary

Accounting for ownership has been reviewed for the sole proprietorship and the partnership. The periodic changes in ownership more often result from the distribution of income than from external changes in investment in ownership.

The four basic rights of ownership are the right to maintain ownership and be represented in management as well as to share in income and the proceeds of liquidation. Nevertheless the claims of owners have lower legal priorities than those of creditors. The simplest theory about ownership is the proprietary theory; this theory is most applicable to sole proprietorships and partnerships. Under it, the all-inclusive income statement is stressed since ownership is the sum of income (less withdrawals or losses) plus the proprietor's original and subsequent investments in the enterprise.

The accounts for ownership are one or possibly two accounts for each owner; these are called capital for permanent investments in the enterprise and current or drawings for temporary investments in and withdrawals from the enterprise.

Both the sole proprietorship and the partnership are established easily and typically have limited lives; in addition, each owner is personally liable for the debts of the enterprise, has the right to act for the enterprise, and, in a partnership, co-owns any enterprise property or enterprise income. In order to avoid disputes among partners, those forming a partnership prepare written partnership agreements which recognize the special characteristics of partnerships.

The special reporting problems associated with a partnership are three: the admission (or retirement) of a partner, the distribution of the partnership's net income (or losses), and the liquidation of the partnership. In all three categories of problems, there are two sets of relationships among the partners. The first is expressed in the ratio of the amounts of capital contributed and maintained by the partners; the second is the ratio by which the partners share partnership income and losses. If not specified, the net income or losses are shared equally by the partners.

The three factors involved in partnership income and loss agreements are: (1) the ratio of partner capital, (2) the quality and the quantity of partner services contributed, and (3) various miscellaneous factors. The first factor has two problems, namely, the measure of capital, and the relevant rate of return or interest. An imputed salary must be set for working partners in recognizing the second factor. Even for the miscellaneous factors such as prestige or risk, it is often desirable to make separate allocations. In applying a partnership income- and loss-sharing plan to the partnership periodic net income, distributions are made according to the plan, even when the net income to be distributed is less than the sum of the stipulated distributions.

When new partners are admitted to an existing partnership or when a present partner retires from a partnership, valuation problems arise. The new partner may *purchase* his interest from a partner, or he may *invest* directly into the existing partnership. When a new partner invests directly into an existing firm, the exact entry made depends upon the interpretation of the circumstances. If the investment differs from the book value, there are three different interpretations and methods for recording the transaction. These are the *revaluation, goodwill,* and *bonus* methods.

When a partnership decides to liquidate, there may be one payment or installment payments to the partners. Before a one-payment liquidation all creditors must be paid, and the entire loss or gain from the disposal of assets must be distributed to the partner's account according to the partnership's income- and loss-sharing ratio. With an installment basis liquidation the same two rules are in force except that the second rule is amended to include not only actual but also potential losses.

A Selection of Supplementary Readings

Brooker, R. P.: "The Background of Garner V. Murray," *Abacus,* August 1968, pp. 73–79.

_____; "The Dissolution of Partnership—Garner V. Murray," *Abacus,* August 1967, pp. 36–54.

Clarke, W. J.: "Partnerships," Education and Training, *Canadian Chartered Accountant* (September 1967), pp. 189–191.

Cockson-Jones, E.: "Partnership Piecemeal Realization—The Third Method," *The Accountant,* Dec. 4, 1965.

Questions

10–1 Three partners share profits and losses in a ratio of 5:3:2. At the end of a very unprofitable year, they decide to liquidate the firm. The partners' capital accounts at this date were as follows: No. 1 Partner, capital $22,000; No. 2 Partner, capital $27,000; No. 3 Partner, capital $14,000. The liabilities shown on the position statement amounted to $28,000 including a loan of $8,000 from Partner No. 2. The cash balance was only $3,280. The partners plan to sell the non-cash assets on a piecemeal basis and to distribute cash as rapidly as it becomes available. If the No. 3 Partner receives $3,000 of the first distribution of cash, how much did Partner No. 2 receive at this time?

10-2   P. Newman and J. Woodward are partners; Newman's capital on January 1 was $30,000; Woodward's, $60,000. Newman invested $10,000 on July 1; Woodward withdrew $10,000 on July 1. The net income was $18,000.

(1) There was no mention made of the distribution of net income in the partnership agreement. Newman's share of the net income would be: (a) $9,000, (b) $8,000, (c) $7,000, (d) $6,000, (e) unknown until the partners reach an agreement.

(2) The partnership agreement states that each partner is to be allowed interest at the rate of 5 percent on the ending capital balances; Newman is to be allowed a salary of $3,000 and Woodward a salary of $2,000; the remainder is to be distributed in the ratio of $\frac{2}{5}$ to Newman and $\frac{3}{5}$ to Woodward. Of the $18,000 net income, Newman's share would be: (a) below $7,400, (b) between $7,400 and $7,700, (c) between $7,700 and $8,000, (d) between $8,000 and $8,300, (e) above $8,300.

(3) If a partnership is incorporated and new books are opened, which of the following partnership accounts usually *would not be* transferred to the corporation books: (a) Cash, (b) Accounts Receivable, (c) Accounts Receivable—Allowance for Bad Debts, (d) Merchandise Inventory, (e) Plant—Accumulated Depreciation.

10-3   Shakespeare and Bacon are partners; Shakespeare has a capital balance of $30,000; Bacon, $20,000. Profits are shared: Shakespeare, two-thirds, Bacon, one-third. Grey is being admitted as a partner:

(1) Grey pays $34,000 into the business for a one-third interest. It is agreed that ownership is to total $84,000 after Grey's admission. Shakespeare's capital will be: (a) $28,000, (b) $30,000, (c) $33,000, (d) $34,000, (e) some other amount.

(2) Grey pays $10,067 into the business for one-fourth interest. Goodwill is to be recorded. Bacon's capital will be: (a) $17,800, (b) $20,600, (c) $22,400, (d) $22,533, (e) some other amount.

(3) Grey pays $40,000 into the business for a one-half interest. It is agreed that goodwill is to be recorded. Grey's capital will be: (a) $30,000, (b) $35,000, (c) $40,000, (d) $45,000, (e) some other amount.

(4) Grey pays $10,000 into the business for a one-fifth interest. This may be an indication that: (a) the partnership assets have a value greater than that shown on the position statement, (b) the partnership of Shakespeare and Bacon has goodwill, (c) the partnership of Shakespeare and Bacon has been very profitable, (d) Shakespeare and Bacon must be good bargainers, (e) Shakespeare and Bacon believe that Grey is contributing something in addition to cash.

10-4   The partnership of Lincoln, Grant, and Lee, all of whom share profits equally, closed its books; the accounts had the following credit balances: Lincoln, capital $9,000; Grant, capital $5,000; Lee, capital $2,000; note payable to Lee $500.

(1) If the loss on liquidation is $3,300, and the cash to be divided among the partners is $13,200, the following amount would be paid Lee: (a) $500, (b) $1,000, (c) $2,500, (d) $4,400, (e) none of these.

(2) If the loss on liquidation is $6,690, and the cash to be divided among the partners is $9,810, the following amount would be paid Lee: (a) $270, (b) $500, (c) $2,500, (d) $3,270, (e) none of these.

(3) If the loss on liquidation is $8,400, and the cash to be divided among the partners is $8,100, the following amount would be paid Lee: (a) $500, (b) $2,500, (c) $2,700, (d) $2,800, (e) none of these.

10–5

Marlborough and Nelson had capital balances of $40,000 and $44,000, respectively. They divided net income and all losses on a 3:2 basis. Mozart was admitted as a partner when he invested $21,000 in the concern. He was to receive a one-seventh interest in the partnership.

(1) If Mozart's admission is to be recorded via the *goodwill* technique, the following amount would be credited to his capital account: (a) $14,000, (b) $15,000, (c) $21,000, (d) $25,000, (e) none of these.

(2) Under the *goodwill* method, Marlborough's capital account would be changed by the following amount: (a) $4,200, (b) $8,400, (c) $16,800, (d) $25,200, (e) none of these.

(3) If the *bonus* technique is used, the following amount should be credited to Mozart's capital account: (a) $14,000, (b) $15,000, (c) $21,000, (d) $25,000, (e) none of these.

(4) If all the facts were the same except that Mozart's cash contribution would be $12,000, the following amount would be credited to Mozart's capital account under the *goodwill* technique: (a) $14,000, (b) $15,000, (c) $21,000, (d) $25,000, (e) none of these.

(5) In the above situation, if Mozart's cash investment was to exactly equal the book value of the interest acquired, he would contribute the following amount: (a) $14,000, (b) $15,000, (c) $21,000, (d) $25,000; (e) none of these.

10–6

	Tunney, Capital				*Buckley, Capital*		
4/1	$3,000	1/1	$10,000	9/1	$2,000	1/1	$5,000
		8/1	3,000			5/1	4,000

(1) Net income is divided in proportion to average capital.

(2) Salaries of $5,500 each to Tunney and Buckley, and any remainder in the ratio 2:1.

(3) Nothing is said about income distribution in the articles of copartnership.

Indicate which of the following answers shows the annual distributive shares of a net income of $8,000 for the Tunney and Buckley partnership according to the various income-sharing agreements listed.

a. Tunney $4,500; Buckley $3,500

b. Tunney $4,000; Buckley $4,000

c. Tunney $5,500; Buckley $5,500

d. Yunney $3,500; Buckley $4,500

e. Some other amount

10–7   Abzug and Dellums are of equal ability and decide to form a partnership. Abzug is to contribute $50,000 and half of his time, while Dellums is to contribute $25,000 and all of his time to the partnership.

(1) In view of the difference in size of the monetary contributions of Abzug and Dellums:

a. Abzug should be given an interest allowance twice that of Dellums: e.g., 6 percent versus 3 percent.

b. Abzug should receive an interest allowance (say 6 percent), and Dellums should receive none.

c. Either Abzug or Dellums should receive an interest allowance (say 6 percent) on the excess of his average invested capital over that of the other partner, and the other partner should receive no interest allowance.

d. Abzug and Dellums should be given the same interest allowance (say 6 percent) on their average invested capital.

e. Either (c) or (d) above should be acceptable.

(2) If Abzug and Dellums agree that $10,000 a year is a reasonable salary allowance for the contribution of full time to the partnership, which of the following is a rational solution, in view of the difference in time contributed by Abzug and Dellums?

a. Abzug should be given a salary allowance twice that of Dellums ($10,000 versus $5,000).

b. Dellums should be given a salary allowance twice that of Abzug ($10,000 versus $5,000).

c. Dellums should be given a salary allowance of $5,000; and Abzug nothing.

d. None of the above is correct.

e. Both (b) and (c) are correct.

(3) Which of the following best states the difference between straight withdrawals and withdrawals authorized under a salary allowance agreement?

a. Straight withdrawals must be debited directly to the partners' capital accounts, whereas salary allowance withdrawals must be charged to their drawing (or personal) accounts.

b. The reverse of (a) above is true.

c. Straight withdrawals may be charged to either drawing or capital, but salary allowance withdrawals must be debited to salary expense.

d. The entire amount of a straight withdrawal by a partner is a charge to that particular partner, whereas a salary allowance withdrawal by a partner is a charge to all the partners.

e. Salary allowance withdrawals must be made monthly, but straight withdrawals need not.

10-8   The following position statement is for a partnership (000's omitted):

Cash	$ 20	Liabilities	$ 50
Other assets	180	H. Fonda, capital (40%)	37
		P. Fonda, capital (40%)	65
		J. Fonda, capital (20%)	48
	$200		$200

Figures shown parenthetically reflect agreed income- and loss-sharing percentages.

(1) If the assets are fairly valued on the above position statement and the partnership wishes to admit D. Reuben as a new one-sixth partner without recording goodwill or bonus, Reuben should contribute cash or other assets of:
   a. $40,000
   b. $36,000
   c. $33,333
   d. $30,000

(2) If assets on the initial position statement are fairly valued, H. Fonda and P. Fonda consent, and D. Reuben pays J. Fonda $51,000 for her interest, the revised capital balances of the partners would be:
   a. H. Fonda $38,500; P. Fonda $66,500; D. Reuben $51,000
   b. H. Fonda $38,500; P. Fonda $66,500; D. Reuben $48,000
   c. H. Fonda $37,000; P. Fonda $65,000; D. Reuben $51,000
   d. H. Fonda $37,000; P. Fonda $65,000; D. Reuben $48,000

(3) If the firm, as shown on the original position statement (except that D. Reuben has replaced J. Fonda as a partner), is dissolved and liquidated by selling assets in installments, the first sale of non-cash assets having a book value of $90,000 realized $50,000 and all cash available after settlement with creditors is distributed, the respective partners would receive (to the nearest dollar):
   a. H. Fonda $8,000; P. Fonda $8,000; D. Reuben $4,000
   b. H. Fonda $6,667; P. Fonda $6,667; D. Reuben $6,666
   c. H. Fonda $0, P. Fonda $13,333; D. Reuben $6,667
   d. H. Fonda $0, P. Fonda $3,000; D. Reuben $17,000

(4) If the facts are as in (3) above except that $3,000 cash is to be withheld, the respective partners would then receive (to the nearest dollar):
   a. H. Fonda $6,800; P. Fonda $6,800; D. Reuben $3,400
   b. H. Fonda $5,667; P. Fonda $5,667; D. Reuben $5,666
   c. H. Fonda $0; P. Fonda $11,333; D. Reuben $5,667
   d. H. Fonda $0; P. Fonda $1,000; D. Reuben $16,000

(5) If each partner properly received some cash in the distribution after the second sale, the cash to be distributed amounts to $12,000 from the third sale, and unsold assets with an $8,000 book value remain, ignoring (3) and (4) above, the respective partners would receive:

    a. H. Fonda $4,800; P. Fonda $4,800; D. Reuben $2,400
    b. H. Fonda $4,000; P. Fonda $4,000; D. Reuben $4,000
    c. H. Fonda 37/150 of $12,000; P. Fonda 65/150 of $12,000; D. Reuben 48/150 of $12,000
    d. H. Fonda $0; P. Fonda $8,000; D. Reuben $4,000

10-9

(1) In a partnership liquidation the final cash distribution to the partners should be made in accordance with the:
    a. Partners' income- and loss-sharing ratio
    b. Balances of the partners' capital accounts
    c. Ratio of the capital contributions by the partners
    d. Ratio of capital contributions less withdrawals by the partners

(2) Partners Pompidou and Heath share net income in a 2:1 ratio, respectively. Each partner receives an annual salary allowance of $6,000. If the salaries are recorded in the accounts of the partnership as an expense instead of being treated as a division of net income, the total amount allocated to each partner for salaries and net income would be:
    a. Less for both Pompidou and Heath
    b. Unchanged for both Pompidou and Heath
    c. More for Pompidou and less for Heath
    d. More for Pompidou and more for Heath

10-10

Each partner in a three-man partnership has a capital balance of $25,000; one partner also has a loan to the partnership for $10,000. The loan note (signed by all three partners) specifies 7 percent interest. Under the partnership agreement, each partner is to contribute to capital and to share in profits equally. What is your reaction to the following adjusting entry on the partnership books?

	Debit	Credit
Dizzy Gillespie, capital	$350	
Bobby Hackett, capital	350	
K. O. Ory, capital		$700
Accrued interest for year on note		

10-11

The largest CPA firms have 600 to 700 partners and operate on an international basis. Why do you suppose such firms use a partnership form of organization?

10-12

When would you expect to see goodwill in the accounts of a partnership? Why?

Problems

10-1

Before Frodo was admitted as a partner, the position statement of the Aragorn-Boromir partnership was as follows:

Aragorn-Boromir
Company
Position Statement
December 14, 1972
(000's omitted)

Assets	$100	*Liabilities*	$ 40
		A, capital	40
		B, capital	20
	$100		$100

No written partnership agreement exists for the firm.

Depending on the circumstances under which Frodo was admitted, some of the following position statements might be prepared after Frodo's admission. Which of these would *not* be valid and why?

A-B-F Company
Position Statements
December 14, 1972
(000's omitted)

(I) *Assets*

	$112	*Liabilities*	$ 40
		A, capital	36
		B, capital	18
		F, capital	18
	$112		$112

(II) *Assets*

	$124	*Liabilities*	$ 40
		A, capital	41
		B, capital	22
		F, capital	21
	$124		$124

(III) *Assets*

	$120	*Liabilities*	$ 40
		A, capital	40
		B, capital	20
		F, capital	20
	$120		$120

(IV) *Assets*

	$100	*Liabilities*	$ 40
		A, capital	25
		B, capital	20
		F, capital	15
	$100		$100

(V) *Assets*

	$190	*Liabilities*	$ 40
		A, capital	50
		B, capital	50
		F, capital	50
	$190		$190

(VI) *Assets*

	$ 80	*Liabilities*	$ 40
		A, capital	20
		B, capital	5
		F, capital	15
	$ 80		$ 80

(VII)* Assets	$100	Liabilities	$ 40
		A, capital	30
		B, capital	10
		F, capital	20
	$100		$100

(VIII) Assets	$240	Liabilities	$ 40
		A, capital	80
		B, capital	40
		F, capital	80
	$240		$240

(IX) Assets	$136	Liabilities	$ 40
		A, capital	44
		B, capital	28
		F, capital	24
	$136		$136

(X) Assets	$ 50	Liabilities	$ 20
		A, capital	15
		B, capital	5
		F, capital	10
	$ 50		$ 50

*This is not a situation where the new partner buys a portion of an old partner's interest.

10-2   A partnership is to be liquidated; the income and loss ratio is 5:3:1. Before liquidation, the firm's position statements is as follows (000's omitted):

Assets	$57	Liabilities	$12
		Soglow, loan	5
		Herblock, capital	15
		Soglow, capital	20
		Darrow, capital	5
	$57		$57

(1) All assets are sold for $30,000 in cash; all is to be distributed.
(2) As in (1), except $2,700 not to be distributed.
(3) All assets are sold for $21,000 in cash; all is to be distributed.
(4) All assets are sold for $75,000 in cash; all is to be distributed.
(5) All assets are sold over several years for $50,000 in cash; the first install-ment to be distributed immediately is $15,000; the second at the end of the first year is $20,000; and the third at the end of the second year is $15,000.
(6) All assets are destroyed in fire except $3,000 in cash.

Show distribution schedules for items (1) to (6); for (6) show what each partner will have to contribute to the partnership to pay the liabilities and apportion the loss.

10-3   Herblock and Soglow have peacefully operated a partnership, The Corn Plant, for years. On April 1, 1972, the firm's total balance is as follows (000's omitted):

Cash	$ 4	Liabilities	$ 2
Other Assets	16	Revenues	16
Expenses	10	Herblock, capital	8
	$30	Soglow, capital	4
			$30

Answer the following questions; each one is independent of the others.
(1) Divide current net income.
(2) Divide current net income, allowing a 10 percent interest on current capital balances.
(3) Divide current net income, allowing a 5 percent interest on current capital balances and a salary to Soglow of $1,000.
(4) Admit Darrow as a new partner for $24,000 invested; record goodwill using a 1:1:1 profit- and loss-sharing ratio.
(5) Soglow sells his interest to Steig for $10,000; the partnership agreement of Herblock and Steig provides for equal sharing of net income and deficits.
(6) Soglow withdraws and leaves the business with Herblock; he receives $3,000 cash and a two-year $7,000 6 percent note.

10-4   A new corporation was formed which acquired the assets of a partnership and assumed its liabilities. In exchange, the partners received 3,000 shares of $10 par-value stock. The trial balance for the partnership on the date of acquisition was as follows (000's omitted):

	Debit		Credit
		Accounts receivable—allowance	
Accounts receivable	$ 4	for bad debts	$ 1
		Building—accumulated	
Inventory	10	depreciation	3
		Equipment—accumulated	
Building	12	depreciation	1
Equipment	3	Accounts payable	2
Supplies	1	Tiny Tim, capital	10
		M. Rock, capital	13
	$30		$30

It was decided that the market value of the building was $15,000 and that the partnership had goodwill of $4,000. Prepare journal entries to close out the partnership books and to open books for the corporation.

10-5

The original condensed position statement of the Ralph and Norton partnership is as follows:

Ralph & Norton Company Position Statement December 31, 1972 (000's omitted)

Assets	$50	Liabilities	$20
		Ralph, capital	20
		Norton, capital	10
	$50		$50

Position statements I, II, III, IV, and V below show the results of the entry of Trixie into the partnership under various situations in regard to the amount paid by Trixie and entry or nonentry of goodwill. In every case assume no revaluation of the assets of the old Ralph & Norton partnership (except possibly goodwill).

R-N-T Company Position Statements December 31, 1972 (000's omitted)

(I)

Assets	$50	Liabilities	$20.0
		R, capital	12.5
		N, capital	10.0
		T, capital	7.5
	$50		$50.0

(II)

Assets	$60	Liabilities	$20
		R, capital	20
		N, capital	10
		T, capital	10
	$60		$60

(III)

Assets	$56	Liabilities	$20
		R, capital	19
		N, capital	8
		T, capital	9
	$56		$56

(IV)

Assets	$62	Liabilities	$20.0
		R, capital	20.5
		N, capital	11.0
		T, capital	10.5
	$62		$62.0

(V)

Assets	$68	Liabilities	$20
		R, capital	22
		N, capital	14
		T, capital	12
	$68		$68

(1) In every one of the five cases above, T is receiving an interest in the new

partnership of exactly: (a) one-sixth, (b) one-fifth, (c) one-fourth, (d) one-third, (e) something else.

(2) Before the entry of T, R and N were splitting profits and losses: (a) equally; (b) two-thirds to R, one-third to N; (c) one-third to R, two-thirds to N; (d) profits were split differently from losses; (e) cannot be determined.

(3) Assuming that R has not withdrawn any assets from the partnership in connection with the entry of T, T has in case I: (a) made an investment in the partnership of $7,500, (b) made an investment in the partnership of some unknown amount, (c) purchased an interest from N by paying him $7,500, (d) purchased an interest from R by paying him some unknown amount, (e) cannot be determined.

(4) In case II, T invested for his percentage interest in the new partnership: (a) exactly what he apparently should have invested, (b) more than he apparently should have, (c) less than he apparently should have, and goodwill was recorded, (d) either a or c above, (e) cannot be determined.

(5) In case III, T paid for his percentage interest in the new partnership: (a) exactly what he apparently should have invested, (b) more than he apparently should have, (c) less than he apparently should have, and goodwill was not recorded, (d) either a or c above, (e) cannot be determined.

(6) In case IV, T paid for his percentage interest in the new partnership: (a) more than he apparently should have, and goodwill was recorded, (b) less than he apparently should have, and goodwill was recorded, (c) more than he apparently should have, and goodwill was not recorded, (d) less than he apparently should, and goodwill was not recorded, (e) either a or d above.

(7) In case V, T paid for his percentage interest in the new partnership: (a) exactly what he apparently should have, (b) more than he apparently should have, and goodwill was recorded, (c) less than he apparently should have, and goodwill was recorded, (d) less than he apparently should have, and goodwill was not recorded, (e) either c or d above.

10-6   Select a classmate for a proposed partnership in public accounting (or for some other professional or business activity). As a team, prepare articles of copartnership including provisions for the following:

(1) Formation:
     a. Names of partnership and partners
     b. Nature and location of the business
     c. Date on which the partnership agreement becomes effective, and its duration
     d. Amount and nature of capital to be invested by each partner, and basis of valuation for assets other than cash

(2) Operation:
     a. Basis of division of income and losses
     b. Duties of each partner and relative amount of time to be devoted to partnership affairs
     c. Limitations, if any, on amounts to be withdrawn in cash (or merchandise or services) from time to time as salary, in lieu of salary, and in addition to salary
     d. Rate and other details concerning calculation of interest, if any, to

be charged each partner on withdrawals and to be allowed on capital
   e. Limitations or restrictions on right of partners to incur partnership debts, or to pay them
   f. Arbitration of differences
(3) Dissolution:
   a. Conditions under which partnership might be terminated before time originally designated
   b. Closing of books and calculation of income or loss upon the death of one of the partners or at some other designated time, such as end of month following death
   c. Payment of liabilities and division of assets among the partners
   d. Withdrawal of assets during process of liquidation if liquidation is by installments

10-7   Alfred N. Whitehead and Christopher Fry are partners in a public accounting firm with a capital ratio of $20,000: $10,000 and an income and loss ratio of 1:1. They decide to admit Tennessee Williams as an equal partner in sharing income and losses. Give the entries (in general journal form) *on the books of the partnership* to recognize the admission of the new partner under the following conditions.
   I. *Exchange:* T. Williams gives A. N. Whitehead personally: (a) $20,000 in cash in exchange for his interest, (b) $25,000, (c) $15,000.
   II. *Exchange:* T. Williams gives C. Fry personally: (a) $10,000 in cash in exchange for his interest, (b) $15,000, (c) $5,000.
   III. *Investment:*
   a. Investment = Book value: T. Williams gives $15,000 in cash to the Whitehead-Fry partnership.
   b. Investment > Book value: T. Williams gives $20,000 in cash to the Whitehead-Fry partnership. Record via:
      (1) Goodwill technique (goodwill to the old partner)
      (2) Bonus technique (bonus to the old partner)
      (3) Asset revaluation

10-8   Natalie Wood opened a retail merchandising firm on January 1, 1973, with the investment of $5,000 cash. During 1973 transactions (all cash) were as follows: sales $41,000, cost of goods sold $16,000, expenses $17,000, withdrawals by Wood $5,000. On January 1, 1974, Wood took in L. Turner as an equal partner, with a contribution of $9,000, goodwill to be recorded.
(1) Prepare a position statement after the admission of Turner. During 1974 transactions (cash again) included $97,000 sales, $38,000 cost of goods sold, and $19,000 expenses. Wood withdrew $11,000, and Turner withdrew $7,000. On January 1, 1975, Wood sold her interest to Davis for $27,000, and Davis and Turner admitted Crawford as a partner with one-third interest for the investment of plant assets valued at $32,000. No goodwill was involved. It was agreed that salaries would be allowed: $14,000 Turner, $9,000 Davis, $8,000 Crawford; interest at 5 percent on average capital balances; remaining profits equally divided (beginning January 1, 1975).
(2) Prepare journal entries for admission of Davis and Crawford. During 1975

sales totaled $127,050, cost of goods sold $46,000, other expenses $28,000, again all in cash. Turner withdrew $4,000 each on July 1, and October 1, 1975. Davis withdrew $8,000 on December 31, and Crawford withdrew $10,000 on December 31, 1975.

(3) Prepare journal entry for net income distribution for 1975.

10–9

The following is the trial balance of the Minnie Pearl partnership on June 30, 1975, the end of their fiscal year (000's omitted).

Cash	$ 2.0	Accounts payable	$ 0.5
		Accounts receivable—	
Accounts receivable	0.9	allowance for bad accounts	0.1
Prepaid rent	0.3	M, capital (July 1, 1974)	2.2
Supplies	0.1	P, capital (July 1, 1974)	1.2
M, drawings	1.2	Sales	11.0
P, drawings	1.8	Interest revenue	0.3
Operating expenses	9.0		
	$15.3		$15.3

(1) Prepare an income statement for Minnie Pearl, and show how the income of the business is to be distributed. The income- and loss-sharing agreement provides that the following allowances are to be made to the partners, whether the income is sufficient to cover them or not. The allowances are not expenses; they are a method of distributing the income to the partners: (a) M is to receive a 1 percent commission on sales; (b) P is to receive a $150 salary allowance per month; (c) interest of 10 percent is to be allowed on the partners' beginning-of-the-year capital balances; (d) the remainder, positive or negative, after allowances (a), (b), and (c) is to be divided equally.

(2) Ford is willing to invest $900 in the partnership for a one-sixth interest in the partnership as of June 30, 1975. With this information prepare journal entries to record F's admission into the new partnership using: (a) the *bonus* method; (b) the *goodwill* method. (c) If F purchased half of M's interest in the partnership for $450, prepare the journal entry necessary to record the admission of F.

(3) On April 24, 1976, the abbreviated trial balance of the partnership appeared as follows (000's omitted):

Total assets	$42	Accounts payable	$ 9
		Wages payable	1
		M, loan (owed to partner)	5
		M, capital	10
		P, capital	10
		F, capital	7
	$42		$42

All the assets are sold on April 25, 1976, for $18,000. The partners share income and losses equally. Prepare the journal entries to record the distribution of cash.

10-10   D. Berrigan, P. Berrigan, and M. Catonsville are partners. In 1973, net income of the partnership was $40,000. For each case below indicate how much of the net income would be allocated to each partner.

(1) The partnership agreement states nothing about income and loss allocation.

(2) Catonsville is to be allowed a salary of 50 percent of partnership net income after the salary allowance. The balance of any income or loss is to be shared equally.

(3) P. Berrigan is to be allowed a salary of $15,000 for running the business. Any balance is to be divided among the partners in the ratio of 2:2:1 to D. Berrigan, P. Berrigan, and M. Catonsville, respectively.

(4) The agreement specifies that income and losses are to be shared according to the capital ratio existing at the start of year. Capital accounts of D. Berrigan, P. Berrigan, and M. Catonsville on January 1, 1973, were $60,000; $70,000; and $20,000.

11 Analysis of Owners' Equity: Corporations

The corporate form has several advantages over the partnership. First, there is the limited liability of corporate owners; second, there is the ready transferability of ownership units that usually are relatively small; third, the corporate structure is long-lived; and finally, capital can be attracted more readily. Unlike the partner, the stockholder has no personal liability for the debts of the corporation; thus in the event of liquidation, the stockholder's losses would be no greater than his investment in the stock. Also unlike the partner, the stockholder usually is able to liquidate his stock at any time. Although the partnership legally can be terminated by any one of the partners, the corporation has virtually an unlimited existence which is not affected legally by either the death or the retirement of any stockholder.

In considering whether to organize in the legal form of a partnership or a corporation, the income tax status of the enterprise may be significant. With a partnership, a federal income tax return is filed but the partnership pays no income tax. Instead all partners must report their share of taxable partnership income and pay individual income taxes on it. A corporation, on the other hand, must file an income tax return and pay income taxes on its reported income. In addition,

*From *Accounting Theory: With Special Reference to the Corporate Enterprise* (New York: The Ronald Press Company, 1922), pp. 472–473.

the individual stockholder must report and pay individual income taxes on dividends declared and received from the corporation in excess of the excluded amount. If the owners of the enterprise find that the applicable individual tax rates would be higher than the corporate tax rates, the tax advantage would be to the corporate form over the partnership. Under special circumstances, a partnership or a corporation may be granted the tax status of the other form of enterprise. For example, a corporation that has ten or fewer stockholders and meets other criteria qualifies as a "tax option" corporation and may elect to avoid income taxes by being taxed as a corporation if the stockholders will report all corporate income or losses on their returns. A partnership also may elect to be taxed as a corporation, but this is seldom done because it offers little advantage. More frequently encountered is the partnership that incorporates but decides to continue being taxed as a partnership.

The Entity and Other Ownership Theories
Unlike the partnership, the corporation is regarded in law as an artificial person, a separate legal entity that has an existence apart from its owners. The theory of ownership which emphasizes this characteristic is called the *entity theory*. Although all ownership theories recognize the existence of the enterprise as being separate from its owners, the entity theory goes the furthest in this regard. It regards the firm as having not only a completely separate existence but also a separate personality. The position statement equation underlying the entity theory is $\Sigma A = \Sigma E$. In this theory, all assets are considered to be the rights of the firm rather than of the owners; similarly all liabilities are considered to be obligations of the firm rather than of the owners. Under the entity theory, income is determined for the enterprise rather than for the stockholders (as implied under the proprietary theory). "Emphasis on the entity point of view . . . requires the treatment of business earnings as the income of the enterprise itself until such time as transfer to the individual participants has been effected by dividend declaration."[1] In short, income is determined before any dividend declarations or other payments to equity holders, and constitutes the income to the corporation or enterprise. All distributions or allocations to equity holders are considered to be allocations of corporate income. Under this concept, revenue is the product of the enterprise, and expenses are goods and services utilized in obtaining revenue. The entity usually is considered to be a separate economic structure which functions chiefly for the benefit of equity holders.

---

[1]W. A. Paton and A. C. Littleton, *An Introduction to Corporate Accounting Standards,* Monograph No. 3 (Chicago: AAA, 1940), p. 8.

In addition to corporations, this theory is relevant to unincorporated enterprises that have a continuity of existence separate from the lives of their owners.[2]

Besides the proprietary and entity theories of ownership, others that have received some support are the enterprise theory, the fund theory, and the commander concept. The *enterprise theory* conceives of the firm as a social institution; ownership is not confined to the economic equity holders found on the position statement (creditors and stockholders) but includes employees, customers, government (both in its taxing and regulating capacities), and the general public. Although this is a broad concept of ownership, it has not been defined rigorously. Under it, however, accounting should be concerned with all groups and not just the interests of investors and creditors. Even the stockholders' equity may be regarded not as representing the claim of the residual stockholders but instead as the residual of all social groups. As the latter, it represents all social groups if this equity is required to provide for expansion, improved productivity, or to maintain the firm's market position. This means that any residual claims of stockholders on the position statement may not be of any specific benefit to the stockholders unless their dividends are raised.

This approach does not focus on the interests of any specific group; instead it attempts to be neutral to all. It seems most applicable to corporations that are large relative to their environment (included would be the firm that is small by national standards but is the dominant employer in its community, as well as national giants such as General Motors). These corporations must consider their social obligations, such as the elimination of air and water pollution, and employment of members of minority groups. The value-added concept of income, discussed in Chapter 9, would appear to be most suitable for this broad approach to ownership. In current accounting practice, applications of this approach seem to be confined to the president's letter in the annual report.

Another theory of ownership, the *fund theory,* also is neutral to the interests of all groups. However, unlike the enterprise theory, the fund theory offers extensive examples in accounting practice. It is the rationale in accounting for nonprofit organizations such as universities, foundations, and government agencies, and in accounting within corporations (for example, pension and sinking funds). Under the fund concept, assets and equities are grouped according to the functions or activities of the organization. Each grouping constitutes a fund; a single organization may have many such funds.

---

[2]A variation of the entity theory is the residual equity theory. Under it, all investors except the common stockholders are considered along with other equity holders. The relevant position statement equation consists of $\Sigma A - \Sigma$ Specific equities $= \Sigma$ Residual stockholders.

Ownership, under this theory, represents restrictions (legal, contractual, managerial, or financial) on the use of the assets. The appropriate equation, as given in Chapter 3, is $A_1 + \cdots + A_n = E_1 + \cdots + E_n$. The emphasis is upon stewardship, or the need for ownership to maintain invested capital.

A final theory to be considered, the *commander concept,* is not developed enough as yet to indicate whether the reports are to be directed to any particular group or all groups. It really emphasizes managerial control of the firm's resources rather than any kind of ownership. As with the fund theory, however, the concern is with stewardship. With this view, the flow statements constitute reports on how management has obtained resources and how it has applied them; the position statement is a report on the resources entrusted to management.

Objectives of Ownership Accounting

Since sole proprietorships and partnerships have only one class of owners (with the only superior claims being those of creditors), there is little need for classification of their ownership equities. Although the distinction between capital and income is made during the period, at the end of each period the income not withdrawn is added to the capital account (but sometimes the drawing account may be kept open). Since there generally is no restriction on the amount of income that can be withdrawn by the owners, the income is usually retained only temporarily. Also, since these forms of organization have limited lives, the firm may be dissolved or liquidated, thereby making any distinction between capital and income irrelevant. Finally, because the owners are personally liable for the firm's debts, external users of financial statements, such as creditors, have less interest in the sole proprietorship and partnership ownership accounts.

For corporate ownership, more information is needed. Since the ownership relationships are more complex, there is greater need for classifying ownership according to its sources. When there are different classes of ownership, there is need to maintain the distinctions between these classes so that priorities in claims can be recognized. Also there are legal restrictions on the distribution of invested capital to stockholders and various restrictions on the distribution of dividends to holders. These latter restrictions may be legal, contractual, managerial, or financial in nature. In practice, corporate ownership usually is presented on the basis of assumed legal and economic relationships rather than on the basis of fulfilling completely the objectives of (1) source, (2) class, and (3) restriction classifications.

If classification by source is the most important classification logically, accountants should concentrate on meeting this objective adequately in the statements and relegate the other objectives to the footnotes or supplementary statements. For a corporation the major sources of capital are (1) the amounts paid in by stockholders and (2) the excess of income over dividends declared and paid to stockholders (or the earnings retained in the business). The former is recorded in the Capital Stock accounts, and the latter is recorded in the Retained Earnings accounts. Minor sources of corporate capital are (1) amounts arising from the revaluation of assets and (2) donations of capital from other than stockholders. If revaluation write-ups result from *specific* price changes, they should be included as part of Retained Earnings; if they result from *general* price changes, this should require a restatement of both the Capital Stock and Retained Earnings accounts. Usually, however, capital arising out of revaluation is classified separately as a total, or added to an existing capital stock account (for example, Capital Stock—Premium or Additional Paid-in Capital).

Although the classification of corporate equity by source appears to be logical, the relevance of this information to the decision making of external users of financial statements is not always clear. In addition, there are problems beyond those related to revaluations which suggest that this classification objective is difficult to achieve. First, maintaining the distinction between the two major sources of corporate capital is made difficult because of the stock dividend transaction (to be discussed later in this chapter), in which an amount is transferred from the Retained Earnings account to the Capital Stock accounts. Second, as long as corporate managers, accountants, and others see little more than a legal distinction between the Retained Earnings and Capital Stock accounts, this classification will not be improved.

In accounting for corporate ownership, the restrictions that have the most influence are those having to do with legal capital. Since corporate owners do not have a personal responsibility for any debts of the corporation, the various state legislatures and courts have established restrictions concerning the amount of corporate assets that can be distributed to stockholders before the liquidation of the corporation. In most states the *legal capital* that cannot be distributed under normal circumstances is defined as the sum of the par values of the shares of stock issued and outstanding. The *par value* of a share of stock is the amount imprinted on the stock certificate as determined by the issuing corporation. Most companies, especially those whose shares are traded publicly, issue par-value stock, usually in rather small denominations of $10 or less per share. (They use par-value stock to minimize stock transfer taxes that are levied upon the stockholder when he sells the shares.) When stock certificates are issued without an imprinted value, they are called no-par stock. With no-par-value stock, most states permit the corporation's board of directors to determine what portion of the amount paid for each share constitutes the *stated value* or stipulated value per share of no-par value (which usually constitutes the legal capital for no-par stock). A few states require that the entire amount paid in on outstanding no-par stock must be classified as the legal capital. In the statutes of many states, however, legal capital is defined vaguely or ambiguously.

The significance of this legal restriction to accounting is that accountants separate the par or stated value of stock from the total amount paid by shareholders when the stock is issued. After the stock has been issued, however, this distinction is not maintained completely, although the accounts are kept open. The result is that legal capital usually is not reported on the corporation position statement. By continuing to carry the separate accounts the corporation may lead statement users to conclude that the balances of the par- or stated-value capital accounts constitute the corporate legal capital. In those states where legal capital is clearly defined, this information could be easily and correctly reported in a footnote, thus improving the reporting of capital stock in the position statement by eliminating any need to report par or stated values separately. The real irony of this situation is that information on the legal capital is most relevant only when the corporation is newly formed or small. Certainly stockholders or creditors in large, established, and profitable corporations would find information on net income, total resources, and financial policies much more relevant for determining dividend or debt payments than information on the relatively small portion of total ownership equity that is legal capital.

Characteristics of Corporation Stock

The stocks of a corporation may have different features or characteristics, and be grouped into different classes. If a corporation has more than one class of stock, one is a common stock. Others have some preference over the common stock and usually are called preferred stock. (Sometimes the issues are designated by letter, such as class A and class B, so that one must examine the stock certificate or other official company statements to determine the applicable restrictions and preferences of each class.) The advantage of preferred stock to stockholders is that it typically has priority over common stock in claims to dividends and to assets in the event of liquidation. However, preferred stock usually is callable (or retirable) at the option of the corporation instead of at the option of the stockholder. The fact that the capital obtained through issuance of callable preferred stock will be available as long as required and can be retired whenever the corporation wishes is a disadvantage to stockholders but an advantage to the corporation. The call price (which is specified on the stock certificate) usually is set above the issuance price; a call price is likely to establish a long-term ceiling on the stock's market price, which would be exceeded only under extreme circumstances and for rather short time periods. Another disadvantage to stockholders of preferred shares is that stockholders usually have only contingent voting rights (that is, they get voting rights usually in increasing proportions, as their dividends are passed).

Preferred stock may be either cumulative or noncumulative. With the cumulative feature if the stipulated dividends are not declared and paid (or are passed) in any year, they accrue to be paid in a subsequent year before any dividends can be declared on the common stock. When the stipulated dividends on cumulative preferred stock are omitted, they are called *dividends in arrears.* Since no liability exists until the corporate board of directors declares the dividend, these omitted dividends do not constitute a liability, but do require a reservation of retained earnings.

Preferred stock also may be either participating or nonparticipating. If it is fully participating, it shares equally with the common stock in any dividend declared after the common shares have received dividends equal to the preference dividends on the preferred stock (or to some other stipulated amount). If it is partially participating, it shares dividends up to a limit established as the maximum amount of dividends that can be received in any one year. Few currently outstanding preferred stocks carry a participating feature.

Like bonds, preferred stock may have a convertible feature. With it, the preferred stockholder may be able to exchange his shares for common stock in a stipulated ratio (or ratios). This gives the holder the option of converting if common stock dividends or other factors make the switch advantageous to him. Although preferred stock is a hybrid that is, in some respects (such as a stipulated rate of return, or lack of voting rights), similar to a liability, it always is classified as ownership. In reporting stock ownership on a position statement, all its special features should be identified.

Stock Issues

When stock is authorized by the corporation's board of directors, a formal journal entry is not warranted; usually only an informal memorandum is recorded. If an authorization account is kept (for example, if there is to be a long delay before all the authorized stock is issued), the companion or related contra account would include "unissued" in the title. At the date of authorization, the amount authorized would be recorded in both accounts; any issue of stock would reduce the balance in the unissued account. The difference between the authorized and unissued accounts at any point in time would constitute the par or stated value of the issued stock (except for any temporary retirements of the stock).

If the stock is issued at its par value, the entry to record this would be as follows:

	Debit	Credit
Cash	×	
Capital stock—par		×
To record issue of stock		

A more typical transaction, however, would be the one in which the stock is issued at a price that is more or less than the stock's par value. If the price received is greater than the par value of the stock, the stock is issued at a *premium* and, as previously explained, this excess is recorded in a separate account as follows:

	Debit	Credit
Cash	×	
Capital stock—par		×
Capital stock—premium		×
To record issue of stock at a premium		

If the price received is less than the par value of the stock, the stock is issued at a discount (a rare occurrence since many state statutes prohibit the issuance of shares at less than their par or stated value), and this deficiency is recorded in a separate account as follows:

	Debit	Credit
Cash	×	
Capital stock—discount	×	
Capital stock—par		×
To record issue of stock at a discount		

Usually these premium and discount accounts are kept open as long as the stock is outstanding. The discount account, however, may be closed occasionally if the stockholders are assessed for this deficiency and this assessment is collected, if later issues are at a premium, or by a transfer from retained earnings.

As the reader will recognize, the premium account is an adjunct account, and the discount account is a contra account to the appropriate par-value capital stock account. Neither account has much meaning without such a comparison. By definition, premium and discount accounts are not applicable in recording the issue of a no-par-value stock. Where different classes of stock are issued (for example, preferred and common), the recommended procedure is to record the premium or discount on the different classes in separate accounts that are adjunct or contra accounts to the par-value accounts for each class of stock. In reporting ownership on the position statement, there is merit in recognizing the adjunct or contra accounts as part of the payment of the stockholders for their stock, as follows:

Preferred stock—par	x	
Plus *premium*	x	x
Common stock—par	x	
Less discount	x	x
		x

The result is that the reader can identify the amount of capital paid in by each class of stockholder. This provides more relevant information than when the premium and/or discount accounts for all classes of stock are combined into a single account called Additional Paid-in Capital.

Stock may be issued in exchange for non-cash assets. In this situation there is a dual valuation problem. The value of the assets received must be measured in order to determine the value of the stock issued. The cash equivalent value of the non-cash assets received is best determined by establishing their fair market value. Only if the market value of the assets received cannot be adequately measured (for example, the promotional and organizational services of the individuals founding the corporation) should the accountant attempt to establish directly the market price of the stock issued. In these situations the accountant should be careful not to assume that the par value (or stated value) of the stock is equal to its market price. Also, the price at which a few shares of stock are issued to individuals, in order that they may qualify as directors of the corporation, does not constitute an adequate test of the market value of a stock. The best evidence of the market value of a stock is the price at which a large number of shares are issued or sold in one or more current or recent arm's-length transactions.

Stock is not always issued for cash, property, or services already performed. Sometimes the buyer pledges to pay for the stock within a stipulated period of time. Stock issued on this basis is said to be *subscribed* or *sold on subscription.* Although the stock is not issued until the subscription is collected, the claim and the reservation of stock subscribed are recorded as follows:

	Debit	Credit
Common stock subscription receivable	×	
Common stock—subscribed		×
To record common stock subscription		

It is possible but not particularly relevant to divide the amount subscribed into two accounts: Common Stock—Par Subscribed and Common Stock—Premium (or Discount) Subscribed. However, it is poor accounting practice to record the par value in a Common Stock —Par Subscribed account and the premium in the premium account for stock already issued, a procedure sometimes followed. When the subscription is collected, the entry to record the change in assets is as follows:

	Debit	Credit
Cash	×	
Common stock subscription receivable		×
To record collection of stock subscription		

and the subsequent entry to issue the stock is as follows:

	Debit	Credit
Common stock—Subscribed	×	
Common stock—par		×
Common stock—premium*		×
To record issue of stock previously subscribed		

*Provided that the stock was issued at a premium.

If originally recorded in two capital stock accounts, the entry is as follows:

	Debit	Credit
Common stock—par subscribed	×	
Common stock—premium subscribed	×	
Common stock—par		×
Common stock—premium		×
To record issue of stock previously subscribed		

The subscription also may be paid in installments, a practice that is common in employee stock purchase plans designed to encourage employees to invest in "their" company. Under these circumstances, the corporation may issue the stock in proportionate basis upon receiving cash for the installment or after the entire subscription has been collected. Occasionally, the stock subscriber may default on his subscription; in such situations and depending upon state laws, the corporation may issue stock to the extent that any shares are fully paid, or it may transfer the amount paid from the Common Stock—Subscribed account to Capital Contributed by Defaulted Subscriber. The unpaid balance in the account would be reversed. The complete entry would be as follows:

	Debit	Credit
Common stock—subscribed	×	
Common stock—subscription receivable		×
Common stock—par		×
*Common stock—premium**		×
To record issue of stock for down payment received on subscription and to cancel balance of subscription		

*Assuming that the stock was subscribed at a premium.

or:

	Debit	Credit
Common stock—subscribed	×	
Common stock—subscription receivable		×
Capital contributed by defaulted subscriber		×
To record capital contributed by defaulted subscriber and cancel the unpaid balance of the subscription receivable		

Infrequently the corporation may receive donations of capital, usually in the form of property rights. Care must be taken to ensure that such donations are recorded on the basis of their current market value. The donation should be entered in a special capital account, Capital from Donation.

Stock Retirements

When a corporation is liquidated, all stock ownership is retired. However, this does not occur frequently since the corporate form of enterprise, compared to the sole proprietorship or the partnership, may continue for a long time, if not forever; however, many corporations are liquidated, in effect, as a result of business combinations. The corporation may decide, even if its lifetime is unlimited, to retire a class of stock in whole or in part, either permanently or

temporarily. Although there is no major difference between the temporary and permanent retirements of stock, they are usually treated quite differently in accounting practice. Permanent stock retirements are recorded as direct reductions of ownership; temporary stock retirements are recorded in special suspense accounts called Treasury Stock. The latter can be confusing to the readers of financial statements; in order to determine the number of shares actually outstanding, the reader must first deduct the number of shares listed in the Treasury Stock account from those listed as outstanding in the regular stock account.

When stock is retired permanently (and the corporation is not liquidated), the specific treatment may vary according to the price paid to retire or redeem the stock. If the redemption price is *greater* than the issue price, the difference usually is charged to the Retained Earnings account. If the redemption price is *less* than the issue price, the difference usually is left in the Capital Stock—Premium account (or transferred to this account to the extent that the redemption price is less than the par or stated value of the shares).

For example, consider a share of stock issued at $110 with a par value of $100. If the share is retired at $120, the entry to record the retirement would be as follows:

	Debit	Credit
Capital stock—par	$100	
Capital stock—premium	10	
Retained earnings	10	
Cash		$120
To record retirement of stock issued at $110		

If the share is retired at $104, the entry to record the retirement would be as follows:

	Debit	Credit
Capital stock—par	$100	
Capital stock—premium	4	
Cash		$104
To record retirement of stock issued at $110		

Note that the $6 of issue price not included in the redemption price is left in the premium account; a less satisfactory treatment would be to transfer this $6 to the Retained Earnings account. If the share is retired at $96, the entry to record the retirement would be as follows:

	Debit	Credit
Capital stock—par	$100	
Capital stock—premium		$ 4
Cash		96
To record retirement of stock issued at $110		

When stock is retired permanently, its authorization is canceled so that the shares are not available for reissue. When stock is retired temporarily, it is not canceled, and the shares are available for reissue. This is not a very significant difference, because increasing the number of shares authorized is a formal, but usually simple, process. Whether stock is retired on a permanent or temporary basis, the reasons for doing so are similar. The corporation may wish to buy out a particular class of stock ownership or a particular stockholder. Sometimes the corporation may wish to settle claims against debtors who also are stockholders. The corporation may also retire stock temporarily in connection with a plan to encourage stock ownership among employees.

Treasury Stock

Although from the viewpoint of readers of financial statements there would be merit in recording temporary retirements in the same manner in the accounts as permanent retirements, this is not done.[3] To add to the confusion, two different methods are used to record temporary retirements.

Furthermore, there are a few companies that make the mistake of reporting their treasury stock (or stock retired temporarily) as a noncurrent asset.

[3]A footnote could be used to indicate what retirements were temporary.

EXHIBIT 11-1
METHODS USED TO RECORD TREASURY STOCK IN 1969

Method	No. of Companies	Percent
Deduct from ownership accounts:		
Cost	358	71
Par	107	21
Noncurrent asset	15	3
Not identified	26	5
	506	100%

NOTE: 20% of the reports did not list treasury stock.
SOURCE: Adapted from Table 2-61, Accounting Trends and Techniques: Annual Survey of Accounting Practices Followed in 600 Stockholders' Reports, 24th ed. (New York: AICPA, 1970), p. 160.

Treasury shares (temporary stock retirements) are virtually the same as unissued shares except that treasury shares may be issued at less than par value without the purchaser being liable for the discount. With treasury stock, the corporation does not have any of the basic rights of stock ownership; such shares give no right to vote, to receive dividends, to share in the assets upon liquidation, or to maintain proportion of ownership (preemptive right). A few corporations that buy treasury stock for their employee stock purchase program will record this stock as an asset This is not a sufficient argument to support this practice. Because a corporation cannot own a portion of itself, neither unissued shares nor treasury stock should be classified as assets.

The two principal methods of recording treasury stock found in practice are the par-value and cost methods. Under the par method, only the par value is recorded in a suspense (or contra-capital stock—par) account with any premium recorded directly as a reduction in the Premium or Retained Earnings accounts. Under the cost method, the entire price is recorded in a suspense account, Treasury Stock, which is a contra account to the entire ownership equity for that class of stock. In both methods, Retained Earnings are restricted or appropriated for the purchase price of the treasury stock (and a footnote indicating this restriction should be reported on the position statement).

To illustrate, a share of stock with a par value of $100 was issued at $110 and reacquired at a price of $115:

	Par-value Method		Cost Method	
	Debit	Credit	Debit	Credit
Treasury stock	$100		$115	
Capital stock—premium	10			
Retained earnings	5			
Cash		$115		$115
To record acquisition of treasury stock				

and if the share were subsequently reissued at a price of $110:

	Debit	Credit	Debit	Credit
Cash	$110		$110	
Retained earnings			5	
Treasury stock		$100		$115
Capital stock—premium		10		
To record reissue of treasury stock				

Occasionally the corporation may receive shares of its stock as donated stock; in this instance, a memorandum would be made only if the cost method were used. With the par-value method, an entry

would be made debiting the Treasury Stock account and crediting the Donated Capital account in the amount of the par value of the shares received.

Stock Rights

In several situations a corporation may issue stock warrants or rights; these certificates convey to the holder the right or option to purchase shares of stock (or a call on the stock) at a specified price. A basic right of stock ownership is the preemptive right to buy a sufficient number of shares of any new issue in order to maintain one's proportion of ownership. The corporation may decide to issue stock rights in the form of stock warrants (1) as a preliminary step to raising more capital, (2) as an inducement to buy another form of equity (for example, bonds or preferred stock) through the exercise of the rights or warrants, and (3) as additional compensation to officers or employees under stock option plans.

When rights are formally granted to existing stockholders, as a preliminary step to raising more capital, they usually expire within a few weeks or months. These rights entitle the holder to purchase stock at a price that almost always is above its par or stated value but lower than its market value. Because these rights are transferable, they may be actively traded in the stock market. However, the issuer need make no formal entry for these rights, because they represent merely an offer relating entirely to the capital stock accounts which may be accepted or rejected within the future; instead a memo is prepared indicating the number of rights granted.

When rights are issued with bonds, notes, or preferred stock, the rights may run for several years or even forever. The longer they run, the greater their speculative value. The separate valuation of these rights usually is ignored on the grounds that their value cannot be determined objectively. The result is that the security is overvalued while the stock rights are not valued. Since stock rights are often traded independently soon after the security is issued, the market price for such rights as compared to the market price for the bond, note, or preferred stock could provide an objective valuation for recording purposes. When the rights are valued separately, they could be recorded in a Stock Warrants account.

For example, consider the following bond issue with warrants attached:

8% debenture bonds, 20-year, maturity value	*$100,000*
Issue price	*105*
Warrants—every $1,000 bond includes 10 detachable	
warrants, each giving the right to subscribe to 1 share	
of capital stock at $40 for the next 10 years	

Current market value of a share of capital stock   *$30*
Soon after issue, the market value of each warrant was $5,
   and that of each bond was equal to its maturity value
   (i.e., a yield of 8%)

This bond issue transaction could be recorded as follows soon after the issue date when market values become known:

	Debit	Credit
Cash	$105,000	
8% debenture bonds payable		$100,000
Capital stock warrants		5,000
To record issue of debenture bonds and warrants		

If the issue price differs from the sum of the market values of the bond (or other security) plus the warrants, the issue price could be apportioned between the bonds and the warrants in the same ratio as the relative market prices of the separable securities.

If the price rises and the warrants are exercised, then the Stock Warrants account is transferred into the Capital Stock—Premium account, as a part of the transaction. If all the above warrants are exercised, the entry to record the issue of the 1,000 shares having a par value of $1 would be as follows:

	Debit	Credit
Cash	$40,000	
Capital stock—warrants	5,000	
Capital stock—par		$ 1,000
Capital stock—premium		44,000
To record exercise of warrants and issue of capital stock		

If the price drops so that the warrants are not exercised, then the Stock Warrants account could be closed into a Capital from Expired Stock Warrants account or other paid-in capital account. Whether or not issued stock rights are recorded in separate accounts, a minimal acceptable standard of reporting practice requires that the position statement disclose the number of shares of stock that are being reserved to provide for the exercising of stock rights and the time periods within which these options may be exercised.

Occasionally the preemptive right is extended to permit existing stockholders to subscribe to a new issue of debenture bonds or preferred stocks that are convertible into capital stock. At the time of issue, the major difference between the convertible debenture bond and the debenture bond with warrants attached is that the

EXHIBIT 11-2
COMPANIES WITH STOCK OPTION PLANS
IN 1969

Type of Business	*Number of Companies*	*Percent with Stock Option Plan*
Manufacturing	647	92
Retail trade	62	81
Life insurance	75	36
Other insurance	49	51
Gas and electric utilities	104	18
Commercial banking	207	31

SOURCE: *Adapted from H. Fox, "Top Executive Compensation," Studies in Personnel Policy, No. 501 (New York: The Conference Board, Inc., 1970), pp. 4-5.*

right or option portion of the convertible bond is not separable; thus, it is not traded separately and must be surrendered if it is to be exercised to acquire capital stock, whereas cash must be given with the warrant if it is to be exercised to acquire capital stock. Thus, the corporation receives cash (an increase in capital) when the warrant is exercised (of course, the debt security would remain to be paid or refunded at its maturity).

The AICPA in APB Opinion No. 14 made a major issue of the separability aspect of these securities and recommends that securities with detachable warrants should be accounted for as suggested above, but that no portion of the proceeds of an issue of convertible debt securities should be accounted for as attributable to the conversion feature. The authors are of the opinion that a security with detachable warrants to acquire capital stock is not different in substance from a security that must be surrendered to acquire capital stock; thus, both these hybrid securities should be accounted for in the same way.

The issue of stock rights under stock option plans to employees or officers has been largely developed and expanded since World War II. In many corporations, key officers and employees are granted stock rights as a form of compensation akin to salaries.[4] In order to be approved by the Internal Revenue Service, the qualified stock option must meet a number of requirements including that it expires five years after it is granted to the employee. The advantage of such an option to the employee is that if all the requirements of the plan

---

[4]As mentioned earlier, there are also employee stock purchase plans which relate to options granted to all corporate employees. These plans require approval of the Internal Revenue Service and the taxability rules are most similar to the restricted stock option plans mentioned in a later footnote.

are met and the shares are held for three years, he will have no taxable income on the shares until he sells them, at which time the gain will be taxed at a capital gain rate, which is lower than the tax rate applicable to his salary. Since the stock right permits the stock to be purchased at a stipulated price for a longer period of time, the employee should be motivated to work to raise the market price of the corporate stock: the greater the increase, the more he can gain by exercising his rights and selling the stock he acquires.

Any compensation cost recognized by the corporation must relate to the values placed on the stock rights. These values would then be matched to the appropriate accounting periods. In measuring the cost of employee compensation that should be recognized, the date on which the measurement will be made must be selected. Significant dates in connection with a stock option plan are those when the:

1. Plan is adopted.
2. Option is granted.
3. Option could first be exercised.
4. Option is exercised.
5. Employee disposes of his stock.

The AICPA argues that the second date, when the option is granted to the employee, is the significant one for measuring compensation, since the value at that date is the one that both employee and employer have in mind. It is also the date on which the corporation forgoes its principal alternative use of the shares subject to option, namely, their issuance. On this date, however, there ordinarily is not a material difference between the market price and the option price of the stock. This is prearranged since one of the requirements of a qualified stock option plan[5] under the Revenue Act of 1964 is that the option price cannot be less than 100 percent of the fair market price at the date of the grant.[6] Without this qualification, some of the employee's gain resulting from the stock option at the date

[5]Some options still outstanding were granted to employees before 1964 under the far more desirable terms of the restricted stock option plans. Since these expire 10 years after the grant is made (as compared to 5 years for the qualified plans), they will go out of existence in 1973.

[6]Among the features and tax consequences of qualified stock option plans that are most relevant to this discussion are the following:

a. The employee has no income for federal income tax purposes at the time when he exercises the option.

b. If the stock is held by the employee for at least three years after he exercises the option, he may sell the stock and treat all the gain or loss as a long-term capital gain or loss.

c. Although the plan approved by the Internal Revenue Service may run for ten years, the employee must exercise his option within five years after it is granted.

d. The corporation may not deduct as a compensation expense any part of the value of the stock that the employee acquires by exercising his option under the plan.

e. The employee must not hold stock plus options to acquire shares of more than 5 percent of the voting stock of the corporation.

of exercise would be subject to the higher ordinary income tax rate instead of the lower capital gain tax rate.[7]

By regarding the date of grant (when there is no difference between the option price and the market price) as the significant date for measurement, most corporations never report any compensation expense under stock option plans for their employees. Instead, in a footnote to the position statement they report the existence of the plan(s) and the number(s) of shares and the price(s) of shares under option to the key employees.

There are at least three more effective alternatives to the prevailing practice. The first and preferable approach would be to recognize that what is granted to the employee under a qualified plan is an option to buy a stipulated number of shares of capital stock at a stipulated price (a call) for five years (or within three months after terminating his employment with the corporation if he leaves before the end of four and three-fourths years). Like an option to buy real property or other tangible or intangible property, these options have value because they are rights, albeit nontransferable rights. Thus, the amount of compensation should be measured in terms of the fair market value of the right, probably at the date when it was granted to the employee. Because of the current state of the art, the valuation problem is difficult, but the fair market value of the option might be measured by comparison with other options possessing established market values. The amount of compensation could be recorded in an asset account and an owners' equity account as follows:

	Debit	Credit
Deferred compensation on		
stock option plan	×	
Stock option credit		×
To record compensation under stock option plan for employees		

The asset account then would be amortized over periods expected to benefit from the given grant. A slight modification of this would be to determine the amount of compensation at the date of the grant, as described above, but to accrue it over the period benefited by charges to compensation expense and credits to the owners' equity account, Stock Option Credit. The balance in Stock Option Credit would be closely related to the Capital Stock—Premium account and might be transferred to it as the options are exercised.

The second approach would be to accrue as compensation periodi-

[7]If the plan is not qualified, the employee would report as ordinary income in the year that he exercises the option the excess of the current market value of the stock over the option price. Under a qualified plan the employee also could have ordinary income if he does not hold the shares for three years after the date when he exercised the option.

cally (the difference between the option price and the market price) from the date when the option is granted to the date when it is exercised. Presumably the market price of the stock rights granted under the plan could be estimated if similar options were being sold in the market. Since these rights offered to employees are nontransferable and may be exercised only if the employee continues to work for the corporation on a satisfactory basis until the date when he may exercise the option, the prices arrived at in the stock market for transferable rights may be far different from those granted under the plan. If this is so, a third approach would be to make a valid measurement at the date when the rights may be exercised. At this date there no longer is any uncertainty about continued employment; also, since the rights once exercised no longer are under corporate control, future changes in their value are irrelevant to the corporation. On this date the compensation cost (the difference in prices) would be recorded as shown below for the first approach.

	Debit	Credit
Deferred stock option compensation	×	
Stock option credit		×
To record compensation under stock option plan for employees		

After this entry, there is the problem of assigning the compensation cost as a periodic expense. If the measurement is made on the date when the rights are granted, the compensation might be allocated on a straight-line basis to the subsequent periods through the date when the rights are exercisable or to a different date which would better span the period to be benefited from the grant. If the measurement is made on the date when the rights are exercisable, the total compensation measurement usually is charged off as an expense in the period in which it is recorded.

The classification of the credit may be either as a liability or as an element of stockholder equity, depending upon the interpretation of the credit. If the emphasis is that the incurring of a cost must be appropriately accompanied by a liability (which will be discharged later by the issue of stock), the credit is classified accordingly. If the emphasis is that the stock will be issued in the future for the services being received currently from the employee, the credit would be classified as part of ownership equity. The latter argument seems to have more substance.

The stock options may not be exercised because of the resignation of the employee before his grant was exercisable and/or the decline of the market price of the stock. The expiration of the options should not affect the compensation cost that already has been allocated. When the stock rights expire and compensation was recorded previously as suggested for the two approaches discussed above, the transaction would be recorded as follows:

	Debit	Credit
Stock option credit	×	
Capital from expired stock options		×
To record the forfeiture of employee stock options		

Stock Splits and Stock Dividends

Corporations often are interested, for both social and economic reasons, in having as many investors as possible hold shares of their stock, even if some hold only a few shares each. If the market price of corporation stock becomes high, many investors seem to be unwilling to purchase it. Such investors seem more unwilling than unable to purchase stock with a very high price per share. In order to accommodate these investors, the company will split its shares. With a stock split, the par or stated value per share is reduced in proportion to the increase in the number of the shares. For example, to effect a 2-for-1 stock split, instead of calling in the old $20 par-value shares and exchanging each for two new $10 par-value shares, the corporation merely issues one new $10 par-value share for each $20 share now held. A stockholder with 100 old shares will hold 200 shares after the split. He will continue to hold the certificate for 100 shares of $20 par. When this certificate is sold or otherwise transferred, the corporation will issue a new one showing a par value of $10. A stock split does not cause any change in total ownership; it merely effects a change in the par value per share since the number of shares outstanding has changed, with no change in the amount in the Capital Stock account. No entry is posted into the accounts for a stock split. A memorandum entry is sufficient.

Sometimes stock splits are confused with stock dividends, particularly large stock dividends. With a stock split, the board of directors issues additional shares of stock in proportion to existing holdings but with lower par or stated values per share. With a stock dividend, the board of directors issues additional shares in proportion to existing holdings listed with the same par or stated value per share as the outstanding stock. The reason for doing this is to avoid declaring and paying cash (or other property) dividends to the stockholders. The cash saved can be reinvested in the company. Really the only change to the stockholder is that his number of shares has increased. Presumably the stockholder can dispose of the additional shares for cash, but the corporation does not have to make the cash payment. Of course, when the stockholder disposes of his additional shares, he reduces his proportionate interest in the corporation. The entry to declare and issue a stock dividend is as follows:

	Debit	Credit
Retained earnings	×	
Capital stock—par		×
Capital stock—premium		×
To record stock dividend at fair market valuation of shares previously outstanding		

If there is a lapse of time between when the stock dividend is declared and when it is issued, a special account, Stock Dividend Declared, could be utilized. This account would constitute part of the ownership equity for statement purposes. For small stock dividends, the value of the shares issued is measured by the fair market price of the shares, not just their par or stated value. This position is supported by the SEC and the AICPA. Small stock dividends are those that do not cause a material price decline in the market value per share. This usually means that to be called a stock dividend the action should increase the number of shares outstanding by less than 20 to 25 percent.

The only accounting effect of a stock dividend is to transfer an amount between ownership accounts. The result is to break down the basic distinction between paid-in capital and earned capital, and thus to make it impossible to classify consistently position statement ownership by source.

Large stock dividends, those that increase the outstanding shares by 25 percent or more, are similar to stock splits, and could tend to be considered as such by the AICPA. Both may be expected to cause a significant decrease in the market price per share. With large stock dividends, only the par or stated value of the shares issued need be capitalized as follows:

	Debit	Credit
Retained earnings	×	
Capital stock—par		×
To record large stock dividend		

Cash Dividends and Retained Earnings
As mentioned in the previous section, stock dividends are not a substitute for cash dividends. They might be considered a partial substitute only in the sense that the same dividend rate may be continued

on the extra shares, thus increasing the total amount of dividends paid. Increasing the dividend rate on the old shares could have the same effect. Cash dividends are the amounts that the stockholder receives on his investment while he holds the stock.[8] Many investors regard cash dividends received as the most significant criterion in judging the effectiveness of their investment. Cash dividends usually are stated as a fixed dollar amount per share of common stock and as a percentage of the par or stated value of preferred stock. Usually cash dividends are declared on a quarterly basis, sometimes with an additional or extra dividend at the end of the year.

Before a board of directors can declare a dividend, it must establish that doing so would not reduce (or impair) the legal capital (as previously discussed), and second that the corporation's cash balances plus anticipated cash inflows are adequate to pay the dividend and to carry out the corporation's operations and future plans. Beyond the legal capital constraint, the board prefers to declare the cash dividend in an amount that is less than the current corporate income. Occasionally, however, cash dividends may be declared in an amount greater than current income; this is referred to as a dividend out of retained earnings. Only in unusual circumstances would the amount impair legal capital; this is referred to as a dividend out of capital. When dividends are declared legally in amounts that reduce or impair legal capital, they must be disclosed as liquidating dividends (as a return *of* capital because such dividends would be refunds of previous investments by owners if there had been no stock dividends or other upward revisions of the owners' capital accounts) and not as cash dividends (as a return *on* capital). This is according to generally accepted accounting practice and the model corporation law (adopted by many states).

In connection with a dividend (cash or stock), three dates are significant: the dates of (1) declaration, (2) record, and (3) payment. For example, the board of directors may declare a dividend on a certain date for the stockholders listed by the corporation as owners on a later date, and payable on a still later date. Because declaration of a dividend for a large public corporation may necessitate payments to hundreds of thousands of stockholders, establishing separate dates for record and payment is necessary. If between the date of declaration and the date of record, the stock is sold to include the right to the dividend declared after the date of record, the stock is sold ex dividend. The entries in connection with a cash dividend are as follows:

---

[8]Recall the valuation ideas presented in Chapter 2. The present value of an investment in stock would be equal to the present value of the annuity represented by the expected cash dividend payments plus the present value of the expected amount of cash to be received when the share is sold.

	Debit	*Credit*
Date of Declaration		
Dividends declared (or retained earnings)	×	
Dividends payable		×
To record declaration of cash dividend		
Date of Record		
No entry except memo—close and post stock ownership		
records to bring them up to date; these owners will		
receive dividend checks.		
Date of Payment		
Dividends payable	×	
Cash		×
To record payment of dividend		

As the reader perhaps realizes, the principal changes in the Retained Earnings account occur with the closing out of income accounts (increases) and the declaration of dividends (decreases). Since the AICPA attempted to enforce an all-inclusive concept of income statement in its APB Opinion No. 9, gains, losses, and adjustments of prior periods are not as likely to be transferred directly to the Retained Earnings account. Apart from income and infrequent causes of changes such as those resulting from stock retirements or deficits, another change in the Retained Earnings account results from the appropriation of retained earnings for special events. By *appropriation* is meant the reservation of retained earnings for anticipated events. The appropriation process may be a voluntary one (discretionary policy) or an involuntary one (legal, or contractual, restrictions). Separate accounts are kept for these appropriations, and the entries to open and close these appropriation accounts are as follows:

	Debit	*Credit*
Retained earnings	×	
Retained earnings appropriated for _____		×
To record the restriction of retained earnings for _____		
Retained earnings appropriated for _____	×	
Retained earnings		×
To record the closeout of retained earnings appropriated for _____		

The entries for the restriction of the Retained Earnings account always are the same. Only the name of the restriction varies. It does not matter whether the anticipated event does or does not occur. The life cycle of these accounts is always the same. Examples of involuntary restrictions on retained earnings are for treasury stock or redemption of bonds; examples of voluntary restrictions are for redemption of preferred stock, expansion of plant, self-insurance, and contingencies.

Although a cash dividend usually is declared out of retained earnings (that is, the Retained Earnings account is to be charged with the amount of the dividend declared and must have a credit of no less than a zero balance after a declaration), it can be paid only with cash, and not with retained earnings. Similarly, although the appropriations are transferred from retained earnings, contingencies and other liabilities cannot be paid with retained earnings, but only with cash, other assets, the incurrence of other liabilities, or the issuance of common or preferred stock. For example, bonds, other liabilities, or stock are retired only with cash or other asset transfers. In short, the appropriation of assets (or funds) for these anticipated events is more significant than the appropriation of retained earnings. The only justification for restricting retained earnings is to indicate that portion of the retained earnings balance which is not available for dividends. But retained earnings not reserved (usually the larger portion of total retained earnings) are not necessarily available for dividends unless cash or other assets are available for that purpose. Involuntary appropriations are required less frequently now because creditors prefer restrictions which directly limit dividends or restrict working capital to certain levels. Furthermore, for mature firms, total retained earnings may exceed the total of the capital contributed by stockholders or at least constitute a large percentage of total ownership equity. Many firms attempt to develop a substantial source of capital from retained earnings; these firms have no intention of declaring dividends that would transfer this (earned) capital to stockholders.

The reporting of information on the voluntary restrictions could be accomplished more effectively (and be less misleading) through footnotes than through ledger accounts. If such appropriation accounts are used, their titles should not include the term "reserve" because these adjunct-retained earnings accounts can be confused with contra-asset or contra-liability accounts. If the corporation deliberately understates its assets or overstates its liabilities, it has effectively established a "secret reserve" (or a hidden asset). Such a practice is unacceptable to all external users of financial statements. If the corporation deliberately overstates its assets or understates its liabilities, its stock is said to be "watered."[9] Such a practice is equally unacceptable to all external users of financial statements.

---

[9]This expression originated with the practice of increasing the weight of cattle before sale by giving them salt and all the water they could drink.

Corporate Ownership—a Summary

Compared to the accounting for both assets and liabilities, the accounting for ownership is not very relevant from the viewpoint of external users of financial statements.[10] Some of the difficulty arises from the residual nature of accounting ownership; by definition, it is the difference between the assets and the liabilities, and thus may be measured indirectly rather than directly. Beyond this, the accounting for ownership has not often been extended beyond the legal requirements for stock ownership. The result is rather sterile accounting. As mentioned earlier, it is not possible to maintain consistent classification of stock ownership to reflect both the legal restrictions and the sources or other bases. Where the most relevant basis of classification of ownership is considered to be source (as previously discussed), other classifications of ownership, particularly legal capital, should be relegated to the footnotes when it is not possible to maintain multiclassifications consistently. Appropriations of retained earnings usually can be shown more clearly in footnotes (or in parenthetical notes) than in the accounts. A major difficulty in accounting for retained earnings is that many, if not most, corporations regard retained earnings as invested capital; this is reflected in the policy of declaring cash dividends only out of current net income. The difficulty is a result of the separation of ownership in public corporations from the managerial control of such corporations. In effect, retained earnings are converted into invested capital without formal actions. Nevertheless, the consistent classification by source would seem to be the most promising way to improve accounting for ownership. Also, it should be remembered that sources of ownership can be classified more clearly in fund-flow statements than in static stock statements.

Investments in Stocks

In addition to accounting for its own stock, the enterprise may have to account for investments that it has made in the capital stock of other corporations. If such an investment is a temporary one, it is classified as a marketable security, a current asset, and is treated as discussed in Chapter 5. If the investment is a relatively permanent one, it is classified as a long-term investment, a noncurrent asset, as explained in Chapter 3. Since investments in stock certificates are not usually a means of activating temporarily idle cash, but are for affiliation or control (as with major customers or suppliers or in corporate joint ventures in which a small group of firms regulates the operations of a separate corporation for the mutual benefit of

---

[10]See "An Evaluation of External Reporting Practices—A Report of the 1966–68 Committee on External Reporting," *Supplement to vol. XLIV, The Accounting Review* (Evanston, Illinois: American Accounting Association, 1969), pp. 103–104.

the group), they are almost always classified as long-term investments. Such investments in stock may be valued on one of three bases of valuation. If the original value of the investment in the stock is to be maintained, the asset is valued on the *cost* or the *legal* basis. If the value of the investment and the current income from it are to be reflected on a more timely basis than cost and the receipt of dividends, the asset might be accounted for on the *market value* basis. If the value of the investment is to reflect changes in the underlying value of the investment (or the net assets of the other enterprise), the asset is valued on the *equity* or *economic* basis.

The rationale for the cost basis is that two separate entities are

EXHIBIT 11-3
VALUATION OF LONG-TERM INVESTMENTS

	Cost or Legal Basis		Market Value Basis		Equity or Economic Basis	
	Debit	*Credit*	*Debit*	*Credit*	*Debit*	*Credit*
When investment is acquired:						
Investment in stock	×		×		×	
Cash		×		×		×
When net income of subsidiary is determined after investment:*						
Investment in stock					×	
Investment revenue						×
When dividends of subsidiary are declared:						
Dividends receivable	×		×		×	
Investment in stock						×
Investment revenue		×		×		
When dividend previously declared is paid:						
Cash	×		×		×	
Dividends receivable		×		×		×
When net losses of subsidiary is determined after investment:†						
Investment loss					×	
Investment in stock						×

	Cost or Legal Basis		Market Value Basis		Equity or Economic Basis	
	Debit	Credit	Debit	Credit	Debit	Credit
When liquidating dividend (i.e., either a dividend from retained earnings accumulated before purchasing the investment or where legal capital of the subsidiary is being reduced) is declared and paid:						
Cash	×				×	
Investment in stock		×				×
When the market value of the investment increases:						
Investment in stock			×			
Investment revenue				×		
When the market value of the investment decreases:						
Investment loss‡			×			
Investment in stock				×		

*The actual amounts would be based upon percentage of ownership. For example, if the parent company owns 30 percent of the investee's outstanding stock, 30 percent of the investee's income would be recorded as an increase to the investment account under the equity or economic procedure.

†If net losses are considered to be indicative of other than a temporary decrease in the value of the investment, then an investment loss and a decrease in the investment in stock would also be recorded under both the cost or legal and the equity or economic bases.

‡A decrease in market value that is considered to be other than a temporary decrease in value also would be recognized under both the cost or legal and the equity or economic bases.

involved, so that a change in the net assets of another corporation (the investee), by itself, may not be sufficient to indicate that a change should be reflected in the value of the investor entity. Beyond this are the basic ideas that underlie cost-based conventional financial accounting.

The rationale for the market value basis (as discussed in Chapter 5 for temporary investments) is that it provides more useful, relevant information than cost for investments that are not large enough either (1) to give the investor significant influence over operating and financial policies of the investee corporation or (2) to significantly affect the market price for the stock in the event of a sale.

The rationale for the equity basis of valuation is that it provides more useful, relevant information than either the cost or market bases if the size of the stockholding is large enough to give the investor the ability to exercise significant influence over operating and financial policies of the investee corporation. This is an extension of the economic entity concept discussed earlier (see Chapter 3), under which any change in the value of the net assets of the investee company should be reflected in the investment account of the investor or parent company.

The choice of measurement procedures depends on whether the market value of the stock or the income (which expresses a change in net assets) of the investee corporation constitutes objective, verifiable evidence of a change in the value of the investor company's investment. If the investment in the stock of the investee corporation is substantial, 20 percent or more of the outstanding voting capital stock, and (or) if the investor has the ability to exercise significant influence over the investor corporation, the authors are in agreement with the recommendations of the AICPA in APB Opinion No. 18 that the investor company's investment should be valued on the equity basis.

The market value basis may be used in certain circumstances where the investor does not have the ability to exercise significant influence over the investee and where the investor's holding could be sold without significantly disturbing the market or depressing the market price of the investee's stock.

If the cost method is used, it is modified to show a reduction of the investment for (1) a dividend declared by the subsidiary on income for periods before the time when the investment was made (that is, a form of liquidating dividend) and (2) any material permanent decline in the value of the subsidiary from operating or other losses.

Entries under the three procedures are shown in Exhibit 11–3.

Consolidated Statements

When one corporation owns a controlling interest in the outstanding voting capital stock of another corporation, statements based on the separate legal entities of the two corporations are not of optimal usefulness, especially to the stockholders and creditors of the parent (investor) company. Instead, the external users of financial statements need to be able to review reports based on the position and operating results of the two companies managed under common control as a unified economic entity so as to complement the reports of the position and operating results of each separate legal entity. Such statements for two or more affiliated companies are called *consolidated statements.* Since most companies whose stocks are listed on the major stock exchanges have one or more subsidiaries (investee companies), the typical financial statements published by the larger corporations are consolidated ones. Although consolidated statements are of primary importance for stockholders and creditors of the parent company, statements of the individual legal entities still have significance to the creditors, stockholders, and other external interests of the subsidiary entities, and should be included in public reports wherever possible. This is not always practical since large corporations may have many active subsidiary companies.

In Chapter 3 the degree of authority specified for a controlling interest (and the usual basis for preparing consolidated statements) is legal control, the ownership of more than 50 percent of the voting stock of the subsidiary corporation. Effective continuing control may be exercised with a much smaller percentage of ownership, particularly where ownership is widely dispersed among stockholders who do not exercise their voting rights. On occasion, effective control may require as much as 75 percent ownership where major decisions must be ratified by this percentage of ownership. In short, the percentage of ownership required to warrant preparation of consolidated statements depends on the particular situation and is a matter of judgment. As a practical matter, there must be persuasive reasons for not preparing consolidated statements when more than 50 percent of the subsidiary's voting stock is controlled by the parent corporation and where the companies operate as an integrated unit. If a subsidiary company's activities do not constitute a part of the integrated area of operations, consolidated statements should not be prepared for it, irrespective of the degree of control. Usually, an integrated area of operations is broadly interpreted to include the performance of any activity that the parent corporation could undertake through a branch or division. Subsidiaries that function as banks and insurance companies and sometimes those that operate in foreign countries are not included in consolidated statements. Banks and insurance companies legally cannot be operated as divisions or branches of corporations, and foreign subsidiaries are sometimes controlled by their governments instead of their legal owners.

The investing company may purchase the stock of a subsidiary corporation for cash or other assets or through exchange of its own securities for the stock of the subsidiary corporation. When other assets are used to acquire the stock, the fair market value of the assets constitutes the measurement of the stock. When securities are given up for the stock, the fair market value of the securities constitutes the measurement of the stock.[11]

When the parent company acquired the investment, the cost of

[11]An alternative procedure is called "pooling." Under it, a new basis of accountability for the subsidiary stock does not arise. Instead the existing book values (of assets, liabilities, and owners' equity including the Retained Earnings accounts) for the two companies are combined. This approach had been much criticized. In APB Opinion No. 16, the AICPA has substantially restricted its use.

the investment would be equal to, greater than, or less than its book value. When a difference exists, this may be due to (1) errors in the subsidiary record or a bargain price and (2) the over- or under-valuation of the subsidiary's net assets in its separate accounts. The latter may result from recorded or unrecorded transactions. One example is unrecorded goodwill or other intangibles. Such goodwill may relate to the subsidiary company, or it may arise from the construction of the affiliated companies into a single economic entity.

In preparing consolidated statements, there always is at least one account of one entity that is the reciprocal of (or interrelated to) one or more accounts of another entity. These reciprocal accounts must be offset or eliminated to avoid double counting. Examples of such accounts are the Investment in Stock account of the parent which is the reciprocal of the stockholders' equity accounts of the subsidiary, the receivables of one entity which are payables of another, or sales of one entity which are purchases of another. Such eliminations are made only on the working papers for the preparation of consolidated statements and are not recorded in the accounts of the separate companies.

In preparing a consolidated position statement, the basic eliminations are the investment account of the parent and the common stock ownership accounts of the subsidiary. If the investment account has been maintained on the equity basis, the pre-elimination entry would be to adjust the investment account (on the parent company books) to reflect the current net income of the subsidiary. If the cost or legal basis of accounting for the investment has been followed, the adjustment would be for all income of the subsidiary since acquisition. If there is no difference in value between the investment account and the subsidiary's common stock accounts, the entry would be as follows on the consolidation work papers:

	Debit	Credit
Subsidiary's capital stock	×	
Subsidiary's retained earnings	×	
Parent's investment in stock		×

If there is a difference, it would be recorded according to its nature. If an error was made in recording the cost of the investment, or if the parent company sustained a loss on the purchase, the investment account and parent company's ownership would be restated by the amount of this difference. If the net assets of the subsidiary are undervalued or overvalued, either collectively or in terms of specific assets or liabilities, whether tangible or intangible, the net assets and ownership of the subsidiary should be restated accordingly. If the parent company paid for goodwill or other intangibles arising from the affiliation of the two companies, the difference is classified as a special intangible asset arising out of the consolidation (in accounts called Consolidated Goodwill or Excess of Cost over Book Value of Interest in Subsidiary). The assumption that the parent company has purchased its interest at a bargain price (and hence made a gain on its purchase) is not generally accepted.

If the controlling company owns less than 100 percent of the capital stock of a subsidiary, the book value of the remainder of the stock (the portion held by parties outside the consolidated group) is classified as minority interests on the consolidated position statement. It is for these interests plus creditors and other interested external parties of the subsidiary that separate legal entity financial statements are prepared.

In addition to offsetting the parent company's investment account against the subsidiary's ownership accounts in preparing a consolidated position statement, there may be other intercompany transactions that result in a double counting of assets and liabilities, or revenues and expenses, from a consolidated viewpoint. These, too, should be eliminated. Also the prices established in intercompany transactions may include income that has not been realized in transactions with outsiders and thus is reflected in the valuation of inventories or other assets. Such intercompany income also must be eliminated. From the viewpoint of the consolidated economic entity, income should not be recognized on intracompany transfers (because the consolidated entity cannot earn income by activities carried on within the entity).

An illustration showing the preparation of consolidated statements is given in the Appendix to Chapter 11.

Summary

The various theories of ownership help answer the question: At whom is ownership accounting directed? The entity theory of ownership regards the corporation as having separate existence and personality from its owners. Assets are considered the rights of the firm, and liabilities are the firm's obligations. In addition, income is determined for the firm. However, the firm or entity is considered to function chiefly for the benefit of the owners or equity holders, and the underlying position statement equation is $\Sigma A = \Sigma E$. The enterprise theory of the firm considers the firm as a social institution with ownership extending beyond the economic equity holders to employees, government, customers, and the general public. Under a third theory of ownership, the fund theory, assets and equities are grouped according to functions of the organization. Ownership represents legal, contractual, managerial, or financial restrictions on the use of assets. The fund theory is used extensively in accounting for nonprofit organizations. As yet not fully developed, the commander concept emphasizes managerial control of the firm's assets instead of ownership.

In the complex relationships of corporate ownership, there is a real need to classify ownership according to its sources and to consider the restrictions on the distribution of invested capital and dividends to stockholders. For a corporation there are two major sources of capital: amounts paid in by stockholders (recorded in Capital Stock accounts), and the excess of income over dividends declared and paid (recorded in the Retained Earnings accounts). Minor sources of capital include amounts arising from revaluation of assets and donations from nonstockholders.

In formulating capital stock and retained earnings accounts there are several areas of interest: (1) the classes of stock, (2) the issuance of stock, (3) the method of stock purchase, (4) stock rights or warrants and stock option plans, (5) stock splits and stock dividends, (6) the retirement of stock, and (7) cash dividends and restrictions on retained earnings. A quick review of these areas follows. Chapter 11 describes in detail the techniques associated with accounting for the areas listed.

1. Stocks are normally classed as common or preferred; the subdivisions of preferred stock include cumulative, noncumulative, participating, and nonparticipating. In accounting for ownership, the accountant should develop a clear picture of the amounts associated with each class or subclass of stock.
2. A stock may be issued at par value, the amount imprinted on the stock certificate, or at no-par value. If no-par-value stock is issued, the firm must determine what amount paid for each share constitutes its stated value. Stock may also be issued at a price less than its par value (at a discount), or at a price greater than its par value (at a premium).
3. Stock may be purchased for cash, in exchange for non-cash assets, on subscription, and in installments.
4. A corporation may issue stock rights or warrants, i.e., the option to buy stock at a price almost always more than its par value but less than its market value during a stipulated period of time. A stock option plan for employees is a special form of stock right (usually for a longer period) and is subject to a number of Internal Revenue Service restrictions.
5. When a stock split is authorized, the firm issues additional shares in proportion to existing holdings but with a lower par or stated value per share. A split usually occurs because investors seem unwilling to purchase stock with a very high price per share. With a stock dividend, the firm issues additional shares in proportion to existing holdings listed but with the same par or stated value per share, usually to avoid declaring and paying cash dividends to stockholders.

6. Stock can be retired permanently or temporarily. Accountants treat permanent retirements as direct reductions of ownership and temporary retirements as special suspense accounts called treasury stock.
7. Cash dividends are the amounts that the stockholder receives on his investment while he holds the stock. Cash dividends are declared out of retained earnings but may be paid only with cash. Similarly, although voluntary or involuntary appropriations from retained earnings (the reservation of retained earnings for anticipated events) are transferred from retained earnings, they can be paid only with cash (or other assets).

The corporation may itself invest in the stock of other legal entities. Such investments are usually long term and may be valued on the cost or legal basis, the market value basis, or the equity basis. When a corporation owns a controlling interest in the outstanding voting capital stock of another corporation, a consolidated statement of the companies under common control as a unified economic entity, as well as statements for each legal entity, are of greatest value to external users. In preparing a consolidated statement, it is necessary to eliminate all intercompany transactions and portions of account balances that reflect internal relationships of the parent company and its subsidiaries. Examples of consolidated statements are given in the Appendix to Chapter 11.

A Selection of Supplementary Readings

American Institute of Certified Public Accountants: "Restatement and Revision of Accounting Research Bulletins," Accounting Research Bulletin No. 43, chap. 1, sec. B, "Profits or Losses on Treasury Stock"; chap. 7, sec. B, "Stock Dividends and Stock Split-ups"; chap. 13, sec. B, "Compensation involved in Stock Option and Stock Purchase Plans." In APB Accounting Principles, vol. 2. New York, pp. 6008, 6023–6026, 6053–6056.

_____: "Consolidated Financial Statements," Accounting Research Bulletin No. 51. In APB Accounting Principles, vol. 2. New York, pp. 6091–6096.

_____: "Business Combinations," Opinions of the Accounting Principles Board No. 16, New York: 1970.

_____: "The Equity Method of Accounting for Investments in Common Stock," Opinions of the Accounting Principles Board No. 18. New York: 1971.

"An Evaluation of External Reporting Practices—A Report of the 1966–68 Committee on External Reporting," Eldon S. Hendriksen, chairman. Supplement to vol. XLIV, The Accounting Review. Evanston, Illinois: American Accounting Association, 1969, pp. 98–104.

Call, Dwight V.: "Some Salient Factors Often Overlooked in Stock Options," The Accounting Review, October 1969, pp. 711–719.

Chambers, R. J.: "Consolidated Statements .˙re Not Really Necessary," The Australian Accountant, February 1968, pp. 89–92.

Landis, Ira M.: "APB Opinion 18 Issued—'The Equity Method of Accounting for Investments in Common Stock,'" The Accounting Forum, Financial Executive, June 1971, p. 64.

McCarten, John: "The Greatest Accountant in the World," *The New Yorker,* December 16, 1939, p. 106.

Paton, W. A.: "Postscript on 'Treasury' Shares," *The Accounting Review,* April 1969, pp. 276–283.

Pusker, Henri C.: "Accounting for Capital Stock Distributions (Stock Split-ups and Dividends)," *The New York Certified Public Accountant,* May 1971, pp. 347–352.

Appendix to Chapter 11
Illustration of Consolidated Statement Preparation

Since an extensive coverage of the issues and techniques of developing consolidated statements becomes extremely complex and is a subject that could be a separate book by itself, the coverage here necessarily will be greatly simplified. The purpose of the presentation will be to introduce enough of the basic concepts and more common practices to facilitate the reading of consolidated statements with some degree of comprehension.

It should be remembered that the underlying objective of the consolidation procedures is to combine the accounts of the parent and the subsidiary into one set for a single entity so that the only accounts remaining are those between this parent-subsidiary entity and outsiders. To do this, it is necessary to eliminate all intercompany transactions and portions of account balances that reflect internal relationships between the parent and the subsidiary. If this were not done, there would be double counting of the interrelated items.

The following data are for the Parent and Subsidiary Companies for the year ended December 31, 1971:

Adjusted
Trial Balance
December 31, 1971
(000's omitted)

	Parent Company Debit	Parent Company Credit	Subsidiary Company Debit	Subsidiary Company Credit
Current assets	$ 225		$125	
Plant (net)	185		55	
Investment in stock of Subsidiary at equity	110			
Current liabilities		$ 90		$ 45
Common stock		340		80
Retained earnings, January 1		71		50
Sales		950		560
Dividend revenue		4		
Cost of goods sold	655		335	
Other expenses	265		215	
Dividends declared	15		5	
	$1,455	$1,455	$735	$735

The following additional information also is available (000's omitted):

1. In 1965, Parent Company paid $94 for its 80 percent interest in Subsidiary Company. At that time the Subsidiary Company equity accounts had the following balances:

Common stock	$ 80
Retained earnings	30
	$110

2. During 1971 Subsidiary declared and paid dividends of $5.
3. During 1971 Parent sold goods to Subsidiary for $150.
4. Parent's Accounts Receivable (and Subsidiary's Accounts Payable) include $9 due on the goods sold to Subsidiary.
5. On December 31, Subsidiary had in inventory goods which it purchased from Parent for $15, but which had a cost to Parent of $13.

Consolidation procedures Usually the worksheet format is used in practice to prepare consolidated statements, but in this simplified situation the worksheet would be of little assistance. Instead, journal entries will be used; but it must be remembered that these entries will be made only in the working papers for preparing the consolidated statements and not in the accounts of the two companies.

Elimination of investment account A usual first step is to eliminate Parent Company's Investment in Stock of Subsidiary account by offsetting it against the Capital Stock and Retained Earnings accounts of the Subsidiary Company to the extent of the Parent's interest. Since Parent is using the equity method, its Investment account includes the initial cost of the acquired stock plus Parent's share of Subsidiary's income, and reduced by Parent's share of Subsidiary losses to January 1, 1971.

The elimination entry for these reciprocal accounts would be as follows:

	Debit	*Credit*
Common stock (of Subsidiary)	$64	
Retained earnings (of Subsidiary)	40	
Consolidated goodwill (or excess of cost over book value of Subsidiary)	6	
Investment in stock of Subsidiary		$110
To eliminate Parent's investment account and its interest in Subsidiary's owners' equity accounts		

Calculation: Initially, Parent paid $94 for book value of $88 (80% of $110). Therefore, there was (and is) consolidated goodwill of $6.

If the investment were on the cost or legal basis, an additional entry would be made to transfer Parent's share of Subsidiary income retained since date of acquisition (80 percent of $20 = $16) from Retained Earnings of Subsidiary to Consolidated Retained Earnings.

Recognition of minority interest Since Parent has less than a 100 percent ownership interest in Subsidiary, there also are minority stockholders. This 20 percent minority interest in Subsidiary at January 1 can be recognized as follows:

	Debit	Credit
Common stock (of Subsidiary)	*$16*	
Retained earnings (of Subsidiary)	*10*	
* Minority interest*		*$26*
To recognize the minority interest in owners' equity of Subsidiary		

Calculation: The minority's share is 20 percent of Subsidiary's January 1 balances of Common stock (20% of $80) and Retained Earnings (20% of $50).

Elimination of intercompany dividend Since Parent's Dividend Revenue is entirely attributable to dividends declared and paid by Subsidiary, this intercompany transaction should be eliminated as follows to avoid double counting:

	Debit	Credit
Dividend Revenue (of Parent)	*$4*	
* Dividends Declared (of Subsidiary)*		*$4*
To eliminate Parent's share of Subsidiary's		
dividends declared and paid		

Calculation: Parent's share is 80 percent of Subsidiary's dividends declared (80% of $5 = $4).

Elimination of intercompany sales-purchases The intercompany sale-purchase transaction now reflected in Parent's Sales account and in Subsidiary's Cost of Goods Sold account should be eliminated as follows:

	Debit	Credit
Sales (of Parent)	*$150*	
* Cost of Goods Sold (of Subsidiary)*		*$150*
To eliminate the intercompany sales-purchases transaction		

NOTE: *Cost of goods sold is calculated by adding purchases to beginning inventory and subtracting ending inventory.*

Elimination of intercompany receivable-payable Since Parent includes a $9 Account Receivable that Subsidiary includes as an Account Payable, these must be eliminated as follows to avoid double counting with the consolidated entity:

	Debit	Credit
Accounts payable—current liabilities (of Subsidiary)	$9	
Accounts receivable—current assets (of Parent)		$9
To eliminate the intercompany receivable-payable		

Elimination of intercompany income in inventory Since Subsidiary still has goods in its inventory for which it paid $15 but which cost Parent $13, the difference of $2 is income that Parent reflects in its accounts, and should be eliminated in the consolidation process, because it arose from transactions within the new entity, not from transactions with outsiders (thus, accountants say that this is unrealized income). This can be done as follows:

	Debit	Credit
Cost of goods sold (of Subsidiary)	$2	
Inventory—current assets (of Subsidiary)		$2
To eliminate intercompany income from the cost of Subsidiary's ending inventory		

NOTE: Again, ending inventory is subtracted in calculating cost of goods sold.

Using T accounts, or simple addition and subtraction, to record the eliminations, the consolidated statements may now be prepared.

Parent Company and Subsidiary Consolidated Statement of Income and Retained Earnings for 1971 (000's omitted)		
Sales (950 + 560 − 150)		$1,360
Less expenses:		
Cost of goods sold (655 + 335 − 150 + 2)	$842	
Other (265 + 215)	480	1,322
Consolidated net income		38
Less: Minority interest share of Subsidiary income		
(20% of $10)	2	
Dividends declared	15	17
Consolidated net income retained		21
Consolidated retained earnings, January 1		71
Consolidated retained earnings, December 31		$ 92

Parent Company and Subsidiary Consolidated Position Statement December 31, 1971 (000's omitted)

Current assets (225 + 125 − 9 − 2)		$ 339
Plant (net) (185 + 55)		240
Consolidated goodwill		6
Total assets		$ 585
Current liabilities (90 + 45 − 9)		$ 126
Minority interest (26 + 2 − 1)	$ 27	
Common stock	340	
Consolidated retained earnings	92	459
Total equities		$ 585

Other considerations It would have been a much simpler task to prepare only a consolidated position statement at December 31, 1971. To verify how easily this could be done and to test his understanding of these basic concepts and techniques, the student may wish to return to the trial balance accounts given at the beginning of this illustration. He should first close the revenue, expense, and dividend accounts into the retained earnings accounts. Then he should adjust Parent Company's Investment and Retained Earnings accounts for their share of Subsidiary's income retained in 1971.

The student also may wish to convert the initial trial balance data to the cost basis and to follow through on the procedures to the consolidated statements given above.

Questions

11–1
Given the following information and the statements of the consolidated entity and parent corporation, reconstruct the statements of the subsidiary.

Parent invested $100,000 in the subsidiary when the latter was formed; it is 100 percent owned.

Subsidiary owes the parent $10,000.
Sales by the parent to subsidiary $50,000.
Purchases by parent from the subsidiary $20,000.
Rent paid by subsidiary to parent $25,000.

	Parent	*Consolidated*
		(000's omitted)
Sales	$400	$730
Cost of goods sold	220	350
Other expenses	120	195
Operating net income	60	185
Other revenue	50	35
Net income	110	220
Investment in subsidiary	100	

	Parent	Consolidated
	(000's omitted)	
Other assets	$250	$490
Liabilities	90	130
Capital stock	210	210
Retained earnings	50	150

11-2

Certain accountants have proposed that the stockholders' equity should be shown as one amount, without being broken up into component parts. Defend this position.

11-3

The position statement of the Kant Company for December 31, 1972, is as follows (with the 000's omitted):

Cash	$ 20	*Liabilities*	$124
Other tangible assets	360	*4% cumulative preferred stock*	
Organization costs	20	*($100 par)*	100
	$400	*Common stock ($50 par)*	100
		Retained earnings	76
			$400

The preferred stock is 4 percent cumulative, nonparticipating, on which the last dividend paid was for 1970.
(1) The book value of each share of preferred stock is: (a) $100, (b) $104, (c) $108, (d) $112, (e) none of these.
(2) The book value of each share of common stock is: (a) $84, (b) $88, (c) $100, (d) $168, (e) none of these.
(3) If Jane Austen owns 50 shares of the Kant Company's common stock, how many shares does her preemptive right entitle her to purchase of a proposed additional issuance of 600 shares? (a) 0, (b) 30, (c) 50, (d) 100, (e) none of these.

11-4

In no more than 50 words, tell (a) why you would prefer to own some preferred stock (as against common stock) in a company or (b) why you would prefer to own some common stock (as against preferred stock) in the same company.

11-5

The Rembrandt Corporation has issued and has outstanding 1,000 shares of $100 par-value common stock. The stock was sold originally at $110 per share and has a current book value of $120 per share. Two hundred shares were purchased by the corporation at a cost of $105 per share.
(1) If the stock retirement is temporary, under the par method the Treasury Stock account would be debited for an amount equal to 200 times the following figure: (a) 100, (b) 105, (c) 110, (d) 120, (e) none of these.
(2) If the cost basis was used, the Treasury Stock account would be debited

for an amount equal to 200 times the following figure: (a) 100, (b) 105, (c) 110, (d) 120, (e) none of these.

(3) If the stock had been preferred instead of common, and if the 200 shares were to be retired permanently, which of the following accounts would *not* be required to record the retirement? (a) Preferred Stock—Par, (b) Preferred Stock—Premium, (c) Retained Earnings, (d) Capital from Retirement of Stock, (e) Cash.

(4) If 10 shares of $100 par stock had been subscribed at $900 and only half collected before the subscriber defaulted, what would be the number of shares issued to the subscriber if the amount collected is applied in full payment? (a) 3, (b) 4, (c) 5, (d) 8, (e) none of these.

(5) In reference to (4) if the amount collected less loss on sale to another subscriber is to be returned to the defaulting subscriber, which of the following amounts would be returned to the defaulter if the 10 shares are sold at $75 apiece net? (a) $50, (b) $150, (c) $350, (d) $400, (e) none of these.

11-6

In auditing a mining company, you find that authorized capital consists of 3 million shares of $1 par-value stock; all these shares were issued initially in exchange for certain mineral properties which were recorded at an amount equal to twice the par value of the shares issued. Soon thereafter owing to the need of additional working capital, 2 million of the shares were donated to the company and immediately were sold for $3 million cash, resulting in a credit to capital of this amount. What adjustment, if any, would you recommend.

11-7

The summarized position statements of the Benjamin Britten Company and the Owen Wingrave Company as of December 31, 1973, are as follows (000's omitted):

	Britten	Wingrave
Assets	$600	$400
Liabilities	150	100
Capital stock	300	250
Retained earnings	150	50
	$600	$400

(1) If the Britten Company acquired a 90 percent interest in the Wingrave Company on December 31, 1973, for $290,000, and the cost (or legal basis) method of accounting for the investment was used, the amount of the debit to Investment in Stock of the Wingrave Company would have been:

a. $360,000

b. $300,000

c. $290,000

d. $270,000

(2) If the Britten Company acquired an 80 percent interest in the Wingrave Company on December 31, 1973, for $210,000, and the equity (or accrual)

method of accounting for the investment was used, the amount of the debit to Investment in Stock of the Wingrave Company would have been:

a. $320,000
b. $240,000
c. $210,000
d. $200,000

(3) If the Britten Company acquired a 90 percent interest in the Wingrave Company on December 31, 1973, for $270,000, and during 1974 the Wingrave Company had net income of $22,000 and paid a cash dividend of $7,000, applying the cost method would give a debit balance in the Investment in Stock of the Wingrave Company account at the end of 1974 of:

a. $285,000
b. $283,500
c. $276,300
d. $270,000

(4) If the Britten Company acquired a 90 percent interest in the Wingrave Company on December 31, 1973, for $270,000, and during 1974 the Wingrave Company had net income of $30,000 and paid a cash dividend of $15,000, applying the equity method would give a debit balance in the Investment in Stock of the Wingrave Company account at the end of 1974 of:

a. $285,000
b. $283,500
c. $276,300
d. $270,000

11-8

Stock dividends and stock splits are common forms of corporate stock distributions to stockholders. Consider each of the numbered statements. You are to decide whether it applies:

a. To both stock dividends and stock splits
b. To neither
c. To stock splits only
d. To stock dividends only

(In each instance, the issuing company has only one class of stock.)

On an answer sheet, print next to the number of each statement below, the single letter of the description which applies to the statement.

(1) There is no change in the total ownership of the issuing corporation.
(2) The individual stockholder's share of net asset is increased.
(3) Subsequent per-share earnings, if any, are decreased.
(4) The retained earnings available for dividends are increased.
(5) The par (or stated value) of the stock is unchanged.
(6) There is no transfer between retained earnings and capital stock accounts, other than to the extent occasioned by legal requirement.
(7) Retained earnings in the amount of the distribution are transferred to capital stock, in some instances in an amount in excess of that required by the law of the state of incorporation.
(8) The total number of shares outstanding is increased.
(9) The distribution is "income" to the individual stockholder for federal income tax purposes.

(10) The distribution is a multiple as contrasted to a fraction of the number of shares previously outstanding.

11-9   At the regular meeting of the board of directors of the Ryan O'Neal Corporation a dividend payable in the stock of the Leigh Taylor-Young Corporation is to be declared. The stock of the Leigh Taylor-Young Corporation is recorded on the books at cost, $75,000; market value of the stock is $90,000. What should be the amount recorded for the dividend? Discuss the circumstances under which each value of the dividend might be acceptable.

11-10   What would be the journal entries for the following events for: (a) a corporation, 75 percent of whose 500 shares of $10 par-value outstanding stock are owned by Frank H. Knight; (b) Frank H. Knight, a single proprietorship; and (c) Knight & Pawn, a partnership, in which F. H. Knight has an 80 percent equity?

Events
(1) Since the business organization needs additional capital, the owners (owner) contribute $4,500 on a pro-rata basis. (400 shares of stock are issued by the corporation.)
(2) The organization distributes $1,000 of prior years' earnings to the owners (owner) in cash.
(3) The net income before income tax for the current period is $12,000. The appropriate tax rates are: Corporation, 25 percent; Mr. Knight, 24 percent; and Mr. Pawn, 22 percent; close books.

11-11   Select one correct answer for each of the following multiple choice questions:
(1) The position of the owner in a single proprietorship with respect to income and personal liability for creditors suggests the _____ theory.
   a. Proprietary
   b. Entity
   c. Commander
   d. Fund
   e. None of the above
(2) If a partnership is similar to a single proprietorship with respect to income and personal liability for creditors, the theory emphasized is:
   a. Proprietary
   b. Entity
   c. Commander
   d. Fund
   e. None of the above
(3) If the partnership is considered separate from the partners to the extent that partnership property is considered owned by the partnership, not by the partners, the relevant theory is:
   a. Proprietary
   b. Entity
   c. Commander
   d. Fund

e. None of the above
(4) In a corporation, creditors often have a greater interest than the legal owners; this is in line with the _____ theory.
   a. Proprietary
   b. Entity
   c. Commander
   d. Fund
   e. None of the above
(5) If the separate concept of the economic unit is emphasized in presenting consolidated statements, the relevant theory is:
   a. Proprietary
   b. Entity
   c. Commander
   d. Fund
   e. None of the above

11-12   Select one correct answer for each of the following multiple choice questions:
(1) Which of the following statements is not a limitation of consolidated statements:
   a. Minority stockholders generally can obtain very little information such as details of assets, liabilities, and income of subsidiary.
   b. Liens on assets that affect the rights of creditors are often difficult to show or explain by footnote.
   c. Since a consolidated statement is a composite, the weak position of one company may offset a strong position of another.
   d. Consolidated statements imply the integration of the activities of two corporations into one economic unit, one business enterprise.
   e. Although the combined assets reported on a consolidated position statement may be a measure of moral ability to pay, the consolidated assets are not legally available (unless specified by agreement) to meet creditor claims of a specific company in the group.
(2) The decision to prepare consolidated statements would not depend upon which of the following criteria:
   a. Freedom from international restrictions.
   b. Similarity of treatment of parent and subsidiary records and statements.
   c. Controlling influence must be present, continuing, and assured.
   d. The percent of stock ownership, particularly a minimum percentage of voting stock ownership.
   e. Similarity of operations and/or related industries to form an integrated unit.
(3) When the book value of the investment account on the books of a holding company is less than the book value of the underlying net assets, the following is not a possible explanation:
   a. Certain assets of the subsidiary are overvalued.
   b. The subsidiary's assets in general are overvalued.
   c. A "fortunate purchase" has occurred; the acquisition has been made at less than true value.

    d. If an exchange of stock has occurred, it may be that a premium received for the stock of the parent company has not been recorded.

    e. All the above are possible explanations.

Problems

11-1

Tony Randall incurred the following transactions in stock of the Klugman Corporation:

(1) January 7, 1972: Purchased 200 shares of $10 par-value common stock at $110 per share.

(2) The corporation was expanding, and as of March 1, 1973 issued to Mr. Randall 200 rights each, permitting him to purchase one-fourth share of common stock at par. No entry was made. The bid price of the stock on March 1, 1973 was 140. There was no quoted price for the right.

(3) Mr. Randall was advised that he would "lose" on his other stock if he did not acquire stock with the rights. He therefore paid $5,000 for the new shares on April 1, 1973, charging the payment to his Investment account. Since he felt that he had been assessed by the company he credited the cash dividends (10 percent in December of each year) to the Investment account until the debit was fully offset.

(4) In December 1974 Mr. Randall received a 50 percent stock dividend from the company. He made no entry for this dividend because he expected to sell the share in January 1975. He credited Revenue for the proceeds.

(5) In December 1975 the stock was split on a two-for-one basis, and the new shares were issued as no-par shares. Mr. Randall found that each new share was worth $5 more than the $110 per share which he paid for his original stock. He debited the Investment account with the additional shares received at $110 per share and credited Revenue.

(6) In June 1976 Mr. Randall sold one-half of his stock at $92 per share. He credited the proceeds to the Investment account.

a. Reproduce the Investment account as it was kept by Mr. Randall in T account form.

b. Prepare the Investment account as it should have been kept by Mr. Randall in T account form.

c. Prepare any necessary adjusting entries.

11-2

	A	B
	(000's omitted)	
Current assets	$ 560	$350
Investment in B bonds (60%)	60	
Investment in B stock (80%)	120	
Plant	260	150
	$1,000	$500

	A	B
		(000's omitted)
Current liabilities	$270	$200
Bonds payable	400	100
Capital stock	200	100
Retained earnings restricted for contingencies		65
Retained earnings	130	35
	$1,000	$500

A purchased 80 percent of the stock of B when B's ownership was $110.
B owes A $30 on open account.
(1) The total assets on the consolidated position statement will be _____.
(2) Goodwill on the consolidated position statement will be _____.
(3) Minority interest on the consolidated position statement will be _____.
(4) Total retained earnings on the consolidated position statement will be

_____.

(5) Total ownership on the consolidated position statement will be _____.

11–3

Following are three different sets of unrelated facts. From the facts stated
in each set you are to answer the two questions that follow it (000's omitted).

(1)	Co. P	Co. S-1	Co. S-2	Consolidated
Investment in S-1	$ 42			
Investment in S-2	270			
Minority interest				$48.8
Capital stock	650	$56	$300	
Retained earnings	95	12	18	

Co. P purchased its interest in Co. S-2 at par when S-2 was organized.
What is Co. P's percentage of ownership in Co. S-1? _____
What is Co. P's percentage of ownership in Co. S-2? _____

(2)	Co. P	Co. S (90%)	Consolidated
Retained earnings	$100	$36	$136

What is the amount of the change in retained earnings of Co. S since acquisition by P? _____
What was the amount of the retained earnings of Co. S at acquisition by
P? _____
(3) Given the following information:

Sales:	
Parent	$1,200.0
Subsidiary A	140.0
Subsidiary B	600.0
Consolidated	1,720.0
Current liabilities:	
Parent	116.0
Subsidiary A	21.0
Subsidiary B	24.0
Consolidated	151.5

The intercompany sales are _____ .
The intercompany liabilities are _____ .

11–4

Prepare journal entries where needed to record the following transactions.
1. The Mick Jagger Corporation receives its charter from the state with the following authorized capital:
   1,000 shares, 6 percent preferred stock, $100 par
   10,000 shares class A common, $10 par
   10,000 shares class B common, no par; to share equally with class A in dividends, convertible to A at 1 for 1
2. Brian Jones acquires 500 shares of class A stock in exchange for Cash $500, Building $3,000, Land $1,000, and Equipment $500.
3. Keith Richard, Mick Jagger, and Charlie Watts each receive 2,000 shares of class B stock for cash of $0.25 a share. The stated value per share is $0.10 per share.
4. Charlie Watts receives 10 shares of class A for organization costs incurred by him.
5. Brian Jones subscribes to 100 shares of class A, paying $100 down.
6. Bill Wyman buys 10 shares of class A and subscribes to 80 shares at par.
7. The first year's business shows a net income of $100,000.
8. The corporation declares and pays a dividend of $1.00 on common stock outstanding.
9. Bill Wyman buys 500 shares of preferred at $110 for cash.
10. The corporation pays stock bonus to Mick Jagger and Watts of 200 shares each.
11. One-tenth of the outstanding class B stock is converted into class A stock for $25 per share.

11–5

A corporation was authorized by its charter to issue 20,000 shares of common stock at a par of $30 per share. Record the following transactions in the company's stock in general journal form:
(1) 7,000 shares are subscribed for at $35; 40 percent of the subscription price was collected in cash at the time when the subscriptions were received. However, none of the 7,000 shares was fully paid for.
(2) $47,000 is received from the subscribers, and 2,500 shares of the 7,000 subscribed are now fully paid. The fully paid shares are issued.

(3) One subscriber defaulted on 220 shares; he has paid $75 in cash to the corporation.

(4) The company reacquired 65 shares issued in (2). The shares were reacquired for $1,800. Use cost method.

11-6

The position statement of a corporation which closes its books annually on December 31 is given below.

Jacques Brel
Balance Sheet
December 31, 1972
(000's omitted)

Cash	$ 200	*Preferred dividend payable*	$ 3
Other	788	*Common dividend payable*	6
Organization costs	12	*Other payables*	191
		6% preferred stock	200
		Common stock (6,000 shares)	300
		Common stock—premium	100
		Retained earnings	200
	$1,000		$1,000

(1) Prepare the entry for the declaration of the dividends shown on the position statement.

(2) Assuming that equal common dividends were declared quarterly, give the amount of dividends declared on each share during the year.

11-7

A corporation purchased 200 shares of its own common stock ($50 par value) on the open market at $80 a share.

	Debit	Credit
Treasury stock	$16,000	
Cash in bank		$16,000

Later in the same year it sold 100 shares at $100 a share and canceled the other 100 shares. The common stock was initially issued at $75 a share.

(1) Record the sale and cancellation of the shares.

(2) Record the purchase, sale, and cancellation by two other methods, identifying each method.

11-8

Indicate the section of the financial statements in which each of the following items should appear.

a. Current assets
b. Noncurrent assets
c. Current liabilities
d. Noncurrent liabilities
e. Ownership—capital stock

f. Ownership—retained earnings
g. Revenues
h. Expenses, losses, and other income statement deductions

(1) Capital stock subscribed
(2) Appropriation for expansion
(3) Interest payable
(4) Capital stock—premium
(5) Goodwill
(6) Union dues withheld
(7) Bonds payable—discount
(8) Treasury stock
(9) Accumulated deficit
(10) Restricted for contingencies
(11) Bonds payable—premium

(12) Retained earnings
(13) Dividends payable
(14) Buildings—accumulated depreciation
(15) Bond sinking fund
(16) Capital stock—discount
(17) Advances to salesmen
(18) Income taxes
(19) Stock subscriptions receivable
(20) Capital from defaulted subscriber

11-9

Following are ten transactions which are to be analyzed in terms of their net effect on the company's position statement equation as it is given on the form below (which should be reproduced in your solution). Use I for increase, D for decrease, and NC for no change. Each transaction is unrelated to every other transaction unless a definite relationship is stated.

Transactions:
(1) Common stock is subscribed at more than par (analyze on the books of the issuing company).
(2) The company sells its own bonds at a discount.
(3) Half of the subscriptions in (1) above are paid in full.
(4) The stock fully paid for in (3) above is issued.
(5) The annual payment is made to the trustee of the bond sinking fund.
(6) A cash dividend is declared.
(7) The cash dividend declared in (6) above is paid.
(8) Retained earnings are restricted for the future retirement of bonds.
(9) The sinking-fund trustee notifies the company of the sinking-fund revenue for the period.
(10) A stock dividend is declared.

Format for solution:

	CA	OA	TA	CL	OL	TL	CS	URE	ARE	TO
1										
2										
3										
4										
5										
6										
7										
8										
9										
10										

Code:

CA	Current assets	TL	Total liabilities
OA	Other assets	CS	Capital stock
TA	Total assets	URE	Unappropriated retained earnings
CL	Current liabilities	ARE	Appropriated retained earnings
OL	Other liabilities	TO	Total ownership

11-10   For each of the following numbered items, select the lettered item that indicates its effect on a corporation's statements. Indicate your choice by listing the appropriate letter for each item, followed by a brief explanatory statement. If more than one effect is applicable to a particular item, be sure to list all applicable letters. (Assume that the state statutes do not permit declaration of nonliquidating dividends except from earnings.)

Item

(1) Declaration of a cash dividend in one month on noncumulative preferred stock
(2) Declaration and issuance of a common stock dividend
(3) Receipt of a cash dividend, not previously recorded, on stock of another corporation
(4) Not declaring dividend on cumulative preferred stock at dividend declaration date
(5) Receipt of common shares as a dividend on common shares held as a temporary investment
(6) Payment of dividend mentioned in (1)
(7) Issue of new common shares in a 5-for-1 stock split
(8) Purchase of treasury stock at a market price in excess of *book value* of common stock

Effect

(a) Reduces working capital
(b) Increases working capital
(c) Reduces the dollar amount of total capital stock
(d) Increases the dollar amount of total capital stock
(e) Reduces total retained earnings
(f) Increases total retained earnings
(g) Reduces equity per share of common stock
(h) Reduces equity of each common stockholder

11-11   Indicate the treatment, if any, which should be given to each of the following items in computing earnings per share of common stock for financial statement reporting:

(1) A provision created out of retained earnings for a contingent liability from a possible lawsuit.
(2) The declaration of current dividends on cumulative preferred stock.
(3) The acquisition of some of the company's outstanding common stock during the current fiscal year. The stock was classified as treasury stock.
(4) A 2-for-1 stock split of common stock during the current year.
(5) The exercise at a price below market price but above book value of a

common stock option issued during the current fiscal year to company officers.

11-12   Each of the numbered items below is a description of a transaction or transactions. Each item is unrelated to the others. Analyze these transactions, and prepare journal entries to record them.

(1) The Matson Corporation was organized on January 1 with authorized capital stock of 1,000 shares, par value $100 per share.

On February 1, 800 shares were subscribed for $110 per share.

On February 2, 100 shares were issued to Mr. M. Lloyd in payment for a patent.

On March 1, the subscribers paid cash for one-half their subscriptions. On April 1, the remaining half of the subscriptions were paid for, and the stock was issued.

(2) The Ables Corporation was organized on January 1 with authorized capital stock of 10,000 no-par-value shares.

On February 1, 8,000 shares were sold for $80,000. An additional 1,000 shares were issued to the founder, Mr. Thomas Ables, for his efforts in organizing the corporation.

(3) The Leavitt Corporation was organized on January 1 with authorized capital stock of 20,000 shares of no-par-value stock. The stock had a stated value of $10 a share.

On February 1, 10,000 shares were sold for $120,000 and 5,000 shares were issued to Mr. L. Leavitt in payment for a building taken over by the new corporation.

(4) The ownership section of the position statement of the Gutter Corporation on December 31, 1972 was as follows:

Preferred stock (10,000 shares, par value $100 per share)	$ 1,000,000
Common stock (1,000,000 shares, no-par value, issued and	
outstanding)	5,000,000
Retained earnings	4,000,000
Total ownership	$10,000,000

The board of directors took the following action:

On December 31, 1972:

a. A 3-for-1 split of common stock was declared.

b. 5,000 shares of outstanding preferred stock were purchased at $120 per share.

On January 1, 1973:

c. The preferred dividend of 6 percent was declared.

d. A cash dividend of $0.10 per share on common stock was declared.

e. A stock dividend of one-tenth of a share was declared on common stock.

On February 1, 1973:

f. The dividends declared in January were paid.

11-13   On January 1, 1973, the partnership of Fetters and Nelson was reorganized as the Nelers Corporation. The accounts of the Fetters and Nelson partnership as of December 31, 1972, showed the following balances:

Cash	$ 5,420	Plant—accumulated	
Accounts receivables	9,932	depreciation	$15,700
Inventory	16,985	Payables	14,946
Plant	24,398	Fetters, capital	10,385
	$56,735	Nelson, capital	15,704
			$56,735

The authorized capital stock of the new corporation was 40,000 shares of $1 par value. The partners agreed to accept the stock at par value in payment for their interest in the partnership.
a. Make the journal entries to close out the partnership books.
b. Make the journal entries to open the books of the new corporation.

11–14 In the following accounts, identify for each numbered amount the other account (accounts) that would have been used to record these transactions. (NOTE: These accounts are not necessarily all kept by the same company. When two answers are required for the same figure, each answer should represent a distinctly different type of transaction or treatment of a transaction. All transactions in any single account are for one accounting period. For each figure, the 000's are omitted.)

Example:

Subscriptions Receivable

(A)	10	(B)	10

(A) Capital Stock Subscribed
(B) Cash

Capital Stock—Discount

✔	0.5	(1)	0.5
		or	
		(2)	

(1) _____
(2) _____

Common Stock Subscribed—Premium

(3)	1	✔	1
or			
(4)			

(3) _____
(4) _____

Notes Payable—Premium

(5)	2		
(6)	1	(7)	3
	3		3

(5) _____
(6) _____
(7) _____

Lease Liability

	(8) 2

(8) _____
(9) _____
(10) _____
(11) _____

Retained Earnings

(9)	5	✔	10
(10)	7	(14)	40
(11)	6	(15)	6
(12)	10	(16)	4
(13)	10		

(12) _____
(13) _____
(14) _____
(15) _____
(16) _____

Retained Earnings—
Appropriation for
Fire Loss

(17)	50	(18)	50

(17) _____
(18) _____

Deferred Executive
Compensation—
Stock Option

(19)	10	(20)	10

(19) _____
(20) _____

Notes Receivable—
Discounted

(21)	1	(23)	1
or			
(22)			

(21) _____
(22) _____
(23) _____

Treasury Stock—Par

(24)	8	(25)	8
or			
(26)			

(24) _____
(25) _____
(26) _____

Stock Dividends Declared

(27)	1	(28)	1

(27) _____
(28) _____

Unrealized Appreciation

(29)	5	✔	100

(29) _____

Income Summary

(30)*	50	(34)	70
(31)*	15		
(32)*	2		
(33)*	3		
	70		70

(30) _____
(31) _____
(32) _____
(33) _____
(34) _____

Each represents a control account for a business function.

Retained Earnings—
Appropriation for
Bond Sinking Fund

(35)	100	✔	90
or			
(36)		(37)	100

(35) _____
(36) _____
(37) _____

Retained Earnings—
Appropriation for
Additional Plant

(38)	100	✔	100
or			
(39)			

(38) _____
(39) _____

Paid in Capital
from Expired Rights

	(40)	5

(40) _____

Capital from Stock
Subscriptions

	(41)	1

(41) _____

Bonds Payable—Discount

✔	10	(42)	1

(42) _____

Capital Stock—Unissued

(43)	10	(44)	10

(43) _____
(44) _____

Treasury Stock—Cost

(45)	0.5	(46)	0.5

(45) _____
(46) _____

Capital Stock—$100 Par

(47)	100	✔	100	(47)

Paid-in Capital from
Lapse of Stock Options

	(48)	0.3	(48)

Paid-in Capital Arising
from Treasury Stock

	(49)	0.3	(49)

H. R. Hatfield, Drawing

(50)	1	✔	1	(50)

11–15   From the following data at December 31, 1971 (000's omitted), prepare a consolidated position statement for the Hair Manufacturing Corporation and its subsidiary, the Hair Sales Corporation.

	Manufacturing Corporation	*Sales Corporation*
Current assets	$150	$110
Investment in stock of Sales Corporation	115	
Plant (net)	100	70
	$365	$180
Current liabilities	$ 60	$ 45
Capital stock	250	120
Retained earnings	55	15
	$365	$180

Hair Manufacturing Corporation accounts for its 90 percent interest in Hair Sales Corporation on a cost (legal basis). At the time when the stock was purchased, the stockholders' equity accounts of Hair Sales Corporation were as follows (000's omitted):

Capital stock	$120
Retained earnings	5
	$125

11–16   Use the position statements given in Prob. 11–15 to prepare a consolidated position statement at December 31, 1971, for Hair Manufacturing Corporation and its subsidiary, but assume that Hair Manufacturing's investment account for the 90 percent interest in Hair Sales Corporation is maintained in the equity basis (i.e., that the $115 investment account reflects not only the initial investment but also any changes since then in the stockholders' equity of the subsidiary).

11–17   Use the following data at January 31, 1972 (000's omitted), to prepare a consolidated position statement for the Roman Company and its subsidiary, the Polanski Company.

	Roman Company	Polanski Company
Current assets	$500	$225
Advances to Polanski Company	50	
Investment in stock of Polanski Co.	175	
Plant (net)	210	195
	$935	$420
Current liabilities	$240	$ 95
Advances by Roman Company		50
Capital stock	560	200
Retained earnings	135	75
	$935	$420

Roman accounts for its 85 percent interest in Polanski on a cost (legal) basis. At the time when the stock was purchased, the Polanski stockholders' equity accounts were as follows (000's omitted):

Capital stock	$200
Retained earnings	0
	$200

11–18   Prepare a consolidated position statement at January 31, 1972, for the Roman Company and its subsidiary, but assume that Roman's 85 percent interest in Polanski is accounted for on the equity basis (i.e., that the $175 investment account reflects not only the initial investment but also any changes since then in the stockholders' equity of the subsidiary).

11–19   From the following information for Robert Company and its subsidiary, Redford Company (000's omitted), prepare a consolidated position statement at March 31, 1972, and a consolidated income statement for the year ended March 31, 1972.

	Robert Company	Redford Company
Current assets	$ 300	$ 245
Investment in stock of Redford Company	310	
Plant (net)	185	95
	$ 795	$ 340
Current liabilities	$ 125	$ 85
Capital stock	540	190
Retained earnings	130	65
	$ 795	$ 340
Sales	$1,200	$ 720
Dividend revenue	9	
Cost of goods sold	(920)	(540)
Other expenses	(244)	(155)
Dividends declared	(25)	(10)
Retained earnings, April 1, 1971	110	50
Retained earnings, March 31, 1972	$ 130	$ 65

Additional information is available as follows:

(1) The Robert Company maintains the account for its 90 percent investment in Redford on the cost (legal) basis. At the time when the shares were purchased, the stockholders' equity accounts of Redford had the following balances (000's omitted):

Capital stock	$190
Retained	20
	$210

(2) During the year Redford sold to Robert for $200 merchandise that cost $170.

(3) At March 31, 1972, Redford had $25 due on its Account Receivable from Robert.

11–20   Use the financial data given in Prob. 11–19 to prepare a consolidated position statement at March 31, 1972, and a consolidated income statement for the year ended March 31, 1972, for Robert Company and its subsidiary; but assume that Robert's 90 percent interest in Redford is accounted for on the equity basis (i.e., that the $310 investment account reflects not only the initial investment but also any changes since then in the stockholders' equity of Redford).

11–21   Prepare a consolidated position statement at May 31, 1972, and a consolidated income statement for the year ended May 31, 1972, from the following information (000's omitted) for the McLuhan Company and its subsidiary, the Bernstein Company.

	McLuhan Company		Bernstein Company	
	Debit	*Credit*	*Debit*	*Credit*
Accounts receivable	$ 53		$ 37	
Inventories	207		118	
Other current assets	215		159	
Investment in stock of Bernstein Company	260			
Plant assets (net)	275		166	
Accounts payable		$ 47		$ 28
Other current liabilities		173		42
Common stock		520		240
Common stock—premium		135		90
Retained earnings, June 1, 1971		95		65
Sales		1,850		975
Dividend revenue		14		
Cost of goods sold	1,200		675	
Other expenses	589		265	
Dividends declared	35		20	
	$2,834	$2,834	$1,440	$1,440

Additional information:

(1) McLuhan Company accounts for its 70 percent interest in Bernstein on a cost (legal) basis. When the interest was purchased, the stockholders' equity accounts of Bernstein were as follows (000's omitted):

Common stock	$240
Premium on common stock	90
Retained earnings	100
	$430

(2) During the year, Bernstein sold to McLuhan for $250 merchandise costing $200.

(3) At May 31, 1972, McLuhan had not paid $30 of the amount due Bernstein.

(4) At June 1, 1971, McLuhan had in its inventory merchandise which it had purchased from Bernstein for $25, but which had cost Bernstein $20. At May 31, 1972, McLuhan had in its inventory merchandise which it had purchased from Bernstein for $40, but which had cost Bernstein $32.

11–22   Using the data given in Prob. 11–21, prepare a consolidated position statement at May 31, 1972, and a consolidated income statement for the year ended May 31, 1972, for the McLuhan Company and its subsidiary; but assume that McLuhan's 70 percent interest in Bernstein is accounted for in the equity basis (i.e., that the Investment account reflects not only the initial investment but also any changes since then in Bernstein's stockholders' equity).

11–23   Select the best answers for each of the following 24 questions. There may be more than one correct answer for each item.

(1) Goodwill should be written off:

    a. As soon as possible against retained earnings

    b. As soon as possible as an extraordinary item

    c. By systematic charges against retained earnings over the period benefited, but not more than 40 years

    d. By systematic charges to expense over the period benefited, but not more than 40 years

(2) If goodwill arising from the consolidation appears among the assets on the consolidated position statement of a parent company and its only subsidiary, this indicates that the subsidiary:

    a. Was acquired at a price that was less than the underlying book value of its tangible assets

    b. Was accounted for as a pooling of interests

    c. Already had goodwill on its books

    d. Was acquired at a price in excess of the underlying book value of its tangible assets

(3) A manufacturing corporation issued bonds with a maturity amount of $200,000 and a maturity 10 years from date of issue. If the bonds were issued at a premium, this indicates that:

    a. The yield (effective or market) rate of interest exceeded the nominal (coupon) rate

    b. The nominal rate of interest exceeded the yield rate

    c. The yield and nominal rates coincided

    d. No necessary relationship exists between the two rates

(4) Assuming that the ideal measure of short-term receivables in the position statement is the discounted value of the cash to be received in the future, failure to follow this practice usually does not make the position statement misleading because:

    a. Most short-term receivables are not interest-bearing

    b. The allowance for uncollectible accounts includes a discount element

    c. The amount of the discount is not material

    d. Most receivables can be sold to a bank

(5) Consolidated statements are used to present the result of operations and the financial position of:

    a. A company and its branches

    b. A company and its subcontractors

    c. A company and its subsidiaries

    d. Any group of companies with related interests

    e. None of the above

(6) Consolidated statements are intended, primarily, for the benefit of:

    a. Stockholders of the parent company

    b. Taxing authorities

    c. Management of the parent company

    d. Creditors of the parent company

    e. None of the above

(7) A consolidated statement for X, Y, and Z is proper if:

    a. X owns 100 percent of the outstanding common stock of Y and 40 percent of Z; Q owns 51 percent of Z

    b. X owns 100 percent of the outstanding stock of Y; Y owns 75 percent of Z

    c. X owns 100 percent of the outstanding stock of Y and 75 percent of Z. X bought the stock of Z one month before the statement date, and sold it six weeks later

    d. There is no interrelation of financial control among X, Y, and Z. However, they are contemplating the joint purchase of 100 percent of the outstanding common stock of W

    e. X owns 100 percent of the outstanding common stock of Y and Z. Z is in bankruptcy

(8) H is the parent company of companies J and K; K would not be considered a consolidated subsidiary in the proposed consolidated statement of H, J, and K if:

    a. H and J manufacture electronic equipment; K manufactures ball bearings

    b. H and J manufacture ball-point pens; K is a bank

    c. K has assets of $1,000,000 and an outstanding bond issue of $750,000; H holds the bonds

    d. Same as (c), except that outsiders hold the bonds.

    e. None of the above

(9) Parent company P has a fiscal year ending June 30, 1972. Subsidiary S's fiscal year ends May 31, 1972. Therefore:

    a. A consolidated statement cannot properly be prepared for P and S

    b. S's May 31, 1972 statement can be used for consolidation with P's June 30, 1972 statement provided disclosure (or some recognition) is made of any June event which materially affected S

    c. If the consolidated statement is permissible, it will be dated June 30, 1972

    d. If the consolidated statement is permissible, it will be dated May 31, 1972

    e. None of the above

(10) In preparing consolidated statements, elimination is necessary for:

    a. Net (intercompany) income or loss on assets remaining within the group

    b. Gross (intercompany) income or loss on assets remaining within the group

    c. Net (intercompany) income or loss on transactions with subsidiaries not consolidated, the investment being carried at cost

    d. Gross (intercompany) income or loss on transactions with subsidiaries not consolidated, the investment being carried at cost

    e. None of the above

(11) P owns 90 percent of the stock of S. W owns 10 percent of S's stock. In relation to P, W is considered as:

a. An affiliate
b. A subsidiary not to be consolidated
c. A minority interest
d. A holding company
e. None of the above

(12) The cost of a parent company's investment in a subsidiary exceeded its equity in the book value of the subsidiary's net assets at the acquisition date. The parent company made the investment because of the subsidiary's ownership of valuable patents which were carried on its books at net cost, $1,000. In the consolidated statements, the excess of the parent's cost over its equity in the book value of the subsidiary's net assets should be shown as:
a. An increase in patents
b. Goodwill
c. Excess of book value over purchase price
d. Capital from consolidation
e. None of the above

(13) P's cost of investment in M exceeded its equity in the book value of M's net assets at the acquisition date. The excess is not attributable to specific assets. In the consolidated statements, this excess should be:
a. Eliminated
b. Allocated proportionately to the subsidiary's fixed assets
c. Shown on the balance sheet as excess of cost of stock of subsidiary over book value
d. None of the above

(14) P's cost of investment in J was less than its equity in the book value of J's net assets at the acquisition date. The difference is related to the decline in value of J's machinery. This difference should be shown on the consolidated balance sheet as:
a. A reduction in machinery
b. Capital in excess of par
c. Capital from consolidation
d. Excess of book value over purchase price
e. None of the above

(15) Company P purchased the outstanding common stock of S as follows:
10 percent, January 2, 1972
25 percent, June 1, 1972
25 percent, August 1, 1972
40 percent, September 30, 1972
The fiscal year of each of the companies ends on September 30. S's stock was acquired by P at book value. Consolidated net income for the fiscal year ended September 30, 1972 would include the following earnings of the subsidiary:
a. 10 percent of earnings, January to May, 1972
b. 35 percent of earnings, June to July, 1972
c. 60 percent of earnings, August to September, 1972
d. 60 percent of earnings, January to September, 1972
e. None of the above

(16) Company P had 300,000 shares of stock outstanding. It owned 75 percent of the outstanding stock of T. T owned 20,000 shares of P's stock. In the consolidated balance sheet, Company P's outstanding stock may be shown as:
 a. 280,000 shares
 b. 300,000 shares less 20,000 shares of treasury stock
 c. 300,000 shares
 d. 300,000 shares footnoted to indicate that T holds 20,000 shares
 e. None of the above

(17) Company P and its subsidiary S filed separate income tax returns. P's tax included $70,000 attributable to profits on sales to S. In preparing consolidated financial statements:
 a. The entire intercompany profit should be eliminated; taxes need not be adjusted
 b. Taxes of $70,000 should be deferred
 c. The intercompany profit should be reduced by $70,000 before elimination, and taxes of $70,000 should be deferred
 d. Income taxes should be recomputed, and a revised return should be filed
 e. None of the above

(18) Combined financial statements are justified for the following:
 a. A group of subsidiaries not consolidated
 b. Corporations engaged in similar or related operations, owned by the same (individual) stockholder
 c. A group of companies under common management
 d. Any group of companies with related interests
 e. None of the above

(19) The preferable method of presenting subsidiaries not consolidated in financial statements is:
 a. At market value, adjusted through income
 b. At market value, adjusted through retained earnings
 c. At cost, plus the parent's share of the subsidiaries' net income (or minus the net loss), since acquisition, adjusted annually through income
 d. At cost, plus the parent's share of the subsidiaries' net income (or minus the net loss), adjusted annually through retained earnings
 e. At consolidated group's equity in net realizable value of assets of subsidiaries not consolidated

(20) It is acceptable accounting treatment to carry investments in subsidiaries not consolidated at cost:
 a. Under no circumstances
 b. With dividends included in income as received
 c. Less provision for any permanent material impairment of the investment
 d. If there is disclosure, by footnote or otherwise, of the equity of the consolidated group in the net assets of subsidiaries not consolidated
 e. None of the above

(21) "Negative goodwill" is:

a. Not acceptable terminology for statement purposes
b. Subtracted from goodwill, if any, for statement purposes
c. Synonymous with capital from consolidation
d. Also known as excess of book value over purchase price
e. None of the above

(22) Company P owns 75 percent of the outstanding common stock of S. During 1960, P's profits on its transactions with S amounted to $50,000. The elimination for intercompany profit is:
a. Not necessary
b. $50,000
c. $37,500
d. Allocated between Company P and the minority stockholders
e. None of the above

(23) P and its subsidiaries, T and V, have issued combined statements for a number of years. In connection with a proposed bank loan, P has been requested to present a statement to the bank which will indicate P's financial position at December 31, 1972. The following will supply the desired information:
a. A copy of the consolidated statement at December 31, 1972
b. A copy of P's financial statement at December 31, 1972 on which the investments in T and V are reported at the current carrying value
c. A copy of the consolidated statement and of the separate parent company (P) statement, both at December 31, 1972
d. A copy of the consolidated statement at December 31, 1972 modified so that one column is used for P and other columns for T and V
e. A copy of separate financial statements of P, T, and V as of December 31, 1972

(24) The stockholders of S sold all its common stock, 1,000 shares, to Company P, receiving in return 5,000 shares of Company P stock. On the day before the sale, P stock sold for $40 per share; S stock sold for $195 per share. P stock has a par value of $20 per share. S stock has a par value of $50 per share. The investment by P may be recorded on its books at:
a. $200,000, only
b. $195,000, only
c. $100,000
d. $50,000
e. Either $200,000 or $195,000

11-24   During the fiscal year ended June 30, 1971, Ayrshire Collieries declared and distributed a stock dividend. Using the Retained Earnings Statement below,

(1) Recreate the journal entry(ies) recorded by Ayrshire to reflect the stock dividend in its accounts. Explain the calculation of each amount.

(2) During each of the preceding six years (1965 to 1970, inclusive) Ayrshire declared and distributed stock dividends. Ayrshire had about 566,620 ($3 par value) shares issued and outstanding at the beginning of the

1965 fiscal year. If, instead of declaring stock dividends annually, Ayr-shire had declared a single 3-for-2 stock split during the 1965 fiscal year, explain or demonstrate (for example, by journal entries) one way in which the stock split might have been accounted for.

Ayrshire Collieries Corporation and Subsidiaries* Retained Earnings Statement for the Year Ended June 30, 1971 (000's omitted)

	Retained Earnings	Paid-in Capital
Balance, June 30, 1970	$24,856	$7,250
Net income, after deducting provision for price-level depreciation	2,846	
	$27,702	
Deduct:		
Cash dividends, $1.00 per share	758	
2% stock dividend, 14,913 shares:		
Par value	45	
Assigned value in excess of par value	750	750†
Cash-fractional shares	12	
Provision for loss on Thunderbird operating property (credited to accumulated depreciation and depletion)	5,000	
	$ 6,565	
Balance, June 30, 1971	$21,137	$8,000

*Other statements are given in Problem 9–21.
†Denotes credit.

12 Auditors, Analysts, and Others

By the end of the 1970s, accounting will be better. Better because we will have more reliable valuation techniques and more knowledge about the ways people use accounting data, but better also because widespread pressures for improvement are certain to be felt.*
SIDNEY DAVIDSON, 1969

In this concluding chapter we shall discuss the following subjects: (1) the role of the auditor and the consequences of the audit and the attest function including the development of "generally accepted accounting principles," (2) the analysis and interpretation of financial data by analysts with special attention to ratio analysis, (3) the uses and usefulness of accounting to external users of financial statements, and (4) the improvements in accounting that might be anticipated during the next decade, given the constraints on accounting due to the "state of the arts."

The Auditor, Audit Reports, and the Attest Function

When an accounting statement is published for external use, it usually is accompanied by a signed auditor's report. As explained in Chapter 1, almost all publicly owned enterprises either voluntarily or involuntarily provide audit opinions with their financial statements. Those concerns that do not now furnish audited statements are under considerable pressure to do so. These reports signify that a CPA, a licensed professional accountant, has examined the statements. The process culminating in the formal authentication of the statements by the auditor is called *attesting;* the CPA's *attest function*

*From "Accounting and Financial Reporting in the Seventies," *The Arthur Young Journal,* 75th Anniversary Edition, Spring–Summer 1969, p. 103.

is his expression of an objective statement of fact or opinion, usually regarding a set of financial statements. The public accountant furnishes this report after he has performed an audit.

In making an examination of the company, usually an annual one, the auditor must satisfy himself that the following specific objectives have been accomplished with respect to the financial statements.

1. No material asset, liability, or ownership item is omitted.
2. No false or untrue statement and no false or untrue item appear in any statement.
3. No material fact is included or omitted which would cause the statements to be misleading.
4. The assets shown at the date of the position statement are owned and the liabilities are amounts actually owing (or contingently owing, in the case of contingent liabilities).
5. The nature, classification, and amounts of capital stock are listed properly.
6. Capital resulting from amounts paid in excess of par or stated values or from net income is classified properly, showing the amount applicable to each class.
7. The income statement reflects fairly the operating results for the audit period.

The auditor begins an audit by planning an audit program or a schedule of audit procedures. The audit program enables the auditor to anticipate the time and assistance needed. With it, he can coordinate the audit and assign tasks to his junior auditors more effectively. The essence of an audit program is a master list of audit procedures which facilitate the audit. Such a program is subject to constant revision as the audit proceeds, based on the examinations of the records. When the audit is completed and the auditor's report written, only then is the audit program in its final form.

Usually accounts are not audited individually; instead, the auditor investigates the various areas of functional activity of the enterprise. The interrelationships among accounts means that one cannot audit as a practical matter any single kind of account without recognizing its effects upon other accounts. For example, accounts receivable is related not only to the revenue account but also to the cash and inventories accounts.

Early in the audit, an evaluation of the firm's internal controls must be made in order to determine the degree of reliability that may be placed upon the company's financial statements. Since it is impractical and often impossible to examine and review all accounting records of the firm, the auditor must judge the extent to which he must test and sample the different kinds of accounting records. The development of scientific sampling methods should improve the basis of determining the degree of testing required.

In carrying out an audit program, the auditor devotes the major part of his attention to an analysis of the company's accounting records. The company's employees may assist in the clerical aspects of this analysis; however, the auditor must closely supervise such activity and must independently verify the changes and the balances of the accounts. The quality of the company's internal controls may minimize the attention he must give to verifying the accuracy of the accounts. In undertaking this internal analysis, the auditor expects to find a good audit trail. An audit trail includes the reference and/or basic documents which accompany and support a transaction entry or posting to source records and documents. Where the trail is satisfactory, the auditor can readily trace transactions to the original documents and their inception.

In addition to making an internal analysis, the auditor also conducts inspections, communicates with those who have dealt with the enterprise, and reviews his findings. His inspections are coordinated with the enterprise's operations and with the auditing analysis. Typical audit inspections (or steps) to verify that the enterprise actually has the assets shown in its accounts include: (1) counting the cash on hand and inspecting the securities held by the client; (2) observing the taking of physical inventories by the employees; (3) inspecting plant assets and enterprise properties.

In forming his independent judgment on the firm's financial statements, direct communications with third parties are most helpful and are undertaken only with the client's permission. The evidence produced from such communications aids in confirming the client's records. Typically, information or confirmations are requested from: (1) banks (to verify the balances of cash on deposit with the bank and the balances of notes owing to the bank); (2) charge customers (to verify the balances of accounts receivable); and (3) trade creditors (to verify the balances of accounts payable). Others with whom the auditor communicates are sinking-fund trustees, corporate transfer agents and registrars, appraisers, attorneys, and sometimes other accountants.

In reviewing his analysis, the imagination and ingenuity displayed by the auditor constitutes much of the difference between a good audit and a poor one. Two types of comparisons are staples of his review process. First, he compares the account relationships as revealed by the records to those shown on the statements. Second, he compares the account relationships for the current period with those of previous periods. Although analysis, inspection, communication, and review are the crux of a standard audit program, the auditor may utilize a great variety of investigative techniques to form his independent professional opinion of the enterprise's financial statements.

The form of the audit report may be short or long. Published statements typically use the short form. The AICPA now recommends that it appear as follows:

To The Board of Directors
The Company
Columbus, Ohio

We have examined the balance sheet of The Company as of December 31, 1971 and the related statements of income and retained earnings and changes in financial position (fund flow) for the year then ended. Our examination was made in accordance with generally accepted auditing standards, and accordingly included such tests of the accounting records and such other auditing procedures as we considered necessary in the circumstances.

In our opinion, the aforementioned financial statements present fairly the financial position of The Company at December 31, 1971, and the results of its operations and the changes in its financial position (fund flow) for the year then ended, in conformity with generally accepted accounting principles applied on a basis with that of the preceding year.

> Sinatra & Martin
> Certified Public Accountants
> March 1, 1972

The first paragraph of this short-form report is called the "scope" paragraph; it emphasizes that the auditor's examination has been carried out in accordance with auditing standards. The second paragraph of the certificate comprises the auditor's opinion or belief concerning the propriety of the financial statements.

A more concise certificate is as follows:

Board of Directors
The Company
Columbus, Ohio

In our opinion, the accompanying financial statements present fairly the position of The Company as of December 31, 1971, and the results of its operations for the year then ended, in conformity with generally accepted accounting principles applied on a basis consistent with that of the preceding year. Our opinion is based upon an examination of the statements which was made in accordance with generally accepted auditing standards and included such tests of the accounting records and such other auditing procedures as we considered necessary.

> Sinatra & Martin
> Certified Public Accountants
> March 1, 1972

Ordinarily, the long-form report is prepared by the auditor principally for the benefit of the client's top management. It includes an opinion; statements of position, income and retained earnings, fund flow; and comments on audit scope in much greater detail than are provided with the short-form audit report. In addition, the long-form report may include comments on and analysis of the financial statements, internal control, and any significant changes from prior years or suggestions for operating improvements or improved accounting procedures. Because there is no established format for a long-form report, its arrangement will depend on its intended purpose and intended recipient; sometimes it is in the form of a letter. Whatever style the long report takes, it supplements, contains, or replaces the short form. In all forms, long or short, the auditor in effect expresses his professional judgment concerning whether the financial statements presented by management are a fair presentation of the actual situation.

Users of financial statements regard the auditor's certificate as advantageous for at least two reasons. First, the CPA exercises his *independent* judgment. By this, it is meant that he must place his professional responsibilities to external users on a higher level than a mere desire to provide services for a particular client company. The external user also values the auditor's skill and competence. If the auditor does not exercise independence and competence in giving an audit report, the user or the client may have legal recourse. The user may recover damages in case of the auditor's fraud or gross negligence; the client may sue for damages from an auditor who has been negligent in the performance of his audit examination.

In 1948 the AICPA established ten standards for an auditor's examination (through its Committee on Auditing Procedure) which were approved by the general membership. These are divided into general, fieldwork, and reporting standards. The general standards are:

1. The examination is to be performed by a person or persons having adequate technical training and proficiency as an auditor.
2. The auditor should maintain an independent mental attitude throughout his audit.
3. The auditor must exercise due professional care throughout the audit and in the preparation of his report.

The standards for fieldwork are:

4. The auditing activities are to be adequately planned, and any assistants are to be properly supervised.
5. The internal controls of the client must be studied and evaluated to determine the extent (a) to which they may be relied upon and (b) to which audit tests may be restricted.

6. Sufficient evidence must be obtained through inspection, observation, inquiries, and confirmations to provide a basis for the opinion to be included in the audit report.

The reporting standards are:

7. The report shall indicate whether the financial statements conform to "generally accepted principles of accounting."
8. The report shall indicate whether such principles have been observed consistently in the current period in relation to the preceding period.
9. Unless otherwise stated, the information disclosed in the financial statements is to be regarded as reasonably adequate.
10. The report shall contain an opinion, qualified where necessary, on the financial statements as a whole. If the opinion is qualified or disclaimed, an explanation must be given.

Many more detailed auditing standards for the examination of various kinds of accounts have been developed. However, these are more appropriately the subject matter of an auditing textbook.

As indicated in the last reporting standard, the opinion may be unqualified, qualified, or disclaimed. If an unqualified opinion is given, the auditor has not indicated any reservations or stated any conditions that are a precedent to his opinion about the fairness of the management's financial statements. In most audit engagements, any conditions that might lead to a restricted or qualified opinion can be eliminated by prior agreement between the auditor and his client company concerning revision of the audit or statements. However, occasionally a qualified opinion may be given. This is done when the auditor does not agree with management regarding the propriety of an accounting method used by the company (for example, the method of counting and valuing inventory). Such a restricted opinion may result, too, when the company is unwilling to permit a specific auditing procedure (for example, letting the auditor observe the counting of inventory). When a qualified opinion is issued by the auditor, the report contains the phrases (1) "except" or "exception" or (2) "subject to," followed by explanations of why the auditor has used the qualifying phrases. Out of 600 company reports in 1969, 90 auditors' reports (or 15 percent) expressed qualified opinions, and none showed a disclaimer of opinion. The 90 auditors' reports with qualified opinions gave 114 instances of qualifications, 55 of which applied to fair presentation and 59 to consistency (in the application of "generally accepted accounting principles").[1]

In addition, the auditor may on rare occasions issue an adverse opinion or a disclaimer (or denial) of opinion. The former may result

---

[1]See *Accounting Trends & Techniques: Annual Survey of Accounting Practices Followed in 600 Stockholders' Reports,* 24th ed. (New York: AICPA, 1970), p. 307.

if the exceptions concerning the fairness of the statements are so material that a qualified opinion would not be justified. In his report the auditor must indicate that the statements "do not present fairly" either the company's position or its operations, and give his reasons in a separate paragraph between the scope and opinion paragraphs. If an adverse opinion is to be given, the company management usually will terminate the audit and attempt to engage new auditors. Similarly, if the auditor refuses to give an opinion because he has not obtained sufficient competent evidence to form one, the company management usually will terminate the auditing engagement. The explanations for a disclaimer, which must be disclosed fully, might be unusual uncertainties about statement amounts or serious limitations on the scope of the audit.

Whatever kind of opinion is issued by the auditor, only part of the financial data is specifically covered by the auditor's opinion. Usually, in the short form, this is limited to the position, income, and retained earnings statements and, in recent years, to the fund-flow statement. All other financial information revealed by the company is not covered. Since the long-form report typically contains more information, it would tend to be more valuable to external users than the short form; however, it usually is provided only to management, special lending agencies such as banks, and to owners of closely held companies. The auditor's opinion is taken to mean that the statements included in his opinion are considered as a whole to "present fairly" and are free from any material bias or misstatement. This should not be interpreted to mean that the auditor certifies that every item or any single statement is correct in any precise or exact sense.

The Principles of Accounting
Of the phrases used by the auditor in his audit opinion, the most controversial one is "generally accepted accounting principles." Despite the extensive use of this phrase in auditing and elsewhere in accounting, there is very little agreement among auditors and accountants about what precisely are accounting principles other than that those used by competent accountants become "generally accepted accounting principles." Many alternative titles and word combinations have been suggested. Some accountants state that many accounting "principles" are not principles; and others state that not all accounting principles have been identified as yet.[2]

Although the reader might assume that accountants always have been interested in accounting principles, this is not so. Despite a

[2]The AICPA Director of Research, Reed K. Story, expressed this view in a monograph: *The Search for Accounting Principles* (New York: AICPA, 1964). His study is utilized in much of the discussion that follows.

background of centuries, public accounting has emerged as a high-level profession only in the twentieth century. As discussed in Chapter 1, accounting has evolved largely from practice; as such, it has always had a strong practical orientation.

The status of accountants and accounting has risen with the development of complex business and government structures. Paralleling this development has been a major movement by accountants and others to try to identify more clearly the objectives and principles (or guides to action or guidelines) that underlie and should underlie accounting practice. This movement has had these general characteristics: It is argued that financial accounting requires improvement because there is a need to limit the number of alternative methods and procedures being used. Some say that this can be best accomplished by establishing principles. This movement, which has been identifiable as such for at least 40 years, has varied in its intensity over that period.

Since 1930, the principles movement has had three peak periods of interest. Although this interest has not resulted in establishing precise accounting principles (despite the formulation of several sets of principles by individuals or committees), accounting practice and accounting theory seem to have improved markedly as a result. For example, in the early 1930s, recognition of the need for accounting improvement resulted in emphasis on (1) cost accounting, (2) relating expenses to revenues, (3) recording depreciation (many firms did not), (4) the need to be consistent, and (5) the desirability of being conservative in accounting. (Remember that this was right after the 1929 stock market crash.) Consequently, the principles activity centered on these problems, with excellent results being achieved in alleviating or solving them, but with no progress in the identification of principles.

The first major period of interest was kindled with the establishment of the SEC, which was given explicit authority to regulate accounting, and with the publication of a report by the CPAs in cooperation with the stock exchanges. Each association turned out reports by committees and individuals. The AICPA's Committee on Accounting Procedures issued the first of its Accounting Research Bulletins in 1939; these prescribed treatment of specific accounting problems. During this time the American Accounting Association's Executive Committee published two broad statements of accounting principles (in 1936 and 1941). The basic approach in these statements was deductive while the AICPA's was inductive, drawing heavily upon accounting practice. The AICPA made little attempt to state the underlying rationale; the AAA tried.

The two studies undertaken by individuals also presented a considerable contrast in approach. The Sanders, Hatfield, and Moore study,[3] under the auspices of the Haskins and Sells Foundation, stressed the best accepted accounting practice of the 1930s although it professed to be an attempt to set forth principles. The study was based on personal interviews and correspondence with prominent accountants, an examination of accounting reports, and a review of the literature and the law. Two members of the Executive Committee of the AAA, Paton and Littleton, published the deductive study referred to earlier which provided theoretical support for the association's committee statement.[4] The study was intended as a coherent, coordinated, and consistent framework for accounting principles. Although the AICPA bulletins immediately influenced CPAs and their clients, the Paton and Littleton study was apparently not influential until later, but its influence continues even now. Much of the theory contained in the study, which was innovative in 1940, is reflected in the improved financial reporting of today.

Although interest in accounting principles slackened during World War II for a variety of reasons, it was revived after the war. The renewed interest was due in part to objectionable practices which certain companies developed during the war (notably the use of net income equalization reserves), but largely to the public confusion about the more readily available and improved but more complex financial statements. (For example, the idea that accounting income need not be equal to taxable income was new and confusing.) This period of activity was shorter than the first; it was also a less fruitful one. However, some improvement in practice did result, and the confidence of the public in financial reporting increased. This period did not produce a major new statement of accounting principles, but in 1948 the AAA issued a second revision of its basic statement (this one was on "Accounting Concepts and Standards," and not on principles as were the two earlier statements), and the AICPA continued to issue bulletins. The general interest in principles declined as accountants became more and more engrossed in the problem of accounting for changing price levels.

In 1957 three events again signaled the reawakening of the concern for principles. The AAA issued a third revision of its basic statement. Leonard Spacek, a partner in the public accounting firm of Arthur Andersen & Co., recommended that an accounting court be established to hear issues involving accounting principles. Alvin R. Jennings, the AICPA president, argued that accountants needed to recognize that the true development of accounting principles necessitated basic research more than applied research based

[3]Thomas Henry Sanders, Henry Rand Hatfield, and Underhill Moore, *A Statement of Accounting Principles* (New York: American Institute of Accountants, 1938).
[4]W. A. Paton and A. C. Littleton, *An Introduction to Corporate Accounting Standards*, Monograph No. 3 (Chicago: American Accounting Association, 1940).

upon practice; and that this task was not one that could be completed immediately, or even within a few years.

Under this impetus, the AICPA organized a new program which continues to the present time. A new committee, the Accounting Principles Board, was given exclusive authority to make public pronouncements on accounting principles. Departures from pronouncements of the Board and its predecessor, the Committees on Accounting Procedures and Accounting Terminology, are to be reported by member CPAs in footnotes to the financial statements or in the auditor's report—a course of action that neither the CPA nor his client can take lightly. However, the Board normally is not expected to act on any issue until it has been investigated by a qualified researcher. This researcher, although advised by the director of accounting research for the AICPA and a committee of authorities on the subject in question, is completely free to interpret his research as he sees fit. After a research report (formally known as an Accounting Research Study) is completed, it is reviewed by the Board, which takes one of three actions: It may issue an opinion accepting the conclusions of the study; it may reject the conclusions of the study and write an opinion stating different conclusions; or it may defer action.

The AICPA's current program is its first major attempt to integrate the logical methods and research approach of the university with the practical experiences of the practitioners. It is also the first AICPA program designed to stress the use of deductive reasoning. In addition, an opinion of the Accounting Principles Board was to state the reasoning and mention the alternatives considered, the arguments in favor of and against each alternative, and why one method is preferred to all others, as well as a conclusion. This process is in sharp contrast with the Research Bulletins which, except for the first few, reported only conclusions.

More than a decade after this program was started, it has produced 11 Accounting Research Studies and 21 opinions. Over the years, this program seems to be diverging more and more from the original plan. Many of the opinions have been issued without prior published studies. The more recent studies have not been undertaken by research-oriented individuals. Even the style of many opinions has been very similar to that of the bulletins.

After recommending one method for accounting for the investment credit in one opinion, the Institute relented in a second opinion, after considerable and well-publicized pressure, to permit the other major alternative method. In two preliminary drafts of a third opinion, the Institute considered but did not revert to its original position. The Institute has suffered damage to its prestige as a result.

In 1966 the AAA issued a completely new statement rather than a revision of earlier statements. This major effort was an attempt to establish a foundation of accounting concepts from which particular practices could be judged. Although the statement was issued while in an early draft stage, it has already had the effect of broadening the definition of accounting (as discussed in Chapter 1).

As previously discussed, there is as yet no meaningful codification of generally accepted accounting principles. Those offered by the AICPA are not comprehensive or integrated, or even principles. A 1965 principles study by a practitioner constituted an inventory of practice with 80 different accounting alternatives for 31 transactions taking up almost 500 pages. Another attempt at codification was published in 1970, as APB Statement No. 4. These attempts and the statements of the AAA (with the exception of the Paton and Littleton monograph) have received only nominal direct attention in practice. Consequently, the current status of accounting principles is a confusing one.

Nevertheless this concern has had significant positive results in improving practice and theory, and even in formulating the principles themselves. Many of these results stem from the improved environment of accounting and from the increased acceptance of certain new ideas about accounting. First, principles are now more commonly understood to refer to guides or rules for selecting methods or procedures, rather than the procedures or practices themselves. Second, more accountants, and others too, now accept the proposition that the purpose of accounting principles should not be concerned with justifying accounting practice. Third, although logical studies of accounting could not solve all the problems of accounting, such studies would be most helpful. Fourth, the formulation of a precise terminology, including one for principles, is the key to the discipline's future development. Fifth, there needs to be additional emphasis upon publishing descriptions of the methods used by companies and accountants in financial reporting—information similar to that submitted to the SEC. Last, although leading accountants have become increasingly concerned about the public status of the accounting profession and its obligations to all social groups, most accountants regard themselves as being responsible primarily to existing shareholders (or an even smaller group—company managers).

On the negative side, some of the past statements on accounting concepts, standards, or principles have contributed to the creation of a multiplicity of generally accepted accounting methods, procedures, and practices; this has served to add to the confusion. The discussion resulting from these studies often has emphasized radical change or no change at all. Whether one considers those who want any change or those who oppose any change, this extremism has not been helpful.

The analogy drawn between accounting and the law which concludes that accounting principles should be developed on a case-by-case basis like common law does not seem to be useful either, since the apparatus necessary for such an approach (such as an accounting court) is not present (or apparently even wanted) in accounting. Furthermore, the historical development of accounting does not suggest that such an approach would be promising—but rather that an analogy to the principles of economics, or statistics, would be more enlightening.

However, since these studies have accomplished a significant improvement of accounting practice; since the development of principles by necessity is a long-run, not a short-run, activity; since the accounting profession is still young; and since there appears to be no real threat of establishing accounting "principles" by statute or edict, one can be hopeful.

The Analysis and Interpretation of Financial Data by Analysts with Special Attention to Ratio Analysis

In recent decades, financial analysts, a group of external users of financial statements, have become increasingly important for at least two reasons. First, this group is the most knowledgeable and sophisticated of the various external groups that use financial statements. Second, the professional services of this user group are made available to others. Thus, financial analysts constitute a very influential group for both users of financial statements and those who prepare them. Financial analysts act as intermediaries between accountants and external users. Expert financial analysts interpret not only accounting information but also local, regional, national, and international economic information. They also are familiar with the financial markets, with management of enterprises, and with relevant governmental activities.

Along with their increasing prominence, financial analysts have been developing professional standards of competence. For example, their members may now take uniform examinations; those who pass the examinations become chartered financial analysts. It seems likely that further improvements in their standards and competency may be anticipated. The principal function of the financial analyst is to determine the status and potential of economic enterprises. More specifically, he is concerned with measuring, evaluating, and predicting the performance of enterprises. For this purpose, he considers audited financial statements as basic tools. Since his clients are often investors and creditors, he often utilizes statements as aids to decision making for external users from these groups.

Two primary techniques of analysis employed by this professional are (1) comparative statements and (2) ratios. As an aid for analysts and other external users, accountants often prepare comparative statements and ratios which are included in published reports.

Comparative statements A comparative statement is often presented as a comparison of the current period with the prior period. Some companies, however, present comparative statements in their published annual reports or in readily available supplementary reports for each year up to ten (or even more) years.

Comparative statements are very useful in identifying trends for an enterprise. Trends are of particular significance in trying to evaluate the performance of a firm. In comparative statements when current results are compared to prior results, the changes or trends may enable the analyst to evaluate either the improvement or the deterioration of the firm.

A financial statement of this sort, whether comparative or for one period or date, is expressed in absolute amounts. The analyst or the accountant may convert the absolute amounts to percentages to show proportional relationships. These percentages may be expressed either (1) vertically or (2) horizontally. For a vertical percentage analysis, each item on a particular financial statement is expressed as a percent or ratio of one specific item, which is regarded as the base. For an income statement, sales is the usual base; only rarely will cost of goods sold be regarded as the base. For the position statement, total assets or equities subgroups of assets or equities are used. Horizontal percentage analysis necessitates the presenting of percentages which indicate the proportionate change in the same item from period to period. The base for horizontal percentages is the earliest year. Statements expressed as percentages are called common-size statements. Percentages based on negative or zero amounts would not result in meaningful percentage increases. Instead, no percentage should be shown, and, where possible, nonrecurring items should be removed from the data before the percentage calculations are made. When horizontal percentages are utilized, it also is possible to be misled if the absolute amounts are small. For example, an increase from $50 to $100 is a 100 percent increase; yet for almost any enterprise this would not be a significant increase.

In utilizing comparative statements, the user should recognize that the earlier period figures may not constitute a good standard of comparison for several reasons. Many factors may have been different in the earlier period from what they are now: the enterprise's internal operations (products, organization structure, manufacturing methods); its volume of activity (sales, production, hours worked); and also the accounting methods and classifications, the industry and the economy, the firm's efficiency, and the general price level.

EXHIBIT 12–1
COMPARATIVE STATEMENTS
PUBLISHED BY 600 COMPANIES IN 1969

Number of Companies with Comparative Statements	1969	Percent
All	478	80
All except fund flow	86	14
Some	36	6
	600	100

SOURCE: *Adapted from Accounting Trends & Techniques: Annual Survey of Accounting Practices Followed in 600 Stockholders' Reports, 24th ed. (New York: AICPA, 1970), p. 4.*

In using and interpreting comparative statements, a reader may be dismayed by the large number of complex tabulations. Only the very sophisticated reader, usually the financial analyst, is sufficiently perceptive to select data that are relevant to his general or specific problems. If he concentrates on differences or variations, the unusual or exceptional items will be revealed. Since the accountant must prepare comparative statements and ratios for many varied external users, he does not find it possible to provide sufficient analytical information for all of them. The best that he can do is try to satisfy the needs of his primary users. For this reason, even if the accountant could prepare financial analysis to suit the needs of any user, the financial analyst is in a more appropriate position to do so. The role of the professional analyst is to service the needs of a few; the role of the professional accountant is a much broader one.

Ratio analysis A ratio is the expression of a relationship between two amounts; it may be computed as a fraction, a decimal, or a percent (which is a decimal multiplied by 100). In preparing a ratio from accounting statement data, one selects two amounts that have a significant relationship to each other and divides one by the other. The amounts are the balances of single accounts or groups of accounts. These amounts may be from the same statement or from two different statements.

Although ratios are used to the extent that many are presented in published statements, their limitations are sometimes overlooked. Since ratios represent averages, they must be interpreted carefully, or else nonsensical conclusions may be reached. Ratios are particularly vulnerable to changes in accounting methods and classifications. Furthermore, one ratio or even a number may not be significant. Favorable ratios may (or may not) indicate that something is right, and unfavorable ratios may (or may not) indicate that something is wrong. But none of them reveals exactly what is right or wrong; further investigation is necessary in order to determine this.

To a considerable extent, a financial analyst is a ratio specialist. It is his primary task to evaluate a specific ratio or a set of ratios for a specific firm in a particular industry in the current economy. In his evaluation, he is likely to compare the ratio(s) with those of preceding years for the enterprise, with those of the enterprise's competitors (when available from published financial statements), with those of the enterprise's industry, and, if possible, with the budgeted or standard ratios for the enterprise.

Industry figures are comparatively easy to come by since trade associations, the United States Department of Commerce, Dun & Bradstreet, Inc., and Robert Morris Associates publish them. The budgeted or standard figures are not generally available. There has been some pressure from analysts and other external users for the inclusion of budgets in published reports; managers and auditors, in general, have opposed this proposed change. Auditors have argued that such information could not be judged fairly by an auditor.

When ratios between two enterprises are compared, extreme caution must be exercised. The statistics may vary because of differences in methods of computing the ratios or differences in accounting or in operations. The size, location, and product lines of the two enterprises may be quite dissimilar too. Notwithstanding their limitations, ratios interpreted by an analyst or an accountant can be very helpful in evaluation. When ratios are presented in published reports, their analysis should include graphs, illustrations, and narrative. Trends and exceptional developments should be clearly identified. The narrative is particularly important for its explanations. Some companies will utilize the president's letter in the report for this purpose.

A further complication of ratio analysis is the lack of uniformity in the appropriate values to be inserted into specific ratio formulas. Analysts do not agree among themselves about the importance of different ratios or about the generally accepted ratio computation methods or ratio valuations. Generally, the precise computation and figures used depend upon the judgment of the analyst or the accountant as to the expected use or interpretation in the particular or general situation.

Although details of their computation may vary among different analysts, the 21 ratios presented below are among those most widely used.

Ratios of overall solvency The first two ratios are those of overall solvency. The first is called the *current* or *working capital ratio.* It is computed as follows:

(1)
$$\frac{Current\ assets\ (net\ of\ contra\ accounts)}{Current\ liabilities}$$

It is a measure of the adequacy of working capital. As the primary test of solvency for a going concern, it gives a measure of the enterprise's ability to meet its current debts from current assets.

The second is a more severe test, one of immediate solvency. The acid-test or quick ratio is computed as follows:

(2)
$$\frac{Current\ assets\ (net\ of\ contra\ accounts)\ -\ inventories\ and\ prepaids}{Current\ liabilities}$$

It tests the firm's ability to meet sudden demands upon its most liquid assets (cash, marketable securities, and receivables). It is also possible to have favorable ratios of both types (even the acid-test ratio, because the receivables or marketable securities may be too high) and still have a shortage of cash. Although the rule-of-thumb standards for some ratios have become traditional (for example, two to one for working capital, and one to one for acid test), peculiarities of the industry and similar factors are more important in evaluating a ratio.

Ratios concerning the movement of current assets The next five ratios concern the movement of the current assets. The usual trading cycle, as discussed in Chapter 5, is from cash to inventories to receivables and back to cash. The frequency of the receivables and inventory turnover is highly significant for the current position of the enterprise. These ratios are called *turnovers*. First, there is the *receivable turnover:*

(3)
$$\frac{Net\ credit\ sales}{Average\ receivables\ (net\ of\ contra\ accounts)}$$

This ratio is an average, a measure of the rapidity of collection of the accounts and notes receivable. It is a test of the efficiency of collection. The computation of this ratio may vary considerably. Total sales may be substituted for credit sales; the ending balance of the receivables may be substituted for an average of the beginning and ending balances. Next, there is the *age of receivables ratio:*

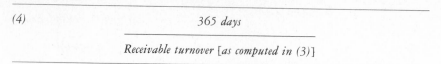

$$(4) \qquad \frac{365 \ days}{Receivable \ turnover \ [as \ computed \ in \ (3)]}$$

This ratio is a measure of the average number of days that it takes the firm to collect its trade receivables. This ratio is really a substitute for turnover (3). Whether the movement of receivables should be measured as a turnover or in terms of days required for collection is the decision of the financial analyst.

The next two ratios are the *average inventory turnover* and the *average number of days' sales in inventory.*

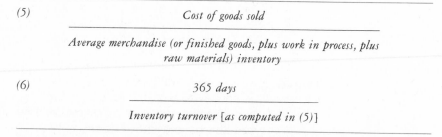

$$(5) \qquad \frac{Cost \ of \ goods \ sold}{Average \ merchandise \ (or \ finished \ goods, \ plus \ work \ in \ process, \ plus \ raw \ materials) \ inventory}$$

$$(6) \qquad \frac{365 \ days}{Inventory \ turnover \ [as \ computed \ in \ (5)]}$$

The inventory turnover gives a measure of the average liquidity of the inventory; the average number of days' sales in inventory measures the same thing. Both give some indication as to whether the enterprise has over- or understocked total inventory; but since it is an average, the enterprise may be understocked in some items and overstocked in others. For comparisons with other firms, sales may have to be substituted for cost of goods in the turnover if the latter is not available. Where this substitution has been made, the inventory figure for the ratio should be restated to retail if possible. If the companies accounting periods are "natural" business years, their turnovers will appear better because the inventory (or receivables) balance will be lower.

The last ratio in this category is the *percent of each current asset to total current assets;* this gives a basis for evaluating the relative liquidity of current assets and is computed as follows:

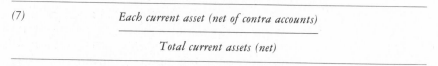

$$(7) \qquad \frac{Each \ current \ asset \ (net \ of \ contra \ accounts)}{Total \ current \ assets \ (net)}$$

Ratios of long-term solvency The next five ratios are particularly helpful in evaluating the long-term solvency and creditor security position of the company. First, there is *ownership equity to total assets:*

(8)
$$\frac{Ownership\ equity}{Total\ assets\ (net)}$$

This ratio of the assets provided by the owners gives a measure of the security provided for creditors. Another often-used equity position ratio is *total liabilities to total assets.* It is the complement of (8) and is computed as follows:

(9)
$$\frac{Total\ liabilities}{Total\ assets\ (net)}$$

This measure is one of "trading on the equity," or the proportion of the assets provided by the creditors. Next there is the *ratio of ownership to total liabilities:*

(10)
$$\frac{Ownership}{Total\ liabilities}$$

This is similar to (8) in that it indicates the relative amount of company resources provided by owners as compared to that provided by the creditors. This measure is helpful in assessing the company's capital structure.

Another ratio, considered by many to be important in measuring the risk of default on utility company bonds, is the *average number of times that interest is earned.* The method of computation usually preferred is as follows:

(11)
$$\frac{Net\ income\ plus\ interest\ and\ income\ tax\ expenses}{Interest\ expense}$$

Next, a closely related ratio, *plant to long-term liabilities,* is considered by many to be very important in evaluating the degree of security enjoyed by the company and the investors for its long-term debt, usually bonds, where plant assets are a major portion of total assets and where plant assets are pledged as security. This ratio is also helpful in determining the company's potential borrowing power; it is computed as follows:

(12)
$$\frac{Plant\ (net)}{Long\text{-}term\ liabilities}$$

When considered together, the last five ratios can be used to evaluate the company's condition of long-run solvency.

Ratios of profitability and efficiency The next three ratios are used to measure the relationships between equities and net income and sales. They are a measure of the return on ownership equity. The first is net *income to ownership equity:*

$$(13) \qquad \frac{Net\ income}{Average\ ownership\ equity}$$

The *ratio of plant turnover* gives a crude measure of the efficiency with which the company utilizes its assets; it is computed as follows:

$$(14) \qquad \frac{Net\ sales}{Plant\ (net)}$$

A ratio that measures the number of dollars of equity at *book value per share of common stock* is computed as follows:

$$(15) \qquad \frac{Common\ stock\ equity}{Weighted\ average\ number\ of\ outstanding\ common\ shares}$$

Since this ratio utilizes book value instead of market value, it has limited significance, despite its general use. When the company has more than one class of stock, the actual computation of this ratio depends on the preferential rights of the preferred stock. For example, if cumulative preferred stock dividends are in arrears, the amount of the arrears should be deducted from the common stock equity.

Ratios of income The last six ratios are on net income.

The first, *ratio of net income to net sales,* is a basic measure of the profitability of each dollar of sales; it is computed as follows:

$$(16) \qquad \frac{Net\ income}{Net\ sales}$$

The *turnover of all assets* (or equities) is an efficiency measure of how well the company resources are employed; it is computed as follows:

$$(17) \qquad \frac{Net\ sales}{Total\ assets\ (net)}$$

The *ratio of net income earned per share of common stock* (or primary earnings per share) is regarded as a measure of the company's ability to pay dividends on its common stock; it is computed as follows:

$$(18) \quad \frac{Net\ income\ before\ extraordinary\ items-preferred\ stock\ dividend\ requirements}{Weighted\ average\ number\ of\ shares\ of\ common\ stock\ outstanding}$$

This ratio is so widely regarded that the AICPA has recommended that it be shown on published income statements. If the corporation has potentially dilutive convertible securities, options, warrants, or other rights that upon conversion or exercise could in the aggregate dilute earnings per common share, the AICPA in APB Opinion No. 15 requires that a second ratio be reported: "fully diluted earnings per share." This would be a pro-forma presentation which reflects the dilution of net income per share that would have occurred if *all* contingent issuances of common stock which would individually reduce net income per share had taken place at the beginning of the period.

Although not as widely utilized as (18), the *average net income per share of common stock based on its market value* is a much more significant measure of profitableness; this is computed as follows:

$$(19) \quad \frac{Net\ income\ per\ share\ before\ extraordinary\ items\ and\ preferred\ stock\ dividend\ requirements}{Market\ price\ per\ share}$$

This same relationship is expressed more popularly as the *price-earnings ratio* and is computed as follows:

$$(20) \quad \frac{Market\ price\ per\ share}{Income\ per\ share\ before\ extraordinary\ items\ and\ preferred\ stock\ dividend\ requirements}$$

The last general ratio, *return on investment*, represents the rate earned by the company on all its assets. As such, it gives a measure of the stock market's appraisal of the ability—the effectiveness and overall efficiency—of company management; this is computed as follows:

(21)   *Net income before interest expense (with adjustment for the tax*
saving on the interest expense)

Total assets (net)

The return on investment considers three principal factors affecting income: namely, sales, costs, and total assets. In practice some analysts deduct intangibles wherever total assets are used. In the case of forced liquidation most intangibles often have had little or no value. But otherwise such assets are valuable and should be included in computing ratios where appropriate.

The Uses and Usefulness of Accounting to External Users of Financial Statements

As discussed in Chapter 1, most companies distribute their published accounting statements widely. However, only the needs of stockholders, potential investors, and creditors have been given special consideration. The objectives of such users as employees, customers, government agencies, and members of the general public have not been well formulated. It is assumed that information that is valuable to the first three groups will also be useful to the others. It is also felt that creditors and government agencies have the means to secure additional information as needed. The result is that the objectives of only two external user groups, stockholders and other investors, are considered in the preparation of accounting statements.

The objectives of the stockholders are to make decisions regarding the employment and compensation of the company managers and in this way exercise control over company management. The objectives of investors (including stockholders) are to make decisions about investments—whether to increase, decrease, or to continue their present holdings. As already pointed out, the objectives of creditors are not considered primary ones for the preparation of accounting statements. Nevertheless financial statements do provide some information indicating whether credit should be extended to the enterprise or not.

In addition to what category of user the reader belongs to, the use and usefulness of financial statements depends to a considerable extent on the reader's knowledge of accounting and his skill in interpreting accounting data. If he is a chartered financial analyst, presumably he would experience no difficulty. Additionally, the reader who has some knowledge of accounting but is not an expert accountant should be able to readily utilize financial statements in making decisions about his investments. However, the reader who is uninformed about accounting and business could not expect to find such statements useful. In order for the statements to be of optimal usefulness to external users, only relevant and material data should be presented. As explained earlier in Chapters 1 and 3, *relevance* refers to the nature of an item with respect to specific or general uses of statements; *materiality* refers to the importance of a specific item in a specific context. Consequently, an item could be relevant in either a general or a specific sense but not material, and vice versa.

An item may be material even though it is quantitative. It is not valid to assume that net income for a given year has about the same probability of error as that for any other year. But if an item is quantitative, some accountants suggest that as a rule of thumb it should be judged material if it exceeds 10 percent of the net income excluding the item. This rule is not very helpful since net income may fluctuate considerably from year to year, and so the same amount might be regarded as immaterial one year and material the next. A better suggestion would be to use the average income for several years or to use revenue or gross margin (both of which are likely to fluctuate less than income). The former would be better since for any given enterprise and set of conditions, the range of probable errors in computing income is likely to be much higher in a poor year than in a good year.

The materiality of position statement items also should be evaluated, even though the position statement generally is not believed to be as useful as the income statement. The materiality of individual asset and liability measurements depends to a considerable extent on the type of asset or liability involved. Informed users of accounting statements expect more accuracy from certain measurements than they do from others. In these situations materiality depends on the relative accuracy expected by readers. For example, measurements of cash items are expected to be very accurate whereas measurements of other intangibles are not considered to be reliable.

When information is not quantified, it is more difficult to evaluate its materiality; different users will weigh the information differently. Whether information is or is not quantified, its relevance may be judged on the basis of its pertinence to the quantitative data to which it is related. In general, information that is not quantifiable but that adds more than it detracts is both relevant and material. Information may be relevant and material even if reaction to it is unfavorable. Such information may range from losses resulting from dishonest actions of managers to the cost of the company's antipollution program. Unfortunately, few firms presently recognize this reporting obligation.

Various methods may be used to report information to the external users. The most important method is in the form and arrangement of the formal statements. The most relevant and material information should be presented in the body of the statements whenever possible. As the authors have stressed throughout this book, certain forms and arrangements (for example, the single-step income statement, the working capital position statement) have more merit than others. The authors have emphasized, too, the value of always using terminology that has a clear, concise, and consistent meaning.

There are also secondary methods of disclosing data in the accounting reports. These are footnotes, parenthetical information, supplementary schedules and statements, the president's letter, and the auditor's opinion (already discussed).

Of these, perhaps the most frequently encountered are footnotes which are used to furnish explanations of accounting techniques or changes in accounting methods, restrictions on dividends, rights or priorities of creditors or stockholders, executory contracts, contingent liabilities, and contingent assets. Although footnotes are a very useful method of presenting secondary data, their use for major information is incorrect. They are often difficult to read and to understand, much less to evaluate.

Parenthetical information is not used as extensively as it might be in published reports. It is a useful way of disclosing specific procedures or methods, alternative valuations, special characteristics, references, and details. Supplementary statements and schedules are methods of presenting additional information (or information arranged differently) which for various reasons does not appear in the body of the statements. The AICPA has recommended that the effect of general price-level changes be reported in supplementary statements. In its Statement No. 2, the APB has recommended that diversified companies voluntarily present supplementary information regarding individual segments of their enterprise as follows: (1) revenues by separate type of activity or by customer, (2) net income or loss for major segments of enterprise or information that certain segments are operating at a loss without disclosing amount of loss, and (3) separate financial statements for segments of the enterprise that operate autonomously and have a significantly different type of equity structure.

A single set of combined statements of a conglomerate company lacks comparability with statements of companies operating in one industry and with statements of other conglomerate firms operating in different combinations of industries. Combined statements also may be less useful to investors in predicting the future of the company. If improved comparability is the objective, segments as small as 5 percent of the total operations of a diversified company should be reported separately. If improved predictability is the objective, separate reports for segments of 15 percent or more may be adequate. Under the rules of the SEC, diversified enterprises must disclose segments that contribute 15 percent. For any segment that contributes 10 percent, the SEC proposes that the approximate amount or percentage of the company's total sales and net income be revealed.

Divisional reporting is opposed by many companies who charge that it may reveal significant information to competitors (but as the alert reader recognizes, this is a two-way information channel—a company also may gain information about its competitors) and that it would not provide equitable reporting among different companies. By the latter is meant that with a percentage rule, small firms would be penalized, and with an absolute dollar rule, large firms would be penalized. Other opposition stems from the necessity of making arbitrary allocations of joint costs and from the treatment of inter-divisional pricing.

Since the auditor's opinion usually does not cover supplementary statements, it is possible for the company to experiment with presenting this type of information. For example, the president's letter could be used to present additional data regarding future expectations for the firm, industry, and economy; plans for growth and change; proposed capital and research expenditures; and all non-financial events and changes during the year that affect operations of the firm. The auditor's opinion does disclose when changes in accounting methods or the use of generally accepted methods have had material effects.

The treatment of poststatement (or subsequent) events in published reports may be of major importance to external users. *Poststatement events* are those material events that occur or become known after the statement date but before the report is completed.

Events that directly affect the amounts reported in the statements are one type. They are caused by inadequate available information during the accounting period, and they result in changes in estimated valuation or allocations because of information acquired after the position statement date. If such information had been available at position statement date and would have been utilized, this information should be recognized directly by adjusting the accounts; the result would be to lengthen the accounting period in the interests of disclosure.

A second type of event consists of those that materially alter the continuing validity of position statement valuations or relationships among equity holders, or materially affect the usefulness of prior years' income as a predictor of income for the current period. Although these events do not have a direct bearing on the statements themselves, they are likely to affect significantly decisions based on the statements. These events may not always require adjustments, but they should be disclosed, usually in footnotes.

Events that might significantly affect future valuations or flows are a third type. The effect of these events is unknown or uncertain. The signing of contracts, changes in market conditions or prices, new management policies, and new legislation are examples of such events. Since it can be argued that disclosure of the events directly in the statements may be more misleading than informative, these events could be disclosed in unaudited sections of the published reports.

Constraints on Accounting Due to the "State of the Arts"

In considering how to improve financial accounting, accountants sometimes feel that users should be able to make meaningful recommendations. But this approach has not had very satisfactory results to date. For example, consider the following typical experience of a prominent Canadian chartered accountant:

When I set out on a sort of crusade for better reporting, I had the naïve and overly optimistic notion that the main problem was to persuade accountants that they should find out what statement-users wanted to know—instead of devoting so much ingenuity to devising ways of telling users what accountants thought they should want to know. I thus took every opportunity to ask investors, analysts, bankers, suppliers, and others who use statements, what they would like such statements to tell them. It was a disappointing experience. Apart from the periods of recrimination which follow, for a brief moment, each recurring financial scandal (during which time everyone is trying, in the interests of his own self-respect, to find someone else to blame for what happened), statement-users appear to be generally satisfied with the statements which they are getting. They have the notion, I think, that any improvement will introduce complexities which they would rather not hear about. They do make some criticisms. But in my experience, I have found that when invited to be specific, even the serious and well-informed analyst comes up with fairly pedestrian suggestions—a little more information here, some clarification there—but nothing really earthshaking . . . .

Users get used to using what they are given. Investors who cannot get by with the information available are, I suppose, eliminated by a sort of Darwinian process—through losing the stuff to invest with.[5]

Another approach would be to consider recommendations of academic scholars. Such a group assessed existing practice recently in accordance with the ASOBAT standards (as given in Chapter 1 and discussed throughout the book). This group study focused on selecting information to permit informed judgments and decisions by investors and creditors.

In reporting on the position statement, they found relevancy for

---

[5]Howard Ross, *Financial Statements: A Crusade for Current Values* (New York: Pitman Publishing Corporation, 1969), pp. 164–165.

the monetary assets but not for some other items. The measurement procedures, in some instances, were considerably biased.

Therefore . . . the balance sheet as presently constituted (does not satisfy) the basic needs of investors. Specifically, improvements of various kinds need to be made in presenting inventories, plant and equipment, and bad debt allowances. Items found to be not relevant such as accumulated depreciation and stockholders' capital investment in most cases could . . . be replaced with different measures which would be significantly more helpful to users of financial statements in their decision making. But irrelevant items should not be included in financial statements merely to make them balance or to make the several statements articulate with each other . . . .

Of the several items generally reported in the income statement . . . only a few meet all the standards of ASOBAT. While many of the items such as sales revenues, cost of goods sold, and selling and administrative expenses are found to be relevant, . . . their relevance could be greatly improved if classifications of the items were presented to indicate the basic behavioral characteristics.

. . . the procedures for all items in the income statement are quantifiable and generally verifiable. The greatest deficiency of these procedures is in their lack of freedom from bias. In most cases, bias occurs because the objectives in selecting procedures are different than the assumed attributes being measured. The influence of taxation, for example, is all too prevalent. Although this situation occurs in many areas it appears most frequently in the allocations of past and future costs.

Our basic criticism of the income statement can be summarized by saying that investors typically extrapolate items in the income statement assuming ceteris paribus. But even a knowledge that other things do not remain constant is of little help to the investor if insufficient information is presented in the statement for him to determine the behavioral characteristics of the several items. With a lack of information to the contrary, the investor is forced to assume that all items in the income statement will change over time in the same way. Some items will vary according to total sales or production while others are committed or result from past or future cash outlays. Other items, unrelated to current operations, might include research and development expenses resulting from management research policies or research commitments, tax reductions because of eligible capital expenditure and tax reductions arising from prior period losses of the firm or its subsidiaries.

. . . Of the historical statements that comprise current reporting, the one that comes closest to presenting relevant information to the investor and creditor is the funds (flow) statement. The attribute of historical cash and (working capital) funds flows in the current and prior periods is a relevant predictor of future cash flows although other information is also necessary to make this prediction. The several items in the (working capital) funds (flow) statement, however, have different degrees of relevance and should be tested separately for the other standards.

The basic source (increase) of (working capital) funds in most statements is net income adjusted by items not involving the expenditure of cash. While this source (increase) of (working capital) funds from operations is relevant . . . the degree of relevance is insufficient because it does not adequately describe the various elements making up (working capital) funds from operations. . . . Traditional (working capital) funds statements do not present adequate information regarding the behavioral characteristics of its elements. . . . The addition of depreciation and other non-fund items to net income is confusing rather than being an aid because it is irrelevant. The methods of computing (working capital) funds from operations also suffer from some of the same basic difficulties as the computation of net income. . . . While the current reporting of funds from operations is found to be relevant, we are of considerable doubt as to the adequacy of the measurement procedures to provide an adequate description of the attribute and, therefore, . . . it is not sufficiently free from bias.

Most of the other sources (increases) of (working capital) funds represent inflows of cash during the prior period or periods, and . . . are relevant for a prediction of future cash flows; . . . this relevance could be improved by a more adequate breakdown of the items. Since these items are usually adjusted to represent actual cash receipts, . . . they do describe the attributes relatively well; . . . most of these sources (increases) of (working capital) funds . . . are sufficiently free from bias. In all cases . . . the items are quantifiable and verifiable.

. . . The cash flow attributes of these items (appearing as decreases in working capital) are relevant for a prediction of future cash flows . . . (and) . . . are relatively free from bias as descriptions of aggregate flows. However, they are generally lacking as general descriptions in that there is usually no attempt to classify the items in any significant way, for example, by management influence, or by functions, such as financing. Therefore, to this extent, their relevance could be improved.

The traditional (working capital) funds statement usually presents only the change in working capital rather than the cash or funds flows of specific current assets and current liabilities. This net figure may be relevant to a prediction of future changes in the investment in working capital. However, . . . other attributes of working capital changes should also be presented. . . . The measurement procedures for determining the amount of change in working capital are not free from bias . . . in that they do not adequately describe the actual change in investment in working capital items particularly because of the wide variety of methods used in measuring inventories and other nonmonetary current items, . . . however, . . . they are quantifiable and verifiable.[6]

In only a few instances, the committee concludes, does current

[6]"An Evaluation of External Reporting Practices—A Report of the 1966–68 Committee on External Reporting," *Supplement to vol. XLIV, The Accounting Review* (Evanston, Illinois: American Accounting Association, 1969), pp. 104, 110–112.

reporting practice meet the four ASOBAT standards adequately. In most cases the relevant information that would permit better predictions of future cash flows is not disclosed. Sometimes the attributes being measured are not sufficiently defined for one to be able to assess the items for relevance. All too frequently the measurement procedure is determined by objectives unrelated to the measurement of the basic attribute. The result is a general lack of freedom from bias.

Although it was unable to develop a complete alternative to current reporting practice, the committee did recommend two alternative statements and several guidelines for the statements. These statements (as shown in Exhibits 12–2 and 12–3) are a statement of resources and commitments and a statement of current monetary flows. The former provides information regarding objects likely to contribute to future cash flows, and the latter information regarding probable future outflows. The changes in resources reported on the statement of resources and commitments would be listed on the current monetary flow statement. Instead of an emphasis only on bookkeeping and balancing, all information meeting the ASOBAT standards should be reported (and not just in dollar terms), wherever possible. For example, current monetary flows should be classified as (1) responsive to sales volume and mix, (2) committed, (3) discretionary, or (4) based on taxable income. Measurement of object attributes should be classified according to the relevant behavior of the components. Finally, where measurements are verifiable and free from bias, budgets should be included in the published reports.

Although these are excellent ways to improve financial reporting, neither the committee nor anyone else anticipates that such improvement could be brought about in the near future. Then, what might be achieved in the next decade? There are likely to be improvements within the present accounting framework. These will result from pressures on and from the SEC, the AICPA's APB, and probably analysts and investors. More reliable valuation techniques and more knowledge about the uses of accounting data will be helpful too. Most of the short-run concern for improvement takes one of two possible but contradictory forms: (1) financial reports are not simple enough, uniform enough, or comparable enough; or (2) financial reports do not provide sufficient relevant information. In the past, auditors have chosen simplicity; improvements were judged on the basis of their auditability, their objectivity, and their uniformity. This is not so likely to happen in the future.

This is not meant to suggest that a radical change will occur. For example, the APB will continue its drive to eliminate alternative accounting treatments not justified by differences in underlying facts on a pragmatic, one-problem-at-a-time basis. But the next decade

EXHIBIT 12-2
THE CORPORATION
STATEMENT OF RESOURCES AND COMMITMENTS
DECEMBER 31, 1972

Resources Available
Monetary:

Cash	$x
Marketable securities—at current market value	x
Accounts receivable—expected net realizable value	x
	$x

Operating:

    Inventory (by major classifications)—at historical cost, current replacement costs, and current selling prices. Units should be expressed where feasible.

    Operating facilities—include data on capacity in terms of physical output and/or sales dollars, estimated economic life of principal facilities where mortality experience is available, relative status of facilities in light of current, and predicted states of technology, and expected cost of replacing facilities in the near future.

Protective:

    Copyrights, trademarks, and patents—include information regarding products covered and duration.

Innovation:

    Description of major research and development programs to meet future needs of consumers. Include data on number and technical skills of research and development personnel.

Investment in other companies:

    Enumeration of companies, date(s) of investment, percent of outstanding stock owned, and current market value or current dividends being received.

Other resources:

    Sales backlog (unfilled orders)
    Selling and administrative facilities

Commitments
Due within one year:

Accounts payable	$x
Taxes payable	x
Lease payments	x
Pension payments	x
Other (to be specified)	x
	$x

Schedule of current commitments due after one year:

	1973	1974	1975	1976	1977	19XX
Lease payments	$x	$x	$x	$x	$x	$x
Pensions	x	x	x	x	x	x
Bonds payable (principal payments)	x	x	x	x	x	x
Notes payable (principal payments)	x	x	x	x	x	x
Other	x	x	x	x	x	x

Schedule of new commitments planned for next three years:

	1973	1974	1975
Lease payments	$x	$x	$x
Capital expenditures	x	x	x
Other (to be specified)	x	x	x

Shareholder's rights:

Number of shares outstanding of each class of stock with information regarding priority rights. Conversion rights of all senior securities and information regarding stock options outstanding or contemplated.

EXHIBIT 12–3

THE CORPORATION

STATEMENT OF CURRENT MONETARY FLOWS

FOR THE YEAR ENDED DECEMBER 31, 1972

Operations—Major

Monetary-asset inflows:

Sales of goods or services (cash and charge)	$x	
Less monetary asset outflows and current cash commitments:		
(1) *Responsive to sales or production volume and mix:*		
Material purchases	x	
Labor services	x	
Other operating costs	x	$x
(2) "Committed":		
Interest on debt	$x	
Employee services	x	
Lease payments	x	
Pension payments	x	
Property taxes	x	x
(3) Discretionary:		
Research and development (outlays by major programs)	$x	
Advertising	x	
Replacement of capacity	x	x

EXHIBIT 12–3 (CONT.)

---

(4) Based on taxable income:

   Federal and state income taxes $\underline{\$x}$

      (classified by applicable rates)

Net change in current monetary accounts resulting from

  major operations $\underline{\$x}$

Operations—Minor

Monetary asset inflows:

  Interest revenue $\$x$

  Sale of securities $\underline{x}$ $\$x$

Less monetary asset outflows and current cash

  commitments:

  Investment in securities $\$x$

  Investment management expenses:

   Salaries $\$x$

   Other $\underline{x}$ $\underline{x}$ $\underline{x}$

Net change in current monetary accounts resulting

  from minor operations $\underline{\underline{\$x}}$

Financing

Monetary asset inflows:

  Sale of stocks and bonds $\$x$

  Borrowing (classified by type) $\underline{x}$ $\$x$

Less monetary asset outflows and current cash

  commitments:

   Retirement of securities $\$x$

   Repayment of debt x

   Management expenses $\underline{x}$ $\underline{x}$

Net change in current monetary accounts resulting from

  changes in capital structure $\underline{\underline{\$x}}$

Operating Capacity

Monetary asset outflows and current cash

  commitments:

  Purchase of additional operating capacity

   (include data as prescribed under "operating

   facilities" in the statement of resources

   and commitments) $\$x$

Less monetary asset inflows:

  Sale of plant, equipment and land (include

   data as prescribed under "operating facilities"

   in the statement of resources and commitments) $\underline{x}$

Net change in current monetary accounts resulting from

  changes in capacity $\underline{\underline{\$x}}$

Distributions
Priority distributions:
   Preferred stock dividends $x
Residual distributions:
   Common stock dividends   x
   Partial liquidation dividends   x
Total distributions $x

SOURCE: Exhibits 12–2 and 12–3 are adapted from exhibits shown in "An Evaluation of External Reporting Practices—A Report of the 1966–68 Committee on External Reporting," Supplement to vol. XLIV, The Accounting Review (Evanston, Illinois: American Accounting Association, 1969), pp. 119–122.

is likely to see an increase in the amount and the relevance of information presented in the reports. One writer has suggested that this will take the following forms:

1. Fund-flow statements further emphasized and developed
2. Line of business reporting for diversified companies
3. Some publication of budgets
4. Further publication of operating statistics
5. Increased experimentation on reporting current values[7]

Apart from the pressures for change, these modest improvements will come about because both producers and consumers of accounting information will be better trained to use such information. As more enterprises develop computer-based record-keeping systems, they will have data inputs from a variety of sources, in addition to the traditional accounting ones (the market transactions of the firm), without prohibitive cost- and time-consuming efforts. The result will be less emphasis on conformity with generally accepted auditing standards, and more emphasis on relevant date for decision-making purposes.

Summary

The use and usefulness of accounting statements is governed in part by the scope and accuracy of the statements, and in part by the skill of the potential users of the statements. This book has placed primary emphasis on the needs of users outside the firm: stockholders,

[7]Sidney Davidson, "Accounting and Financial Reporting in the Seventies," *The Arthur Young Journal*, 75th Anniversary Edition, Spring–Summer 1969, pp. 106–109.

potential investors, creditors, employees, customers, government agencies, and the general public. In actual practice, this emphasis is narrowed to stockholders and other investors.

An accounting statement published for external use generally is accompanied by the report of a competent auditor (a licensed CPA) who places his professional responsibilities (to the public) above his desire to provide a service to the client company. The auditor authenticates—attests—the financial statements of a firm through analysis, inspection, and review of the firm's operations, and through communication with management and those who deal with the firm. He states his opinion in an audit report as to whether the financial statements present fairly the financial position of the firm and the results of its operations in accordance with generally accepted accounting principles.

Unfortunately, the phrase "generally accepted accounting principles" is, at best, ambiguous since there is little agreement about what the principles of accounting are. A myriad of attempts to state precisely the principles of accounting has resulted primarily in helpful descriptions of accounting methods, procedures, and practice. Such attempts have markedly improved accounting practice by emphasizing theory, by refining and developing new practices, and by calling attention to the ambiguities of current practices.

Perhaps the most knowledgeable and sophisticated external user of published accounting statements is the financial analyst. The function of the financial analyst is to measure, evaluate, and predict the performance of enterprises. In employing his primary analysis techniques of comparative statements and ratios, the financial analyst uses audited accounting statements as a basic tool. Comparative statements of the current results with prior results for a firm are useful to the financial analyst in identifying trends for an enterprise. Ratios of amounts that have a significant relationship also serve as a means of making year-to-year comparisons for a firm and comparisons among firms. The most widely used classes of ratios are those of overall solvency, the movement of current assets, long-term solvency, profitability and efficiency, and net income and operating results.

In order that accounting statements be of optimal value to all external users, only relevant and material data should be presented. To be relevant, the data must bear upon the intended use of the accounting statement. To be material, data must be important in a specific context.

The method of presenting the information in an accounting statement also affects its usefulness. Information considered most relevant and material should be presented in the body of the statement instead of in footnotes, as parenthetical information, or on supplemental schedules or reports. All information should be clear, concise, and consistent.

A Selection of Supplementary Readings

Albrecht, Philip E.: "Analyst Views Financial Reporting Problems," *Financial Executive,* September 1966, p. 12.

American Accounting Association: *A Statement of Basic Accounting Theory,* Evanston, Illinois, 1966, pp. 63–79.

"An Evaluation of External Reporting Practices—A Report of the 1966–68 Committee on External Reporting," Eldon S. Hendriksen, chairman. *Supplement to vol. XLIV, The Accounting Review.* Evanston, Illinois: American Accounting Association, 1969, pp. 79–122.

"Annual Reports," *World,* Peat, Marwick, Mitchell & Co., Spring 1971, pp. 39–41.

Backer, Morton: *Financial Reporting for Security Investment and Credit Decisions.* New York: National Association of Accountants, 1970, chap. 13. Reprinted as "Financial Reporting for Security Investment and Credit Decisions," *The New York Certified Public Accountant,* November 1970, pp. 885–892.

Barr, Andrew: "The Influence of Government Agencies on Accounting Principles with Particular Reference to the Securities and Exchange Commission," *The International Journal of Accounting Education and Research,* Fall 1965, pp. 15–33.

Beams, Floyd A., and Paul E. Fertig: "Pollution Control Through Social Cost Conversion," *The Journal of Accounting,* November 1971, pp. 37–42.

Bevis, Herman W.: "The CPA's Attest Function in Modern Society," *The Journal of Accountancy,* February 1962, pp. 28–35.

———: "Accounting and Auditing Comparability: Fact and Fiction," *Banking,* February 1967, p. 54.

Brenner, Vincent C.: "Financial Statement Users' Views of the Desirability of Reporting Current Cost Information," *Journal of Accounting Research,* Autumn 1970, pp. 159–166.

Broster, E. J.: "Business Ratios to Combat Creeping Inefficiency," *The Accountant,* Nov. 27, 1969, pp. 721–724.

———: "Business Ratios," *Certified Accountants Journal,* July–August 1971, pp. 403–406.

Burton, John C.: "'Criticism with Love': An Educator Views the Public Accounting Profession," *The Arthur Young Journal,* Winter–Spring 1971, pp. 17–22.

Caplan, Edwin H.: "Relevance—A 'Will-o'-the-Wisp,'" *Abacus,* September 1969, pp. 48–54.

Chambers, R. J.: "Fact, Symbol, and Feedback in Accounting," *The New York Certified Public Accountant,* January 1970, p. 43.

———: "What's Wrong with Financial Statements?" *The Australian Accountant,* February 1970, pp. 19–28.

Corcoran, A. Wayne, and Wayne E. Leininger, Jr.: "Financial Statements—Who Needs Them?" *Financial Executive,* August 1970, p. 34

Craswell, Allen T.: "Accounting Reports . . . Do They Communicate?" *The Chartered Accountant in Australia,* December 1969, p. 4.

Davidson, Sidney: "Accounting and Financial Reporting in the Seventies," *The Arthur Young Journal,* Spring–Summer 1969, pp. 101–109. An adaptation using the same title also appears in *The Journal of Accountancy,* December 1969, pp. 29–37.

"In Defense of the APB," editorial summary, *Financial Executive,* February 1971, p. 48.

Defliese, Philip L.: "The Accounting Principles Board and Its Recent and Pending Opinions," *The New York Certified Public Accountant,* April 1971, p. 279.

Eiteman, Dean S.: "Critical Problems in Accounting for Goodwill," *The Journal of Accountancy,* March 1971, pp. 46–50.

Estes, Ralph W.: "An Assessment of the Usefulness of Current Cost and Price-level Information by Financial Statement Users," *Journal of Accounting Research,* Autumn 1968, pp. 200–207.

Goetz, Billy E.: "Return on Investment: Garbage in, Garbage out," *The Florida Certified Public Accountant,* June 1970, pp. 24–28.

Grenside, John P.: "Accountants' Reports on Profit Forecasts in the U.K.," *The Journal of Accountancy,* May 1970, pp. 47–53.

Haack, Robert W.: "Viewpoints in Corporate Disclosure," *Financial Executive,* February 1969, p. 19.

Hawkins, David F.: "Behavioral Implications of Generally Accepted Accounting Principles," *California Management Review,* Winter 1969, pp. 13–21.

Hendriksen, Eldon S.: "Toward Greater Comparability through Uniformity of Accounting Principles," *The New York Certified Public Accountant,* February 1967, pp. 105–115.

Hobgood, George: "Increased Disclosure in 1969 Corporate Annual Reports," *Financial Executive,* August 1970, pp. 24–33.

Horngren, Charles T.: "The Accounting Discipline in 1999," *The Accounting Review,* January 1971, pp. 1–11.

Horrigan, James O.: "A Short History of Financial Ratio Analysis," *The Accounting Review,* April 1968, pp. 284–294.

Kell, Walter G.: "The Auditor's Responsibilities in Financial Reporting," *Michigan Business Review,* March 1967, pp. 26–32.

Knortz, Herbert C.: "Economic Realism as a Reporting Essential," *Financial Executive,* March 1969, p. 21. Also in *The New York Certified Public Accountant,* December 1969, pp. 929–937.

Layton, LeRoy: "Accounting Principles Board in the 1970's," *The Ohio CPA,* Autumn 1970, pp. 168–174.

Maloan, W. T.: "What Bankers Are Now Looking for in Financial Statements," *The Practical Accountant,* January/February 1970, pp. 40–45.

Mautz, Robert K.: "An Approach to the Uniformity-Flexibility Issue in Accounting," *Financial Executive,* February 1971, pp. 14–19.

Moonitz, Maurice: "The Accounting Principles Board Revisited," *The New York Certified Public Accountant,* May 1971, pp. 341–345.

_____: "Why Is It So Difficult to Agree upon a Set of Accounting Principles?" *The Chartered Accountant in Australia,* November 1968, pp. 439–449. Also in *The Australian Accountant,* November 1968, pp. 621–631, and *The New York Certified Public Accountant,* May 1969, pp. 347–352.

Nicholson, H. N.: "The Role of the Security Analyst," *The Australian Accountant,* November 1970, pp. 490–492.

Norr, David: "What a Financial Analyst Wants from an Annual Report," *Financial Executive,* August 1970, pp. 20–23.

Powell, Weldon: "Putting Uniformity in Financial Accounting into Perspective," *Law and Contemporary Problems,* Autumn 1965, pp. 674–689. Also reprinted as "Putting Accounting Uniformity into Perspective," *Financial Executive,* October 1966, p. 18.

Rappaport, Alfred, and Eugene M. Lerner: "Public Reporting by Diversified Companies," *Financial Analysts Journal,* January–February 1970, pp. 54–64.

Richards, D. G.: "Modern Presentation of Information in Balance Sheets and Accounts for Shareholders," *Accountancy,* December 1969, pp. 900–906.

Savoie, Leonard M. "The Accounting Principles Board: What It Is, How It Works and What Its Role in Business Is," *Financial Analysts Journal,* May–June 1965, pp. 53–57.

_____ : "Financial Communication: The Public's Right to Know," *Financial Executive,* December 1968, p. 20.

_____ : "Raising Accounting Standards," *Empirical Research in Accounting: Selected Studies, 1969,* supplement to vol. 7, *Journal of Accounting Research,* pp. 55–62.

_____ : "What Issues Will Challenge CPAs in the 1970's?" *The Ohio CPA,* Summer 1969, pp. 97–104.

Silverman, Edward J.: "Common Weaknesses in Financial Reports and How to Avoid Them," *The Practical Accountant,* May–June 1970, pp. 28–35.

Stamp, Edward: "Accounting Principles: Challenge and Response," *The Accountant,* November 5, 1970, pp. 628–631.

_____ : "Establishing Accounting Principles," *Abacus,* December 1970, pp. 96–104.

Vance, Lawrence L.: "The Road to Reform of Accounting Principles," *The Accounting Review,* October 1969, pp. 692–703.

_____ : "Changing Responsibilities of the Public Accountant," an address presented at the Stanford University Graduate School of Business under sponsorship of the Price Waterhouse Foundation, June 5, 1970, privately printed.

Vatter, William J.: "Progress in the Pursuit of Principles," *The International Journal of Accounting Education and Research,* Fall 1969, pp. 1–15.

Weston, J. Fred: "Financial Analysis: Planning and Control," *Financial Executive,* July 1965, p. 40.

Willingham, John J., Charles H. Smith, and Martin E. Taylor: "Should the CPA's Opinion Be Extended to Include Forecasts?" *Financial Executive,* September 1970, p. 80.

Wright, M. G.: "Dividend Rate in the Strategy of the Company," *The Accountant,* December 2, 1967, pp. 715–717.

Questions

12-1 A key criterion for evaluating almost any discipline today is the one of relevance. Prepare an outline (or an essay) on one of the following subjects:

The limited relevance of accounting

The unlimited relevance of accounting

12–2   *Thus, the one basic accounting postulate underlying accounting principles may be stated as that of fairness—fairness to all segments of the business community (management, labor, stockholders, creditors, customers, and the public), determined and measured in the light of the economic and political environment and the modes of thought and customs of all such segments—to the end that the accounting principles based upon this postulate shall produce financial accounting for the lawfully established economic rights and interests that is fair to all segments.**

Evaluate this principle as providing an adequate foundation for accounting.

*The Postulate of Accounting—What It Is, How It Is Determined, How It Should Be Used (Arthur Andersen & Co., 1960), p. 31.

12–3   Contrast the essential differences between the approaches used by the AICPA to formulate principles and those used by the AAA. Consider procedures, philosophic differences, and end results.

12–4   Why is it important for a discipline to have a codified set of principles? *Alternate question:* Defend the proposition that accounting is a discipline.

12–5   One recommendation for improving accounting reports is to include a statement of taxable income and a reconciliation with reported income. Defend a pro or con position on this recommendation.

12–6   The creation of an accounting court has been suggested; it has not been developed, however, although many accountants and external users of financial statements consider it an excellent idea. If you favor this recommendation, explain how you think it could be implemented. If you don't favor this recommendation, explain why not.

12–7   It has been argued that a principal source for determining whether an accounting practice has substantial authoritative support is "common business practice." Do you agree? Give your reasons for agreeing or not agreeing.

12–8   What uses would you make of accounting reports:
a. As the owner-manager of a service garage for the repair of automobiles?
b. As the financial analyst for a large mutual investment fund?
c. As a prospective investor in the stock of a leading automobile manufacturer?

12–9   Briefly describe the major uses of accounting reports for each of the following:
a. A nonmanagerial shareholder who owns 75 percent of the outstanding shares of the reporting firm
b. An insurance company that has loaned the reporting firm $25 million for 10 years at 5 percent
c. Determining whether the firm should invest $10 million in a program of research and development of new uses for its products

12-10   The owner of a business, planning to sell it, has requested his certified public accountant to prepare statements for the information of prospective buyers. "Don't use your regular statements," he instructs the CPA, "because I want to get a high price for my business. Make it look as good as possible." Would it be proper for the CPA to prepare statements different from those he ordinarily prepares for his client at the end of the year? If so, what form would they take?

12-11   A large manufacturing corporation with thousands of stockholders throughout the country is studying its financial reports with the idea of eliminating unnecessary duplication in them. One recommendation is to eliminate duplication by preparing a single set of reports to be used by department managers, division heads, corporate management, and the stockholders. Would this recommendation be desirable and practicable?

12-12   The following information is provided (with 000's omitted):

Cash	$ 2	Current liabilities	$16
Receivables	10	Long-term debt	10
Inventory	12	Stockholders' equity	8
Plant (net)	10		
	$34		$34

Sales	$100.0
Cost of goods sold	60.0
Other expenses	34.9
Interest charge	0.7
Income taxes	2.2
Dividends	2.2
Increase in stockholders' equity	0.0

(1) The most important measure of profitability is (approximately): (a) 27.5 percent, (b) 6.5 percent, (c) 12.9 percent, (d) 2.2 percent, (e) 15.0 percent.
(2) A measure of the length of time merchandise stays in stock is (approximately): (a) 5.0, (b) 8.3, (c) 0.6, (d) 0.4, (e) 2.9.
(3) A measure of current liquidity is (approximately): (a) 1.5, (b) 0.7, (c) 0.4, (d) 10.0, (e) 8.3.
(4) A measure of long-run solvency is (approximately): (a) 7.3 percent, (b) 2.2 percent, (c) 0.5 percent, (d) 55 percent, (e) 25 percent, (f) 0.4 percent.

12-13   Ownership is $120,000, liabilities $60,000, noncurrent assets $30,000. The current ratio is 3.75; the acid test, 0.75. Sales are $500,000.
(1) The current liabilities are: (a) less than $25,000, (b) $25,000 to $34,999, (c) $35,000 to $44,999, (d) $45,000 to $54,999, (e) above $55,000.
(2) Prepayments are zero. The inventory is approximately: (a) $80,000 to $94,999, (b) $95,000 to $117,999, (c) $118,000 to $132,999, (d) over $132,500, (e) an amount that cannot be determined.
(3) Cash and marketable securities $5,000. The receivable turnover is approximately: (a) 20, (b) 15, (c) 12, (d) 10, (e) 5.

(4) The gross margin is 28 percent of sales. The inventory turnover is approximately: (a) 3, (b) 5, (c) 8, (d) 10, (e) 12.

12-14   Usually the CPA is engaged by the board of directors of the company whose statements he is to audit and paid from company funds. How can the CPA justify this practice when he has public responsibilities to the general or investing public and to other external users of financial statements?

12-15   *To summarize, accounting information on profits represents the results of an imperfect measuring system manned by imperfect human beings. Valuable as the information may be, it is subject to misuse, and among the individuals most likely to misuse it are imperfectly informed scholars and practitioners in economics and finance.**

Comment.

*Carl L. Nelson, George O. May Professor of Financial Accounting, Columbia University, in "An Accountant's View of Profit Measurement," from H. W. Stevenson and J. R. Nelson, eds., *Profits in the Modern Economy* (Minneapolis: University of Minnesota Press, 1967), p. 81.

12-16   *Accountants are basically concerned with three measurement questions. What? When? How? The answer to the first question seems to be to ignore many events, namely, those that do not affect directly the accounting entity considered or those that cannot be measured objectively or in monetary terms. The answer to the second question is largely a matter of deciding upon the most appropriate accounting period. The answer to the third question is the central problem of financial accounting.*

Comment. Illustrate.

12-17   Consider the extent to which alternative methods of valuation should be reported in financial statements.

12-18   *Ringling's Board of Directors believes that the proposed merger is advantageous to Ringling and its shareholders and therefore recommends its approval. Mattel's and Handfeld's obligations under the agreement are conditioned upon delivery to Mattel (or its nominee) on or before January 30, 1971, of proxies, which are to be irrevocable prior to February 27, 1971, to vote at least 90% of the outstanding stock of Ringling in favor of the agreement and the merger contemplated thereby. The purpose of this condition is to comply with Accounting Principles Board Opinion No. 16 relating to pooling of interests.**

What is the required condition? What other conditions are required too?

*From "Notice of Special Meeting of Shareholders of Ringling Bros.—Barnum & Bailey Combined Shows, Inc., to Be Held on February 23, 1971," p. 2.

12-19   *Accounting has always been a highly practical discipline. Accountants have been faced with the problem of making immediate decisions in order to* *meet the exigencies of practice. They have not had the luxury of extensive reflection before taking a position. In addition, they were not much more than specialized craftsmen when an almost overwhelming responsibility was rather suddenly thrust upon them. They were asked to become the stewards of the community's wealth. They were required to make public what had previously been jealously guarded private information. They were asked to make independent judgments about the affairs of persons who had previously directed their activities. They were asked to provide information via a device that had sometimes been used to misinform or conceal. They were required to have integrity when deceit was not uncommon. As a consequence of these factors, there were twin developments: (1) problems were solved in isolation; and (2) the solutions became accepted and rather rigid. . . . In the absence of a cohesive theory, in the absence of police power, in the presence of ignorance and apathy of the community, his only defense was precedent and persuasion. Precedent soon became rule, and the rigid application of rules was his primary weapon. It is easier to accuse someone of breaking a rule than to accuse him of not telling the truth.**

Comment on this statement on the position of the accountant.

*Robert R. Sterling, *Theory of the Measurement of Enterprise Income* (Lawrence: The University Press of Kansas, 1970), pp. 255–256.

12–20   Select the best answer choice for each of the following seven items which relate to a CPA's standards of professional conduct and responsibility.

(1) A CPA should reject a management advisory services engagement if:
   a. It would require him to make management decisions for an audit client.
   b. His recommendations are to be subject to review by the client.
   c. He audits the financial statements of a subsidiary of the prospective client.
   d. The proposed engagement is not accounting-related.

(2) Bubbles, Inc., an audit client of Ted Williams, CPA, is contemplating the installation of an electronic data-processing system. It would be inconsistent with Williams' independence as the auditor of Bubbles' financial statements for him to:
   a. Recommend accounting controls to be exercised over the computer
   b. Recommend particular hardware and software packages to be used in the new computer center
   c. Prepare a study of the feasibility of the computer center
   d. Supervise operation of Bubbles' computer center on a part-time basis

(3) The CPA should not undertake an engagement if his fee is to be based upon:
   a. The findings of a tax authority
   b. A percentage of audited net income
   c. Per diem rates plus expenses
   d. Rates set by a city ordinance

(4) The CPA ethically could:
   a. Perform an examination for a financially distressed client at less than his customary fees

      b. Advertise only as to his expertise in preparing income tax returns
      c. Base his audit fee on a percentage of the proceeds of his client's stock issue
      d. Own preferred stock in a corporation which is an audit client

(5) If a CPA is not independent, his auditor's report should include a:
      a. Qualified opinion
      b. Description of the reasons for his lack of independence
      c. Description of the auditing procedures followed
      d. Disclaimer of opinion

(6) The essence of a CPA's independence is:
      a. Avoiding significant financial interest in the client
      b. Maintaining a mental attitude of impartiality
      c. Performing the examination from the viewpoint of the stockholders
      d. Being sure that no relatives or personal friends are employed by the client

(7) The CPA would issue an adverse auditor's opinion instead of a qualified opinion if:
      a. His exception to the fairness of presentation was so material that a qualified opinion was not justified.
      b. He prepared the financial statements from the client's records without completing an audit.
      c. The client limited the scope of his examination.
      d. He did not confirm receivables or observe the taking of the physical inventory.

12-21

The president of the AICPA has called for the development of a system of "social accounting" as a means of assessing costs and benefits of current social and environmental problems. In a speech in Los Angeles Mr. Armstrong said: "We must find better methods than we now have for measuring the cost/benefit ratios in the social field and for establishing criteria for gauging the quality of life."

What recommendations for fulfilling this objective do you think that the AICPA should consider?

12-22

Economics Professor Paul A. Samuelson, Nobel Prize Winner for 1970, said (in discussing investing in the stock market):

With common stocks, it's earnings. That's the name of the game.

Keynes always looked at balance sheets. By and large, people I admire and who do well and who should be nameless, do make money in, say Toni hair products, which had no book value but had a new idea, and they jumped on it. Or on Avon. Intrinsic value in terms of balance sheet.

The fundamentals are future earnings. There are disputes, whether it should be dividends or earnings, but most people in high brackets don't want dividends except as far as it is a test to earnings . . . .

The sophisticated investor can also see through accounting methods . . . .

This year it's expensed, last year it's capitalized. The purpose of public ac-

counting should be to everyone's use. Instead, we've had this conglomerate business with phoney instant earnings. You get $10,000 for your dogs, giving them two $5,000 cats. *

Prepare a profile of the Samuelson investor and how he utilizes financial statements; are there any surprises in his view of financial statements?

*From "Paul Samuelson, Investor," The New York Times, March 14, 1971, sec. 3, p. 18.

12–23 Lord Justice Buckley made the statement that every balance sheet is a matter of estimate and opinion. Illustrate.

12–24 The argument is frequently made that accounting statements should be prepared so that they can be read on the run or that the external user of financial statement is in the best position when he has a minimum amount of information. Support or criticize this argument.

Problems

12–1

(000's omitted)

Cash	$ 12	Current liabilities	$ 80
Marketable securities	60	Bonds payable	60
Receivables	40	Preferred stock (6%)	20
Inventories	60	Common stock ($100 par)	80
Prepayments	4	Retained earnings	26
Plant (net)	90		
	$266		$266

Sales	$400.0
Cost of goods sold	360.0
Gross margin	$ 40.0
Other operating expenses	13.4
	$ 26.6
Interest charges	3.6
	$ 23.0
Income taxes	6.9
Net income	$ 16.1

Assume that the average of all balance sheet items is equal to the year-end figure and that preferred dividends have been paid currently.
(1) The current ratio is: (a) less than 1.80, (b) between 1.80 and 1.99, (c) between 2.00 and 2.18, (d) between 2.19 and 2.39, (e) over 2.39.
(2) The ownership equity ratio is: (a) less than 0.30, (b) 0.40 to 0.50, (c) 0.60 to 1.00, (d) 1.25 to 1.75, (e) over 3.00.
(3) The rate of return on common stock equity is: (a) less than 14 percent, (b) 14 to 15 percent, (c) 15 to 16 percent, (d) 16 to 17 percent (e) over 17 percent.

(4) The merchandise turnover is: (a) less than 6.5, (b) 6.5 to 7.5, (c) 7.5 to 8.5, (d) 8.5 to 9.5, (e) over 9.5.

(5) The book value per share of common stock is: (a) $100, (b) $110 to $120, (c) $130 to $140, (d) $150 to $160, (e) some other amount.

(6) The quick assets ratio is: (a) 1.00, (b) 1.15, (c) 1.25, (d) 1.35, (e) some other amount.

(7) The number of times interest is earned is: (a) less than 5.0, (b) 6.0 to 6.5, (c) 6.5 to 7.0, (d) 7.0 to 7.5, (e) over 7.5.

(8) The net income per share of common stock is: (a) $18.00 to $19.00, (b) $19.00 to $20.00, (c) $20.00 to $21.00, (d) $21.00 to $22.00, (e) $22.00 to $23.00.

(9) All sales are on account. The average collection period is approximately: (a) 27 days, (b) 30 days, (c) 33 days, (d) 36 days, (e) 39 days.

12–2   Obtain from your library a copy of the most recent annual report of a corporation engaged in manufacturing or merchandising. If you have a special interest in a particular company, why not select it for this particular exercise? If the report is not available at your school or public library, please secure it directly from the corporation, allowing yourself sufficient time so you may use it in this exercise.

(1) Verify the ratios that are given in the report for the current year and the previous year. Compute any others that are not given.
(2) Prepare common-size statements.
(3) Follow any special instructions of your instructor.
(4) What information is disclosed by your analysis?

12–3   On the basis of the following financial statement data, compute the specified ratios.

Cash	$ 100	Current liabilities	$ 200
Accounts receivable (net)	100	Long-term debt	400
Inventory	200	Common stock*	800
Plant (net)	1,600	Retained earnings	600
	$2,000		$2,000

Sales	$1,000
Cost of goods sold	500
Gross margin	$ 500
Other expenses	200
Net income of enterprise	$ 300
Federal income taxes	50
Net income to investors	$ 250
Interest charges	10
Net income to stockholders	$ 240

*80 shares—$10 par.

Rate of return on total capital _____
Rate of return on stockholder's equity _____
Net income per share on common stock _____
Inventory turnover _____
Collection period _____
Turnover of plant _____
Current ratio _____
Quick ratio _____
Working capital _____
Ownership equity ratio _____
Times interest earned _____

(1) Compute two ratios to measure current liquidity.
(2) Compute two ratios to measure long-run solvency.
(3) Compute three ratios to measure profitability and efficiency.

12-4

In conducting the first audit of the Hot Lunch Program at a private school, the accounting firm uncovered the following situations. Prepare a letter for the accounting firm, making recommendations to the school board.

(1) No lists of the equipment used in the program and owned by the school had been made.
(2) Several bills from suppliers were long overdue.
(3) The program's board of overseers had met only once during the year, on a picnic with the program staff.
(4) The milk used in the program totaled 2 quarts per child per school day although each child received only a pint per meal to drink.
(5) There was no record of which children had paid for their lunches although the program director said she knew which ones had not paid.
(6) The total of outstanding bills exceeded the balance in the program's bank account.
(7) No budget had been prepared for the coming year.

12-5

We have examined the position statements of Kate Smith, Inc., as of January 31, 1972, and the related income statement to the extent we considered necessary in the circumstances.

The accompanying financial statements do not reflect a fee of $100,000 for the year ended January 31, 1972, due to a 100 percent stockholder. Payment of the fee is subject to the working capital restrictions referred to in the footnote. A fair presentation of the financial statements would require the inclusion of the $100,000 fee as a noncurrent liability and, accordingly, an increase of the loss for the year ended January 31, 1972, and the accumulated deficit as at January 31, 1972.

Since the amount omitted as described in the preceding paragraph is material, we are of the opinion that the financial statements do not present fairly the financial position of Kate Smith, Inc., at January 31, 1972, or the results of its operations for the year then ended in conformity with generally accepted accounting principles.

FOOTNOTE: Certain agreements entered into during the year between the company and its stockholder provide, among other things, that the company pay an annual fee of $100,000 a year for 10 years, and $10,000 a year for 5 years thereafter for services to be performed by one stockholder.

The above annual fees will be paid only if the working capital of the company is in excess of $125,000. To the extent an annual fee is not fully paid, the unpaid balance will be carried over to subsequent years subject to the working capital limitation. At January 31, 1972, the working capital of the company was less than $125,000; accordingly the annual fee of $100,000 for the year ended January 31, 1972, has been neither accrued nor included in the accompanying financial statements.

(1) What type of opinion is the above? Why?
(2) Is the $100,000 a contingent liability?

12–6

A substantial part of the criticism of accounting is concerned with the limitations of historical transaction-based data to serve a significant number of desired uses. At the same time, the proposed replacement of historical transaction-based information by current values (however defined) fails to satisfy a number of other uses. Our standards provide an approach to the solution of this conflict. Historical transaction-based information has been verified by a market transaction, and hence is of great usefulness when verifiability is emphasized. Current values, on the other hand, reflect not only the transactions of the firm but also the impact of the environment on the firm beyond the completed transactions. Thus they possess a high degree of relevance for many uses in which prediction is prominent. The presentation of the historical information alone excludes the full impact of the environment on the firm; presentation of current cost information alone obscures the record of consummated market transactions. The committee recommends that both kinds of information be presented in a multi-valued report, in which the two kinds of information appear in adjacent columns. This has the added advantage of revealing the impact of environmental changes, since the historical information reflects market transactions, the current-cost information reflects market transactions plus "unrealized" market influences, and the difference shows the effect of unrealized environmental influences. Inclusion of the environmental information in what is reported better enables the accountant to meet the standard of relevance.*

Prepare a commentary or critique of the above statement.

*From *A Statement of Basic Accounting Theory* by AAA Committee (Evanston, Illinois: AAA, 1966), pp. 30–31.

12–7

Following is an excerpt taken from the Silver Bell, Inc., statement of consolidated income and retained earnings for 1970.

Silver Bell, Inc.
Statement of
Consolidated Income
and Retained Earnings

Income before extraordinary item	$ 5,412,844
Loss from discontinued operations—net of related income reduction	1,058,240
Net income	$ 4,354,604
Retained earnings at beginning of year	22,790,896
Total	$27,145,500
Deduct cash dividends ($1.35 per share):	1,830,870
Pooled company (before merger)	51,018
Total	$ 1,881,888
Retained earnings at end of year	$25,263,612

With no preferred stock or convertible securities outstanding, show the net income per share calculation as it must have appeared on the income statement if this calculation had been made in accordance with "generally accepted accounting principles." You must show calculations, but you may round to significant digits.

12-8

In each of the following ten *independent* situations offer any comment which you believe pertinent. The situation may deal with accounting concepts or techniques. Assume that the accounting period coincides with the calendar year in each situation.

	Debit	*Credit*
(1) In the process of adjusting and closing the books, the A Company made an entry:		
Cost of goods sold	$ 3,000	
Merchandise inventory		$ 3,000
(2) The B Company made the following entry to record the sale of some merchandise:		
Cash	$25,000	
Merchandise inventory		$20,000
Revenue		5,000
(3) The C Company made the following entry:		
Delivery expense	$20,000	
Cash		$15,000
Estimated delivery expenses		5,000
(4) The D Company made the following entries:		
Investments	$12,000	
Revenue from investments		$12,000
and then for a cash dividend received:		
Cash	$2,000	
Investments		$2,000

	Debit	Credit
(5) The E Company made the following entry:		
Accounts receivable	$50,000	
Inventory		$50,000
(6) The F Company made the following entry:		
Cash	$25,000	
Marketable securities		$25,000
(7) The G Company made the following entry:		
Delivery expense	$10,000	
Prepaid delivery expense	5,000	
Delivery equipment—		
accumulated depreciation		$15,000
(8) The H Company made the following entry:		
Land	$10,000	
Merchandise inventory		$10,000
(9) The I Company made the following entry for the cash sale of some of its product:		
Cash	$25,000	
Loss due to fluctuations in product price	25,000	
Inventory		$50,000
(10) The J Company uses a perpetual inventory approach in determining Cost of Goods Sold. On December 31, 1973, after taking a physical inventory they made the entry:		
Cost of goods sold	$ 2,000	
Merchandise inventory		$ 2,000

On January 20, 1975, an error was found in the computations made in the December 31, 1973 physical inventory. The error had understated the inventory by $2,000. No physical inventory was taken after December 31, 1973.

12-9

Jackie Gleason
Trial Balance
December 31, 1973

Cash	$ 36,860	$ 34,950
Accounts receivable	32,150	30,050
Accounts receivable—allowance for doubtful accounts	200	322
Inventory	25,500	21,750
Supplies	375	
Prepaid insurance	400	
Land	1,500	
Building	8,500	
Building—accumulated depreciation		255
Accounts payable	23,150	26,275
Salaries payable		175
Interest payable		180
Note payable (6%)		6,000
Jackie Gleason, capital		?
Jackie Gleason, current	3,000	
Sales		32,150
Sales—returns and allowances	490	
Sales—doubtful accounts	322	
Cost of goods sold	21,750	
Other operating expenses	?	
Interest charges	360	
	$154,557	$152,107

The Gleason trial balance is a trial balance of totals—that is, for each account the total debits and the total credits are listed. No balance is listed for Jackie Gleason, Capital or Operating Expenses because these two ledger accounts have been misplaced, although it is known that the former had no debits and the latter had no credits. On January 1, 1973, Gleason commenced business by purchasing the building and land for cash and the 6 percent note. The purchases of inventory, supplies, and insurance were made on account. Determine the balance of each of the two missing accounts. As a preliminary step, set up in general journal form or in T accounts the entries that were made during the period.

12-10

The following four statements have been taken directly or with some modification from the accounting literature. All of them either are taken out of context, involve circular reasoning, and/or contain one or more fallacies, half-truths, erroneous comments, conclusions, or inconsistencies (internally or with generally accepted principles or practices).

Statement 1
Accounting is a service activity. Its function is to provide quantitative financial information which is intended to be useful in making economic decisions about and for economic entities. Thus the accounting function might be viewed primarily as being a tool or a device for providing quantitative financial information to management to facilitate decision making.

Statement 2
Financial statements that were developed in accordance with general accounting principles, which apply the conservatism convention, can be free from bias (or can give a presentation that is fair with respect to continuing and prospective stockholders as well as to retiring stockholders).

Statement 3
When a company changes from the Lifo to the Fifo method of determining the cost of ending inventories and this change results in a $1 million increase both in income after taxes and in income taxes for the year of change, the increase would stem from the elimination of Lifo reserves established in prior years.

Statement 4
If the value of an enterprise were to be determined by the method that computes the sum of the present values of the marginal (or incremental) expected net receipts of individual tangible and intangible assets, the resulting valuation would tend to be less than if the value of the entire enterprise had been determined in another way, such as by computing the present value of total expected net receipts for the entire enterprise (i.e., the resulting valuation of parts would sum to an amount that was less than that for the whole). This would be true even if the same pattern of interest or discount rates were used for both valuations.

Evaluate any *one* of the above numbered statements as follows: (a) list the fallacies, half-truths, circular reasoning, erroneous comments, or conclusions, and/or inconsistencies; and (b) explain by what authority and/or reasoning each item listed in (a) can be considered deficient. If the statement (or a portion of it) is merely out of context, indicate the context(s) in which the statement would be correct.

12–11   You have been asked by the board of trustees of a local church to review its accounting procedures. As a part of this review you have prepared the following comments relating to the collections made at weekly services and record keeping for members' pledges and contributions:

The church's board of trustees has delegated responsibility for financial management and audit of the financial records to the finance committee. This group prepares the annual budget and approves major disbursements, but is not involved in collections or record keeping. No audit has been considered necessary in recent years because the same trusted employee has kept church records and served as financial secretary for 15 years.

The collection at the weekly service is taken by a team of ushers. The head usher then counts the collection in the church office after each service. He then places the collection and a notation of the amount counted in the church safe. Next morning the financial secretary opens the safe and recounts the collection. He withholds about $100 to meet cash expenditures during the coming week and deposits the remainder of the collection intact. In order to facilitate the deposit, members who contribute by check are asked to draw their checks to "cash."

At their request a few members are furnished prenumbered, predated envelopes in which to insert their weekly contributions. The head usher removes the cash from the envelopes to be counted with the loose cash included in the collection and discards the envelopes. No record is maintained of issuance or return of the envelopes, and the envelope system is not encouraged.

Each member is asked to prepare a contribution pledge card annually. The pledge is regarded as a moral commitment by the member to contribute a stated weekly amount. Based on the amounts shown on the pledge cards, the financial secretary furnishes a letter to members who request it to support the tax deductibility of their contributions.

Describe the weaknesses and recommend improvements in procedures for
a. Collections made at weekly services
b. Record keeping for members' pledges and contributions
Organize your answer as follows:

Weakness	*Recommended Improvement*

A   Compound Interest Tables

Table 1:
*Amount of $1 Due
in n Periods*

$$a_{\overline{n}|i} = (1 + i)^n$$

				Rate of Interest, %				
n	1.0	2.0	3.0	4.0	5.0	6.0	8.0	10.0
1	1.0100	1.0200	1.0300	1.0400	1.0500	1.0600	1.0800	1.1000
2	1.0201	1.0404	1.0609	1.0816	1.1025	1.1236	1.1664	1.2100
3	1.0303	1.0612	1.0927	1.1249	1.1576	1.1910	1.2597	1.3310
4	1.0406	1.0824	1.1255	1.1699	1.2155	1.2625	1.3605	1.4641
5	1.0510	1.1041	1.1593	1.2167	1.2763	1.3382	1.4693	1.6105
6	1.0615	1.1262	1.1941	1.2653	1.3401	1.4185	1.5869	1.7716
7	1.0721	1.1487	1.2299	1.3159	1.4071	1.5036	1.7138	1.9487
8	1.0829	1.1717	1.2668	1.3686	1.4775	1.5938	1.8509	2.1436
9	1.0937	1.1951	1.3048	1.4233	1.5513	1.6895	1.9990	2.3579
10	1.1046	1.2190	1.3439	1.4802	1.6289	1.7908	2.1589	2.5937
11	1.1157	1.2434	1.3842	1.5395	1.7103	1.8983	2.3316	2.8531
12	1.1268	1.2682	1.4258	1.6010	1.7959	2.0122	2.5182	3.1384
13	1.1381	1.2936	1.4685	1.6651	1.8856	2.1329	2.7196	3.4523
14	1.1495	1.3195	1.5126	1.7317	1.9799	2.2609	2.9372	3.7975
15	1.1610	1.3459	1.5580	1.8009	2.0789	2.3966	3.1722	4.1772
16	1.1726	1.3728	1.6047	1.8730	2.1829	2.5404	3.4259	4.5950
17	1.1843	1.4002	1.6528	1.9479	2.2920	2.6928	3.7000	5.0545
18	1.1961	1.4282	1.7024	2.0258	2.4066	2.8543	3.9960	5.5599
19	1.2081	1.4568	1.7535	2.1068	2.5270	3.0256	4.3157	6.1159
20	1.2202	1.4859	1.8061	2.1911	2.6533	3.2071	4.6610	6.7275
25	1.2824	1.6406	2.0938	2.6658	3.3864	4.2919	6.8485	10.8347
30	1.3478	1.8114	2.4273	3.2434	4.3219	5.7435	10.0627	17.4494
40	1.4889	2.2080	3.2620	4.8010	7.0400	10.2857	21.7245	45.2593
50	1.6446	2.6916	4.3839	7.1067	11.4674	18.4202	46.9016	117.3909

Table 2:
Amount of an Annuity
of $1 per Period

$$A_{\overline{n}|i} = \frac{(1 + i)^n - 1}{i}$$

Rate of Interest, %

n	1.0	2.0	3.0	4.0	5.0	6.0	8.0	10.0
1	1.0000	1.0000	1.0000	1.0000	1.0000	1.0000	1.0000	1.0000
2	2.0100	2.0200	2.0300	2.0400	2.0500	2.0600	2.0800	2.1000
3	3.0301	3.0604	3.0909	3.1216	3.1525	3.1836	3.2464	3.3100
4	4.0604	4.1216	4.1836	4.2465	4.3101	4.3746	4.5061	4.6410
5	5.1010	5.2040	5.3091	5.4163	5.5256	5.6371	5.8666	6.1051
6	6.1520	6.3081	6.4684	6.6330	6.8019	6.9753	7.3359	7.7156
7	7.2135	7.4343	7.6625	7.8983	8.1420	8.3938	8.9228	9.4872
8	8.2857	8.5830	8.8923	9.2142	9.5491	9.8975	10.6366	11.4359
9	9.3685	9.7546	10.1591	10.5828	11.0266	11.4913	12.4876	13.5795
10	10.4622	10.9497	11.4639	12.0061	12.5779	13.1808	14.4866	15.9374
11	11.5668	12.1687	12.8078	13.4864	14.2068	14.9716	16.6455	18.5312
12	12.6825	13.4121	14.1920	15.0258	15.9171	16.8699	18.9771	21.3843
13	13.8093	14.6803	15.6178	16.6268	17.7130	18.8821	21.4953	24.5227
14	14.9474	15.9739	17.0863	18.2919	19.5986	21.0151	24.2149	27.9750
15	16.0969	17.2934	18.5989	20.0236	21.5786	23.2760	27.1521	31.7725
16	17.2579	18.6393	20.1569	21.8245	23.6575	25.6725	30.3243	35.9497
17	18.4304	20.0121	21.7616	23.6975	25.8404	28.2129	33.7502	40.5447
18	19.6147	21.4123	23.4144	25.6454	28.1324	30.9057	37.4502	45.5992
19	20.8109	22.8406	25.1169	27.6712	30.5390	33.7600	41.4463	51.1591
20	22.0190	24.2974	26.8704	29.7781	33.0660	36.7856	45.7620	57.2750
25	28.2432	32.0303	36.4593	41.6459	47.7271	54.8645	73.1059	98.3471
30	34.7849	40.5681	47.5754	56.0849	66.4388	79.0582	113.2832	164.4940
40	48.8864	60.4020	75.4013	95.0255	120.7998	154.7620	259.0565	442.5926
50	64.4632	84.5794	112.7969	152.6671	209.3480	290.3359	573.7702	1163.9085

Table 3:
Present Value of $1
Due in n Periods

$$p_{\overline{n}|i} = \frac{1}{(1 + i)^n}$$

Rate of Interest

n	1.0	2.0	3.0	4.0	5.0	6.0	8.0	10.0	15.0	20.0	25.0
1	0.9901	0.9804	0.9709	0.9615	0.9524	0.9434	0.9259	0.9091	0.8696	0.8333	0.8000
2	0.9803	0.9612	0.9426	0.9246	0.9070	0.8900	0.8573	0.8264	0.7561	0.6944	0.6400
3	0.9706	0.9423	0.9151	0.8890	0.8638	0.8396	0.7938	0.7513	0.6575	0.5787	0.5120
4	0.9610	0.9238	0.8885	0.8548	0.8227	0.7921	0.7350	0.6830	0.5718	0.4823	0.4096
5	0.9515	0.9057	0.8626	0.8219	0.7835	0.7473	0.6806	0.6209	0.4972	0.4019	0.3277
6	0.9420	0.8880	0.8375	0.7903	0.7462	0.7050	0.6302	0.5645	0.4323	0.3349	0.2621
7	0.9327	0.8706	0.8131	0.7599	0.7107	0.6651	0.5835	0.5132	0.3759	0.2791	0.2097
8	0.9235	0.8535	0.7894	0.7307	0.6768	0.6274	0.5403	0.4665	0.3269	0.2326	0.1678
9	0.9143	0.8368	0.7664	0.7026	0.6446	0.5919	0.5002	0.4241	0.2843	0.1938	0.1342
10	0.9053	0.8203	0.7441	0.6756	0.6139	0.5584	0.4632	0.3855	0.2472	0.1615	0.1074
11	0.8963	0.8043	0.7224	0.6496	0.5847	0.5268	0.4289	0.3505	0.2149	0.1346	0.0859
12	0.8874	0.7885	0.7014	0.6246	0.5568	0.4970	0.3971	0.3186	0.1869	0.1122	0.0687
13	0.8787	0.7730	0.6810	0.6006	0.5303	0.4688	0.3677	0.2897	0.1625	0.0935	0.0550
14	0.8700	0.7579	0.6611	0.5775	0.5051	0.4423	0.3405	0.2633	0.1413	0.0779	0.0440
15	0.8613	0.7430	0.6419	0.5553	0.4810	0.4173	0.3152	0.2394	0.1229	0.0649	0.0352
16	0.8528	0.7284	0.6232	0.5339	0.4581	0.3936	0.2919	0.2176	0.1069	0.0541	0.0281
17	0.8444	0.7142	0.6050	0.5134	0.4363	0.3714	0.2703	0.1978	0.0929	0.0451	0.0225
18	0.8360	0.7002	0.5874	0.4936	0.4155	0.3503	0.2502	0.1799	0.0808	0.0376	0.0180
19	0.8277	0.6864	0.5703	0.4746	0.3957	0.3305	0.2317	0.1635	0.0703	0.0313	0.0144
20	0.8195	0.6730	0.5537	0.4564	0.3769	0.3118	0.2145	0.1486	0.0611	0.0261	0.0115
25	0.7798	0.6095	0.4776	0.3751	0.2953	0.2330	0.1460	0.0923	0.0304	0.0105	0.0038
30	0.7419	0.5521	0.4120	0.3083	0.2314	0.1741	0.0994	0.0573	0.0151	0.0042	0.0012
40	0.6717	0.4529	0.3066	0.2083	0.1420	0.0972	0.0460	0.0221	0.0037	0.0007	0.0001
50	0.6080	0.3715	0.2281	0.1407	0.0872	0.0543	0.0213	0.0085	0.0009	0.0001	0.0000

Table 4:
Present Value of
an Annuity of $1
per Period

$$P_{\overline{n}|i} = \frac{1 - \dfrac{1}{(1 + i)^n}}{i}$$

Rate of Interest, %

n	1.0	2.0	3.0	4.0	5.0	6.0	8.0	10.0	15.0	20.0	25.0
1	0.9901	0.9804	0.9709	0.9615	0.9524	0.9434	0.9259	0.9091	0.8696	0.8333	0.8000
2	1.9704	1.9416	1.9135	1.8861	1.8594	1.8334	1.7833	1.7355	1.6257	1.5278	1.4400
3	2.9410	2.8839	2.8286	2.7751	2.7232	2.6730	2.5771	2.4869	2.2832	2.1065	1.9520
4	3.9020	3.8077	3.7171	3.6299	3.5460	3.4651	3.3121	3.1699	2.8550	2.5887	2.3616
5	4.8534	4.7135	4.5797	4.4518	4.3295	4.2124	3.9927	3.7908	3.3522	2.9906	2.6893
6	5.7955	5.6014	5.4172	5.2421	5.0757	4.9173	4.6229	4.3553	3.7845	3.3255	2.9514
7	6.7282	6.4720	6.2303	6.0021	5.7864	5.5824	5.2064	4.8684	4.1604	3.6046	3.1611
8	7.6517	7.3255	7.0197	6.7327	6.4632	6.2098	5.7466	5.3349	4.4873	3.8372	3.3289
9	8.5660	8.1622	7.7861	7.4353	7.1078	6.8017	6.2469	5.7590	4.7716	4.0310	3.4631
10	9.4713	8.9826	8.5302	8.1109	7.7217	7.3601	6.7101	6.1446	5.0188	4.1925	3.5705
11	10.3676	9.7868	9.2526	8.7605	8.3064	7.8869	7.1390	6.4951	5.2337	4.3271	3.6564
12	11.2551	10.5753	9.9540	9.3851	8.8633	8.3838	7.5361	6.8137	5.4206	4.4392	3.7251
13	12.1337	11.3484	10.6350	9.9856	9.3936	8.8527	7.9038	7.1034	5.5831	4.5327	3.7801
14	13.0037	12.1062	11.2961	10.5631	9.8986	9.2950	8.2442	7.3667	5.7245	4.6106	3.8241
15	13.8651	12.8493	11.9379	11.1184	10.3797	9.7122	8.5595	7.6061	5.8474	4.6755	3.8593
16	14.7179	13.5777	12.5611	11.6523	10.8378	10.1059	8.8514	7.8237	5.9542	4.7296	3.8874
17	15.5623	14.2919	13.1661	12.1657	11.2741	10.4773	9.1216	8.0216	6.0472	4.7746	3.9099
18	16.3983	14.9920	13.7535	12.6593	11.6896	10.8276	9.3719	8.2014	6.1280	4.8122	3.9279
19	17.2260	15.6785	14.3238	13.1339	12.0853	11.1581	9.6036	8.3649	6.1982	4.8435	3.9424
20	18.0456	16.3514	14.8775	13.5903	12.4622	11.4699	9.8181	8.5136	6.2593	4.8696	3.9539
25	22.0232	19.5235	17.4131	15.6221	14.0939	12.7834	10.6748	9.0770	6.4641	4.9476	3.9849
30	25.8077	22.3965	19.6004	17.2920	15.3725	13.7648	11.2578	9.4269	6.5660	4.9789	3.9950
40	32.8347	27.3555	23.1148	19.7928	17.1591	15.0463	11.9246	9.7791	6.6418	4.9966	3.9995
50	39.1961	31.4236	25.7298	21.4822	18.2559	15.7619	12.2335	9.9148	6.6605	4.9995	3.9999

B Worksheet or Working Papers

What Are They?
Worksheets or working papers are a columnar device employed by professional accountants as a convenient and orderly way of organizing the accounting data to be used in the preparation of statements and in the analysis of data.

What Are They Used For?
They are used in the preparation of position statements, income statements, fund-flow statements, consolidated statements, departmental and branch operation reports, schedules of cost of goods sold, budgets, interim reports, or any accounting report and statement.

Why Are They Used?
Worksheets or working papers are employed by professional accountants in situations where they will facilitate the preparation of the information required. As explained above, they are basically a simple statistical device by means of which adjustments and reclassifications are calculated before they enter the permanent books of account. The information is accumulated in separate columns for convenience in preparing statements.

How Do They Work?
For example, consider the preparation of two periodic financial statements: the position statement and the income statement. During the course of the accounting period, many events will have occurred that will have altered the figures appearing in the relevant accounts appearing on these two statements. In almost every company, these will be such that the balance in each particular account may be increased or decreased several times. To save work, and to save the necessity of making piecemeal adjustments, transaction by working papers or worksheets is employed.

Basically, the relevant accounts (all the accounts on the position and income statements) and their balances are entered on the left-hand side of a ten-column page. The particular adjustments are debited or credited to the appropriate accounts in the next two columns, the figures net of the adjustments are then determined, the accounts are classified according to the statement on which they belong, and all the individual columns are summed.

Several features of the procedure are noticeable.

First, as each adjusting entry is made to a particular account, be it debit or credit, the corresponding adjustment of credit or debit is made to the appropriate account; consequently, the effect of each adjustment is readily visible. Each adjusting entry should be annotated so that when the journal entries to record the adjustment are made from the worksheet, the procedure is not hindered by the need to retrace the effect of each adjustment.

Second, it can be seen that balancing of entries and final account figures is facilitated for the process ensures that corresponding entries are made for each item. The system is not error-proof, for there is no certainty that the entries will be made to the correct accounts, but where a number of transactions are to be recorded, the method provides a number of checks, by comparison of column totals, so that reasonable *arithmetic* accuracy is assured.

Third, in a situation where a large number of adjustments are to be made and worksheets are not used, it is difficult to envision the scope of the adjustments, and thus to ensure their accuracy, if they are made directly one by one into the ledger accounts. Furthermore, where several adjustments to particular accounts are required, the continual process of altering ledger accounts increases the possibility of inaccuracy.

Finally, the use of this method provides management with a concise report on operations soon after the close of the accounting period, in a form that explains changes, and enables analysis of particular accounts to be readily undertaken. Changes in account balances and the reasons for them are readily discernible from the working papers; if these were not prepared, extra time and effort would be required to provide management with a meaningful report on the period.

The procedures used in this worksheet illustration can be adapted for the preparation of any accounting report or statement. For consolidated statements or interim reports, be they monthly, quarterly, or semiannually, worksheets or working papers per se are particularly valuable. They present the required information without the necessity of altering the permanent books of account, by dispensing with the formality of making adjusting and closing entries.

Since there is no single method of preparing a worksheet or working paper—or even a best format—every company (or public accounting firm) tends to develop its own format. For this reason, and because it is cumbersome, this device does not prove to be as effective as T accounts for learning accounting.

Illustrations of Various Kinds of Worksheets

EXHIBIT B-1

AN EIGHT-COLUMN PARTIAL WORKSHEET

Account No.	Account Name	Trial Balance		Adjustments		Income Statement		Position Statement	
		Dr.	Cr.	Dr.	Cr.	Dr.	Cr.	Dr.	Cr.
	Merchandise inventory	1,000		(B) 1,500	(A) 1,000			1,500	
	Purchases	1,500			(A) 1,500				
	Cost of goods sold			(A) 2,500	(B) 1,500	2,000			

Explanation of Adjustments:

A. To transfer cost of goods available for sale (beginning inventory and net purchases) to Cost of Goods Sold.

B. To set up the ending inventory as an asset and reduce the Cost of Goods Sold accordingly. The debit here could be placed below the trial balance captions as a new item.

EXHIBIT B-2

A TEN-COLUMN PARTIAL WORKSHEET

(WITH SEPARATE COLUMNS FOR COST OF GOODS SOLD)

Account No.	Account Name	Trial Balance		Adjustments		Cost of Goods Sold		Income Statement		Position Statement	
		Dr.	Cr.	Dr.	Cr.	Dr.	Cr.	Dr.	Cr.	Dr.	Cr.
	Merchandise inventory	1,000				1,500	1,000			1,500	
	Purchases	1,500				1,500					
						3,000	1,000				
	Cost of goods sold						2,000	2,000			
						3,000	3,000				

EXHIBIT B-3
A TWELVE-COLUMN PARTIAL WORKSHEET

Account No.	Account Name	Trial Balance Dr.	Trial Balance Cr.	Adjustments Dr.	Adjustments Cr.	Adjusted Trial Balance Dr.	Adjusted Trial Balance Cr.	Cost of Goods Sold Dr.	Cost of Goods Sold Cr.	Income Statement Dr.	Income Statement Cr.	Position Statement Dr.	Position Statement Cr.
	Merchandise inventory	1,000		(B) 1,500	(A) 1,000	1,500		1,500	1,000			1,500	
	Purchases	1,500			(A) 1,500			1,500					
				(A) 2,500	(B) 500	2,000			2,000	2,000			

C   Journals

What the Journal Is
The journal is the book of original entry in which the details of each accounting transaction are recorded.

Description
The procedure of recording in the journal under the double-entry system of accounting, whereby each debit or credit entry is offset by a corresponding credit or debit entry, is fairly straightforward. The journal page is divided into a series of columns. Generally, from the left-hand side of the page, they are: date of transaction, names of accounts charged plus an explanation of details of the transaction, posting reference, debit amount, and credit amount.

How They Are Used
Each transaction of the enterprise is entered daily or weekly into the journal, depending on the frequency of occurrence, by the following method. The date is entered; the account names to which the corresponding debit and credit are to be made, as well as an explanation of the transaction, are entered into the next column; then the appropriate dollar amounts are entered as debits or credits opposite the account involved.

An important feature is that each transaction is posted as both a debit and a credit, so that each one is balanced, thus preserving the essence of the double-entry system of bookkeeping.

Types of Journals

In any enterprise larger than a one-man business, with many diverse types of transactions taking place each day, it is uneconomical to maintain simply one journal in which all these events are recorded.

Since there is a fairly easily discernible line between the different types of transactions, the normal procedure is to maintain a number of special journals, one each for events of a similar type.

For example, there may be four special journals, and one general journal in which to record items that are not classifiable into one of the special journals. Such special journals are likely to be: a sales journal, a purchases journal, a cash receipts journal, and a cash disbursements journal. The purpose of each is self-explanatory.

One complication of a special journal system is that some transactions may be recorded in more than one journal. One solution to this problem is to specify which type of transaction is to be recorded in each journal. For example, only charge sales may be recorded in the sales journal; all cash sales might be recorded in the cash receipts journal. Another solution would be to journalize the transaction in two journals but post only once to the particular ledger account. Under this procedure all sales would be recorded in the sales journal, and all cash sales in the cash receipts journal; there would be no posting to cash from the sales journal, and no posting to sales (for cash sales) from the cash receipts journal. The duplication would thus be eliminated in the posting process.

Two types of entries are made into a journal: simple entries when only one debit and one credit per entry is made; and compound entries when more than two accounts are involved in recording a transaction.

Points to Watch

If three rules are followed, journals will always provide a chronological record of the transactions of an enterprise and will balance:

First, account names and numbers consistent with the chart of accounts of the enterprise must always be used, so that the effects of each entry are readily traceable through the accounts.

Second, a clear and concise explanation of each transaction must be provided, so that the reasons why the particular accounts named were charged can readily be seen.

Finally, care must be taken, particularly with compound entries, to ensure that the offsetting charge or charges exactly balance the initial charge recorded.

Illustrations of Various Kinds of Journals

EXHIBIT C-1
GENERAL JOURNAL (PARTIAL)

Date		Accounts and Explanation	Posting Reference	Debit	Credit
1973					
Jan.	1	Cash	100	10,000	
		Johnny Cash, Capital	300		10,000
		Proprietor invested in business			
	5	Supplies	150	500	
		Accounts Payable	200		500
		Supplies purchased on account			

EXHIBIT C-2
PURCHASES JOURNAL (PARTIAL)

Date		Account Credited	Invoice No.	Terms	Posting Reference	Accounts Payable Credit
1973						
Jan.	4	Pearl Bailey	11	1/10, n/30	205	100
	5	Hazel Scott	12	2/10, n/30	207	500
	6	Adam Powell	13	30 days EOM	203	300
						900

EXHIBIT C-3
SALES JOURNAL (PARTIAL)

Date		Account Debited	Invoice No.	Terms	Posting Reference	Sales Credit
1973						
Jan.	2	George C. Scott	33	2/10, n/30	119	50
	4	Lee Grant	34	on account	127	100
	6	Dan Duryea	35	n/20	118	100
	31	Debit Accounts Receivable				250

EXHIBIT C-4
CASH RECEIPTS JOURNAL (PARTIAL)

Date		Account Credited	Explanation	PR	Cash	Sales Discount	Accounts Receivable	General Ledger
1973								
Jan.	2	Jackie Gleason, Capital	Invest	300	5,000			5,000
	11	George C. Scott	On account	110	49	1	50	
	18	Sales	Cash sales	400	300			300
	20	Sales	Cash sales	400	100			100
	30	Sales	Cash sales	400	50			50
	31				5,499	1	50	5,450
					Dr.	Dr.	Cr.	Cr.

EXHIBIT C-5
CASH DISBURSEMENTS JOURNAL (PARTIAL)

Date		Account Debited	Explanation	PR	General Ledger	Accounts Payable	Purchase Discount	Cash
1973								
Jan.	3	Miscellaneous Expense	Miscellaneous	500	30			30
	7	Advertising	In the Dispatch	501	50			50
	10	Pearl Bailey	Paid in full	205		100	1	99
	15	Purchases	Cash purchases	550	75			75
	15	Hazel Scott		207		500	10	490
	31				155	600	11	744
					(✔)	(200)	(550)	(100)
					Dr.	Dr.	Cr.	Cr.

EXHIBIT C-6
CHECK REGISTER (PARTIAL)

Check Number	Date 1973		Payee	Voucher Number	Vouchers Payable Dr.	Purchase Discount Cr.	Cash Cr.
53	Jan.	3	Jack Jones	21	100	1	99
54		4	Shirley Jones	22	150	3	147
55		6	Alan Jones	23	100	1	99
56		7	Paul Jones	24	50	1	49
					400	6	394
					(200)	(550)	(100)

EXHIBIT C-7
VOUCHER REGISTER (PARTIAL)

Voucher Number	Date 1973		Payee	Date	Payment Check Number	Vouchers Payable Cr.	Purchases Dr.	Other
21	Jan.	1	Jack Jones	Jan. 3	53	100	100	
22		2	Shirley Jones	4	54	150	150	
23		3	Alan Jones	6	55	100	100	
24		4	Paul Jones	7	56	50	50	
						400	400	
						(200)	(500)	

D The Organization, Examination, Regulation, and Practice of CPAs

The American Institute of Certified Public Accountants (AICPA) is the national professional organization of CPAs in the United States. Its membership is restricted to holders of valid CPA certificates from one of the 54 jurisdictions (the 50 states, the District of Columbia, Guam, Puerto Rico, and the Virgin Islands), who have passed the Uniform CPA Examination (or an accounting examination considered to be an equivalent), who have two years of public accounting experience (or the equivalent), and who are engaged in work related to accounting at the date of application.

Associate memberships in the AICPA also are granted to CPAs who meet the major membership criteria but who have less than two years of qualifying experience or who are not engaged in public accounting on the date of application. Associate memberships automatically advance to membership after completion of a predetermined waiting period.

Of special interest to foreign students who study (or intend to study) accounting at accredited United States universities is the International Associate membership in the AICPA for which they may qualify by passing the Uniform CPA Examination.

CPA certificates are awarded in the public interest to qualified candidates in accordance with the statutes of one of the 54 jurisdictions. The certificate is granted to meet the public's need for assurance that persons offering professional accounting services are competent. It is not granted for the private benefit of any person or special-interest group holding the certificate(s). The state (or jurisdiction) boards of accountancy which administer the state accountancy laws carefully investigate the qualifications of candidates for the CPA designation. The candidate must demonstrate his professional competence by passing the comprehensive two and one-half day Uniform CPA Examination. This indicates that the candidate has adequate technical knowledge in accounting practice, accounting theory, auditing and business law; skill in applying such knowledge; and an understanding of professional responsibility.

All the jurisdictions now use the AICPA's Uniform CPA Examination and the Advisory Grading Service, both of which are the responsibility of the board of examiners and are staffed by the Examinations Division.

The state boards must rely on personal interviews, reference letters, and employment affidavits to determine whether the candidate has the necessary character attributes to practice as a CPA. Many state boards also require that the candidate demonstrate knowledge of the rules of professional conduct by passing an ethics examination.

In many jurisdictions the accountants' rules or code of professional ethics, so important to a mature profession, has been enacted as a part of the accountancy law.

Regulatory versus Permissive Certification

All the jurisdictions have statutes regulating the awarding of the CPA certificate. These statutes are either regulatory or permissive. In the 42 *regulatory* jurisdictions only holders of valid CPA certificates may offer their services as public accountants. In general, most regulatory statutes contain "grandfather" clauses that permit those who were engaged in public accounting when the statute was passed to continue offering their accounting services. After the passage of the regulatory statutes, anyone wishing to offer public accounting services in his name must be a CPA.

In the 12 *permissive* jurisdictions anyone awarded a license may practice as a public accountant, but only CPAs (that is, those who have passed the CPA examination and have met all the requirements of the accountancy laws in their jurisdictions) are licensed to use the title CPA.

Typical Requirements

Substantial progress has been made in recent decades to reduce the differences among the 54 jurisdictions in the requirements for becoming a CPA, but differences continue to exist. Typical requirements in a majority of jurisdictions are: (1) some formal education beyond high school, (2) two years or less of accounting experience of a type specified by statute, (3) successful completion of the CPA examination, and (4) be 21 years of age, a U.S. citizen or intend to become one, a resident or office holder in the jurisdiction awarding the certificate, and of good moral character. The trend in recent years has been to increase the education requirement to a college degree, with a concentration in accounting, and to reduce the experience requirement—often to permit college education to substitute partially or wholly for experience. Those interested may learn of the examination and certification requirements of a particular jurisdiction from one or more of the following sources:

1. University or college library: Request the most recent editions of one of the following compilations on all 54 jurisdictions for which the most recent editions available in 1970 are cited:
   a. Robert P. Behling, *CPA Requirements,* 2d ed. (Whitewater, Wisconsin: Wisconsin State University, 1968).
   b. The *Accountancy Law Reporter,* a looseleaf service giving changes in state accountancy laws, published by Commerce Clearinghouse, Inc.
   c. *Provisions in CPA Laws and Regulations,* prepared by United States Army Audit Agency in cooperation with AICPA, July 1, 1970.
2. State (or jurisdiction) board of accountancy: Write (or call) for the information.

Success Factors

Although AICPA data indicate that only about 10 percent of all candidates pass all four sections of the examination the first time they attempt it, other studies indicate that 70 to 85 percent of the serious candidates complete the examination within five years. Eliminated from the latter studies are those candidates who sit for the examination once, fail it, and do not try it again.

An AICPA study of candidates in a recent examination indicates that about 95 percent of all candidates have at least a baccalaureate degree, and that 10 percent of these also have a postgraduate (masters, doctors, or law) degree. As might be expected, the percentage of first-time candidates with postgraduate degrees who pass all four sections of the examination is substantially greater than the national average of 10 percent. For several years the examination passing percentages for candidates from the states of Colorado, Illinois, Minnesota, Missouri, and Wisconsin have regularly been higher than the national average, even though all candidates from all states are graded by the same uniform standards.

Education and Experience Recommendations

After an extensive study, the ad hoc Committee on Education and Experience Requirements for CPAs recently submitted its report, which the AICPA has adopted as policy. The following resolutions were among those included in the report that the AICPA is recommending for inclusion in state accountancy rules and statutes:

1. The CPA certificate is evidence of basic competence of professional quality in the discipline of accounting. This basic competence is demonstrated by acquiring the body of knowledge common to the profession and passing the CPA examination.

2. *Horizons for a Profession*[1] is authoritative for the purpose of delineating the common body of knowledge to be possessed by those about to begin their professional careers as CPAs.

3. At least five years of college study are needed to obtain the common body of knowledge for CPAs and should be the education requirement. For those who meet this standard, no qualifying experience should be required.

4. The states should adopt this five-year requirement by 1975. Until it becomes effective, a transitional alternative is four years of college study and one year of qualifying experience.

5. Candidates should be encouraged to take the CPA examination as soon as they have fulfilled education requirements, and as close to their college graduation dates as possible. For those graduating in June, this may involve taking the May examination on a provisional basis.

6. Student internships are desirable and are encouraged as part of the educational program.[2]

In addition to increased formal education, the AICPA reports that major factors contributing to success on the CPA examination are intelligence and academic ability, motivation, a thorough review and preparation for the examination, and timing—taking the examination as soon as jurisdictional laws permit after completing the accounting education.

Much information on the content, the taking, and the grading of the CPA examination is provided in *Information for CPA Candidates* which is published by the AICPA and which its board of examiners revises every few years. One copy of this publication is given free (1) by the AICPA to members upon request, and (2) by state boards to each first-time applicant taking the CPA examination.

Growth and Status of the Profession

The number of CPAs has approximately doubled in each decade since 1920, with some 119,270 certificate holders at August 31, 1970; and only about 63 percent of these certificate holders (or 74,413) were members of the AICPA. Many CPAs are not members of national organizations because they are certified to practice by state boards, they practice in a single state, and/or they are members of their state's CPA society. Many other CPAs are not members because they do not engage in public practice; these are certified as CPAs but have chosen to serve mainly in government or private industry positions, or as university or college professors. It is very common for accountants who do not wish public accounting careers, however, to first become certified public accountants because the CPA

[1]Robert H. Roy and James H. MacNeill, *Horizons for a Profession* (New York: AICPA, 1967).
[2]*Report of the Committee on Education and Experience Requirements for CPAs*, Elmer G. Beamer, chairman (New York: AICPA, 1969), pp. 6–7.

certificate is widely regarded as a standard of excellence in all fields of accounting and business.

Public accounting, because of the great diversity of services that it can perform, is often undertaken by two or more professional accountants, CPAs, working together, with staff assistants, in a partnership. Many CPAs, however, continue to function as one-man professional firms. In 1970 the AICPA's 46,184 members who were in public accounting practice constituted 14,950 practice units; of these, 20.3 percent of the total (or 9,400) were in one-member practice units, and another 33.6 percent (or 15,500) were in practice units with two to nine AICPA members. Only 258 firms have ten or more AICPA members, and the 25 largest firms had 38.6 percent of the total, or nearly 18,000 AICPA members. Many of these firms are the world's largest partnerships, especially the "Big Eight" firms: Arthur Andersen & Co.; Arthur Young & Co.; Ernst & Ernst; Haskins and Sells; Lybrand, Ross Bros. & Montgomery; Peat, Marwick, Mitchell & Co.; Price Waterhouse & Co.; and Touche Ross & Co. In a recent study of the 639 largest corporations in the United States 92.7 percent were audited by one of these eight firms.[3] (See page 580.) Firms often specialize in the accounting problems of certain industries, such as oils, autos, chemicals, or financial institutions.

According to a 1966 article, the largest of these partnerships, Peat, Marwick, Mitchell & Co., had over 600 partners in 248 offices on 6 continents and in 50 nations with annual revenues of $150 million on a $50 million capital. In the United States, this firm had 87 offices, 345 partners, 6,000 employees, and annual revenues of $100 million based on a $30 million capital. The average annual income for a Peat, Marwick, Mitchell partner in 1966 was estimated to be $50,000.[4]

The Roles of Accounting and Professional Accountants

Recent studies indicate (1) that incomes of CPAs rank about fourth in a list of the professionals behind physicians and surgeons, dentists and dental surgeons, and practicing lawyers; and above architects and engineers; (2) that CPAs have an increasing share of top management positions in business and industry; and (3) that demand is increasing for qualified entrants into the accounting profession.

Because of its current and potential role in the effective, efficient, and equitable allocation of resources, the accounting profession can be interesting, stimulating, challenging, and rewarding to those who qualify.

[3]See Stephen A. Zeff and Robert L. Fossum, "An Analysis of Large Audit Clients," *The Accounting Review*, April 1967, pp. 298–320.
[4]See T. A. Wise, "The Very Private World of Peat, Marwick, Mitchell," *Fortune*, July 1, 1966, pp. 88–89, 128–129.

200 Ernst & Ernst offices throughout the world: Ernst & Ernst operates with well-established policies worldwide through one United States partnership and, where required by the laws of other countries, through related partnerships. It is one of the "Big Eight" firms.

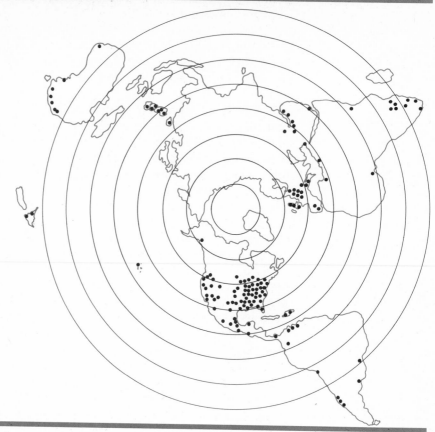

A Selection of Supplementary Readings

Brown, William J., Donald E. Kieso, and Robert L. Thistlethwaite: "Accounting Graduates not among the Disenchanted," *The Illinois CPA,* Summer 1969, pp. 45–49.

Carey, John L.: "What Is the Professional Practice of Accounting?" *The Accounting Review,* January 1968, pp. 1–9.

Frishkoff, Paul: "Chandler on Accounting," *Canadian Chartered Accountant,* January 1969, pp. 28–31.

Lawler, John: "The Quest for Accounting Philosophers," *Empirical Research in Accounting: Selected Studies, 1967,* supplement to vol. 5, *Journal of Accounting Research,* pp. 86–92.

Smith, E. J.: "The Illinois CPA Examination: Its Production and Its Candidates," *The Illinois CPA,* Winter 1969, pp. 18–30.

Williams, Doyle Z.: "A Profile of CPA Candidates," The Teachers' Clinic, *The Accounting Review,* January 1969, pp. 153–164.

E

An Accountant's Profile

The Strong Vocational Interest Inventory has been of great value in revealing an individual's interests, as distinct from his aptitudes and achievements. When analyzed in connection with actual tests, it indicates whether a candidate shares the interests of those who have found satisfaction in a given occupation and, therefore, whether he is likely to be content in his work.

This inventory has been used by the AICPA since 1945. There are 399 items or questions on the test. There are 22 basic interest scales dealing with broad subjects and 55 occupations. In the nonoccupational scales of the inventory, academic achievement contrasts the interests of those who do well in school with those who do not. The AICPA special profile for CPAs is reproduced on page 582. The lightly shaded area represents the interest ratings of the middle 50 percent of 1,000 accountants. The dark oblongs show the interest ratings of men in general. The score of a person who takes the inventory can thus be compared with both the interest ranges indicated for accountants and those for applicants in general.

In a 1947 study that compared the median scores of students of accounting and accountants, it was found that the general median interest ratings of the students bears considerable similarity to those of employed accountants. The profile was compiled from blanks filled in by 1,000 public accountants whose 115 firms cooperated in the project. Forms were completed by 250 each of partners and managers, seniors, semiseniors, and juniors.

The profile shows that the five occupations with which CPA reflect the greatest similarity of interests—much greater than for candidates in general—are in this order: senior CPA, credit manager, CPA owner, Chamber of Commerce executive, and computer programmer. The five occupations with which accountants display the least similarity of interests, as compared with successful practitioners, and reading from the bottom of the list up, are: minister, physicist, mathematician, biologist, and dentist.

This profile for CPAs serves as a useful supplement to the information obtained from the aptitude and achievement tests administered in the AICPA testing programs. The inventory results provide indications concerning the suitability for a career in accounting to students themselves, as well as to their prospective employers. These tests can be secured from the AICPA.

NAME _____   DATE _____

AICPA SPECIAL PROFILE FOR CPA'S

REPORT FORM – STRONG VOCATIONAL INTEREST BLANK – FOR MEN

OCCUPATION	STD. SCORE	C			C+	B–	B	B+	A	
		0	10	20	30		40		50	60
SENIOR CPA										
CREDIT MANAGER										
CPA OWNER										
CHAMBER COM. EXEC.										
COMPUTER PROGRAMMER			10	20	30		40		50	60
PUBLIC ADMINISTRATOR										
ACCOUNTANT										
BUS. ED. TEACHER										
PERSONNEL DIRECTOR										
LAWYER			10	20	30		40		50	60
ARMY OFFICER										
REHABILITATION COUNSELOR										
COMM. REC. ADMIN.										
BANKER										
PHYSICAL THERAPIST			10	20	30		40		50	60
YMCA SECRETARY										
PRESIDENT – MFG.										
SOCIAL WORKER										
ENGINEER										
PSYCHOLOGIST			10	20	30		40		50	60
OSTEOPATH										
ARCHITECT										
CHEMIST										
PHYSICIAN										
ARTIST			10	20	30		40		50	60
DENTIST										
BIOLOGIST										
MATHEMATICIAN										
PHYSICIST										
MINISTER			10	20	30		40		50	60
OCCUPATIONAL LEVEL		20	30	40	50		60		70	80
MASCULINITY, FEMINITY	F									M
ACADEMIC ACHIEVEMENT										
SPECIALIZATION LEVEL		20	30	40	50		60		70	80

   The lightly shaded area extending diagonally across the page marks the general trend of interest ratings found for one thousand public accountants (250 partners and managers, 250 seniors, 250 semi-seniors, 250 juniors). This area shows the range of the middle 50 per cent of the scores on each scale for this group. Thus, for the scale of senior CPA, the ratings of 50 per cent of the one thousand public accountants fall between the scores of 39.3 and 53.5; for the scale of credit manager, between 34.8 and 49.5, and so forth. On the whole, it is desirable for one who is considering accountancy as a profession to have scores which follow the general trend of this lightly shaded area to the extent that ratings for occupations listed at the top of the chart are relatively high, while the lower ratings occur for scales appearing at the bottom of the list.

   For further information about the interpretation of your scores, see the back of the standard report form.

Digests of AICPA Accounting Research Studies and APB Opinions

The following are brief highlights of the AICPA Accounting Research Studies and the APB Opinions which have been published to date.

Accounting Research Studies

Author	Number	Date
Maurice Moonitz	*No. 1*	*1961*

This was meant to serve as a summary of broad accounting postulates upon which the AICPA would base subsequent pronouncements.

These consist of three sets of 14 postulates: the environment (quantification, exchange, entities, time period, and unit of measure); the field of accounting (financial statements; market prices—with two corollaries: namely, recording initially at exchange prices and that accounting is "cost-based"—and entities); and the imperatives (what ought to be: continuity, objectivity, consistency, stable unit, and disclosure).

Perry Mason	*No. 2*	*1961*

A fund-flow statement should be included as a major financial statement; the concept of funds preferred is "all financial resources." There should be interpretive comments related to the funds statement. The format is one that begins with net income, making sure not to give the impression that depreciation and other such adjustments are "sources" of funds. Although cash-flow information may be helpful, isolated cash-flow data should be avoided because such data may be misleading.

Robert T. Sprouse and Maurice Moonitz	*No. 3*	*1962*

This is an extension of ARS No. 1, summarizing basic accounting principles that should be applied to business enterprises.

Principles should not be formulated for purposes of validating policies established in other fields. Valuation of plant and equipment should be restated in terms of current replacement cost at periodic intervals (or when a significant reorganization occurs), perhaps every five years. Inventories should be valued at replacement cost (when net realizable value is not determinable).

John H. Myers   *No. 4*   *1962*

With respect to both the lessor and the lessee, to the extent that leases give rise to property rights, those rights and related liabilities should be incorporated in the position statement by discounting the rentals that constitute payments for property rights. To the extent, however, that rental payments are for items such as maintenance and insurance which are not property rights, this portion of the payments should not be discounted and reflected in the position statement.

Arthur R. Wyatt   *No. 5*   *1963*

The purchase method of accounting for business combinations should be utilized since all business combinations result from exchange transactions. When equities are used to effect the exchange, the assets received should be valued at the fair value of the equities given up.

Staff   *No. 6*   *1963*

Price-level changes should be provided as supplementary data to all conventional financial statements. These supplementary data should be introduced through the use of a single index of general price level such as the GNP Implicit Price Deflator, which is reliable enough for accounting purposes.

Paul Grady   *No. 7*   *1965*

This "Inventory of Generally Accepted Accounting Principles for Business Enterprises" is extensive. With an emphasis on practical applications, this study discusses and summarizes accepted accounting practices.

Ernest L. Hicks   *No. 8*   *1965*

Provision for the normal cost of a pension plan should be made annually; and past service cost should be charged to expense in a rational, systematic manner over a reasonable period after the adoption of the pension plan.

Homer A. Black   *No. 9*   *1966*

The accounting for the "Interperiod Allocation of Corporate Income Taxes" considers the three methods: liability, deferral, and net of tax. Where income taxes are charged to expense before paid, an expense and liability should be accrued, and the tax rate used should be that rate anticipated for the payment date. A subsequent change in the tax rate should be reflected as an adjustment to prior periods. Where income taxes are paid before accrued, a prepayment exists, which should be deferred and subsequently amortized in the period of reversal, the current tax rate being used for the deferral.

George R. Catlett and
Norman D. Olson   *No. 10*   *1968*

The purchase method of accounting should be used in accounting for business combinations, and the excess of the amount of consideration given up over the fair value of the separable resources and property rights acquired should be assigned to purchased goodwill and should be treated as a reduction of the shareholders' equity.

Robert E. Field   *No. 11*   *1969*

Firms in the extractive industries can best solve their accounting problems by adhering to traditional concepts of realization and matching, the similarity of inventory to minerals in the ground being significant. Preferred accounting practices are those that would restrict the number of alternative treatments to those that occur only because of differing circumstances. More information should be in financial statements, including adequate notes which would explain accounting procedures, and supplementary data which would aid investors.

APB Opinions

Number   *Date*
No. 1   *November 1962*

In considering the Depreciation Guidelines and Rules issued by the United States Treasury, useful lives of broad classes of depreciable assets are suggested which attempt to conform asset lives for income tax purposes more toward actual experience.

No. 2   *December 1962*

The investment credit would be reflected in the income statement over the useful life of the assets. The opinion recommends the reflection of the credit as a reduction in asset cost.

No. 3   *October 1963*

A fund-flow statement should be presented as supplementary to the published financial statements. The "all-financial-resources" concept of funds and the format which begins with net income and adjusts for "non-fund transactions" are recommended.

No. 4   *March 1964*

This is an amendment to Opinion No. 2. The APB found that practice largely ignored the recommendation of Opinion No. 2. Upon reflecting that its pronouncements are based upon general acceptance, the Board now allows the method commonly found in practice, the treatment of the investment credit as a reduction of federal income taxes in the period in which the credit arises, although it reaffirms its previous recommendation as preferrable.

No. 5   *September 1964*

With the subject of leases, the nature of some lease agreements is such that assets and related liabilities should be shown on the position statement. The criteria for determining whether a lease agreement should be shown on the position statement is dependent upon whether the lease is in substance a purchase of property. Lease agreements which merely cover the right to use property in exchange for a promise for future rental payments are nothing more than executory contracts and should be treated as such, and information in the financial statements should be limited to notes and schedules. Noncancelable leases in which the payments in the initial life of the lease are substantially greater than the decline in economic value of the property are purchases in substance and should be recorded as such. The opinion criteria for treating lease as a purchase are so constraining that relatively few lease agreements will qualify.

No. 6   *October 1965*

This is an Omnibus Opinion. It covers the following areas: treasury stock; current assets and current liabilities; intangible assets; stock dividends and stock split-ups; depreciation on appreciation; foreign operations and foreign exchange; unamortized discount, issue cost,

and redemption premium on bonds refunded; declining-balance depreciation; business combinations; and deferred income taxes.

No. 7   *May 1966*

In accounting for the revenue and expense related to the lessor in a
lease agreement, two different methods are discussed: the financing
method and the operating method. The financing method treats the
total rental receipts over the life of the investment as a repayment for
the property, the amount above cost being compensation for the use
of the invested funds. The operating method treats each rental receipt as the revenue unless payments differ radically among periods.
The financing method should be used when the lessee has most of
the ownership rights and responsibilities, and the operating method
should be used when the lessor retains the risks or rewards of ownership. Leases qualifying for the financing method should be capitalized on the position statement, using an appropriate title denoting
its status as a receivable, whereas under the operating method, a
physical asset would be shown on the position statement. This
opinion establishes different criteria for the lessor than it did for
the lessee in Opinion No. 5.

No. 8   *November 1966*

In accounting for pensions, the entire cost of the pension plan
should be charged to expense subsequent to the adoption of the
plan. The accrual of such costs should be based upon an acceptable
actuarial method which is rational and systematic and which is consistently applied. The annual provision for pension costs should be
no less than the sum of the normal cost, an amount equivalent to
interest on any unfunded prior service cost, and a provision for vested
benefits, if indicated, and no less than the sum of the normal costs,
10 percent of the past service cost, 10 percent of the amounts of increases or decreases in prior service costs from plan amendments,
and interest equivalents. In addition, such variations as funded plans
and insured plans are considered.

No. 9   *December 1966*

The "all-inclusive" view of net income is adopted to a great extent,
namely, that the net income figure for a period reflect all items of
income and loss during the period with the exception of prior-period
adjustments. While extraordinary items would be included in net income, they should be segregated from the remaining items. Prior-
period adjustments which are material, which can be specifically
identified with prior periods, which are not attributable to economic

events subsequent to the financial statement, which depend for determination upon persons other than management, and which could not previously be subject to reasonable approximation should be adjusted to beginning retained earnings. Examples of prior-period adjustments are material, nonrecurring settlements of income taxes and of significant amounts from litigation. The renegotiation of utility rates may also constitute prior-period adjustments. Net income per share based upon a weighted average of shares outstanding during the period (excluding treasury shares) should be disclosed on the income statement. The disclosure of net income per share should include pro forma information pertaining to potential dilutions.

No. 10   *December 1966*

This is an Omnibus Opinion covering the following areas: consolidated financial statements; pooling of interest; tax allocation accounts; offsetting securities against taxes payable; convertible debt and debt issued with stock warrants; liquidation preference of preferred stock; and the installment method of accounting.

No. 11   *December 1967*

Intraperiod income tax allocation and interperiod tax allocation are required. For the latter, the deferred method is recommended whereby the tax effects of timing differences are deferred currently and allocated to income tax expense of future periods, while loss carryforwards (except in cases where realization is beyond doubt) not be recognized until realized, the realizable loss carrybacks should be recognized in the period of the loss.

No. 12   *December 1967*

This is an Omnibus Opinion covering the following areas: classification and disclosure of allowances; disclosure of depreciable assets and depreciation; deferred compensation contracts; capital changes; convertible debt and debt issued with stock warrants; and amortization of debt discount and expense or premium.

No. 13   *March 1969*

This amends Opinion No. 9 to include commercial banks.

No. 14   *March 1969*

This relates to Opinion No. 10. No portion of the proceeds from the issue of convertible debt or securities with nondetachable warrants be accounted for as attributable to the conversion feature but that part of the proceeds from the issue of securities with detachable warrants should be attributed to the warrants.

No. 15   *May 1969*

Earnings per share should be presented on financial statements for all the periods covered by the income statement, adjusting for prior-period corrections. The methods of computing primary and fully diluted net income per share and the methods of disclosure in financial statements are described.

No. 16   *August 1970*

While both the purchase method and the pooling-of-interest method are acceptable means of accounting for business combinations, rigid criteria for the use of the pooling-of-interest method are specified. All business combinations which do not qualify for pooling using these criteria should use the purchase method.

No. 17   *August 1970*

The costs of intangible assets acquired from others, including goodwill acquired in a business combination, should be recorded as an *asset;* the costs of developing intangible assets which are not specifically identifiable should be recorded as *expenses.* All intangible assets should be amortized by systematic charges to expense over the period to be benefited not, however, to exceed forty years.

No. 18   *March 1971*

Investors should account for investments in unconsolidated subsidiaries by the equity method. In addition, investors should use the equity method for investments in an investee in which the investor has 20 percent or more of the voting stock.

No. 19   *March 1971*

A fund-flow statement must be presented as a basic statement in financial reports of businesses. The need is for each entity to pick the definition of funds most relevant to its operations; however, the "funds" statement should disclose all important aspects of investing and financing activities. The fund-flow statement may begin with either net income or revenue, but funds provided by operations must be shown. Whether working capital is the definition of funds adopted, each change in a working capital element should be disclosed either in the statement itself or in a supporting schedule.

No. 20   *July 1971*

For a change in an accounting principle (and practice or the methods of applying it), most changes should be recognized by including the cumulative effect, based on retroactive computation, of changing to a new accounting principle in net income of the period of the change. In support of this position, the Board believes that public confidence in financial statements would be diluted if prior-period financial statements were restated routinely. But for special changes, the prior-period statements should be restated; these include any change from the Lifo method of inventory pricing, and in accounting for long-term, construction-type contracts or the "full-sort" method (used in the extractive industries). Another exception is where the change results in a different reporting entity. In this situation too, all prior-period statements should be restated. Pro forma effects of retroactive application should be shown for all changes in accounting principles.

For a change in an accounting estimate, most changes should be accounted for in the period of change and possibly future periods. There should not be a restatement of prior-period statements or of the pro forma amounts. The exception is where the change meets all the conditions for a prior-period adjustment (Opinion No. 9). If it is not possible to distinguish between a change in principle from a change in estimate, the change should be reported as the latter.

No. 21   *August 1971*

Interest must be imputed to most long-term receivables and payables bearing no interest or an interest rate much lower than the prevailing current rate for a comparable note. The difference between the present value and the face amount is to be amortized over the life of the note at a constant rate of interest on the unamortized principal outstanding at the beginning of any given period.

Note: When this book was going to press, the following opinions were at draft stage: extractive industries, marketable securities, and tax allocation—special situations. Those at a preliminary development stage are: diversified companies, accounting policy (statement), leases, non-cash transactions, interim financial statements, components of a business enterprise, common stock equivalents, stock compensation, and retirement of debt.

G How to Study Accounting

When you study the first course in a discipline, it may prove difficult. This may be so for several reasons. Until you understand the overall structure or approach of a discipline, it is difficult to comprehend any part of the subject. It is similar to the blind men trying to comprehend the shape of an elephant by one feeling only its trunk, another its tail, and a third its tusks. During the first six or seven weeks, while you adjust to the subject, you may worry about and feel overwhelmed by accounting, and you will probably lack perspective about your progress. You should be careful not to underrate yourself or worry unduly, particularly if you are a "worrier." If you are studying as your instructor directs, these feelings of inadequacy will be overcome as you grasp the general nature of financial accounting, which will be partially accomplished when you understand the use and preparation of the basic financial statements: the income, the position (or balance sheet), and the fund-flow statements. Once you comprehend reasonably well the fundamental structure of these statements, your preliminary adjustment to the subject will be near completion. In this text, Chapters 4 and 6 are the key for accomplishing this objective, since they deal with the general aspects of these statements. Even if you are an excellent student, you will need to study these two chapters very thoroughly, and after you go on to other chapters, you will still find it worthwhile to review the subject matter of these two chapters frequently. Sometimes it is quite useful to work problems in addition to those assigned (which your instructor or an advanced student may be willing to check out). *In any event, during this period of adjustment, try to avoid excessive anxiety, and let your instructor, rather than yourself, judge your status and progress in the course and subject.* Also, you should keep in mind that it is normal not to understand the subject matter of Chapters 4 and 6 as thoroughly when you first study it as you will after you complete your study of the next chapters, or as you progress through the text.

If some students seem not to need a period of adjustment, it may be because they had had sufficient work in the subject before, perhaps in high school. So, bear this in mind when they seem to be learning the subject more readily than you are.

There are also a few lucky students without prior experience in accounting who will seem to learn it readily from the start. These are usually students who have prior learning experience in other abstract and intangible subjects, especially those of a quantitative nature (for example, mathematics). If the beginning student has unusual abilities, training, or experience of this sort, he may learn accounting without much initial strain.

Accounting is an abstract subject in at least two ways: first it consists of sets of labeled *numbers* organized according to certain patterns, and second, its numbers refer to economic abstractions whose physical properties (if they exist) are less significant. For example, money has physical properties, but these are greatly overshadowed by its economic properties. Similar observations could be made about almost every topic in accounting.

Many students find abstractions difficult. This may be because when a subject is abstract it is often expressed very compactly: this means a single figure or a single expression may symbolize complex relationships. In studying an abstract subject, one must study its expressions very carefully and thoroughly to gain real insight into the subject. In reading a text on an abstract subject, one must read rather deliberately and very closely. In this text, only Chapter 1 (and perhaps parts of Chapter 12) uses ordinary language to describe accounting and hence can be read rather quickly; the rest of the book deals with the abstractions of accounting and must be read and reread (and reread again) for optimal understanding.

In fact, a student typically achieves real understanding in an abstract subject most effectively when he solves problems which help him to apply and reinforce what he has learned and also to discover what he has not learned. Practice in problem solving is the key to learning mathematics or financial accounting. Problem solving is not an activity that can be pursued successfully without complete concentration. There are problems at the end of each chapter; the complete documentation of each problem solution is at least as important as a "correct answer." If you take the trouble to organize and structure the form of each solution most effectively, not only will you solve the problem accurately but you will find your understanding improved. For a proper solution, you must show how every figure was derived (if not taken directly from the problem), and every significant figure should be labeled in your solution. With a logical and complete approach to problem solving, both you and your teacher will more readily understand your solution.

The most valuable part of problem solving, however, is not your documentation, but your thinking, for the thinking you do in solving textbook problems should be invaluable in helping you solve real-life problems. You should be careful to do your own thinking in solving problems and not rely too much upon the thinking of your instructor or your classmates.

There are perhaps three levels of problem solving. The first is the general subject matter of the problem; usually you will have little difficulty at this surface level. Typically you will retain from your reading (or classroom discussion) sufficient knowledge to know how to approach this aspect of the problem. For example, in preparing a position statement, you would know from reading the text that the assets (resources) are kept separate from the equities (claims).

The second level of problem solving requires more thinking. Here you must determine which of the various accounting alternatives can be adapted most effectively for a solution within the constraints of the problem. This can be difficult, yet good thinking here is of crucial importance, for its value in learning accounting extends far beyond its use in solving a single problem. At this level, there are a finite number of alternatives or approaches that could be used to solve not only a particular problem but most problems of a particular type. Consequently, the thinking undertaken at this level for one problem probably will be repeated in a second problem, a third problem, and so on. For example, there are a limited number of ways assets (resources) may be shown on the position statement. Because this selection process is a recurring one, this aspect of problem solving is the most important one; you should devote considerable effort to this process, particularly in the first problems of any type you solve.

The third level of problem solving, since it is nonrecurring, is a less important one. For example, a company may have overdrawn its checking account; on its position statement while this situation exists, the overdraft would be shown as a liability and Cash in Bank would not be shown. Since a firm could continue this insolvency only briefly (unless it wishes to go out of business), the asset Cash in Bank is likely to reappear on any subsequent position statement.

Often you may become quite concerned when you are unable to solve (correctly) this aspect of a problem. Although it is natural that you should feel this way, it is also natural that you should have more difficulty with this level of the problem, since guidelines may not be available (or as apparent). Although often this nonrecurring part of a problem may be the most perplexing, you should not be unduly concerned if you do not solve it correctly in every problem, since it is nonrecurring.

Although financial accounting is regarded as a problem solving discipline, much can be learned, even by beginning students in accounting, from the solving of cases too. For this reason, some cases have been included in this text. Problems consist of structured situations; cases consist of unstructured situations. In a case or unstructured situation, you must determine what the problem is before you can solve it. Since real-life accounting practice includes unstructured situations, selected cases are a valuable aid in learning accounting, and since accounting consists of both language and figures, some writing assignments also can be most helpful in learning accounting.

Accounting is not a subject that you learn by last-minute cramming; it is one that is learned on a day-by-day basis. Although you may have had subjects in which last-minute cramming improves at least your examination record, these are not usually abstract subjects.

The best overall preparation for accounting examinations is to keep up to date on all your assignments. If you fall behind, you are not likely to be able to catch up with your classmates. If, however, you persist in disciplining yourself to do each homework assignment as required, you receive numerous benefits. First, you should be able to follow your instructor's lectures and the classroom discussion without much difficulty. Second, you should be better able to formulate questions to your instructor about those things that still puzzle you. Finally, you will be in a better position to satisfy yourself, your instructor, and others that you have learned some financial accounting.

In accounting, as with other abstract subjects, one does not learn without becoming involved. Passive students do not learn accounting, and if such is your nature and you don't want to change it, you should avoid accounting. On the other hand, students who read the subject carefully, do the analytical thinking and well-organized documentation required in problem solving, and take part in discussion of the subject, both in and out of the classroom, will become good students of accounting. Perhaps it is not too surprising, given the extent of the involvement required of the student, that otherwise ordinary students frequently find accounting turns out to be their best subject, not only in the grade received but in the learning achieved.

When you have completed your first accounting course and this text, you will have made a good start, but it is important to realize that the successful completion of the first course should mean a change, not a conclusion, to the process of learning accounting. Now it should become possible for you to start concentrating on those subjects in or related to accounting that you really enjoy learning or doing the most, the things in which you find you can best express yourself and those in which your usefulness can become optimal.

Those who stop learning and thinking about accounting after they complete the final examination of the course will quickly get left behind. Accounting is not a stationary subject; since its environment of organizations continually changes, it must change too.

Glossary

AAA American Accounting Association, an organization of accounting practitioners and college teachers.

AICPA American Institute of Certified Public Accountants (or the Institute) (formerly American Institute of Accountants), the authoritative professional organization of certified public accountants in the United States.

APB Accounting Principles Board, a committee of the American Institute of Certified Public Accountants that determines accounting principles for its members and member CPA firms.

ASOBAT *A Statement of Basic Accounting Theory,* a monograph prepared by a special committee of the American Accounting Association and published in 1966.

Account receivable Amount due from (or a claim against) a debtor, generally on open account. Usually uncollected amounts due on completed sales of goods or services.

Accounting control Procedures and system used to maintain accurate financial records and to safeguard the assets of the entity. See also internal control.

Accounting cycle Steps in the processing of accounting data during an accounting period: (1) occurrence of the transaction, (2) classification of the transaction in chronological order (journalizing), (3) recording the classified data in ledger accounts (posting), (4) preparation of financial statements, and (5) closing of nominal accounts.

Accounting entity or unit Activity or resource or group of activities and/or resources for which an accounting system is designed and maintained.

Accounting equation Truism that expresses the fundamental financial relationships of double-entry accounting in money amounts: Assets (in dollars) = Liabilities (in dollars) + Ownership (in dollars), or Assets (in dollars) = Equities (in dollars).

Accounting income Period revenue less period expense.

Accounting information Quantified economic data and reports provided by the accounting system.

Accounting measurements For profit-seeking enterprises, the primary measurements are of performance or activity (income and other fund flows) and financial condition or status. For government units and not-for-profit enterprises, the primary measurements are of activity (fund flow) and financial condition. Also see fund accounting.

Accounting period Arbitrary interval of time chosen for an accounting entity (usually one year) (1) for which income, fund-flow, and other activity or performance reports are prepared regularly and (2) at the end of which a position statement or other financial status report is prepared. It also is the time interval during which the accounting cycle is completed. Also called fiscal period or fiscal year.

Accounting system Formal network of accounts, personnel, records, and equipment that carries out the process of identifying, measuring, and communicating economic information that is relevant and an aid to users in making decisions.

Accrual basis of accounting Method of accounting in which revenues are recognized when realized and expenses are matched with either the revenue or the period in which the revenue is recognized.

Accrue To accumulate, to grow, to increase. Also to recognize the increase, such as interest receivable or payable on a debt, usually at the end of the period.

Accumulated Depreciation Real account contra to a plant asset account (or accounts) showing the amount of plant value that has been charged to depreciation as of the statement date.

Actuarial Relating to insurance mathematics and statistics which include the use of probabilities based on statistical records and compound interest.

Actuarial gains (or loss) Effects on pension costs of (1) differences between actual experience to date and the actuarial assumptions used or (2) changes in actuarial assumptions as to future events.

Adjunct account Type of account that is used for increases (or to accumulate increases) in another account (a principal account). Also called a valuation account. For example, Merchandise Inventory—Freight In is an adjunct to Merchandise Inventory, and Bonds Payable—Premium is an adjunct to Bonds Payable.

Adjusting entry Entry to record an internal transaction that is usually made at the end of the accounting period. The major types are allocations of an asset to expense or of a liability to revenue, accruals of an asset to revenue or of a liability to expense, or corrections of errors.

All-changes-in-financial-position con-cept Fund-flow concept that requires the reporting of all important aspects of financing and investing activities regardless of whether fund accounts are directly affected; may be applied with cash, cash and temporary investments, net quick assets, or working capital definitions of funds.

All-financial-resources concept Fund-flow concept that requires the reporting of the financial aspects of all significant transactions, even non-fund transactions, for example, the exchange of capital stock for plant assets, usually applied with the working capital definition of funds. Superseded by all-changes-in-financial-position concept.

All-inclusive concept Income concept under which all transactions that involve a change in ownership during the period (excluding dividend declarations and capital retirement or investment transactions) are reported on the income statement.

Allocate To transfer or charge a part (or all) of the value of an asset item or group of items to expense (or revenue), or to transfer or credit a part (or all) of the value of a liability item or group of items to revenue (or expense).

Allowance Permitted reduction in a measurement in the settlement of a debt, a deduction granted or accepted by the creditor for causes such as damage, delay, imperfection, or shortage, but excluding returns. For example, sales allowances.

Allowance for Cash Discounts Real account contra to Accounts Receivable showing the amount of outstanding available cash discounts that are expected to be taken when accounts are paid in the next accounting period.

Allowance for Uncollectible Accounts Real account contra to Accounts Receivable showing the amount of outstanding accounts that are not expected to be collected. Also called Allowance for Bad Debts and Allowance for Doubtful Accounts.

Amortize   To write off or allocate a part of the cost of an asset. Usually applied only to intangibles, such as patents, bond discount or premium, and leaseholds.

Annuity   Loan to be repaid (or collected) in installments at regular time intervals. In an ordinary annuity, the installments are at the end of each time interval; in an annuity due, the installments are at the beginning of each time interval.

Appraised value   Money value for property, determined by appraisal. Usually the replacement or reproduction cost less observed depreciation.

Appropriation of retained earnings   Reservation or restriction of all or part of the Retained Earnings account as a result (1) of discretionary managerial actions (for example, as a way of informing stockholders through the accounting records that cash dividends are being reduced or not increased because the cash is needed to finance plant expansion); (2) of statutory requirements (for example, when treasury stock is acquired, many state laws require that retained earnings be restricted to protect legal capital); or (3) of contractual restrictions (for example, a bond indenture may place restrictions on retained earnings which may have the effect of reducing cash dividend payments and giving greater assurance that cash will be available to pay the bonds' interest and principal).

Articles of incorporation   Document prepared by the persons establishing a corporation in the United States and filed with state authorities; thus it becomes the agreement between the corporation and the state. Also called the corporation charter.

Assessed value   Money value placed on property for taxation and other purposes by a governmental official, the assessor.

Asset   Economic potential secured by law from which there is a reasonable expectation that the accounting entity will receive a positive benefit or service in the future.

Attention-directing function   Accountant's task of supplying information that focuses on problems, imperfections, or inefficiencies in the entity's operations.

Attest function   Express an objective statement of fact or opinion, usually relating to a set of financial statements. Also see independent audit.

Audit report   Public accountant's statement, following an examination (audit) made by him, of his judgment or opinion as to the propriety of financial statements.

Auditing   Branch of external accounting that is concerned primarily with the periodic, independent examination of the financial data of enterprises and the expression of opinions on the fairness of their financial statements.

Balance sheet   See position statement.

Basket purchase   Acquisition of a group of assets, usually plant assets, at a single negotiated price.

Bond   Debt security, usually issued initially for long periods of time in the form of either coupon (or bearer) bonds, bonds registered in the name of the owners for principal only (registered coupon bonds), or bonds registered in the name of the owner for both principal and interest (registered bonds). Examples are debenture bonds and mortgage bonds.

Bond indenture   Agreement between the bondholder and the issuing entity.

Book value   When applied to assets, the amount at which an asset or group of assets appears in the accounting records. This is the historical cost of the asset(s) less any applicable contra account such as accumulated depreciation or allowance for doubtful accounts. When applied to capital stock, the net asset amount (historical cost, less contra accounts, less all liabilities, and less the agreed liquidation value of any outstanding preferred stock) applicable to the capital stock.

Budget   Financial plan of action expressed in numbers to facilitate control over future activities or operations.

CPA Certified Public Accountant, a professional accountant in the United States who has passed the Uniform Certified Public Accountant Examination and who has satisfied experience, character, and other requirements of one of the 54 states, districts, and territories.

Capital Term used in many different ways, so that its meaning must be inferred by considering both the adjectives used with it and the context in which it appears. The usual meanings are (1) total assets or total equities (all or total capital), (2) current assets less current liabilities (working capital), (3) a noncurrent asset (capital asset), (4) long-term liabilities plus owners' equity (long-term capital), (5) owners' equity (invested capital), (6) the amount directly invested in the entity by its owners, that is, usually Capital Stock plus Capital Stock—Premium (paid-in capital or capital contributed by stockholders), or (7) part of a corporation's ownership equity either (a) established by statute and restricted as to use to protect creditors (legal capital) or (b) allocated to the Capital Stock account when no-par-value stock is issued (stated capital). Also see capital stock.

Capital Stock Real owners' equity account for the ownership shares of a corporation authorized by its articles of incorporation. Also see Common Stock and Preferred Stock.

Capital Stock—Discount Real owners' equity account for accumulating the excess of the par value of shares issued and the amounts actually received for them.

Capital Stock—Premium Real owners' equity account of a corporation for accumulating amounts in excess of par or stated value of shares (1) from contributions by stockholders when initially acquiring stock, (2) from capitalization of retained earnings, as when a stock dividend is distributed, (3) from revaluation of assets, or (4) from donations of assets. Also called Capital in Excess of Par (or Stated Value).

Capitalize To add to an asset account (for example, when a plant asset is acquired, or when a cost incurred is transferred to an inventory or prepayment account) or to transfer from a Retained Earnings account to the Capital Stock accounts (for example, when a stock dividend is declared).

Cash basis of accounting Usually refers to the accounting method under which revenue is recognized when cash is collected, but expenses are recognized on an accrual basis in which major expense items are matched with revenues. In the simplest and most extreme form of the cash basis, revenues are recognized when cash is collected and expenses are recognized when cash is paid (with owner investments and disinvestments excluded).

Cash discount Allowance for settling a debt before it is due; a deduction from the invoice price.

Cash Fund Flow (External) Nominal clearing account used in fund-flow T-account analysis to which the nonfund account change balances are transferred (or closed). After these transfers have been made, the account reflects the data for the fund-flow statement. The balance in this account is transferred to the Net Cash Change (Internal) account, thereby closing both accounts.

Cash items Cash accounts and temporary investments (or marketable securities).

Clearing account Account used to accumulate amounts that are to be transferred later to another account(s). Examples are Revenue and Expense Summary and a construction account that is transferred to one or more plant asset accounts when the construction is complete.

Closing Transferring the balance in a nominal account (for example, revenue, expense, gain, and loss) to the real account to which it relates (for example, Retained Earnings or Owner, Capital).

Commander concept Ownership theory that emphasizes managerial control of the corporation's resources.

Common Stock Basic ownership class of capital stock of a corporation; usually referred to as the residual equity in the corporation, meaning that all other claims rank ahead of those of the common stockholder.

Comparative statements Usually income or position statements in which data for two or more dates or periods are presented in a single format.

Comparison See intrafirm comparison and interfirm comparison.

Compound interest Time cost of using money, computed by adding the simple interest of a period to the principal to establish the base for computing interest for the next period. Also called compound discount.

Conservative Accounting practice of "recognizing all possible losses and anticipating no possible gains" that tends to result in the understatement or minimizing of asset values and the overstatement of liabilities.

Consistency Practice of applying the same accounting rules, methods, and procedures in each similar case so as to avoid manipulating the end result and to facilitate comparisons over time (intrafirm comparisons) and among different entities (interfirm comparisons).

Consolidated statements Single set of position, income, and fund-flow statements for two or more separate corporations (legal entities) that operate as a single economic entity so that their accounts can be combined into a single accounting entity.

Contingent liability Obligation from a past transaction that will come into existence if an unlikely future event occurs.

Continuity concept Aspect of disclosure that requires modification of the presentation of financial data in the event of a possible discontinuance of the activities of the accounting unit.

Contra account Type of account that is used for offsets (or to accumulate deductions) from another account (the principal account). Also called a valuation account. For example, Allowance for Doubtful Accounts is contra to Accounts Receivable, and Discount on Bonds Payable is contra to Bonds Payable.

Control Continuous process of conforming the activities of an entity or organization to a plan of action and of conforming the plan to the achieved level of entity or organization activities.

Controlling interest Usual (legal) interpretation is ownership of 50 percent plus one share of the outstanding voting shares of a corporation, but there are exceptions to this. Accounting prefers the (economic) interpretation which requires control of a sufficient number of voting shares to enable the holder to direct the operations of a corporation on other than a temporary basis. Controlling interest must be present and continuing to justify preparing consolidated statements.

Convert In price-level accounting, to adjust historical-cost-based financial data for changes in the general or specific price level by using the appropriate price index.

Convertible bond Bond that can be exchanged for common stock or another security at the option of the holder but subject to the time, rate of exchange, and other conditions stipulated in the bond indenture.

Corporation Legal form of business organization that operates under a grant of authority from a state or other political jurisdiction and that is owned by stockholders who have limited liability for corporation debt.

Cost See historical cost.

Cost center Smallest unit of activity or area of responsibility for which costs are assigned and accumulated.

Cost of Goods Sold Expense account for the total cost value of merchandise sold during the period. Also called Merchandise Expense.

Coupon interest rate Rate of interest stated on the face of a bond certificate that is the basis for determining the promised amount of periodic interest payments. Name derives from coupons attached to the bond certificate that must be submitted to receive the periodic interest check. Also called the nominal interest rate.

Credit Accounting term indicating either (1) an increase in equity (including revenue) and contra-asset accounts or (2) a decrease in asset and contra-equity accounts; usually recorded on the right side of an account.

Creditor Person or organization to whom amounts are owed on a debt.

Current asset Liquid assets that can be expected to be directly or indirectly converted into cash within one year or the operating cycle of the entity, whichever is longer.

Current cash equivalent Market selling price or realizable price of an asset; a direct valuation measure, an exit price.

Current liability Obligation that falls due and should be paid within one year or the operating cycle of the entity, whichever is longer. Also includes obligations whose liquidation is expected to require (1) the use of existing current assets or (2) the creation of other current liabilities.

Current (normal) service cost Pension plan costs of providing retirement benefits for services performed following the inception of the plan.

Current operating concept Income concept which attempts to distinguish clearly the current, operating, and normal events of the period from other events that are not, to compute an income measure that is a better indication of the current period's relative efficiency and performance. Noncurrent, nonoperating, and nonnormal items usually are recorded directly to Retained Earnings.

Customers' ledger Form of subsidiary ledger for customer accounts receivable.

Cutoff Interruption in the continuity of recording transactions and in the flow of cash, goods, and transactions, generally at the end of the accounting period, for the closing of the books and audit purposes. The interruption date is called the cutoff date.

Debit Accounting term indicating either (1) an increase in asset, expense (equity deduction), and contra-liability accounts or (2) a decrease in liability, owners' equity, and contra-asset accounts; usually recorded on the left side of an account.

Debtor Person or organization who owes an amount, a debt.

Decision making Choosing between alternative courses of action.

Depletion Physical exhaustion of a natural resource (for example, timber or a petroleum deposit).

Depreciation Expired usefulness of a limited-life plant asset as a result of (1) physical use, (2) technological change, (3) unusual damage (for example, from inadequate maintenance), or (4) economic obsolescence or inadequacy for intended purpose (for example, an electric generator becoming too small because of growth in demand for electricity).

Depreciation accounting Process of allocating the cost of a long-limited-life asset to expense (or production) over its useful life.

Direct valuation Process of measuring an object or event in terms of the future output or exit prices that are expected from it. Also see current cash equivalent and liquidation price.

Disclosure Secondary concept relating to the presenting of financial reports that contain adequate, clearly expressed, factual data to fairly disclose the operating results and financial condition of the accounting unit and to not be misleading to the user.

Discount Term used in several different ways: (1) the difference between the estimated future amount and present value of a future benefit, a compensation for waiting (simple or compound discount); (2) an allowance given for the settlement of a debt before it is due (cash discount); (3) an allowance that stands without reference to date of payment (trade and quantity discounts); or (4) the excess of face, par, or stated value of a security over the amount paid or received for it (bond discount or stock discount).

Discount on bond (investment or payable) Excess of face value of bond over the issue (or later selling) price. Arises because the effective (or yield or market) interest rate is greater than the coupon (or nominal) interest rate promised on the face of the bond.

Discount rate See interest rate.

Discounted money receipts See present value.

Discounted value See present value.

Dissolution of a partnership Legal term for the point at which the regular activities of a partnership end but the partnership continues to liquidate and wind up its affairs. A partnership is legally dissolved by the (1) death, (2) retirement, (3) bankruptcy, or (4) incapacity of a partner or (5) the admission of a new partner.

Distribution of income Deduction from income. For example, when stockholders are viewed as recipients of a corporation's income, dividends declared become a distribution of income.

Dividend Distribution to stockholders of a corporation of (1) cash (cash dividend or liquidating dividend), (2) property (property dividend or dividend in kind), (3) debt certificates, usually promissory notes (scrip dividend), or (4) shares of the corporation's capital stock (stock dividend).

Divisional income reporting Practice of presenting income data on divisions or segments of the enterprise for both internal and external users. Also called segment income reporting.

Double-entry accounting Method of accounting (used throughout this book) that recognizes the dual aspect, source and disposition, of each transaction and that is manifested in any of the several forms of the accounting equation, of which the traditional form is: Assets (in dollars) = Liabilities (in dollars) + Ownership

(in dollars). An essential aspect of double entry is that the owners' equity balance is determined within the system of accounts rather than by "plugging," as is the case when single entry is used.

Doubtful accounts Receivable accounts that are likely to never be collected.

Earning Process or series of events that must be completed to create, furnish, and collect for the good or service to become entitled to the revenue.

Effective interest rate Actual rate of interest earned on a bond that may be more than, equal to, or less than the coupon or nominal rate, depending upon whether the bond was issued at a discount, at face value, or at a premium. Also called the yield or market interest rate.

Enterprise theory Ownership theory in which the corporation is viewed as a social institution operating for many interested groups.

Entity theory Ownership theory that emphasizes the view of the corporation as a separate legal entity having an existence apart from its owners.

Equity Right or claim, including those of both creditors and owners of the entity.

Executory To be performed, completed, or executed in the future.

Expected value Weighted average of all the conditional values of an act or alternative. Each conditional value is weighted by its probability.

Expense Expired cost, asset, or value. A cost incurred directly or indirectly in the earning of revenue.

External accounting Branch of accounting, usually called public or financial accounting, that is concerned primarily with the accounting of many enterprises and providing information that is useful to external parties (for example, existing and potential investors, creditors, stockholders) in making decisions about the firm.

External transaction Financial event that arises in relations with an outside person or organization. Also called a business transaction.

FICA Federal Insurance Contributions Act, the act under which taxes are levied on the income of individuals to support the retirement, death, dependent, Medicare, and Medicaid benefits of the Social Security program. When individuals are employed by others, an equal amount of tax is levied on both the employer and the employee.

Fifo First-in, first-out, a method of determining the cost of inventories of goods or investments in which it is assumed that the costs of the goods purchased first are the costs of the first goods sold or transferred.

Factory overhead Costs incurred at the factory or plant level for items that do not go directly into the product. Examples are supplies used, superintendence, and factory depreciation.

Finished Goods Cost of completed product inventory held for sale by a manufacturer. A real account.

Fiscal period Accounting period, usually a part of a fiscal year, which is any accounting period of 12 successive months, 52–53 weeks, etc.

Flow-through Method of accounting for the investment credit in which the entire amount allowed as a reduction in income tax payable is also reported as a reduction in the period income tax expense.

Foreign exchange index or rate Statistical average or rate that expresses the value relationship of one national monetary unit to another.

Freedom from bias Requirement that accounting reports exclude information that is beneficial to one group of users but detrimental to others.

Fund accounting Theory of accounting, of greatest usefulness in governmental and not-for-profit institutions, in which a separate accounting entity, a fund, consisting of cash, other assets, and/or liabilities, is established for each operational or activity-oriented unit. Each fund has a separate budget and a double-entry set of balancing accounts that are the basis for preparing operating and position statements.

Fund-flow statement Financial report of sources and uses in some definition of funds (usually cash, cash items, net quick assets, or working capital) for the period.

Fund-flow statement account format Arrangement in which increases in funds are shown on the left side of the statement and decreases are shown on the right.

Fund-flow statement balanced account format Arrangement in which increases in funds are shown on the left side of the statement, decreases are on the right, and the net change in funds is presented as the balancing figure so that the totals for both sides are equal.

Fund-flow statement complete report format Arrangement in which revenues are shown at the top in the increases in funds section and expenses are shown below in the decreases section, with the net change in the fund shown on the last line.

Fund-flow statement long-form analytical format Arrangement that attempts to match specific fund increases with specific decreases; revenues are shown first, with expenses shown next and deducted directly to yield funds provided from operations; the net change in funds is shown on the last line.

Fund-flow statement reconciling report format Arrangement that begins with period net income, then adjusts it for non-fund items that appeared on the income statement. Decreases in funds are shown as the second section below the increases, with the net change in funds shown and added to or subtracted from the beginning fund balance to yield the ending fund balance.

Fund-flow statement remainder report format Arrangement that begins with period income, then adjusts it for non-fund items that appeared on the income statement. Decreases in funds are shown as the second section below the increases, with the net change in funds shown on the last line.

Fund theory Ownership theory that is neutral to the interests of all groups and emphasizes an activity-oriented unit as the basis for accounting; the rationale for accounting in not-for-profit organizations.

Funded Portion of pension cost that has been paid into an agency fund to provide retirement benefits.

GNP Gross national product, the market value of the nation's production of goods and services for a calendar year.

GNP implicit price deflator Gross national product implicit price deflator, an appropriate index of general price-level changes compiled quarterly by the United States Department of Commerce.

Gain Excess of revenue over the related cost, usually used in the accounts only for a transaction or group of transactions that may be classed as extraordinary or nonrecurring.

General journal Form of the journal, a chronological record of transactions containing two money columns. Used as the only journal or in conjunction with specialized journals for recording transactions not provided for in the specialized journals.

General ledger Form of the ledger, a book containing the principal real and nominal accounts of an accounting system. Also see subsidiary ledger.

Governmental accounting Branch of accounting that may be either externally or internally oriented but is concerned primarily with the accounting of federal, state, or local governmental units.

Gross margin Net sales less Cost of Goods Sold expense.

Gross margin inventory method Process of estimating the cost of the ending inventory (or of verifying the reasonableness of results obtained by others) without taking a physical inventory. This is done by applying the average cost–selling price ratio for previous periods (the complement of the ratio of the gross margin to sales for these periods) to the total sales of the current period. This result, an estimate of the cost of the goods sold, is then subtracted from the cost of the goods available for sale during the period (cost of beginning inventory plus net purchases cost); the residual is the estimate of the ending inventory.

Historical cost Exchange or entry price paid for goods or services at the time of acquisition. It is measured as of the date of acquisition by the cash outlay, indebtedness incurred, or cash equivalent (when non-cash assets are exchanged).

Implicit cost Incurred cost that is not stated separately. For example, the interest cost in an installment contract, or a long-term lease in which the interest portion of the payments is not expressly stated.

Imprest system Method under which imprest petty cash is disbursed and later restored to its original amount by making reimbursements equal to amounts expended.

Imputed cost Cost that does not appear in conventional accounting records and does not require dollar outlays. For example, the inclusion of "interest" on ownership equity as an element of operating expenses.

Income statement Financial report on the entity's performance or activity for the period; an accounting flow report.

Income statement multistep format One of several possible arrangements in which there usually are one or more revenue sections and about three groups of expense items with separate subtotals in each section, and in which the net income appears near the bottom.

Income statement single-step format Arrangement in which revenues are presented first and summed; all expenses are then itemized, summed, and deducted as a single total to arrive at the net income in one step.

Income tax allocation Apportioning federal income taxes between different statements (intraperiod alloca-tion) or between different periods (interperiod allocation), so that the income tax expense (or refund) is matched with the reported income (or loss).

Independent audit Examination and investigation by a public accountant of the internal control and accounting records of an entity for the purpose of expressing an opinion on the pro-priety and fairness of the entity's financial statements. Also see attest function.

Indirect valuation Process of mea-suring an object or event in terms of entry or input prices (for example, historical or replacement costs).

Installment Periodic payment or rent.

Intangible Having no physical exis-tence; a right such as the cash, re-ceivables, most prepaids, patents, copyrights, trademarks, and goodwill assets of an entity.

Intangible assets Classification used for items such as patents, copyrights, trademarks, and goodwill that have a useful life longer than one year.

Interest Rent or service charge for the use of money for a period of time. A compensation for waiting. The dif-ference between an estimated future amount and its present value.

Interest rate Percent to be paid per unit of time for the use of money. The rate which equates a future amount or benefit and its present value.

Interfirm comparison Approach to interpreting and analyzing financial data by considering similar elements of different entities at the same mo-ment in time or for the same time period.

Interim statement or report Financial report for less than a full fiscal year or for less than the customary report-ing period. For example, a report for a quarter or three months or thirteen weeks.

Internal accounting Branch of ac-counting, usually called managerial accounting, that is concerned pri-marily with accounting within the enterprise and with providing man-agement with information that will be useful in making decisions.

Internal check Coordinated methods and measures within an organization designed to check the accuracy and validity of organization data and safeguard assets. These are elements (3) and (4) of the more inclusive in-ternal control concept.

Internal control Coordinated methods and measures within an organization designed to (1) promote efficiency, (2) encourage adherence to manage-ment plans and policies, (3) check the accuracy and validity of organiza-tion data, and (4) safeguard assets.

Internal rate of return Interest rate at which the present value of an in-vestment cash inflow equals the pres-ent value of its cash outflow.

Internal transaction Financial event that is initiated within the firm, often by the accountant. Also called an ac-counting transaction. Examples are the expiration of the cost of plant assets, the transfer of the cost of goods in process to finished goods, or the amortization of an intangible. The major categories are recorded as adjusting and closing entries.

Interval estimate Estimate which states that a characteristic of a popu-lation lies between two points or within a given range. For example, an estimate that the arithmetic mean of a population (a group of numbers or values) lies between 10 and 12.

Intrafirm comparison Approach to interpreting and analyzing financial data trends over time for a single entity by considering similar items at different moments in time or for different time periods.

Inventory Stock of raw materials, goods finished and in process, sup-plies, and/or merchandise which is on hand, in transit, in storage, or consigned to others. A current asset of the accounting entity.

Investee Entity that issued the long-term debt or stock held by another.

Investment credit Permanent reduc-tion in income tax payable computed as a percent of the purchase price of qualifying machinery, equipment, or other property.

Investments Classification used for securities, long-term receivables, cash value of life insurance policies, and other long-term holdings of intangible assets. Also see monetary and nonmonetary current assets and marketable securities.

Investor Person or entity that holds an investment in another, usually in the form of long-term debt or stock.

Journal Accounting book where transactions are classified and recorded first in chronological order; thus a chronological record of transactions. Often called a book of original entry.

Journalize To classify and record transaction data in a journal.

Kiting Method of overstating the total cash balance by cashing an unrecorded check drawn on one bank and depositing the cash in a second bank.

Lifo Last-in, first-out, a method of determining the cost of inventories of goods or investments in which it is assumed that the costs of the goods purchased most recently are the costs of the first goods sold or transferred.

Locom Lower of cost or market (or cost or market, whichever is lower), an indirect valuation method that is commonly applied to inventories and marketable securities under which the items are carried at their historical cost, but may be written down to approximately their current replacement costs when these prices decline.

Lapping Theft, usually by a cashier, of cash collected from one customer, whose account is credited at a later date by the theft of cash collected from a second customer.

Lease Conveyance of the use of property from one person or entity (lessor) to another (lessee) for a specified period of time in return for rent or other compensation.

Leasehold Interest in land conveyed under a lease agreement, normally classified as a tangible plant asset.

Ledger Book in which transaction data are classified by account; thus a book of accounts. Often called a book of final entry. Also see general ledger and subsidiary ledger.

Legal capital Part of corporate ownership equity that is established by statute and restricted as to use to protect creditors (for example, it cannot be distributed to common stockholders as a dividend). Often, the sum of the par values of the common shares issued and outstanding.

Lessee Person or entity using the property of another under the terms of a lease agreement.

Lessor Person or entity owning property, the use of which has been conveyed to another under the terms of a lease agreement.

Liability Debt or obligation of the accounting unit.

Limited liability Liability limited by law or contract. Examples are a special (limited) partner in a partnership whose liability is limited by contract, the partnership agreement; the liability of a stockholder in a corporation whose liability is limited by law; neither can lose more than his initial investment (plus any additional contributions that he may voluntarily make).

Liquid In cash or easily converted into cash without material loss of principal. Also used to refer to the state in which an entity has a substantial amount of cash and near cash assets.

Liquidating dividend Distribution of cash or other property to stockholders by an organization that is in liquidation.

Liquidation Part of the winding-up stage at the end of the life of an enterprise when regular activities have ended, assets are being sold, debts are paid, and remaining assets are distributed to owners. Also called the winding up.

Liquidation price Price that can be obtained from assets in a forced sale or liquidation proceedings; a direct valuation measure; an exit price.

Long-term liabilities Classification for obligations of the entity that are not due within one year or one operating cycle, whichever is longer.

Loss Expired cost, expense, or value for which there is no offsetting revenue.

Macroeconomics Branch of economics dealing with the broad and general aspects of the economy of an entire country.

Marketable Securities Real account for amounts invested temporarily in monetary (notes and bonds) and nonmonetary (capital stocks) securities that are frequently and widely traded.

Matching Conventional accounting concept under which income determination is a process of first recognizing revenue and then matching against that revenue the direct and indirect costs of bringing about the revenue.

Materiality Statistical concept applicable to accounting which implies that items that are not significant should not be given the same emphasis or consideration as significant items because insignificant items cannot and should not influence decisions or confuse decision makers.

Measurement Assignment of numbers to objectives and events. Measurement in accounting is concerned primarily with providing financial information that is relevant for specified user purposes.

Merchandise Inventory Cost of the inventory of goods held for sale by a retailer or wholesaler. A real account.

Microeconomics Branch of economics dealing with particular aspects of an economy, usually for a single enterprise.

Minority interest The portion of owners' equity in a subsidiary company that is not owned by the controlling (parent) company.

Monetary item Money or a claim to a specified amount of money. Examples are all liabilities, cash, receivables, and investments in notes and bonds.

NSF Nonsufficient funds, refers to a check which has been presented for payment but not paid by the drawer's bank because the account of the drawer (maker) had a balance that was smaller than the amount of the check.

Natural business year Accounting period of 12 months (or 52–53 weeks), ending (and starting) with the annual low point of business activity. Also called a fiscal period.

Net Cash Change (Internal) Nominal clearing account used in fund-flow T-account analysis to which the fund account change balances are transferred (or closed). The balance in this account is transferred to Cash Fund Flow (External), thereby closing both accounts.

Net quick assets See net short-term monetary assets.

Net realizable value Current selling price less costs to complete, sell, deliver, and collect for the good; the amount of proceeds from the sale of an item less all necessary costs of completing sales–collection process.

Net selling price See net realizable value.

Net short-term monetary assets Monetary current assets (cash, receivables, and temporary investments in monetary securities) less current liabilities.

Nominal account Temporary account, one that is used to accumulate detailed information on a real (position statement) account for a period of time. Examples are revenue, expense, gain, and loss accounts that accumulate information for the period income statement and are closed at the end of the period to the owners' equity account to which they relate, either Retained Earnings or Owner, Capital.

Nominal interest rate Rate of interest stated on the face of a bond certificate that is the basis for determining the promised amount of periodic interest payments. Also called the coupon interest rate.

Normative Based on the norm, best, or ideal standard of correctness.

Notes Receivable—Discounted Real

account, usually classified as a contra to the asset. Notes Receivable, used to record notes discounted (sold) to a bank with recourse; that is, the entity has a contingent liability to the bank, because if the maker of the note defaults, the entity becomes liable.

Objectivity and verifiability Required attribute of accounting measurements and information that permits qualified individuals working independently to develop similar measures or conclusions from the same evidence.

Operating Related to the normal buying, selling, and administrative functions of a trading or service enterprise; a manufacturing function would be added for manufacturing enterprises.

Operating cycle Cash to cash cycle for the activities of the entity. For the trading firm, the cycle is a continuum of many transactions that begin with cash that is used to acquire merchandise that is later sold to customers, usually in exchange for receivables which are later collected in cash to complete the cycle.

Opinion See audit report and APB Opinion.

Opportunity cost Maximum amount that might have been obtained if the good or service has been used in an alternative way.

Option Legal right to buy or sell something at a specified price, usually within a specified period of time.

Overhead General term for costs of materials and services not easily or directly identifiable with the major product or service. Also factory overhead.

Owners' equity Classification for the claims of the owners of the entity.

Par value Amount imprinted on the certificate of each share of a corporation's stock by the terms of the articles of incorporation and that often determines the minimum at which the corporation can initially issue the share.

Parent company Company controlling one or more (subsidiary) corporations.

Partnership Legal form of business organization in which the entity is owned by two or more persons, each of whom has unlimited liability for partnership debts.

Payable Liability, debt, or obligation of the entity.

Payroll taxes Taxes levied upon the employer and the employee to support the Social Security program.

Pension costs Prior service costs plus current (normal) service costs plus actuarial gains and losses.

Periodic inventory method Process of accounting for inventoriable goods by maintaining a record of the beginning inventory and purchases, and of verifying goods that remain by a physical count and valuation at the end of the accounting period; all goods not still on hand are presumed to be sold (or issued). Under this method, the real account, purchases (and related adjunct and contra accounts), is charged when goods are purchased; after the final inventory valuation is determined, the purchases and related accounts are closed out, and the ending inventory recorded with offsetting charges to Cost of Goods Sold.

Perpetual inventory method Process of accounting for inventoriable goods by maintaining a continuous detailed record of purchases, sales (or issues), and balances for each item. Under this method, the real account, Merchandise (or other) Inventory, is charged when the good is purchased and is credited when the good is sold (or issued). Actual quantities on hand are verified by a physical count at least once during each year.

Petty cash Fund of cash, usually small, that is kept on hand to facilitate the paying of small accounts that cannot be settled (efficiently or by request of the supplier) by check.

Plant assets Land, buildings, equipment, furnishings, and fixtures used by the entity that have a useful life longer than one year or the operating cycle of the entity.

Point estimate Single number estimate of a characteristic of a population. For example, an estimate of the arithmetic mean of a population (a group of numbers or values).

Position statement (or balance sheet) Report of financial condition or status of the accounting entity at a given date; an accounting stock report.

Position statement account (or horizontal) format Traditional, most popular arrangement for the body of the statement, in which assets are on the left and equities on the right.

Position statement report (or vertical) format Arrangement for the body of the statement in which current assets are presented at the top, with owners' equity below.

Position statement sequence version of the report format Vertical arrangement for the body of the statement in which current assets are presented first; current liabilities follow, and their total is subtracted from the current asset total, giving the amount of working capital; plant assets and intangibles follow, and from their total are subtracted any long-term liabilities; a grand total then is taken for net assets (working capital plus net noncurrent assets); owners' equity constitutes the final section of the statement (with the total equal to that for the net assets).

Posting Process of transferring dollar amounts from the journal or other basic record to a ledger account.

Preemptive right Right of a stockholder to subscribe to additional shares of the same class of stock that he holds in a subsequent issue of new shares for cash.

Preferred Stock Class of capital stock of a corporation having two or more classes of stock that is given a preference over the common stock, usually in claims to dividends and/or to assets in the event the corporation is liquidated. When a corporation has two or more classes of common stock (for example, Class A and Class B), one of them will have some preference over the other.

Premium on bond (investment or pay- able) Excess of issue (or later selling) price over the face value of the bond. Occurs because the coupon (or nominal) interest rate promised on the face of the bond is greater than the effective (or yield or market) interest rate.

Present value Estimated worth now of future payments (or receipts) from which interest (or a discount) has been deducted.

Price index Statistical, weighted average of prices of goods and/or services. May be either general (that is, covering a broad spectrum of items) or specific (that is, covering a group of more homogeneous items). An example of a general index is the GNP price index, the wholesale price index, and the composite construction cost index.

Principal Sum on which interest accrues; it may or may not be the amount stated in an investment or loan contract.

Prior service cost Pension plan costs of providing retirement benefits for services performed before the inception of the plan or before a change in plan benefits.

Problem solving function Accountant's task of supplying information in concise quantified terms on the relative advantages to the entity of pursuing (1) a possible future course of action or (2) one of several alternative methods of operation.

Production cost Cost of factors that contribute directly or indirectly toward completing the manufacture of a product.

Profit center Unit of activity that is responsible for both revenue and expense.

Proprietary theory Ownership theory that focuses interest upon the proprietor, the owner and manager of the firm's assets.

Public accountant or auditor Independent accountant having no financial stake or other interest in the person or entity on whose statements he is expressing his professional opinion.

Purchasing power Ability to purchase goods and services. The purchasing power of the dollar is its value in terms of what it can buy at one time as compared to what it could buy in some base period.

Quantifiable Attribute of a transaction, event, or activity that permits the assignment of numbers that obey arithmetic laws and procedures (for example, they can be added, subtracted, etc.).

Real account Permanent account that appears on a position statement (balance sheet).

Realization Concept which requires the recognition of revenue (1) when there is objective evidence of the market value of the good or service and (2) when the earning process is substantially completed.

Realize Traditional meaning is to convert into cash or a receivable.

Receivable Amount due from customers, officers, and employees. Usually called an account or note receivable and classified as a current asset.

Refinance or refund To provide for the payment of a debt by issuing a new loan or debt.

Relevance Necessary characteristic of accounting information that it be useful to the user in making decisions about investing in the entity.

Rent Compensation for the use of property. Also one of a series of annuity installments or payments.

Replacement cost Current cost at which asset could be acquired.

Retail inventory method Process of accounting for inventoriable goods (usually in retailing establishments) by maintaining a continuous and detailed record in terms of selling prices (and changes in them) for beginning inventory, purchases, and sales. The physical inventory on hand at the end of the period is also taken on the basis of the selling price tags attached to the merchandise. The cost record is kept on a periodic inventory basis, with data available only on the beginning inventory plus purchases. The cost of goods sold is determined after the ending inventory is converted from selling price to cost by applying an appropriate cost–selling price ratio (usually cost of beginning inventory plus purchases in the numerator, and the selling price of beginning inventory plus purchases and additional mark-ups in the denominator).

Retained Earnings Real account that appears on the position statement of a corporation to accumulate net income less distributions to stockholders and transfers to the capital stock accounts.

Return on investment Measure of an entity's operating efficiency; the ratio of net income to the amount invested.

Revenue Value inflow expected from the furnishing of goods or services. Examples are interest, rent, sales, and service revenue.

Revenue and Expense Summary Nominal clearing account often used in the closing of revenue and expense accounts.

Risk Exposure to chance of injury or loss. See uncertainty.

SEC Securities and Exchange Commission, the federal government agency that regulates the issuance and trading of securities.

Sales—Allowances Nominal account contra to Sales Revenue for amounts granted for damages, delays, imperfections, or shortages which are related to period sales of goods or services.

Sales—Cash Discounts Nominal account contra to Sales Revenue for the amount of cash discounts on this period's sales that have been taken during the period, plus those that the entity expects will be taken (if the adjusted gross method is used).

Sales—Cash Discounts Not Taken Nominal account adjunct to Sales Revenue that is used when the net method is used for recording cash discounts.

Sales—Returns Nominal account contra to Sales Revenue for the sales value of goods sold and returned to the entity.

Sales—Uncollectible Accounts Nominal account contra to Sales Revenue for the portion of the period sales of goods or services on accounts that the entity does not expect to collect. Also called Sales—Bad Debts and Sales—Doubtful Accounts.

Satisfice Term used to describe the many, usually unquantifiable, types of behavior that may result when an entity adopts as its primary objective an objective other than (and that would tend to conflict with) maximizing profits. Examples of such objectives are to maintain sales at a given percent of the regional, national, or international market for the entity's products or to sell only the most advanced, technologically superior products.

Scorekeeping function Accountant's data-accumulation activity in the task of supplying information for both internal and external evaluation of the entity's financial performance.

Security General term for a transferable certificate of ownership (capital, common, or preferred stock) or debt (bond or note).

Segment income reporting See divisional income reporting.

Selling price See net realizable value.

Serial bond Type of bond contract that provides for repayment of the face amount in a series of periodic installments.

Simple interest Time cost of using money, usually for short period(s) of time, computed only on the initial principal. Also called simple discount.

Single-entry accounting Method of accounting (or bookkeeping) in which only one side of many transactions is recognized and in which the total of owners' equity is determined by "plugging," that is, the amounts of assets and liabilities are determined, then owners' equity is determined as the difference.

Sinking fund Cash and other assets restricted, such as for the retirement of a debt or the redemption of a stock.

Smoothing Use of an accounting method or treatment to remove irregularities in net income.

Sole (or single) proprietorship Legal form of business organization in which the entity is owned by one person who has unlimited liability for debts of the business.

Solvent Ability to pay legal debts when they come due. Also used to refer to a situation in which the value of an entity's assets exceeds its liabilities.

Specialized journal Form of the journal, a chronological record of transactions that are similar in type and that occur frequently within the accounting period. Examples are cash receipts journal, purchase journal, and sales journal.

Stated value Nominal amount assigned to a share of no-par-value stock, usually at the discretion of the board of directors.

Statement of affairs Statement of assets, liabilities, and owners' equity for an enterprise in financial difficulty or liquidation. Statement usually shows book and liquidation values of assets and estimated amounts to be recovered by the various classes of creditors.

Statement of income and retained earnings Period financial report that combines the income statement with a reconciliation of the Retained Earnings account.

Stock dividend Issuance to present stockholders of additional shares of a corporation's capital stock in proportion to present holdings, in which the total amounts in the Capital Stock accounts are increased by a transfer from Retained Earnings. The par or stated value per share usually remains unchanged.

Stock option Right to purchase shares of a corporation's stock within a stated period at a specified price per share; usually granted as a nontransferable option under a stock option plan for motivating and partially compensating officers and employees.

Stock purchase warrant Detachable certificate issued with a bond or preferred stock, giving the holder the right to purchase at his option an indicated number of shares of stock at a specified price within a stated period of time.

Stock right Transferable right or option to purchase shares of a corporation's stock within a stated period at a specific price, issued to stockholders in connection with the preemptive right.

Stock split-up Issuance to present stockholders of additional shares of a corporation's capital stock in proportion to present holdings without changing the total amounts in the Capital Stock accounts. The only effects are to increase the number of shares outstanding and to reduce the par or stated value and book value per share.

Stock warrant See stock right and stock purchase warrant.

Straight-line method Assignment of equal amounts of the service cost of any item to equal time periods. An example is the straight-line method of depreciation.

Subsidiary company Corporation controlled by another (parent) company.

Subsidiary ledger Form of the ledger, a book of homogeneous accounts that constitutes the detailed record supporting a principal or general ledger account. Used where there are many accounts of one type to reduce (1) the size of the general ledger, (2) the length of the trial balance, and (3) the amount of time needed to get summary data. Examples are the customers' (or accounts receivable) ledger, the plant ledger, and the accounts payable ledger.

Substitution transaction Financial event that might be either internal or external and that does not affect the totals of the major categories (assets and equities) of the accounting equation. Thus, a transaction in which either (1) an asset item is exchanged for another asset or (2) an equity item is exchanged for another equity.

T account Form of the ledger account that is used to illustrate the effect of

a transaction or series of transactions or for solving accounting problems.

Tangible Having a physical existence, such as the inventory or plant asset items of an entity.

Trade discount Allowance given to a customer because of his classification (wholesaler or retailer) or order size (also called a quantity discount) that is deducted in arriving at the invoice price.

Transaction Economic or financial event or condition. Accountants use selected transactions as the basis for an entry in the accounting records.

Translate In accounting for foreign operations, to adjust financial data from foreign currency amounts to domestic currency amounts by using the applicable foreign currency index.

Treasury stock Shares of the capital stock that have been reacquired by the issuing corporation. Shares that are retired temporarily are recorded in Treasury Stock, a real account that is contra to either Capital Stock—Par or to all of owners' equity, depending upon the method of accounting used.

Trial balance List of account titles and their debit and credit balances that is used internally to determine whether posted debits and credits are equal and to establish a basic summary for financial statements.

Turnover Number of times that an asset or group of assets is replaced, usually during a year. Also the ratio of sales to the net book value of (1) total assets and (2) plant.

Uncertainty State that makes the outcome of an event doubtful or unpredictable as to the occurrence, amount, and timing of future cash flow, future interest rates, and the contribution of individual inputs that function only jointly.

Unemployment compensation tax Tax levied on employers by both federal and state governments to support the unemployment benefits of the Social Security program.

Unexpired cost Asset.

Unit of measure Basic monetary or nonmonetary quantity in which accounting information is accumulated. Most accounting reports are in terms of the local monetary unit (for example, the United States dollar in the United States).

Unlimited liability In the sole proprietorship and partnership forms of organization, the owner's and partners' (general) liability for proprietorship and partnership debts is not limited to their investments, but extends to their personal assets as well.

Valuation Process of determining the number of nonmonetary units of the attribute of the object or event and applying the relevant money amount (or price) to these units.

Valuation account See contra account and adjunct account.

Vested pension benefit Employee's right to the pension benefit is not contingent upon his continuing to be employed under the plan.

Work in Process Cost of uncompleted goods inventory still in production. A real account.

Working capital Net assets used in the current operations of an entity. The excess of current assets over current liabilities.

Index